FROM TODAY TO ETERNITY

A STUDY OF BIBLICAL PROPHECY AND END TIMES

VOLUME 2

WALTER R. SCARBOROUGH

Inks and Bindings
888-290-5218
www.inksandbindings.com
orders@inksandbindings.com

Even so, when
you see
these things happening,
you know that
the kingdom of God
is near.

Jesus as recorded in Luke 21:31

PREFACE

It seems as if every book, past and present, written about prophecy and end times begins with a characterization of just how difficult, perilous, uncertain, hostile, chaotic, violent, dangerous, horrible, unrighteous, immoral, and evil the times are in which we live. We do live in unprecedented times -- times in which the world seems to be degenerating into chaos. The authors of the earlier books are trying to paint a picture of all the things that are wrong about the world, the nation, society, the church, believers, and non-believers. The picture is usually disturbing, dismal, depressing, and discouraging. This book will be no different because the times in which we live are worse than when the earlier books were written. As predicted in the earlier books, our world continues in a downward spiral. Many people believe that humankind is heading for a devastating disaster.

The purpose of a picture such as those painted in words is to remind the reader of just how far away from God's righteousness our world has drifted. For most of the last century, our nation slipped away from the godly principles on which our nation was founded, our laws, our society, and our values. Now, immorality runs rampant, yes means no and no means yes, violence continues unabated, and everything seems to be turned upside down. It seems every day we must face yet another situation that stands defiantly in opposition to God.

Consider the following observations by John F. Walvoord in several of his books:

- "By every standard of measurement, the twentieth century will go down in history as the incredible century. The century began with limited use of electricity and without radio, television, planes, missiles, computers, modern weapons, and atomic bombs. Technology has moved man into a modern era that now witnesses more rapid change in the course of a year than formally took place in a century."[1]
- "In our modern world the human race is desperately trying to forget that God exists. The media constantly report scientific findings that seem to show that the human race has existed for millions of years, even though alleged proof for it is highly questionable."[2]

Some churches seem to be forming a doctrinal theology that includes everything under the moral, cultural and social sun, with the astounding exclusion of God and the Lord Jesus Christ. We hear reports and read that churches all over the world are either empty or have become apostate. Consider the following observations:

- "The spiritual fog that so clouded the minds of the religious leaders in Jesus' day still hangs over our theological landscape today."[3]
- "... [C]hurches are not offering prophetic teaching, since they perceive that people do not want it (and they have geared their programs to offer what people want, not what they need)."[4]

- "Tragically, many pastors today know little or nothing about Bible prophecy because it wasn't taught in their seminary; consequently, they do not teach about prophecy from the pulpit. This leaves many Christians ignorant of the exciting plans God has for the future."[5]
- "Not only do theologians tend to avoid eschatology, but also courses of instruction in theological seminaries often include little instruction on eschatology."[6]

Most pictures painted by these book authors seem to be based on conditions in the United States, but in reality they exist all over the world. The United States does not have a corner on the market for bad things. Churches in Britain and Europe are largely empty; Christians are punished, imprisoned, and killed for their beliefs in many nations. Nations that do not consider the United States as an ally have nuclear weapons they threaten to use, some countries are run by tyrants, and life carries little value.

There are many problems today, and people are scared. They are scared because they do not understand why some things are the way they are and why bad things happen. They are scared because of the senseless violence that seems to be close, and sometimes they feel angry because some things, once thought as sacred, are now swallowed up in apostate events, beliefs, and people. Evil seems to have an oppressive, and ever growing, grip on the vast majority of humanity; things we thought were unbelievable just a few years ago, are now accepted today.

Many are desperately searching for answers. A number of individuals suspect there is a spiritual aspect to many things that are happening and many of them believe that the answers are buried in Biblical prophecy. However, most Christians do not have a general understanding of Biblical prophecy, nor do they have the interpretative skills to adequately find the answers in the Bible. Most believers do not have the time and opportunity to study the Word at the same level as theological authors and scholars, so we have to depend on books such as this one to gain our understanding of prophecy and end times.

That's where this book and many of other books about Biblical prophecy come in. The intent of this book is to assist in making prophecy and end times more understandable to the serious student.

The subject of prophecy and end times cannot be studied casually. As can be seen from the Table of Contents and the size of this book, prophecy and end times consists of numerous events which occur in a specific order, and with characters having specific roles to fulfill. Because of its extensiveness, the study of prophecy and end times requires commitment, time and a strong desire to understand a multifaceted portion of one-quarter of the content of the Bible. The student should not be discouraged with the time commitment required because this time is time spent with the Lord, and the subject is worth understanding.

SEARCHING FOR A THEME

One of the things that serious students that mine the depths of the Bible, are searching for is something that unifies the revelation - someway of understanding the picture that the Bible paints. As we are commanded, we read and study the Bible to bring ourselves closer to the God of the universe, a closeness that sustains us throughout our lives. But many students of Scripture are looking for that theme that brings the Bible into a unified whole. I believe that books like this book go a long way to tell the story that unifies the Bible. Of course, there are other pieces that are necessary, but books like this book can establish the framework that might be necessary for some believers to understand the big picture of "His Story."

Pentecost, in the Preface of one of his books, *Thy Kingdom Comes*, says this about how the kingdom of God that unified the Bible for him: "It became possible to trace the development of that kingdom through Scripture from Genesis to Revelation, and that theme provided a unifying structure that bound all the Bible together into a unit, and by which all the history recorded there could be understood and related."[7] The theme for me is prophecy and end times, and unbelievably it has opened the entire Bible up for me to see How God works through Israel, the Church, and the world.

TABLE OF CONTENTS

28

THE RAPTURE

One of the most controversial subjects among all the characters and events of prophecy and end times is the Rapture. Many Christians have trouble understanding the Rapture because, first, there is the question of if it is real or not, and then, second, there are five major views of the timing of the Rapture. The idea of the Rapture is quite simple; the Lord comes and instantly snatches away those people, both alive and dead, that believe in him. It is the contention of this book that the Pretribulational timing is the most consistent view with Scripture and the other aspects of God's eschatological program.

28.1 THE DEFINITIONS

Rapture: "The word *rapture* is from *rapere*, found in the expression "caught up" in the Latin translation of 1 Thessalonians 4:17."[1] The Rapture consists of the translation of living believers in Christ and the resurrection those believers in Christ that have died since the day of Pentecost in which they will each receive immortal bodies suitable for an eternity. The type of eternal beings that believers will be patterned after is the being that Jesus Christ was after His resurrection - an eternal, imperishable, and immortal being with physical body, mind, and soul. The Rapture also is the movement of these believers from their mortal earthly homes to the immortal heavenly house of the Father as indicated in John 14:2-3, who will then spend eternity with God and Jesus Christ without fear of separation.

Resurrection: This is the event when the first of two groups of believers in Christ, who have previously died after Pentecost and before they are raptured, who are raised from their earthly graves and instantly changed into eternal, imperishable, and immortal beings as indicated in 1 Corinthians 15:51-54. These bodies will be reunited with their souls that have been in heaven with Christ since their own individual, personal, physical death.

Translation: This is the event when the second of two groups of believers in Christ, who are living at the time they are raptured, who are instantly changed into eternal, imperishable, and immortal beings as indicated in 1 Corinthians 15:51-54.

28.2 INITIAL UNDERSTANDINGS

The Rapture occurs prior to Daniel's 70th Week (Pretribulationalism) and there are several initial understandings, which are necessary to comprehend in order grasp more fully the contrasts between Pretribulationalism and the other views.

THE RAPTURE IS NOT REVEALED
IN THE OLD TESTAMENT

First Observation

There are a number of interactions between the leadership of Israel and Jesus that provide insight into the Jewish understandings and expectations of the times, as evidenced by the following examples:

- The nature of the questions that were asked of Jesus during His First Advent by His disciples and by others revealed no perception of a coming interruption in God's dealings with Israel.
- The Jews of the time were expecting their Messiah and Deliverer, as anticipated by Old Testament prophecies, to bring in the Kingdom on earth; there was no expectation of anything other than the Kingdom.
- When Jesus came to them, the Jews did not understand who He was, what He was doing, and why He was before them. Because of this blindness, Israel rejected Jesus as their Christ and killed him.

Therefore, Israel was not expecting the Church much less the Rapture.

Second Observation

Because Israel rejected Jesus as their Messiah, the possibility of the Kingdom coming to them was now gone. Because of the rejection, Jesus introduced another entity to occupy divine center stage, as Israel would be put aside for a while. The Jews did not understand that Israel was being set aside, nor did they understand that there would be an interruption in God's program with Israel, bracketed by two different advents of Jesus Christ. As we know this other entity, the Church or the body of Christ, was not revealed in the Old Testament, however, Jesus provided the necessary theological structure before and after His resurrection. Since the Church was to be an interim program, it seems appropriate that God would need to remove it before He turned His divine attention back to Israel. The method of removal, revealed in the New Testament, is the Rapture, which is the translation and resurrection of those who believe in the Lord Jesus Christ as their personal Savior and Messiah, which will occur at a particular point in time in the future. This aspect of the Church was not revealed until the night before Jesus' crucifixion in John 14:1-3.

NO SPECIFIC NEW TESTAMENT SCRIPTURE UNEQUIVOCALLY ESTABLISHING THE TIMING OF THE RAPTURE

"One of the problems that face both pretribulationism and posttribulationism is the fact that their point of view is based on an introduction of scriptural facts rather than an explicit statement of the Bible."[2] This 'problem' actually faces anyone that attempts to look for specific Scripture to support any of the Rapture views. In spite of the fact that there are many doctrines clearly defined and described in the Bible, the doctrine of the Rapture has to be established with the available Scriptures as they are related to the greater context of God's plans for the end of this present age, the notion of imminency, the Day of the Lord, and Daniel's 70th Week.

Before one can decide on one view over the others it is necessary to consider all the evidence that is available in the Old and New Testament and to not base a conviction on only one or two passages, at the exclusion of others. There are a considerable number of Bible verses that could be construed to contribute to an understanding of the Rapture, however, a doctrine of the Rapture has to be based on all the available verses, in their respective contexts, and how they fit together to establish a comprehensive fact that is consistent with all of the Bible. Doctrines cannot be doctrines if some passages are ignored or are not included because they may not support the doctrine.

It should be pointed out that one's belief in the timing of the Rapture is not crucial to one's salvation and standing before God. There are many devoted Christians, wholly committed to Jesus Christ, whose views of the Rapture stands in disagreement with fellow believers.

THE MEANING OF THE CHURCH

The Church is the divine entity that was created by Jesus Christ during His Advent to be the object of His divine attention in a parenthesis of time between Daniel's 69th Week, that are now history, and Daniel's 70th Week, that is yet future. The Church is not found before its creation at Pentecost, and it is not found in any Biblical passages after its Rapture. Also, nowhere in Scripture is the Church and Israel stated to be the same thing, nor are there any references to Israel ceasing to exist or to be important, nor, that the Church replaces Israel.

THE WORK OF THE HOLY SPIRIT
IN THIS PRESENT AGE

Prior to the Holy Spirit coming to indwell those that comprise the membership of the True Church, as stated by Jesus Christ in John 14:16-17, the Holy Spirit only dwelled among those Old Testament personalities that were true believers in God. After the True Church is removed in the Rapture, prior to Daniel's 70th Week, the Holy Spirit will dwell among tribulation saints in the same way as He did prior to the advent of the Church. There is no evidence in the Bible that the methodology of the Holy Spirit will be the same in both the Church Age and Daniel's 70th Week.

In 2 Thessalonians 2:6-8, Paul indicates that the Restrainer of Sin will be removed prior to the lawless one being revealed. We know from other passages that the lawless one is first the Ruler to Come, and then later, the Antichrist. "The ultimate decision on the reference to the restrainer goes back to the larger question of who, after all, is capable of restraining sin to such an extent that the man of sin cannot be revealed until the restraint is removed. The doctrine of divine providence, the evidence of Scripture that the Spirit characteristically retrains and strives against sin (Genesis 6:3), and the teaching of Scripture that the Spirit is resident in the world and indwelling the church in a special sense in this age combine to point to the Spirit of God as the only adequate answer to the problem of identification of the restrainer. ... If, therefore, the restrainer of 2 Thessalonians 2 is identified as the Holy Spirit, another evidence is produced to indicate the translation of the church before the final tribulation period will begin on earth."[3]

THE NECESSITY OF INTERVENING EVENTS

According to 2 Corinthians 5:10, all Christians have to appear before the judgment seat, or the bema seat, of the Lord Jesus Christ to be judged individually for what was, or was not, done while on earth. This is not a general judgment, it does not include Old Testament saints, it is not for punishment for sin, and it is not associated with judgment predicted for Christ's Second Coming - it is for determining rewards for the good works done in the name of Christ. "The point is that this judgment, important as it is, precedes the return to earth and could hardly be accomplished during the process of the Second Advent itself."[4]

There will be mortal human beings who will survive the seven years of Daniel's 70th Week that will live on into the Millennium; therefore, time is necessary for people to come to new faith in Jesus Christ after the Rapture in order for them to be ready to go into the Millennium. If the Rapture occurs prior to Daniel's 70th Week, then the required time will occur; however, it the Rapture is not until the end of Daniel's 70th Week, then there is not enough time to develop another group of believers with mortal bodies as required for the Millennium.

Judgment of the Survivors of Daniel's 70th Week:

- The Judgment of Israel: According to Ezekiel 20:34-38, the believers and non-believers of the nation of Israel that survive Daniel's 70th Week still in the flesh, not translated nor resurrected, will be gathered together for individual judgment. Those that are believers will enter into the Millennial Kingdom in bodies of flesh (not immortal bodies), and those that are non-believers will be put to death. It should be noted that if the translation of the Church took place at the time of the Second Coming, there would not be sufficient time for the gathering and judging to take place, nor would the judgment even be necessary because believers and non-believers would have been separated by Rapture at the time of the Second Coming, "…[A]n interval is required between the translation of the church and the judgment of Israel during which a new generation of Israelites who believe in Christ as Savior and Messiah comes into being and is waiting for His second advent to the earth to establish the millennial kingdom."[5]

- The Judgment of the Gentiles: Similar to the judgment of Israel, there will be a corresponding judgment of the Gentiles. According to Matthew 25:31-46, the believers and non-believing Gentiles will be gathered and will be separated into two groups. As with the judgment of Israel, these will be people still in their mortal bodies. One group will be the sheep, those that did the good work during Daniel's 70th Week of befriending the brethren, the Jewish people, who will then enter into the Millennial Kingdom keeping their mortal bodies. The other group will be the goats, those that did not do the good work of befriending the brethren; these will be put to physical death in the everlasting fire.

- Observations of These Judgments:
  + The reference to works is not in regard to eternal salvation by works; instead, it acknowledges that believers in Jesus Christ will express their belief by the fruits of their labor. In this case, the labor that is important here are the acts "… of kindness which no one but a believer in Christ would perform during the Tribulation when Christians as well as Jews is hated by all the world."[6]
  + Both judgments are for purging unbelievers from among Israel and the Gentiles.
  + Individual people will be judged, not nations of people.
  + Neither the Ezekiel nor the Matthew passages mention resurrection or translation within the context of the gathering and judging of the survivors of Daniel's 70th Week.
  + These judgments occur after the Second Coming of Jesus Christ, and after He has established His throne from which to rule.
  + These judgments are entirely different events from the translation and resurrection of the Church.

"… [T]he interval between the translation and the Second Coming is absolutely necessary for the creation of a new generation of believers in Christ, composed of both Jews and Gentiles who retain their national identification and who will await the second advent of Christ and the millennial kingdom to follow."[7]

28.3 THE PROMISE OF JESUS CHRIST'S RETURN

The teachings of Jesus Christ two thousand years ago as recorded in the Gospels and the writings of His followers, tells of His intent to return to earth at some point in the future to judge those that have rejected Him, to redeem those that have accepted Him and to carry them into His eternal kingdom. The entire theology of Jesus Christ as the living Son of God is based on the fact that He will come to earth again to restore the relationship between the Triune Godhead and the creatures that were created thereof. The integrity and veracity of the Scriptures depend upon Jesus Christ coming again.

The following passages establish that the Lord will come again, which is in opposition to those that deny that the Lord will return. There can be no denial that Jesus Christ will come again, however, as is the topic of this chapter, there are a number of views as to just how and when this return will occur.
- The three I Wills of Jesus:
  + John 14:16-17: I will send My Spirit.
  + Matthew 16:13-19: I will build My Church.
  + John 14:1-3, 14:28, and 16:22: I will come again.
- The New Testament is dominated by the fact that Jesus Christ will return again because reference is made to the event 318 times.
- Matthew 24 - 25: Matthew recorded Jesus' responses when questioned by the disciples regarding the end of the age, and He provided considerable detail about the events that will surround the time of His Second Coming.
- Acts 1:11: Immediately after His ascension, two unidentified men tell the disciples who had just witnessed the awesome event that He would return in the same way He departed.
- 1 Corinthians 16:22: A call by Paul, who obviously would know if Jesus Christ was to come again or not, for the Lord to come.
- Colossians 3:4: A reference to believers being revealed as Christ when He appears in the future.
- 1 Thessalonians 4:15: Paul tells the Thessalonians that those believers that are living at the time of the coming of the Lord will follow those believers who had previously died and are raised from the dead when they are all taken away.
- 1 Timothy 6:14: Another reference to a future appearance of the Lord.
- Hebrews 9:28 and 10:37: Specific verses that indicate that Jesus Christ will come again.
- 2 Peter 3:9: Before He considers His promise fulfilled, the Lord is waiting patiently until all that are destined to come to Him have done so.

The time when Christ comes is of great importance to believers. If He comes prior to Daniel's 70th Week, then the Rapture represents hope for the believer because he or she will not have to fear the horrors of that time. If, however, the Rapture is not until the middle or end of Daniel's 70th Week, or, only some believers will be taken out, then believers are not near as hopeful because the Church will have to endure some or all of the horrors of the time. "The question of whether the church must continue on earth through the predicted time of trouble is obviously a major problem of Christian faith."[8] Any believer that comes to even a basic understanding of God's Plan looks at the future with trepidation - in spite of the fact that we are not to fear about the future, but instead trust God. Second only to personal judgment before Christ, the fear of Daniel's 70th Week is probably one of the most serious anxieties that believers endure.

28.4	A BRIEF HISTORY OF THE DOCTRINE OF THE RAPTURE

It needs to be understood at the outset that the history of the doctrine of the Rapture is much debated among theological scholars, conservative and liberal, as to which of the various views of the Rapture were held by the early church. Adherents of each view lay claim to their view being the one believed at the time. If does not seem plausible that the early Christian scholars would have a complete and detailed understanding of the eschatological aspects of God's Plan sufficient enough to formulate a view that would be as fully developed as the views today (we have the advantage of almost 2,000 years of history, study, and discussion). While they might understand the pieces and parts, how they went together was probably still a mystery to them. Without including an extended description of the history of the doctrine of the Rapture, suffice it to say that there is sufficient evidence that the early church did anticipate an imminent return, at any moment, of Jesus Christ, which is greatly substantiated by Paul's epistles, especially his letters to the Thessalonians. Also, there is evidence that the church of the first several centuries anticipated a future time of great distress, and a lengthy millennium to follow. While there is dispute regarding which view of the Rapture they held, they appeared to expect the Lord's return at virtually any moment.

The notion of a future beyond their lifetimes was probably far from detailed; in fact, it would not be surprising to learn that the eschatology of the Bible may not have been given much consideration since the second and third centuries AD were a torturous time for the Church because of Roman persecutions. Most of the theological doctrines of Christianity have taken centuries to develop, and we need to keep in mind that the Biblical canon did not get completed until sometime after the early church. "If major doctrines like the Trinity and the procession of the Spirit took centuries to find acceptable statement, it is likely to be expected that the problems of eschatology would be all settled in the early centuries."[9]

7

"The early church was far from settled on details of eschatology, though definitely premillennial. ... In a word, the early Fathers were not specifically pretribulational, neither were they all posttribulational in the modern meaning of the term. They simply had not raised the questions involved in the controversy."[10]

28.5 THE IMMINENCY OF THE RAPTURE

Of all the Biblical concepts that influence the development of a doctrine of the Rapture, imminency of the expectation of the return of Jesus Christ is the most influential. As will be seen below in the Pretribulational Rapture view, Jesus Christ's return is seen as imminent - it could occur at any moment, at any time, without any signs pointing to its occurrence (there are no signs, events, or conditions that are necessary for something to be imminent). All of the other views have to deny that imminency is of significance because each of the other views place the Rapture at some point within the span of Daniel's 70th Week, which thus eliminates the need for imminency for it is now predictable because Daniel's 70th Week is predictable.

Predicted in numerous locations of the Bible are signs for Israel to watch in anticipation of the coming of their Messiah and Deliverer, such as given in Matthew 24 - 25, in order to restore the people to their nation and enter into the long-awaited Kingdom. However, those signs point to Jesus Christ coming for His Second Coming. In contrast, the Church has been given no signs for the coming of the Lord Jesus Christ to remove them before the time of great distress and trouble that Israel will have to endure before their Messiah and Deliverer does come for them. The Church is told simply to live in expectation of the imminent return of Jesus instead of looking for signs of His return. Thus, unrighteous Israel should watch for the signs of the Lord coming for them (which would be His Second Coming at the end of Daniel's 70th Week), but the Church is not to watch for signs of the lord coming for them (which would be the Rapture before Daniel's 70th Week). "The hope of the Church is to be taken to heaven; the hope of Israel is Christ returning to reign over the earth."[11]

THE BASIS OF IMMINENCY

The Scriptural basis of imminency involves the following New Testament passages. Be particularly attentive to the exhortations that are written to *look* for, *watch* for, *wait* for the soon coming of the Lord Jesus Christ, and to *comfort* one another with the hope of His quick return. Also, be attentive to the sense of imminency that is threaded throughout these passages, as can especially be seen in Paul's writings.
* John 14:3:
    + Jesus previously had told His disciples that He was going to leave them for now, but here He is telling them that He will return in the future to take them with Him from earth to heaven. Thus, He provided substance to the idea of His coming for a Rapture, which will later be

seen to be in addition to His Second Coming where no one goes from earth to heaven. This was a new concept for His disciples, because they were still expecting an earthly kingdom as can be seen in the question asked in Acts 1:6. As established by the various epistles, this became a new concept representing a new hope for the disciples at the time, and eventually for the Church.

+ This verse seems to clearly indicate a Pretribulational Rapture. In order for the other views to be viable, the idea of going from earth to heaven has to be spiritualized because if the Rapture is denied, or the Rapture occurs simultaneously with the Second Coming, then where is Jesus talking about taking the disciples? Some believe that Jesus will return for each individual believer at death to take them to His Father's house, a teaching that is not supported by Scripture. Also, some believe that this is a reference to each believer being a part of Jesus' body (i.e. the Father's house), again, a belief without Scriptural basis.

+ The hope of this passage is one of imminency because there are no other passages that teach of any intervening events, or perquisite signs, before this particular event. If the church were to go through Daniel's 70th Week, then it seems logical that Jesus would have included such a reference to the coming time of trouble within the context of this passage. When this verse is compared to Matthew 24:15-22, we can see that Jesus has not mentioned the time of trouble in John when talking about the church, but He did mention it in reference to the Jewish nation in Matthew. Thus, missing the times of trouble becomes the hope of the Church. If the True Church is to go through Daniel's 70th Week, then there is no imminent return by Jesus Christ because we now know when He comes; therefore, there is no hope or comfort for the Church.

- Acts 1:11: As the disciples watched Jesus ascend into the heavens, they were told by the two men (angels) that the Lord would return in the same way that He departed - without warning or notice.

- 1 Corinthians 1:4-8: In his greeting to the Corinthians, Paul observes that they are waiting on Jesus Christ to be revealed in His glory to the Church at the Rapture - the day of Christ.

- Philippians 3:20: Believers, as citizens of heaven, are to await the coming of the Savior from there.

- 1 Thessalonians 1:10: Paul expresses the hope that comes from waiting for the coming of the One raised from the dead as He will deliver believers from the wrath to come.

- 1 Thessalonians 4:18: After detailing the nature of the Rapture, those dead will be resurrected and those living will be translated. Paul concludes with an exhortation to tell others about Jesus' soon return for believers and the comfort that comes from that belief. Notice that Paul continues in the epistle to describe the coming Day of the Lord (which is *after* the description of the Rapture) where he points out that the sons of the light will not suffer the wrath to come, and in that there is hope. Again, hope would not be necessary if the Church was to pass through Daniel's 70th Week.

- 1 Thessalonians 5:2-10: Paul likens the coming Day of the Lord to a thief that comes in the night and a drunkard being a creature of the night, and then he encourages believers by pointing out that they are not vulnerable to the night if they keep alert while waiting on the return of the Lord.
- 1 Thessalonians 5:6: The Thessalonians are exhorted to be alert and sober (self-controlled in the NIV), "… hardly a realistic command if the coming of Christ was greatly removed from their expectation."[12]
- Titus 2:13: Again, the promise of the happy fulfillment of the hope that believers are to wait for Jesus. If the Church is to go through Daniel's 70th Week, then this verse is now not consistent with the notion of hope and comfort that is established by other passages. It is not inconceivable that Jesus Christ will appear to His bride, the Church, to become her bridegroom at a different time than when He will appear to Israel, to become their long-awaited Messiah. The Bible records a number of signs preceding the Second Coming, but no signs for the Rapture.
- James 5:8: An exhortation to be patient in waiting for the Lord's return, which is near.
- 2 Peter 3:10: A statement that the Day of the Lord will come as a thief, therefore, if the coming of a thief is imminent then the Rapture has to be imminent as well.
- 1 John 3:1-3: While not directly related to imminency, John is looking forward to an experiential event that is yet to be revealed where believers will be purified to be as the purity of Christ.
- Book of Revelation: The Greek words used throughout the book to qualify the emphasis on time makes a case for the immediate return of Jesus Christ, and, "… these literary devices show why the church from its beginning until the present has viewed end-time events, including the coming of Christ, as something that could occur or begin to occur at any moment."[13] The following is a summary of the English translations of the Greek literary devices regarding the dimension of time[14]:
  + 1:1: With Speed.
  + 2:16; 3:11; 22:6; 22:7; 22:12; and 22:20: Quickly.
  + 1:3 and 22:10: Near.
  + 3:3 and 16:15: Use of the thief simile.
  + 1:7: He comes.
  + 2:5; 2:16; 3:11; 16:15; 22:7; 22:12; and 22:20: I am coming.

"The teaching of the coming of the Lord for the Church is always presented as an imminent event that should occupy the Christian's thought and life to a large extent. … By contrast, the exhortation to those in the Tribulation is to look for signs first and then, after the signs, to look for the return of Christ to establish His kingdom."[15]

The significance of imminency is that if it is true, then the Lord has to extract believers out of the world before the peace treaty between the Ruler to come and Israel, which is prophesied as the beginning of the seven-year period of Daniel's 70th Week. If imminency is not true, then the extraction by Christ can occur at any time during Daniel's 70th Week. However, one still has to reconcile this with other Pretribulational passages that contradict this timing, such as the fact that the Restrainer, widely believed to be the Holy Spirit, will be removed prior to the Ruler to Come coming on the scene. Then the question: How can the Holy Spirit be removed if the Church is not removed?

28.6 THE PRETRIBULATIONAL RAPTURE VIEW

THE ESSENCE AND BASIS

The Essence of Pretribulational Rapture and Posttribulational Second Coming

"The pretribulational interpretation regards the coming of the Lord and the translation of the church as preceding immediately the fulfillment of Daniels's prophecy of a final seven-year period before the Second Advent. Based on a literal interpretation of Daniel's prophecy, it is held that there has been no fulfillment of Daniel 9:27 in history and that therefore it prophesies a future period, familiarly called 'the Tribulation.' The seven years of Daniel, bringing to a close the program of Israel prior to the Second Advent, will, therefore, be fulfilled between the translation, before the seven years, Christ will return to meet the church in the air; at the Second Advent, after the seven years, it is held that Christ will return with His church from heaven to establish His millennial reign on earth."[16]

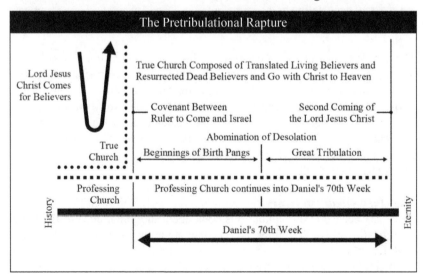

The Pretribulational Rapture

Lord Jesus Christ Comes for Believers

True Church Composed of Translated Living Believers and Resurrected Dead Believers and Go with Christ to Heaven

Covenant Between Ruler to Come and Israel

Second Coming of the Lord Jesus Christ

Abomination of Desolation

True Church

Beginnings of Birth Pangs

Great Tribulation

Professing Church

Professing Church continues into Daniel's 70th Week

History

Eternity

Daniel's 70th Week

11

"Pretribulation rapturism rests essentially on one major premise - the literal method of interpretation of the Scriptures. As a necessary adjunct to this, the pretribulationist believes in a dispensational interpretation of the Word of God. The church and Israel are two distinct groups with whom God has a divine plan. The church is a mystery, unrevealed in the Old Testament. This present mystery age intervenes with the program of God for Israel because Israel's rejection of the Messiah at His first advent. This mystery program must be completed before God can resume His program with Israel and bring it to completion."[17]

The Historical Basis
One of the reasons the Posttribulationists are fond of attacking Pretribulationalism is the idea that it is one of the newest views of the Rapture; apparently for the weak reason that if the view is new, then it is not solid, is undeveloped, or is not worthy of consideration (Posttribulationalism especially enjoys attacking John Nelson Darby, who is incorrectly held by them to be the first theologian recorded as preaching or teaching Pretribulationalism). It is unfair to expect any Biblical doctrine to have a history of completeness dating from the early church; the fact is few solid doctrines of today were fully developed at the time of the early church. Granted, the concept of Pretribulationalism was not even remotely developed at that time as it is today, however, what Posttribulationalists seem to not to realize is that their view was not developed at that time either. "It is certainly an unwarranted generalization to require a detailed and systematic Pretribulationalism as in existence for the apostolic age in order to accept the doctrine as true."[18]

Pretribulationalism is forever built around the belief that the return of Jesus Christ for His Church is imminent. If a fully developed, systematic theology of Pretribulationalism is not found as part of the early church's understandings, the constant expectation of the immediate Lord's return is found as a prominent theme of those times. Imminency is not new and it is not an unheard-of doctrine.

The simple fact is that the appeal to the historical dimension of theological development does not really provide sufficient insight into understanding what the early church writers believed to be the correct interpretation of the Scriptures. Trying to figure out a far distant, future time did not seem to be one of the more important things that needed doing. "In any event, the thesis that the early fathers were omniscient and once-for-all defined every phase of theology is an unjustified limitation on the liberty of the Spirit of God to reveal the truth of Scripture to each generation of believers."[19]

The Hermeneutical Basis
Much has been said throughout this book about the importance of the literal interpretation of the Scriptures, and the interpretation regarding the Rapture is no different. In fact, the differences in interpretation between the amillennialism and premillennialism is that amillennialism relies on the spiritualized method of

interpretation, while premillennialism relies on the literal method of interpretation - conclusions of both are radically distinctive.

There is also a radical distinction between posttribulationalism, which also relies on the spiritualized method of interpretation, and Pretribulationalism. There are two principal realms of the differences between the two views:

- Posttribulationalism sees no distinction between Israel and the Church, because in spite of the fact that there are no specific tribulation passages mentioning the Church, then the view has to spiritualize Israel to become the Church. In contrast, Pretribulationalism sees Israel and the Church as two very different institutions.
- Posttribulationalism spiritualizes Daniel's 70th Week by minimizing the severity so they can avoid a detailed exegesis. Pretribulationalism very much sees Daniel's 70th Week as a time of trouble, as the world has never seen, and holds literally to the way it is described in the Bible.

The Imminency of the Rapture

As was discussed above, the Pretribulational Rapture view is the only one that is based on the imminent return of Jesus Christ. All the other views have to eliminate the doctrine of imminency in order to establish their theology.

28.7 THE PRETRIBULATIONAL RAPTURE VIEW AND THE DAY OF THE LORD

One of the ways we learn the details about a topic is to contrast that topic with another corresponding and related perspective. Therefore, Pretribulational Rapture View will be discussed and contrasted with the Posttribulational Rapture View in order to establish the details and understanding of the Pretribulational Rapture View.

IS THE RAPTURE IN MATTHEW 13?

Posttribulationalism: Some see a reference to the Rapture because some of the parables describe judgments and separations of the unrighteous from the righteous.

Pretribulationalism: The parables are descriptive of the nature of this present age as it stands in contrast to the kingdom to come, and do not refer to the Rapture.

IS THE RAPTURE IN MATTHEW 24 - 25?

The interpretation of this significant passage is a major factor in determining one's view of the Rapture and Daniel's 70th Week. The Olivet Discourse is unparalleled in the prophetic importance of requiring an accurate interpretation. "A careful study of Matthew 24 - 25 will reveal that the subject matter is the end of the age,

13

and the age in view is the same as that of Matthew 13, namely, the whole period between the first and second advents of Christ. This is brought out in the exegesis of the passage itself, describing as it does the general course of the present age, culminating in the Great Tribulation and the second coming of Christ."[20]

Contemporary Posttribulationalism, who do not give Israel its rightful place in God's Plan, finds the Rapture mentioned in the following passages:
- Matthew 24:31:
    + Posttribulationalism: Because of descriptive similarities with some of Paul's writings in 1 and 2 Thessalonians, the gathering of the elect (remember they substitute the Church for Israel) is equated with the Rapture.
    + Pretribulationalism: This is a reference to the regathering of Israel for judgment after the Second Advent of Christ, and also, neither translation nor resurrections are mentioned.
- Matthew 24:40-41:
    + Posttribulationalism: Because of the similarity with the separation of the wicked from the righteous in judgment at the time of Noah and the Flood, the belief is that this is also a reference to the separation of the wicked from the righteous in judgment at the Rapture.
    + Pretribulationalism: Those taken away in the in judgment to die in the flood, those that were left behind were the righteous. In this passage the same is true - those taken away are taken in judgment, those that are left are the righteous. In order for this to apply to the Rapture, those left behind would have to be left for judgment, which is not true of the context of this passage. "At the second coming of Christ, indeed, many will be taken in judgment and some will be left to enter the millennial kingdom. This is exactly the opposite of what happens at the Rapture."[21]
    + Luke 17:34-37: This passage puts to bed, so to speak, the notion of being taken away as being taken in Rapture, because it teaches that those taken are taken to another place for judgment - the verse paints the picture that they are dead and are surrounded by vultures.
- Matthew 25:31-46: Posttribulationalism avoids this passage because it so explicitly establishes the separation of the wicked, the goats, from the righteous, the sheep, immediately after the Second Coming of Christ (however, some move this judgment to the end of the Millennium, which is a violation of the what the passage states, that is, that the judgment will occur when Christ comes). The purpose of avoidance is that if the Rapture occurs at the same time as the Second Coming, who is taken and who is left behind if the goats and sheep judgment occurs within a short time later? Who is left to be judged if a Posttribulational Rapture removes the righteous?

THE IMPLICATION OF RAPTURE IN JOHN 14:1-3

Core Scripture: John 14:1-3

Posttribulationalism: This is another passage that is avoided because it does not support this view. Some will spiritualize this by saying that the Father's House is Christ's Body and the coming to get is a reference to coming to faith in Christ. Posttribulationalism has to deny this passage because it the Rapture that is immediately before the Second Coming, and only the righteous will enter into the Millennial Kingdom, then there is no need for a separate "house" in heaven.

This passage is not held by many to be a reference to Christ coming to take individual believers to heaven at the point of their own personal death, not does the context favor this perspective.

Pretribulationalism: This is a major supporting Scripture:
- "… John's record of the statement of Christ in the upper room the night before His crucifixion is taken by many to be the first clear mention of the Rapture from a chronological point of view."[22]
- The event described by this passage stands in significant contrast to the Coming of Christ described in Matthew 24:27-30, and seems to describe a much different event. Because of the reference to the Father's house, translation of those living at the time, and resurrection of those dead at the time, is implied.
- These verses seem to be clear that there will come a day in which Jesus Christ will come and snatch away His children and carry them to another place that He has been preparing for them since the first time He was on earth, so that they are in His presence as well as the Father's presence.

THE RAPTURE IN 1 THESSALONIANS 4

The Book of 1 Thessalonians is unique among the passages dealing with the Rapture. It contributes more to the Pretribulational view of the Rapture than any other New Testament book, yet it is a thorn in the side of Posttribulationalism because they do not know what to do with what is stated, therefore, it is generally ignored.

The Rapture as an Imminent Event
The Book of 1 Thessalonians definitely emphasizes we are waiting for the imminent return of the Lord Jesus Christ as can be seen in the following passages:
- 1:10: Paul recognizes that the Thessalonians were diligent in waiting on the Lord to return, and also, points out that when the Lord does come, He will deliver them from the coming wrath.
- 2:19-20: Paul expresses the joy he will feel when he and the Thessalonians will stand before the Lord at some time in the future.

- 3:13: Paul indicates that as the Thessalonians love one another they will be strengthened in holiness for when they stand before God the Father as Christ returns with them from earth after to Rapture.
- 5:23: Paul summarizes his desires for the Thessalonians and prays that their spirits, souls, and bodies will be kept blameless in anticipation of the Lord's Coming.

THE COMFORTING HOPE OF 1 THESSALONIANS 4:13-18

Core Scripture: 1 Thessalonians 4:13-18

This is the first of two major Biblical passages (the other being 1 Corinthians 15:51-58) that establishes a Pretribulational Rapture that addresses the question as to if "… those who had died in Christ would have the same benefits and experience as those that were translated."[23]

Pretribulationalism
The setting of the Thessalonians was that they were probably relatively new to the faith, they did not have written Scriptures for reference other than the various letters in circulation at the time, and they did have what had been previously taught them by Paul, Silas, and Timothy. They seemed to have an awareness of the imminency of Jesus' Coming because they were concerned about the destiny of their believing friends and relatives that had recently died. They apparently knew of the resurrection of the dead associated with the Lord's return, as well as the translation of the living when the Lord returned, but what they did not seem to understand was the relationship between the resurrection and the translation as discussed in 1 Thessalonians:

- 4:13: Paul wanted the Thessalonians to completely understand what would happen to those that had previously died and those that would be alive when Jesus Christ came to gather the members of His body. Paul did not want them to be ignorant of these spiritual matters as those that were not of the faith.
- 4:14: For as Jesus' death and resurrection was a certainty, it was also just as much a certainty that Jesus would return for them and He would bring with Him from heaven the souls of those believers that had already died. What was once a prophecy was now fulfilled and formed the basis of their faith.
- 4:15-16: Paul instructed them that when Christ comes from heaven, he would bring with Him the souls of those that had previously died. As Jesus said in John 5:25, when He comes, He will come with commanding authority to raise dead believers by the sound of His shouting voice. The voice of the archangel will sound representing victory over death for the many, and the trumpet of God will call signaling the importance

of the event. Then, the resurrection of the physical bodies of the dead will occur, and the bodies will be rejoined with their respective souls, to form new, immortal beings.

- 4:17: After the resurrection of the dead, those living at the time will be translated instantly into new immoral bodies and souls. Finally, all that are resurrected, and all that are translated will rise to meet the Lord Jesus Christ in the clouds, and from that point on, believers will be with the Lord forever.
- 4:18: Paul concluded with a command to comfort one another with the hope of this glorious future.

Notice that Paul's description of this event is imminent, and is without any mention of preceding events being necessary.

A major strength of this passage is that it contains descriptions of the two essential aspects necessary for the Rapture - the translation of the living in Christ, and the resurrection of the dead in Christ - distinctive and differing events that occur simultaneously.

Posttribulationalism
The pretribulational view is based on the belief that the Thessalonians were afraid that they would not see their loved ones who had previously died until the dead were resurrected after Daniel's 70th Week (the Thessalonians believed that the living would be translated when the Lord returned imminently before the wrath came, but the resurrection of the dead would be delayed until after Daniel's 70th Week). The Posttribulational Rapture view is that if the Rapture occurs immediately before the Second Coming, then the fear the Thessalonians felt for their loved ones would be because the loved ones would not be seen until after the Millennium. This is not supportable by Scripture because there is no evidence that the Thessalonians were even aware of the idea of a thousand-year Millennium. It seems logical that if the Thessalonians had to go through Daniel's 70th Week, as Posttribulationalism says, they would have been more concerned with the wrath to come instead of when they would see their deceased loved ones.

Posttribulationalism takes its support for the Rapture after Daniel's 70th Week from the phrase *will come down* in 1 Thessalonians 4:16, meaning that Jesus Christ will make a complete, uninterrupted descent, stopping in the air in route to receive the Church unto Himself, but then continuing on to earth. The passage says nothing about Jesus' descent continuing on to earth, however, when confronted with this point, Posttribulationalism argues that the Bible is silent about it. Why can it be silent about Jesus continuing straight on to earth and it be a reasonable interpretation, but it is not reasonable if the Bible is silent about Jesus turning, and going back to heaven?

Also, why do the saints have to leave the earth, just to immediately return to earth with Jesus (why the trip up into the air then back to earth)? Posttribulationalism argues that those that go to meet Jesus in the air is a delegation sent to meet Him much as in antiquity, delegates went out to meet returning kings and then escorted them back to the city. Again, the text says nothing like this, and, Posttribulationalism does not have an adequate answer for this question. There is no need for such a gathering in the air if Posttribulationalism is the correct view.

This passage is an embarrassment to Posttribulationalism, "… because in none of the accounts of resurrection related to the second coming of Christ is any translation of living saints mentioned."[24] After the Rapture, all the resurrections that follow (the tribulation saints in Revelation 20:4, and, the Old Testament saints in Daniel 12:2) are immediately after the Second Coming, and they mention nothing about the translation of any of the body of Christ.

This passage is the only passage in which a translation is to occur at the same time as a resurrection occurs. If Posttribulationalism is correct, and they acknowledge a translation occurring at some time then how do they account for this since there is no mention of a translation at the same time as any of the other resurrections? Why is it that this is the only time of resurrection in which there is mention of a translation of living saints?

How is 1 Thessalonians 4:18 to be explained if the Church is to experience Daniel's 70th Week? Why would Paul encourage the Thessalonians to be comforted and to comfort one another, if they would not be raptured until they had gone through the horrors of Daniel's 70th Week?

If the Thessalonians had believed that they were to go through Daniel's 70th Week and that most of them would be martyred, it is reasonable to expect them to be joyful that their loved ones that had previously died would not have to experience Daniel's 70th Week; why is nothing said about that?

This passage in 1 Thessalonians is a major problem for Posttribulationalism to explain.

THE RAPTURE AND THE DAY OF THE LORD IN 1 THESSALONIANS 5

Core Scripture: 1 Thessalonians 5:1-11

This section of Scripture, that immediately follows the strongest evidence in the Bible for a Pretribulational Rapture, presents interesting problems yearning for resolution. "The center of the problem is, first of all, the question of what the "the Day of the Lord" means. A second question is why the day of the Lord is introduced immediately after discussion of the Rapture. A third question is the meaning of specific statements relating to the time of the Rapture."[25] Instead of telling the Thessalonians that the Rapture would occur at the end of the time of distress, Paul describes the day of the Lord, and suggests that its beginning is tied to the Rapture. He also indicated that the time of beginning is uncertain by using the 'thief in the night' metaphor.

The Meaning of the Day of the Lord

There is an extensive group of references to the Day of the Lord in the Old Testament yet a small number in the New Testament. When all are analyzed, the following categorizations surface[26]:

- Generally, the Day of the Lord refers to any period in the past or the future when God directly judges human sin. Examples would include Old Testament instances of judgment.
- The narrower sense of the definition would be certain specific future events. The best example is 2 Thessalonians 2, as will be seen below.
- The broader sense of the definition would be when God deals with the full spectrum of the human situation, both in judgment and in blessing. The best example is the passage under consideration.

The analysis also reveals that the use of the word 'day' is symbolic in many instances. The time period involved may be a single, twenty-four-hour period, or it may refer to an extended period of time lasting many centuries.

In some instances, like the passage under consideration, the article 'the' is not found, therefore, the phrase could be interpreted as 'a' Day of the Lord. This is especially true when there are past Day of the Lord occurrences.

There are many references to the day of 'something,' and we have to let the context determine if any day of 'something' is really a Day of the Lord. Not every mention of the word 'day' is referring to a Day of the Lord. Posttribulationalism tends to be guilty of this hermeneutic violation. Whenever 'the,' or 'a,' Day of the Lord is used, it is done so to describe an event, or series of events, that occurs in a sequential pattern that is similar to the twenty-four-hour (hence the use of the term day) sequence of events in the life of a human being.

Under the symbolism of a day, Pretribulationalism sees the Day of the Lord, in which God will judge human sin, as beginning as soon as the Rapture closes the day of grace.

As previously discussed, many prophecies have a near fulfillment (partially fulfilled in the context of the time the prophecy is given) and a far fulfillment (more completely fulfilled at some event of the distant future).

The Old Testament Doctrine of the Day of the Lord
There are many passages in the Old Testament that provide details of the divine judgments of the Day of the Lord.

- Isaiah:
  - + 2:12-21: The prophets describe a time in which pride, arrogance, things considered of value, and things considered the strength of humankind will be judged by God. Yet at this same time the Lord alone will be exalted, as the wicked try to escape His dreadful judgment. This judgment could be in reference to ancient captivities, or it could be applied to future judgments awaiting fulfillment. It is clear that the time of this day is longer than a twenty-four-hour span.
  - + 13:9-16: This passage paints a sorrowful picture coming for sinners and unbelievers. That day will be a day of judgment, cruelty, and savage, raging anger by the Lord as He punishes the evil world. The earth will be destroyed and there will also be heavenly, cosmic events as well. The fury of the Lord will again bring down those that are prideful and arrogant. This could be said to have been fulfilled to some extent since the verses that follow this passage refer to the destruction of the Jewish nation by the Medes. However, as indicated above, it could also refer to future judgments in which the prophecy is more completely fulfilled.
  - + 34:1-8: Because of His furious anger with all nations, God will take His revenge by judging and then annihilating them. The dead will remain unburied, the heavenly elements will change, and much blood will be shed.
- Joel:
  - + 1:15 - 2:11, 28-32: Almost the entire Book of Joel is about the Day of the Lord. In this passage, Joel talks about how food and water become scarce to non-existent, and the means to produce food goes away. Then an army, or possibly locusts as mentioned in Joel 1, will come and devastate everything in front of them. Eventually the Lord will pour out His Spirit on all. In Acts 2:17-21, Peter acknowledges that on that day of Pentecost, portions of Joel's prophecy were being fulfilled.
  - + 3:9-12: Joel calls the armies of the nations to assemble to meet the judgment of the Lord on that day.
- Amos 5:18-20: Amos responds to those that call for the Day of the Lord to come by advising them of how terrible it will be, how it will not be escapable, and how death and destruction will be common.
- Obadiah 15-17: The prophet points out that on that day, whatever was done by one nation will be done to them in return.
- Zephaniah 1:7-18: The day of judgment is described as a sacrificial meal. Included will be the punishment of the wicked and their wealth and possessions will not buy anything, and there will be terrible destruction.

Why is the Day of the Lord Introduced After the Rapture in this Passage?

It is believed that this portion of Scripture is the beginning of a new subject, but it still has a connection with the previous portion about the Rapture. The two subjects seem to be distinguished from each other, as one is not referring to the other, yet they are complementary of each other. This portion of 1 Thessalonians is about eschatological aspects of the end times and both parts are companions of the bigger context.

- 5:1: Paul indicates that it is not necessary for him to tell the Thessalonians about some aspects of the Day of the Lord; the implication is that they already know of some of the details as apparently the Day of the Lord is not a new idea to them. The use of the world 'times' suggest duration, while the use of the word 'dates' suggests a particular time. See adjacent table of word

1 Thessalonians 5:1	
NIV	*dates*
NASB	*epochs*
NET	*seasons*
KJV	*times and the seasons*
NKJV	*seasons*
AMP	*seasons and dates*

comparison of several translations. Both are interchangeable and since two words are used, the idea is a reference to the multiple eschatological events that comprise the bigger program, with the Rapture and the Day of the Lord being two of the many.
- 5:2: As indicated above, the use of the metaphor 'thief in the night' is a reference to the fact that the date of the coming is not known nor is it predictable.
- 5:3: The reference to an existing 'peace and security' before the travail seems consistent with the peace that exists in Israel during the first half of Daniel's 70th Week, and could be 'the calm before the storm.' Then the storm comes, in the same developing sequence, surprising speed and growing severity as the delivery process comes over a pregnant woman - an event that is not escapable.
- 5:4-5: However, Paul points out the Thessalonian will not be overtaken like a thief in the night because they know it is coming, therefore they are expecting the event. They do not belong to the night, so the coming thief is not surprising to them because they belong to the day that precedes the darkness. This has much to do with understanding God's Plan for humanity, which apparently the Thessalonians had the benefit of having been previously taught by Paul.
- 5:6-8: Paul then describes the contrast between those that are part of the night, the wicked, and those that belong to the day, the righteous.
- 5:9: Here, Paul states that the believer in Christ is not destined for the coming wrath of God - the thief cannot overtake the Church because the Church will not be here to be overtaken. This is a strong statement of support for the Pretribulational view for the Rapture, its coming is imminent, and it is a period of time rather than a specific event.

21

- 5:10: Paul adds the Gospel message to the paragraph to round out the distinctions that characterizes those that will not face the coming wrath.
- 5:11: Again, as in verses 4:18, Paul encourages the Thessalonians to comfort one another in the knowledge that they will not be present for the wrath.

The Posttribulational Interpretation of the Day of the Lord

Generally, Posttribulationalism puts the Day of the Lord at the extreme end of Daniel's 70th Week immediately before the Second Coming. In order to justify this arrangement, the Church is said to still not go through the wrath of God, because the wrath of God is removed from Daniel's 70th Week and placed as a very short period of time immediately before the Second Coming. Even a casual reading of the Book of Revelation reveals that the recorded judgments are so severe and terrible that the Day of the Lord must extend over the entire Great Tribulation. "The promise to be kept from wrath, accordingly, is a promise to be kept from the future time of wrath, that is, the Great Tribulation. It is characteristic of Posttribulationalists that, while they must take the church through the Tribulation, they try to eliminate it as a time of wrath, especially as a time of divine wrath, and usually minimize the effect of this on the saints."[27]

- As a means of apparently justifying their view, Posttribulationalism accuses Pretribulationalism of appealing to the emotions of people by stressing that believers will avoid the tribulation of Daniel's 70th Week if they believe the Pretribulational view. It is not what believers want; it is what the Scriptures say? Nevertheless, why should Pretribulation lists be ashamed of wanting to avoid a terrible time such as the Great Tribulation, which the Bible says is a judgment that is unprecedented? The hope to avoid the Great Tribulation is not unlike the hope to avoid hell.
- Denial of Divine Wrath in the Great Tribulation:
  + Posttribulationalism goes to great lengths to make the Great Tribulation a time of satanic wrath only because they deny that it is a time of divine wrath. If this denial can be made, the severity of the Great Tribulation is watered down and weakened, and, as the Church goes through this time, it can be said that the Church is experiencing satanic wrath only and not God's divine wrath. The attempt by Posttribulationalism to reduce the amount of suffering by the saints during the Great Tribulation is a false assumption that is not supported by Scripture.
  + Even if the premise is supportable by Scripture, what makes Posttribulationalism think that satanic wrath alone makes believers comforted in the knowledge that they do not have to face divine wrath. Ask Job if the wrath of Satan made him feel less severely afflicted. The notion that the absence of divine wrath would make believers feel less travail during the Great Tribulation is absurd.
  + In response, the following passages establish that it is a time of satanic wrath and divine wrath that extends over the entire three and one-half years of the Great Tribulation, which is the second half of Daniel's 70th Week:

- o Satanic Wrath: The fact that satanic wrath is present during the Great Tribulation is not disputed as can be seen by the following:
  - Revelation:
    - 6:9-11: This passage tells of the tribulation saints martyred by Satan during Daniel's 70th Week, which indicates that the satanic wrath will be the persecution of the tribulation saints. Posttribulationalism tries to make the believers in this passage to be members of the Church, however, the context of the passage indicates they are saints that have been martyred during Daniel's 70th Week.
    - 7:9-17: This is another reference to the martyrs of the satanic persecution of tribulation saints. In the effort to reduce tribulation suffering by the saints, Posttribulationalism moves this passage out of the Great Tribulation into the eternal state - a move that has no Scriptural support at all. Another reason for moving this passage is that if the Church enters Daniel's 70th Week, then there is a strong possibility that a large number will be martyred, and if so, then the Church does not really go through Daniel's 70th Week.
    - 12:12: Satan is thrown out of heaven down to the earth (12:9) and is filled with terrible anger.
  - o Divine Wrath: The Posttribulational belief that divine wrath is not present during the Great Tribulation is contrary to the Scriptures, as can be seen by the following:
    - Revelation 6:16: Even though the first mention of the wrath of God in this verse (actually it says *the wrath of the Lamb*) does not occur until the Sixth Seal is opened, the verses before this, beginning at 6:1, record other devastating divine judgments - war, famine, death, and martyrdom.
    - "It is clear ... from the nature of the judgments poured out that these last three and one-half years are also a time of divine wrath on earth. This is evident by the disturbances in heaven, great earthquakes, and the catastrophes described under the trumpet judgments and the bowl judgments."[28]
- + Posttribulationalism states that God's wrath, which is poured out on the world between the translation of the Church (and the Second Coming, takes place over a short period of time of unspecified length. Pretribulationalism disagrees with this view and holds that the judgments given in the Book of Revelation cannot possibly take place in as short a period of time as suggested by Posttribulationalism. We know from Daniel 9:27 that the Abomination of Desolation occurs at the middle of Daniel's 70th Week, and in Matthew 24:15-28, Jesus Christ Himself specifies that the Abomination of Desolation begins the time in which *... there will be great distress, unequaled from the beginning of the*

world until now – and never to be equaled again (Matthew 24:21), therefore, the Great Tribulation has to be at least three and one-half years in length.

+   Assume for a moment for the sake of argument that the Church does go through the entire seven years of Daniel's 70th Week, because of the scope and severity of the seal, trumpet, and bowl judgments, which does not distinguish between believers and non-believers, it is extremely improbable that all members of the Church could survive all of the horrendous events that take place - surely some would have to fall victim to some of the catastrophes that are said to occur by the Book of Revelation. "A major problem with Posttribulationists is that they must get the church through the Tribulation relatively unscathed, but the only way they can do this is to deny or ignore the plain teachings of the Book of Revelation ..."[29]

"If pretribulationists are right that the Great Tribulation is a time of divine wrath and 1 Thessalonians 5 promises that Christians will not enter the time of divine wrath, it is an express refutation of posttribulationalism."[30]

THE RAPTURE AND DANIEL'S 70th WEEK IN 2 THESSALONIANS 1:5-10

Core Scripture: 2 Thessalonians 1:5-10

A common theme of both letters to the Thessalonians is that they were undergoing much persecution during their times, and in the passage Paul is assuring them that the believers will someday be rewarded, and the persecuted will be punished.

Posttribulationalism uses this passage to say that the Thessalonians would be delivered from their persecution at the end of Daniel's 70th Week, and that this passage is evidence against Pretribulationalism. Since the Thessalonians died prior to either the Rapture or Daniel's 70th Week, Posttribulationalism then says that they are symbolic of the last generation of believers that will live through Daniel's 70th Week.

The Pretribulational view is that God will punish the persecutors in His own time. The Thessalonians will be raised from the dead at the Rapture and will participate in the various Body of Christ events, however, their persecutors will not be resurrected until the end of the Millennium, at which time they will be judged and then cast into the lake of fire.

With all due respect to the Posttribulationalists, this passage makes no contribution to the debate over Daniel's 70th Week.

THE RAPTURE AND THE DAY OF THE LORD IN 2 THESSALONIANS 2:1-12

Core Scripture: 2 Thessalonians 2:1-12

This particular passage is claimed by both Posttribulationalism and Pretribulationalism as supporting their respective Rapture views, and, the interpretation is further complicated because many other end time activities are included in the verses, so how these events are viewed could help or hinder the interpretation. "The only reason posttribulationalists bring up this passage is that it is a major proof for pretribulationalism and, as such, needs to be refuted by posttribulationalism."[31]

The Posttribulationalism view is that 2 Thessalonians specifically places the Great Tribulation before the Rapture, and it deals with the Day of the Lord as it relates to one of its primary actors - the man of lawlessness.

- 2:1-2: Apparently the Thessalonians were being falsely taught that the Day of the Lord had already arrived and that the Church was going through it (there is evidence that Posttribulationalism was taught in the early Church, and, as is true with this letter, many of Paul's letters are intended to correct doctrinal errors of the early Church), therefore, Paul exhorted them to not be so easily persuaded away from what he had taught them earlier about the Rapture preceding the Day of the Lord. Notice that Paul was essentially disputing Posttribulationalism in this passage.
- 2:3: Paul proceeds to identify the focus of their anxiety (they were in the Day of Lord) as false doctrine and then reiterates true doctrine by telling the Thessalonians that the following two things must happen before the Day of the Lord can come. Paul is essentially saying that they should not be deceived because there is no evidence that either of these two things have occurred, and that they are also the signs that have to be fulfilled in order for the Day of the Lord to occur.

2 Thessalonians 2:3 – First to Come		2 Thessalonians 2:3 – Second to Come	
NIV	*the rebellion*	NIV	*the man of lawlessness*
NASB	*the apostasy*	NASB	*the man of lawlessness*
NET	*the rebellion*	NET	*the man of lawlessness*
KJV	*a falling away*	KJV	*the man of sin*
NKJV	*the falling away*	NKJV	*the man of sin*
AMP	*the apostasy*	AMP	*the man of lawlessness*

- 2:4: Paul describes the activities of the man of lawlessness.
- 2:5: A reference to what Paul had previously taught the Thessalonians.
- 2:6-8: Paul tells the Thessalonians that whatever is holding the man of lawlessness back has to be taken away before the he can be revealed and the Day of the Lord can begin.

25

- 2:9-12: The things in these verses will be covered in other Chapters:
  + There is much division among Posttribulationalists about the identity of the restrainer, all of the following have been suggested: God, the Antichrist, Satan, the Roman Empire, the government itself, and finally, in agreement with the Pretribulationalists, some believe it is the Holy Spirit.
  + "Pretribulationalists generally hold that if the Holy Spirit is removed from His present state indwelling the church, then the church itself must also be removed, and hence the Rapture must take place at the same time. ... If this removal of the Holy Spirit in the church takes place *before* the lawless one can be revealed, it points to an event that must precede the Tribulation."[32]

"Paul taught in 2 Thessalonians 2 the important fact that the man of sin, or the lawless one, cannot be revealed as such until the Rapture, that is, the removal of the church indwelt by the Holy Spirit."[33]

THE RAPTURE IN 1 CORINTHIANS 15:51-58

Core Scripture: 1 Corinthians 15:51-58

This is the second of the two major Biblical passages (the other being 1 Thessalonians 4:13-18) that establishes a Pretribulational Rapture that addresses the question as to it "... those who are translated will have the same experience and benefits as those who have died and who are resurrected."[34]

This passage provides strong support for the Pretribulationalism view. Posttribulationalism only deals with this passage in order to refute it being used by Pretribulationalism, it contributes nothing to their own view. After having presented the aspects of the resurrection earlier in 1 Corinthians 15 prior to this passage, Paul indicates that the translation of believers at the time of the Rapture is the only exception to the normal rule of death followed by resurrection as further recorded in 1 Corinthians 15:
- 15:51: Paul presents the idea that it is a mystery (a truth not revealed in the Old Testament) that there will not be death for a generation of believers, but instead they will be translated into immortal beings in an instant. Posttribulationalism agrees with Pretribulationalism that translation is a mystery, but because the Old Testament clearly teaches that the resurrection of the dead is not a mystery, then they ask why the Rapture is a mystery. They continue by saying that the time of the Rapture is not important, but it is the fact of the Rapture that is important.
- 15:52: Posttribulationalism wants to identify the sounding of the trumpet in this verse with the seventh trumpet of Revelation 11:15 and the loud trumpet blast of Matthew 24:31. Most see these as three entirely different

events. "In Revelation, the trumpets relate to the judgments and events of the end time and are declared to be trumpets of angels. For the most part, they relate to the unsaved world. The great trumpet of Matthew 24:31 deals with the saints of all ages who are assembled at the time of the second coming of Christ, but it says nothing of either resurrection of translation, though for some resurrection may be involved."[35] Posttribulationalism does not have Scriptural support for all three trumpet blasts to be the same thing.

- 15:52-55: An interesting characteristic of this passage is that these three verses do something that no other Biblical passage regarding the Rapture does - there are references to both translation and to resurrection in the same passage. Paul is saying that those that are translated and those that are resurrected are given the same immortal, imperishable, eternal bodies. Paul goes on to point out that the translation of the Church and the resurrection of dead believers will be a partial (in the sense that not all of the dead will be resurrected) fulfillment of Isaiah 25:8 and Hosea 13:14.

- 15:58: "The doctrine of the Rapture, whenever mentioned in the Bible, is always related to practical application. In John 14:2, it is to the point that we should not be troubled in view of the coming of the Lord. In 1 Thessalonians 4, it is a comforting or encouraging hope. ... Here the Rapture is used as an exhortation to us to be faithful, standing firm in our faith, letting nothing move us, and giving ourselves at all times fully to the work of the Lord."[36]

THE RAPTURE IN THE BOOK OF REVELATION

The Book of Revelation serves a unique purpose in the Bible. While the Gospels relate the events of, and the historical significance of, Christ's First Advent, the Book of Revelation anticipates Christ's Second Advent and specifies what will happen before, during and after blessed event. Posttribulationalism has great difficulty with this book because nowhere is the Rapture after Daniel's 70th Week mentioned; in fact quite the opposite is true as the apparent emphasis is that the Church is not present during the various seal, trumpet, and bowl judgments. It would seem crucial that if Posttribulationalism is the correct view, that the Book of Revelation would contain at least some, if not considerable detail about the experiences of the Church during the time and that the descriptions of Christ's Second Coming would at least mention it, however, neither translation nor resurrection (in the sense of the Rapture) are mentioned at all. "There is absolutely nothing in Revelation 19 – 20 to support the idea that there is a rapture of the church involved in the second-coming process."[37] In spite of the fact that the book is not really about the Rapture, there are some passages in the book of Revelation that supports and harmonizes with the Pretribulational view as will be seen below, and the best that Posttribulationalism can do, as is done with so many other passages supporting Pretribulationalism, is to attack those passages supporting Pretribulationalism, and attempts to argue away the support they provide.

- 2:25: While not specific enough to be justified as significant, this verse could support Pretribulationalism.
- 3:10-11: In the message to the Church at Philadelphia, Christ makes no condemnation of them because the Church has stood firm on their faith and have not succumbed to the world. Because of this faithfulness in Jesus Christ, they will not have to face the hour of testing of Daniel's 70th Week.
    + Posttribulationalism: As is common with many Posttribulational interpretations, they hold that the meaning of the Greek word that is translated as 'from' in verse 10, means 'out from within', therefore, when coupled with the word 'keep' they create the meaning 'of keep out from within'. Because of this interpretation, the view can then be articulated to mean that the Church will not be raptured before the Great Tribulation, but it will be protected from the terrible events of the time. So rather than using the word in its literal interpretation, this view changes its meaning to serve the purpose of placing the Rapture after the Great Tribulation. It seems logical that if John wanted to say that the Church went through Daniel's 70th Week, he would have chosen other previews to communicate that fact, however, he did not.
    + Pretribulationalism: This passage is not as strong for Pretribulationalism as many believe. The essence of concern is if Christ's letter is addressed to the specific Church at Philadelphia, or is it addressed to the Church at large? When the letter was written, the church at Philadelphia was in the midst of Roman persecution, and the promise could be that they would be kept from that particular persecution. The argument however, is that the Bible says they will be kept from the 'time' of persecution, rather than from a particular persecution; the sense of the verse seems to rule out the Roman persecution of their time. "While this passage may not be decisively in support of pretribulationism, it offers no support at all for posttribulationism and is another source of embarrassment."[38]
- 5:8-10: The identity of the twenty-four elders is controversial because it is not clear as to if the elders are part of the angelic group, or it they are Raptured believers.
    + One View: They are men because they refer to themselves as the redeemed, as seen in the KJV. This view is given some validity because in verse 4:4, the elders are in white clothing and have golden crowns on their heads, implying that they have already been Raptured, judged, and rewarded. Pretribulationalism believes it provides no support for Posttribulationalism.
    + Another View: They are angelic beings because they refer to the saved in the third person, as seen in the NASB, NIV, and NET.
- 6 – 18: As indicated already, this point is a major asset to Pretribulationalism, but a major liability for Posttribulationalism, mainly because there is a total absence of mention anywhere with these chapters of a local Church or of a universal Church. If Posttribulationalism is true, surely the Church would

have been mentioned in the portion of the Bible that tells about the things the Church would have to either endure, or be protected from, depending on which Posttribulational views is held. This issue cannot be ignored, nor does changing the meaning of words cover this fact.

- 7:1-8 and 14:1-5:
  - Yet again, this is another passage in which the interpretation depends on one's view on the nation of Israel and the Church.
    - Posttribulationalism: This view tends to spiritualize this passage and replaces Israel with the Church and makes the 144,000 representatives of the Church instead of Israel. This is done so that the Church can be said to go through Daniel's 70th Week. This twist has no Scriptural merit at all.
    - Pretribulationalism: This view sees Israel and the Church with distinct entities and destinies, and sees the 144,000 as saved Jews. Again, the Church is not seen in Daniel's 70th week as described in Revelation 4 - 18.
  - Taken in its proper context, Revelation 7:1-8 pictures twelve tribes of Israel miraculously preserved through the Great Tribulation because the Church is not seen in Daniel's 70th Week as described in Revelation 4 – 18.
- 12: This chapter indicates that the nation of Israel, *the woman*, is the object of Satan's fury because she produced Jesus Christ, *the child*, which was to eventually defeat Satan and set His own rule of the world. The Church must be gone during the Great Tribulation, otherwise why would Satan attack unrepentant Israel when the Church would be available for him to persecute. Why attack Israel, the sense of their condition is that they are apostate during the time of testing because one of the purposes of Daniel's 70th Week is to prepare Israel for the reception of Jesus Christ. "The reason Satan turns against Israel can only be explained by the absence of the church from that scene."[39]
- Armageddon in Relation to the Rapture:
  - Posttribulationalism sometimes adopts a strange interpretation of the sequence of events that can only be necessary in order to (desperately?) prevent Posttribulationalism from being proven false. As indicated in the 1 Thessalonians 5 discussions above regarding the Day of the Lord, Posttribulationalism places the Day of the Lord, a time of God's wrath, after the Great Tribulation, a time of Satan's wrath, in order to justify the Church going through Daniel's 70th Week so that it can be a Posttribulational Rapture. The Day of the Lord would begin with the Battle of Armageddon, therefore the Church would have to be raptured immediately before the battle in order to escape God's wrath. The problem here is that many theologians and scholars place the sixth bowl, the battle of Armageddon, late in the Great Tribulation and immediately before the Second Coming. The Posttribulational view would have all of the seal, trumpet, and up to the fifth bowl

> judgment as not being part of the *great suffering unlike anything that has happened from the beginning of the world*, Matthew 24:21.
>
> + Pretribulationalism holds that the Rapture occurs prior to the beginning of Daniel's 70th Week and the seal, trumpet, and bowl judgments happen in the order shown in the Book of Revelation, with the battle of Armageddon occurring just before the Lord sets foot on earth for the Second Coming.

- 19:1-10: This passage is the announcement of the wedding feast between the Lamb and His bride, and contains descriptions of the events in heaven prior to the feast, and includes a description of the bride. In Jewish culture a wedding had three parts:
    + First, the arrangement of the marriage between the parents of the bride and the bridegroom.
    + Second, the bridegroom coming to claim the bride.
    + Third, the celebration of the wedding feast.
- The Pretribulational view is that at this point in the Book of Revelation, the first and second parts of the wedding have taken place and the third part is pending; as can be seen the announcement is occurring immediately before Christ's Second Coming. Posttribulationalism simply casts this interpretation aside without sufficient explanation except to say there is a misapplication of the use of metaphors.
- 19:11 - 20:6: The significance of this description of the Premillennial Lord's Second Coming accompanied by the saints and angels in relation to the Rapture is that it supports Pretribulationalism, and provides no support for Posttribulationalism, because in all of this description, there is absolutely no mention of a translation or resurrection of believers from the dispensation of grace. Those resurrected in Revelation 20:4-5 are the tribulation saints, and the event probably occurs several days after the Second Coming.

"When all this evidence is put together, one must conclude that in the most comprehensive and detailed account to be found anywhere in the Bible of the second coming of Christ, there is no resurrection or translation mentioned as an event occurring in the Second Coming itself. The Posttribulational Rapture, which should have been a prominent feature in the Book of Revelation if it were indeed a part of the great climax of the second coming of Christ, is totally missing in the narrative."[40]

28.8	THE RAPTURE AND AN EARLY MEDIEVAL CITATION

One of the oft-debated aspects of the Rapture question concerns what the Church of the early centuries believed and taught about the removal of the Church prior to, during, or after the time of great distress. There is a tendency for each Rapture view to attempt to claim the early Church as among their respective view. It is the contention of this book that the early Church probably did not have a sophisticated doctrine of the Rapture, but instead were only aware that Jesus Christ would come again at any moment. Thus, the belief that was apparently present was the belief that the early Church may have had, and it is found within a sermon of the Middle Ages written by Pseudo-Ephraem titled "On the Last Times, the Antichrist, and the End of the World" or "Sermon on the End of the World", written sometime between the fourth and seventh centuries.

Contemporary critics are quick to attack Pretribulationalism on the basis that the view is of recent origin, primarily since the early 1800s. As indicated above, this is a weak argument and as far as this book is concerned is of little consequence. Also, there is evidence that the Church of the first few centuries held to a premillennial view of a future Kingdom, yet with the advent of the Augustinian method of allegorical interpretation, apocalyptic thought favored the view that the future as described in the Book of Revelation was of symbolic relevance only. It is in this context that the statement under consideration was found.

Pseudo-Ephraem's "Proto-Rapture" Statement is as follows:

> "All the saints and elect of God are gathered together before the tribulation, which is to come, and are taken to the Lord, in order that they may not see at any time the confusion which overwhelms the world because of our sins."

According to theologians and scholars, the entire message of the sermon appears fairly consistent with the general style of sermons from the medieval period, and it is considered as a stable manuscript. It includes topics such as the end of the world is near according to the signs; the predictions of Matthew 24 have been fulfilled; the coming of the evil one is near; condemnation for rejecting the invitation of Christ; the world being deluged by wars, disasters, plaques, and fear; great traumas that will overwhelm people; the appearance of the Antichrist; the rebuilding of the temple in Jerusalem; the attraction of the Antichrist to the world's remaining population for a time; the 1,260 days of great distress; the coming of the prophets Elijah and Enoch to announce the Second Coming of Jesus Christ and to denounce the Antichrist; the end of the Antichrist; the coming of the Lord Jesus Christ with a host of angels; and finally the judgment of the unrighteous and the everlasting life of the righteous.

The importance of this sermon and this statement is that it is from a written document that is anywhere from 1400 to 1700 years of age and, it speaks of a promise to deliver believers from a coming tribulation of a defined interval of three and one-half years, it emphasizes imminence, and it recognizes two separate events regarding Jesus Christ. In fact, the Pseudo-Ephraem sermon is reasonably similar to the contemporary view of a Pretribulation Rapture.

29

THE CHURCH AFTER THE RAPTURE

Thus far, we have explored the nature of the True Church as the body of Christ, and then, we saw how the Church essentially will evolve into two distinct parts, one the True Church and the other the Professing Church, as it progresses down through 2,000 years of history. We saw that the preponderance of Scripture points to a Rapture that occurs immediately before Daniel's 70th Week, and now in this Chapter, we will identify the two events that will happen to the True Church after the Rapture while she is in heaven.

This Chapter poses the question of what happens to the believers after they are raptured from earth to heaven to be with Christ. The answer is that there are two sequential events that will occur while the True Church is in heaven.

29.1	THE BEMA, OR JUDGMENT SEAT, OF CHRIST

THE FIRST OF TWO HEAVENLY EVENTS

Each individual believer of the True Church will stand before the Judgment Seat, or Bema, of Jesus Christ, not to be judged for their salvation in Him, but instead so that each may give an account for their own life, service and ministry while on earth, as can be seen from the following passages:
- 2 Corinthians 5:10: *For we must all appear before the judgment seat of Christ, so that each of us may receive what is due us for the things done while in the body, whether good or bad.* This judgment is only for Christians.
- Romans:
  + 13:12: *The night is nearly over; the day is almost here. So let us put aside the deeds of darkness and put on the armor of light.*
  + 14:10-12: In this passage regarding tolerance for other spiritual brothers and sisters, Paul points out there should be mutual forbearance in judging one another because *we will all stand before the judgment seat of God* so that *each of us will give an account of himself to God.* Believers will stand before Christ and be examined for their own spiritual work done, or not done, on earth.

THE MEANING OF THE BEMA OF CHRIST

There are two words that Paul uses in his New Testament epistles that are translated as 'judgment seat' that are relevant to this event.
- *criterion*: The idea of this word suggests "justice and judgment."[1]
    + Strong's Reference Number: 2922, and means a rule of judging ("criterion"), by implication a tribunal.
    + Vines Expository Dictionary: Primarily a means of judging, then, a tribunal, law-court, or lawsuit.
    + Scriptural Usage:
        o James 2:6: *and personally drag you into court.*
        o 1 Corinthians 6:2: *the smaller courts.*
        o 1 Corinthians 6:4: *If then you have law courts.*
- *bema*: The idea of this word is " … prominence, dignity, authority, honor, and reward …"[2]
    + Strong's Reference Number: 0968, and means by implication, a rostrum, i.e. a tribunal.
    + Vine's Expository Dictionary: Denotes a raised place or platform, reached by steps, from which orations were made.
    + Scriptural Usage:
        o Romans 14:10: *stand before the judgment-seat of God.*
        o 2 Corinthians 5:10: *appear before the judgment-seat of Jesus.*
- So as can be seen from the above, Paul specifically chose the word *bema*, rather than *criterion*, to characterize the event of the believer's standing/ appearing before the throne of Jesus Christ and being examined.

The bema is not to determine if any of those standing before Him will enter heaven or hell or to punish sin. That issue was resolved at the moment each person believed in Jesus Christ as his or her personal Savior from sin.

PREPARING FOR THE BEMA OF CHRIST

Since we know that the bema of Christ is in our future, we should live our lives in such a way that we can answer every question by Christ in an exceptional way. Hitchcock[3] has comprised a list of the main areas that will be examined when we stand before Christ:
- Psalm 90:9-12 (cf. Ephesians 5:16; Colossians 4:5; and 1 Peter 1:17): How did we spend our time?
- Daniel 12:3 (cf. 1 Thessalonians 2:19-20): How many souls did we witnesses to and win for Christ?
- Matthew:
    + 5:11-12 (cf. Mark 10:29-30; Luke 6:27-28, 35; Romans 8:18; 2 Corinthians 4:17; and 1 Peter 4:12-13): How did we handle mistreatment and endure personal injustice?

+ 6:1-4 (cf. 1 Timothy 6:17-19): In what spirit did we use the money we were entrusted with?
+ 10:40-42: How did we support others in the ministry?
+ 10:41-42 (cf. Hebrews 6:10): How did we treat other believers?
+ 12:36 (cf. James 3:1-12): How did we use our tongues?
+ 25:14-29 (cf. Luke 19:11-26; 1 Corinthians 12:4, 7; 2 Timothy 1:6; and 1 Peter 4:100: How did we use our God-given talents and abilities?
+ 25:35-36 (cf. Luke 14:12-14): How hospitable were we to strangers?
- Acts 20:26-28 (cf. 2 Timothy 4:1-2; Hebrews 13:17; James 3:1; 1 Peter 5:1-2; and 2 John 1:7-8): How faithful were we to God's people and God's Word?
- 1 Corinthians:
  + 9:24 (cf. Philippians 2:16; 3:12-14; and Hebrews 12:1): How did we run our own particular God-given race?
  + 9:25-27: How well did we control our fleshy appetites?
- Colossians 3:22-24: How faithful were we in our vocation?
- 2 Timothy 4:8: How much did the Rapture mean to us and shape our lives?
- James 1:12 (cf. Revelation 2:10): How did we endure our personal trials and sufferings?

THE TIME OF THE BEMA OF CHRIST

There are several ideas that have been presented regarding the timing of the judgment as being between the Rapture and the Second Advent.

- Luke 14:14: Jesus points out that the reward for good work will occur at the time of the resurrection of believers as an integral part of the Rapture.
- Revelation 19:7-8: When the Bride, the Church, accompanies Jesus back to earth at the Second Advent, her state is seen as *dressed in bright, clean, fine linen* indicating that the Bema of Christ has already taken place and she has been rewarded for her righteousness. The verb tense of *the marriage of the Lamb has come* indicating that the event has already occurred prior to this passage that describes the Second Advent. Note that the sense of this passage is that the Church is already in heaven with Jesus when He comes to earth at His Second Advent, which supports Pretribulational Rapture.

THE PLACE OF THE BEMA OF CHRIST

If believers are caught up into the clouds to meet the Lord at the Rapture, as indicated in 1 Thessalonians 4:17, and the Bema examination takes place after the Rapture but before the Second Advent, then the place of the Bema of Christ must be in the presence of Jesus Christ who is within the heavenly realm.

THE JUDGE OF THE BEMA OF CHRIST

As was seen in Romans 14:10-12, this judgment will take place before the presence of God, however, God has given the authority to judge all of humankind to Jesus as indicated in John 5:22, 27 and 2 Corinthians 5:10. The authority to judge is part of the exaltation of Jesus by God. "Revelation 4 - 5 demonstrates Jesus' authority to judge. He is both the Lion from the tribe of Judah and the Lamb of God who dies and rose again. He who was judged has the right to judge all humanity because He is both the Sovereign and the Savior. The Bible says that Jesus is the "righteous Judge," and therefore all judgments will be fair and final (2 Timothy 4:8). Like the Father, Jesus will also judge "without respect of persons" (1 Peter 1:17 KJV). The attributes of Jesus Christ as the Sone of God guarantee that all the evidence will be gathered and carefully evaluated."[4]

THE SUBJECTS OF THE BEMA OF CHRIST

Those who will stand before the Bema of Christ in heaven are the New Testament believers exclusively, unbelievers will not be judged at the time. The punishment that everyone deserves for sins has been paid by Jesus Christ on the cross.
- Romans:
  + 5:1: Peace with God through Jesus Christ is the result of justification by faith.
  + 8:1: A person will never be condemned for personal sins if they have trusted in Jesus Christ for salvation.
- 2 Corinthians 5:21: Jesus was made to sin with our sins so that we can be made righteous with His righteousness.

THE BASIS OF EXAMINATION OF THE BEMA OF CHRIST

When those who believe in Jesus Christ as Savior and Lord are examined at the Bema of Christ, the examination is not about their salvation, as can be seen from the following passages:
- John 5:24: Jesus indicates that those that hear His message and believe they will have eternal life and will not face the same judgment as those that do not believe what they have heard.
- Romans 8:1: Paul says that there is not condemnation for those that believe in Christ Jesus.
- 1 John 4:17: The love a believer has for God, and the love God has for the believer, provides the believer the basis that he or she will not face judgment.

"To bring the believer into judgment concerning the sin question, whether his sins before his new birth, his sins since his new birth, is to deny the efficacy of the death of Christ and nullify the promise of God that "their sins and iniquities will I remember no more" (Heb. 10:17)."[5]

The phrase *we must all appear before* in 2 Corinthians 5:10 might be better rendered, as indicated in Strong's (Reference Number 5319) and in Vine's Expository Dictionary, to manifestly declare, or to manifest one's character, which is a much broader concept than just an appearance. Also, the context of the passage suggests that it is single individuals who are manifesting their character for examination by Jesus Christ, rather than groups of people.

All of the earthly works of every believer will be examined for quality, not quantity, and every action, thought, or motivation, will be determined to be of one of the following classifications:
  • Those that are good in character, of benefit to the glory of God and Jesus Christ, and therefore are acceptable because they are worthy.
  • Those that are bad in character, or of no benefit to the glory of God and Jesus Christ, and therefore are unacceptable because they are unworthy.

The image is that after all believers are raptured into the presence of Jesus Christ in heaven, each believer will appear before Him, and will publicly reveal, or manifest, his or her own personal character for Christ to determine if their individual deeds are worthy, resulting in rewards, or unworthy, resulting in loss of rewards. Apparently each believer, being imperfect in earthly life, will be rewarded for some things, but will not be rewarded for other things.

THE RESULT OF EXAMINATION OF THE BEMA OF CHRIST

Core Scripture: 1 Corinthians 3:10-15

The Work of Believers
Paul uses the metaphor of the construction of a building to describe the work of the believer while on earth. Jesus Christ is the only one that can place the foundation within a person, and it is that person that is to build on that foundation using either indestructible building materials, like *gold, silver, precious stones…* or, destructible building materials, like *wood, hay, or straw.* The work of the believer while on earth is motivated by either pleasing the Lord, or satisfying personal fleshly desire.

The Test by the Lord
Then Paul uses the metaphor of test by fire to describe the mechanism of examination, which will determine the inner character and motivation of the believer for every deed. The fire will reveal the deed to either be of indestructible building materials, or, of destructible building materials. What is not burned away

is indestructible and will be rewarded, what is burned away is destructible and any potential reward will be lost.

- Loss of Reward: Rewards that will not be received by the believer are those that are motivated by the flesh. In fact, Paul on several occasions expresses his own frustration with his body and his attraction to fleshly desires, as indicated in Romans 8:13, 1 Corinthians 9:27, and Colossians 3:5-11. It seems that throughout Paul's ministry, he was cognizant of the importance of remaining in control of his own physical body and its desires.
- Rewards Bestowed: The New Testament records five conditions under which there is mention of a heavenly reward, or a crown, for earthly work by the believer:
  + 1 Corinthians 9:25 - Crown of the New Man over the Old Man: For mastery and victory by exercising self-control; for those that have learned to successfully live the Spirit-filled life.
  + 1 Thessalonians 2:19 - Crown for Rejoicing: For winning souls for Christ; for those who do the work of evangelism and witnessing.
  + James 1:12 and Revelation 2:10 - Crown of Life: For not giving in to the persecution of the body of Christ; for those enduring trials, testing, persecutions, and martyrdoms.
  + 2 Timothy 4:8 - Crown of Righteousness: For those who keep the faith doctrinally and morally; for those who love His appearing and look longingly for it.
  + 1 Peter 5:4 - Crown of Glory: For those that faithfully shepherd the flock of Christ.

In each instance of the use of the word *crown* in the five passages listed above, Paul used the Greek word *stephanos* rather than the word *diadema*. *Stephanos* denotes the victor's wreath, the symbol of triumph over something and belongs to believers, while *diadema* is always the symbol for kingly or imperial dignity and belongs only to Jesus Christ. Even though the English word crown is translated for both *stephanos* and for *diadema*, they are actually two distinctly different concepts.

1 Corinthians 6:20 tells all believers that their redemption by Christ is for the purpose of bringing glory to God, as can be seen in the bestowal of crowns for their good works. However, there is a more profound observation that can be made. Pentecost astutely observes that "… it may be that the reward given to the believer is a capacity to manifest the glory of Christ throughout eternity. The greater the reward, the greater the bestowed capacity to bring glory to God."[6] Since this is an eternal gift of the Kingdom, then some of this capacity is exercised while here on earth as expressed in 1 Peter 2:9.

In Revelation 4:10, we see the Twenty-Four Elders cast their own crowns to the feet of the One who sits on the throne, thus indicating that believers only temporally possess the crown because all glory belongs to the Triune God.

THE QUESTION OF CONFESSION OF SIN

If the sin of believers is already forgiven when the believer gets to the Bema of Christ in heaven, then why is it necessary to seek forgiveness of sin while living on earth as commanded by 1 John 1:9? Why is the confession of sin necessary? While it is true that the death of Christ on the cross assures God's forgiveness of human sinfulness in the ultimate sense, there is still the issue of being in fellowship with God while the believer is living on earth. The context of 1 John is in regard to fellowship while the believer is alive on earth, and the command to believers to confess sinfulness is in order for a harmonious relationship between the believer and God to be maintained. Disobedience and departure from God yields a decrease in fellowship with God, so the confession of sin is the mechanism that the believer uses to restore that fellowship and maintain it throughout the believer's earthly life.

PAUL'S DESCRIPTION OF HOW TO LIVE BEFORE APPEARING BEFORE THE BEMA OF CHRIST

Paul uses three examples to paint the visual image of what believers should do in this life on earth before ultimately standing before the Bema examination.

- Romans 14:10-12 – Life as a Stewardship: Paul explains that human judgment by one believer of the quality of another believer is essentially usurping Christ's authority of divine judgment of all people. It is not the role of believers to judge others, it is Christ's. When believers judge, it is with bias, it is subjective, and it is motivated by the fleshly desire to take advantage over the other believer – to step on a brother or sister in order to improve one's own view. A believer is not judged on the basis of what other believers have done or not done, but on what the believer has done or not done. Each believer is uniquely equipped with spiritual talents, natural abilities, and intellectual capabilities that they can use when the opportunities are presented, and the issue is what each believer did with what they were uniquely given.
- 1 Corinthians:
  + 3:10-15 – Life as a Building: The foundation of Jesus Christ, given by God, is the same with every believer, and the building materials that are available for use are the same for every believer. What is different is what the believer builds with those materials on the foundation of Jesus Christ. Every believer is the architect of their own life structure, by either listening to the Holy Spirit and building with indestructible materials, or resisting the Holy Spirit and building with destructible materials.
  + 9:16-27, especially 24-27 – Life as a Race: In an apt description of disciplined competition against oneself, Paul describes how he adapted to whatever condition was necessary in order to be an effective witness to the diversity of people he encountered through the course

39

of his ministry. The use of his spiritual talents, natural abilities, and intellectual capabilities through his personal spiritual work was executed in such a manner that he set for himself the personal goal of not losing any potential eternal rewards to be given him by Christ. It seems apparent that Paul very much understood the nature of the spiritual work required of him and the potential for reward in the future, as can be seen by his emphatic declarations that he did whatever was necessary, within righteous reason, to spread the Gospel and win souls for Christ. Additional observations that can be gleaned from this passage include the following:

- o Paul was physically, spiritually, mentally, emotionally, and intellectually conditioned in order to run the race to win souls.
- o Paul understood his responsibilities and was disciplined and determined.
- o Paul did not let obstacles obstruct his path of endeavor.
- o Paul did not let himself settle for anything less than accomplishment.
- o Paul kept his focus on the ultimate goal of pleasing Christ by focusing on the earthly goal of winning races.
- o Paul ran the race to spread the Gospel according to the divine rulebook.
- o Paul kept his future in mind rather than dwelling on his here and now.

29.2   THE MARRIAGE OF THE LAMB

THE SECOND OF TWO HEAVENLY EVENTS

Core Scripture: Revelation 19:7-9

After each individual believer is examined as to the quality of their spiritual work on earth, there will be a marriage between the bride, the True Church that was snatched off of the earth into heaven, and the bridegroom, Jesus Christ. In a number of New Testament passages, the figure of the bride and bridegroom relationship is revealed:

- • John 3:29: The bride belongs to the bridegroom.
- • Romans 7:4: Paul speaks of the view believers have in that they have died to the law through Jesus Christ so that they will be joined to, or will belong to, the One that was raised from the dead, so that they will do the Lord's work on earth.
- • 2 Corinthians 11:2: Paul reveals his motivation for his ministry, and that is to witness to people about Jesus so that he might disciple them to live as righteously as possible so that they would be a chaste virgin promised in marriage to Jesus Christ. This verse indicates that Paul's ministry included discipleship as well as witnessing.

- Ephesians 5:25-33: Paul uses the analogy of marriage between a man and a woman to effectively describe the relationship between Jesus and the Church. Just as there should be love, trust, fidelity, and ultimate commitment between a man and a woman in human marriage, so should be the same in the marriage between Jesus and the Church.
- Revelation:
  + 19:7-8: John describes the rejoicing that occurs after the wedding ceremony when Jesus comes to earth for the Second Advent, and the Church accompanies Him as His wife, having been examined and rewarded. We know from other passages that Jesus and the Church remain married throughout the one-thousand-year Millennium.
  + 21:1 – 22:7: John is shown the ultimate destiny, in the eternal state, that awaits the wife of Christ after the Millennium; the dwelling places in the Father's house that Jesus spoke of, as recorded in John 14:2-3, are described in majestic detail. Thus, the intimate relationship between Jesus and the Church, which was confirmed by the marriage of the Lamb, continues through the Millennium and into eternity.

THE JEWISH WEDDING CUSTOMS OF THE NEW TESTAMENT

Since the specifics of the Marriage of the Lamb are being investigated, it might be helpful to outline the Jewish marriage tradition of the times in which the New Testament was written. It should be pointed out that, unlike the wedding customs of our time, the emphasis of a marriage then was on the bridegroom rather than the bride.

- The Selection of the Bride: The father of a son considered it his cultural duty and fatherly prerogative to secure a wife for his son, thus a father would present his son with a bride that was chosen for him.
- The Payment of the Bride-Price: Money, property or possessions were given to the bride's parents by the bridegroom in the form of a dowry.
- The Betrothal: The selection was followed by a formal espousal proceeding that could last for weeks, months, or years, undertaken by a representative of the bridegroom in concert with the parents of the bride. The betrothal was celebrated, and in some cases a ring was placed on the finger of the bride to represent fidelity and acceptance into the bridegroom's family.
- The Wedding Ceremony: The ceremony would generally begin when the bridegroom, in appropriate wedding attire, would lead his groomsmen from his father's house to the house of the bride's father, where the bride and her bridesmaids anxiously expected the bridegroom's appearance. The actual wedding ceremony appears to consist of the act of fetching the bride from her father's house.
- The Wedding Feast: The bridegroom would then lead the entire procession back to his father's house, with friends of the bridegroom and the bride

41

joining in the procession as it passed. At the house of the bridegroom's father, a feast was prepared to which all were invited. The feast lasted from seven to fourteen days, the guests were given fitted robes, and there was food and entertainment. At this time the bridegroom and the bride converse (possibly for the first time). The last act of the ceremony was when the bridegroom would lead the bride to the bridal chamber.

THE TIME OF THE MARRIAGE

As discussed above regarding the timing of the Bema of Christ, the verb tense of *has come* in Revelation 19:7-8 indicates that the Marriage of the Lamb has already occurred prior to the Second Advent. The marriage is seen to follow the Bema of Christ.

THE PLACE OF THE MARRIAGE

Also as already seen, the Marriage follows the Bema of Christ and is before the Second Advent, so the Marriage must occur in heaven.

THE PARTICIPANTS IN THE MARRIAGE

Based on what has been seen thus far in this chapter, it is apparent that the only participants in the ceremony are Jesus Christ and the Church, the collective body of believers.

THE WEDDING SUPPER

While the Marriage of the Lamb takes place in heaven between Jesus and the Church, the wedding supper does not occur until after Jesus Christ and His bride come to the earth for the Second Advent. There will be other saints in attendance at the Wedding Supper as can be seen by the following:
- The Old Testament Saints:
  + Daniel 12:1-3: The angel Michael tells Daniel that the resurrection of *your people*, Israel, will not occur until after the *time of distress* of seven years of tribulation.
  + Isaiah 26:19-21: The prophet indicates that the Old Testament saints will not be raised from their graves until after the *indignation runs its course*.
- Revelation 20:4-6 - The Tribulation Saints: John saw that those that died for Christ during Daniel's 70th Week did not because they *had not worshipped the beast or its image and had not received its mark on their forehead or their hand*, so they were not raised until the time of the Second Advent.

- Jewish and Gentile Survivors of Daniel's 70th Week: It is obvious that there will be some that are the survivors of the time of great distress, the righteous of which (the sheep of Matthew 25:31-46) will proceed into the Millennium in their earthly bodies.

"... [S]ince the marriage supper consistently is used in reference to Israel on earth, it may be best to... view the marriage of the Lamb as that event in the heavens in which the church is eternally united to Christ and the marriage feast or supper as the millennium, to which Jews and Gentiles will be invited, which takes place on the earth, during which time the bridegroom is honored through the display of the bride to all His friends who are assembled there."[7]

THE STEPS OF THE MARRIAGE OF THE LAMB CLARIFIED

The divine parallel of the Marriage of the Lamb can be established in the same pattern as the traditional Jewish wedding custom delineated above:
- The Selection of the Bride: God the Father is the host of the wedding ceremony and selected the bride for His Son, Jesus Christ. Those who live in the age of grace and who come to believe in Him through His Son will be the bride.
- Payment of the Bride-Price: God the Father paid the dowry with the blood of His Son, as can be seen in Ephesians 5:25-27.
- The Betrothal: Just as a period of time elapsed for the betrothal in a Jewish marriage, so also a long period of time has elapsed in the betrothal of the True Church to Jesus Christ, in this case 2,000 years so far. God the Father also has presented the bride with the gifts, especially the gift of eternal life with His Son.
- The Wedding Ceremony: The Rapture is the fetching of the bride by the bridegroom from her father's house, the earth, to His Father's house in heaven, as can be seen in 1 Thessalonians 4:13-18, where the wedding ceremony then takes place, which is indicated by Revelation 19:6-8 to have already happened when Christ comes in His Second Advent.
- The Wedding Feast: The wedding feast will take place on earth after the bride accompanies Christ at His Second Advent, and will be attended by the resurrected Old Testament saints, the survivors of Daniel's 70th Week, and the resurrected Tribulation saints.

30

THE SEVEN GREAT PERSONAGES
OF THE END TIMES

In the panoramic flow of the Book of Revelation, Chapters 12 and 13 identifies the seven great personages that will be the primary actors during Daniel's 70th Week. "About these main actors swirls the tremendously moving scene of the great tribulation."[1] Therefore, it is helpful to identify each individual personage:
- First Personage - Revelation 12:1-2 - Woman Clothed with the Sun: This is the nation of Israel, God's chosen people.
- Second Personage - Revelation 12:3-4 – Great Red Dragon with Seven Heads and Ten Horns: This is Satan.
- Third Personage - Revelation 12:5-6 - Male Child: This is Jesus Christ.
- Fourth Personage - Revelation 12:7-12 - Archangel Michael: This is obviously Michael, and his role is to cast Satan out of heaven.
- Fifth Personage - Revelation 12:13-17 - Offspring of the Woman: This is the people of Israel – the remnant; God's chosen people persecuted by Satan.
- Sixth Personage - Revelation 13:2-10 - Beast Out of the Sea: This is the future world dictator, the Antichrist.
- Seventh Personage - Revelation 13:11-18 - Beast Out of the Earth: This is the false prophet.

30.1	FIRST PERSONAGE - THE WOMAN CLOTHED WITH THE SUN

Core Scripture: Revelation 12:1-2

Revelation 12:1-2 introduces the woman clothed with the sun, with the moon at her feet, and with a crown of twelve stars on her head, who is pregnant, suffering in pain and struggling to give birth to the male child of verse 5. While there is great diversity of interpretation among theologians regarding the identity of the woman - there are some that believe the woman is Jesus Christ, the Church in general, the leader of a sect, or the Virgin Mary - however, because of the verses that follow these, Israel as a nation is the entity that is in the most harmony with the Scriptures. Pentecost[2] proposes the following considerations as support for this conclusion:
- The context of this portion of the Book of Revelation is in regard to the nation of Israel, so the context speaks for the chosen nation.
- Throughout the Old Testament, the nation of Israel is presented as the wife of Jehovah, often in a state of unfaithfulness, so it would be consistent that the wife of Jehovah would symbolically give 'birth' to the Son of Jehovah.

- The sun/moon/stars description is a reference back to Genesis 37:9-11 regarding Joseph's dream where his family, Jacob (sun), Rachel (moon), and the other eleven sons of Jacob (stars), are symbolically described by this imagery, "… thereby identifying the woman with the fulfillment of the Abrahamic Covenant."[3] In fact, there are several Old Testament instances where heavenly bodies are used to describe Israel. Also, Isaiah 40:27, 49:5, and Jeremiah 30:10 are among numerous passages that clearly links Jacob as Israel as one person.
- "The number twelve not only represents the twelve tribes of Israel, but is used in Scripture as the governmental number."[4]
- The word *woman* is used eight times in Chapter 12, and is referred to as *she* or *her* an additional eight times, and in the Old Testament, Israel is frequently referred to as *she* or *her*. "While the church is called a *bride*, or a chaste *virgin*, we never find the church referred to as a *woman*."[5]
- The theme of a dragon as the adversary that pursues Israel is common in the Old Testament, and it seems appropriate that the persecuted people here should also be Israel.
- The word wilderness has a peculiar connection to Israel. There are several other Old Testament instances where Israel is turned away from her land and into another land identified as wilderness for discipline on account of unbelief. These include Ezekiel 9:20 regarding being turned back into the wilderness for an additional forty years of wandering during the Exodus; and Hosea 2 where God will be gracious to Israel during her time in the wilderness associated with her repentance and restoration.
- The parallelism of the woman being in labor to give birth to a king recorded in Micah 5:2-3 also supports the idea that the woman is Israel and the king is Jesus Christ.
- Romans 9:4-5 indicates that Christ came from Israel supporting the fact that the male child in the passage before us comes from Israel.
- Any time the length of time for the Great Tribulation - 1,260 days, forty-two months, three and one-years, or time, times, and half a time is used, it is always in reference to Israel; it is used twice in Revelation 12.
- The fact that the angel Michael appears in the context of Revelation 12 "… indicates that God is again dealing with the nation of Israel …"[6] just as Michael *stands guard over the sons of your people*, Israel, in Daniel 12:1.
- The woman arrayed in the sun, moon, and stars is clearly Israel.

30.2 SECOND PERSONAGE - A GREAT RED DRAGON WITH SEVEN HEADS AND TEN HORNS

Core Scripture: Revelation 12:3-4

Revelation 12:3-4 introduces a great dragon with seven heads and ten horns who appears in heaven which is confirmed by Revelation 12:9 and 20:2 to be none other than the antithesis of goodness, Satan. From these two verses we can make the following observations:

- Satan first appears in heaven before he is thrown to earth. This substantiates the notion that, in spite of the fact that he is trying and will continue to try to replace God, Satan has access to the heavenly realm, and from other passages can communicate directly with God. However, as we will shortly see, the angel Michael and Satan will battle each other and Satan will be cast out of heaven to the earth, the idea being a permanent ousting, which he begins to pursue and persecute the nation of Israel (The Male Child).
- Regarding the seven heads represent the three kingdoms, if the ten, that will have been subdued by the Antichrist.
- Regarding the ten horns, based on Revelation 17:12-13 they are seen to be ten kings who have the sole purpose of giving their power and authority to the beast, the Antichrist. It is interesting to note that Satan possesses the symbolic image of what the Antichrist receives as indicated in Revelation 13 and 17, thus establishing the fact that the Antichrist derives his authority from Satan.
- "The seven crowns point to a concept of conquest. Satan wrestles authority over the earth from man, and the Gentiles empires wrestled authority from Israel."[7]
- Verse 12:4 appears to be a parenthetical remark that, in a reference to events of history forming the character of Satan, also discloses his goal of devouring the Son of the Living God. The first part of the verse indicates that Satan's action caused a third of the angles (stars) to be swept to earth, the implication being that Satan caused something to occur that resulted in the dejection of the angels, and as we know these became the demonic forces on earth thus giving an account of the origin of sinfulness on earth. The idea also is that the demons were to assist Satan in his efforts to kill the child. The second part of the verse indicates that Satan attempted to destroy the Son of God at the point of His human birth.

Walvoord expands the interpretation to a much broader level by associating the dragon with the restored Roman Empire as governed by Satan; the third of the stars in heaven are those that oppose him that he has gathered under his power; and, the situation where the dragon is waiting for the birth is the Roman Empire, via Herod, waiting to kill Jesus immediately after His birth.

30.3 THIRD PERSONAGE – THE MALE CHILD

Core Scripture: Revelation 12:5-6

Revelation 12:5-6 introduces a male child who will be born to the woman clothed with the sun, who will rule over the nations of the world with an iron rod, however, the child was caught up to God and His throne, the implication being that he ascended up to the presence of God prior to his rule over the nations. The phrase, *to rule all the nations with a rod of iron*, is from Psalm 2, a Messianic Psalm, and indicates that the male child of Revelation is the same one that is spoken of in the Psalm passage - Jesus Christ. "The fact of the birth, the fact of the destiny of this child, for He is "to rule all nations with a rod of iron," and the fact of the ascension, since he is "caught up unto God, and to His throne," all cause the identification to point to one person, the Lord Jesus Christ, for of none other could all three statement be made."[8]

Revelation 12:6 indicates that after the woman gives birth to the male child, God snatches him up to heaven, and then the woman will flee the place of the birth and into the wilderness to a place prepared by God where she will be cared for and reside for 1,260 days. There is a significant amount of time between verse 5 and verse 6, however, one of the characteristics of the prophecy is that two events, widely spaced in time, can be contained in one sentence or thought.

It should also be noted that there are some theologians that believe the male child to be someone, or something, other than Jesus Christ - some believe it is the New Testament Church destined to reign with Jesus and the catching up is a reference to the Rapture, and others believe the woman is the Virgin Mary, neither of which are supported by Scripture.

30.4 FOURTH PERSONAGE – MICHAEL CASTS SATAN OUT OF HEAVEN

Core Scripture: Revelation 12:7-12

Revelation 12:7-12 introduces the angel Michael and documents the victorious battle he will have with Satan, which will result in Satan's expulsion from heaven down to earth.

When the particular topic of Satan being in heaven is introduced, most people express utter surprise at the idea that the evil one, the serpent of the Garden of Eden, the old dragon has been in heaven all this time seems to be incongruous to everything that many believers thought they had known all their spiritual lives, and that was that Satan has been in hell since the beginning. It is difficult for many to rationalize that Satan currently has a place in heaven, or his third abode - the atmospheric heavens as Fruchtenbaum refers to it, The Third Abode of Satan described in Section 13.5, and has direct access to God on His throne as the Book of Job clearly indicates. Satan will continue to reside in heaven until the future great battle with the angel Michael predicted in the Book of Revelation to occur sometime around the middle of Daniel's 70th Week, which will result in Satan being permanently thrown out of heaven to his fourth abode - the earth.

"The casting of Satan to the earth also marks the beginning of the most awful periods in human history, the Great Tribulation."[9] The event is also one of the principal milestones events that cause great changes to occur in the way of life for the inhabitants of the earth during the seven years of Daniel's 70ᵗʰ Week. In order to begin to understand this critical event, we should examine Revelation 12:7-12 and look over John's shoulder to see what he observed.

- The passage begins abruptly - a war breaks out between the forces of good, the archangel Michael and his holy angels, and the forces of evil, the dragon and his wicked angels. The sense of verse 7 is that Michael is on the offensive, while Satan is on the defensive. The passage quickly concludes that the forces of evil were not strong enough to prevail and there was nowhere left in heaven for them to go. This portion of the passage connects to that described in Daniel 12:1 which indicates that Michael, the great prince that protects the people of Israel, will stand up for them.

- Then, recording all of his important titles that have been used to identify him throughout the Bible, Satan and his demon angels are thrown down (notice the use of the word 'down' to indicate direction, and to suggest status and hierarchy) to earth.

- "Five names are given to Satan, all describing his person and his work. In the *great dragon,* his fierceness and ferociousness is seen. The *old serpent* points back to the Garden of Eden where, due to his temptation, man fell, bringing sin and death into human experience. The Great Tribulation is a judgment of man's sin. In the word *devil*, Satan is viewed as the accuser of all of God's children. *Satan* means adversary, and in this he is seen as the opponent to God's program. As the *deceiver,* he is pointed out as the great master counterfeiter by which he attempts to deceive elect and non-select alike."[10]

- Finally, John hears a loud, unidentified voice acknowledging the significance of the casting of Satan to the earth by pointing out the following things of importance:

  + The power of God and the ruling authority of Christ will be completed, and the salvation (the sense of deliverance) and the kingdom (the sense of the completing of the divine program that is about to start) will also begin to come in, because the one that had been accusing the believers day and night before God had been thrown out of heaven.

  + Additionally, in spite of the evil influence that Satan had exerted on the believers they will be able to victoriously overcome him because of their faith in the ultimate sacrifice and their commitment and testimony to the Christ will be so strong that they will not be afraid to die in the Name of all that is good and righteous. "The victory of the saints in that hour is revealed in verse 11, where it is declared that they overcame Satan by the blood of the lamb, by the word of their testimony, and by the facts that they loved not their lives unto death. The accusations of Satan are nullified by the blood of the Lamb which renders the believer pure and makes possible his spiritual victory."[11]

+ So, while the heavens will be rejoicing at that time, the earth and the sea (its inhabitants) will be trembling in awfulness and fear because Satan and his evil dominions will be terrorizing them because he will then know that the time left to accomplish his demonic plan will be extremely limited.

Two observations can be made regarding Satan's departure from heaven:
- First, Satan no longer has access to heaven and the throne of God, so he can no longer accuse the brethren, for this there is rejoicing in heaven. Satan's heavenly activities have now closed, and his earthly terrorizing is to begin.
- Second, Satan is now full of anger and will focus his wrath on anyone who believes in God because he knows that he has such a small amount of time left. It is important to understand that the word *woe* is used to describe the significance of what is about the come. It goes without much explanation that whenever the word woe is used, that is one of the Bible's most powerful ways of identifying the coming of something that will be very destructive.

Regarding the time in which Satan is cast out of heaven, most believe that it will be sometime near the middle of Daniel's 70th Week for the following reasons:
- The context of Revelation 12 indicates that Satan will pursue the woman, Israel, while God is providing protection for a period of 1,260 days. This amount of time aligns with the time of the Great Tribulation, so in order for this to occur, the pursuer has to start the pursuit before, which would put this event no later than the middle part of the Week.
- The individual that begins as the Ruler to Come becomes the Antichrist because he will be empowered by Satan, and since it is the Antichrist that causes the Abomination of Desolation in the Tribulation Temple, again this event will have to have occurred prior to the mid-point of the Week.
- It should be noted that even though this passage is after the seventh trumpet judgment, those things such as this that are parenthetical descriptions of things of Daniel's 70th Week, do not necessarily occur chronologically as given, More specifically, if we hold that all of the seal, trumpet, and bowl judgments occur in the second half of the Week, then casting out of heaven would occur much later in the second half which would not accommodate the sense of Revelation 12 and its timeline of 1,260 days of Israel's pursuit. So, this is one of the reasons that the parenthetical events are not taken to be in the chronological flow of the various judgements

30.5	**THE FIFTH PERSONAGE – OFFSPRING OF THE WOMAN, AND SATAN'S REIGN OF TERROR AND HIS PERSECUTION OF THE JEWS**

Core Scripture: Revelation 12:13-17

Revelation 12:13-17 introduces what Satan will do after he is cast to earth - he will pursue the woman who had previously given birth to the male child, but now has been given the ability to flee to the place prepared in the wilderness in order for God to provide divine protection for a period of time identified as a time, times, and half a time. Satan will attempt to destroy the woman, however, he will not be successful because some who will help the woman survive the onslaught will resist him. Unable to fully succeed, Satan will then turn his attention to the other of the woman's children, those *who keep the commandments of God and hold to the testimony of Jesus*, and will make war with them. The identity of the woman in this passage is again the nation of Israel, but this time it is clear that there are two personages that are Israel, however, there is a distinction between the two, where 12:1-2 is in reference to Israel as a nation, and here in 12:12-17 it is a reference to the Godly remnant of Israel.

Walvoord suggest that the event of Satan being cast to earth is one of the first events of the Great Tribulation, the second half of Daniel's 70th Week. In fact, Walvoord makes two additional observations about the relationship between Israel and Satan: "The persecution of Israel is a part of the satanic program to thwart and hinder the work of God. ... Israel is hated by Satan not because of any of its own characteristics but because she is chosen of God and essential to the overall purpose of God for time and eternity."[12]

From this passage, the following observations and interpretations may be made:
- The significance of the two wings of the great eagle is to illustrate God's faithfulness in caring for His children.
- The woman will flee to a protected place (some believe it to be Petra), which is consistent with Jesus' words in Matthew 24:16, where God will care for her, possibly using supernatural means.
- Again there is a time reference, which again suggests these events occur during the Great Tribulation.
- The description of Satan's attack, spewing water from his mouth but resulting in the earth swallowing it up, is best taken as a symbolic description rather than a literal interpretation. "The flood cast after Israel is the total effort of Satan to exterminate the nation, and the resistance of earth is the natural difficulty in executing such a massive program."[13] Satan will apparently expend considerable effort trying to destroy Israel, but will ultimately fail.
- Satan will become angry at Israel, as anti-Semitism will probably reach its peak against Jewish believers. He will then turn his terrorizing attention

to the faithful remnant and will persecute them; undoubtedly, many will be killed in the names of God and Christ.

This passage in Revelation brings to mind a portion of the Olivet Discourse where Jesus states that an event will happen in Jerusalem that will be a signal to the Jews that they should flee the city and surrounding nation immediately and without possessions in order to avoid what comes after the event. More specifically, Matthew 24:15-28 has much to say regarding the conditions following the Abomination of Desolation. Rome's sacking of Jerusalem in 70 AD partially, but not ultimately, fulfilled the various prophecies in Matthew 24:15-28. It was a partial fulfillment because not all aspects of the prophecy were fulfilled in 70 AD - the terrible events of 70 AD were only a foreshadowing of the ultimate fulfillment of the prophecies yet to occur at some time in Israel's future. Therefore, it might be helpful to examine portions of Matthew 24:15-28 again from the perspective of crucial happenings in Jerusalem:

- 24:15: Jesus indicates that an event will occur in the Temple that will be an abomination of Judaism and God. At the middle of Daniel's 70th Week, the Antichrist will enter the Holy of Holies, take God's rightful earthly place, and declare himself to be god. And it is this single event that sets in motion a chain of events that will go on until the Lord comes three and one-half years later.
- 24:16-19: Whether these verses are literal instructions for the Jews to follow, or they are just symbolic, the passage sufficiently conveys the importance for a speedy exit of the city of Jerusalem. However, the character of the passage is that the people of Israel are to leave their land, homes, possessions, their lives, possibly even their families (?) and flee for their own personal safety and security. They are not to even consider collecting and taking possessions - there is a sense of immediacy and urgency that is not often found in prophecies. The reference to women that are pregnant or nursing babies gives an indication of just how difficult the time will be in all likelihood.
- 24:20: This verse also gives an insight to just how difficult the fleeing might be. The context of the passage suggests there would be a good time in which to quickly flee the area, and a bad time to do so. Either way, there is an uncertainty about the timing of the Antichrist's abominable act, so Israel should be ready for its eventuality. Until then, Jesus warns that the Jews are to pray for their situation - they are to pray that they do not have to flee in the winter or on a Sabbath, two times in which travel would be very difficult and noticeable.
  + Fleeing in the Winter: Travel, especially a hurried exodus of a large number of people, during the winter months in Israel would be treacherous at best and life-threatening at worst. The escape routes out of Jerusalem to get to the hills and mountains to the east, is usually through wadis, or dry riverbeds at the bottom of canyons and valleys. While rain is infrequent in the Middle East, when it does rain, it is

mostly in the winter (October through April), and flash flooding of the wadis is a common occurrence resulting in difficult navigation during perilous traveling.

+ Fleeing on a Sabbath: The reason traveling would be difficult on a Sabbath is because there is no public transportation on the Sabbath. Essentially, only those that could travel by foot or by automobiles (if they have access to them) would be moving on that day. The Jewish laws associated with the Sabbath would impair the Jews' ability to quickly leave the city. Also, as the Sabbath is a day or worship, a large number of Jews moving about in and around the city would be noticeable and could possibly result in the forces of the Antichrist resisting the movements

- 24:21: This verse seems to have a dual end time application. While it supports that possibility that the Great Tribulation will be in the second half of Daniel's 70th Week following the Abomination of Desolation, it also indicates that there will be such a state of suffering as never has existed before. This verse seems to suggest that anti-Semitism will again become prevalent and the Jews will be severely persecuted for the remainder of Daniel's 70th Week.
- 24:22: This verse provides the hope that in spite of the severity of the end times, it too will someday end and the Lord will step in to resolve the situation before humankind literally destroys itself.
- 24:23-28: The outline of the future ends with Jesus advising the Jews that, in the end times, there will be *false Christs and false prophets* [that] *will rise and will show great signs and wonders, so as to mislead, if possible, even to elect*. Jesus admonishes the Jews to be aware of this future effort of deception that will be conducted by Satan. They are not to be drawn out of their hiding by someone that declares himself to be a messiah or prophet - they are to exercise wisdom and discernment.

While most theologians are reluctant to attempt to determine the place of refuge for Israel during their last exile from Jerusalem, Fruchtenbaum[14] advances an idea of where the Jews will spend three and one-half years.

- Fruchtenbaum believes there are three clues that are given in the Bible:
  + Matthew 24:16: The Jews that are in Judea are to flee to the mountain.
  + Revelation 12:6: The woman fled into the wilderness.
  + Revelation 12:14: God will have prepared the place in the wilderness beforehand, and it will be sufficient to hide Israel from Satan.
- While inconclusive, Fruchtenbaum proposes that Isaiah 33:13-16 may contribute to determining the location because the passage indicates that at some point in Jewish history, they will occupy a mountainous stronghold that is easily defendable.
- Fruchtenbaum contends that the location is specifically indicated in Micah 2:12 - ... *I will put them together as the sheep of Bozrah* ... (KJV).

+ While the original Hebrew word was translated as Bozrah in the KJV, it was translated as *fold* in the NASB and the NIV, thus creating a slightly controversial issue. The issue here is how the original Hebrew word is translated. A text-critical note in the NET indicates that the Masoretic Text uses the word *basrah* (Bozrah) here, but that it should be amended (to edit or change, to free or correct from errors) to *bassirah* (into the fold) for a reason contained in a particular commentary used as a reference.

+ Fruchtenbaum contends that the context of the passage is in regard to the Lord's restoration of the nation of Israel in the end times as He brings them together like sheep in a place identified as Bozrah. The ancient city of Bozrah was located in the region of Mount Seir, which just happens to satisfy the location requirements of mountains, wilderness, prepared by God, and defensible. Mount Seir is located southeast of the Dead Sea in what is now the nation of Jordan.

+ Fruchtenbaum continues by favoring a place now known as Petra as the exact location of ancient Bozrah. He continues to justify the view by indicating that Petra "... is totally surrounded by mountains and cliffs. The only way in and out of the city is through a narrow passageway that extends for about a mile and can only be negotiated by foot or horseback. ... The name *Bozrah* means "sheepfold." An ancient sheepfold had a narrow entrance so that the shepherd could count his sheep. Once inside the fold, the sheep had more room to move around. Petra is shaped like a giant sheepfold, with its narrow passage opening up to a spacious circle surrounded by cliffs."[15]

+ In addition, Fruchtenbaum believes that Daniel 11:40-45 supports this theory because the passage indicates that as the Antichrist conquers the world, the nations of Edom, Moab, and Ammon will escape his domination - these three nations comprises modern-day Jordan. It seems logical that the Jews would flee from their land to this place. "Thus, God will provide a city of refuge outside the Antichrist's domain for the fleeing Remnant."[16]

30.6 THE SIXTH PERSONAGE – THE BEAST OUT OF THE SEA

Core Scripture: Revelation 13:1-10; 15-18

Revelation 13:1-10 introduces a beast that will arise out of the sea (also identified as the First Beast), who will have ten horns, seven heads, and ten crowns - the same description used for Satan in Revelation 12:3. The identity of this beast as the Antichrist is in harmony with many other Old and New Testament passages as well as the entire context of Daniel's 70th Week. This beast is described as possessing the following characteristics:

• A blasphemous name will be on the heads.

- John describes this beast as being like a leopard, with feet like a bear, and a mouth like a lion.
- The dragon, Satan, gives this beast *his power and his throne and great authority*.
- One of this beast's heads appears to have been killed, but is brought back to life, thus causing the world to follow this beast in amazement, worship the dragon and this beast, and to yield authority to this beast.
- This beast blasphemes against God, the name of God, God's dwelling place, and the saints that dwell therein.
- This beast is given ruling authority for forty-two months.
- This beast is allowed to persecute the saints and conquer them.
- This beast is given ruling authority over every people and nation.
- And the passage concludes with the observations that those whose names have not been written in the book of life will follow this beast.

30.7	THE SEVENTH PERSONAGE – THE BEAST OUT OF THE EARTH

Core Scripture: Revelation 13:11-18

Revelation 13:11-18 introduces a beast that will arise out of the earth (also identified as the Second Beast), who will have two horns like a lamb, but will speak like a dragon. As with the beast out of the sea, the identity of this beast as the False Prophet is in harmony with many other Old and New Testament passages as well as the entire context of Daniel's 70th Week. This beast is described as possessing the following characteristics:

- This beast will exercise ruling authority on behalf of the other beast, the Antichrist.
- The beast will make all on the earth worship the Antichrist.
- The beast will perform signs, including making fire come down from heaven, and he will deceive everyone.
- This beast will direct that an image (a statue?) be constructed of the Antichrist, at which time this beast will give it life.
- This beast will kill those who do not worship the Antichrist.
- This beast will force all on earth to either take the mark of the beast, or else be killed, in order to conduct business and daily living; the mark of the beast will be the number 666 (note however that his passages does not actually state that the number 666 will be the actual mark on people's forehead or hand; it states that the beast's number is 666).

31

INTRODUCTION TO DANIEL'S 70th WEEK

We have previously examined in detail the removal of the True Church of the Lord Jesus Christ from the physical realms of the earth. We now turn our attention to the cataclysmic period that will be the most profound period of time in the entire span of human history. The seven-year period, identified as Daniel's 70th Week, that follows the Rapture will make the evilness, the unrighteousness, the lawlessness, the wickedness, the sadisticness, the meanness, the inhumanness, the oppressiveness, and the cruelness humans have shown others throughout the span of human history will look like a walk in the park during this time which will be the world's darkest hour.

Daniel's 70th Week, or the Tribulation as it is called by many Christians, will be *a great tribulation, such as has not occurred since the beginning of the world until now, nor ever shall*, as Jesus states in Matthew 24:21 (cf. Daniel 12:1). Refer to the adjacent table for a comparison of several translations that describe the time that is yet still to come. So you can see that the English words chosen to translate the Greek are those that are used to describe life-changing,

Matthew 24:21	
NIV	*great distress*
NASB	*great tribulation*
NET	*great suffering*
KJV	*great tribulation*
NKJV	*great tribulation*
AMP	*great tribulation (affliction, distress, and oppression)*

earth-changing, and beyond comprehension events in human life.

31.1   THE VARIOUS WAYS THE BIBLE REFERS TO ISRAEL'S TIME OF GREAT DISTRESS

There is no shortage of passages in either testament that indicates there will be a future time of trouble for Israel; and, as can be seen from the multitude of verses listed below, it is obvious that it will be a significant time in the history of the world and the nation of Israel.

By far the most common way that the coming time of tribulation, suffering, distress, and misery are referred as the phrases *the day of Jehovah* or *the day of the Lord*. This is true of both the Old and New Testaments. In addition, there are dozens of other instances where *that day*, or some similar phrase occurs. Notice that, (a) many times the phrase will be qualified by some indication of either timing or manner in which action will occur, and (b), there will be some mention of the effect the time will have on the earth or humankind.

- Deuteronomy:
    + 4:30: *in distress and all these things have happened to you.*
    + 32:35: *their day of disaster.*
- Isaiah:
    + 2:12: *The Lord Almighty has a day in store for all the proud and lofty, for all that is exalted (and they will be humbled).*
    + 13:6 and Joel 1:15: *the day of the Lord is near... it will come like destruction.*
    + 13:9: *the day of the Lord is coming – a cruel day, with wrath and fierce anger.*
    + 21:3; 26:17-18; 66:7; Jeremiah 4:31; 30:6; and Micah 4:10: Old Testament imagery of woman in the pain of childbirth as the description of the coming time.
    + 24:1-3: *the Lord lays the earth waste, devastates it, distorts its surface, and scatters its inhabitants... the earth will be completely laid waste and completely despoiled.*
    + 24:21: *in that day the Lord will punish the powers in the heaven above and the kings of the earth below.*
    + 26:20: *until his wrath has passed by.*
    + 28:15 and 18: *When an overwhelming scourge sweeps by.*
    + 28:21: *to do his work, his strange work, and perform his task, his alien task.*
    + 34:1-3: *The Lord is angry with all nations; his wrath is on all their armies. He will totally destroy them; he will give them over to slaughter.*
    + 34:8: *the Lord has a day of vengeance; a year of retribution.*
    + 35:4: *he will come with vengeance; with divine retribution.*
    + 61:2: *the day of vengeance of our God.*
    + 63:4: *the day of vengeance.*
- Jeremiah 30:7: *How awful that day will be! No other will be like it ... time of trouble for Jacob.*
- Ezekiel:
    + 13:5: *the battle on the day of the Lord.*
    + 30:3: *the day of the Lord is near – a day of clouds... a time of doom for the nations.*
- Daniel:
    + 9:27: The foundation of Daniel's 70th Week.
    + 12:1: *a time of distress such as not happened.*
- Joel:
    + 1:15: *the day of the Lord is near; it will come like destruction from the Almighty.*
    + 2:1: *the day of the Lord is coming. It is close at hand.*
    + 2:2: *a day of darkness and gloom, a day of clouds and blackness... such as never was in ancient times nor ever will be in the age to come.*
    + 2:11: *The day of the Lord is great; it is dreadful.*

+ 2:31: *the coming of the great and dreadful day of the Lord.*
+ 3:14: *the day of the Lord is near in the valley of decision.*
- Amos 5:18-20: *the day of the Lord... will be darkness, not light... Will not the day of the Lord be darkness, not light – pitch-dark, without a ray of brightness.*
- Obadiah:
  + 12-14: *in the day of his misfortune... day of their destruction... day of their trouble... day of their distress... in their calamity; in the day of their disaster.*
  + 15: *the day of the Lord is near for all nations.*
- Zephaniah:
  + 1:7: *the day of the Lord is near.*
  + 1:1-18: *will sweep away everything... man... beast... birds... fish... idols... will stretch out my hand... the day of the Lord is near... the Lord has prepared a sacrifice... the day of Lord's sacrifice... that day I punish... punish those who are complacent... great day of the Lord is near – near and coming quickly... a day of distress and anguish, a day of trouble and ruin; a day of darkness and gloom; a day of clouds and blackness – a day of trumpet and battle cry... I will bring such distress... the day of the Lord's wrath... In the fire of his jealousy the whole earth will be consumed, for he will make a sudden end of all who live on the earth.*
- Zechariah 14:1: *A day of the Lord is coming.*
- Malachi 4:5: *that great and dreadful day of the Lord comes... I will come and strike the land with total destruction.*
- Matthew:
  + 24:21: *there will be great distress – unequaled from the beginning of the world until now – and never to be equaled again.*
  + 24:29: *the distress of those days.*
- Acts 2:20: *the coming of the great and glorious day of the Lord.*
- 1 Thessalonians:
  + 1:10: *the coming wrath.*
  + 5:2: *the day of the Lord will come.*
  + 5:9: *wrath.*
- 2 Thessalonians 2:2: *the day of the Lord.*
- 2 Peter 3:10: *the day of the Lord will come like a thief... heavens will disappear ... elements will be destroyed by fire... earth and everything done in it will be laid bare.*
- Revelation:
  + 3:10: *the hour of trial that is going to come on the whole world to test the inhabitants of the earth.*
  + 6:16-17: *wrath of the Lamb... great day of their wrath has come... who can withstand.*
  + 7:14: *great tribulation.*
  + 11:18: *your wrath has come.*

+ 14:7: *the hour of his judgment has come.*
+ 14:10: *the wine of God's fury, which has been poured full strength into the cup of his wrath.*
+ 14:19: *great winepress of God's wrath.*
+ 15:1, 7 and 16:1: *God's wrath.*
+ 16:5: *these judgments.*
+ 16:7: *Lord God Almighty, true and just are your judgments.*
+ 16:19: *the cup filled with the wine of fury of his wrath.*
+ 19:2: *true and just are his judgments.*

The preponderance of the Biblical evidence listed above indicates that there will be a time of extreme difficulty at some point in the future. The fact that it is in the future is established because there is no historical evidence that suggests there has been such an event in the past that measures up to the magnitude indicated in the passages. Christians are to be comforted because believers are not destined for a future time of distress as is indicated in 1 Thessalonians 5:9-10.

31.2	THE DISTINCTION BETWEEN GENERAL TRIBULATION AND THE GREAT TRIBULATION

"The future time of great tribulation and distress in the world is often confused with the stress that has characterized the human race from its beginning."[1] Therefore, before we begin the exploration of the theology of Daniel's 70th Week, a crucial clarification is necessary – there are two different forms of tribulation in the Bible that differ in concept, character and extent. This is of importance, because one's view on whether there are one or two forms of tribulation greatly influence their view of many things, including their view of the Rapture, the structure of Daniel's 70th Week, and their millennial perspective.

GENERAL TRIBULATION

The first form of tribulation is the kind that is common and personal to every believer and person of God and includes the general trials and sufferings of the individual lives of believers. "The concept of tribulation implies a time of pressure, affliction, anguish of heart, and trouble in general. A situation of tribulation is, accordingly, a common experience of the human race resulting from its sin and rebellion against God and from the conflict between God and Satan in the world."[2] "Tribulation characterizes the human race."[3] This can be seen by many of the passages referenced in this chapter, as well as the following passages:

- Old Testament: When they were disobedient to God, His chosen nation of Israel faced national tribulation throughout their existence.
- Genesis 3:17-24: As part of the curse for the original sin, Adam and Eve were judged and subsequently banished from the Garden of Eden, the

implication being that human life will be difficult for all, and there will be a struggle between those that are righteous before the Lord and those that are unrighteous.

- Nehemiah 9:32: An acknowledgement that trouble has followed Israel during part of their history.
- Job 5:7 and 14:1: Job recognizes that humankind is destined to be in trouble throughout life.
- Psalms:
  + 32:7: David recognizes that as a child of God, he faced trouble and distress, and found his hiding place in God.
  + 34:17: *The righteous cry and the Lord hears, and delivers them out of all their troubles.*
- Matthew 13:21: In the parable of the sower and the soils, Jesus points out that when trouble or persecution comes some that confessed belief will fall away, while others will endure. The essence is that it is personal tribulation that tests one's faith.
- John 16:33: Jesus tells his disciples that they will have peace when in Him, but when they are in the world they are to have courage because they will experience trouble and suffering.
- Romans 8:35: Paul points out that tribulation, distress and persecution are the challengers of faith in Jesus Christ.

THE GREAT TRIBULATION

The second form of tribulation is unique to the world as a whole. This form of tribulation occurs one time and is of such magnitude as to be characterized as unprecedented and not having happened on the earth before its occurrence, as can be seen from the descriptions above, especially Matthew 24:21. This form of tribulation is the Great Tribulation (the second half of Daniel's 70th Week) and lasts for the three- and one-half-year period immediately before Christ's Second Advent.

31.3 THE DAY OF THE LORD

" "The Day of the Lord" is a key biblical phrase in understanding God's revelation about the future... The day of the Lord is one of the major strands woven throughout the fabric of biblical prophecy."[4] The essential passages that support the day of the Lord are the following:

- Acts 2:20: *The sun will be turned to darkness and the moon to blood before the coming of the great and glorious day of the Lord.*
- 1 Thessalonians 5:2: Paul tells the Thessalonians that the day of the Lord *will come like a thief in the night.* This means that the date is not known nor is it predictable.

- 2 Thessalonians 2:2: Paul encourages the Thessalonians to not be *easily unsettled or alarmed by the teaching allegedly from us* concerning if the day of the Lord had already come.
- 2 Peter 3:10: Peter reiterates that the day of the Lord will come like a thief and when it does there will be cataclysmic changes to the earth and sky.

THE DAY OF THE LORD DEFINED

The Day of the Lord is a time, a single day, an extended period of days, weeks, months or years, in which God directly and dramatically intervenes in human affairs and in human history with events of judgment followed by events of blessing.

THE TIME AREAS WITHIN THE DAY OF THE LORD

There is debate among theologians and scholars at what events and times will be included in the span of the day of the Lord. There are two basic schools of thought regarding the duration of the Day of the Lord:

- First View: The Day of the Lord begins at the Pretribulational Rapture and ends at the end of the one-thousand-year Millennium when the earth is renewed by fire.
- Second View: The Day of the Lord begins at the Second Advent and ends at the end of the one-thousand-year Millennium when the earth and heavens are purged in anticipation of the new heavens and the new earth.

There are several beliefs as to the extent of the Day of the Lord, and when it terminates:

- Pentecost: "… [T]he Day of the Lord is that extended period of time beginning with God's dealing with Israel after the rapture at the beginning of the tribulation period and extending through the second advent and the millennial age unto the creation of the new heavens and new earth after the millennium."[5]
- Fruchtenbaum: "Others wish to extend the period of the Day of Jehovah to include the Millennium and the Aftermath, but a study of the term uses in every passage will show that it is never used in any context except that of the Tribulation."[6]
- Walvoord: "Scripture bears witness to a future Day of the Lord that will begin at the time of the Rapture, continue through the Great Tribulation, and include the thousand-year reign of Christ."[7]
- Jeremiah: "The day of the Lord… encompasses the Tribulation, the Second Coming of Christ, the Millennium, and the final judgments (1 Thess. 4:13-18; Rev. 4 – 16, 19, 20)."[8]

It is the view of this book that the day of the Lord begins immediately after the Rapture, will extend through Daniel's 70th Week and Christ's Second Advent, the one-thousand-year Millennium, and concludes with the Great White throne Judgment.

THE EVENTS OF THE DAY OF THE LORD

If the Day of Lord includes the events and judgments of Daniel's 70th Week, the Second Advent of Christ, and the one-thousand-year Millennium, then there are a considerable number of events that have to be examined in order to fully understand the time. Because of space limitation they will not be listed here, however, the remaining Chapters will include many of them.

THE RELATIONSHIP OF THE DAY OF THE LORD TO THE DAY OF CHRIST

Many confuse the Day of Christ with the Day of the Lord and try to say they are the same things.
- The Day of the Lord: As discussed in Section 28.7, the Day of the Lord refers to the entire period of time encompassing Daniel's 70th Week and the Messianic Millennium.
- The Day of Christ: Since the mystery of Jewish and Gentile salvation in one body was not seen in the Old Testament, the Day of Christ is a uniquely New Testament term. The context in which it is used refers to the time in which Jesus will come for the church at the Rapture, as can be seen by the following passages:
  + 1 Corinthians:
    ○ 1:4-9: Paul points out that Jesus strengthens those that will be gathered to Him on His day.
    ○ 5:5: An example of the effort that may be expended to save the lost so that they will be saved.
  + 2 Corinthians 1:14: Paul expresses confidence that the Corinthians that have responded to him will be saved when Christ comes to take the Church.
  + Philippians:
    ○ 1:6, 10: Paul tells the Philippians that the One that saved them will perfect them in anticipation of the Rapture.
    ○ 2:16: Again, a reference to being blameless on the Day that Christ comes for His Church.
  + 2 Thessalonians 2:2: The KJV incorrectly uses the Day of Christ, when it should be the Day of the Lord.

"In each case in which the Day of Christ is used it is used specifically in reference to the expectation of the Church, her translation, glorification, and examination for reward."[9]

31.4	THE SCOPE OF TRIBULATION DURING DANIEL'S 70TH WEEK

There can be no question that the scope of Daniel's 70th Week will see God's wrath poured out on the entire world, on all that are living during the seven-year time, and it will especially be focused on Israel. We have also seen that the True Church, of Body of Christ, will be absent from the earth at the time. It is interesting to note that the Church did not come into existence until after Christ's death, resurrection, and ascension, therefore, it was not part of the sixty-nine weeks, then it is reasonable to expect that it will not be part of Daniel's 70th Week.

31.5	THE SOURCE OF TRIBULATION DURING DANIEL'S 70TH WEEK

IIn order for those that do not hold to the Pretribulational Rapture view to make their respective theological constructs work they have to have Satan and humankind be the source for the tribulation that is to occur, thereby replacing God as the source for some portions of the seven-year period (your attention is called to the Pre-Wrath Rapture View in which the first half of Daniel's 70th Week is a time of man's wrath, and the first half of the second half of Daniel's 70th Week is a time of Satan's wrath, with God's wrath occupying the balance of the seven years). Efforts to arrange Daniel's 70th Week in this way is not supported by Scripture – Satan and humankind do not replace God's wrath in order to justify the location of the Rapture.

It is true that Satan and humankind will make a contribution to the time of distress, but neither are assigned a particular time period of Daniel's 70th Week as some believe.
- Revelation:
    + 1:12-17: During Daniel's 70th Week, Satan is thrown down out of heaven to the earth, and he realizes that his time is short and that he has much to accomplish if he is going to win over the Lord. So he immediately begins pursuing the nation of Israel, and when he discovers that the nation is divinely protected, he turns his attention to the saints that have become born-again believers (tribulation saints) after the True Church was removed in the Rapture.
    + 13:7: The Antichrist is permitted to persecute the tribulation saints, and he is given governing authority over the peoples of the earth, which as we know leads to profound distress for those alive at the time.

However, there are no passages that describe that the wrath of Satan or humankind will be of the same magnitude as that ascribed to the Lord. As can be seen from scrutinizing the Scriptures above, "… it cannot be denied that this period is peculiarly the time when God's wrath and judgment fall upon the earth. This is not wrath from men, nor from Satan, except as God may use these agencies as channels for the execution of His will; it is tribulation from God. This period differs from all preceding tribulation, not only in intensity but also in the kind of tribulation since it comes from God Himself."[10]

31.6   THE PURPOSE OF TRIBULATION DURING DANIEL'S 70TH WEEK

As has been indicated throughout this book, the profound events of Daniel's 70th Week will be world-wide in scope and will affect the entire living population, as the purposes that follow will describe (which are not listed in any order of importance). As with everything He does, God has specific purposes for the tribulational events of Daniel's 70th Week.

FIRST PURPOSE – TO COMPLETE PUNISHMENT FOR JUDICIAL HARDENING

"The Tribulation will complete the decreed period of national Israel's judicial hardening as punishment for her rejection of the Messianic program, which the partial return from exile did not remove, and which culminated in the national rejection of Jesus …"[11]
- Isaiah:
  + 6:9-13:
    o At his commissioning as a prophet of God, Isaiah is taken to heaven into the very presence of the Preincarnate Christ (who must have been the sovereign master sitting on the throne, since no man has ever seen the Lord God and lived; refer also to John 12:41), where he was told that the message that he was to preach to his people would not be believed because the Jews were not able to believe the message that the Lord was their God (in another sense, Isaiah is also being told his ministry would not produce much fruit). He was told that the people would not be able to see, hear, or comprehend the essence of their Lord.
    o When asked by Isaiah as to how the callous unbelief and lack of response to the message would continue, he was told that it would last until the land of his people, including the heart of their land (a reference to Jerusalem) was ruined, devastated, and abandoned. He was also told that all would not be lost or destroyed, but that a remnant of Jews would survive and remain in the land.

- ○ While the Babylonian Exile fulfills this prophecy, it is indicative that in fulfillment of Deuteronomy 4, the pattern continued in which God, judges Israel by removing them from the land and dispersing them in other countries before He calls them back and restores them to their land and to Himself. This passage could also be a foreshadowing of the final restoration of Israel to their land during Daniel's 70th Week in preparation for national acceptance of Jesus Christ as their Messiah.
  - + 24:1-6: Isaiah tells Israel that because of the rampant human sinfulness in the world (laws that have been transgressed, and the everlasting covenant broken – essentially, people have refused to live according to the Word of God), the Lord has decreed that He will judge the whole world, and he is ready and willing to do so. He will lay the earth waste, devastate it, distort its surface, and scatter its inhabitants, the earth will wither and dry up, and obviously there will be mush suffering – all of society, regardless of wealth, status, or position, will be affected. God's earthly judgment is the consequence for the guilt of human sinfulness.
- • John 12:37-41: The outcome of Jesus' public earthly ministry was that Israel still refused to believe Him because of their hardened hearts and minds, thus fulfilling the prophecy given in Isaiah 6.
- • Romans 11:7-10: Paul writes that the most important point about Israel's collective hardened heart and mind is that salvation has come to the Gentiles, thus establishing the *elect* (verse 7). This aspect is to also make Israel jealous so that in the future they will return to the Lord.

SECOND PURPOSE – TO PREPARE THE NATION ISRAEL FOR HER MESSIAH

It is interesting, as can be seen from the description of this purpose below, how the Lord works with His chosen nation is not that much unlike how He works with individual people. Through circumstances that are unique to each individual, the Lord brings each person to a point in their life in which they have to willfully choose between Him, or the world led by the antithesis of Him, Satan. The Lord has been bringing Israel to these points, and there are many, throughout her history, and each time she has rebelled and turned away from Him, thus resulting in judgment and punishment. Now at the end of human history, He will restore the tiny nation from worldwide dispersion and will bring about circumstances in which enough individual Jews will recognize Jesus Christ as their Messiah and will turn to Him to constitute a national return to the Lord – not all Jews will turn to the Lord, in spite of the horribleness of times, some Jews will continue to rebel.

We know that when Christ comes for His Second Advent, He will bring the Church Age believers with Him, and it is obvious that there will be people that will live during the one-thousand-year Millennium, that have survived the Great

Tribulation, however, how will the Jews get to the Millennium? They will get there because of what the Lord does to the nation Israel during Daniel's 70th Week, and because there are many covenant promises to Israel that are yet to be fulfilled. Thus, "God's purpose for Israel in the Tribulation is to being about the conversion of a multitude of Jews, who will enter into the blessings of the kingdom and experience the fulfillment of all Israel's covenants. ... It is also God's purpose to populate the millennium with a multitude of saved Gentiles, who are redeemed through the preaching of the believing remnant. ... God's purpose then, is to populate the millennial kingdom by bringing a host from among Israel and the Gentile nations to Himself."[12]

THIRD PURPOSE – TO PREPARE THE NATION ISRAEL FOR HER MESSIAH BY CONVINCING HER OF THE NEED FOR THE MESSIAH

In anticipation of national repentance and restoration, Israel will need to be convinced that the One they called the Prophet that came to earth nearly two thousand years ago is indeed the One that will deliver them to the kingdom.

- Isaiah 59:20-21: Isaiah points out that a future redeemer (a reference to Jesus Christ) will come to Israel to provide protection for those that repent of their rebelliousness, and those that turn to God will receive the Spirit of God who will be with them forever.
- Jeremiah 31:31-34: The ultimate provision of the Lord for His chosen nation is that He will make a new unconditional agreement with them at some time in the future in which, after He restores them back to their land, He will put His law within them and there will be not further need for evangelization. He will be their God, and they will be His people in the true sense that was intended from the beginning of the nation.
- Ezekiel:
  + 20:34-38: [34] *I will bring you from the nations and gather you from the countries where you have been scattered – with a mighty hand and an outstretched arm and with outpoured wrath.* [35] *I will bring you into the wilderness of the nations and there, face to face, I will execute judgment upon you.* [36] *As I judged your ancestors in the wilderness of the land of Egypt, so I will judge you, declares the Sovereign Lord.* [37] *I will take note of you as you pass under my rod, and I will bring you into the bond of the covenant.* [38] *I will purge you of those who revolt and rebel against me. Although I will bring them out of the land where they are living, yet they will not enter the land of Israel. Then you will know that I am the Lord.*
  + 36:25-27: Again, a message of restoration. God will gather the scattered Jews, will cleanse and purify them, will remove their hardened hearts and give them a new fleshy heart, will give them His Spirit, and they will walk in His statues and ordinances.

+ 37:1-14: Ezekiel 33 - 39 emphasizes the new life that Israel will eventually have at some time in the future, and this passage symbolically describes the conditions of restoration. The nation of Israel, exiled to Babylonia at the time the Book of Ezekiel was written, is seen as a valley full of disconnected, dry, sunbaked bones, indicating that the nation is only a dried-up carcass of a nation with no life. Then, at the will of the Lord He will breathe new life (in the same sense as life was breathed into Adam, refer to Genesis 2:7) into the bones, and the nation will come to life again and will be rebuilt into a fully functioning collection of people with a national identity. The Israelites that live in the Middle East at this time is not a fulfillment of this prophecy, because this prophecy will be fulfilled at the Second Coming of Christ.

- Daniel 12:5-7: The Daniel 11:36-45 passage chronicles the 70th week of Daniel where the ruler to come, the Antichrist, is said to have governing control for the time of the 70th week. In Daniel 12:5-7, Daniel is told that the earth-shattering events described will last for three and one-half years. This passage establishes that there will be a time in Israel's future that will challenge them as they have never been challenged.

- Zechariah 12:9 - 13:2: This passage indicates the Lord will destroy the nations that have persecuted Israel and that the Jews will cry and mourn for the One they pierced, Jesus.

FOURTH PURPOSE – TO BRING ABOUT A WORLDWIDE REVIVAL

Price writes that "[t]he Tribulation will produce a Messianic revival among the Jewish people scattered throughout the world ..., and also will result in a massive return to the Land of Israel ... in preparation for nation repentance."[13]

- Deuteronomy 4:27-30: In a prophecy that is one of the most important aspects of the relationship between God and His elected people, Israel, Moses tells the young nation just before they enter Canaan, their Promised Land, that if they are disobedient to God, they will be judged and will be scattered in small numbers into other nations where they will worship other gods of human origin. However, if they seek the Lord, then in the distress of the last days, the Lord will not let them down or destroy them. Verse 4:30 establishes the idea that there will be a time of distress that will occur at the end of the period of time.

- Ezekiel 36:24 and 37:21: Ezekiel records the Lord saying He will take the Jews from the nations and restore them to their land, an obvious indication that they had been scattered prior to their restoration, and that the Lord had opened their eyes as they were returning to their land because of Him.

- Zechariah 36:24 and 37:21: *Thus says the Lord of hosts, 'Behold, I am going to save My people from the land of the east and from the land of the west;*

and I will bring them back, and they will live in the midst of Jerusalem, and they will be My people and I will be their God in truth and righteousness. '

Fruchtenbaum[14] points out that for what seems like the Lord's last offer to bring sinners to saving faith, 144,000 Jews are sent out to evangelize to the unbelieving world that is in the midst of severe tribulation.

- Matthew 24:14: Immediately before Jesus describes the Abomination of Desolation in Matthew 24, He prophesies that the Gospel of the Kingdom will be proclaimed to the world just before the end, with 24:15 being the beginning of the end. From their efforts, there will be a revival that will be associated with the return to the land.
- Revelation:
  + 7:1-8: This passage presents the means of evangelization:
    o 12,000 believing Jews will be commissioned from each of the 12 tribes of Israel, and collectively, the 144,000 will be sealed in order to be the evangelists for Daniel's 70th Week. They are sealed for two reasons, first the sealing provides protection from the judgments poured out by God and, second the sealing indicates that they will serve the Lord by proclaiming the Gospel during the time of tribulation.
    o The fact that Jews were chosen is interesting and the reason is a logical choice.
      - While it usually takes a number of years to train evangelists, the Jews that have come to Jesus Christ apparently already know much of what is necessary without much additional training and study - Jews have to in order to recognize who Jesus really is. The Jews are significantly knowledgeable of the Old Testament and the events surrounding Jesus' First Advent, so it is safe to say that regardless if individual Jews believe in Jesus Christ, they have a substantial knowledge of Him and His Gospel.
      - The Jews are currently scattered all over the world and are integrated into many cultures and societies, also, they speak most, if not all, the predominant languages of the world.
    o Thus the 144,000 Jews will evangelize the world in fulfillment of Matthew 24:14 and essentially bring about a worldwide revival of sorts. There is no indication of the number that will come to Jesus except as described in the following passage.
  + 7:9-17: John describes the results of the evangelization of the tribulation world when he sees an innumerable multitude of martyred Jews and Gentiles that surround the throne of God and worship Him.

FIFTH PURPOSE – TO DELIVER THE JEWISH PEOPLE FROM GENTILE DOMINATION IN PREPARATION FOR THE MESSIANIC KINGDOM

The Gentile nations that have ruled Israel for so many hundreds of years will be judged.

- Isaiah:
    + 24:21-23: At some point in the future, earthly political kings will be judged for their disobedience to God, thus delivering the Jews from Gentile rulership.
    + 59:16-20: Isaiah records attributes of God, the desire for justice and righteousness and the punishment for injustice and unrighteousness. While this passage speaks in the sense of worldwide justice and righteousness, God especially focuses on those nations that have persecuted Israel.
- Matthew 24:29-31 (cf. Mark 13:24-27): This passage follows the portion of Matthew 24:15-28 that describes the second three and one-half years of Daniel's 70th Week. The fruit of the evangelism that has been taking place during Daniel's 70th Week will be harvested.

SIXTH PURPOSE – TO POUR OUT JUDGMENT ON AN UNBELIEVING WORLD BY PURGING THE WICKED IN PREPARATION FOR THE MESSIANIC KINGDOM

As can be seen from the following passages, the Lord will judge all the living that remain on the earth after the Rapture and who do not come to saving faith in Jesus Christ.

- Isaiah:
    + 11:9: The Lord will bring the world into universal knowledge of Him which leads to universal submission.
    + 13:9: A verse that succinctly states that a worldwide day of judgment is coming from the Lord against those who are in opposition to Him.
    + 26:21: The Lord will come down from heaven to punish the sinfulness of humankind, and to exact justice.
- Jeremiah 25:32-33: During Daniel's 70th Week, the wrath of God will move from the destruction of one nation to the destruction of others by a military force from another part of the world; the dead will not be mourned for or buried.
- Ezekiel:
    + 20:33-38: Refer to commentary above.
    + 37:15-23: Ezekiel is directed by God to use two sticks to symbolically demonstrate the eventual restoration of the two divided kingdoms, Judah and Israel, into one unified people in which He will not allow them

to remain focused on the world, but instead will bring them to Him. Again, the statement, *they will be My people, and I will be their God.*

- Zechariah:
    + 13:2: God will remove idolatry, false prophets, and unclean spirits from the land of Israel at the time He restores the nation to their land.
    + 14:9: In the future, the Lord will be the one and only king that rules the earth and those that live during that time.
- Matthew 25:31-46: Immediately after Jesus Christ returns to earth for His Second Advent, He will purge the survivors of the seven-year tribulation of rebellious Gentiles, thus completing the judgment of the human unrighteousness that had occurred to that time.
- 2 Thessalonians 2:12: As Paul concludes the description of the Day of the Lord, he points out that many will have been deceived by satanic deception, and they will be judged for having turned from the truth to delight in evil.
- Revelation: Many individuals and nations will be deceived and will follow the false teachings of the harlot system lead by the false prophet, and will worship the Antichrist - for this they will be judged.
    + 3:10: Jesus points out the faithful will not have to endure the time that will come in which those that are focused on the world, rather than God, will be judged for their sinfulness.
        o Note that Jesus said that those that dwell on the earth would be tested, He did not say that the True Church would be tested; in fact Jesus says that those He was speaking to, the Philadelphian Church of true believers, would be spared from the wrath that is to come.
        o The Greek word used for dwell gives a sense of permanence, and suggests those that dwell on the earth are those that have aligned themselves with the earthliness of the world.
        o It just seems as if the True Church was to experience Daniel's 70th Week, that somewhere in the New Testament there would be a specific statement of such, or at least an implication - the New Testament gives no indication that the True Church will experience the time.
    + 6 - 18: These chapters of Revelation describe the times that have been characterized as being like no other time on earth. In the same context as Revelation 3:10, the following passages make reference to those that dwell on the earth as the ones that suffer tribulation at the exclusion of a reference to the True Church:
        o 6:10: Those who dwell on the earth cry out asking how much longer the judgment is to continue.
        o 11:10: Those who dwell on the earth will celebrate the death of the two witnesses sent by God. The verse does not say that all who dwell on the earth rejoices over their death.
        o 13:8: All who dwell on the earth will worship the beast. Again, no specific reference to the True Church is made. Some could say

71

that the remainder of the verse about being written in the book of life could be a reference to the True Church, however, the verse indicates a time period that extends back to the foundation of the world and is not limited to the seven-year period.

- o 13:12: The other beast forces those who dwell on the earth to worship him. If the True Church were present then it would be worshipping the beast, again, this is not consistent with Scripture.
- o 13:14: The other beast deceives those who dwell on the earth; again, if the True Church were present it would be being deceived.
- o 14:6: An angel preaches the gospel to those who live on the earth. If the True Church were present, it would not have to wonder, it would know about the beast.
+ 19: The ultimate battle between the forces of earthly evil, led by Satan, and the forces of heavenly good, led by King Messiah; the ultimate effort by the created to eliminate the Creator. The Campaign of Armageddon becomes the ultimate conclusion of the apostasy of humankind that has completely saturated the world and those that have survived the judgments of Revelation 6 - 18.

THE COMPLETE LACK OF EVIDENCE FOR THE PRESENCE OF THE TRUE CHURCH IN DANIEL'S 70TH WEEK

"… [A] careful and literal exegesis of the Scriptures reveals no evidence whatever that the church of the present age will go through the Tribulation. … In the Old Testament the tribulation passages refer to both Israel and the Gentiles and to the saved among either group but never to a corporate body of Jews and Gentiles combined as they are in the church."[15]

One of the Biblical substantiations that the Rapture of the True Church will be Pretribulational is the lack of any references to the True Church in passages dealing with Daniel's 70th Week. There are some, especially those of the Posttribulational Rapture view, that try to say that any used of the following New Testament words are for the purpose of establishing that the Rapture will be after Daniel's 70th Week (posttribulational).

- *elect*: Matthew 24:22 and 24:31 both use this word, and postribulationalists believe that the True Church is referred to each time. However, this view is borne out of the idea that Matthew 24 and 25 concerns the Church rather than Israel. It should be noted that these two chapters of Matthew refer specifically to Israel and not to the Church. By taking this view, posttribulationalism denies the possibility that the word elect can refer to other of God's children in addition to those of this present age. In fact, the nation of Israel is an elect nation, and we know that Israel is not the Church, so the word elect does not always refer exclusively to the Church.

- *gathering*: Again, posttribulationalism does the same thing with this word. They believe that its use in Matthew 24:31 means the same things as its use in 1 Thessalonians 4:16-17 and 2 Thessalonians 2:1. The context of the passages indicate that the use of gathering in the Matthew passages is in reference to the elect of Israel that are being restored to the Promised Land according to the multitude of Old Testament passages indicating such. The context of the Thessalonian passage clearly indicates a reference to the True Church at the Rapture.

31.7 THE TIMING OF THE GREAT TRIBULATION

A point of clarification is necessary at this point to discuss the relationship between the Daniel's 70th Week and the Great Tribulation. There are many who hold that the events described in Revelation 6 through 18 all occur within the seven years of Daniel 9:27. But wait… the sense of Revelation 6 through 18 is that the events all seem to happen during a three- and one-half-year period instead of during a seven-year period, as we will see shortly.

Above, Daniel's 70th Week, the Tribulation First Half, and the Great Tribulation were respectfully defined, and the point has been asserted since then that the two halves, while they both comprise Daniel's 70th Week, will be distinctively difference from each other.

- Pre-Daniel's 70th Week - A Time of Preparation: It is the position of this book that this undefined period of time between the Rapture of the True Church and the beginning of Daniel's 70th Week (the signing of the covenant of peace) will be characterized by the preparatory convergence of the conditions and situations required for humankind and the world to travel the most unique seven years of history culminating in the Messiah's Second Advent.
- The Tribulation First Half - A Time of "Peace": It is also the position of this book that this period will be characterized by the following:
  + The first half of Daniel's 70th Week will be a time of "relative" peace and calm, relative because the general tribulation that had been occurring prior to Daniel's 70th Week will continue as the evolution of the almost godless world society escalates to its logical conclusion of being a fully godless society ruled by the Antichrist who is empowered by the antithesis of God - Satan.
  + The Ruler to Come, signifies the beginning of Daniel's 70th Week, and by preparing for his rulership of the world as the Antichrist. This individual is not identified as the Antichrist until the middle of Daniel's 70th Week, and the implication is that the first half will be relatively quiet and somewhat uneventful as the Ruler to Come / Antichrist develops his power base and manipulates the various governmental and religious institutions to serve his goals, which are also Satan's goals.

- + The latter stages of the Times of the Gentiles will be fulfilled and the world will move to the required setting necessary for the Antichrist to steal control of the world government from others by sinister means.
  + The Professing Church, which was not raptured with the True Church, will continue to devolve into the Christ-less shell that is predicted. This provides the required setting necessary for the Antichrist to desecrate the Jewish Temple and falsely establish himself as God.
- The Great Tribulation: - A time of Hell on Earth: It is also the position of this book that this period will be the second half of Daniel's 70th Week and will be characterized by the following:
  + It will be a time that will be the darkest time of all of human history, and unlike any other time.
  + All those that believe in anything related to God will be severely persecuted; this includes those that come to faith in Jesus Christ during Daniel's 70th Week, and it includes the nation of Israel because she becomes the focus of the wrath of the Antichrist and his god, Satan, because the True Church is not present to persecute.
  + All of the seal, trumpet, and bowl judgments of Revelation 6 through 18 will take place.

The aspect of Daniel's 70th Week that provides the Scriptural basis for the above position can be found in how the timing of the Great Tribulation is explained within the context of Israel.

- Daniel:
  + 7:25: A concise prophecy about the impact that the Antichrist will have for a time, times, and half a time. He will speak out against God, he will persecute God's chosen nation, he will attempt to change the culture and laws, and many will be delivered into his hands.
  + 12:7: In a vision to Daniel, Jesus Christ indicates that the Antichrist will persecute the Jews for a fixed period of time - time, times, and half a time.
- Revelation:
  + 11:2: The Gentiles will occupy the city of Jerusalem for forty-two months.
  + 11:3: The two witnesses will perform their functions for 1,260 days.
  + 12:6: The nation of Israel, represented by the Woman, will hide in the wilderness and be taken care of by the Lord for 1,260 days.
  + 12:14: Another passage indicating that the nation of Israel will be given the ability to flee the persecution of the Antichrist to a place prepared by God away from Satan, where she will be cared for by her Lord, for a period of time indicated to be time, times, and half a time.
  + 13:5: The beast, the Antichrist, will be permitted to blaspheme the Lord and rule the earth for a period of forty-two months.

What all this means is logically laid out in the following:

- The Antichrist will be active for a fixed period of time that is identified as time, times, and half a time; therefore, as the Antichrist does not actually come into the scene until the desecration of the Tribulation Temple at the middle of Daniel's 70th Week, it is logical that the time of the Antichrist's operations will be during the Great Tribulation.
- The outer court of the Jewish Temple, and the city of Jerusalem will be occupied by the Gentiles for forty-two months; therefore, it is logical that this occupancy will occur during the Great Tribulation, as it is the time after the Antichrist desecrates the Jewish Temple, and, since the Antichrist is Gentile, he will command the necessary military and governmental forces in order to do so.
- The two witnesses will testify for 1,260 days; therefore, since they are testifying against the Antichrist during his reign, it is logical that his reign will occur during the Great Tribulation.
- The Antichrist will persecute the nation of Israel, causing the Jews to flee for protection, for 1,260 days or for a time, times, and half a time; therefore, it is also logical for this time of persecution of Israel by the Antichrist to be during the Great Tribulation.

31.8   THE PROMISE OF THE TRUE CHURCH NOT GOING THROUGH DANIEL'S 70TH WEEK

Throughout this book, the point has been made repeatedly that the True Church is not destined to experience the seven years of Daniel's 70th Week. "Not only is there no mention of the church in any passage describing the future Tribulation, but there are specific promises given to the church that deliverance from that period is assured."[16] The following passages attest to this:

- Luke 21:34-36: Following the passage about the Coming of the Son of Man, verses 25-28, and the Parable of the Fig Tree, verses 27-33, Jesus then admonishes that people should be ready and stay alert for the coming of that day which will overtake all who live on the face of the earth. Jesus continues by advising that it is possible to escape the terrible things that must happen and instead appear before the Son Man.
- Romans 5:9: Another statement, this time by Paul, that indicates the saving work of Jesus Christ will deliver believers from God's wrath.
- 1 Thessalonians:
  + 1:10: A specific indication that Jesus Christ is the deliverer from the coming wrath.
  + 5:9: God did not destine the True Church for the wrath of a future time, but instead for salvation made available by Jesus Christ.
- 2 Peter 2:4-9: Using the examples of angels, Noah, and Lot, Peter points out that God knows how and when to separate the righteous from the unrighteous destined for punishment. A general principle is at work here, "… God characteristically delivers believers from wrath designed for judgment upon the unbelievers."[17]

- Revelation:
    + 3:10: "… the Philadelphia church, representing the true and faithful church, is promised deliverance before the hour comes."[18]
    + 6:17: John indicates that the wrath will be terrible and asks the rhetorical question of who would be able to stand against it. "The only way one could be kept from that day of wrath would be to be delivered beforehand."[19]

31.9   THE REMOVAL OF THE RESTRAINER

Another important aspect that needs to be understood about Daniel's 70th Week is that there exists a restrainer of sin who will, at the right time, be removed from the earth prior to the beginning of that terrible time. Second Thessalonians 2:7-8 clearly indicates that the (*hidden* in NET, *mystery* in NASB, and *secret* in NIV) power of lawlessness will be held back, or restrained, by someone or something until it is take out of the way. Part of the purpose of Paul's second letter to the Thessalonians was to clarify their misunderstanding that they were already in the Day of the Lord. In his response, as recorded in 2 Thessalonians 2, Paul comforts them by establishing a sequence of events that are to take place before the Day of the Lord comes:

- 2:1: The context of the passage is regarding the Second Coming of Jesus Christ in its relationship with the Day of the Lord.
- 2:3: The Second Coming of Jesus Christ will not happen until the rebellion, or apostasy, comes first and the man of lawlessness, the one destined to destruction, is revealed.
- 2:4: The man of lawlessness is described as one that exalts himself as the object of worship, and who will attempt to display himself as God's replacement at some time in the future.
- 2:7: Paul points out that the man of lawlessness is already at work even at that time, but his identity cannot be revealed until the restrainer is removed. The implication here is that when the restrainer is removed, then the man of lawlessness will be revealed and the Day of the Lord will ensue.

So, just who, or what, is the Restrainer? What has the power and ability to restrain, or limit, the power of Satan? There are a number of views as to the identity of the restrainer that can be seen below. However, before the views are explored, it should be established that the Bible is not explicit about the identity. This is another instance in which a theological view has to be developed based on the evidence given in the Bible and how it fits within the larger context.

- First View: This book holds that the most plausible view is that the restrainer is the Holy Spirit because it is the most consistent with the Scriptures.
    + Satan is a spiritual personality, so if there were a restrainer, it would seem probable he would also be a spiritual personality capable of operating within the same realm of Satan.

+ As lawlessness is a function of Satan, and the man of lawlessness will be a person empowered by Satan, the restrainer must have the ability to resist the power of Satan, thus it must be a part of the Triune Godhead. Also, the restrainer cannot be limited by time and space, thus the divine attributes of eternality and omnipresence must be characteristics.
+ Since the current dispensation is one of Grace, as manifested by the Spirit of God, then the Holy Spirit is already at work within this period. Since the Holy Spirit has abided spiritually with the body of the True Church from its beginning (Pentecost), then it is conceivable that it will be removed when the True Church is removed in the Rapture. Refer also to John 16:7-11 and 1 John 4:4.

- Second View: Some theologians of church history believe that the Roman Empire, and its ability to make laws and exercise justice, is the restrainer. However, this idea does not have any direct Scriptural support.
- Third View: Many others believe that the concept of government and law is the restrainer based on Romans 13:1 that says, the powers of government are ordained by God. However, since God ordains the government, then it is not the government that restrains lawlessness, it is the One that ordains the institution – God. This view also does not have any direct Scriptural support.
- Fourth View: This view holds that the restrainer does not have to be from the good side of things – it can be from the bad sides of things, Satan. This idea is based on the notion that if God can have His Son, then Satan can manifest his son of perdition. This would put the Lord into the view of working His Plan by Satanic power, which is contrary to His name. If the restrainer were of Satan, why would it be necessary for it to be removed? Also, the idea of the passage is that things get worse after the restrainer is removed. Thus, this view seems implausible, as it does not agree with Scripture.
- Fifth View: The view that the church is the restrainer seems to be more possible than the previous second, third, and fourth views, however, it also has its own weaknesses. This view is based on the premise that believers are both the salt of the earth and the light shining in the darkness, the implication being that salt and light resists the powers of Satan. While there is obvious truth to this idea, it is God through the Holy Spirit that empowers believers to resist Satan's power, therefore, like the third view above, God is behind the power of government and the believer, so it seems unlikely that either of these is the restrainer.

The notion that the restrainer has to be removed prior to Daniel's 70th Week, and the probability that the restrainer is in all likelihood the Holy Spirit, lends credibility to a Pretribulational Rapture of believing saints. Removal of the restrainer at the time of the Rapture seems to be the only logical conclusions to the believer-indwelling work of the Holy Spirit that began on the day of Pentecost. It seems the best scenario for the removal to occur at the Rapture.

31.10 SALVATION DURING DANIEL'S 70TH WEEK

The logical question that occurs at this point is: If the Holy Spirit is the one that brings people to saving faith in Jesus Christ, and He is removed before Daniel's 70th Week begins, then how will people become believers between the Rapture and Christ's Second Advent as the Bible clearly indicates? We can see in Revelation 7 that there will be many Gentiles that come to saving faith in Jesus Christ, and that there will be 144,000 Jews that will be divinely sealed, or protected against harm from the Antichrist, that will globally witness for Christ. Therefore, the Holy Spirit must have some role or responsibility during this time. The Bible does not indicate that the Holy Spirit's role during this time will be indwelling of believers as it has been during the Dispensation of Grace. "Once the body of Christ has been caught away or raptured to heaven, the Holy Spirit's ministry will revert back to what He did for believers during the Old Testament era."[20]

There is an important qualification that should be understood regarding salvation:
* It should be recognized that salvation throughout all of human history and regardless of dispensation, is always by the grace of God. While the process and methodology might vary somewhat, the grace of God is always at the core of the forgiveness of sin and the bestowal of eternal life to those that believe in Him. There are not several plans of salvation, only the one plan of God's grace. The manifestation of the grace of God is the giving of His Son to be *the one and only true sacrifice* for all of human sin.
* "The *basis* of salvation in every age is the death of Christ; the *requirement* for salvation in every age is faith; the *object* of faith in every age is God; the *content* of faith changes in the various dispensations."[21] It is this last point that is important here. The revelation of God to humankind was revealed progressively, and until Christ's actual earthly, human birth, the people of the Old Testament could not see Him as their future Messiah in the same manner as we can see Him as our Messiah in our past. This is not to say that they did not anticipate, or look forward to, a coming Messiah, they just did not know that the Son of the Living God would come to earth as a human, be crucified, and then be resurrected. Stated another way, they did not have specific knowledge that the forgiveness of their sins and the bestowal of eternal life would be from Jesus Christ.

SALVATION DURING THE OLD TESTAMENT ERA

Jewish Salvation
There are two separate and distinct aspects of Jewish salvation in the Old Testament – individual and national.
* Individual:

+ Essentially, because of their belief in God as evidenced by faithfulness based on blood sacrifice to cover their sins; specific individuals were declared to be righteous by God in His sight. God considered them as saved as a principle of faith because of the future sacrifice of Jesus Christ. Thus, salvation became an inheritance to be received at a future time, rather than a present possession as would occur during the time of the Church. Individual Israelites were saved if they believed in God, but the fullness of that salvation was a future experience. The perspective of salvation as an inheritance can be seen by the following passages:
    o Daniel 12:2: Note that this verse is the only undisputed reference to saint resurrection found in the Old Testament.
    o Luke 10:25-29: When asked by *an expert in the law* as to what he should do *to inherit eternal life,* Jesus turned the question back on him. The expert answered, *Love the Lord your God with all your heart and with all your soul and with all your strength and with all your mind.* Jesus responds by pointing out that the answer was correct.
+ During the time of the Church, when a believer physically died, their soul went immediately into the presence of Jesus Christ however this was not true of Old Testament saints. Obviously, if Jesus Christ had not come to earth as their Savior, then when an Old Testament saint died, they could hardly go immediately into His presence. The Old Testament experience of the eternal life aspect of their personal salvation waits on the Work of Christ; their resurrection will be at Christ's Second Advent.
+ When presented in the context of dispensationalism, salvation during all dispensations can be seen as follows: "In examining salvation under the Mosaic law the principal question is simply, how much of what God was going to do in the future did the Old Testament believer comprehend? According to both Old and New Testament revelation it is impossible to say that he saw the same promise, the same Savior as we do today. Therefore, the dispensationalists' distinction between the *content* of his faith and the content of ours is valid. The basis of salvation is always the death of Christ; the means is always faith; the object is always God (though man's understanding of God before and after the incarnation is obviously different); but the content of faith depends on the particular revelation God was pleased to give at a certain time."[22]
• National:
    + Romans 11:25-32 summarizes this aspect of salvation very succinctly. After the full number of Gentiles has come to salvation, an opportunity provided to them because of Israel's disobedience, Jesus Christ the Messiah will restore the nation to its status as the elected nation of God. This national salvation is related to the full history of Israel as seen in the Bible and her covenantal relationship with God in which

God's graciousness will ultimately restore Israel in the future regardless of her iniquities.

+ The salvation of the nation of Israel will be assured by God, and it will depend on the salvation of the people of Israel. While the individual Israelite who believed God was himself saved, that salvation was assured to him on the basis of a future work which God was going to do for the entire nation at the Second Advent, at which time the Messiah would make a final dealing with the sins of the people.

+ There are many passages that speak to the promised salvation of the nation of Israel:

  o Jeremiah 30:7: The return of Israel and Judah to the promised land will come after a time of national distress. They will be delivered by God.

  o Ezekiel 20:37-38: Israel will know that God is their God because those that revolt and rebel against Him while being scattered among the nations will not be allowed to enter the promised land.

  o Daniel 12:1: A very terrible time of distress is coming, but those Jews whose names are written in the book will be delivered.

  o Joel 2:31-32: The Jews that are living in other nations that call on the name of the Lord will be saved.

  o Zechariah 13:1, 8-9: At some point in the restoration process one-third of the Jews will call on the Lord's name and they will be refined like silver.

SALVATION DURING DANIEL'S 70TH WEEK

God's dealing with Israel was temporarily postponed after the crucifixion of Christ as He turned His attention away from Israel and to the Church. After God determines the fullness of the Church is completed, He will then close His program with the Church and will return His attention once again toward the nation of Israel. The content of faith prior to Christ's First Advent during the Old Testament times was different than the content of faith during the Church Age. It is the Old Testament version of the content of faith that will be returned to during Daniel's 70th Week as God resumes His program with Israel. Salvation during Daniel's 70th Week will be according to the principle of faith. This principle can be seen in Hebrews 11:1-40 where those that were saved were those that believed in God – this principle is not limited to any age or dispensation.

Even though the Holy Spirit did not indwell believers in the Old Testament, God still indicates that those saints were saved by the work of the Holy Spirit. As is true of the time before the Church Age will also be true during Daniel's 70th Week. The Holy Spirit, who is omnipresent, will do the work of regeneration as He did when God was previously dealing with Israel, but without an indwelling ministry.

The indwelling today is related to empowerment, but the indwelling is entirely distinct and separate from the work of the Spirit in regeneration. Thus, it should be clearly seen that even though the Spirit is not indwelling in the tribulation, He may still be active in regeneration.

31.11 THE THRONE OF GOD

The Book of Revelation is divided into three sections as defined in verse 1:19:
- *Write therefore the things which you have seen* (Revelation 1)
- *and the things which are* (Revelation 2 and 3)
- *and the things which shall take place after these things* (Revelation 4 through 22)

In the transition from the second to the third vision of things, John is transported into heaven (Revelation 4:1) to be shown the things that compose the third grouping of things. The very first observation John makes is the throne of God that he describes in Revelation 4:2-11. It should be noted, before this topic is detailed, there are some who hold to the premillennial and pretribulational rapture views are seen in Revelation 4:1-2. However, this is unlikely because the context does not seem to support this idea.

John's body was not translated physically; it is more accurate that John was transported spiritually to heaven while his body remained on earth (a text note in the New English Translation (NET) for Revelation 4:2 says, "a state of spiritual exaltation best described as a trance"). If he had been translated physically, he must have been returned to earth after the visions because he wrote the Book of Revelation describing his experiences and observations, and lived out the remainder of his natural life on the Isle of Patmos. Revelation 4:1 seems to just be the response to the invitation to come up to heaven. Also, this is seen as the future event according to the futurist interpretive view above, rather than as a past event according to the preterist interpretive view, because the events described in Revelation 4 – 19 has not occurred in history.

The significance of this fourth chapter of Revelation is that we are given a glimpse of the grandeur of heaven with the Lord sitting on His throne, as well as the environment that will exist at some point between the Rapture and the Great Tribulation. We know the scenes seen by John are after the Rapture because of what will be pointed out below concerning the twenty-four elders. It is the position of this book that the other end of the potential time frame is the Great Tribulation rather than the beginning of Daniel's 70th Week. This belief is based on the idea that all of the seal, trumpet, and bowl judgments, listed in Revelation 4 – 19, will occur during the second three- and one-half-year period of Daniel's 70th Week, rather than throughout the seven years as many premillennialists and pretribulational rapturists believe.

From the fourth chapter of Revelation we can make the following observations of what John was shown:

- 4:2-3: Walvoord sees this passage as "… a general expression of the glory of God."[23] The occupant on the throne must be God, because Jesus is seen as the Lamb later on, and John uses references to precious stones possibly as a connection between God and Old Testament Israel. The high priest, when interceding for Israel, wore precious stones representing, one for each of the twelve tribes of Israel, on his chest as part of his priestly garments. Beyond this, the purpose of the stones is uncertain.
- 4:4: Refer to discussion below concerning the twenty-four elders.
- 4:5: The glory of God is further described by references to forms of nature that express the powerful and awful judgments about to descend upon the earth. The seven flaming torches representing the seven spirits of God are representatives of the Holy Spirit.
- 4:6-9: As part of the throne area, John sees a sea of glass and four living creatures, whole descriptions seem to be far removed from anything familiar. The meaning of the sea of glass is also uncertain, however, it may be a reference to aspects of the tabernacle and temple. "There has been much speculation concerning the identity of these living ones and the significance of their presence and ministry in this heavenly scene."[24] Walvoord[25] recognizes there are several possible views:
  + First View: It is the position of this book, that probably the best explanation, according to Walvoord, is that the living creatures are representative of the attributes of God, with the lion referring to majesty and omnipotence, the calf referring to patience and continuous labor, man as the most majestic of His creations, and the eagle symbolic of His sovereignty and supremacy.
  + Second View: The four living creatures are compared to the four Gospels that represent Christ in four major aspects of His person. The lion refers to Christ as the King of the tribe of Judah (Matthew), the calf refers to Christ as the Servant of Jehovah (Mark), the man refers to the Humanity of Jesus (Luke), and the eagle refers to the Divinity of Christ (John).
  + Third View: The four living creatures indicate a general representation of God that would be visible to humans, such as the manner in which the tribes of Israel pitched their tents on the four sides of the tabernacle during Old Testament times.
  + Fourth View: The four living creatures represent four angels whose function is to bring glory and honor to God. This view is somewhat plausible because of other Biblical references to angels performing this purpose elsewhere as well as the fact that the living creatures were described as having wings.

| 31.12 | **THE TWENTY-FOUR ELDERS** |

Because of its important implications, the discussion regarding the twenty-four elders has been pulled out of the larger context as detailed above and given its own place in the list of events and situations. The identity of these throne attendants has been much debated throughout church history, and there are three views. Before the various views are listed, it is helpful to understand the meaning of the word *elder*. "In the New Testament the basic concept of elder is that of a representative of the people, one who rules or judges on behalf of God over the people (Acts 15:2; 20:16)."[26] "The very use of the word 'elder' suggests this maturity in spiritual understanding, for the Scriptural concept of an elder was one mature either in years or experience. The promise of such maturity, as indicated in 1 Corinthians 13:12, is now actual."[27] The number of twenty-four has significance with its possible connection to the Old Testament priesthood with twenty-four order of priests. The elders seem to be representative of a larger group, and are seen sitting in repose on their thrones glorifying the Lord, and celebrating the flow of history to the consummation of the ages.

The three primary views of the identity of the twenty-four elders are:
- First View: It is the position of this book that they are the exclusive representatives of the saints of the Dispensation of Grace, or, the Church Age. This view is the most plausible explanation that is also the most supportive of the pretribulational rapture view.
- Second View: They are celestial, or angelic, beings.
- Third View: They are representative of saints of all ages.

The view that the twenty-four elders are representative of church saints, translated and resurrected into heaven derives its strength from the following:
- The elders are clothed in *white garments*. Throughout the Book of Revelation, white garments represent salvation, redemption from sin. Since redemption is only necessary for humans, this would eliminate the option that the elders are angels – angels do not need salvation because they are not spiritually lost. The idea here is that the elders were once lost, but then were redeemed. Also, consider the following:
  + Isaiah 61:10: A reference to believers in God being clothed in certain garments.
  + Revelation 3:4-5: Christ tells believers of Sardia they will be clothed in white.
- The elders are wearing *golden crowns*:
  + These crowns are not *diadem* crowns, which are only worn by royal sovereign or ruler signifying governmental authority. Instead, they are *stephonos* crowns that are worn by overcomers or victors (the crown was usually made of leaves, or metal representing leaves, awarded the victors of the Greek games), which is the type of crown given by

Christ at the Bema Seat Judgment. The notion that the crowns are of gold suggests victory and accomplishment.

+   As seen in Revelation 4:10 and 5:8-10, the elders will later return their victory crowns to Christ in an act of worship.

+   Throughout the Bible, only humans are said to wear crowns, not angels – there is no need for an angel to wear a crown. Angels are not in ruling positions, nor are they rewarded with victor's crowns.

+   The title of elder is only used in the Bible for human leaders as described above; it is never used for angels.

+   The elders appear to have already been judged which would eliminate Israel and angels because their respective judgments occur at a time subsequent to this event. Also, the elders are associated with the pretribulational rapture that is not part of God's Program with Israel.

+   The elders are seated on thrones which are specifically promised to the Church in Matthew 19:28 and Revelation 3:21. No such reference is made in the Bible regarding the angels seated on thrones, and it cannot refer to Israel because she will be subjected to the authority of the throne rather than being associated with the rule from the throne.

+   The elders appear to have intimate knowledge of God's Plan as shown Revelation 5:5 and 7:13-14 which suggests that they have been taken into His confidence.

+   The elders seem to be ministering to Jesus Christ as priests in Revelation 5:8.

32

GENTILES IN DANIEL'S 70ᵗʰ WEEK

We know, from Section 31.6, of God's divine purposes for the seven years of Daniel's 70ᵗʰ Week. The natural question that occurs is how will those years play out in human history on the world stage? What will be the form of the period of time between the Rapture and the Second Coming of Christ? What will the human conditions be like? Most Christians have at least some marginal understanding that the seven-year period will be extremely difficult, however, that understanding is limited to the basic idea that there will be severe judgments and they will be worldwide in scope. While we know of those judgments and agree that they will be worldwide and severe, there are many other things that will characterize Daniel's 70ᵗʰ Week, as well as the time before the seven years begin.

The time between the Rapture and Christ's Second Coming will be a tumultuous and terrible time, it will also be devastating and destructive, and it will be a time of much death and misery. The people that will experience this time after the removal of the True Church will be Gentiles that will remain unsaved, Gentiles that will come to faith in Jesus Christ, Jews that will remain unsaved, and finally, Jews that will come to faith in Jesus Christ.

32.1 | SEVERAL OBSERVATIONS

Before we explore the Gentiles in Daniel's 70ᵗʰ Week in detail, it might be helpful to make a couple of observations regarding the history of humankind in order to set the perspective for this chapter. We might describe the history of humankind as a metamorphic slide from God-centeredness to human-centeredness as can be seen by the following:
- God created human beings in His image and there was a divine harmony that originally existed between them.
- His creatures sinfully rebelled, and thus a disharmony developed.
- Throughout history, humans have either turned to God, or, led by Satan, away from Him and apostasy grew, as sin and rebellion evolved it increased in scope, influence, and strength. If it could be measured somehow, we might find that sinfulness and rebellion increases with time, as darkness increases with the setting sum, to virtually cover the earth.
- God sent His only Son to earth to be the one and only sacrifice for human sin, and make it possible for the divine harmony to be partially restored for those that lived after Him, and to justify those that lived before Him.
- Sin and rebellion continued to evolve and increase, and the apostasy became very prevalent, as humans tend to continually try to go it alone.

- When human history comes finally to an end, after the faithful have been removed, those left behind during the seven years of Daniel's 70th Week are so apostate that they will ultimately shake their fist in God's face in rejection and denial as they ignore their own Creator. It is now complete, the world and its inhabitants are now totally to Him. In fact, at the last battle they will actually go up against Jesus Christ with the full expectation of victory, but instead hundreds of millions will be destroyed by His words.
- Thus the divine harmony that existed in the Garden of Eden will again dominate the earth and those that live thereon.

When viewed from the global perspective, the seven years of Daniel's 70th Week can be seen as follows:

- A covenant, for what is believed to be a treaty of peace, will be made between the nation of Israel and a national leader only identified as a Ruler to Come, supposedly to end a time of conflict.
- For the next three and one-half years, the sinful and rebellious nature of humankind, that began at the Fall and progressed over the centuries, will have fully developed into a humanistic worldview that will attempt to replace the Living God of the Universe. The logical conclusion of turning away from God will be manifested in the world during this time. It will be seen in the form of government that will exist, in the form of religion that will exist, and in the human morality that will exist. Also during these three and one-half years, events will transpire that will allow the Ruler to Come to gain considerable power and influence. The humanistic worldview, headed by the Ruler to Come, will see government and religion merge into a final and logical form of apostasy. It should be recognized that this will be a time of preparation for the Ruler to Come, a time in which the antithesis of God, led by Satan, prepares to reveal himself as the Antichrist.
- At the midpoint of the seven years the Ruler to Come, now with the necessary power base, will declare himself to be god and will demand worship from the world. Religion and government will have now merged. The Ruler to Come is now the Antichrist and will set up the Abomination of Desolation as he desecrates the rebuilt Temple in Jerusalem.
- The second three- and one-half-year period will be a time in which the world will be dominated by the Antichrist, presenting himself as god, and the True God will be pouring out judgements on Israel, him and the apostate world. There will be a chain of unprecedented, cataclysmic events that will be so bad that, when Christ comes, the world will have been on the very knife-edge of destroying itself. During this time the Antichrist will be in full control of the world, however God will pour out the seal, trumpet, and bowl judgments onto the unbelieving world.
- The seven years will be terminated by the return of the Lord Jesus Christ who comes so that the world does not destroy itself.

Human beings are interesting creatures. While most people today will say that they do not like change, change has been a constant companion for individuals as well as for nations down through time. In fact, change is one of the most common denominators for the history of humankind as it continually changes - nothing remains static. This is important because humans, as they grow in age and maturity, change with the times in which they live, albeit subtly.

- Individually, every person evolves during his or her own life. We have considerable insight into this evolution because of what the Bible tells us about humankind and what makes human beings 'tick.' Without fail, every single person that has ever lived, either grows toward the Lord, or walks away from Him - a function of changing their lives to fit their focus and orientation. There is no middle ground regarding the Lord, either we are with Him, or, we are against Him. When individuals who are leaders of nations walk away from God, they contribute to the condemnation of their nation; after enough of this kind of leadership, nations collapse. Human beings have an incredible propensity to not see the obvious and purposefully step into situations that can either hurt at the time, or harm them at some time in their future.
- Nationally, every nation evolves during its life. Nations develop, struggle through infancy, grow into maturity, reach a state of strength, then begin the slide into complacency and lethargy, and eventually collapse. If this were not true then why would there be such an extensive recorded history full of nations that no longer exist? The collapse of nations is replete in history, and the primary reasons for the collapse almost always include the fact that the citizenry devolved into degeneracy and depravity. Invariably as nations get past the struggle to survive, they begin to focus on self-gratification and self-delusion - they believe they are invincible. They become convinced they can endure whatever comes their way, and they either collapse from within, or, are conquered by another nation because of their internal weakness due many times to moral weakness. It is without debate that the strength of any nation is directly proportional to the strength, or weakness, of its citizens. Also, every nation grows either toward God, or away from God, based on the orientation of its leaders and citizens. Nations are only as strong as the moral heritage of the leadership.

32.2 THE REVIVAL OF THE IMPERIALISTIC (ROMAN) EMPIRE

Previously, in Section 20.4, we examined the prophecies of the Book of Daniel, and we saw that there will be a fourth empire, of the Times of the Gentiles, that would dominate and govern over the nation of Israel that is identified as the Imperialistic (Roman) Empire. We further saw that this empire would be manifested in five, sequential and chronological stages:

- Stage 1 - United: 63 BC until AD 285.
- Stage 2 - Two Division: AD 264 until sometime in the future.

- Stage 3 - One World Government: Future.
- Stage 4 - Ten Kingdoms: Future.
- Stage 5 - Antichrist: Future.

One of the reasons we can pinpoint where we are in the stages of the fourth empire is by what has not happened. Historically, there has never been a one world government, nor have historians ever established a ten-nation alliance that fits the Biblical description. "... the principal reason for believing in the revival of the ancient Roman Empire is the fact that prophecies dealing with the latter part of this empire have not been fulfilled ... The anticipated revival of Rome is related, first, to its geography, second, to indications of its political character, and, third, relationship of the political revival to the last form of apostate religion which will appear before the second advent of Christ."[1]

Based on this timeline we find our world in the midst of Stage 2. Since the fall of Rome, and Stage 1, the world has been dominated and governed by a balance of power in the form of two political ideologies that for the most part have been rivals if not outright enemies. For the last 1,600 years, history has recorded an eastern school of thought and a western school of thought, with many political, economic, social, and religious differences between eastern and western philosophies. Because of recent events, the prospect of Stage 3 starting soon may be coming upon us.

32.3 THE BOUNDARIES OF THE LAST FORM OF THE IMPERIALISTIC (ROMAN) EMPIRE

"Geographically the ancient Roman Empire at the height of its power extended from the Euphrates River to the east [actually it should be west] across Northern Africa and Southern Europe and included a portion of Great Britain."[2] Thus, there are really only three views as to the geographical boundaries of the revived Imperialistic (Roman) Empire. The Bible does not specifically indicate the geographical size of the empire; it only establishes that the empire that existed at the time of Christ will be revived to some undefined extent of its former glory.

- First View: The revived empire will occupy an area less than Stage 1.
- Second View: The revived empire will occupy the same land mass as Stage 1 did in antiquity.
- Third View: Held by Pentecost[3], and this book, is that there is a strong possibility that the Bible establishes a larger land mass than Stage 1, which is based on the following:
    + The Ten Kingdoms, having never been proven to exist before, are said to the outgrowth of the original stage of the empire and does not necessarily have to conform to the original empire size. Also, stage 1 of the empire was an expansive and conquered force and it seems logical that the later stages could also be granted the full land mass of the ten nations.

+ Revelation 13:7 indicates that the first beast, the Antichrist, that rises out of the sea is given authority over every nation, and we know that he conquers three of the ten kingdoms which would suggest that in addition to the power he receives from Satan, he could also be granted the full land mass of the ten kingdoms.
+ Revelation 17 describes the relationship between the woman and the beast and indicates their control extends over the world of Christendom, so a case could be made that the land mass under control would be the realm of the professing believers.

32.4   THE ONE WORLD GOVERNMENT

The Bible is not really clear concerning Stages 2 and 3 as described above. Other theologians researched for this book do not necessarily see these two stages in the fourth empire in the same way as Fruchtenbaum does. It should now be considered uncertain if the Bible supports these two stages, however, the Bible does support Stages 1, 4, and 5. The course of history does seem to give credibility to these two stages however they have been included in the current discussion. Events such as these are not clearly marked with specific beginnings or endings. It would be better to say that they overlap somewhat as they evolve from one to the other. This is important for reasons that will become obvious.

Our current world situation is one in which the east/west balance of power is being significantly challenged on many fronts and is truly characterized by the fact that the east seems to be rising up in revolt against the west. While this tension has shifted back and forth between the two for centuries, it is different today because the west is not beginning to call for, and work toward, a strengthened position by consolidating many nations into one superpower nation. The idea of globalization has become a common idea that has converged on the world since World War I, and strengthens with each passing day. For many reasons the world seems to be moving in the direction of a one world government.

It is at this point that the uncertainty of Stages 2 and 3 becomes necessary to evaluate. While the Bible only marginally supports Stage 2 in Daniel 2:33b, history does seem to fully support the idea of an east and west division of power. Stage 3 has its only Biblical support in Daniel 7:23b, and history seems to be beginning to provide support for a one world government as a legitimate stage of the fourth empire. Part of what makes this uncertain is not whether there will be a one world government, but instead if it will occur before Stage 4 - Ten Kingdoms, or the Ten Nation Confederacy. It is without doubt that Stage 4 and 5 are predicted because it can be seen in Daniel 2 and 7, and Revelation 13 and 17. Either one or the other of the following scenarios will occur:
• First View: The sequence of Stages 2, 3, 4, and 5 will occur as indicated. The east/west division of power (Stage 2) would soon give way to a one world government (Stage 3), which in turn would evolve into the Ten

Nation Confederacy (Stage 4), and would culminate in the time of the Antichrist (Stage 5).
- Second View: The sequence of Stages 4 and 5 will occur, however, the one world government aspect of Stage 5 could actually begin before the Ten Nation Confederacy becomes formalized (which would actually support Stage 3 in a way) and become fully manifested by the time the Ruler to Come becomes the Antichrist at the midpoint of Daniel's 70th Week.

Nevertheless, a one world government appears to be on the horizon for humankind, and when we look out our windows we could very well see the beginnings or either Stage 3 specifically, or Stage 5 informally. When Daniel 2 and 7, and Revelation 13 and 17, are combined to form the Times of the Gentiles timeline, it becomes obvious that human history will end in a form of one world government with the ruling control residing in one person. The notion that makes this so intriguing is that our own world seems to be rapidly heading to a one world government at the same time so many other events are transpiring that seem to point to the idea that we are very close to the Rapture and Daniel's 70th Week. World War I seems to be the line of demarcation where a one world government begins to be within reach of humankind. What started after World War I as a response to the extent of the war, gained additional momentum after another world war, now has a fully developed a head of steam and is racing toward a destiny that is in complete agreement with Biblical prophecy. Consider the following examples of human efforts toward establishing a one world government, which are only a few chosen from a multitude of actualities.
- After World War I, a League of Nations was established for the effort of preventing the devastation of another world war, but was ultimately unsuccessful because the world shortly found itself in World War II.
- After World War II, the United Nations was established to continue the efforts begun by the League of Nations, and it gained a foothold in world politics. While it has been inept to a large extent, it nevertheless has attempted to exercise some degree of rulership over the conflicts of the world, which have been considerable.
- After the Cold War, the nations of Europe rearranged themselves into an alliance that is known as the European Union for the purposes of economic and political survival. Now that the European Union is in place, it is beginning to assume leadership in the world at large, it is considering the formation of a military force, and has recently challenged the world by establishing what can be seen as a world court, identified as the International Criminal Court (ICC) whose purpose is to try individual soldiers, from anywhere in the world, for war crimes.

What makes all this so critically important is that the nature of this time was predicted by God and recorded by several of His prophets thousands of years ago, and seems to be coming together at the same time so many other predictions also seem to be happening. Also, it is critically important because if we are close to the end of the age, then it has implications for believers. If indeed the one world government develops prior to the Rapture, which is a distinct possibility, then our individual ministries could be influenced by it in the following ways:

- We could use current events as the means of entering in a conversation about the Lord with an unbeliever.
- Because we have an insightful understanding of the global perspective of the Bible, each of us should become an apologist for the Lord.
- Our personal evangelistic effort could be motivated by the coming events.

Hindson makes the following observation concerning the current times in which we live and face as our future: "We're forming a new civilization, a global civilization, distinct from those that arose before this era. It's not just a Western civilization forcing itself on others. It's not a resurgent Chinese civilization struggling to reassert itself after years of being thwarted. It's a strong blend of both, and the others. It's something different, something still being born. ... In many ways, it's a civilization of civilizations. We're building a framework that will enable all the world's civilizations to exist side by side and thrive - where the best attributes of each can stand out and make their unique contributions, where the peculiarities of each are cherished and allowed to live on. We're entering an age where diversity is truly valued - the more options, the better. Our ecosystem works best that way. Our market economy works best that way. Our civilization, the realm of ideas, works best that way, too."[4]

32.5 THE TEN KINGDOMS, OR, THE TEN NATION CONFEDERACY

The next stage that will be seen is Stage 4 - Ten Kingdoms, or the Ten-Nation Confederacy, and will be the form of world government by which the Antichrist takes control of the earth. The concept for a Ten-Nation Confederacy originates in the imagery of those of the statue in Nebuchadnezzar's dream and the imagery of horns on a terrible beast.

- Daniel:
  + 2:41-45:
    o While the description of the statue in Nebuchadnezzar's dream does not specifically mention the statue's toes, it is mentioned when Daniel interprets the dream. The passages indicate that the composition of the material mixture of the feet and toes will be partly iron, which will be strong, and partly clay, which will be fragile. Actually, the Hebrew word used for the clay indicates a formed pottery object. Notice that the feet and toes are described in the same manner, suggesting that both Stage 2 - Two Divisions and Stage 4 - Ten Kingdoms will be a mixture of strength and weakness. The mixture could be:
      - An intermarriage of two things.
      - Several forms of government.

- A union between democracy and imperialism.
  - ○ A key aspect of this passage lies in the idea that the composition of the mixture includes something of strength and something of fragility, at the same time; the mixture is unified, yet it is also divided. Obviously iron and clay will not combine well or adhere to each other - they can co-exist, but they will not blend together to form a third mixture. The mixture suggests a situation in which an entity has to exist that is possibly in conflict with itself, or, endures success and failures due to whichever material, iron or clay, is subjected to a force.
  - ○ Verse 43 sheds additional light on the topic. The iron and clay are symbolic representations for peoples of differing persuasions. This "… form of the kingdom will include diverse elements whether this refers to race, political idealism, or sectional interests; and this will prevent the final form of the kingdom from having a real unity."[5]
- \+ 7:7-8, 19-25: In this passage, Daniel himself has a dream in which he sees four beasts rising for the sea, with the sea being symbolic of the Gentile peoples. In turn, an angel interpreted Daniel's dream. In this dream, a beast is seen as the Fourth Empire and only strength is included in the description at the exclusion of fragility. On this beast are ten horns, which verse 24 indicates are ten kings that will reign simultaneously.
- Revelation 13:1; 17:7, 12-14:
  - \+ John also sees an image of a beast with ten horns that are indicated to be ten kings who will be the authority to rule, along with the beast, for a short period of time.
  - \+ Verse 13 goes on to point out that the single purpose for the ten kings will be to give the authority and power to rule invested in them to the Antichrist.
  - \+ Ultimately the ten kings will be led by the Antichrist to make war with Christ when he returns. "These kings will seek together to prevent the reign of Christ on earth. They will make His defeat their one purpose, but because He is the Almighty Lord and King, their efforts will all come to nothing (see 19:15-19)."[6]

As outlined above, we really do not know whether the one world government or the Ten Nation Confederacy will come into being first. Historians have made many attempts to find a ten-nation alliance in history however, there does not appear to have been such a confederacy, so the only conclusion can be that it has never existed. However, we can see an increasing effort by the peoples and nations of today's world to relinquish national sovereignty in favor of a global government in order to allegedly make themselves safe and secure. It seems the most plausible scenarios are first, the seeds of a one world government could be the genesis of the Ten Nation Confederacy, or second, the two could be co-dependent during the time. The Bible is not specifically clear of what happens after the Antichrist conquers three of the ten rulers regarding if the Ten Nation Confederacy ceases to exist entirely, or, continues to exist as the puppets of the Antichrist. The most plausible explanation is that they will continue to exist and be the mechanism by which the Antichrist implements his sinister program of demonic terror.

Regarding the identity of the future Ten Nation Confederacy, the Bible has nothing to say. "The identity of the nations has not been revealed and with this we may be content. The probability is, however, that the ten nations will include not only portions of Southern Europe and Northern Africa, but also some nations in Western Asia, inasmuch as the revived Roman Empire to some extent is viewed as including the three preceding empires, which were largely Asiatic. As the Holy Land is the center of Biblical interest, it would only be natural for the empire to include this area, especially when it is taken into consideration that the Holy Land becomes a part of the area of influence of the Roman Empire as demonstrated in the covenant with Israel (Daniel 9:27) and in the later warfare described as being in this area (Ezekiel 38 - 39; Daniel 11:4--45; Zechariah 14:1-3)."[7]

32.6 THE FINAL FORM OF RELIGION – APOSTATE WORLD CHURCH

After the True Church are removed from the earth at the pretribulational Rapture, evil, sinfulness, and apostasy will run rampant over all the peoples, cultures, and societies of the world. While the True Church is absent from the earth, the Professing Church will proceed into Daniel's 70th Week and will be characterized as the antithesis of the True Church. The Professing Church will be anything but a Biblically based institution with the goal of worshipping and glorifying God and Jesus Christ. The Bible paints the picture that the Professing Church will be a theological rendition of who God is and is not as seen through human eyes - religion will be about what humankind wants God to be. This stands in direct opposition to what God has revealed to His creation in the revelation of His Word.

Throughout human history, sinfulness has manifested itself in the form of individual disobedience that in some instances has led to national sinfulness, and in response, God has judged and admonished those individuals and nations because of the disobedience. However, the Bible emphasizes the fact that the final form of religion will be a worldwide rejection of Him and what His Son has done. So it can be said that part of what will happen during Daniel's 70th Week will be God's response to sin that is manifested on a global scale, rather than on an individual or national scale. Humankind has evolved over the centuries to the point that there is global sinfulness, because the earth is mostly sinful nations composed of mostly sinful individuals. Just as we see in the Bible and in our own lives, God responds in judgment of individuals and nations, He will respond in judgment in a global dimension at some point in the future. The ultimate conclusion of the original sin of individual disobedience to God that occurred in a paradise so long ago will be the disobedience to Him over the entire globe.

32.7   FIRST BEAST - THE ANTICHRIST

Eventually, a single human being, possessed by Satan, will wrestle political and religious control to assume dictatorial governing dominance over all the earth as the citizens of the world give him the power to do so and to worship him as a deity. As part of his government, the Antichrist will impose a special form of economic buying and selling restriction that will effectively and publicly separate believers in God from believers in the Antichrist. And the Antichrist will persecute and kill those that reject him to follow God and Jesus Christ. At this point the world stage will be set for the final conflict between good and evil. The Lord God, the Creator of the Universe and the very being that he created that stands in ultimate opposition to Him, will be in heaven prepared to draw human history to a close. The Antichrist, rejecting the fact that he was created by God, will be on earth making every effort possible to bring Satan's counterfeit plan to fruition of replacing God and stealing His glory and rightful possessions.

THE ANTICHRIST'S RESURRECTION APPEARANCE

Core Scripture: Revelation 13:3

The Antichrist will have the appearance that he has been miraculously healed from some event that occurs during his reign, thus making him appear to the world to be the resurrected messiah. It is this aspect of his life that causes the world to falsely worship him as the savior to the world. He will suffer a head wound that will appear to be fatal, but he will recover. It is thought, that since Satan does not have the power to resurrect those that have died, that the event will be a ruse in order to gain the adoration of his worshippers. Because the Antichrist is a counterfeit of Jesus Christ, the course of the existence of the False Messiah will mimic the life of the True Messiah in all its events of importance and significance.

THE ANTICHRIST'S GOVERNING RULE

Core Scripture: Daniel 11:36

He will rule with absolute authority as he exercises his will, rather than the will of God. Again, the Antichrist, led by Satan, will mimic the absolute governing authority of Jesus Christ.

THE ANTICHRIST'S PERSECUTION OF GOD'S HOLY PEOPLE

The Antichrist becomes the great adversary and persecutor of Israel. He will subdue and conquer many people including powerful and mighty people, and will also pursue and attempt to destroy... *the holy people*... the Jews.
- Daniel:
    + 7:21: He will wage war against the holy ones and will defeat them.
    + 7:25: He will continually harass the holy ones.
    + 8:24: He will destroy the people of the holy ones.

THE ANTICHRIST'S PERSECUTION OF THE TRIBULATION SAINTS

Core Scripture: 2 Thessalonians 2:4; Revelation 13:7; and 17:14

He becomes that adversary to the person, work, and people of Jesus Christ by brutally persecuting any who come to saving faith in Jesus Christ during this time.

THE ANTICHRIST'S ATTEMPT TO CHANGE THINGS

Core Scripture: Daniel 7:25

He intends to change times, possibly things associated with religious events, and laws, possibly replacing existing laws with his own demonic oriented laws.

THE ANTICHRIST'S DECEPTIVE INFLUENCE OVER THE WORLD

- Daniel 8:25: Just as Antiochus was his foreshadow, the Antichrist will successfully exercise a prolific deceptive influence on the world and many people will suffer greatly because of his superior sinister scheming and ability to draw unsuspecting people into his clutches.
- 2 Thessalonians 2:9-11: As the leader of the demonic and lawless governmental system, his claim to political power and religious deity will be shown by miracles, signs, and false wonders, all derived from Satan's power. Those that have turned away from the truth and do not desire to be saved will be the receivers of his deception. Because of their spiritual blindness that makes them susceptible to deception, the citizens alive at the time will receive him and his demonic governing rule without objection.

THE ANTICHRIST'S USE OF THE APOSTATE CHURCH

Core Scripture: Revelation 17:3, 16-17

The apostate church will be instrumental in the Antichrist's journey to the top of satanic political power, and will attempt to dominate him. However, because the apostate church will be an obstacle in his path, he will destroy it to remove the hindrance.

THE ANTICHRIST'S WORSHIP BY THIS WORLD

The world will worship the Antichrist because of his popularity and because he will appear to be the resurrected Messiah that the world expects. Standing here today, it is hard to image that there will be millions of people that will be misled about who the true Messiah will be.

- Ezekiel 28:2, 9-12 (cf. Daniel 8:25; Revelation 13:4): He, as well as the dragon (Satan) who energizes his prideful ruling authority over the earth, will be worshipped by the people of the world.
- Revelation 13:8: His influence will extend over the entire world, because, he will be worshipped by who dwell on earth that have not been written in the Lamb's Book of Life.

THE ANTICHRIST'S ECONOMIC RULE

In addition to the Antichrist's political rule over the world, probably one of the most significant and opposition characteristics of his dictatorship will be his method of economic rule. This method of control is also one of the most unique aspects of the worldwide demonic government that is told in the Bible. While it seems subtle the Biblical description of this method just so happens to be so unique that for the first time in human history there is now a process available that makes this method possible and feasible. It was not until the late 1990's that a technological capability was put in place to serve as the means of exercising economic rule over the geographic scope of the Antichrist's rule.

THE ANTICHRIST'S MILITARY PROWESS AND ACTIVITIES

- Ezekiel 28:7 (cf. Daniel 11:40-45): There will be numerous military campaigns by the Antichrist and against him by an alliance of nations that will raise up to challenge his political rulership. As a result of the ensuing

conflict, he will gain control over Israel and make Jerusalem the capital of government.
- Revelation 19:19: The final conflict will be a military campaign in Israel arrayed against the returning Jesus Christ.

THE CONCLUSION OF ANTICHRIST'S RULE

At the end of Daniel's 70th Week, the Antichrist will meet the end decreed for him.
- Divine Destruction:
  + Daniel:
    o Daniel 7:26-26; 9:26-27; and 11:36: After the decreed time has come to completion, his ruling authority will be quickly removed, destroyed and abolished forever, and the kingdom will be turned over to Jesus Christ and the kingdom of the saints will begin.
    o 8:25: Unlike Antiochus, the Antichrist will rise up against Christ … *the Prince of princes* …, but will be destroyed by Him without the assistance of any human contributions.
  + 2 Thessalonians 2:8: He will be destroyed by the breath of Jesus Christ at His Second Advent.
- God's Judgment:
  + Daniel:
    o 7:22: This judgment will take place as Christ returns in glory to earth in His Second Advent.
    o 7:22, 26; 9:27; 11:45 (cf. Revelation 19:19-20): His satanic rule of the world will end during the final military campaign by a direct judgment from God.
  + 2 Thessalonians 2:12: Those that accept the evil of the Antichrist, and turn away from the good of the Lord, will be judged for their rejection to the truth.
  + Revelation 11:15: Christ's judgment of him, at the seventh trumpet, will be a manifestation of Christ's Messianic authority over the kingdom to come.

THE ANTICHRIST'S ULTIMATE DESTINY

Core Scripture: Revelation 19:20

God will cast the ultimate human manifestation of evil into the lake of fire burning with sulfur, along with his master, the Dragon (Satan), and the Second Beast, the False Prophet.

THE ECONOMY OF DANIEL'S 70ᵀᴴ WEEK

Thus far in this book, we have explored the political and ecclesiastical character of Daniel's 70th Week which includes the Antichrist seizing governing control over the world and establishing himself as the object to be worshipped by those that live during this time. We now turn our attention to another significant characteristic of this period of time - how the Antichrist will rule from his worldly position by setting in motion an oppressive and brutal economy. It will be this very economy that will serve as the Lord's 'line in the sand' that will distinguish between those that are for the Lord and those that are for the Antichrist. Much has been written in recent years regarding the Antichrist's economy most likely because the necessary technological mechanism to achieve worldwide economic control over humankind appears to be already available today. Just as we see our world rapidly evolving into a one world governmental structure, we also see the disparate and diversified world economy beginning an unmistakable trend toward globalization, a trend that is facilitated by sophisticated technology. In addition, just as the world will see a one world government and a one world religion both administrated absolutely by the Antichrist, it also will see a one world economy that will severely impact the times.

There are several Scriptural passages that describe the nature of the economy during this terrible time:
- James 5:1-3: This passage indicates that the monetary standard, essentially for all of gold and silver of human history, will no longer be of value to anyone, and will not protect the wealthy from the coming economic collapse. This seems to be the logical conclusion for those that serve the god of money instead of the True God; theirs will just become worthless and will not 'save' them from the time of trouble.
- Revelation:
  + 6:5-6: Associated with the third seal judgment (known as the third horseman of the Apocalypse), this passage indicates that there will be a time of what appears to be severe famine. This is supported by the facts that the breaking of the first seal judgment marked the beginning of the First Beast's formal reign as the Antichrist, and the breaking of the second seal judgment yields peace being removed from the world and replaced with war. The idea here is that when the Antichrist comes to power, there will be worldwide war and turmoil, which will cause a significant scarcity of food and an inflation of the value of money (which is always common during war). Essentially, "… the price of food in the famine will be so great that an entire day's wages (a denarius) will be required to purchase enough wheat (a quart) for meals for one day or enough barley (three quarts) for three meals."[8] The idea here is that because of famine, survival will be dependent on the small amounts of the most basic foodstuffs that can purchased using all the money that people have.

+   13:16-17; There will be a requirement placed on economic relationships of the time that everyone will be required to bear a physical mark on their foreheads or hands in order to buy and sell goods and services. The passage also indicates that this requirement will be for everyone, apparently no one will be exempt from possessing the mark of the beast. Revelation 14:9-10 makes very clear that anyone that accepts this mark, which signifies acceptance and worship of the Antichrist, will be subject to the wrath and anger of God and will spend eternity in torment.

32.8   SECOND BEAST – THE FALSE PROPHET

"The Antichrist will not rise to power alone. His success will result from a worldwide spiritual deception perpetrated by the False Prophet. This religious leader's ability to perform miraculous signs will enable him to convince the public that the Antichrist is the leader for whom they have been looking. ... The False Prophet serves as the spokesperson for the Antichrist. Satan's program will culminate in the two beasts' corporate enterprise. The first beast will directly oppose Christ, and the second beast will assume the place of religious leadership that rightly belongs to Christ."[9]

THE ROLE OF THE FALSE PROPHET

Just like John the Baptist publicly prepared the way for the public ministry of Jesus Christ, the False Prophet will prepare the way for the Antichrist. The False Prophet will not accept worship for himself, but will direct it to the Antichrist after his fraudulent attempt of having been resurrected. Once the False Prophet is possessed by Satan, he will then have supernatural power to deceive the world into believing in the Antichrist.

THE FALSE PROPHET WILL PERFORM
SIGNS AND MIRACLES

Because the Jews will be looking for the prophet Elijah, part of the reason that they will be taken in by the Unholy Trinity is because the False Prophet will give the appearance that he is capable of performing the very miraculous signs and miracles that they are anticipating. The calling down of fire from heaven is a specific reference to Elijah himself calling down fire from heaven in order to consume King Ahab and his fifty military officers as recorded in 2 Kings 1:10. "Satan will use the Jewish expectation of Elijah to encourage many to accept the false messianic claims of the Antichrist. The False Prophet's satanic miracles will lend credibility to his diabolical claims that the Antichrist is their long-awaited Messiah."[10] The Bible indicates that the people that live during Daniel's 70th Week will be especially deceived by the signs and miracles performed instead of testing things according to doctrinal truths.

THE IMAGE OF THE BEAST

After the Antichrist appears to have been resurrected, the False Prophet will direct those that live on the earth to make an image of the one that they believe to be their Messiah, the Antichrist. This statue or image will be something that will be mysterious because it will be something that is a physical object that represents the Antichrist, but the False Prophet will have the supernatural ability to animate it and make it appear alive. And because of his special efforts, the image will overwhelm many people and they will be forced to worship it or be killed instead. "In some supernatural manner, this 'image' will both speak and cause the destruction of men who refuse to worship the image. Thousands of years of idol worship will culminate in this diabolical creation of Satan, the "image of the beast".[11] Thus, idolatry finds its logical and ultimate conclusion in an image of a fraudulent savior, which signifies that the religion of Satan is now fully developed and established on earth, even though it will only be for a short period of time.

THE FALSE PROPHET AND THE MARK OF THE BEAST

The false Prophet will be the one that will introduce the mark of the beast to the world and will then administer the demonic program as economics is used as the means to force compliance with the requirements for worship of the Antichrist.

THE FALSE PROPHET WILL PERSECUTE THOSE THAT RESIST

Through comprehensive political, economic, social, religious, and cultural control, the False Prophet will put to death all those who defiles or resists the Antichrist, including those who resist receiving the mark of the Beast. In spite of the sentence of death, many, perhaps millions, will choose death and martyrdom instead of accepting the mark of the beast.

THE FALSE PROPHET WILL SEND THE WORLD TO WAR

The False Prophet will be instrumental in bringing the military forces of the world to the great final battle between evil and good in the Campaign of Armageddon.

THE FINAL DESTRUCTION OF
THE FALSE PROPHET

Because the Antichrist and the False Prophet will have willingly assisted Satan in his final effort to overcome God in spiritual rebellion, all three of these beings are destined for eternal damnation in the lake of fire.

33

ISRAEL IN DANIEL'S 70th WEEK

Part of the purpose of Daniel's 70th Week is not so much for God to judge Israel for her history of disobedience, but for God to prepare her for the promised, and long-awaited, Messiah. Because God is true to His promises and commitments, He must fulfill all of the outstanding unconditional covenant obligations to Israel. Daniel's 70th Week is the conclusion of God's dealing with His chosen people, so He draws them to Him by causing them to discover that they need their Messiah, thus accepting Jesus Christ as the true Son of their God, Yahweh.

33.1 THE MIDDLE EAST AND JERUSALEM AS THE CENTER OF WORLD ATTENTION

"God has placed Jerusalem in the eye of the storm. As we approach the days leading up to the second coming of Jesus Christ, Jerusalem and the Temple Mount will be the center of the conflict."[1]

One of the more interesting aspects of the times in which we live is the fact that the Bible indicates Israel, Jerusalem and especially the Temple Mount will be the center of worldwide attention during the last days, and it just so happens that this is also the very area that is under intense news media scrutiny continuously. There seems to be one or more reports, stories, or news report on the Middle East, usually about politics, bloodshed, conflict, or bombings in every daily television news broadcast, newspapers, magazines, or website devoted to end times matters. There is an overwhelming abundance of news that goes out every day from the Middle East, and it continues unabated. The world seems to have an insatiable hunger for information about Middle Events and happenings. Is this a coincidence, or, are current world events aligning with Biblical prophecy? Why does the world seem to be obsessed with this particular political conflict?

The attention of the world is focused on this portion of the world at a variety of levels:
- Regionally, the Arab and Muslim nations surrounding Israel outsize them geographically and outnumber them demographically many times over. Quite simply, in spite of the publicly debated reason given for the violent conflicts between the Israeli's and the Palestinians being possession of the land, the battles are actually over the continued existence of Israel itself. The Arab world wants to drive the Israelis into the Mediterranean Sea and scrub them from existence, yet the Jews are fiercely protecting their nation as they struggle to maintain their existence.

- Civically, the city of Jerusalem is a constant battlefield in the continuing struggle between Jewish rights to control of the city and Palestinian rights to control the city. Being crucial to all three of the world's great religions, Christianity, Judaism, and Islam, Jerusalem is under unique and unusual pressures because all three religions lay claim to this ancient city, albeit that the Christian 'side' is not near as pronounced as the other two.
- Religiously, violence between the Jews and the Muslims can spill out into the streets at the slightest provocation, and it does not even have to be based on honest and truthful reasons. All three religions have an enormous amount invested in the state of the Temple Mount, Jerusalem, Israel, and the religion itself.

Part of the world's attraction involves an intriguing human condition that has existed for almost as long as the Jews have existed. Throughout the full span of her history, they have been the victims that have been persecuted by others for centuries - it is part of God's judgment that they are to suffer for Him in this manner. The Jews have been, and continue to be, the ones other nations bully; they have been victimized by the Gentile world for just about every political, economic, cultural, or social cause and for any unsavory, undesirable, unwanted, unnecessary, unsolicited thing that has happened to someone. It is part of their existence to be held guilty by the Gentile world for an unsavory, undesirable, unwanted, unnecessary, unsolicited thing that has happened to someone. Even after almost two thousand years of national non-existence, the nations of the world still watch for opportunities to bully them for one reason or the other.

The world also watches Israel because this comparatively tiny group of people has accomplished something that no other group has ever accomplished - they have come back from a two millennia national extinction to a world recognized national existence again, a feat without historical precedent. For centuries, many have believed that Israel ceased to exist in 70 AD, and no one could have ever conceived that the nation would someday be back. In actuality, Christianity even now includes a theological system, known as replacement theology, which believes the church has replaced Israel on the basis that God turned His back on her and destroyed the nation forever. The fact remains however, that the Jews have been re-established politically in the land of their forefathers, the nation has a legitimate government, a superior military, a robust economy, and, she once again occupies her ancient capital of Jerusalem. There is a crucial distinction that should be kept in mind, this current regathering so far, is physical only and not spiritual - Israel is back in the land in unbelief.

There is another important attraction to watching Jerusalem. Since Jerusalem is sacred to three world religions, the world is watching to see which religion will ultimately own the city. Jerusalem is the most important city to Judaism, and for all practical purposes single-handedly the city represents the essence of the Jews, their history and their heritage. In addition, Jerusalem is the third most sacred city in the Muslim faith and currently has a mosque on the Temple Mount that is accessible only to the Muslims. And finally, Jerusalem is very important to Christendom because Jesus Christ lived and ministered there. While the Christians are not fighting for ownership and control of the city and the Temple Mount, the Jews and the Muslims are locked in a bitter and violent struggle; a struggle that is witnessed by the world.

For those of the world that have a prophetic understanding of the Bible, the attraction of watching Israel is that three-thousand-year old prophecies will be, or, are being depending on one's theological framework, fulfilled during our lifetimes and before our very eyes. It has been the contention of this book that there is a high probability that we are living in the latter days and that the next prophetic event, the Rapture, could occur at any moment. In fact, most of the scholars whose books and articles consulted for this book are of the belief that we are the terminal generation and that the Rapture will be in our lifetimes.

There are several events that are predicted to occur in Jerusalem that are part of the end time scenario, which includes the following:
- A New Temple in Jerusalem: As will be considered in greater detail later, because there will be a specific event at the mid-point of Daniel's 70th Week that involves temple worship, a new temple must be planned, constructed, consecrated, and activated for sacrificial worship.
- A Covenant will be Signed in Jerusalem: As will be considered in greater detail below, a covenant will be proposed, by the one that will become the Antichrist, and accepted, by Israel, and will be signed in Jerusalem. The treaty will herald the official beginning of Daniel's 70th Week, and the seven-year countdown until Christ's Second Advent comes.
- Jerusalem as the City of Choice for the Antichrist: Daniel 11:36-45 describes some of the Antichrist's activities, which include invading and occupying the land of Israel, and establishing his headquarters near or at Jerusalem or the Temple Mount, identified as the *beautiful Holy Mountain* (verse 45). We have already seen that the Antichrist will represent himself as, and will mimic the True Christ in every possible way, so it is not inconceivable that the Antichrist will use Jerusalem as his center of evil operations.
- The Abomination of Desolation in the Temple in Jerusalem: In Matthew 24:15-16, Jesus predicted that there would be a desolation that causes an abomination in the Temple in Jerusalem.
  + While this has been partially fulfilled by Antiochus Epiphanes less than two hundred years before Christ's First Advent, its complete fulfillment will be at the mid-point of Daniel's 70th Week when the temple will be defiled by the Antichrist. This is based on two passages in Daniel, 9:27 and 12:11, which indicate that their daily sacrifice and offering will be abolished by the Antichrist, and that it would last until Christ came again 1,290 days later (which places it at mid-week).

+ "This prediction is most significant, as it anticipates a rebuilding of the Jewish Temple in Jerusalem by orthodox Jews and the renewal of ancient forms of worship prescribed in the law of Moses."[2]
+ Also, another aspect that is implied by this passage is that another Jewish temple will have to be in Jerusalem in order for the defilement to occur, something that does not exist yet, but as will be seen below, something that intense preparations are underway for accomplishing.
• An International Siege on Jerusalem as Part of the Campaign of Armageddon:
+ In Psalm 2, the Lord indicates that it is His intention to have the Messiah return to earth and take His place on David's throne in Jerusalem (verses 2 and 6), but yet the leaders of the world's nations will unite and plot against Him (verses 1-3). However, the Lord laughs at the puny efforts expended by the human rulers, and He will deliver them into the hands of His King, Jesus Christ.
+ Zechariah 12:1-9 and 14:1-3 tells us that the Gentile nations of the world, including those surrounding Israel, will become intoxicated with the possibility of possessing Jerusalem (Zechariah 12:2) and will lay siege against it. The Lord will make Jerusalem a cup that makes them reel (Zechariah 12:2) and a heavy burden, or immovable rock, (Zechariah 12:3) for all the nations, and as they try to carry it away, they will be seriously injured. The nations will wage war to some extent (Zechariah 14:1-2) and there will be some destruction, however, the sense is that this will be an initial victory that will not last. Eventually, Christ will destroy the nations upon His Second Advent (Zechariah 12:9 and 14:3). This prophecy could not have been fulfilled in 70 AD because it was only one nation, Rome, that destroyed the city of Jerusalem and the state of Israel, and this passage indicates that there will be many nations that will unsuccessfully lay siege to the city (Zechariah 12:6 and 14:2). The political situation that exists today in Jerusalem could very well be the beginning of the surrounding nations contending for the City - it is the Arab and Muslim nations that are backing the Palestinian effort to establish a Palestinian state in opposition to Israel.
• Jesus will Return to Earth at Jerusalem: As will be considered in greater detail later, when Jesus Christ returns to earth He will do so at Jerusalem and He will establish His throne and rule His Kingdom from there.

33.2 WILL ELIJAH COME AGAIN?

Core Scripture: Malachi 4:5-6

In the last three verses of the Old Testament, Malachi 4:4-6, we see that God first admonishes Israel to remember and therefore be obedient to the rules and regulations He had given them, and, second that He will send Elijah to witness, evangelize and encourage belief in God before the judgment of the great and terrible Day of the Lord that will come in the future. These verses are the concluding remarks that follow a portion of Scripture that outlines a time to come when goodness and righteousness will overcome evilness and wickedness.

By way of review, Elijah was a prophet to the Northern Kingdom of Israel, during the Davidic Kingdom period, specifically during the reign of the wicked King Ahab and his wife Jezebel. Among the many things that make Elijah important to the Bible, there are specifically three that have special prophetic importance. First, Elijah cried in the wilderness of Israel a message of repentance, judgment and hope. Second, Elijah was responsible for withholding rain from the land because of Israel's wickedness. Third, Elijah is one of only two Old Testament individuals (the other being Enoch) who were raptured, or translated, to heaven without physically dying first. This is the context to which the prophecy recorded in Malachi 4:4-6 is juxtaposed.

An exposition of the prophecy in Malachi 4:4-6 would yield the following observations regarding a future Elijah:
- 4:4: Appropriately the Old Testament ends with an exhortation for Israel to remember, or to recall, the law that was given to the nation, and to obey, or act according to, the one that gave the law. The reference to Moses makes a connection back to the faithfulness of God's designated human instrument as the leader of an ancestral exodus out of persecution by the grace of God, which was the condition and setting by which God's law came to the Jews at Horeb (Mount Sinai).
- 4:5: God promised to send the Prophet Elijah to minister before the great and terrible Day of the Lord (this is the only Old Testament passage that speaks of a future ministry for Elijah) thus pinpointing the time in which the fulfillment of this prophecy will occur.
  + Notice that Malachi indicates that there is a qualification for Elijah's appearance; he will come before the Day of the Lord, the idea being immediately before. As will be discussed in greater detail below, this fact along disqualifies John the Baptist from fulfilling the future ministry for Elijah. The Bible does not indicate that Jesus came the first time as part of a Day of the Lord time, while it does indicate that He will come a second time that is associated with the Day of the Lord.
  + Many have linked this passage with Malachi 3:1 which indicates that God will send a messenger to be a forerunner to clear the way for God's coming to His people. However, Jesus' words in Matthew 11:7-10 identify John the Baptist as the messenger thereby indicating that John fulfills Malachi 3:1, but not Malachi 4:5. Then the obvious question becomes, should John the Baptist also be considered as fulfilling Malachi 4:5? This question will be answered shortly.
  + A future coming of Elijah provides a reference point to which the Jews can watch for in anticipation of the terrible Day of the Lord that the Bible predicts to come over them. Given the fact that Elijah was

raptured from earth without partaking in the inconvenience of physical human death, his rapture made him the second most watched for person by the nation of Israel (the first being the Messiah). While this verse implies that the actual person of Elijah will be sent, passages in the New Testament, discussed below, indicate that the one that will come will be in the spirit and power of Elijah and will not actually be Elijah.

- 4:6: The purpose for Elijah's coming is to be God's messenger to encourage salvation and restoration so that the covenant curse of the purifying judgment detailed Malachi 4:1-3 will not be necessary; Fruchtenbaum refers to this event as "... a Jewish family reunion program ..."[3]. Thus, the Old Testament closes with a final concluding statement reaffirming the continual Old Testament theme of the certainty of a coming judgment of all of existence, a judgment that can only be avoided by God's gracious offer of salvation. It is interesting that the New Testament concludes in the same manner as can be seen from Revelation 22:12-17.

There are three views as to the interpretation of this prophecy of a future ministry of Elijah, the first view being the position of this book.

- First View – One with the Power and Spirit of Elijah: The theory that is the most harmonious with the Scripture is that one will come in the spirit and power of Elijah.
  - + Malachi 3:1, as well as Isaiah 40:3-5, predicted a messenger who would come to clear the way for the Lord, a prophecy that was fulfilled by John the Baptist as the forerunner for Christ's First Advent as can be seen in Matthew 3:1-6 (a reference to Isaiah), 11:7-10 (a reference to Malachi), and John 1:23 (also a reference to Isaiah).
  - + Matthew 17:9-13 supports the notion of the one that will come prior to the Lord will be one that comes in the spirit and power of Elijah. Responding to the disciples' questions after the Transfiguration, Jesus make two points with His answer:
    - ○ First, Jesus indicated that John the Baptist would have been the one to fulfill the prophecy had Israel accepted His offer of the kingdom, but they did not - John being the one to fulfill Malachi 4:4-6 was contingent on Israel accepting the offer of the kingdom by accepting Jesus as the Son of God.
    - ○ Second, Jesus essentially indicated that the one who will come before Him will come in the spirit and power of Elijah as stated in Malachi, which excludes the possibility that an actual return of the person Elijah is intended by the prophecy. This is based on the idea that had Israel accepted Jesus' offer of the kingdom, then John the Baptist would have fulfilled the prophecy, but only in the spirit and power of Elijah.
- Second View – Actual Person of Elijah will not Come Again: This view holds that Elijah will not come again because John the Baptist fulfilled

this prophecy since Jesus referred to him as Elijah in Matthew 11:14. This is not supportable by Scripture for the following reasons:

+ Malachi refers to Elijah coming before the Day of the lord, which is a specific reference to God's first intervention in the affairs of humankind, usually in judgment before a later restoration. Obviously, Jesus did not come the first time to judge the world in the sense of the Day of the Lord; therefore the Malachi prophecy may not even apply to Christ's First Advent. The Day of the Lord is associated only with Christ's Second Advent.

+ Malachi 3:1 and Isaiah 40:3-53 both predict a forerunner will herald the arrival of Isaiah's Messiah. When the angel appeared to Zechariah, John's father, to tell him of the forthcoming birth, he tells him that his son will be the forerunner before the Lord ... *in the spirit and power of Elijah* ... (Luke 1:17); the angel does not say that John will actually be Elijah. Matthew 3:1-6; 11:7-10; and John 1:23 confirm that John the Baptist was the forerunner of Jesus; the passages do not indicate that he was the Elijah.

+ One of the strongest arguments for this view is found in Matthew 11:14 and 17:12, where Jesus Himself connects John to Elijah. One of the reasons Jesus came to earth the first time was to offer the kingdom to Israel, and in order to accept the kingdom, the Jews had to accept Jesus as the Son of God and their Messiah. However, the Jews rejected Jesus; therefore they did not inherit the kingdom, which precluded John the Baptist from being the one to fulfill the Elijah prophecy. John would have been Elijah only if the Jews had accepted Jesus.

• Third View – Elijah Himself will Come and Minister: This view acknowledges that John the Baptist does not fulfill Malachi's prophecy, and an extreme literal interpretation holds that the actual person of Elijah has to come in order for the prophecy to be fulfilled. This is based on the notion that since Elijah was removed from his original time on earth without dying, then, he can return again in a normal human body in order to be the forerunner for the coming Messiah. Notice that the Malachi prophecy does not necessarily indicate that Elijah will be in a spiritual body - the sense is that he will be a normal human.

+ In Luke 1:17, John is identified as coming in the spirit and power of Elijah and he is not specifically identified as the actual person of Elijah. Therefore, because of this view, John is not seen as the one to fulfill Malachi's prophecy since he is not specifically identified as such in Luke 1:17.

+ John himself denied being Elijah in John 1:19-23, but instead connected himself to Malachi 3:1 and Isaiah 40:3-6.

In conclusion, the Old Testament Book of Malachi predicts that there will be one who will come prior to the Day of the Lord, possibly before Daniel's 70th Week begins, to evangelize Israel, or possibly the world.

- Regarding Christ's First Advent, John the Baptist did not fulfill the prophecy because Christ's offer of the kingdom to Israel was rejected, thereby eliminating the need for one to fulfill the Elijah prophecy.
- Regarding Christ's Second Advent, the one that will come to fulfill the prophecy will in all likelihood be someone, alive at the time with a strong conviction in the Lord, which will come to call sinners to salvation so they will avoid the coming judgment about to climax to human history.

33.3 FOUR GROUPS OF JEWS

There are four distinct groupings of Jews that can be seen in the Bible that will struggle to survive the tumultuous sequence of events that will occur during Daniel's 70th Week.[4] Each group will be explored in further detail throughout this book.

- First Group – The "Many" of Daniel 9:17: These are the Jews that will, on behalf of national Israel, make a covenant with the Ruler to Come (eventually becoming the Antichrist), and are distinguished from those that will see the covenant for what it is, a covenant with death. This will comprise approximately two-thirds of the peoples of Israel and they will die during the seven-year period.
- Second Group – The 144,000 Jews: As part of the one-third of the people of Israel that will survive the seven-year period, these are the Jews that at some point after the Rapture will be supernaturally saved (12,000 from each of the twelve tribes of Israel) and sealed (protected from persecution by Satan and the Antichrist) that will evangelize for Jesus Christ in worldwide revival.
- Third Group – Hebrew Christians: These are the Jews that will come to Jesus Christ because of the work of the 144,000 Jews; however, they will not be counted among the divinely protected 144,000. Some will be part of the two-thirds that will die during the seven-year period, and some will be part of the one-third that will survive.
- Fourth Group – Faithful Remnant: These are the Jews that are faithful and obedient to God, however it will not necessarily be in faith to Jesus Christ, who will be divinely protected from persecution by Satan. They will be part of the one-third of the people of Israel that will survive the seven-year period.

33.4 JERUSALEM UNDER JEWISH CONTROL

The essence of the prophetic thrust of the Bible presupposes a number of things that will exist in the future, including, but not limited to, a restored number of the descendants of Abraham living in the land given to the Jewish patriarchs, the ancient city of Jerusalem being under Jewish control to some sufficient degree, and the existence of a politically recognized Israeli nation among the nations of the world. A detailed study of Biblical prophecy prior to 1947 AD would have to ultimately conclude that Israel would have to exist again no matter how inconceivable the thought might have been - it is a true testimony to the Lord that there were many scholars who had come to this very conclusion.

The most crucial land area that Israel has to possess in order for so many of the other events to occur is the Old City of Jerusalem, the ancient area that also contains the Temple Mount. After the War of Independence in 1948-49, the previously united city of Jerusalem was divided, with the west side retained by the Israeli, and the east side (with the Old City and the Temple Mount) remaining under Jordanian control. In spite of the fact that the United Nations was supervising the region, the Jordanians unrightfully denied Jewish access to the area under their control. On June 7, 1967, as a result of the Six-Day War that was caused by a Jordanian attack on West Jerusalem, East Jerusalem and the Temple Mount finally fell under Jewish control. The significance of this event should not be missed: 2,000 years after the destruction of the Temple and Jerusalem by the Romans, the city was now united and under Jewish control for the first time. However, ten days later, Israel returned the Temple Mount to Islamic sovereign control as a gesture of peace, under the eventually unfulfilled premise that the Jews could have access to it. The Temple Mount remains today the very epicenter of the Arab-Israel conflict, with the Muslims declaring that the Jews will never possess the Temple Mount.

Possession, to some extent, of the Temple Mount by the Jews is important largely because of the prophecies that presuppose the existence of another Jewish Temple during Daniel's 70th Week. The specific passages are examined in other locations; however, suffice it to say that there will be another Temple, a physical building structure, which will be functioning in much the same manner as the Temple of Jesus' time.

33.5 THE SIGNING OF THE SEVEN-YEAR COVENANT

Core Scripture: Daniel 9:27a

"The world stands by and holds its collective breath whenever Israel and her neighbors are at war, because it fears two things. First, it fears that the Arab world will retaliate against the West by withholding oil and creating another economic crisis in the industrialized countries that are so dependent on oil from the Middle East. Second, it is afraid that Israel will feel threatened enough to unleash its nuclear arsenal … and draw the rest of the world into nuclear war."[5] Hence this explains the intensity that drives the continuous efforts by the United States, the United Nations, and others that propose plans of peace for the turmoil in the Middle East. Thus far all treaties promising peace have failed. However, sooner or later, a plan for peace in the Middle East will be proposed by a Gentiles political leader that will be accepted by Israel and the surrounding nations.

The literal interpretation of Israel's Seventy Sevens Prophecy given to Daniel concludes that only sixty-nine of the seventy weeks were fulfilled at the time of Christ's First Advent. The seventieth week has been postponed until it is started by a particular covenant that is established between a coming prince of the Roman Empire and Israel, as indicated in the first sentence of Daniel 9:27. It is necessary to understand that the person making the covenant is identified as the coming prince, the Ruler to Come, and it not yet the Antichrist. It is the theological view of dispensationalism that this covenant has not yet occurred in history, which is substantiated by the fact that the many events prophesied to occur during this seventieth week have also not been recorded as having happened in history.

There are a number of observations that can be made regarding this particular covenant and the role it is to have as the starting point of the seven years that concludes with the return of Jesus Christ to earth.

- In Daniel 9:27, the ... *he* ... is the key to the interpretation of this covenant, and it refers to the ... *prince who is to come* ... in verse 26 because it is the nearest preceding possibility (the normal interpretative rule). "This is the normal premillennial interpretation which postulates that the reference is to a future prince who may be identified with the Antichrist who will appear at the end of the inter-advent age just before the second coming of Christ."[6] There are other interpretations of the identity of this individual, such as Antiochus Epiphanes, however they do not harmonize with other prophetic events. He also fits the characteristics described in verse 26. The context of the paragraph indicates that this person will be a political ruler of an unidentified state, or, possibly even a powerful organization or other entity.
- In Daniel 9:27, the ... *many* ... is a reference back to ... *your people* ... in verse 24 which are identified as Daniel's people, or, the Jews, which is also true in Daniel 11:39 and 12:2. This passage presupposes that Israel will exist again politically, and that the Jewish leadership, because of their unbelief, will enter into an agreement with a Gentile world leader. Also, the many does not mean that all will support the covenant; the implication is that there will be a remnant that will object.
- The details of the covenant are not disclosed. While it is not identified as a covenant of peace as in Ezekiel 37:26, the sense is that it will be a treaty, agreement or understanding of some sort that will provide for an end to military conflict and will provide some measure of peace to the Jews living in their land. This is not difficult to comprehend due to the fact that Israel will always suffer for the Lord, and that they are completely surrounded by hostile Arabic and Islamic nations that have only one desire - to see Israel's complete extinction as a nation and expulsion from the land. At the current time, it seems as if Israel only wants peace rather to occupy the full extent of God's promised land.
  + Walvoord[7] puts forth the idea that such a covenant could fix Israel's borders, establish trade relations with her neighbors, and provide

protection from attacks by others. In addition to bringing peace to Israel, the covenant might also bring peace to the world.

+ This covenant could be the mechanism that facilities the condition of peace that exists in Israel as indicated by the following passages:
  - ○ Ezekiel 38:11: At the time of the attack by Gog, Israel will be living quietly and safely in unwalled cities.
  - ○ 1 Thessalonians 5:3: Prior to the coming of the Day of the Lord and its associated sudden destruction, Israel will be in a state of peace and security.
  - ○ Revelation 6:4: The horse that comes out of the second seal will take the peace away for the earth.
+ Price[8] suggests that the covenant may allow for the rebuilding of the Temple, on the Temple Mount, and the restoration of sacrificial worship.
+ It is also possible that the covenant may include the Ruler to Come / Antichrist locating his headquarters, or governmental authority, in Jerusalem because of what is stated in Daniel 11:45. The two seas in all likelihood are the Mediterranean Sea on the west, and the Dead Sea on the east sides of ... *the beautiful holy mountain ...*, or Jerusalem. This notion is supported by the fact that in just three and one-half years the Ruler to Come is will become the Antichrist and will declares himself to be divine by desecrating the Jewish Temple.

"This covenant, which will guarantee Israel the possession of their land and the restoration of their religious and political autonomy, is to be viewed as a false fulfillment of the Abrahamic covenant. This covenant deceives many in Israel into believing this "man of sin" is God (2 Thess. 2:3)."[9]

33.6	THE 144,000 JEWS SEALED BY GOD

Core Scripture: Revelation 7:1-4

Now that the True Church has been raptured from the earth and is therefore absent from the tribulation of Daniel's 70th Week, God again begins working with a remnant of Israel, " ... setting them apart to national identities, and sending them as special representatives to the nations in place of the witness of the church ..."[10] The divine sealing of the 144,000 Jews is another instance when God supernaturally protects a remnant of His chosen nation, this time from the catastrophes befalling the world at the time, just as He had numerous times in biblical history with such people as Noah and his family, and Rehab when He destroyed Jericho.

REVELATION 7:1-8

Prior to the four angels, acting as God's instruments to dispense judgment on the earth, proceed with the commission of God to damage the earth and sea, a separate angel tells them to wait until 144,000 Jews are sealed against the forthcoming adverse effects of the Tribulation. A number of observations may be made from this passage:

- The composition of this unique Jewish group includes 12,000 men from each of the twelve tribes of Israel, which puts to rest several untruths regarding Israel as the literal descendants of Jacob:

  + First, this substantiates that God is again working with regenerated Israel which is another reason the Church does not replace Israel. For all those who believe that Israel ceased to exist in 70 AD and was subsequently replaced by the Church literally or figuratively, this passage remains a significant stumbling block.

  + Second, this also substantiates that the ten tribes of northern kingdom of Israel prior to the Babylonian Captivity are not permanently lost. Representatives of all tribes participate in this effort. This makes plain that all of the tribes of Jacob will persevere through the centuries and come out at the end of this age intact and with their original tribal identity.

- Since this event is between the sixth and seventh seals, it seems logical to ask if anyone can or will be saved during this time, given that the Holy Spirit was removed at the time of the Rapture to allow sinfulness to achieve its ultimate conclusion (1 Thessalonians 2:7) during Daniel's 70th Week. The sealing of the 144,000 Jews is a testament to the fact that the Holy Spirit will still be active to some extent in bringing people to Christ - the idea being that the Holy Spirit will operate in much the same omnipresent manner as it did before Pentecost when individuals were indwelt for specific purposes during specific events or times. Salvation during Daniel's 70th Week can be seen in the 144,000 Jews as well as in the second half of Revelation 7 concerning the innumerable Tribulation saints in heaven at the time of John's vision.

- The 144,000 Jews will have a physical seal placed on their foreheads by God. The purpose of the seal is to make them as God's own servants and to set them apart from the mass of humanity that lives through Daniel's 70th Week as a special remnant that testifies of God's grace and mercy. Also, they will be supernaturally protected from death and are thus immune from the terrible events taking place all around them. It is not unreasonable to conclude that the seal of God will stand in opposition to the mark of the beast that will be on the foreheads or hands of those that follow the Antichrist.

- There is much debate about the itemized list of the twelve tribes mentioned in this passage. Each time the tribes are listed in the Bible, because the tribe of Joseph became two tribes, one tribe has to be eliminated so that Israel may be referred to as having twelve tribes in both the Old and New Testaments. Most of the time it is the tribe of Levi that is omitted, most probably because the tribe is a special tribe, however, in this listing it is the tribe of Dan that is omitted, and the omission is without explanation.

- Many believe that these 144,000 Jews will be evangelists for Christ during Daniel's 70th Week, mainly for two reasons. First, being evangelists would be consistent with all the other New Testament instances when believers are called to witness for Christ throughout the world is spite of the times. Second, the passage that immediately follows this passage about the 144,000 Jews indicates that there will be many martyred saints in heaven during Daniel's 70th Week, and the proximity of the two passages suggests highly the associated linkage of evangelists with tribulation believers. Having made this point, the Bible does not specifically indicate that the 144,000 Jews will be evangelists, however, "[t]he Scriptures clearly indicate that a great multitude of both Jews and Gentiles will trust in the Lord after the church is caught up to glory."[11] It is also interesting to note that the word 'church' is never used of any collection of believers during Daniel's 70th Week, however, it is obvious that there will be groupings of believers-in-Christ during this time, and they are referred to as servants and saints.
- Regarding the timing of this event, most scholars believe the sealing of the 144,000 Jews will occur during the first half of Daniel's 70th Week.

A POINT TO CONSIDER

Are the 144,000 of Revelation 7 the same 144,000 of Revelation 14? While there are some that contend that they are distinctly different groups, the sequence of Daniel's 70th Week events are the most harmonious when both passages are seen as regarding the same group, but seen at two different times. There does not appear to be any Scriptural reason for these two passages to refer to anything other than the same group. Walvoord says, "… it would be unlikely to have two different groups of 144.000 each, especially when the original 144,000 is based on 12 tribes of 12,000 each in order to arrive at this number."[12]

REVELATION 14:1-5

In the second of the two passages addressing the sealing of 144,000 Jews, the following observations may be made to complete our understanding of this particular event:
- One of the first questions to arise regards the identification of Mount Zion: Is it earthly or heavenly? This is a difficult question to answer because of the reference of standing with the Lamb (verse 1), along with the reference that the 144,000 have been redeemed from the earth and are standing before the throne of God and other heavenly beings (verse 5). However, an examination of the passage would suggest that it is the literal earthly Mount Zion that is seen here for a rather obvious reason - if the 144,000 are sealed and protected by God and will not die or be martyred during Daniel's 70th Week, the implication is that they will live through the chaos

115

of the Week to enter the Millennium as living human beings. Therefore, this scene cannot be in heaven since none of the 144,000 will die as tribulation saints. "Preferable is the interpretation that in prophetic vision John sees the triumph of the Lamb following His second coming and the 144,000 on Mount Zion as tokens of His keeping power and their induction to the millennial reign."[13]

- This passage pictures 144,000 Jews that were originally sealed and protected by God during the first half of Daniel's 70th Week as standing pure and redeemed Messianic Jews in the presence of Jesus Christ at the time of His Second Coming, victorious and triumphant over the sinister and evil elements of Daniel's 70th Week, specifically Satan, the Antichrist, and the unrighteous portion of humankind.

- This passage solves the mystery as to what the seal will be that will be placed on their forehead - it will be their respective names along with the name of God, their Father's name.

- Again, as pointed out in the other Revelation passage discussed above, there is nothing in this passage suggesting that the 144,000 Jews are evangelizing the world during this time, or for that matter, exercising any special spiritual skill or unique prophetic ability. However, since they will demonstrate the power of the Triune God, it would not be surprising to discover that they witnessed and testified to the saving power of Jesus Christ during this, the darkest hour of humankind.

- The sound that John hears is described as the combined sound of many waters, loud thunder, and the music of many harps. Along with the instrumental music and natural sounds, the 144,000 that have been redeemed from earth have learned a new song to sing, a song that they sing before the throne of God, the four living creatures, and the twenty-four elders. Some believe the sound of the waters and thunder is the music of a heavenly choir, however, this is only speculation.

- This passage also provides an insight into the character of the 144,000 Jewish Christians - they are obviously all men who are virgins because they have kept themselves pure by not having been defiled with women. The Bible does not indicate if any of them are married or not, however, given their commitment to Jesus Christ (they follow Him wherever He goes) and the turmoil of the times, a normal married life might be virtually impossible. Further, they are considered as men of moral integrity because they are honest and without blame. In fact, this ever so brief of character description in these few verses paints the picture that these 144,000 human beings are a portrait of who, and what God wants His children to be. Throughout the Bible, sexual purity is symbolic of spiritual purity as can be seen in Jeremiah 18:13 and 2 Corinthians 11:2.

- Another of God's purposes for sealing and protecting these men during Daniel's 70th Week is revealed in this passage - they are to be the firstfruits of humankind before God and Jesus Christ. These representatives of the tribes of Jacob could very well be the first converts of Israel to turn to Jesus Christ as foreseen in Zechariah 12:10 and Romans 11:15, 26-27.

- "The 144,000 constituted an amazing testimony of the holiness of God in the midst of a generation that was utterly wicked and worshipping Satan,"[14] Living as a testimony to the Lord could very well be the most important reason for the existence of the 144,000 Jewish Christians.

33.7	THE MARTYRED TRIBULATION SAINTS IN HEAVEN

Core Scripture: Revelation 6:9-11 and 7:9-17

In three places in the Book of Revelation, John records seeing a great multitude of believers who are in heaven in the presence of the Lord. These few verses tell us much about the destiny of those that come to belief in Jesus Christ during Daniel's 70th Week.

This event of martyred believers in heaven is included in this chapter about Israel instead of any of the other chapters because of the possibility that the 144,000 sealed Jews of the first half of Revelation 7 were the evangelists that harvested them for Jesus Christ. As discussed above, this connection is indirect because there is not a specific Scriptural linkage between the two; therefore, the possible relationship is one of proximity and reasonable implication. Nevertheless, it is an important passage because we can see that those killed for Christ during Daniel's 70th Week receive their reward immediately by going spiritually into presence of the Lord - just as the True Church saints, they do not have to wait until a future resurrection as do the Old Testament saints.

REVELATION 6:9-11

Unlike the other of the other seal, trumpet, and bowl judgments, the opening of the Fifth Seal, detailed in this passage, is a bit unusual because it does not bring a catastrophic judgment onto the earth or its inhabitants. Instead, it introduces us to the events that will transpire in heaven during the second half of Daniel's 70th Week, the Great Tribulation. While Satan and the Antichrist are wreaking havoc, fostering chaos, and terrorizing the earth during this time and the Lord is dispensing global judgment onto the earth, the Bible describes what will become of those who are killed, murdered, and martyred for their belief in Jesus Christ. As examination of this passage reveals the following observations of the nature of this yet to be fulfilled prophecy:

- After Jesus opens the Fifth Seal, a heavenly scene is revealed where those that have been slain, see adjacent table for other words used in several translations, for their testimony of the word of God, are seen as being underneath the heavenly altar. This is the ultimate manifestation of the Old

117

Testament ritual of pouring out the blood of the sacrificed animal that remained after all the other rituals had been fulfilled, as can be seen in Exodus 29:12 and Leviticus 4:7.

- The martyrs are petitioning the Lord and asking Him how much longer the children of God on the earth will be persecuted and martyred before He brings humankind and its troubled history to a close in order to bring judgment against those that have been disobedient and rebellious to Him. The martyrs know what is to come, and their righteous impatience propels them to

Revelation 6:9	
NIV	*slain*
NASB	*slain*
NET	*violently killed*
KJV	*slain*
NKJV	*lain*
AMP	*sacrificed*

ask the Lord to bring the suffering to a close and avenge unrighteousness.
- Each martyred believer is given a long while robe, to signify their eternal salvation, and told to remain patient until the full number of those that were to be martyred had come about. This indicates that the Lord has a specific number of His children that will suffer and pay the ultimate human price for His glory and name.
- Since this is the first of the three relevant passages in the chronology of the Book of Revelation, the idea here is this scene may be during the early part of the Great Tribulation. If so, this could also substantiate that this Fifth Seal, as well as the remaining seal, trumpet, and bowl judgments will occur during the second half of Daniel's 70th Week. As will be seen in a future chapter, it is the position of this book that, based on Walvoord's belief, all of the seal, trumpet, and bowl judgments will occur during the Great Tribulation. This stands in contrast to the respective positions of many of the theological scholars consulted for this book, as their position is that some or all of the seal and trumpet judgments occur during the first half of Daniel's 70th Week.

REVELATION 7:9-17

An examination of this passage also reveals the following of the experience of believers during Daniel's 70th Week:
- After witnessing the supernatural sealing of 144,000 Jewish men for a special purpose of God, John witnesses a heavenly scene in which he sees an innumerable group of martyred people surrounding the Lord God on His throne with the Lamb, Jesus Christ, standing adjacent. The aspect of this scene regarding so vast a collection of people stands in contrast to the earlier portion of this chapter where the number of believers is specifically identified.
  + It is interesting to note that these martyrs are described as being *from every nation and all tribes and peoples and tongues*, an uncontestable

acknowledgement of the universality that the Gospel is for the entire world.

+ Just in the short span of a few years, people all over the earth will be exposed to the Gospel of Jesus Christ, will accept it, will be martyred for their belief, and will find themselves before the God of the universe. Imagine the commitment that must develop during these turbulent times, so much so that these infant believers will hold to their newly found faith so much so that they eventually are killed for it, and because of it.

+ It is interesting that nothing is said about if the martyred are of Jewish or Gentile origin. It only indicates that they were people that had believed in Jesus Christ and are now in the presence of both God and Jesus Chris in their spiritual bodies.

- The martyred, dressed in long white robes, are holding palm branches, and are worshipping both God and Jesus Christ in loud voices and are proclaiming that God (alone) provides for eternal salvation. Also the passage links the One on the throne and Jesus together as their God.

- They apparently are surrounding an inner circle of angels that itself surrounds God on His throne, Jesus the Lamb, the twenty-four elders, and the four living creatures. As a group they are all giving praise and glory to the Trinity, and they are acknowledging many of the supernatural attributes of the Trinity - sovereignty, omnipotence, omnipresence, and eternality.

- After being asked a rhetorical question by one of the twenty-four elders. John is then told that all of those that he sees outside the circle of angels received Jesus during the Great Tribulation, and by their presence in heaven had been martyred for that belief.

- Then the same elder explains the scene, and its significance, to John and indicates that what he is seeing is the ultimate conclusion of belief in God. Think back to the unconditional covenants between God and Israel, the people chosen by God to His representative to humankind as well as from humankind as well as from humankind, what was the essence of the promise? Also, what is one of the central messages of God's revelation to humankind in the Bible? The reality of the answer to both of these questions is before John's eyes - if the created believes in the Creator, the Creator will provide for the created. The elder explains to John that the martyred saints are present with God because they believed in Jesus Christ, are serving them both, and now God and Christ are providing for their every need, the implication being for eternity.

- "It is obvious that they are martyrs who died in the Great Tribulation. Because they would not worship the world ruler, they were killed, but they will be subject to resurrection on the return to Christ in order to enter the millennial kingdom as stated in Revelation 20:4."[15]

- The provision by God that brought forth martyred believers in heaven is explained symbolically using the basic human needs of the provision of food and protection for the physical part of our humanness, and spiritual guidance and emotional comfort for the non-physical part of our humanness.

119

It is not likely that the supernatural bodies that these martyrs obviously possess have the need for physical and non-physical provision; the picture painted here implies that, as in eternality of heaven, God will provide for those that believe in Him.

• The idea here is that this event occurs at some point in the process of the Great Tribulation.

REVELATION 20:4

In a passage that describes a scene after the return of Jesus Christ, the ultimate destiny of the great multitude of believers that were martyred during the Great Tribulation is revealed.

• There will be many who come to faith in Jesus Christ that will take a stand against the evil global ruler of Daniel's 70th Week and will not worship him, nor will they receive his mark on their forehead or their hand. Combined with the other two passages, this passage substantiates that here will be much persecution of believers and there will be much death as a result.

• The destiny of these tribulation saints is that their physical bodies will be raised, joined with their spiritual souls, and, in their resurrection bodies will reign with Christ for the one-thousand-yearlong Millennial Kingdom. This is identified in verses as the first resurrection.

• This passage is also significant in that it refutes any tribulational view of when Christ will come other than at the end of Daniel's 70th Week, and any millennial view other than premillennial. This portion of the Book of Revelation indicates that Christ will return at the end of the Great Tribulation, which is also the end of Daniel's 70th Week, and before the beginning of the one-thousand-year Millennium.

GENERAL OBSERVATIONS

An examination of all three primary passages reveals the following general observations:

• In the above study of the 144,000 sealed Jews, the conclusion is that the probable timing for the occurrences is the first half of Daniel's 70th Week. If there is a direct link with the martyrs in heaven, then the connection is strengthened because Revelation7:14 indicates that the saints that John sees in heaven come out of the Great Tribulation.

• The passages substantiates that there will be many people, unsaved at the time of the Rapture, that will understand the realities and truths of their condition and those of the world situation, and will come to belief in Jesus Christ.

• As we have previously studied, there is much in the Bible that points to the Rapture being pretribulational, and this passage is included in the group. As is true of all of Revelation 4 through 18, this passage makes no mention, specific or implied, of these saintly martyrs being a part of the True Church. While they receive the same reward as those in the True Church, that being immediately in the presence of the Lord, at the moment of death, they are not referred to as being of the True Church. This also indicates that the Holy Spirit will still be functioning in some capacity during Daniel's 70th Week, as they obviously come to faith in Jesus, and the Holy Spirit is the only One that can make that happen.

- As there have been millions martyred for Christ in human history prior to the Rapture, these passages indicated that the martyrdom of Christians will continue , with the possibility that the quantity of those martyred during Daniel's 70th Week have the very possibility of being vastly more than all of the other time of human history.

33.8 MEASURING THE TEMPLE

Core Scripture: Revelation 11:1-2

In Revelation 11:1-2, we find an unusual account of where John is directed to be an actor in addition to being an observer. He is given a measuring rod and directed without explanation from God to measure the temple of God. This passage discloses two things, first, the measuring exercise symbolizes an assessment of the spiritual quality of Israel, and second, the time length of the Great Tribulation is revealed and a connection to the Old Testament's account of the Times of the Gentiles is established.

First, John is told to measure the temple of God, altar, and those worshipping within using a measuring rod that is likened to the Old Testament method of using a ten foot long, lightweight reed from a plant that grows in the Jordan Valley. Thus he is to measure the holy place and the holy of holies within the inner court, access to which is limited to the priests.

- At this point in Daniel's 70th Week, the temple has been already been desecrated by the Antichrist, the sacrificial worship rituals have been discontinued, and worship of the Lord has been transferred to the Antichrist. While the temple belongs to God, it is now in possession of the Antichrist as can be seen by the following passages:
  + Daniel 9:27; 12:11-12: The Ruler to Come will make a seven-year covenant with Israel, but will put an end to the sacrifice and offering the middle part of the covenant and will place an abomination in the Temple. Then from the time the sacrifice is abolished and the abomination that causes desolation is set up will be 1,290 days, and the ones that wait for and reach the end of the 1,335 days will be blessed.
  + Matthew 24:15: Jesus says, *So when you see standing in the holy place 'the abomination that causes desolation,' spoken of through the project Daniel – let the reader understand –*

+ 2 Thessalonians 2:4: Paul explains to the Thessalonians what the Antichrist will do: *He will oppose and will exalt himself over everything that is called God or is worshiped, so that he sets himself up in God's temple, proclaiming himself to be God.*
+ Revelation 13:14-15: The beast out of the earth was given power to act on behalf of the first beast, it deceived those that live on the earth, the first beast was wounded but lived. The second beast was given power to give breath to the image of the first beast.
- Regarding the purpose for measuring the temple, Walvoord concludes, "[m]easuring the temple will indicate the apostasy of the nation of Israel and their need for revival and restoration."[16]
- The act of measuring physical property has Biblical precedence and is symbolic of an evaluation of possessions as can be seen in the following:
+ Ezekiel 40: The Millennial Temple is measured.
+ Zechariah 2: Jerusalem is measured.
+ Revelation 21: The New Jerusalem is measured.
- The picture painted here is the implication that John will measure the physical temple and the worshippers, and will find the nation of Israel lacking and not measuring up to God's divine standard.

Second, John is told to not to measure that outer court of the temple because this part can be accessed by anyone, including the Gentiles.
- The passage goes on to indicate that the Gentiles are in controlling dominion of the outer court as well as being in control of the holy city (Jerusalem) for forty-two months.
- These verses brings dimension to the time in which this event occurs. The reference to forty-two months is consistent with all the other time references in the Book of Revelation, and lends considerable credibility to the idea that if Revelation 6 thorough 18 concern events that occur during a forty-two-month time span, this makes these events take place exclusively during the Great Tribulation, and does not allow for any to occur during the first half of Daniel's 70th Week. It stands to reason that, if all the events of Revelation 6 through 18 were to occur over a seven-year time span, then the time reference in verse 2 would have seen the Gentiles trample the holy city for seven years instead of how it is actually written. Also, since the Times of the Gentiles cannot end until Christ returns, the three- and one-half-year period before His return aligns with the Great Tribulation.
- This verse also corresponds to Christ's statement in Luke 21:24 where He predicted that Jerusalem would be trampled down by the Gentiles. It is also connected to the Old Testament prophecies of the Times of the Gentiles.

| 33.9 | GOD'S TWO WITNESSES |

Core Scripture: Revelation 11:3-13

Another of the several parenthetical intervals in the flow of God's judgments explained in Revelation 6 through 18 regards two supernaturally protected witnesses that will be present during Daniel's 70th Week as end time prophets, as can be seen in Revelation 11:3-13. Serving God and standing in opposition to the events ensuing around them, these two individuals will bring frustration to the dark forces of Satan and the Antichrist operating at the time, and they will again prophesy truth, for a fixed period of time, to a world under divine punishment.

As is the case with many prophecies of the Bible, this account of God's two witnesses can be interpreted from two, entirely different, perspectives:
- First, it can be interpreted literally, and the Bible will provide considerable support. It is the literal interpretation that his book holds to be in harmony with Scripture.
- Second, it can be interpreted symbolically, but the Bible will not provide sufficient support for it to be a credible view.

REVELATION 11:3-13

John is introduced to two individuals who are granted the authority by God to prophesy for 1,260 days. These individuals are unnamed and are unidentifiable, they are dressed in sackcloth, and the passage does not indicate if the two are men that were living at the time, or if they have been placed there supernaturally. Parenthetically, they are likened to the two olive trees and the two lampstands that stand before the Lord.
- The 1,260-day period of time is of interest because this is also the same time period that is mentioned in other passages referring to the length of the Great Tribulation.
  - + There is debate as to when these two witnesses will serve God. Some believe that the witnesses will be present during the Tribulation First Half, while there are others who believe they will be present during the Great Tribulation.
  - + This book holds to the position of Walvoord who offers that, "[t]heir prophecy will cover 1,260 days, or forty-two months, the same length of time that the world ruler will possess the temple and turn it into a religious center for the worship of himself."[17] This will be during the Great Tribulation.
  - + Walvoord goes on to say, since "… the two witnesses pour out divine judgments upon the earth and need divine protection lest they be killed, it implies that they are in the latter half of the seven years when awful persecution will afflict the people of God, as this protection would not

123

be necessary in the first three and one-half years. The punishments and judgments the witnesses inflict on the world also seem to fit better in the great tribulation period."[18]

That they were dressed in sackcloth is significant. Sackcloth was woven from either goat or camel hair, hence it was a dark color and it was of a coarse texture, and, depending on the situation it was either worn over or under other clothing. In the Old Testament, the act of girding oneself with sackcloth was symbolic of enduring heavy afflictions; also, prophets wore it to signify the sincerity of their calling. Most likely these two witnesses will be wearing sackcloth in the same manner as the Old Testament prophets because they are testifying of doom that is soon to come from God. Refer to Isaiah 37:1-2 and Daniel 9:3 for two examples of people wearing sackcloth for specific purposes.

The identity of these two unnamed witnesses has caused much speculation among theologians and scholars. Pentecost proposes the following possibilities as to who these individuals will be.
- Witnesses Who Lived Previously Placed There by God: There are essentially three Old Testament men who have been proposed to be the witnesses:
    + The First Witness: Regarding the identity of the first of the two witnesses, more often than not, Elijah is the first man proposed.
        o Supporting Reasons:
            - The predictions in Malachi 3:1-3 and 4:5-6 are that Elijah will precede Christ's Second Advent.
            - Old Testament Elijah did not experience real human death as evidenced in 2 Kings 2:9-11, therefore, he could come back and then be killed.
            - Old Testament Elijah possessed the prophetic sign of having the ability to withhold rain as can be seen in 1 Kings 17:1.
            - The period of time that the drought prevailed for Old Testament Elijah, 1 Kings 17:1, is the same as the length of time in Revelation 13:1.
            - Old Testament Elijah appeared along with Moses at Jesus' transfiguration, Matthew 17:3, thus establishing a precedent for appearing after his rapture.
        o Difficulties: There do not appear to be any difficulties with Elijah being one of the witnesses under this view.
    + The Second Witness: Regarding the identity of the second of the two witnesses, there have been two men that have been proposed as possibilities, Moses and Enoch.
        o Moses:
            - Supporting Reasons: If Moses is to be the second person of the two witnesses, this would be the joining of the law (Moses) and the prophet (Elijah) during the announcement of the coming of the King.

- Moses appeared along with Elijah at Jesus' transfiguration.
- Moses had the ability to turn water into blood as seen in Exodus 7:19-20.
- Deuteronomy 18:15-19 requires Moses to reappear.
- The body of Moses was preserved by God, according to Deuteronomy 34:5-6 and Jude 9, so that he might be restored.
- Difficulties:
  - The phrase like Deuteronomy 18:15 suggest that God will raise up a future prophet that is like Moses, rather than Moses himself.
  - The similarity of signs and miracles do not constitute identification as the same person.
  - Just because Elijah and Moses appeared at Jesus' transfiguration does not mean that there is a connection to either Daniel's 70th Week or the ministry of the two witnesses, however, Peter does indicate in 2 Peter 1:16-19 that the transfiguration did have a connection to the Millennium. Also, just because they appeared at the transfiguration does not mean that they are to be the two witnesses.
  - It cannot be argued that Jude 9 indicates that Moses' body was preserved so that he could die later, because his body at the transfiguration was not his resurrection body nor an immortal body.
- Enoch:
  - Supporting Reasons: According to Genesis 5:24, Enoch was translated without experiencing human death.
    - When both of Elijah and Enoch were translated at the end of their respective Old Testament lives, they would have had to have been supernaturally preserved if they were to come back in the future to serve and then to die. Translation of the human body results in the discarding the mortal body and putting on an immortal body, as indicated in 1 Corinthians 15:53, however, according to 1 Timothy 6:16, Jesus Christ is the only one who possesses an immortal body at this time. Therefore, Elijah and Enoch are eligible to be the two witnesses because they are still in their preserved original human bodies.
    - Enoch, as well as Elijah, were both prophets of judgment.
  - Difficulties:
    - Hebrews 11:5 indicates that Enoch was originally taken up so that he would not see death; therefore, it seems unlikely that he would be returned in order to see death.

- It seems unlikely that a prophet that lived before the Flood would be sent to such a future time as Daniel's 70th Week when God is dealing with the nation of Israel, which Enoch would know nothing about.
- Just because Enoch and Elijah were translated does not make them any different than any of the other Old Testament saints that are before the Lord by their own physical deaths; nor does it necessarily mean they are destined for a future event in which they will die.

• Witnesses Living at the Time and Supernaturally Protected by God: Because the Bible is silent regarding who these two witnesses will be, then it is best to conclude there is insufficient evidence as to their identity and therefore they cannot be identified. Concerning the several theologians consulted for this topic, the following is offered:

+ Pentecost concludes, "[i]t would seem best to conclude that the identity of these men is uncertain. They, in all probability, are not men who lived before and have been restored, but are two men raised up as a special witness, to whom sign-working power is given."[19]

+ Walvoord concludes, "… it is probably safe to recognize them as two witnesses who will appear in the end time who are not related to any previous historical character."[20]

+ Fruchtenbaum concludes, "[i]t is best to take these men to be Jewish prophets whom God will raise up during the Tribulation itself. They are purely future persons and not two men from the past. … The Two Witnesses will be simply two Jewish men living in that time whom God will elevate to the office of prophet and will endow with miraculous powers. Their exact identity, then, awaits the tribulation."[21]

• The reference to the two olive trees and the two lampstands may be a reference to Zechariah 4:1-14, where the witness of Zerubbabel was empowered by the oil from the olive tree, which was symbolic of being empowered by the Holy Spirit. "The olive oil from the olive trees in Zechariah's image provided fuel for the two lampstands. The two witnesses of this period of Israel's history, namely Joshua the high priest and Zerubbabel, were the leaders of Israel in Zechariah's time. Just as these two witnesses were raised up to be lampstands or witnesses for God and were empowered by olive oil representing the power of the Holy Spirit, so the two witnesses of Revelation 11 will likewise execute their prophetic office. Their ministry does not rise in human ability but in the power of God."[22]

They obviously represent a threat to the world at the time because the implication is that they are speaking things that cause others to want to harm them. However, they are supernaturally protected against harm, for a period of time of God's choosing, and they have the ability to kill any attackers by fire from their mouths that consumes them. This is, at the same time, a judgment from God and the means by which they protect themselves.

In addition to their other powers, they are given the following additional abilities that can be used during their prophesying: they have the power (a) to prevent rain from falling, (b) to turn water into blood, and (c) to strike the earth with any and every kind of plague whenever they so desire.

- These two witnesses are empowered to perform the same miracle as Elijah was, including calling fire down from heaven in order to kill his enemies, and preventing rain from falling on Israel for, curiously enough, three and one-half years.
- Also, they are like Moses in that they have the power to turn water into blood.
- It goes without much debate that these two witnesses have been furnished with the combination of the greatest powers ever given to prophets.

After the time God had allotted them to perform their functions, the beast from the abyss, we know as Satan, will make war against them, will conquer them, will kill them, and will let their bodies remain in the street of a city that is symbolically named Sodom and Egypt and is also identified as the city where the Lord was crucified, we know as Jerusalem, for three and one-half days.

- Because of the world's reaction to the death of the two witnesses, the notion that comes to mind is that the witnesses, and the inability to kill them, will be a significant problem for the Antichrist and his evil government.
- When the Antichrist kills the two witnesses it will be after he himself appears to have been killed and raised from the dead, which is signified by the words in verse 7, *the beast that comes up out of the abyss*. The fact that the Antichrist is responsible for the death of the two witnesses may increase the world's worship of, and allegiances to, him.
- It is also not surprising that the fate of these two witnesses is the same as the respective fates of the long line of prophets in Israel's history.
- The death of the two witnesses seems to give credibility to the notion that death is the only means that the wicked have in order to silence those speaking the truth.

We then find an interesting situation is described regarding the dead bodies of these two individuals - they are allowed to remain in the street for the entire world to see instead of being buried. Also, because these two individuals have been killed, the entire world rejoices and celebrates their death because all in the world believed the two witnesses had been responsible for their torment. The world rejoices so much that they give gifts to one another as if it were Christmas.

- This particular aspect of the prophecy has an important contemporary implication. If you were reading the Book of Revelation, say a hundred years ago, what would you make of the fact that the world will see the two witnesses lay dead in the streets of Jerusalem for three and one-half days? Needless to say, this passage would not be interpretable because you would not be able to even imagine such a possibility. Now however, with today's sophisticated technology and the fact that it is now possible to that the news can be seen by the entire world as it is actually occurring, the prophecy is

127

not so hard to imagine - in fact, it is not an issue of imagination as much as it is of accepted fact and expectation.

After the three and one-half days, God resurrects them by breathing life into them, and they will stand on their again. This brings tremendous fear into those who have been watching all of the previous events. The Lord then calls to them to come up to heaven, which they will in a cloud while their enemies watch.

- "The resurrection of the two witnesses becomes an important testimony to the world at a time when the world was given to the worship of the world ruler, and Satan seemed to be reigning supreme."[23]
- Walvoord summaries the ministry of the two witnesses thusly, "[a] righteous prophet is always a torment to a wicked generation."[24]
- There are some who believe that the Lord's call to the witnesses to come up to heaven also means that this is the time that the Church will be raptured (this is the mid-tribulational rapture view, and it would require the ministry of the witnesses to occur during the Tribulation First Half). This view is not supportable by Scripture - the sense of the passage is about the witnesses, not the Church.
- Immediately thereafter, an earthquake occurs in the city with a tenth of the city collapsing and seven thousand dying; and many were terrified and gave glory to God. While those that are unmoved by the events associated with the two witnesses continue to worship the Antichrist, in all likelihood there will be many who will give gory to their God in heaven.

In conclusion, these two witnesses will herald the coming of the Second Advent of Jesus Christ the Messiah and Son of God to the nation of Israel as well as the world in much the same fashion John the Baptist did prior to Christ's First Advent. Unlike the first time in which Israel did not accept John the Baptist's announcements nor Jesus' offer the kingdom, the second time, Israel will accept the offer because of the punishment being poured out on them.

33.10 THE SEVEN-YEAR COVENANT BROKEN

Core Scripture: Daniel 9:27b

Daniel 9:27 states that *the prince who is to come*, identified in this book as the Ruler To Come, will make a covenant with Israel that will signify the beginning of Daniel's 70th Week, but at the middle of the seven-year period, now the Antichrist, he will desecrate the Temple and bring the restored Jewish sacrificial worship system to an abrupt end. At the point that the covenant is broken, everything will change - the breaking of the covenant marks the time of transition between the 'relative' peace of the first half of Daniel's 70th Week and the world's worst time of the second half, the Great Tribulation. Jesus Christ confirms Daniel's 9:27 prophecy and also acknowledges that the desecration of the Tribulation Temple will be a milestone event that will usher in a change in the way the world goes, as can be clearly seen in Matthew 24:15.

The Bible however does not indicate what will be the cause, or causes, that will precipitate the Ruler to Come / Antichrist to desecrate the Temple. The idea that can be gleaned from the various prophecies is that after making a covenant with Israel, the Ruler to Come will manipulate a ten-part collection of national governments to the most advantageous position so that he can assume dominance by seizing political control, then changing from the Ruler to Come to Antichrist, he will break the same covenant that in all likelihood made him famous to the world audience. The Bible suggests that the Antichrist will be seen by all those living at the time as the savior of the world, the one who will bring peace to what will be a world of the continued escalation of terror, chaos, suffering, death, destruction in all realms of human existence - personal, social, cultural, racial, economic, political, and international. After stealing more political control than ever held by any one human being, the Antichrist will sweep aside the false religion and professing church because the institutions are no longer important to him as they have served his purpose by providing him the vehicle that he will need to propel himself to the self-designated position of god. What more effective manner of doing so than by pronouncing himself deity in the centerpiece of the Jewish religion, located in the place that most certainly still commands world attention.

As already mentioned, the Bible indicates no specific reasons behind the Antichrist breaking the covenant, however, Daniel 11:40-45 does mention a couple of events that might be associated with the time. Before we examine that passage, the Bible seems to present, and geopolitical logic seems to support, the notion that the Antichrist will have a significant presence in Jerusalem at the time of the breaking of the covenant that dates back to the origination of the covenant. The signing of the covenant accomplishes several things - first, it brings a 'relative' peace to Israel and the possibly the Middle East by protecting Israel; second, it allows the restoration of Jewish worship in the Temple if the Temple has already been built, in fact, the covenant may even allow the construction of the Temple itself; third, whatever military forces that are commanded by the Antichrist may be deployed in Israel that provides the protection; and finally fourth, the Antichrist himself may live in or around Jerusalem during this time.

- Daniel 11:1-45: Walvoord[25] contends that there are two major sections representing two different time periods in Daniel Chapter 11:
  + Daniel 11:1-35: This first section prophetically describes a course of historical people and events, which at the time of Daniel's inspired writing of his book was in the future. The passage is in regard to the history of that part of the world that "... describes the major rulers of the Persian Empire and then gives in great detail some of the major events of the third empire following Alexander the Great, concluding with Antiochus Epiphanes (BC 175-164)."[26] Keep in mind that the information contained in these verses were given to Daniel nearly

four hundred years before its fulfillment as recorded in history, it is this specific passage that critics point to when they declare that the Book of Daniel is a forgery on the basis that the prophecies happened exactly as predicted.

+ Between Daniel 11:35 and 11:36: "The entire period from the death of Antiochus Epiphanes to the time of the end is skipped over with no reference to events of the present church age…"[27] Chronological gaps in the Bible, such as this, are common and are characteristic of God's plan for humankind. One of the most significant gaps concerns the Church itself - it's as if the Church was not anticipated prior to the time of Christ's First Advent.

+ Daniel 11:36-45: This second section then, "… deals with the last Gentile ruler who will be in power when Christ comes in His second advent."[28] This view is based on the fact that the prophetic fulfillment of the verses in this section cannot be found in recorded history.

• Daniel 11:40-43: An examination of this passage reveals the following observations that are relevant to the setting of the Antichrist's breaking of the covenant according to Walvoord[29]:

+ The phrase *at the end time* (also mentioned in Daniel 11:35) establishes that the events that will be described will be associated with the activities of the Antichrist, and because of what is written, the place, the state of Israel, and the time, generally the end of the age, more specifically the second half of Daniel's 70th Week, will be characterized by military actions of nations against the Antichrist.

   ○ It is also obvious from this passage that the Antichrist does not actually govern the entire world, as we commonly believe, but will apparently dominate a major part of the world, resulting in other nations moving against him militarily. In fact, there is debate as to what the interpretation should be when the Bible indicates that the world will be ruled by the Antichrist. One view is that he will dominate the entire world, while the other view is that he will dominate the restored Fourth (Roman) Empire only. This portion of Daniel, as well as others, indicates that the Antichrist has enemies of sufficient size to deploy large armies against him from multiple directions.

   ○ Regarding the king of the south, earlier in Daniel 11 Egypt is identified as the southern king in a war that occurred during the third and second centuries BC, but, in this passage it seems that this king would need to rule something larger than contemporary Egypt, most probably this is in reference to a larger army that may be African in origin.

   ○ Regarding the king of the north, again earlier in Daniel 11 Syria is identified as the northern king of the third and second centuries BC, and again this passage suggests a king commanding a nation larger than contemporary Syria, therefore, this king may be in reference to a multitude of nations to the north of Israel. Naturally, the question arises if this passage refers to the Gog-Magog (northern) invasion led by Russia described in Ezekiel 38 - 39, however, because that invasion occurs when Israel is living in peace. So, the Gog-Magog invasion will be toward the end of the first half of Daniel's 70th Week, and the invasion in this passage is believed to occur during other military activity during the second half of the week; most conservative scholars believe the two are not related.

The referent of the word *he* in verse 41 is most likely to the world ruler of verse 36 rather than the king of the south or the king of the north. If so, this verse indicates that the Antichrist, along with his armies, will invade lands and will easily pass through them, suggesting overwhelming military capability and power and weak resistance. The Antichrist's dominance and rule will prevail until disposed of by Christ.

- o *The Beautiful Land* in verse 41 that is invaded by the Antichrist is taken as a reference to his invasion of the Holy Land of Israel that is supported by verse 42, which indicates that the Antichrist will go *against other countries*. The Antichrist's victories are such that he captures much of the wealth of the lands that he invades and adds it to his possessions.
- o Finally, the end of verse 43 implies that as the Antichrist invades nations, he is also being closely pursued by other nations, identified here as the Libyans and Ethiopians.
- Daniel 11:44-45: Again, the context of this passage indicates that the military activities become more pronounced, suggesting that the various conflicts are prolonged, and will end with the Antichrist being defeated by Christ as prophesied in numerous places.
  - + Regarding the king from the east, this may be the force associated with the sixth trumpet found in Revelation 9:13-21 and 16:21.
  - + Again for a second time, the king of the north will go up against the Antichrist's empire.
  - + "Against both of these invaders, the king [the Antichrist] launches counterattacks which result in many perishing; and he succeeds in establishing his tent-palace "between the seas in the glorious holy mountain," best understood as being a reference to Jerusalem situated between the Mediterranean Sea and the Dead Sea. Actually, the struggle goes on without cessation right up to the day of the second advent of Christ as brought out in Zechariah 14:1-14."[30]

Thus, we find that at the time that the Antichrist terminates the covenant with Israel at the mid-point of the seven-year covenant, military conflict will be prevalent throughout the region surrounding Jerusalem; therefore, there is a strong likelihood that the desecration of the Temple by the Antichrist will have its basis in the geopolitical events occurring at the time.

34

THE THIRD JEWISH TEMPLE

Without doubt, the most observable prophetic situation on the world stage that can be personally witnessed is the current events surrounding the Temple Mount in the very heart of the Old City of Jerusalem. The Temple Mount, a relatively small, elevated stone platform, has a history that is crucial to three of the world's great religions - Judaism, Islam, and Christianity - and has been the focus of reverence as well as conflict between those religions throughout its history. Now, after several millennia of existence, those that pay attention may very well be seeing prophecies that are several thousand years' old beginning to come to fruition.

The condition that makes the Temple Mount significant is that the Bible says there will be a Jewish Temple in Jerusalem, complete with sacrificial worship, during the time of Daniel's 70th Week. To hasten the construction of a new Temple is that there have been activities in progress within the nation of Israel for the last several years with the sole and express purpose of building a new Jewish Temple and starting sacrificial worship! While there is controversy over many aspects of this project, there is no controversy about the scope and intent of this effort.

34.1	A BRIEF BIBLICAL HISTORY OF THE TEMPLE

The Bible outlines a succession of sanctuaries throughout the history of the nation of Israel that represents God's presence with His chosen people.

- A Heavenly Temple: All the earthly temples are based on the existence of a heavenly temple (Exodus 25:40; Psalm 11:4; Micah 1:2-4; and Revelation 11:19).
- Tabernacle: During the Exodus out of Egypt and through the conquest and settlement period of Israel's history (BC 1446 until 960), God commands Moses to build a sanctuary so that He might live among His people; the design is directed to be according to a heavenly pattern (Exodus 5:8-9). The Shekinah Glory of God fills the Holy of Holies.
- First Temple: Solomon builds the first permanent structure for worship and the Shekinah Glory moves into its Holy of Holies; it exists throughout the monarchy period until it is destroyed by the Babylonians (BC 960 until 586). The sanctuary is ultimately defiled by idols (2 Kings 21:7 and Ezekiel 8:5-17), and the Shekinah Glory departs prior to Israel going into exile (Ezekiel 11).
- Second Temple: After seventy years of exile, a new Temple is built by Zerubbabel (Ezra 6:23-25); it exists throughout the Gentile domination until

the Romans destroy it in BC 538-515 until 70 AD. During its existence, it is desecrated by Antiochus Epiphanes (Daniel 11:31) in BC 168, and it is enlarged by King Herod (John 2:20) in BC 20 and defiled by him.

- Dome of the Rock: While not part of the succession of God's sanctuaries, an Islamic shrine is built over the sites of the First and Second Temples on the Temple Mount during Israel's absence from their land. The nation of Israel is re-established (1948 AD) and the Temple Mount returns to Jewish control (1967 AD), however, a few days after it was regained, Israel gave administrative control of the Temple Mount back to the Muslims, and now the Jews only have access to the Western Wailing Wall but not to the platform.
- Tribulation Temple: The Bible indicates there will be a fully functioning Jewish Temple in Jerusalem during Daniel's 70th Week (Daniel 9:26; 2 Thessalonians 2:4; and Revelation 11:1-2). At the midpoint of Daniel's 70th Week, the Antichrist will desecrate the Temple and sacrifices will cease (Daniel 9:27; Matthew 24:15; Mark 13:14; and 2 Thessalonians 2:4).
- Millennial Temple: There will be a Millennial Temple (Ezekiel 40 - 48 and Haggai 2:6-9) that will be much grander than any previous Temple and it will be built by the Messiah with assistance from the Gentile nations (Isaiah 56:6 and Zechariah 6:12-15) and will exist for the one-thousand-year millennial reign of Jesus Christ. There is a resumption of animal sacrifices and festival worship (Zechariah 14:16), and God's divine presence returns to the Temple (Ezekiel 43:7).
- New Jerusalem: After all is completed and the New Heavens and New Earth come into being, the Lord Himself will be the Temple (Revelation 21 - 22).

34.2 THE PURPOSE OF THE TEMPLE

Regardless of which it is, the Jewish Temple occupies a very large area of the nation of Israel's view of their being, nationality and heritage. It has always been a large part of their culture and is on the mind of each Jew that still holds to Judaism, and finally, it is inseparably linked to the coming of the future Kingdom of God. In addition to the creatures' connection to the Temple, the Creator is connected to His creatures through the Temple as will be seen below. David acknowledges as much in 1 Chronicles 29:1, when he says that, "... *the temple is not for men, but for the Lord God*. Price clearly explains, "... that while the Temple would certainly be a place where the needs of man were met, it was first and foremost a witness to the fact of God's existence, His covenant with Israel, and His purpose though the Nation of Israel as a kingdom of priests to manifest God's glory to the world."[1] Thus the purpose of the Temple can be seen from the following list, all of which are predicated on Israel fulfilling her role as God's kingdom of priests that are to witness to the unbelieving world.

The Temple served as the visible place where the invisible God, who cannot be contained within any human structure, dwelled in His divine transcendent manifestation that caused His name to dwell there - hence the Shekinah Glory of God. In fact, the following passages delineate the sense of His dwelling:

- Exodus 15:17: God chose His dwelling, or sanctuary.
- Deuteronomy 12:11: The place God selected as the place of residence for His name.
- 2 Chronicles 7:16: God chose and consecrated the Temple as His permanent home.
- 1 Kings 8:27: If God cannot be contained in the sky and highest heavens, a structure on earth will never suffice.
- Ezra 6:12: God made His name to dwell there.
- Nehemiah 1:9: God referred to the Temple as the place He chose for His name to reside.
- Jeremiah 7:12: The place where God allowed Himself to be worshipped.
- Matthew 23:21: Jesus indicated that the Temple was the dwelling place for the Lord.

The Tabernacle first, then the Temple later, functioned as the witness to the covenant promises made between God and Israel exemplifying the suzerain-vassal treaty where the sovereign rule conditionally protected and provided for a subject people. Each covenant can be seen as having a connection to the Temple.

- Abrahamic Covenant: The Temple was founded on the Mount of the Lord, or the Land of Moriah, the one place where the Lord would provide spiritually for Israel, Genesis 22:14.
- Mosaic Covenant: The Temple was built to house the Ark of the Covenant, which contained the tablets of the law (Exodus 25:9 and 2 Samuel 7:2, 5).
- Davidic Covenant: The Temple confirmed that Solomon would build God's house and God would establish the throne of the son of David, with Solomon as the first son, permanently and forever (1 Chronicles 17:14).
- New Covenant: During the Millennial Age, the Temple will serve humankind as the place from which the Lord Jesus Christ will dispense truth and justice (Isaiah 31:27-40; Ezekiel 16:60-63; 36:26-27; and 37:21-28).

The Temple, and the associated expression of worship, served as Israel's central sanctuary as established in Deuteronomy 12:9-11, and signified that the nation was at rest in the inheritance of the Lord, the land, and any exile had ended. This is found in Solomon's dedicatory prayer for the First Temple (1 Kings 8:56), and the prophets indicated that there is a future rest after Israel's last exile (Isaiah 11:10; 14:3-4, 7; 28:12; 32:17; 63:11-14; and Ezekiel 44:30). "Just as the destruction of the Temple caused a loss of rest, so will its rebuilding restore that rest."[2]

The Temple fulfilled a socio-political function; it was prominent in the Jewish culture and was of political significance. In times of exile, the Jews sought to send contributions to Jerusalem and the Temple, during life in the land the Temple served as the glue of national unity, and after the destruction of the Second Temple, the synagogue was established as the temporary substitute until the Temple could be restored. "The Temple, then, governed the daily life of the Jew, since this life was lived in view of the festivals, the pilgrimages, the sacrificial rites, and the reading and studying the Torah - all of which centered on the Temple."[3]

The Temple was the unifying institution that was the symbol of Israel's national sovereignty and unity. As pointed out above, when Israel was at rest in the land, the Temple existed, when Israel was in exile, the Temple laid in destruction, thus, there was a direct relationship between the existence of the Temple, obedience to the Lord, rest in the land, and, the Temple destroyed, disobedience to the Lord, and exile from the land. One of the possible reasons that there will be a Tribulation Temple is that it will be an attempt by the nation of Israel to restore their national sovereignty and unity by their own will without the Lord's assistance; while in the future the Millennial Temple will again serve as the unifying institution that will bring national sovereignty and unity to Israel.

The Temple was connected to Israel securing national blessings from God as can be seen in Solomon's dedicatory prayer for the First Temple (1 Kings 8). There was a cause-effect relationship between the Temple and the bestowal of blessing, such as relief from nature, relief from famine, relief from military attack, and relief in foreign distress (1 Kings 8:35-49; 2 Chronicles 6:24-30; 7:12-14). The Millennial Temple will fulfill the portion of the Abrahamic Covenant in which blessing will come onto all the people of the world (Ezekiel 47:1-12 and Zechariah 14:8, 16-17).

One of the purposes of the Temple, not fulfilled during the time of the Frist and Second Temple periods, is that the Temple is to be a source of universal appeal and blessing for all the world. The prophets indicate that the Millennial Temple will be the place which Jesus Christ will dispense international blessings, it will be the center of world renewal drawing all people to Temple worship, it will serve as a sacrificial center and a house of prayer (Isaiah 2:2-4; 11:1-11; 56:6-7; 60 - 66; 65:25; Zechariah 8:23; 14:16; and Micah 4;1-5).

The Temple will serve as the focal point of prayer. While in the history of ancient Israel prayer was to be part of Temple worship for the nation (1 Kings 8:29, 41-43), the Millennial Temple will again fulfill this purpose for all in the world (Zechariah 14:16-19).

34.3 THE ANTICIPATION OF THE NEXT (TRIBULATION) TEMPLE

The Bible looks forward to another temple on the Temple Mount in the Old City of Jerusalem, and can be seen in many passages below (the passages listed below are only those that predict the Tribulation Temple - those predicting the Millennial Temple are not included). However, the Bible does not provide enough informational evidence in order to establish the date of when the next Temple will be constructed, it only indicates that there will be a fully functional Jewish

Temple in Jerusalem, complete with sacrificial worship according to the Mosaic Law, at the time of the mid-point of Daniel's 70th Week.

- General Anticipation: Both the Old and New Testaments testify that the architectural structures that have existed previously, and will exist in the future, as the Jewish Temples are the earthly sanctuaries based on a design that is heavenly in origin and divinely inspired - this can especially be seen in God's command to Moses to build a sanctuary (Exodus 25:8-9, 40; 26:30; 27:8; Numbers 8:4; 1 Chronicles 28:11, 19; Hebrews 8:2, 4-5; 9:23-24; Revelation 15:5). Therefore, it is not unreasonable that the two yet to be constructed Temples of the future will comply with the same design as the previous two Temples.
- Isaiah 66:1-6: Many theologians believe that this passage refers to the Tribulation Temple and cannot refer to either the First and Second Temples, nor the Millennial Temple. The passage makes clear that unlike the First and Second Temples, God will not sanction the Tribulation Temple. The Tribulation Temple will be one of Israel's last activities of misplaced effort - Israel believes that they should build a Temple when all that God desires is for Israel to come to Him.
  + Isaiah 6:1: God protests and says that no temple built at this time will be acceptable to Him, He will not come and reside within it.
  + Isaiah 6:2: God wants Israel to come to Him, not build Him a temple.
  + Isaiah 6:3: God will not accept the reinstated Levitical sacrifices performed by the same ones that are guilty of murder, bringing swine into the sacrificial process, and idolatry.
  + Isaiah 6:4: God will punish those that are disobedient because of their failure to listen to Him and respond in faith to Jesus Christ.
  + Isaiah 6:5: Isaiah draws a distinction between those that build the temple, and those that do not participate in the construction effort and remain part of the faithful remnant.
  + Isaiah 6:6: Isaiah indicates that the new temple will end in judgment rather that acceptable sacrifice or forgiveness of sin.
- Daniel 9:27: This passage clearly establishes that there will be a temple in existence at the middle point of the last week of Daniel's Seventy Sevens prophecy, on the basis that sacrifice and offering can only occur within a temple. Also, the verse indicates that there will be an abominable desecration of severe magnitude at this time, again, only a temple can be desecrated.
- Matthew 24:15: In a reference to Daniel's prophecy, Jesus indicated as well that there would be an abominable desecration in the holy place at some point in the future.
- 2 Thessalonians 2:3-4: Paul indicates that a future man of lawlessness and destruction will reveal himself (i.e. the Antichrist) and will defile the Temple by setting himself up and declaring himself to be God.
- Revelation 11:1-2: John the Apostle is told to measure, or spiritually assess, the temple existing at the time but to not include the Court of the Gentiles because Jerusalem had been given to them to trample for forty-two months.

34.4	THE PRESENT IMPORTANCE OF THE TEMPLE MOUNT

The current situation surrounding the Temple Mount brings considerable complexity to the question of how God will articulate the course of history to bring the Tribulation Temple to fruition. This can be summarized in the various perspectives of the three principal religions present in Jerusalem.

THE JEWISH PERSPECTIVE

In spite of the fact that there is now a new political state of Israel and there has not been a Jewish temple in existence for almost two thousand years, there is a considerable range of beliefs present today among those Jews, there are many non-observant Jews that are identified as secular by Orthodox Judaism.

- Orthodox or Traditional Judaism: While there is disagreement whether the next temple will be divinely or humanly built, most are committed to waiting for Elijah and the Messiah to resolve outstanding issues, questions, and unknowns. There are many that believe they should not construct a sanctuary for God based on the Biblical injunction. This is the only officially recognized group in Israel.
- Ultra-Orthodox Judaism: Jerusalem and the Temple are seen as spiritual and physical entities. Essentially, on the material level the Messiah will physically build the Temple after the Jews have attained a spiritual level of godliness that brought Him in the first place for redemption. They continue to strive for a state of spirituality that they deem proper as they await the Messiah.
- Conservative Judaism: Distinctly an American movement, those that hold to this view see Judaism as evolving with the times and approach their religion pragmatically and interpretatively according to individual congregations. The possibility of a next temple is seen in terms of the contribution it can make socially to strengthen national cohesion.
- Reform or Progressive Judaism: The most literal of the group, these do not regard a vertical relationship between God and humans, but instead follow a horizontal relationship between humans - they have moved in the opposite direction from traditional Judaism. This view is driven by whichever wind is blowing and from whichever direction it comes - they follow the evolution of contemporary culture. They have eliminated references to a future temple and have no interest in restoring the historical Jewish faith and culture surrounding a new temple.

At this time there are several reasons why the next Temple has not been built in Jerusalem:

- There is not sufficient population in Israel to do so; this is based on the idea that most Jews have to be in the land before the Temple can be built.

- There is a condition of ritual impurity that exist because the Jews have been unable to enter the Temple Mount, considered defied, in order to rebuild.
- The presence and prominence of the Muslims on the Temple Mount and in the region precludes any attempt at construction; which is the fuse on the dynamite of the Middle East.
- The current policy of the Israeli government is that they are unwilling to disrupt the current 'peace' that exists between the Muslims and the Jews on the Temple Mount.
- The complacent mindset of Orthodox Judaism.
- The belief by many that the Jews must wait for God to come and build the Temple.

THE ISLAMIC PERSPECTIVE

Islam stands in complete opposition to Judaism; so much so that Muslims believe that the Jews were never in possession of the Temple Mount, much less that a Jewish Temple once stood on the same site as the third most important site to Islam now stands. Islam contends that the Temple Mount is holy ground and that anything Jewish will defile it. They also contend that once a parcel of land is under Muslim control, it can never be returned to another's control - once Islamic, always Islamic.

Islam's goal is to dominate the world for Islam, either by conversion or by force. To the Muslims, there are only two kinds of people, those that are Muslims, and those that are not Muslims which are considered infidels ripe for conversion or elimination. There is no tolerance for other beliefs, especially Judaism and anything Jewish. The current Middle Eastern situation of struggle is fueled by an intense hatred of the Jews by the Arab Muslims.

THE CHRISTIAN PERSPECTIVE

This perspective is much more complex than either of the other two. There is an extreme range of beliefs among Christianity, ranging from those that believe that Christianity should support Jewish effort to build a new Temple, to those that side with Islam in the elimination of Israel from existence. While the United States Government does not have a policy position on the construction of the next Temple on the Temple Mount, it does support Israel's right to exist as a nation, but cautions are actions that might upset the efforts to bring peace to the Middle East, and the construction of a temple would most definitely bring an end to peace.

34.5 THE CURRENT EFFORTS TO CONSTRUCT A TEMPLE

Simply stated, there is a concerted Jewish effort, not officially sanctioned by the Israeli government, to bring the next Temple into existence within the immediate future. In fact, there have been efforts in recent years to actually set a cornerstone on the Temple Mount!

- Problems with the Temple Location: There are currently three theoretical locations for the next Temple. The first is immediately north of the Islamic Dome of the Rock, the second is on the same site as the Dome of the Rock, and the third is immediately south. Because any Jewish presence is prohibited on the Temple Mount, archeological efforts to determine the exact location of the First and Second Temples have been non-existent. All efforts to determine the location have been from a distance. Nevertheless, access to the Temple Mount, the presence of the Dome of the Rock, official sanction by the Israeli government, and the lack of knowing the exact site of the previous temples remains the primary obstacles to proceeding with the effort.
- Current Activities: There is a string commitment by several groups to construct the new Temple and restore the traditional sacrificial worship system, as can be seen from the following examples:
  + There are those that are pursuing and searching for the proper site.
  + There are those that are hunting around the world for the red heifer, the ashes of which are necessary for the ritual purification of the priests.
  + There are those that are preparing for the priesthood, including the search for the required purity of priesthood and the training for priesthood.
  + There are those that are researching the historical Jewish past in order to restore the tools of the temple and the apparel of the priests.
  + There are those that are pursuing the development of the architectural design and necessary documentation to construct the temple.
- Groups Involved in Current Activities:
  + There are a number of Jewish groups that have goals such as the following:
    o Pursuing the right to access the Temple Mount via the courts.
    o Facilitating the return to the Temple Mount.
    o Arousing interest and consciousness, including the religious leadership, of the importance of the next Temple.
    o Preparing for the Third Temple era.
    o Registering qualified priests and Levites on an international level.
    o Education regarding the laws governing the Temple and its worship services.
    o Training priests for priesthood.
    o Purchasing the property surrounding the Temple Mount.
    o Seminaries to train student of the Temple.
    o Researching the architectural design of the previous Temples.

- o Designing and constructing the various vessels and implements that were used.
+ Just a few of the Jewish groups involved in these activities include the following:
  - o Temple Mount and Land of Israel Faithful Movement - www.templemountfaithful.org.
  - o Alive and Existing - www.chaivekayam.org.
  - o The Temple Mount Center - www.virtual.co.il/org/org/temple/.
  - o The Crown of the Priesthood Rest (with) Levi - www.houseoflevi.org.

35

THE INVASION OF ISRAEL
BY A CONFEDERACY

Perhaps the most intriguing of all the multitude of prophecies of end times is the prophecy in Ezekiel 37 - 38 that there will be an invasion of the state of Israel by a confederation of greedy nations from the land to the north of Israel. Unlike so many other prophecies that are clearly identified and defined within the Scriptures, this prophecy is mind-bogglingly intricate and complex, not so much regarding what will happen, but more of when it will happen - this eschatological event is virtually impossible to accurately locate before, during or after the many varied events of Daniel's 70th Week.

The current state of political, social, economic, militaristic, and religious conditions around the east end of the Mediterranean Sea gives this prophecy a crucial importance, not only because it is predicted in the Bible, but because we may actually witness the various events and conditions moving into the view that will be necessary for an invasion of Israel. In short, it seems as if the nations surrounding Israel, and extending far to the north, are quickly arranging themselves to become more and more aligned with the scenario that is painted by Ezekiel's prophecy, written 2,500 years ago.

An interesting factor to notice in this prophecy is that there is no mention of an actual battle between the invaders and the nation of Israel - only the military confederation from the enemies of Israel are identified as suffering divine destruction. The prophecy indicates that the Lord will defeat the invaders by severe natural forces, and the subsequent reactions of the individual soldiers. Surprisingly there is also no mention of Israeli casualties, the implication being that there have been none - the invading forces have apparently been defeated without causing injury to Israel. The picture that is painted by Ezekiel 38 and 39 is that Israel may be unaffected by the invasion, because God uses this event to demonstrate to Israel that He can protect them if He so chooses.

While the Bible does not really connect this invasion with other seventieth week events well enough to accurately establish it's time of occurrence, it will in all likelihood have a deciding effect on some other event because it is part of the overall scenario of how the Lord will draw this portion of human history to a close. For example, the invasion could shape the course of nations and history in that part of the world to facilitate the formation of the ten-nation confederacy, or conversely, actions by the ten-nation confederacy could become the impetus for the invasion.

The invasion could somehow have a part in the one world government that will develop during this time, or, it could be the means by which the Ruler to Come / Antichrist either comes into power, or invades the land of Israel to fulfill other prophecies about his activities. Quite frankly, there are a number of possibilities that this invasion could have for Daniel's 70th Week.

Twice within this passage, Ezekiel 38:17 and 39:8, the Lord mentioned that He would send the invasion according to the prophecies of earlier prophets. However, a prophetic connection is difficult to clearly determine, and there are many diverse opinions about it. A protracted discussion of the various views would be counterproductive because there does not appear to be a dominant view, nor a dominant connection. We will let the following quotation be the view of this book: "It is possible that there is no direct reference to any specific group of prophecies (elsewhere in the Old Testament) but to a general concept that permeates prophecy. Earlier prophets, in speaking of eschatological times, foretold catastrophic events and God's judgment on Israel's enemies, though the specific name of Gog did not appear in their prophecies."[1]

35.1 THE TIMING OF THE INVASION

There is very little agreement among theologians, scholars and believers as to the timing of this prophecy, it remains elusive and unsettled, and probably will be so until the event actually happens. Both Pentecost[2] and Fruchtenbaum[3] more than adequately examines the various positions and their associated strengths and weaknesses, and can be summarized in the following evaluations and observations.

It is the contention of this book that the most favored time for the invasion of the land of Israel by a northern confederacy led by the nation of Russia will be at some point near the end of the first half of Daniel's 70th Week, just before the desolation of the Temple by the Antichrist which is the Fourth View below. A less favored time is that the invasion will occur prior to Daniel's 70th Week.

FIRST VIEW - IN THE HISTORICAL PAST

As is true of any prophecy, it is logical to ask if this invasion has already occurred in history. "A search of history finds no such battle or outcome."[4]

SECOND VIEW - AT SOME TIME DURING THE CHURCH AGE PRIOR TO THE RAPTURE

One of the principal reasons for this view is that it is based on the process of elimination - those that hold this view believe the invasion cannot occur at any other time. However, there are difficulties with this view that includes the following:

- One of the main justifications for a pretribulational Rapture is that it is imminent; there are no other prophetic events that are required to be fulfilled before the saints are taken by Christ. If the invasion were to occur prior to the Rapture, then this would constitute an outstanding prophecy that would need to be fulfilled first, and would be inconsistent with the doctrine of imminency.
- The invasion is said to occur in the latter years, however, these are the latter years of Israel, not the Church - the invasion has no relationship with the Church.
- While the Bible is not specific about a relationship between the seven-year covenant and the invasion, many believe it will be the covenant that establishes the time of peace and security in the land of Israel that is required by the prophecy, however, we know that the covenant that starts the seven-year period of Daniel's 70th Week occurs after the Rapture. This point causes an arrangement of events that are inconsistent with other prophecies.

THIRD VIEW - BEFORE DANIEL'S 70TH WEEK
- The various descriptions given in Ezekiel of Israel fits well with the state as it exists before Daniel's 70th Week, and includes the following conditions:
  + Israel has been brought back from the sword (Ezekiel 38:8). "After 1900 years, 46 invasions, the War of Independence, the land is Jewish again and free from foreign domination."[5]
  + The nation has been gathered from many nations (Ezekiel 38:8, 12). Actually from eighty to ninety nations.
  + The waste place are now inhabited (Ezekiel 38:8, 12).
  + Ancient places are being rebuilt and turned into towns and cities.
  + The Jews dwell securely in the land (Ezekiel 38:8, 11, 14). Fruchtenbaum makes a strong case for this not necessarily meaning living in the land in peace because the Hebrew word used for securely means "… security due to confidence in their own strength …," not "… security due to a state of peace …"[6]
  + Israel is dwelling in unwalled villages (Ezekiel 38:11), which is an apt description of kibbutzim in Israel.
- It is significant that the very nation, Magog, predicted in the Bible to be the leader of a confederation of other like-minded nations, is the ancient name of the modern-day nation of Russia, which is a major world power that just happens to not like Israel's struggling presence.
- The problem of the seven months to bury the dead and seven years to burn the weapons of war is an important aspect of this prophecy, and more particularly this view of the timing.
  + The invasion will occur at least three and one-half years before the beginning of Daniel's 70th Week, so that there will be sufficient time for both fixed time events to come to completion before the events

145

of the second half. The conditions that shape this belief include the following:

+ Israel will be in flight during the second half of Daniel's 70th Week and will not have the resolve and time to bury their own dead, much less the multitude that die during this invasion. Nor will they have need for the burning of the weapons of war.

+ If any of the seven years of the burning of the weapons of war were to extend into the one-thousand-year Millennium, it would not be consistent with the Scriptural descriptions of that time. Also, Israel just might need these weapons during the second half of Daniel's 70th Week for their own use in battling the forces of the Antichrist.

+ If the invasion occurred too near the end of Daniel's 70th Week, burial of dead bodies would be pointless if their resurrection for judgment were to occur at the time of the Lord's return.

+ Expressing another opinion, some discount the importance of the seven years being fully completed prior to the Lord's return by contending that Israel will also need fuel for their fires after the Lord returns much the same as they did before His return.

• In opposition, there are several objections to this view that are answered by Fruchtenbaum[7]:

+ The description of this invasion is included within the restoration section of the Book of Ezekiel, therefore we have to discern which restoration, the first in unbelief or the second in belief? In response, the context of the passage suggests that it will be the first restoration in unbelief, and if the purpose of God is to use the invasion as a means of demonstrating to Israel His omnipotence, then the restoration in faith would have to be subsequent to the invasion.

+ The idea of dwelling safely or securely in the land usually refers to a time of peace and safety that will only be found in the Millennium. In response, there are a number of Old Testament instances when this idea is used where it does not have reference to the Millennium.

+ Should the invasion occur prior to Daniel's 70th Week, it would conflict with the doctrine of imminency. In response, even though the Rapture precedes rather than starts Daniel's 70th Week, it also can precede this invasion - there is nothing in the Bible that indicates the invasion has to precede the Rapture.

FOURTH VIEW - DURING THE FIRST HALF, OR, IMMEDIATELY BEFORE THE MID-POINT OF DANIEL'S 70TH WEEK

It is interesting to note that Pentecost[8] believes that this invasion, even though it occurs at the mid-point of the seven-year period, will also signal the opening of the conflict between the forces of God and the forces of the Antichrist that culminates in the Campaign of Armageddon. The following are Scriptural justifications as well as some objections for this view:

- The invasion occurs when Israel is dwelling in their land (Ezekiel 38:8), the occupancy is on the basis of, as Pentecost believes, the covenant of Daniel 9:27 provides the authority to do so.
- The invasion occurs when Israel is living securely in their land (Ezekiel 38:8 and 11). The notion of living securely is debated among theologians:
  + The only real time that a peace will exist after the beginning of Daniel's 70th Week will be in the first half of the seven-year period. It might be helpful to note that the degree of peace that will exist will in all likelihood be relative to the conditions that prevailed prior to the state of peace - it could very well mean that there is an absence of conflict that might otherwise be considered an extended cease-fire or stalemate between forces. There will be no peace in the second half when the seal, trumpet, and bowl judgments are in progress, and in fact Zechariah 13 - 14 indicates that the land will be destroyed and the people scattered at the end of the seven years. Peace will exist during the Millennium as promised by the Messiah, however, the context of Ezekiel 38 - 39 is not characterized as occurring during the Millennium. There is a strong possibility that the seven-year covenant will foster a time of peace and security in the land of Israel for a short time immediately after its execution and before it is ended by the Antichrist at the middle of the week.
  + Some theologians disagree by making the point that living securely does not necessarily mean they are living in peace.
- The use of the time concepts of ... *latter years* ... in Ezekiel 38:8, and ... *last days* ... in Ezekiel 38:18 places the event in the end times of Israel's existence on earth, not the Church's time on the earth. Pentecost contends the following support for the two-time concepts that establishes the event occurring during Daniel's 70th Week:
  + *latter years*: This "is related to the time prior to the *last days* of the millennial age, which would be the tribulation period."[9]
  + *last days*: While the singular form of day is in reference to the resurrection and judgment program (John 6:39-40, 44, 54; 11:24; 12:48), the plural form "... is related to the time of Israel's glorification, salvation, and blessing in the kingdom age (Isa. 2:2-4; Micah 4:1-7)."[10]
- Pentecost[11] links Daniel 11:41 to this invasion as the necessary event to which the Antichrist can terminate the seven-year covenant and begin the persecution of Israel that is predicted in so many places of the Bible.
- Revelation 12:7-13 indicates that there will be a great battle in heaven between the angel Michael and Satan the dragon, and Michael will be victorious by permanently throwing the dragon out of heaven to earth where he will expel his wrath onto Israel and the world. One of the dragon's first acts may be to move Gog to lead a confederacy of nations again Israel,

as described in Ezekiel 38 - 39, which will be initial event of a three- and one-half yearlong campaign that concludes at Armageddon.

- In Ezekiel 38:23 and 39:21-22, the Lord indicates that His destructive actions against the invaders from the north will be a sign to many nations, including Israel, of His ability to control the affairs of humankind as well as of nations, and provide protection for His chosen people. This condition could very well be one of the many things that will cause those living during Daniel's 70th Week and witnessing the events to come to a saving trust in Jesus Christ as predicted in Revelation 7:4-17.

- Why would God intervene for Israel at this point in Daniel's 70th Week when He immediately will allow the catastrophic events of the second half of the week to commence? This could be answered with God's purpose for the invasion in the first place - to give Israel as well as other nations the opportunity to witness His omnipotence before all the other unfathomable events occur.

FIFTH VIEW - END OF DANIEL'S 70TH WEEK

This view is based on the association of the invasion of Israel with the events of the Campaign of Armageddon, however, a comparison of the two events[12], as can be seen in the table below, reveals them to be distinctly separate events. The invasion prophecy does not appear to be associated with the Campaign of Armageddon because there is no indication in Ezekiel 38 and 39 that there will be conflict between the nations associated with the invasion (this prophecy required the nations to be allied), which is a major characteristic of the Campaign. The invasion passage says that God Himself will destroy the invaders through the forces of nature. Also, when Jesus Christ returns it will be in the midst of a battle between armies of the Campaign, but that is not what is described in Ezekiel.

Invasion by Gog Ezekiel 38	Battle of Armageddon Revelation 16
Specific allied nations are included Ezekiel 38:5-6	All the nations of the world are included Joel 3:2; Zephaniah 3:8; Zechariah 12:3 and 14:3
Gog comes from the north Ezekiel 38:6, 15; 39:2	Armies come from the whole world
Invasion takes place while Israel is living securely	Event takes place when Israel is in flight and in hiding
Gog comes to take spoils Ezekiel 38:11012	Intend to destroy the peoples of God
Protest against the invasion Ezekiel 38:13	No protest - all nations participate

Gog will be the leader Ezekiel 38:7	The Antichrist will be the leader Revelation 19:19
Forces destroyed on the mountains	Forces destroyed in area between Petra and Jerusalem
Forces destroyed by nature Ezekiel 38:22	Forces destroyed by sword from Christ Revelation 19:15
Armies arrayed in open fields Ezekiel 39:5	Armies in the city of Jerusalem Zechariah 14:2-4
Lord calls for assistance Ezekiel 38:11	Lord treads the winepress alone Isaiah 63:3-6

SIXTH VIEW - AT THE BEGINNING OF THE MILLENNIUM

The reasoning for this view is based on the belief that Ezekiel 38:8 refers to the restoration (... *restored from the sword* ...) of Israel in belief (... *gathered from many nations* ...) at the time of the Second Advent of Christ. However, this reasoning is somewhat weak; the following are the difficulties with this view:

- The magnitude of death that ensures defiles the land until all burials are completed seven months after the destruction of the invading forces. An existing defilement of the land does not correspond to the cleansing that occurs as part of Christ's return.
- Jeremiah 25:32-33 and Revelation 19:15-18: Passages indicate that the wicked on earth will be judged at Christ's return; therefore, for this view to be true, it would mean that there would be a large number of ungodly warriors that would raise up to invade Israel almost immediately after Christ's judgment. Such an event seems inconsistent with the judgments that will occur at the end of Daniel's 70th Week.
- Likewise, it seems inconsistent that there would be such unsaved Gentiles (which they would have to be in order to participate in the invasion), as needed for this invasion, on earth after the judgment between the sheep and goats that is defined in Matthew 25:31-46.
- Where would the invaders at the beginning of the Millennium get the weapons necessary for the invasion? The armaments and weapons of war will be destroyed at the beginning of the Millennium.
- Likewise, Isaiah 2:1-4 also tells us that the Lord will resolve disputes between nations, again which makes this view inconsistent with Scripture.
- It seems obvious that Satan is the motivator behind Gog and the Confederacy, however, now can this be if Christ has bound Satan at the beginning of the Millennium?

SEVENTH VIEW - AT SOME TIME
DURING THE MILLENNIUM

As listed under the view that the invasion may occur at the beginning of the Millennium, any view associated with the invasion at any time during the Millennium can be dismissed fairly quickly on the same reasoning.

EIGHTH VIEW - AT THE END OF THE MILLENNIUM

Those that hold to this view do so on the basis that Gog and Magog in Ezekiel 38 - 39 is the same Gog and Magog indicated in Revelation 20:7-9. This is not supportable by Scripture for the following reasons:

- Ezekiel mentions that the participants for the invasion as being from the nations north of Israel, while Revelation indicates that all the nations of the earth will be gathered for battle.
- Ezekiel does not mention anything about a one-thousand-year binding of Satan, while Revelation indicates that the battle will occur after the binding is finished.
- The context of the portion of Ezekiel containing the prophecy of a northern invasion does not seem to be within the Millennium, while Revelation specifically indicates that the event is after the one-thousand-year have elapsed.
- The dead in the Ezekiel passage are buried over a period of seven months, while Revelation indicates that those dead are devoured by fire making burial unnecessary.
- The chapters of Ezekiel following the prophecy of a northern invasion are about situations and conditions within the time of the Millennium, while the context of Revelation indicates that the new heavens and new earth will be after that battle. Also, the new earth cannot be defiled by dead bodies lying about for the seven months required for their burial.

35.2 GENERAL OBSERVATIONS

There are many intriguing aspects about this invasion and its purpose as can be seen from the following:

- "Gog's attack on Israel will actually be orchestrated by God."[13]
- "We can rightly identify the modern nations listed in Ezekiel 38:2-6 as nations hostile to Israel and supportive of the Islamic Arab agenda and of the Palestinian plan in particular."[14]
- Is it interesting that of all the times in human history for an anti-Semitic (as well as anti-West) concentration of militant power, similar to as described in Ezekiel's prophecy, to develop to the north of the newly restored state of Israel that there is now such a condition that is in place in Russia and

the adjacent Arabic states? This simply cannot be a mere coincident in the span of human history.

35.3 | EZEKIEL 38

This chapter outlines the prophecy against Gog, the leader of the land of Magog to the north of Israel, who will lead a confederacy of nations in an invasion of the land of Israel at some point after it's restoration as a nation has started.

THE COMMISSIONING OF THE CONFEDERACY

Core Scripture: Ezekiel 38:1-6

The first of four commands by the Lord to the Prophet Ezekiel is to tell the powerful ruler of a kingdom, that is north of Israel, that He is wrathfully opposed to him and what he is about to do. Ezekiel proceeds to deliver God's threatening prophecy by writing that Gog is about to bring him, and the armies of his nation, out of their land fully armed for conflict.

There are several place names and titles used in verses 1and 2 that need to be clarified as there is not only much debate, opining, and controversy regarding them, there is considerable confusion as to heir meaning. There is a tendency to associate some of the following place names and titles with modern countries (Russa for Ros, Moscow for Meshechh, Tobolsk for Tubal), however similarity of sounds is not an appropriate or proper interpretative method alone - these are historical places of Ezekiel's time and should be interpreted in that perspective.

- Gog: This appears to be a title rather than a proper name (in much the same way as pharaoh was the title of the leader of Egypt) of the leader of the land of Magog as well as the chief prince of Meshech and Tubal, which will lead the confederacy of nations in the invasion.
  + Due to a lack of Biblical and non-Biblical evidence, the name is not connected to the Antichrist, it is most likely not a derivative of Magog (Gog appears in 1 Corinthians 5:4), nor has a relationship been established to Gagaia (an Egyptian connection) or Gyges (a Lydian king).
  + There are no clues of the identity of Gog, so the world will have to wait until the invasion to discover who this person will be.
- Magog: Not found outside the Bible, Magog appears to be attached to the land of the Scythians tribes between the Caspian and Black Seas north of the Caucasus Mountains in the southern portions of modern-day Russia, according to Jerome as well as Josephus.
  + Genesis 10:2 and 1 Chronicles 1:5 indicate that Magog was a descendant of Japheth.

+ Price attaches Magog to "… the former Soviet republics of Kazakhstan, Kirghiza, Uzbekistan, Turkmenistan, and Tajikistan …"15, all of which in addition to Azerbaijan have become independent Islamic nations because of the speed by which Islam has spread to dominant the region.

+ "Russia could easily fulfill the role of Gog [Price may have meant Magog here], for its current economic hardships and political instability have led Russian to forge military alliances with Islamic powers that continually call for Israel's destruction."[16]

+ The use of the words … *remote parts of the north* … in 38:15, and the … *remotest part of the north* … in Ezekiel 39:2 is a reference to the land that is at an extreme distance from Israel, which is Russia. Many scholars make the point that Moscow, the capital of Russia, is due north of Jerusalem, the capital of Israel.

+ The consensus seems to be that Russia will fulfill the role of Magog as the leader of the Confederacy. But the obvious question occurs: Why would Russia do all that is predicted? Couch[17] offers several ideas:

  o Anti-Semitism is alive and well in modern-day Russia, and has been for decades; all one has to think about is the current exodus of tens of thousands of Jews out of Russia. Also, Russia may want to regain the world superpower status they enjoyed in the second half of the Twentieth Century.

  o It is not difficult to believe there are still many people in Russia that want to go back to the way things were in the past.

• Rosh and the Chief Prince: The original Hebrew word has been variously translated as the proper noun 'Rosh' (NASB), or as the common noun 'chief prince' (KJV, KIV, and NET).

+ Rosh: In spite of disagreement, many have connected this to modern-day Russia.

+ Chief Prince: This seems to be the favored interpretation because while all the other names and places are included elsewhere in the Bible, a land, nation, or people by the name Rosh is not.

• Meshech: Genesis 10:2 and 1 Chronicles 1:5 indicates that Meshech was a descendant of Japheth. This has been identified as the land of Phrygria. Classical Greek writers referred to these people as Moshoi, and Assyrian records referred to them as Muski, who settled in Armenia in the area where the border of Russia, Iran, and Turkey converge.

• Tubal: Genesis 10:2 and 1 Chronicles 1:5 indicate that Tubal was a descendant of Japtheth. This has been identified as the land of Cappadocia. These people were located in what is now central Turkey that was west Togarmah.

Ezekiel then lists the nations of the confederacy:

• General Observations: An analysis of each nation revels an intriguing continuity among them that would make all the listed nations, including Magog, fit the role as the protagonist of this prophecy.

- + They all share an intense hatred for Jews, as people, and Israel, as the most democratic nation in the region.
- + An Islamic fundamentalist government, that is sometimes harsh and oppressive, is common among these nations as some are fully developed while some are in the process of building such a society.
- + They all are consistently hostile to Israel, in specific, and the West, in general.
- + Many of the nations are building significant military forces, and some are seeking nuclear capability.
- + There is substantial persecution of Christians that varies in intensity among the nations.
- + Most, if not all, of the nations are under severe economic hardship and political instability which could serve as the catalyst for the need for an invasion of Israel in order to acquire whatever it is that the prophecy refers to regarding spoils.
- Countries included in the Bible and their present-day locations:
  - + Persia: Old Testament Persia is now where Iran is located today.
  - + Ethiopia or Cush (NIV): Old Testament Ethiopia is now where Sudan is located today.
  - + Put or Libya (KJV): Old Testament Put is now where the contemporary state of Libya is located today.
  - + Gomer: Genesis 10:2 and 1 Chronicles 1:5 indicate that Gomer was a descendant of Japheth, however, there seems to be divergent opinions as to the present-day identity of Gomer. Some believe Gomer is located where modern-day Germany is today, or where Turkey is.
  - + Beth Togarmah: Old Testament Beth-Togarmah is now where east Turkey is located today.
- *many people with you*: This phrase could possibly refer to additional unnamed nations that will participate in the confederacy.
- Feinberg observes that the passage suggests that Gog will, first, be unwillingly diverted from some earlier plan to invade Israel instead, and second, Gog will be powerless to resist the diversion by God as suggested by "… *I will turn you about, and put hooks into your jaws, and I will bring you out* …" Thirdly, Gog will proceed with the invasion a prophesied.
- The various references here, and in the remainder of the prophecy, regarding ancient implements and weapons of war are difficult passages to interpret. Obviously, Ezekiel's vision was of conditions that were consistent with his day as is indicative of the terms that were used. The problem develops with applying this prophecy to the current times, or some future time. Contemporary warfare does not use the type of weapons described in the passage, therefore only two possible interpretations exist. First, the words used are symbolic, and the invasion will use modern implements, or second, some condition will prevail which will cause the invading forces to use weapons exactly as described. There is the additional clue that the

weapons left after the battle will be used by Israel as fuel for wood burning purposes for seven years.

THE INVASION OF ISRAEL BY THE CONFEDERACY

Core Scripture: Ezekiel 38:7-9

Ezekiel tells Gog, as the commander of Magog and the Confederacy, to be ready for the invasion of Israel when He calls for them to do so. Several observations may be made regarding the Confederacy:
- Crucial to this prophecy is the fact that the state of Israel had to exist before this prophecy could be fulfilled - an activity that has been true for just over three-fourths of a century.
- The idea appears to be that the Confederacy is to prepare for the invasion and … [*a*]*fter many days you will be summoned* … which indicates they will be called to attack after a long period of preparation has elapsed.
- The confederacy will be summoned, indicating a call by the Lord to begin the invasion operation.
- The phrase …[*i*]*n the latter years* … indicates the invasion will be part of end time events. In the Old Testament, references to the latter or last times or days is always associated with the fulfillment of prophecies at the termination of human history it looks forward to when all is concluded and righteousness if glorified and unrighteousness is judged. The reference to this occurs several times in this prophecy, here and in verse 16. References to the prophecy being fulfilled on the last day occurs in Ezekiel 38:14, 18 and Ezekiel 39:8, 11.
- The invading multitudes of the Confederacy will swarm over Israel and cover the nation as storm clouds move over the land and cover it in the darkness that proceeds the ravages of nature; the Confederacy will have numerical superiority.

Several observations may be made about the land the Confederacy is to invade:
- The Confederacy is to invade a specific and very real land - a figurative interpretation is not called for here - which is described as people living after having been restored from the sword, or, as having been restored from the effects caused by earlier persecution and violence. This appears to be connected to earlier references in Ezekiel regarding the final restoration of Israel to their promised land.
- The people living in the land … *were brought out from the nations* …. Since the word nation is plural, this passage is more in harmony with the people being restored from the long-awaited worldwide dispersion after the fall of Israel and Jerusalem to the Romans, rather than their short-lasting captivity by the Babylonians.

154

- The people are seen to be living in the mountains of Israel that had been a continual waste land. Again this passage seems to be more in harmony with the land being a waste land for nineteen hundred years of the dispersion rather than the seventy years of the captivity.
- The people are living in the land securely and at peace - they do not seem to be expecting an invasion. There is no mention of an Israeli military response to the invitation.

THE REASON FOR THE INVASION

Core Scripture: Ezekiel 38:10-13

For the purpose of material gain - seizing spoils and plunder - is the reason given for the invasion.
- Again, conditions in Israel are described - the people are living quietly and safely in unwalled villages, and without protective enclosures, or fortifications. Something will have happened that will cause the Jews to believe that they did not need to fear an attack from outside their borders. It is based on this passage that many today believe that there will be a provision that is part of the seven-year covenant with the Ruler to Come that will guarantee security for the land of Israel. While this is a possibility, the two are not specifically connected in the Bible. Nevertheless, there will be some sense of national, social, religious, and economic security in the land.
- While specifics are not provided regarding what is to be seized, there will be something in Israel that will be of such value to justify a confederacy of nations to invade and attempt to conquer a much smaller nation. Will territorial expansion be the reason for the invasion? Or will it be to obtain wealth (Isaiah 60:5-9 indicates that those restored form dispersion will possess great wealth), a natural resource (minerals of the Dead Sea?), something essential to national survival (oil?), greater economic opportunities, national prestige, envy, or could it be just for revenge? Verse 13 provides some clues which all focus on wealth. Also, the end of verse 10 suggests that Gog will devise a reason for the invasion.
- Interestingly, since God set the boundaries of the nations of the earth, as explained in Deuteronomy 32:8, He designated Israel as the center of the world; literally the naval of the world (cf. Ezekiel 5:5). As Israel is the center of God's Plan for humankind, the land is the center of the world in which the plan is played out.
- In addition to the nations indicated in verses 1-6, there is a list of three additional nations that this passage does not seem to clearly explain. To a few these three appear to be nations that are added to the list of the Confederacy; however, to most others these nations will come to the defense of Israel by protecting the move by the Confederacy to invade Israel.

+ Sheba: Old Testament Sheba is now where northern Arabia is located today.
+ Dedan: Old Testament Dedan is now where northern Arabia is located today.
+ The Merchants of Tarshish: This is an interesting reference to a nation that will have an important role in this invasion. The word merchants is English for a Hebrew idiom which means young lions, and this passage indicates that they come out of Tarshish. One interpretation could mean that three young lions will be other nations that come out of a greater region identified as Tarshish. According to Fruchtenbaum[18], Tarshish could be one of any of the following three locations:
  ○ Somewhere on the east coast of Africa, but its location is not known.
  ○ Spain, which could include nations from Central and South America.
  ○ England, which by extension could include the United States of America, Canada, Australia, possibly the British Isles, and other western democracies.

GOD'S INTENTION FOR THE CONFEDERACY

Core Scripture: Ezekiel 38:14-16

The second of four commands by the Lord to the Prophet Ezekiel is one in which Ezekiel is to tell Gog of God's intentions to use the Confederacy for His purposes of judging Israel. In this paragraph Ezekiel reiterates much of what has already been explained about the prophecy, and again emphasizes that this invasion will occur in the latter times of Israel's existence. However, there are a couple of new observations that can be made:
  • Notice that the Lord's sense of possession where He refers to the Jews as, *my people* in verses 14 and 16, and the land of Israel as, *my land* in verse 16.
  • Notice also in verse 16, that God indicates, that He will bring Gog and the Confederacy up against Israel. It should be understood that God does not instill evil into anyone's heart, but instead will permit a course of events that will be the logical conclusion of the evil desires that are already within their heart - God will not cause Gog to sin, but will allow the Confederacy to pursue their own evil desires as indicated in verse 10.
  • The Lord reveals His purpose at the end of verse 16. It is God's intent for the course of these events to be to be the mechanism where the nations of the world will know God's holiness.

GOD DEFEATS AND DESTROYS THE INVADERS

Core Scripture: Ezekiel 38:17-23
- Verse 17 is difficult to interpret because there are no specific prophetic utterances by earlier prophets regarding the activities of Gog and a Confederacy; some believe this verse is a general prophetic reference to God's future judgment of the ungodly nations of the world.
- In spite of the fact that God will bring the Confederacy against the land of Israel, He will become jealously enraged and furious that the apple of His eye is being attacked. Feinberg summarized thusly, "The reaction to the audacity and effrontery of the invasion of Gog and his forces was stated in bold terms and a vivid anthropomorphism (see Ps. 18:8). The picture is of the breath which an angered man inhales and exhales through his nose. God's patience would be exhausted with the repeated attempts of Israel's enemies, choosing to use no secondary agent, for this is to be a final and irrecoverable judgment."[19]
- Without the aid of military forces from other nations, God will bring forces of nature to bear against the invaders and will destroy them.
  + An earthquake, or more specifically, a violent shaking, that is described as great in the land of Israel will affect humankind and the animal kingdom not only on the land, but in the sea and in the sky.
  + The earthquake will cause significant change to the geography of the land as well as much property damage, and subsequently there will be pestilence.
  + There will be torrential storms of rain, hail, fire, and brimstone.
  + This cataclysmic occurrence will cause confusion, panic, distress, and strife among the invaders as they fight among themselves resulting in much bloodshed.
- Verse 23 concludes with God's declaration that because of the course of events of this chapter, He will be known before the nations of the world, and He will be exalted and sanctified.

35.4   EZEKIEL 39

In spite of the fact that there are some that believe that Ezekiel 39 is the record of another event not associated with Ezekiel 38, it is the belief that they are inextricably linked together and are two viewpoints to the same series of events. Also, the question of whether these will be literal or symbolic events come into consideration again, however, it is the contention of this book that they will be literal events. Finally, some associate the events of Ezekiel 39 with events in the distant past of Israel, however, the passage seems to describe events that clearly occur in the times of Israel's future restoration.

GOD'S JUDGMENT OF THE INVADERS

Core Scripture: Ezekiel 39:1-10

The third of four commands by the Lord to the Prophet Ezekiel, given in verses 1 and 2, is essentially the same as given in 38:3-4, and does not communicate any new information - God is against Gog and the Confederacy.
- God will strike the bows and arrows from the hands of the invaders; He will render them weaponless.
- The invaders will all die in the mountains and open fields, and will become food for the animals of the region, because as will be seen in subsequent verses, it will take seven months to bury all the dead.
- God again expresses His reason for bringing the invasion to the land of Israel in verse 7 - He will no longer allow His name to be profaned, the nations of the world will know that He is the God of Israel, and finally, Israel itself will know that He is their Sovereign God.
- The magnitude of the invading armies can be seen in the description of the results of God's judgment described in this portion as well as the following portion. The weaponry of the Confederacy will be the primary source of fuel for Israel for seven years, and they will not have to take wood from the surrounding countryside. Also, Israel will then take the loot and plunder from the invaders - the plunderers will be plundered.

THE MAGNITUDE OF DEATH

Core Scripture: Ezekiel 39:11-16

In a succinct and graphic description of the carnage left after God's judgment, Ezekiel indicates that it will take seven months for the people of Israel to cleanse their land by burying all the dead invaders. The location is a valley of the Jordan River above the Dead Sea and is apparently on a frequently traveled path as the description further clarifies that travel through the area will be difficult, and it will be renamed Harmon-Gog to commemorate God's victory over Israel's enemies. The idea here is that the land will have to be purified before it becomes defiled, not to mention the health crisis that will be caused by the magnitude of unburied dead bodies putrefying in the sun and weather. There will be people that will be designated to survey the land in search of bones that are still in need of burial. Finally, a memorial will be established in the city of burial to remind Israel of God's protective cover over them.

A SACRIFICIAL FEAST

Core Scripture: Ezekiel 39:17-20

The fourth of four commands by the Lord to the Prophet Ezekiel is for him to speak to the birds and wild beasts and tell them of a great feast that is to come for them. The idea is that there will be much for the animal world on which to feast. Feinberg observes, "It is a vivid figure to bring out the idea of vast carnage, deserved judgment and irrevocable doom."[20] Notice that the passage indicates that the judgment will be a sacrifice and the feast will be at the Lord's table.

GOD DISCLOSES HIS PURPOSE FOR THE INVASION

Core Scripture: Ezekiel 39:21-29

The concluding passage contains much regarding God's declared purposes for the invasion of Israel by a northern Confederacy.
- His judgment and glory will be displayed among the nations of the world.
- The house of Israel will know that He is the Lord their God.
- The world will understand that Israel's earlier captivities occurred because of their iniquity, uncleanness, and transgressions, and that He hid His face from them.
- God will ultimately have mercy on Israel and will restore them to their fortune after the invaders are defeated, judged, and buried; they will bear the shame of their disobedience as the Lord their God gathers them from their exile to the nations of their enemies to which they have been scattered, and finally sanctifies them in the sight of the nations of the world. These verses seem to provide support for the notion that the invasion by Gog and a Confederacy will occur between the first restoration to the land in unbelief and a second restoration in belief.
- God will restore the glory of His name.
- God will no longer hide His face from Israel and will pour out His spirit onto them.

THE OBJECTIONS TO A LITERAL INTERPRETATION

The following reasons have been presented by those that hold that this prophecy should not interpreted literally, however, the merits of each is not sufficient to justify a non-literal interpretation. Regarding the interpretation of this passage, which also applies to all Biblical interpretation, Feinberg succinctly observes that, "(i)t is either grammatical, literal, historical interpretation or we are adrift on an uncharted sea with every man the norm for himself."[21]

- The unlikelihood of the nations listed to confederate because they are neither contiguous nor immediately adjacent to Israel.
- Israel does not have sufficient plunderable resources to justify the size of the forces that will come against them.
- Some have estimated that there could be 350 million people that will die during this engagement (based on an estimated number of people that can be buried in one day times the number of days in seven months), a quantity that is inconceivable.
- The carnality of the event does not fit into the Messianic times.

36

THE ABOMINATION OF DESOLATION

While the breaking of the covenant of peace between the state of Israel and the Antichrist will in all likelihood be just another in what will undoubtedly be a long series of failed attempts to bring peace to Israel and the surrounding nations, it is another associated event of that time that will be the thing that brings devastation to restored Israel, and in addition, devastation all of humankind. Empowered by Satan to achieve Satan's ultimate goal, the Antichrist will make a feeble human imitative attempt to usurp the Holy Being, divine authority, and righteous glory of the True God, in an act that will be the logical conclusion of human apostasy - the replacement of the Creator of the Universe by one of His creatures - by declaring himself, in the most holy place of the restored Jewish Temple in Jerusalem, to be god. While in the grand scheme of God's Plan, the attempt will be feeble, it will nonetheless bring considerable misery and suffering to millions of human beings that have the misfortune to be alive during the earth's darkest "week." The desecration of the Temple seems almost like the last straw, from which God pours out His wrath upon the earth.

The role that the Antichrist will play in the end times is inextricably linked to what he will accomplish at the mid-point of Daniel's 70th Week - it is the defining moment that finally discloses his true identity to the world - the one human being that Satan will use in his "doomed-from-the-beginning" attempt to dispense with the True God of heaven and insert his puny puppet in His place on earth. It is interesting to note that Satan, no longer a resident of the heavenly realm, will endeavor to create his replacement realm on the earth.

The Jewish Temple, combined with the various furnishings within, can be seen as an Old Testament type that looks forward to and testifies of the future advent of Christ, the Messiah of Israel. As one of the many revelatory methods that God has chosen to communicate with His creation, He has determined that each major part of the physical structure represents major spiritual aspects of the One (Christ) that He (God) will send as His personal ambassador to humankind. So, it is within the newly restored physical structure of the type of Jesus Christ, that the Antichrist, as the human imitator of true deity, will declare himself to be the one of which the Temple itself testifies.

36.1   RELEVANT SCRIPTURE

Let's examine those passages associated with the Unholy Trinity's slap of God's face.

- Isaiah 14:13-14: Set in the context of the Babylonian and Assyrian Captivities, verses 4b through 12 record a taunt (song) that will be sung by those who will be freed from fear of the king of Babylon. The king that the reference is believed to be to is Sennacherib, who was the king of Assyria (and Babylon since it was conquered by the Assyrians earlier) from BC 705 until 681 and thought of himself as godlike. Verses 12-14 seem not to refer to Sennacherib, but instead seems to refer to Satan, as the one that aspires to *make himself like the Most High* because of arrogant pride. The maxim, for every action there is a reaction, is also true about God and His creation - there will be those, with Satan as their leader, who will react to God in opposition and will endeavor to be like Him, but not in the sense of *with* Him, but in the sense of *instead* of Him. Again, this is the logical conclusion of human apostasy. Note that Isaiah 14 seems to look forward to God's restoration of His chosen people, but the timing could apply to more than one time. Aspects of the passage seem to also apply to a future time that is yet to occur which suggests an ultimate restoration.
- Ezekiel 28:2-19: In this passage widely believed to be directed to the ultimate prideful being of Satan, God directs the prophet Ezekiel to give a particular message to the ruler of Tyre (with Satan being the ultimate ruler of an earthly empire).
  - + Speaking for God, Ezekiel is to let the ruler know that, seeing into his soul, God acknowledges that the pride and arrogance that this ruler possesses will someday lead him to do blasphemous things against God that are doomed to fail. Nothing that a created being, spiritual or human, will ever possess includes the ability to displace or replace its Creator - the created can never be greater than its Creator.
  - + The prideful ruler arrogantly declares *I am god, I sit in the seat of gods,* yet God recognizes that he is *a man not God* in spite of the attempts to make himself like God.
  - + The ruler becomes prideful because in his pursuit to make his heart like God's heart he acquires wisdom, wealth, skill, and beauty. These passages attest to the fact that this ruler had been successful in his pursuits and had achieved vastly more than any other. Verse 6b suggests the same attributes of wisdom, wealth, skill, and beauty exists in the heart of God, however, the words *made* and *like* are used suggesting the superiority of God's attributes and the inferiority of the ruler's attributes.
- Daniel:
  - + 7:25: In the previous verses, the angel interprets Daniel's dream to mean that here will be a fourth empire that will come and will foster who will speak out against the Most High.

+ 9:27: In one of the most potent Scriptures regarding Israel's future, Daniel records that in the middle of the seventieth week, one will come who will first, put a stop to the sacrificial worship of the Jews (which presupposes the existence of the Temple in Jerusalem), and then second, will desolate the Temple with an abomination. The nature of the abomination is that disclosed.
+ 11:36-37: Daniel records a number of actions that the Antichrist will take at the end times:
    o He *will do as he pleases*; there is no mention of anyone restraining his actions and activities.
    o He will *exalt and magnify himself* to be superior to every other deity or god; he *will show no regard for the gods of his fathers*; he will declare himself above them all.
    o He *will speak monstrous things against the God of gods.*
    o He *will prosper* until he comes to his end.
+ 12:11: Daniel records a simple scene in verses 5 through 13 where there are two beings standing on either side of a river and a man dressed in linen (Jesus Christ) in the air above the waters. Near the end of the experience, Daniel is told that there will be a 1,290-day period associated with the removal of the sacrifice and the abomination of desolation. Again, the nature of the abomination is not revealed.
- Matthew 24:15 (cf. Mark 13:14): Referencing the prophet Daniel, Jesus Christ tells the disciples that an abomination of desolation *standing in the holy place* (notice that the word standing is used) in the Matthew passage, and *standing where it should not be* in the Mark passage; however, there is no mention of when this event will occur in either passage. Again, the nature of the abomination is not disclosed.
- 2 Thessalonians 2:4, 9, 10: Paul records in verse 4 that the man of lawlessness, the son of destruction will come someday and will oppose and exalt himself, the above all other gods and objects of worship, and *takes his seat in the temple of God, displaying himself as being God.* Paul expands his description in verses 9 and 10 by indicating that the coming of *the lawless one will be by Satan's workings* (NET) and will be accompanied with miracles, signs, false wonders, and evil deceptions.
- Revelation:
    + 13:1, 4-6: John the Apostle records that the first beast that arises out of the sea, the Antichrist, will be given ruling authority by the dragon, Satan, for forty-two months, and will again speak proud words and blasphemies against the name of God as well as against those who dwell in heaven.
    + 13:11-15: John then records the second beast that arises out of the sea, the False Prophet, who will make those poor souls who inhabit the earth at the time to worship the Antichrist. This beast will perform miracles, and will appear to give life to an image of the Antichrist, previously wounded by a sword, that will have been constructed by

the people, and thus will deceive the world by promoting the Antichrist to the office of deity.

So what can we conclude from these passages? Basically, there will be a human being that will come on the scene at some point in the future that will be empowered, or energized, by Satan to possess ruling authority for 1,290 days, which is 30 days beyond the length of the 1,260-day Great Tribulation, but yet still in harmony with it (no reason is given for the additional 30 days). Because of pride, he will bring desecration to the Jewish Temple by placing, or standing, an abomination within the most sacred place of the Temple, the Holy of Holies, which will occur at the mid-point of Daniel's 70th Week. He will exalt, magnify, and declare himself to be above all gods including the True God. And finally, this man will speak out against God, and those that believe in God, in blasphemous ways, he will display counterfeit miraculous signs, and will deceive many by his evilness.

36.2 THE TEMPLE WILL ONCE AGAIN EXIST

As has been already been established, there will be another Jewish Temple on the Temple Mount in the Old City of Jerusalem during Daniel's 70th Week. While the Bible does not indicate how this Temple will get there, or who will build it, a Temple will once again stand in its historical place. There are several theories as to how this Temple will once again exist, including the following:

- Obviously many in Judaism believe the Messiah is yet to come the first time, so when the Antichrist comes on the scene in history there are many who will believe that he is the Messiah. Since Zechariah 6:12 indicates that the Messiah will build the Temple, it is believed that the covenant of peace between the Ruler to Come / Antichrist and Israel will contain a provision allowing the Antichrist, the false Messiah, to rebuild the Temple under the pretense that it is for Israel. However, since the Antichrist is the counterfeit Messiah, if he does build the Temple for Israel, it will be actually for himself, in much the same way that Herod refurbished, embellished, and enlarged the Second Temple ostensibly for the Jews, but it was for himself.
- Some believe that Judaism will join the ecumenical world religion headed by the Antichrist, and the next Temple will be for that variation of religion. However, the fallacy of this view is that the Temple is for the observance of the Jewish law, but if many in Israel are not Jews, the need for a Temple is no longer necessary.
- Finally, some will believe the Temple will be rebuilt because the Antichrist will be Jewish, and he will build it because he has the ability to do so. However, as we have already established previously, the Antichrist will be a Gentile out of a nation subsequent to the Roman Empire.

36.3   THE ANTICHRIST AND THE TEMPLE

During Israel's Second Temple Period there had been a number of the leaders of Israel's enemies that had desecrated the Temple, and rendered it defiled. These men were antichrist types in the history of Israel that are lesser than the greater antitype yet to come - the Antichrist who will, during Daniel's 70th Week, desecrate the Temple with an abomination.

- The Syrian-Greek Ruler Antiochus IV Epiphanes erected an abomination in the area of the Temple. In fact, it is this abomination that is spoken of in Daniel 11:31.
- The Greek World Conqueror Alexander the Great attempted to approach the Temple.
- The Roman Emperor Pompey actually entered the Holy of Holies.
- The Roman Emperor Gaius Caligula attempted to place Roman images in the court.
- The Roman Emperor Vespasian and his military son Titus destroyed the Temple itself.

In the context of temple desecration, Price has this to say about the nature of an antichrist, "[t]he designation "Antichrist," appears only in the epistles of John (1 John 2:18, 22; 4:3; 2 John 7), is made up of the Greek words *anti* ("against, in place of") and *christos* ("Christ," "Messiah"), and indicates any agent of the veil one (Satan) who acts contrary to or seeks to usurp the place of God's Anointed who is destined to rule the world (Psalm 2:2, 6-8; 110:1-2; Isaiah 9:6-7, et al)."[1]

36.4   THE BIBLICAL PATTERN OF THE DESECRATION OF THE TEMPLE

Price makes the point that there are instances of temple desecration that are recorded in the Bible, and an examination of some of these will provide some insight as to the significance of the desecration that will happen in the end times. Once a desecration occurs in the temple, the sacrificial worship becomes inoperative because the temple is ritually impure. There are two types of events that can happen that cause ritual impurity in the Temple:

- Defilement - The Lesser Degree of Violation: "[A] transgressor is in a persistent and deliberate condition of defiling."[2]; with the following being examples:
  + Leviticus 15:31: The Israelites were to avoid uncleanness by neglecting purification, so they do not die in that condition and defile the tabernacle.
  + Numbers 19:13, 20: An Israelite that touches a dead body becomes unclean and defiles the tabernacle if the person fails to be purified.
  + Jeremiah 7:30; 16:18; 32:34: The presence of idols within the Temple causes defilement.
- Desecration - the Higher Degree of Violation: "The chief agent ... is the invasion of a foreign element into the Temple."[3] Generally, the desecrations

indicated in the Old Testament involve non-Israelite people, regardless of if they are clean or unclean, who enter areas of the Temple; with the following being examples:

+ Psalm 74:7 (cf. Ezekiel 25:3): The Babylonians desecrated the Temple.
+ Ezekiel 7:21-24: Foreigners and the wicked of nations are cast as robbers that enter the holy place of the temple.

36.5 THE BIBLICAL LANGUAGE OF "ABOMINATION"

Price's examination of the Hebrew words reveal the following observations:

* The general word group of abomination reveals three related terms that are used in the Old Testament and have the following meanings:
    + *piggul*: An abomination, detestable thing usually used in the context of edible meats that have become inedible, not necessarily limited to becoming rotten.
    + *to'egah*: An act that was foreign to Israelite ethical standards because it was detestable, offensive, or repulsive; or, it was repugnant to God.
    + *zimah* from the root *zaman*: An abominable act or wicked device used during lewd or criminal action.
* The related words associated with the use of the root word *shaqatz* used for abomination in the Book of Daniel have the following two meanings:
    + *sheqetz*: Something related to unclean animals, especially loathsome creatures.
    + *shiqqutz*: Idols, and the associated practices, were detestable things.

The root word *shaqatz* used throughout the Old Testament is a technical term that refers to an animal or other detestable things used in idolatrous practices that renders an Israelite unclean.

"From this technical survey of terms it can be seen that acts of ritual impurity and especially the threat of foreign invasion of the Temple were viewed by the Israelite as ultimate violations of sanctity and as a sign of judgment. For this reason, they were extremely careful to prevent such acts, and in the time of the Second Temple had erected a boundary fence, the *Soreg*, between the Court of the Gentiles and the Court of the Israelites, with a warning inscription promising death to any non-Israelite who passed beyond it into the Court of the Israelites."[4]

36.6 THE MEANING OF THE PHRASE "ABOMINATION OF DESOLATION"

In the Old Testament, "[t]he form of the Hebrew term … has a range of verbal meanings: "devastate, desolate, desert, and appall," with nominal derivatives: "waste, horror, devastation, appalment.""[5] "When combined with the Hebrew term for "abomination" (*shiqqutz*), the idea of the forcible intrusion of idolatry into a place of sanctity in order to defile it is significantly intensified."[6]

In the New Testament, the Greek word used for abomination, including in the Septuagint, "... has the basic idea of something that makes one feel nauseous, and thus by transference, is psychologically or morally abhorrent or detestable... and is applied particularly to idols or associated with idolatrous practices..."[7] The Greek word used for desolation comes from the "...root which signifies "to lay waste, make desolate, bring to ruins"..."[8]

Of a special note, Price indicates that "[i]n both Jeremiah and Ezekiel, frequent mention is made of "abomination" and "desolations" ..., idolatry that has desecrated the Holy Place, and foreign invaders who will further desecrate and destroy the Temple..."[9]

36.7	**THE ABOMINATION OF DESOLATION IN DANIEL 9:27**

As we have already examined the meaning of the words "abomination" and "desolation," we should now examine the additional contribution made by Daniel 9:27 to this concept, and that being the word "wing". "It is clear that this term (Hebrew *k^enaf*) has a direct association with the "abomination of desolation" and most likely describes that place where it will occur in relation to the Temple. The word has been the subject of extensive controversy and fanciful interpretation in both ancient and modern commentaries."[10]

- Jewish commentaries have interpreted it in such a manner as to say that the abomination has been either self-imposed, or caused by the Gentiles, and has spread desolation over all of the Jewish nation and people.
- Christian commentators have been just as creative in their interpretations, including such things as having to do with flight, eagles winged statues, or other deities.
- As already indicated, Price contends that this word is a reference to the place in which the abomination of desolation is to occur, especially "... in the Holy of Holies in relation to the winged cherubim of the Ark of the Covenant."[11]
  + Price develops this conclusion based on the idea that the words Greek chosen to translate the Scripture into the Septuagint, the use of the word sacrifice before the word wing in Daniel 9:27, Paul's statement in 2 Thessalonians 2:4 that the Antichrist *takes his seat in the temple of God, displaying himself as being God*, the precedent set by Old Testament desecrators, and the archeological presence of winged thrones, all converge to suggest that the Antichrist will indeed enter the inner holy sanctum of the Temple and seat himself on the throne of God and declare himself to be god. "Therefore, for the Antichrist to

usurp "the throne of the Lord" as his own would certainly be the height of blasphemy, desecration, and defilement for God and the Temple."[12]

+ The logical question that now occurs, regards how the long last Ark of the Covenant will come to be in the Temple again? There are only possibilities that exist:

  ○ First Possibility: The lost Ark will be found and returned to its proper place in the Temple (remember that there are many Jewish historians and archeologists that believe the Ark is buried within the Temple Mount and the construction of the new Temple will reveal its secret location).

  ○ Second Possibility: Since the Antichrist is the counterfeit opposite of Christ, he will construct his own Ark of the Covenant (which consists of winged cherubim on the top forming a throne seat) and place it within the Holy of Holies. This makes his taking of a seat in the Holy of Holies even more abominable because he brings his own winged throne with him (this idea is even more plausible if the construction of a counterfeit Ark of the Covenant is the result of the earlier covenant of peace made between Israel and the Ruler to Come / Antichrist).

+ Another interesting observation of this event is the fact that the Antichrist does not die if he approaches and touches the Ark, therefore, he will appear to be deity to the gullible world of unbelievers, which gives additional credence to the idea that the Antichrist might construct his own ark.

36.8	THE IDENTIFICATION OF THE ABOMINATION OF DESOLATION

There have been several individuals who have been proposed as responsible for the abomination of desolation depending on how the view of the future is interpreted. [Randall Price, *The Temple and Bible Prophecy*, pages 488-491]

• Individuals Not Supportable by Scripture and History: Price identifies a number of people and situations that have been offered that are either, not supportable by the multitude of passages associated with this time in history, or, are not supportable by the course of the historical record. While parallels and consistencies are undeniable, exact fulfillment of the prophecy is incomplete. Price summaries all of these views in this manner, "… we are left with unresolved details that either must be harmonized by reading the Bible in other than a literal, historical manner or by dismissing details altogether."[13]

+ The desolator most commonly proposed is Antiochus IV Epiphanes, who in, "167 BC committed a desolation in the Temple by setting up an idolatrous image and sacrificing an unclean animal on the altar."[14] While Walvoord[15] believes that Antiochus is the one that literally fulfilled the prophecies in Daniel 11:21-35 that are recorded in history before the time of Christ. The passage that follow, Daniel 11:36-45 were not completed before the time of Christ, but instead will happen in the future.

+ There are still yet other desolators and the abomination of desolation of the Temple, that have been proposed as having already fulfilled the prophecy in history:
  o A statue of Titus that was erected at the side of the desolated Temple.
  o Statues that may have been erected by Pilate and Hadrian; or, the standards containing medallions of the emperor that were brought into the Temple.
  o The Roman army that destroyed the Temple in 70 AD.

• The One Individual Supportable by the Scriptures and His Absence from History: So, just who is the one that will make desolate? The only possibility left is an eschatological one - the desolator will be a future person that is identified in the Bible as the Antichrist. The conclusion is based on the following reasons:
  + The passage from Jesus and Paul associated with this event references back to Daniel 9:27 in which the subject of the passage is the Antichrist.
  + The spirit and essence of Daniel 9:27 is fully contained within Paul's description of the Day of the Lord in 2 Thessalonians 2:3-9.
  + "One factor in favor of the eschatological view is that it has the precedence of types that await their antitype to ultimately fulfill them."[16]
  + In referring to Daniel 9:27, Jesus' Olivet Discourse seems to outline the order of events of Daniel's 70th Week concludes with a future fulfillment.
  + In 2 Thessalonians 2, Paul corrects a misapplication of his earlier teaching of preparation for the last days, and indicates that before the Lord comes again, the Antichrist must come first and be destroyed as part of the Day of the Lord.

In conclusion, all of the relevant Scriptures are in harmony if the Antichrist's is seen as the one who will desolate the Temple with an abomination.

36.9　THE DESECRATION OF THE TEMPLE

• The Nature of the Desecrator: 2 Thessalonians 2:3-4 and 9 establishes the nature of the desecrator:
  + 2:3: Paul indicates that the Antichrist will have the following characteristics:
    o He will be the son of lawlessness - he will stand in opposition to the divine order.
    o He will be the son of destruction - his destiny will ultimately be destruction in judgment.

169

- o He will be revealed - he will be manifested to the world for who he is. Some believe his revealing is better explained as the Antichrist being revealed as the son of Satan, in the same manner as Jesus was revealed as the Son of God.
  + 2:4: The idea here that the Antichrist stands in opposition in much the same way that Satan stands as the adversary to God and the saints.
  + 2:9: Paul specifically states that the Antichrist will come in accordance with Satan's activities.
- An Analysis of the Desecration: When the various key passages are combined and analyzed they point out that the Antichrist will literally fulfill the prophecies stated in the Bible and will deify himself over the True God as well as any and all other gods (an idol), will make himself the object of worship in the literal Temple (an idolatrous practice), will do as he pleases, and will monstrously blaspheme the True God.
  + In order for the Temple to be desecrated, it will have to literally exist and be recognized as God's temple as indicated in 2 Thessalonians 2:4. Also, the Antichrist's action of self-exaltation as deity, self-elevation as the supreme being, and self-display as God will have to be a literal, actual event. Both of these aspects would then be the ultimate fulfillment of lesser significant physical events that have happened historically as types of the Antichrist; "… the historical figures who desecrated the Temple in the First and Second Temple eras committed *physical* acts against a *material* Temple."[17]
  + In making himself the object of worship, in addition to his declaration of deity, the reference may be to his replacing the Temple itself as well as the sacred vessels as the object of worship.
  + An interpretation of Revelation 13:6 could include the desecration of the Temple by the reference to the Tabernacle as the earthly dwelling place of God. Also, the reference to God's name could be to His Shekinah (His earthly manifestation of His glory). The idea here is that as the Antichrist is attacking God in heaven as the source of authority, and the saints that reside in heaven, he is also attacking the earthly Temple by usurpation.
  + "The desecration (*chalal*) of the Temple does not necessarily *render* the Temple unholy (by the addition of the element of uncleanness), but only *deprives* it of holiness."[18] In the history of the First and Second Temples, both desecrations and defilements occurred, however, desecration did not require purification, but when followed by defilement, the Temple had to once again be purified. "[T]he presence of idols or idolatrous practices is an "abomination" (*shiqqutz*) that brings both desecration and defilement to the Temple and the Land, which has harbored such abominations. … When the Antichrist enters the Holy of Holies, blasphemously establishes himself as god (an idol), and accepts worship (an idolatrous practice), then the Temple complex and the entire Land of Israel will be put into a state of ritual defilement. It is the immense

gravity of the Antichrist's act that demands restoration and ritual purification, and which results in the Messiah's advent to destroy the desecrator (Daniel 9:27; Zechariah 14:3-4, 12-13; Revelation 19:17-21), restore the Land (Zechariah 14:10), and rebuild and consecrate the Temple (Zechariah 6:12; Daniel 9:14)."[19]

37

THE SEVEN SEALED SCROLL
AND SEAL JUDGMENTS

Thus far, we have examined the people, places, and events of the seven-year Daniel's 70th Week, and have found the prophecies to be indicative of the darkest time in all of human history. We now come to the various physical events that, during the second half of Daniel's 70th Week, will befall the earth, unbelievers Gentiles, unrepentant Jews, as well as those that were saved during the Daniel's 70th Week, as God exercises His wrathful and righteous judgment. All of the warnings that God has given throughout human history, through the prophets and His Son, will now come true as the prophecies of a final day of reckoning will be fulfilled - all things will be brought to their final conclusion as good triumphs over evil

The fulfillment of the vast majority of the unfulfilled prophecies regarding the conclusion of human history that have been made throughout the Bible are explained and described in the Book of Revelation beginning in Chapter 4. Many hold that Revelation 1:19 forms the outline for the last book of the Bible, and the third part of the verse is Christ's direction for John to record an account of what he sees as he is shown the events that will take place as God draws human history to a close. All will be resolved as the longsuffering Creator or the universe first permits Satan to seemingly accomplish his demonic purposes where evil reaches its logical conclusion of shaking its fist in the face of God, and then second as He swipes His eternal hand over His creation in judgment and demonstrates, unquestionably for all of eternity, His power, His sovereignty, and His ownership of the earth and its creatures.

37.1	THE PRELUDE TO THE TRIBULATION - SEVEN SEALED SCROLL AND THE WORTHY LAMB

As the first act of the Revelation judgments drama of history opens, the Apostle John moves from the earth to heaven spiritually and begins the Revelation of Jesus Christ by describing, in Revelation 4, a wondrous scene taking place in the heavenly throne room of God. As best as can be recorded in finite words, John sees the Lord in His holy majesty, in His entire glorious splendor, sitting in His holy and rightful place.

173

THE SCROLL

Core Scripture: Revelation 5:1-4

As Revelation 5 opens, the focus of the scene narrows to an object in God's right hand, a scroll. While it may seem odd that such a common object as a scroll can have a role in this drama, this scroll ultimately becomes one of the most significant objects of God's Plan as it holds the mysteries of God's judgment of all that has been wrong with His creation for so many thousands of years.

- The scroll begins its role of significance prominently held in the right hand of God as He sits on His throne amidst the royal splendor of the heavenly throne room, surrounded as we are told in Revelation 4, by the twenty-four elders, crowned, dressed in white, and sitting on their respective thrones, and the four living creatures.
- The scroll (the Greek is *biblion*) is described as having writing on the front and the back and sealed with seven seals. Johnson[1] extensively examines the description of the scroll and makes the following observations:
  + Books (papyrus codices) did not originate until the second century AD; therefore, this scroll is a roll of papyrus and was used in ancient times for public and private documents. Normally, documents that were salable contained writing arranged in vertical columns on the inside surface of the roll. However on some occasions, when the document was not for sale and was used for private purposes, the writing was on both sides of the papyrus, and it is known as an 'opisthograph.'
  + There seems to be several opinions as to how the seals would be arranged on the scroll, with some believing that all of the seals have to be broken before the scroll can be opened, and others believing that the seals are broken one at a time. The Scriptures indicates that the seals are broken one at a time as the seal judgments are successively disclosed.
  + In ancient times, a seal on a document was considered something of importance. Once a document was sealed, an impression was made in a wax blob thus closing a legal document. The document could only be subsequently opened by either the owner, or by one that had the right, power, authority to do so, by breaking the wax seal.
  + Regarding the significance of the scroll, Johnson indicates that Jesus Christ is the only one that can disclose the several aspects of the scroll: the unveiling of what the prophets had foretold (cf. Revelation 10:7), the coming of God's judgments, the inheritance of the kingdom (cf. Revelation 11:15), and the unfolding consummation for all things, or the end of the world and human history. There are additional theories that have been proposed, however, while each view contains some truth, none are sufficient to explain the significance of the scroll:
    o Roman wills or testaments were sealed by six different people, each with their own seal, who were the only ones that could

later break the seal.[2] This notion gives rise to the idea that the scroll of Revelation 5 is, "... the testament of God concerning the promise of the inheritance of his future kingdom."[3]

  ○ This scroll is similar to the scroll in Ezekiel 2:9-10 that expresses lament, mourning, and woe.
  ○ The breaking of each seal is the progressive unfolding of the history of the world.
  ○ The scroll is the Old Testament law, the Torah.

- An angel powerfully proclaims, or actually heralds a challenge, asking if there is anyone that is worthy to open the scroll, break the seals, and look inside.
- There is a moment of silent, motionless drama - no one can be found that is worthy to open the scroll. Interestingly, verse 3 indicates that within the realms of heaven, the earth, and under the earth, there is no one worthy to open the scroll - the idea being in all of God's creation - no one can be found that has the right, authority, or power to open the scroll. LaHaye makes an important observation: "It is evident at the outset that this is a scroll intensely related to the human race, for angelic beings are excluded from opening it. Instead the angel is looking for a human being. We therefore conclude that the book has something to do with human beings and their relationship to the earth, the home of the human race. In spite of that fact, no redeemed person in heaven, on earth, or under the earth (in Hades) is considered worthy to open the book."[4]
- The first few verses of Revelation 5 emphasize the significance of the scroll, as can be seen in the following observations:
  + It is seen in God's right hand, indicating its relevance as containing something of considerable importance; as we will see in the developing vision being disclosed to John, the scroll contains the prophecies of the judgmental events that are about to unfold in the final few years of the history of this present age.
  + An angel calls, almost rhetorically, across the vast expanse of creation for one to come forward that has the authority to open the scroll.
  + The Apostle John, Spirit-filled, lifted into heaven, and entrusted with the Revelation of Jesus Christ making him a person of considerable importance to the Triune Godhead, weeps bitterly at what seems to be an absence of anyone to come forward.
  + Finally, as will be seen in the following verses, one of the elders stops John's weeping by pointing out that there is only one that is worthy to open the scroll.
- LeHaye summarizing the event, states, "[f]or all intents and purposes the seven-sealed scroll is the title deed to the earth. This title deed was given by God to Adam, who lost it through sin to Satan; for that reason Satan is in control of the world from the time of Adam until the glorious appearing of Christ. John weeps because he knows that this scroll represents the title

deed to the earth and that as long as it is left sealed, Satan will remain in control of the earth.

- It should also be pointed out that the forthcoming judgments (seals, trumpets, and bowls) are all from this single scroll sealed with seven seals. This notion lends support to the seven trumpet judgments issuing from the seventh seal, and the seven bowl judgments issuing from the seventh trumpet.

THE LAMB THAT IS WORTHY

Core Scripture: Revelation 5:5-7

As John stands in the midst of the throne, surrounded by the twenty-four elders and four living creatures, bitterly weeping over the absence of one that can open the scroll, one of the twenty-four elders tells John to stop weeping because there is one that has the right and authority to take the seven-sealed scroll from God, open it by breaking the seven seals, and pouring out the divine judgments upon the earth. The elder identifies the One that is worthy by describing him as *the Lion of the tribe of Judah, the root of David.* He is further qualified to do so because he has overcome as indicated by the adjacent table of various translations. The two titles, lion and root, are used because they are familiar Old Testament messianic names, and they directly connect the Jews to God as His chosen people. As such, "…Christ is completely worthy and has full authority in respect to the contents of the seven-sealed book."[5]

Revelation 5:5	
NIV	*triumphed*
NASB	*overcome*
NET	*conquered*
KJV	*prevailed*
NKJV	*prevailed*
AMP	*won (overcome and conquered)*

- The names Lion and Root are established in the following passages:
    + Genesis 49:9-10: The prophecy that the future ruler of the earth will be from the tribe of Judah, the lion tribe.
    + Isaiah 11:1, 10: The prophecy that there will be one that will come from the line of King David, who will be the leader of nations.
    + Jeremiah 23:5: The Lord promises a new day will come when He will raise a descendant of King David to wisely and righteously rule in the land.
    + Revelation 22:16: As the visions revealed to John conclude, Jesus declares Himself to be the descendant of King David.
- What Jesus, the Son of God, has overcome is disclosed in Revelation 5:9 - He paid the price for the redemption of the people for God by being killed and shedding His blood as a sacrifice.
- The portrayal as the Lion suggests the Second Coming of Jesus in sovereign majesty as the Judge and Ruler of the world.

As John continued to look at the scene, he saw *a Lamb that appeared to have been killed. He has seven horns and seven eyes, which are the seven spirits of God.*

- The image of the Lamb:
  + Refers to the First Coming of Jesus.
  + Expresses His responsibility as Savior.
  + Meekly demonstrates the fullness and the redemptive aspects of the grace of God.
  + Forms the connection of Jesus being the Lamb in heaven with Him being the sacrificial Lamb on earth under the judgment of God for human sinfulness.
  + Forms a direct connection between Jesus and the True Church.
  + Represents, "… as one sovereign in His own authority, omnipotent in power, and worthy as the Redeemer who died."[6]
  + Portrays, "… sacrificial death and links the Messiah to the OT Passover lamb (Exod. 12:5f; Isa. 53:7; John 1:29; Acts 8:23; 1 Peter 1:19)."[7]
- "The horns seem to speak of the prerogative of a king (cf. Dan. 7:24 and Rev. 13:1). The seven eyes are identified as "the seven Spirits of God" sent forth into all the earth (cf. Zech. 3:9 and 4:10)."[8]
  + The number seven is the sign of divine perfection and completeness.
  + Horns are seen as the symbol for ruling power.
  + The "… eyes speak of the judgment of our Lord, including the seven characteristics of the Holy Spirit that rests on Him without measure (Isa. 11:2 and John 3:34)."[9]

Notice the implications of the symbolism expressed in verses 5 and 6. In verse 5, the one that is worthy to open the scroll is referred to as the Lion of the nation of Israel and the Root of the ruling dynasty of the nation; then, in verse 6, the one that is worthy is referred to as the Lamb that had been sacrificed. These two verses pull together God's Plan for humankind and connects two distinct groups of chosen people, the Hebrews of the Old Testament and the Believers of the New Testament, to His only Son, Jesus Christ. There may be no other passage of Scripture in the entire Bible that so succinctly establishes the separateness of Israel and the Church as do these two verses. Jesus Christ is described from two different perspectives that combine to form the single focus of God's Plan for all of humankind - Believers see Jesus as the Savior Lamb, and non-believers see Jesus as the Judging Lion.

"Symbolically, the one on the throne thus authorizes the slain messianic King to execute His plan for the redemption of the world because in and through the Lamb, God is at work in history for the salvation of humanity."[10]

THE WORSHIP OF THE LAMB

Revelation 5 closes with the worship of Jesus Christ by three different heavenly angels singing three hymns of praise and acknowledgement. Each hymn is directed specifically at the Lamb, with the third hymn also including praise for God.

Worship by the Living Creatures and the Elders
Core Scripture: Revelation 5:8-10

In the first hymn, twenty-eight beings give praise to the Lamb accompanied by harps and bowls of incense representing the prayers of the saints. In this hymn, the earthly work of the Lamb is acknowledged as the qualification necessary in order to take the scroll from the hand of God. Jesus' universal act of love serves as the means to victory over death and is the ransom that was paid for the priests that will inherit the Kingdom to come.

Worship by the Angels
Core Scripture: Revelation 5:11-12

In the second hymn and in addition to the living creatures and the elders, *myriads of myriads, and thousands* of angels are singing loudly and declaring the worthiness of the Lamb *to receive power and riches and wisdom and might and honor and glory and blessing*. The image of thousands of angels before the throne of God can also be seen in Daniel 7:10, and these same seven characteristics stated of Jesus are also said about God in Revelation 7:12.

Worship by All Creation
Core Scripture: Revelation 5:13-14

In the third and final hymn, all of creation sign their praise of Jesus Christ and the Lord God by acknowledging their sovereign power and eternality. The worship of the Lord and Jesus conclude with the living creatures proclaiming Amen, and the elders throwing themselves to the ground and continuing to worship.

37.2	THE CHRONOLOGY OF THE SEAL, TRUMPET, AND BOWL JUDGEMENTS

Before we start examining details of the seal, trumpet, and bowl judgments, we should understand several aspects regarding the chronology. As would be expected of prophetic and end times matters, there are several interpretations that have been proposed over the decades to answer two essential questions:
- When do the seal, trumpet, and bowl judgmental events begin?
- In what order do the seal, trumpet, and bowl judgmental events occur?

While the Bible indicates that the trio of seven judgments will be complete by the time Jesus Christ returns to earth at His Triumphal Second Advent, other than their place in the sequence of events in the last book of the Bible there are no specific passages in Revelation, or the entire Bible for that matter, that indicates when the judgments actually start. Therefore, it is left to the interpreter to determine their start, and the only effective manner to do so is to base the decision on the relationship between the first seal and the other personages, as well as the other events taking place at the time. Walvoord has noted that, "[a]t least fifty different systems of interpretation have arisen from the historical view alone."[11]

- The Historic View: While acknowledging that all of the judgments are comprehended in the seven seals (i.e. seven trumpets from the seventh seal, and seven bowls from the seventh trumpet), this theory holds that the twenty-one judgments represent the progress of the Church through two thousand years of the twists and turns of world history. The most significant weakness of this view is that history does not substantiate the events with actual happenings.
- The Futuristic View: Those holding to a literal interpretation contend that all of the judgments occur within the confines of Daniel's 70th Week, however, the specific amount of time necessary and their order is very much debated and there are multiple interpretative theories, with only four shown here:

Various Views of the Timing of the Seal, Trumpet, and Bowl Judgments		
View	First Half of Daniel's 70th Week	Second Half of Daniel's 70th Week The Great Tribulation
A		7 Seals, 7 Trumpets, and 7 Bowls
B	7 Seals and 7 Trumpets	7 Bowls
C	7 Seals	7 Trumpets and 7 Bowls
D	First 4 Seals	Last 3 Seals, 7 Trumpets, and 7 Bowls

+ View A – View of this Book: Walvoord[12] contends that all of the seal, trumpet, and bowl judgments occur during the second three and one-half years. His own words suffice to explain this view:
  ○ Sequence of Events - Progressively and Telescopically: "Though many have attempted alternate views, probably the best approach is the view that the seven seals are the major events, or time periods, that out of the seventh seal will come a series of events described as the seven trumpets, and out of the seventh trumpet will come a series of seven bowls of wrath: judgments on the world just preceding the Second Coming."[13]

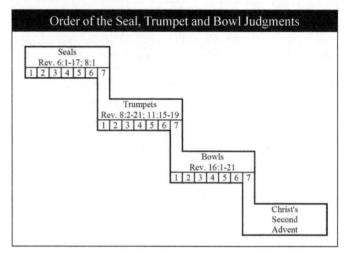

○ Time of Occurrence - The Great Tribulation (Second Half of Daniel's 70th Week): "Expositors ... have usually taken for granted that the book gives a panoramic view of the entire seven years even though there is no explicit proof of this in the book itself. There is some evidence, however, that the events pictured in the seals, trumpets, and vials are instead a concentrated prophecy of the latter half of the week, i.e., a period of three and one-half years, designated as a time of wrath and the great tribulation, and constituting the introduction of the second coming of Christ."[14]

The conclusion that seems to make the most sense scripturally, and to be the most consistent with the whole of the Bible, especially the many aspects of prophecy, is the view of Walvoord, View A. In order for this interpretation to be accurate, the rider of the white horse in the first seal has to be the Antichrist. This view seems to be in harmony with other end time prophecies according to the following logic:

- The Prince to Come starts the seven-year Daniel's 70th Week by making a treaty with Israel.
- Since the first half of the Week appears to be a time of relative peace, this would be the appropriate time for the Prince to Come to develop the political and military power base that will serve as the launching pad for eventual global domination. The idea would be that the developments would be secretive clandestinely.
- The one that is the Prince to Come at the beginning of the Week will be the Antichrist by the midpoint of the Week, at which time several other events converge to signify the beginning of the second half of the Week:
  + The Abomination of Desolation of the Jewish Temple occurs.
  + The Unholy Trinity is formalized because Satan is thrown to earth, and the False Prophet appears on the scene.

180

+   The Antichrist assumes control of the false religion.
+   The Antichrist begins his governance of the world.

Many scholars believe that the time of the Antichrist's global rule will be limited to the second half of Daniel's 70th Week. Therefore, when a man is presenting himself to the world as the Messiah, the Holy Trinity will respond by exercising their authority over the world, the rebellious Gentiles, the irreverent Jews, and the Unholy Trinity by opening the seven-seal scroll, thus dispensing a tirade of terrible judgments.

One other aspect of the seal, trumpet, and bowl judgments is that, as can be seen from even a casual reading of the relevant passages, is that the judgments increase in severity - the bowl judgments are more severe than the trumpet judgments which are in themselves more severe than the seal judgments.

The unique imagery disclosed in many of the passages do not seem to be directly interpretable by the remainder of Scripture therefore, it will be necessary to interpret some of them based on the immediate context, the sense of the passages, and by a general knowledge of the prophetic aspects of Scripture. This raises the concern for caution because it is extremely easy to "see" things in the passages that are not there, and the propensity to speculate has to be resisted so as to not distort the interpretation. Be it known that nothing written below, or anywhere in this book, is intended to alter the Bible in any way, and the interpretation will be attempted only in the sense of the nature of the times, personages and events as established by other prophetic Scripture.

While not necessarily in regard to the chronology of the judgments, there is yet another interesting observation that can be made. For the first time in the history of the world, humankind now possesses on a wide scale basis, the means to inflict the magnitude of death and destruction indicated in the various judgments. In spite of the fact that the Bible does not always indicate the manner that the predicted death and destruction will be accomplished, it is quite plausible that the arsenal of weapons and implements of war that currently exists could somehow fit into these judgments. It does not seem to be just a coincident that humankind now possesses the weapons that it does at the same time that the judgments of Revelation appear to be on the threshold of the conclusion of history.

37.3   WRATH OF GOD - THE SEAL JUDGMENTS

And the wrath of God begins.

GENERAL OBSERVATIONS OF THE SEALS

Notice that the Lamb, or Jesus Christ, is the One that breaks each of the seven seals on the scroll, thus making the origin of the judgments from the Holy Trinity, which is consistent with these judgments being considered as God exercising His righteous wrath on sinfulness and rebellion.

Regarding the four horses, it is very difficult to determine if they are actual horses with riders, or, they are symbolic of something else.
- Couch makes the point that, "[a]s animals of war, horses signified the ability to attack swiftly and with frightening results against the enemy's foot soldiers."[15]
- Johnson suggests that the imagery of the four horses of Revelation 6 may be found in the four horses of Zechariah 1:8ff and 6:1-8, where they are "… divine instruments of judgment on the enemies of God's people, while the colors represent geographical points of the compass. This may also be the best interpretation of the horses and their riders in Revelation 6, where each is sent by Christ through the instrumentality of the living creatures."[16]
- These horses, with unidentified riders that come out onto the world with differing powers, are commonly known as the Four Horsemen of the Apocalypse, and have historically represented the beginning of God's final judgments of humankind.

There is a noticeable alignment between the events described in Christ's Sermon on the Mount and the seal judgments as can be seen in the following comparison[17]:

Comparison of Olivet Discourse and Seal Judgments		
	Matthew	Revelation
War	24:6-7	6:3-4 - Second Seal
Famine	24:7	6:5-6 - Third Seal
Death	24:7-9	6:7-8 - Fourth Seal
Martyrdom	24:9-10, 16-22	6:9-11 - Fifth Seal
Sun and Moon Darkened, Stars Falling	24:29	6:12-14 - Sixth Seal
Time of Divine Judgment	24:32 - 25:26	6:15-16

The similarities are striking, thus causing some to believe that the words of Christ in the applicable portions of Matthew 24 and 25 refer to the seal judgments of

Revelation 6. However, if this were the interpretation, then the first through the fifth seals would have to occur during the first half of Daniel's 70th Week, which would not be consistent with the idea that the first half is a time of relative peace. Therefore, it is the position of this book that in spite of the fact that they are similar, they are not the same things - there does not seem to be an appropriate harmony for the two passages to be in reference to the same thing, not to mention that the first and seventh seals are not included in Matthew.

The following is a summary of the seal judgments:

The Seven-Seal Judgments	
First	White horse – brings the peoples of the world under conquest
Second	Red horse – brings warfare to the peoples of the world
Third	Black horse – brings famine to the peoples of the world
Fourth	Pale horse – brings death to an enormous number of the peoples of the world
Fifth	Reveals the abode of the saints that are martyred during Daniel's 70th Week
Sixth	Brings catastrophic terror to the people of the world
Seventh	Brings the seven trumpet judgments to the people of the earth

FIRST SEAL

Core Scripture: Revelation 6:1-2

Interpretation
White Horse: A conquering military commander riding a white horse, either into battle or in his triumphal return home from a victory, has been a part of military tradition spanning from ancient times up until today; so, the opening of the first seal revealing a rider on a white horse does not seem unusual from what would be expected given the imagery and symbolism of the Book of Revelation. In fact, Christ returns to earth with His angels on white horses as can be seen in Revelation 19:11-21.

Rider: The rider is not identified, nor, with the exception of the bow, is he described.
- The interpretation that is in the most harmony with Scripture supports the Antichrist as the rider because he soon appears in the Book of Revelation in Chapters 11 and 13. This would be consistent with the idea that part of the nature of the Antichrist during this time is to mimic Jesus Christ by misrepresenting himself to the world as the long-awaited Messiah. As Jesus will make His appearance riding a white horse, the Antichrist will imitate Him by riding into his time on a white horse. The Antichrist as the first rider is also supported by the fact that bringing conquest to the

world is in character with the other riders bringing war, famine, and death into the world.

- There are some who believe that the rider is Christ and is connected to Revelation 19:11, and the victory of the Gospel. However, neither the context (rider comes to conquer), nor the sequence of activities (Christ breaking the seals on the scroll, and later riding a white horse at His Second Advent) supports this notion. Also, this rider is one of four bringing judgment, and the concept of Jesus bringing the sort of trouble as the other three riders is inconceivable. Further, it would be inappropriate for an angelic being to call forth Jesus on a horse, and it would also be inappropriate for Christ to need a bow to accomplish any of His purposes. Finally, the crown is not the kind of crown that belongs to Christ.
- Still others believe that the rider is not a person at all, but instead the spirit of military conquest that has been dominate in human history.

Arrowless Bow: It is interesting that there is no mention of the rider also having arrows to go with the bow. The absence of arrows has led to theological debate, however, it might be more accurate to not read an interpretation into something that is not specifically mentioned in the Scriptures (which is the positions taken in this book). The most plausible explanation is that the bow signifies bloodless conquest, victory without warfare possibility by diplomacy.

Crown: The rider will be given the crown of the victor (Greek *stephanos*), not of sovereignty or royalty (Greek *diadem*), from the unidentified source.

- Since the rider is believed to be the Antichrist, the source of the crown could be the recognition by the world for having made the treaty of peace with Israel (as the Prince to Come) at the beginning of the seven years, and having desolated the Jewish Temple at the midpoint of the seven years, thus firmly establishing him as the world ruler that the Bible says he is to become. Another plausible idea is that Satan is cast from heaven to earth at the midpoint of the Week, he crowns the Antichrist as his principal representative to rule the world.
- The passage does not indicate when the crown will be given, when the rider first comes out, or at some point later. It would seem logical that the crown would come later after the rider, the Antichrist, has conquered to whatever extent necessary for the world to bestow the honor.

Conquering and To Conquer: The passage makes no statement about who is conquered and to what extent the conquests will be. The picture painted by the context of the magnitude of the various judgments suggests that the conquering will be on a global scale, and also suggests dominance of peoples, tribes, and nations, which would make sense if the rider were the Antichrist. Larkin makes an interesting observation: "This is a picture of a brilliant, strategical, and irresistible conqueror, whose victories will dazzle the world, and elevate him to a leadership …"[18]

What This Seal Means
This first seal will be the Antichrist that will appear on the scene and will conquer many nations of the earth and, because of this, will be considered a victor.

SECOND SEAL

Core Scripture: Revelation 6:3-4

Interpretation
Fiery Red Horse: Again, a horse is part of the scene, however, this time it is a fiery red horse. The color red seems to symbolize military war and bloodshed.

Rider: Like the rider of the white horse, this rider is not identified nor described. One possibility is that the rider is an associate of the Antichrist.

Take Peace from the Earth: In a sense, the rider is given permission to take peace from the inhabited earth by causing wars, possibly such as civil unrest, governmental oppression, and international conflict. The phrase used for what humankind will do to itself is presented in the adjacent table.

Revelation 6:4	
NIV	make people kill each other
NASB	that men would slay one another
NET	people would butcher one another
KJV	that they should kill one another
NKJV	people should kill each other
AMP	that men slaughtered one another

Large Sword: The Greek word used (*machaira*) indicates that it is a short sword or dagger, however, it is further qualified as being great in size, and used for violence, or destruction of peace. Great numbers will be killed with great severity.

What This Seal Means
The second seal, as a continuation of the first seal, will be that peace will turn to warfare on a global scale that will lead to much death by violence.

THIRD SEAL

Core Scripture: Revelation 6:5-6

Interpretation
Black Horse: The color black is the symbol of suffering, sorrow, sadness, and mourning.

Rider: Again the rider is not identified nor described, and the only thing that can be surmised is that he is an associate of the Antichrist.

Pair of Scales: The symbolism here is that the scales represent balances that are used for measuring the food and commodities that are to be sold during this time.

Voice: Unlike the other three horses and riders, John hears an interpretation coming from the midst of the four living creatures, explaining the monetary impact that the results of this rider, famine, will have on the earth.

Famine: While the passage does not specifically mention that this horse and rider bring famine to the world, it does suggest that a devastating famine will occur that will be a severe challenge for people as they struggle just to take care of the bare necessities of daily living. Many theologians believe that this will be the aftermath of the war introduced by the second seal, however, the Bible seems to imply that the entire Great Tribulation will be characterized by warfare the entire three and one-half years, therefore, it might be plausible to see the famine as occurring at the same time as the warfare rather than following it. It is also historically characteristic for devastating monetary inflation to occur during and after wars.

- Quart, Wheat, and Barley: The unit of measure of the time was equivalent to a modern-day quart which was about the amount of food consumed by a person for one meal. Wheat was a more expense grain than barley, so one denarius could buy one quart of wheat for one meal, or three quarts of barley for three meals.
- Denarius: Workers during the time in which the Book of Revelation was written received a daily wage of one denarius (sometimes called a penny or a cent), which in today's currency is just about fifteen cents.
- Oil and Wine: Traditionally a part of the ancient world's dietary customs, oil, and wine were usually reserved for the more wealthy people, which suggests that those of substantial means are not affected by the famine, while the common people are greatly affected.

What This Seal Means
This third seal continues the sense of the first and second seals and means that there will be much suffering due to a famine.

FOURTH SEAL

Core Scripture: Revelation 6:7-8

Interpretation
Pale Horse: The translator's note in the NET indicates that the color of this horse is "… [a] sickly pallor, when referring to persons, or the green color of plants."[19] Several theologians have referred to the color as being a ghastly and unearthly color; also found in Mark 6:39, Revelation 8:7 and 9:4 in reference to the color of grass.

Rider: Unlike the other three riders, the identity of this rider is specifically mentioned – it is named Death. And behind Death is Hades, or the abode of the dead, ready to swallow those that are killed. It seems unusual that Death and Hades would be personified as they are, since one is a state of being and the other is a spiritual place.

Authority: This seal means one of two things. First, the obvious results of the judgments dispensed by the other three horses and riders (conquest, war, and famine) are summarized in this judgment. Second, the judgment of this seal is in addition to the other three making the totality of all four massively horrendous. Nevertheless, this rider is given the power to kill one fourth of the earth's population by the sword (same as the second seal?) and famine (same as the third seal?), however is the addition of pestilence, and wild beasts.

- The scope of the word earth suggests the entire, inhabited world.
- The fact that one fourth of the earth's population is killed under these circumstances is a strong indication that the effect of this seal is within the second half of Daniel's 70th Week. The number of dead can only be described as a staggering amount. While there is no possible way to determine the number of people that will be raptured prior to Daniel's 70th Week, if the earth's remaining population is set at 6 billion people, then this judgment will result in the death of one and one-half billion people – a truly awesome and awful event without precedent since the Flood.
- he mechanisms of death certainly seem plausible if the Antichrist is exercising his illegitimate power over the nation of Israel, those that do not receive the mark of the beast, those that do not worship him, and those that have the misfortune to be found in opposition to the brutal regime. The four mechanisms also seem to be connected to Ezekiel 14:21, where the Lord says that He will send the four severe and evil judgments against Jerusalem – sword, famine, wild beasts, and plague.
- If not begun by any of the previous three seals, certainly by the time of this seal Christ's prophetic words of unequaled distress recorded in Matthew 24:21-22 will have started to be fulfilled. Also, this could begin the fulfillment of Old Testament prophecies in Jeremiah 30:7 and Joel 2:1-3. And yet this is only the beginning of the distress. "Though the book of Revelation itself does not state specifically what event begins the great tribulation, the characteristics unfolded in the fourth seal would indicate the great tribulation is underway at the time."[20]

What This Seal Means

This fourth seal indicates that one fourth of the world's population will be killed by violent means, thus, concluding the judgments to be carried out by the Four Horses of the Apocalypse.

187

FIFTH SEAL

Core Scripture: Revelation 6:9-11

Interpretation

Altar: The scene shifts from observing the four horses and riders on earth to seeing the holy altar in heaven. When Israel practices sacrificial worship in their Temple, after using some for specific purposes, the remaining blood of the sacrifice was poured out under the altar as can be seen in Ezekiel 29:12 and Leviticus 4:7. As the earthly Temple was a replica of the heavenly Temple, this passage seems to indicate that those that were killed for their testimony during Daniel's 70th Week, the Tribulation Saints, were sacrificed in the same sense as Old Testament sacrifices.

Slain Souls and Their Testimony: As the souls of those that believed in Jesus Christ as the Son of God during the Dispensation of Grace were raptured before to the beginning of Daniel's 70th Week. Matthew 24:14 also records Jesus saying that the Gospel will be preached at the end of the age before the end comes, therefore the disembodied souls seen here must be those that are martyred during the Week in fulfillment of Christ's prophecy.

- The more accurate rendition of the manner of death are souls of those that had been murdered because of their conviction that God and Jesus Christ are the only Ones entitled to govern humankind.
- These martyrs are the results of the persecution of believers that stand up for God rather than worshipping Satan and his illegitimate 'son'. These are the ones that the Antichrist will pursue with a vengeance in Satan's final effort to wrestle power and glory from God.
- This passage is significant proof that there will be some sort of temporary body for these people because they are not shown to be in their resurrection body.
- This appears to be the same group alluded to in Revelation 13:15; 18:24; and 20:4.

The Searching Question: The essential question being asked is how much longer will the time of unprecedented events, including persecution of believers, last before the Messiah returns to fulfill His promise to return before the earth destroys itself.

- The fact that the martyrs ask a piercing question regarding the fulfillment of promises and prophecies indicates a conscious expression of the emotional sense of long-suffering – How much longer does unrighteous persecution have to afflict the children of God? As those that were previously raptured concludes the persecution of the Church, this passage indicates the believers during Daniel's 70th Week will also be persecuted and killed.
- The passage also indicates that the persecution is still underway and is not ended yet.

- "Their cry for righteous judgment is in the same spirit as the Psalmist's call to God to vindicate His holiness and righteousness in dealing with the injustice and oppression which characterize the human race."[21]

White Robe: The significance of the white robe is that it is symbolic of the righteous approval by Jesus of the victory over the world by those martyred. This also seems to support the idea that these souls are not yet in their permanent resurrected form.

The Divine Response: The cry of the martyrs for an end of the persecution of God's children is responded to with a message that they are to continue being patient until the designated end comes and those elected to be martyrs for their beliefs will have been completed. This is also consistent with the end of this present age, where the Bible indicates that not even Jesus knows when it will end, only the Father knows and it will be when the number that is elected to come to faith is complete.

What This Seal Means
This fifth seal indicates that there will be a great soul harvest during this time, as it is the destiny of many of the believers of the time will be martyred for their belief in God and Jesus Christ in lieu of Satan and the Antichrist. They will be given a temporary body until they receive their permanent body; otherwise, why the need for a robe, or for a continuation of rest. This seal could also anticipate that those 144,000 Jews to the supernaturally sealed in Revelation 7 will be ministers of the Word during Daniel's 70th Week.

SIXTH SEAL

Core Scripture: Revelation 6:12-17

Interpretation
Catastrophic Natural Events: This passage reveals that God will cause a significant response by nature to the evil prevailing on the earth at the time. As the earth groans under the weight of the sinfulness of humankind beginning with Adam, evidenced by Genesis 3:17, the earth now seeks vindication.
- Earthquakes: This is the first mention of a natural event that will be repeated in future judgments. One of the more visible happenings of God's final judgment of the world is the devastating earthquakes that are predicted in the Bible. Physical and violent shakings of the earth have traditionally been used by God to demonstrate the gravity of human sinfulness and to get the attention of those being dealt with at the time.
- Blackened Sun: The normal sunlight impacting the earth will be turned into a lack of sunlight by something can only be one of two things – first, something could happen to the sun itself (unlikely), or the appearance of the sun as seen by humans could be affected (more likely).

189

+ The Old Testament prophets frequently spoke and wrote about the sun being darkened at the time of the Day of the Lord as can be seen in Isaiah 13:10; 24:33; Ezekiel 32:7-8; Joel 2:10, 31; Amos 5:20; 8:9; and Zephaniah 1:15.
+ It is not unusual at all for there to be volcanic activity during the time of the earthquakes, and if so at this time, then the ash that is spewed into the air could blot out the ability of sunlight to reach the earth thus giving it a blackened appearance.
+ Sackcloth was a rough cloth that was made of the hides of goats and camels, and was usually worn as a tunic or loincloth to signify mourning or anguish. In addition, fasting and ashes on oneself accompanied the mourning. Refer to Isaiah 58:5 and Daniel 9:3.

- Blood Red Moon: Again volcanic ash in the atmosphere could give the moon a reddish color.
- Falling Stars and Fig Trees: The Greek word used not only refers to the conventional notion of stars, but it also can refer to asteroids or meteors. Nevertheless, something will happen in the sky, maybe a meteor shower, to give the impression that the stars are falling. The magnitude of falling stars is likened to a strong wind causing unripened figs to fall from the fig tree.
- Sky Split Apart: Reminiscent of Isaiah 34:4, there will be events taking place in the sky at will give the appearance that it is splitting apart and rolling away, maybe even suggesting that the universe is falling apart.
- Mountains and Islands Moved: The obvious result of the earthquakes and volcanic activity, the topography of the landscape will be changed, so much so that the mountains and the islands will have appeared to have moved from their original locations.

Wrath of the Lamb: While there are some theologians that believe that the wrath of God does not start until later in the trio of judgments, this passage clearly indicates that the catastrophic events taking place now will originate with the Holy Trinity. This strongly suggests that those living at the time will understand that the events transpiring are the part of the Lord's final judgments.

Fear of the Lord: "Great fear will grip human hearts, but because of their stubborn, willful, rebellious ways, instead of turning to God in the hour of peril they will hide in the rocks and the dens of the earth. The cataclysm will be so gigantic in proportion that even the great people of the earth will have no place to hide."[22]

What This Seal Means
Following the wide spread persecution of the children of God revealed by the fifth seal, this sixth seal brings massive and devastating natural catastrophes to the earth, causing non-believers to fear for their lives and hide instead of turning to God. In spite of that the worst is yet to come, everyone alive at the time are most likely aware that they and the earth are experiencing unprecedented happenings caused by the Lord because of human sinfulness.

SEVENTH SEAL

Core Scripture: Revelation 8:1-5

Interpretation

As is true of the seventh trumpet and the seventh bowl judgments also, there is an interlude in the text before the seventh seal. Here the seal judgments conclude by the appearance on the scene of seven trumpets in the hands of seven angels.

- Silence: There was a heavenly silence for about half an hour, reasons for which are unclear. The potential theories include the following:
    + To allow the prayers of the suffering saints in verses 3 and 4 to be heard.
    + To allow the cries of the persecuted saints of Revelation 6:10 to be heard.
    + To allow for a Sabbath pause at this time.
- The Angel and the Censer: The belief here is that an unidentified angel takes a golden censer to, "… offer incense in the altar in behalf of the prayers of all God's people."[23] The angel then takes the censer, fills it with burning coals from the altar and pitches it down to earth representing righteous answer to the prayers.

What This Seal Means

This seventh seal, while causing a pause in the flow of judgments to respond to the need for righteous intervention, forms the transitions from the seal judgments to the trumpet judgments.

38

INTERVALS AND TRUMPET JUDGMENTS

In the flow of Revelation's passages, there are several parenthetical intervals before and after the trumpet judgments that discuss other aspects of the end times and do not advance the narratives about the seal, trumpet, and bowl judgments. Also the seventh seal judgment opens the seven trumpets, which are more severe than the seal judgments but less severe than the bowl judgments.

38.1 THE FIRST PARENTHETICAL INTERVAL IN THE BOOK OF REVELATION

Chapters 6 through 16 of the Book of Revelation are a logical, progressive, and linear sequence of judgmental events – seals, trumpets, bowls – however, there are several places where the flow is interrupted in order to address other topics that are closely related to the time of the end. These interruptions are identified as parenthetical intervals. These parenthetical interval topics create a measure of interpretative difficulty, or more positively interpretive challenge. This chapter will include mention of these intervals for purposes of completeness, and to allow the reader to make the appropriate connections to other places within this book where the topics are explored.

The related topics that are included in the first parenthetical interval that occurs between the sixth and seventh seal judgments include the following:
- Revelation 7:1-8: 144,000 Jews Sealed by God – previously explored in Section 33.6.
- Revelation 7:9-17: Martyred Tribulation Saints in Heaven – previously explored in Section 33.7.

38.2 THE UNIQUENESS OF THE SEVENTH SEAL AND THE SEVENTH TRUMPET

Each seal, trumpet, and bowl judgment originates with a direct act – Christ breaking the seals, the angels sounding their trumpets, and the angels pouring out the bowls – that results in a unique judgmental event, or series of events. However, the seventh seal and the seventh trumpet form unique transitions between the seal and trumpet judgments, and then between the trumpet and bowl judgments.
- In Revelation 8:2, after the seventh seal is broken, John indicates that more of God's wrath is to come when he sees seven angels each being given a

trumpet representing judgements; thus, a direct connection is established between the seventh seal and the seven trumpets.

- That the seventh trumpet contains all of the seven bowls is not as clearly stated in the Book of Revelation, however, a connection is established in the context of what is to occur at the time of the sounding of the seventh trumpet.
  + 11:15: Loud voices state that the kingdom of the world will change to become the eternal kingdom of the Lord and His Christ.
  + 11:17-18: As they worship the Lord, statements by the twenty-four elders indicate that, in spite of the continued rebellion of the nations, all of creation is at a particular milestone in the Plan of God. It is time for the:
    o Wrath of God to come upon the earth.
    o Long-awaited reign of the Lord to begin.
    o Judgment of the dead to come to pass.
    o Saints to receive their reward.
    o Righteous justice of God to be dispensed onto those that seek to destroy all that God has created.

Then, after it is established that there are still judgmental events yet to come, the events associated with the seventh seal and the seventh trumpet each end with crashes of thunder, the roar of the coming storm, flashes of lightening in the skies, a severe earthquake on the earth, and unique to the seventh trumpet, a great hailstorm. But the end is not yet – as foretold in Revelation, another series of seven judgments will fall onto humankind and the earth that will be more severe and more cataclysmic than those before.

38.3	**WRATH OF GOD – THE TRUMPET JUDGMENTS**

And the wrath of God continues.

GENERAL OBSERVATIONS OF THE TRUMPETS

The sound of trumpets were common in the life of the Israelites of the Old Testament, and it is not surprising that the trumpet would be used as a symbol of judgement in Revelation.

- Purpose of Trumpets: Shofar trumpets, usually made from the horn of a ram, were used as instruments for signaling information over distances longer than can be called across by voice (similar to smoke signaling used by Native Americans).
- Trumpets in the Old Testament: Trumpets were traditionally used for a variety of purposes and can be found associated with specific events during the history of Israel:

+ Exodus 20:18: The infant nation of Israel was called by trumpet to Mount Sinai to receive the Ten Commandments.
+ Numbers:
    ○ 10:1-18: Trumpets were used to call the nation (two blasts) and leaders (one blast) to the tabernacle in anticipation of moving to a new location.
    ○ 10:9: Trumpets called the nation to war.
    ○ 10:10: Trumpets called for attendance at special events.
+ Joshua 6: Trumpets were used during the conquest of Jericho.
+ Judges 7:19-20: Trumpets were used to cause panic among Israel's enemies.
+ 1 Chronicles 15:24: Trumpets were used for ceremonial processions.
+ Isaiah 27:13 (cf. Joel 2:1; Zephaniah 1:16; Matthew 24:31; 1 Corinthians 15:53; 1 Thessalonian 4:16): Trumpets were used to announce the coming of the Day of the Lord.

Couch[1] makes the following observations regarding the purpose of the trumpets in Revelation, which are somewhat different from the traditional uses:
• The trumpets were given to angels for announcing great calamity.
• The trumpets are related to the breaking of the seven seals.
• There are no expectations for a response to the trumpet blasts.

For the most part, the seal judgments deal with the world in general, the trumpet judgments deal with one-third of the world, while the bowl judgments will deal with the entire world. This point provides strong support for the seal, trumpet, and bowl judgments being successive and sequential rather than simultaneous. When this point is combined with the fact that the judgments increase progressively in intensity and severity, the support for sequence is further validated.

Just as the first four seals form a unit that is somewhat separate from the other three, the first four trumpets also seem to form a complimentary unit of events that are separate from the other three.

The question of literalness is asked frequently in the Book of Revelation, and the interpretation of the trumpets is no different. There is another Old Testament situation that is strikingly similar to some of the judgments in Revelation. Five of the ten plagues that rocked Egypt and caused the Pharaoh to let God's people leave are also found among the judgments of the Great Tribulation. So if the plagues of Egypt were literal events, there is no reason not to expect the judgments in Revelation to be literal events as well.

The following table is a summary of the trumpet judgments:

The Seven Trumpet Judgments	
First	Brings destruction to one third of the land vegetation of the earth
Second	Brings destruction to one third of the seas, its creatures, and its ships, of the world
Third	Brings destruction to one third of the rivers of the world
Fourth	Brings a significant change in the amount of sunlight, moonlight, and starlight that reaches the earth by a reduction of one third
Fifth	The first woe, brings an incredible physical suffering to those who do not worship God
Sixth	The second woe, brings death to those that do not worship God to the awesome extent of one third of humankind
Seventh	The third woe, before bringing the seven bowl judgments (plagues) onto the satanic civilization led by the Unholy Trinity, acknowledges that the wrath of The Lord God has come and that final judgment is at hand

FIRST TRUMPET

Core Scripture: Revelation 8:7

Interpretation
Hail, Fire, and Blood: It is very likely that the hail and fire should be taken as literal weather phenomenon; the relationship with blood is unclear, however, with supernaturally driven events, anything is possible. The God that rained down burning sulfur on Sodom and Gomorrah is certainly capable of throwing a mixture of hail, fire, and blood down onto the earth. Precedence for such an event can be found in the seventh plague on Egypt found in Exodus 9:18-26 (cf. Ezekiel 38:22).

Earth, Trees, and Grass Burned Up: The effect of the hail, fire, and blood thrown down to earth is that one-third of the earth will be burned up, and all of the green grass will be destroyed. While this judgment does not directly affect humanity, its impact will be devastating because crops and food sources will be affected. The limitation of this judgment to only vegetation is based on the fact that two of the three destructive effects (to the trees and grass) are specifically mentioned, while the third of the three (to the earth) is more generalized; therefore, the sense of the passage is that the judgment only impacts the vegetation.

What This Trumpet Means
This first trumpet will be that a supernatural weather event, consisting of hail and fire mixed with blood, which will rain down on the earth and destroy a significant portion of the earth's vegetation – one-third of the vegetation, one-third of the trees, and all of the green grass.

SECOND TRUMPET

Core Scripture: Revelation 8:8-9

Interpretation

A Great Mountain: There are a number of instances in the Bible where a mountain is used as the symbol for a government, however, that does not seem to be the sense of this passage – a literal interpretation seems to be in order. Here, a large object, only described as something like a burning mountain falls into the sea, or actually is thrown into the sea. There is no mention of the size and composition of the object, however, because the word mountain is used, soil and rocks come to mind. The identity of the one doing the throwing is not indicated, nor is its identity discernible. This trumpet judgment is similar to the sixth seal where heavenly objects fall out of the sky to the earth.

Sea Became Blood: Similar to the first plague on Egypt found in Exodus 7:20-21, the results of this trumpet is that one third of the sea becomes blood – the sense of the passage is that the water actually changes into blood rather than the water appearing to be blood (cf. Zephaniah 1:3). The implication is that the bodies of salt water across the earth are affected by this judgment.

Sea Creatures Died: Again, similar to the first plague, one third of the creatures that live in the sea die.

Ships Destroyed: While this effect of the judgment does not seem to fit with the other effects, it seems logical that should a large object fall into a body of water, there would result such sufficiently destructive turbulence and tidal waves that watercraft would be swamped and sink, in this case, one third of them.

What This Trumpet Means

This second trumpet will be that a large burning object will fall out of the sky and into a major body of water (or maybe it breaks apart and falls into several bodies of water) that will result in one third of the water becoming blood, one third of the water creatures dying, and one third of the ships will be destroyed. This obviously results in a catastrophic impact on humankind.

THIRD TRUMPET

Core Scripture: Revelation 8:10-11

Interpretation

"In interpreting this third trumpet, expositors have had a field day in assigning symbolic meaning to the components of this judgment. If the meaning is symbolic, there is no clear indication as to the interpretation of this judgment except that the great star can be assigned to some personage such as the Antichrist or Satan himself and the waters could be regarded as symbolic of the peoples of the earth."[2]

Great Star Named Wormwood: This passage indicates that a large celestial body will fall to the earth from the heavens, or from the sky. The origin of the star is not identified, nor are the circumstances of it falling to earth indicated. All that is mentioned is that it is burning like a torch (KJV uses the word lamp) and that it falls onto a third of the rivers and springs. It appears that it is named Wormwood for no other reason than to describe its effect on the earth. Wormwood refers to a non-poisonous herb that is known in the Middle East for its bitterness; it is used symbolically in the Old Testament to emphasize bitterness and sorrow. Interestingly, the effect of Wormwood in this context is that many people will die from what it does to the drinking water.

Rivers and Springs: The implication is that the bodies of fresh water are affected by this judgment.

What This Trumpet Means

This trumpet means that something will fall to the earth from above, which is burning like a lamp, which will have a poisonous influence on the potable water of the earth thereby causing many people to die.

FOURTH TRUMPET

Core Scripture: Revelation 8:12-13

Interpretation

Celestial Changes of the Sun, Moon, and Stars: While a symbolic interpretation would see these as the disruption of human government, it is probably best to see these events as a disruption of the various lights of the sky. Actually, the question that comes to mind is, could this be the fulfillment of Luke 21:25-26?

- Smitten: The Greek word used here is similar to a plague, stripe of wound.
- Darkened: The Greek word used here suggests being deprived of light.
- Cause of the Darkness: A specific cause for the darkness is not indicated, suggested, or implied; however, something will happen that will deprive the earth of one third of the light from the sun, the moon, and the stars.

The possibilities range from a supernatural intervention by God of the actual luminous bodies to an event caused by humankind, such as a nuclear explosion, or explosions, of such magnitude (in spite of the fact that such an event is not mentioned) as to cause environmental pollution to be thrown into the earth's atmosphere to such an extent as to render a reduction of light reaching the earth by one third.

- Change in Day and Night: Most likely due to the reduction in light passing through the earth's atmosphere, the normal day and night sequence will be affected – the average sixteen-hour days could be shortened to eight hours, while the eight-hour nights could be lengthened to sixteen hours. The impact on humankind could be significant, as this change will have an adverse effect on agriculture.
- Similar Biblical Events: "The heavens are struck with partial darkness, reminiscent of the ninth plague (Exod. 10:21-23). ... In the OT the darkening of the heavens appears in connection with the theophany of God in judgment (cf. Isa.13:10; Ezek. 32:7-8; Joel 2:10; 3:15; Matt.24:29). An unusual darkness also attended the crucifixion of Christ (Matt. 27:25)."[3]

The Warning of Woes to Come: This trumpet also includes something not found in the other trumpet judgments, John sees an eagle flying through the sky loudly warning of the remaining of the remaining three trumpet judgments to come that, by implication, will be more severe than the previous trumpet judgments.

- Eagle or an Angel: Due to a subtle difference in the Greek words used in the various ancient manuscripts, the KJV and the NKJV translate the Greek into the word angel, while the NASB, NIV, and the NET translate use the word eagle in this verse. Whether the creature flying through the sky is an eagle or an angel is of no significant importance. The better translation would be that the creature is an angel on the basis that eagles do not talk, and there are other occasions in the Bible where an angel is flying through the air, or proclaiming a coming event.
- The creature warns those on earth that the three trumpets yet to be sounded signifying worse judgmental events are yet to come. "The Greek word *ouai* is what one might scream when under intense pain or suffering."[4]

What This Trumpet Means
This trumpet means that something will happen that will cause the light given by the sun, moon, and stars to be reduced by one third in quantity and quality thus causing a change in the time of day and time of night and a reduction of visual clarity. Also, a creature pronounces that the remaining three trumpets will be woefully more devastating to the earth and humankind.

FIFTH TRUMPET - THE FIRST WOE

Core Scripture: Revelation 9:1-11

Interpretation

Heavenly Star Fallen to Earth, Abaddon, and Apollyon: Rather than this being an actual celestial body, star, or meteor, in contradiction to previous seal and trumpet judgments, the *star* in this passage appears to be a literal, intelligent being for the following reasons: it is later referred to in a personal manner ("him" in verse 1, "he" in verse 2, "king" in verse 11, and by the personal names Abaddon and Apollyon also in verse 11), it seems to be in control of the portal to the bottomless pit, and it is given authorities and responsibilities. The star being an angelic being rather than a human being is more consistent with the sense of the passage, however, while the specific identity is not disclosed, there are several theories worthy of notice:

- Some believe it is an elect angel given control of the bottomless pit, as is the same angel that binds Satan in Revelation 20:1. This view would be inconsistent with the responsibilities given the being of this passage as well as the assigned names.
- Walvoord contends that this being is Satan who was cast out of heaven in Revelation 12, and thus has fallen to earth. We have previously established that the most appropriate sense of Satan being cast out of heaven is for the event to occur at the midpoint of Daniel's 70th Week, therefore, if this star were Satan, this trumpet would be sounded at the midpoint of Daniel's 70th Week. This would then be inconsistent with the interpretation that all of the seal, trumpet, and bowl judgments are seen to occur during the Great Tribulation in the second half of Daniel's 70th Week.
- The interpretation that seems to agree with the context of the passage, as well as the general sense of end time prophecy, is that it is a fallen angel from Satan's realm that is also the king of the Bottomless Pit.

Bottomless Pit: Also known as the Abyss, the bottomless pit is referred to in several other places in the Bible as a place that is distinct from hell or Hades as described in Luke 16:19-31.

- The place where demons (i.e. fallen and wicked angelic beings) are held in detention, according to Luke 8:31; 2 Peter 2:4; and Jude 1:6.
- This is also the place where, according to Revelation 20:1-3, Satan will be confined for the one-thousand-year Messianic Reign.
- According to Revelation 11:7 and 17:8, this is the place of origin for the beast from the sea, or the Antichrist.
- "Romans 10:7 implies hypothetically that Christ descended into the spirit world between His death and resurrection."[5]

Key to the Bottomless Pit: As in other locations of the Bible, those that possess keys have the authority to open and release something that is locked away, in this case a terrible judgment from the bottomless pit.

Rising Smoke: The imagery here is that, once the portal to the bottomless pit is opened, smoke (products of combustion) rises as if from a great furnace, thus contaminating the atmosphere with residue and, like the previous trumpet judgment, rendering the air more obscure and darker than normal. "It seems to portend the spiritual corruption which will be caused by these demons released from their confinement, and it identifies the character of the judgment involved in the fifth trumpet as that of demonic and satanic oppression."[6]

Locusts: Coming from out of the smoke are strange and horrifying creatures that, because of their demonic nature, will bring incredible misery to those that are not divinely protected. "Though they took on the appearance of locusts and were given the power of scorpions, they actually were neither."[7] Their description seems to be more along the line of some sort of demonic creatures rather than natural insects.
- Their Heritage: In the Old Testament, locusts were used by God as a divine judgment on a sinful people, the most commonly known instance being when locusts were one of the ten plagues that God used against Egypt in Exodus 10. Such a plague is also seen in Joel 1:4-7.
  + "Locust plagues are one of the severest plagues of mankind. The imagery of locusts, appearing like armies, advancing like cloud, darkening the heaves, and sounding like the rattle of chariots, goes back to Joel's vision of the locust army that came on Israel as a judgment of God (Joel 1:6; 1:4-10)."[8]
  + "[L]ocusts were a greatly feared plague because they could strip the country of every green leaf and sprout, leaving man and beast alike to die for lack of food."[9]

Their Title: Quite possibility they may be called locusts more because of what they will do to the earth and humankind as a divine judgment on a wicked world rather than the insect they appear to resemble.

Their Power: The locusts are given a power that is compared to the power possessed by scorpions in that they have a sting that will be capable of causing the most extreme pain and suffering that can possibly be experienced by human being. "The torment they inflict may be physical, spiritual, or psychological or all of them. But whatever it is, people will seek death but will be unable to die (v. 6)."[10]

Their Responsibility: The locusts are directed, by an unidentified authority (would it be God or Satan?). to not harm any of the earth's vegetation, but instead are to torment for five months, but not kill, those people who do not have the seal of God on their forehead. The non-fatal torment that people will experience is compared to the sting of a scorpion. The ironic fact that the locusts are not to eat the grass, as is their natural inclination, implies they could be creatures that only resemble the nature of ordinary locusts.

Their Time: There is no explanation for the five-month time period, it could be the lifespan of the creatures, it could be the time of the year in which locusts are normally active, or it could just be the limit of time decreed by God.

Their Effect: Those that will be stung by the locust will be in such pain, agony, and suffering that they will seek ways to die. However, they will not be able to escape their fate, but instead will just have to endure the tormenting affliction. "This is a horrible picture of domination by demons to such an extent that men lose their ability of free choice and are in agony of body and soul."[11]

Their Appearance: The locusts are described as having an unnatural appearance - actually the Biblical description sounds entirely demonic. It is not discernible from the passage if these creatures will be the size of actual locusts or if they will be larger than normal. It seems plausible that in order for people to see their physical features, a size somewhat large than normal would be expected.

- Like Horses Prepared for Battle: In the times of antiquity, it was normal practice for armies to dress their horses in protective coverings as well as symbolic accessories suitable for battle. Also, horses were fearsome beasts to soldiers on foot, with the battle dress adding to the display of power. This seems to be the sense here as well, the locusts are dressed for battle and they have a fearsome appearance.
- Golden Crowns: The passage says that there appeared to be crowns on their heads, ordinary a symbol, here however, it is more of a decoration of headdress.
- Faces as Men: This could possibly speak of an intelligence that is greater than normal insects.
- Hair as Women: The only idea that surfaces for this is a reference to the antenna of insects.
- Teeth as Lions: While a lion is a beast worthy of being feared, it is the power and strength of their teeth that is the most fearsome aspect to be avoided. Being bitten by a fierce creature capable of inflicting death and/ or unbelievable pain is a universally held human anxiety.
- Breastplates of Iron: This indicates that the locusts might be protected from destruction and resistant to counterattack.
- Wings as the Sound of Chariots: Being equipped with wings gives the locusts a mode of mobility suitable for a quickness of attack and necessary speed to avoid counterattack. Another aspect of warfare that is usually not noticed, are the sounds that are made by an advancing and/or attacking army. Loudness and the intensity of a rushing army can intimidate even the strongest soldier.

Their Leader: The name of the leader of the army of locusts is Abaddon (Hebrew for destruction) and Apollyon (Greek for destroyer), who is the angel of the Abyss. Some believe this is Satan himself, however, the more plausible option is that it is a demon that is a leader within the demonic empire. Nevertheless, the name of the leader is a personification of death.

God's Seal of Protection: The only people that are specifically mentioned to be divinely protected by God's seal are the 144,000 Jews of Revelation 7. The Bible does not indicate that those that come to faith in Jesus Christ during Daniel's 70th Week are to also receive a seal, which presents somewhat of a problem. "The question as to whether those who are saved who were not protected by the seal of God would be under this judgment is not answered, but it would seem to be contrary to God's purpose to allow this judgment which comes from God to strike a man who had actually been born again."[12]

What This Trumpet Means

This trumpet means that those inhabitants of the world that do not worship the Lord God, the implication being those that do worship the Antichrist, will be stricken with terrible pain and unbearable suffering, so much so that they will unsuccessfully seek to die, by unnatural demonic creatures released for the depths of the bottomless pit.

SIXTH TRUMPET - THE SECOND WOE

Core Scripture: Revelation 9:12-21 and 11:13

Interpretation

Woes to Come: As horrifying as the first woe will be, there will be two more times to come that will be much worse than the first woe, any previous seal judgment, any trumpet judgement, or for that matter, any event in the history of humankind to that time.

- When Jesus spoke the words recorded in Matthew 24:21 when He told the disciples that there would be a future time of suffering that would be greater than ever known by humankind before, it is difficult even today, much less then, to imagine just how terrible life on earth could possibly ever get. Try to visualize someone having lived through the tragic times up to and including the fifth trumpet judgment, who also understands what is going on, when they realize that a much worse global catastrophe is still ahead in the world's future.
- "The tribulation period unmasks human wickedness and also demonstrates the true character of Satan. In our modern day while Satan is still restricted it is easy to forget the great conflict which is raging between the forces of God and the forces of Satan referred to in Ephesians 6:12. In the great tribulation, and especially in the time of the fifth trumpet, with the release of the confined demons the full character of Satan will be starkly manifested. For the first in history all those who do not know the Lord Jesus Christ as Savior will come under demonic possession and affliction."[13]

203

The Voice and the Golden Altar: In the heavenly temple pattern, and as followed in the earthly tabernacle and temple, there is a sacrificial altar that stands in the outer court that is used for blood sacrifices, and there is a golden altar that stands in The Holy Place that is used for incense offerings. The altar of the fifth seal, Revelation 6:9, is believed to be the sacrificial altar, while the golden altar of the seventh seal, in Revelation 8:3, and this sixth trumpet is the golden altar. The purpose of the golden altar during Old Testament Jewish worship was to burn incense as an offering to God, while in seventh seal the burning of incense is accompanied by the prayers of the tribulation saints. In this trumpet judgment, a voice comes from the heavenly golden altar instructing the angel that sounded this trumpet to release four angels that had previously been bound.

Four Angels Bound at the Euphrates River: The question that immediately comes to mind is, why would there be four angels bound at the Euphrates River?
- These four angels do not appear to be the same four angels mentioned in Revelation 7.
  + The four angels of Revelation 7 who hold the four winds of the earth are instructed not to damage the earth or sea until the 144,000 Jews have been supernaturally sealed and protected. The sense seems to be that these angels are holy angels acting in behalf of God as instruments of judgment.
  + The four angels of the sixth trumpet are described as being bound, which according to Jude 1:6, the implication being that the only angels that are bound are wicked angels. As there is no reason to bind holy angels, then the sense is that the four angels of this trumpet judgment are demon angels. Also, keep in mind that Satan himself will be bound for one thousand years in the future.
- There is no legitimate reason to consider the reference to the Euphrates River to be anything but the literal river. The possible significance is that it is from the Euphrates River, as the eastern extremity of the region, that the enemies of Israel came in ancient times. "..[I]t formed one of the boundaries of the Garden of Eden. It was also a boundary for Israel (Gen. 15:18), the easternmost boundary of Egypt, and the boundary of the Persian Empire. It is used in Scripture as a symbol of Israel's enemies."[14] Interestingly, human sin originated in this area at the beginning of human history (the Fall, Babylon, and the Tower of Babel), and now at the end of human history, the area again plays a crucial part in God's judgment of human sin (this trumpet judgment and the destruction of rebuilt and spiritual Babylon).
- The reference to a particular hour, day, month, and year for the release of the angels indicates that God is in sovereign control of human history, and He will determine when the proper moment comes for this judgment to take place.
- Therefore, the picture painted by the Bible is that these four wicked angels are bound at the Euphrates River waiting for the exact moment in the future

when their bindings will be loosed and they will execute this judgment as God's agents.

Kill a Third of Mankind: Once the four wicked angels are released, one third of those remaining alive in the world will be slain. Previously the fourth seal eliminated one fourth of the earth's population (the 6 billion was reduced to 4.5 billion), and as this judgment causes the death of one third of those remaining, the population of the earth will now be about one-half (3 billion) of the amount that were alive at the time that Daniel's 70th Week began. This does even take into account the deaths that are the indirect result of the previous seal and trumpet judgments. Not since the time of Noah has the earth seen this magnitude of destruction of human life. Also, there is no indication as to how long this extermination will take; it is feasible that it could continue until the time of Christ's return rather than before the seventh trumpet sounds.

An Army of Two Hundred Million Horsemen:
- Scripture does not indicate the origin of this army, however because the angels are associated with a river that is at the eastern edge of Israel; the implication is that the army originates in that geographical region. Later in the Book of Revelation, we will see an army move into the area of Israel from the east.
- Scripture also does not explain the relationship between the four angels and the enormous army; the implication is that they are in command of the forces.
- There is debate as to if the two hundred million number is to be taken literally or figuratively.
  + Some believe the number should be taken figuratively on the basis that it is such an absurd and unreasonable number of people that would be in a military force, which would only be possible via a disruption of the structure of society on a global scale. "Thus it seems better to understand the vast numbers and description of the horses as indicating demonic hordes. Such large numbers do occasionally indicate angelic hosts elsewhere in Scripture (Ps. 68:17; Rev. 5:11; cf. 2 Kings 2:11-12; 6:17). This would not eliminate the possibility of human armies of manageable size also being involved. But the emphasis here (vv. 16-19) is on their fully demonic character, utter, cruel and determined, showing no mercy to man, woman, or child. These demons might also be manifest in pestilences, epidemic diseases, or misfortunes as well as in armies. Such would explain the use of "plague" to describe these hordes (vv. 18, 20; cf. 11:6; 16:9, 21)."[15]
  + There is no valid reason to not take the amount as a literal number.
- As a point of reference and comparison, all of the Allied and Axis forces combined in World War II comprised about 70 million people.

Horses: Again, like the locusts of the fifth trumpet, there is debate as to if the horses will be real horses with riders, or it the use of the horse motif is for symbolic purposes. Again, also like the locusts, the sense of this prophecy is that John describes the instruments of death in the only way he knew how to, by using words and concepts that were common of his day and time. It is very possible, and may be probable, that the locusts of the fifth trumpet and the horses of this sixth trumpet will be modern day implements of war and contemporary weaponry, including nuclear, biological, and chemical weapons. The sense of this passage seems consistent with this view.

- Their Heritage: Until the beginning of the twentieth century, horses were the primary means of transportation for armies when they were not walking or marching. Equipping combatants with horses gave a military force an extreme, so much so that it could change the outcome of a battle. Foot soldiers confronting an enemy mounted on horses, not only had to deal with the enemy soldiers, but they had to deal with the horses as well. Horses are powerful and superior assets in warfare.

- Their Title: The use of the idea of horses is most probably symbolic because the sense of the passage describes attributes and actions that are not natural to horses; and, the concept of horses may be used because a horse is a means of carrying a soldier along with the associated accessories of war.

- Their Power: The passage indicates two unique powers possessed by the horses.
    + The horses are capable of breathing fire, smoke, and brimstone (associated with sulfur) out of their mouths as individual plagues that will kill many human beings. The combination of these three things is highly suggestive of large-scale destruction by elevated temperatures of heat.
    + The horses also possess tails that are described as being like serpents with heads, however, because it is not stated what method of destruction proceeds from them, it is assumed that they are capable of also breathing out fire, smoke, and brimstone.

- Their Responsibility: Unlike the locusts, the horses are not given limitations to the execution of their responsibilities. The passage only says that there is an army of two hundred million, that one third of the world's population will be killed, and that those are not killed are still unrepentant. The implication is that the enormously large army kills an unbelievable number of people that had previously worshipped idols.

- Their Time: Unlike the locusts of the fifth trumpet, no time period for this judgment is given.

- Their Effect: The horses will kill people by spreading fire, smoke, and brimstone (NIV and NET use the word sulfur) that will affect them as do plagues. "God's [first] purpose for the plagues is first of all a judgment on man for his willful choice of idolatry and the corrupt practices that go with it (v. 21)." His second purpose, "… is to bring societies to repentance (cf. 19:9, 11)."[16] This description comes the closest to an ancient description of modern day biological and/or chemical warfare as any in the Bible. While the passage does not disclose the actual symptoms experienced by the victims, the sense is that the fire, smoke, and brimstone is suggestive as any unstoppable diseases of history that resulted in massive amounts of casualties.

- Their Appearance: While the description of the horses seems partially plausible, it is the actions that they take that are not natural to horses. Similar to the locusts, the Biblical description sounds almost demonic. It is not discernible from the passage to establish the size of the horses.
    + Riders: There is no identification of the rider, nor is there mention of the number of riders for each horse. The only detail is in regard to the breastplates worn by the riders, which are described as having three colors, fiery red, dark blue, and sulfurous yellow. There is no mention of the significance of the rider, only the implication that as the one in control of the horse, it is the rider that is the intelligence behind the release of the fire, smoke, and brimstone.
    + Heads of Horses Like Lions: This destructive aspect may be more to emphasize the fierceness of the horses' action, terrorizing (Revelation 10:3) and destructive (Revelation 13:2), rather than in their actual appearance.
- Idols: The passage indicates that the people of the world have reached the logical conclusion of a godless culture. In addition to worshipping demons, there are still many who are worshipping inanimate, cultic idols that they have been made from gold, silver, brass, stone, and wood. "'Demons' may mean either pagan deities (Deut. 32:17; Ps, 106:37) or malign spirits (1 Cor. 10:20-21; 1 Tim. 4:1). ... John no doubt shared Paul's concept of demons as evil spirits (Rev. 16:14; 18:2). Hence, there is a twofold evil in idol worship; it robs the true God of his glory (Rom. 1:23) and it leads to consorting with evil spirits that corrupt man."[17]
- Lack of Repentance: Interestingly, in spite of knowing that the death of one third of humankind, those that survive the extermination are still pridefully stubborn, staunchly defiant, persistently rebellious, and without any desire to repent of their sinful behavior or unrighteous beliefs. "Such is the hardness of the human heart even though faced by worldwide destruction and divine judgment from God and a clear testimony of God's power to deal summarily with every human soul. ... They do not repent of the evil works of their hands. They do not repent of their worship of devils, or demons, and the worship of idols which their hands have formed ... Their worship does not change their lives ... they do not repent of their murders, their wicked sorceries, their fornication, nor their thefts. Though the power of satanic false religion is evident in the world, it does not have the transforming, purifying, redeeming quality found only in the power and grace of God."[18]
- Condition of Humankind: The passage indicates that those that died as well as those that survived this judgment were guilty of murder, magic spells, sexual immorality, and stealing. As these are the only sins specifically

mentioned, it is obvious that sinfulness has reached its logical human conclusion where the world society, with the exception of those trying to follow God during this dark time, has collapsed and there is not restraint on evil.

Earthquake, Death, Destruction, and Repentance: Most of the prophecy associated with the sixth trumpet is contained within Revelation 9:12-21, however, it is the position of this book that there is one more verse, Revelation 11:13, that really belongs to the sixth trumpet even though it is at the end of the passage regarding the Angel with the Little Scroll (discussed below) and the Two Witnesses (discussed in Section 33.9).

- Timing of the Event: While there is a tendency to associate Revelation 11:13 exclusively with Revelation 11:1-12 describing God's Two Witnesses, the context seems to suggest that the earthquake not only follows God's call for the Witnesses to come up to heaven, it seems to also close-out the sixth trumpet as well; which is also supported by Revelation 11:14.
- Scope of the Event: While the context of the passage seems to support the notion that the earthquake is localized in the city of Jerusalem, it is possible that because the world will have just witnessed the life, death and resurrection of God's Two Witnesses, that the repentance will be worldwide rather than limited to the city.
- Earthquake: As with the sixth seal, a *great* (NASB) earthquake occurs. The context of the sixth seal passage that the earthquake will be global in scale, however, the sixth trumpet passage only indicates that the resulting damage is restricted to Jerusalem.
- Death: The earthquake will kill seven thousand people.
- Destruction: The earthquake will destroy one tenth of the buildings of Jerusalem.
- Repentance: Unlike the aftermath of the earthquake of the sixth seal in which the Bible does not record repentance, the aftermath of this earthquake results in an unquantified number of people that give glory to God. This also is the opposite response of the people that will live through the fourth bowl judgment; cf. Revelation 16:9.

What This Trumpet Means
This trumpet means that God will eliminate a massive number of unrepentant people by means of an unbelievably large military force of mounted horses with the ability to spew fire, smoke, and brimstone as plagues on humankind. After the massive amount of deaths, humankind still remains unrepentant. A massive earthquake strikes Jerusalem, which is associated with God's call for His Two Witnesses to come to heaven, which causes a significant number of dead and a sizeable portion of Jerusalem lying in destruction. Those that survive the earthquake become terrified realizing that God has just acted in history, which results in them giving glory to Him.

SEVENTH TRUMPET - THE THIRD WOE

Core Scripture: Revelation 10:6c-7 and 11:14-19

Interpretation

As is true of the seventh seal and seventh bowl judgments also, there is an interlude in the text before the seventh trumpet. As the time for Christ's dramatic return draws, judgment of sin and resolution of injustice continues to increase in magnitude and intensity; and the spiritual realm begins to celebrate.

- Delay No Longer: An angel will come down from heaven, different from the angel sounding either the sixth or seventh trumpets, in the course of events associated with the little scroll to pronounce something of great importance to the seventh trumpet and the destiny of humankind, especially for the sinful and evil angelic and human realms. Throughout human history the children of God have petitioned Him to replace the worldly kingdom with the holy kingdom, and to judge the unrighteous, the ungodly, the disobedient, and the sinful - to bring them to their predicted fate. There have been an innumerable number of prayers sent to God requesting the suffering, the persecution, and the misery of the human condition to come to its final and predicted end. Saints throughout time have looked forward to when they will find rest and comfort in the presence of the Lord - they have believed fervently in the coming of a time of peace. Finally, after decades and centuries of God's Plan marching to its predetermined completion, a powerful angel announces that God has determined that time has run out and that there will be no more delay. He is about to close history, as the world has known it for not less than six millennia. Time will not cease, but the dominance of sinful thought, behavior and action will. While not specifically stated, Jesus Christ is about to return to resolve and reign!

- The Mystery of God: All that has been recorded in the Bible by the prophets about the long-awaited future is about to come into being - prophecies given by the powerful, majestic, and holy God to His people will be finally and completely fulfilled at the Advent of Jesus Christ. Quotes by Walvoord from three different books will suffice in interpreting this concept:

  + "… John was informed that when the seventh trumpet sounds, it will introduce the mystery of God, apparently a reference to details about the second coming of Christ not previously revealed. The prophecy to be fulfilled will be the full revelation of the glory of God which will fulfill what the prophets had predicted."[19]

  + "This mystery had been previously announced to God's prophets. The reference, therefore, is not to hidden truth but to the fulfillment of many Old Testament passages which refer to the glorious return of the Son of God and the establishment of His kingdom of righteousness and peace on earth. While God's purposes are not necessarily revealed in current events where Satan is allowed power and manifestation, the time will come when Satan no longer will be in power and the predictions of the Old Testament prophets will be fulfilled. Then all will know the Lord and the truth about Him (Jer. 31:34)."[20]

+ "The prediction is related to the full manifestation of the divine power, majesty, and holiness of God which will be evident in the glorious return of Christ, the establishment of His millennial kingdom, and the creation of the eternal state which will follow. The ignorance of God and the disregard of His majestic person which characterize the present age as well as the great tribulation will exist no longer when Christ returns and manifests Himself in glory to the entire earth. In that day all, from the least to the greatest, will know the Lord, that is, know the important facts about Him (cf. Jer. 31:3)."[21]

- Third Woe is Coming Quickly: Just as was done before the second woe (the sixth trumpet) there is an announcement of the something terrible about to commence - the horses for the unbelieving citizens of the world continues.

- Celebration in Heaven: Upon the sounding of the seventh trumpet, celebration breaks out in the heavenly realm.

    + A symphony of voices loudly proclaim that the ownership of the world will change from the temporal satanic realm to the eternal godly realm - the world will now be governed by - God the Father, Jesus the Son, and the Holy Spirit - the eternal Holy Trinity.

    + The twenty-four elders fall prostrated face down to symbolize ultimate surrender to the Lord God, at the same time giving thanks, presumably on behalf of all other saints as well as themselves, that the Lord, by His great power and eternally, will now reign above all others in fulfillment of Psalm 2.

- Kingdom of the World Has Become the Kingdom of the Lord: The logical question that occurs is, how can this transition be made before the seven bowls of judgment are poured out? The answer is that the transition really started when God's wrath began with the first seal judgment, and now that all seven-seals and six of the trumpet judgments have been dispensed, the transition has progressed to the point where the outcome is within sight, not to mention inevitably destined. In the beginning the lordship of the earth belonged to the Lord, however because the will of humankind rejected the Creator in favor of the imitator it was given over to humankind under Satan's evil influence and allowed to run an historical and rebellious course resulting in its logical conclusion of self-destruction, at which point, the Lord brings the repentant to Himself and restores His lordship over the unrepentant by judging them. Humankind will not give control of the world back to the Lord, as we are incapable of such a possibility, God has bought it back eternally by the saving sacrifice of His Only Begotten Son. Never again will the world be governed by the lordship of humankind or Satan.

- Nations Enraged at God's Wrath: The nations of the world become angry with the Lord, which is consistent with the anxiety felt by the nations as recorded in Psalm 2:1-4, and the political leadership become fearful of the Lord, as suggested by Revelation 6:15-17, when He exercises His wrath out on the world. This implies that the nations understand that the catastrophic events taking place are judgments by the Lord.

- Dead to Be Judged: Given the context of the passage indicating rewards for both the good and the bad, this could be a reference to both - give everyone what is due them based on their decision regarding Jesus Christ.
- God's People Rewarded: The time has come for all of the servants of God, the prophets of God, and the saints of God are to receive the reward promised them by the Bible.
- Destroy the Destroyer: Also, the time has come to those that endeavor to destroy all that is good and right to be judged and condemned to their due punishment.
- God's Temple: In spite of the fact that God's earthly temple has been desecrated temple and the ark of His covenant still manifest His righteousness and majesty.
- Drama of Nature: At the time the heavenly temple is opened, another display of nature's fury, superintended by God, occurs indicating that God will now pour out onto the world the severest of His wrath. For yet another time, lightning and thunder set the stage for coming attractions, and again an earthquake rattles the world. In addition this time a hailstorm drains terror down on humankind, without indication of its severity. It is hard to fathom that there could still be people alive during this period that are resisting what seems to be apparently clear to civilization that all the calamity going on is God pouring out His wrath on an unbelieving people.

What This Trumpet Means

This trumpet seems to be the prelude to the coming of the seven bowl judgments and emphasizes that the time has come for the righteous to be rewarded, the unrighteous to be judged and punished, Satan and his dominion to be disposed of, and for God's holy justice to be established. The trumpet concludes with another display of nature's fury as history draws to a climatic close.

38.4	THE SECOND PARENTHETICAL INTERVAL IN THE BOOK OF REVELATION

The related topics that are included in the second parenthetical interval that occurs between the sixth and seventh trumpet judgments include the following:
- The Angel with Little Book | The Seven Thunders | Anticipation of the Seventh Trumpet - Revelation 10:1-10: Refer to Chapter 39.
- God's Two Witnesses - Revelation 11:1-12: Refer to Section 33.9.

38.5	THE THIRD PARENTHETICAL INTERVAL IN THE BOOK OF REVELATION

The related topics that are included in the third parenthetical interval that occurs between the trumpet judgments and the bowl judgments include the following:

- The Seven Great Personages of the End Times - Revelation 12:1 - 13:18: Refer to Chapter 30.
- 144,000 Jews Sealed by God - Revelation 14:1-5: Refer to Section 33.6.
- Pronouncements of Coming Conclusions: Refer to Section 39.2.

39

THE LITTLE BOOK, PRONOUNCEMENTS, AND BOWL JUDGMENTS

Revelation records several passages containing information about other activities and events not associated with the trumpet or bowl judgments. John records an angel with a little book, and then he is shown the seven thunder judgments but is told to not record anything about them. Then seven pronouncements are seen that further explains the coming seven bowl judgments. Finally, the seven bowls are poured out in God's wrath on the earth.

39.1	THE ANGEL WITH THE LITTLE BOOK AND THE THUNDER JUDGMENTS

Nestled between the sixth and seventh trumpet judgments is a seemingly unusual and out-of-place narrative (one of two such narratives in the second parenthetical interval) about an angel that confronts John, tells him about seven thunder judgments and the coming seventh trumpet judgment, then makes him eat a small scroll the angel is carrying.

REVELATION 10:1-3

John encounters another angel coming down out of heaven whose appearance seems to be different than the others previously met. In his hands is a little book that is open, the contents of which is not disclosed.

Some believe that because of the majestic description the angel is actually Jesus Christ, however, this notion is not in harmony with the sense of the events and times. There is no evidence elsewhere in the Bible of Jesus coming down to earth during Daniel's 70th Week in the manner stated in this verse; also when angels are mentioned in the Book of Revelation, they are always angels, rather than a representation for Christ. Others believe the angel is Michael because he is seen shortly in another context. The angel's specific identity is not really relevant to the event, except that he is a holy angel apparently of considerable stature in the angelic realm.

The use of the word another suggests that it is not the angel that recently sounded the sixth trumpet, and is probably not the angel about to sound the seventh trumpet, and in fact may be an angel not previously encountered.

- This angel is identified as being strong (which also suggests mighty and powerful). Again this supports the idea that this angel has been entrusted with substantial authority to perform the task assigned him. The implication is that this angel is of a high rank.
- Unlike most of John's encounters with angels, the appearance of this angel is described using terms typically used for majesty and divinity.

The angel holds a little, opened book in his hands. Since the contents of the book are not revealed, we can only speculate about its purpose, with the following being options:

- There is no evidence that this little book is in any way connected to the Lamb's scroll of Revelation 5 - 7. The Greek word used here suggests a form that is somewhat less important than the word used for the scroll.
- The purpose of the book seems, "… to represent in this vision the written authority given the angel to fulfill his mission."[1]
- "The contents of the Little Book is prophecy, especially the prophecy of the middle and the second half of the tribulation."[2]
- An option of reasonable possibility is that the little book here is the book that Daniel was told to seal up in Daniel 12:4 and 9 after he had written about end time events that were not to be known until the end.
- It is feasible that the little book is related to the seven thunders mentioned in verses 3 and 4. The book is open in the angel's hand, who then cries out in a loud voice - is it possible that the angel is reading what is written and he is calling out the next judgments? Many of the seal, trumpet, and bowl judgments begin with an angel doing something - calling forth the horses, sounding a trumpet, and pour out bowls, respectively. So, is it not possible that the prophecies of the seven thunders are contained within this little book?

The angel stands with his left foot on dry land and his right foot on the sea suggesting that the message contained in the little book may be, meant to be heard by the entire world. The "sea is mentioned before earth, though the normal order in the Book of Revelation is to mention earth before sea (cf. 5:13; 7:1-3; 12:12; 14:7). John is more impressed by the fact that the angel stands on the sea than upon earth, but the symbolism in either case indicates compete authority over the entire earthly situation."[3] The angel then cried out in a loud voice, which is compared to the roar of a lion, something the specifics of which are not recorded.

REVELATION 10:4 - THE SEVEN THUNDERS

After the seven thunders had spoken and John was about to write what was spoken, but a voice from heaven directed him to not write the messages down, but instead to seal up the things that were spoken. Only John knows what the seven thunders are and what impact they have on the earth.

This seems to be a very unusual condition to be put on a message, which is apparently about a specific series of end times judgments, when it is one of the many parts of a larger message in regard to the events that will occur when God calls an end to human history. Why seal these up when all the other events are being predicted in sufficient detail?

This notion of knowing things about God and the heavenly realm and then not being able to communicate them to a larger audience is not unusual in the Bible.

- In Daniel 12:4 and 9, after certain things had been revealed to Daniel, but he is told to not write them down because they will not be needed until the time of the end. The impression is that the information is not for humankind to know at this time, as we should wait until the right time to be revealed.
- Also, in 2 Corinthians 12:4, Paul indicates he was shown some things during his theological education in the wilderness when he *heard things too sacred to be put into words, things that a person is not permitted to speak.*

Regarding what the seven thunders will be, we can only speculate. Because the context of this portion of the Book of Revelation is about judgments, seven seals and six trumpets thus far and one trumpet and seven bowls to go, it seems logical to consider the seven thunders as seven additional judgments, the subject of which will remain a mystery until it is time for them to occur. "Either the seven thunders were intended for John's illumination and were not essential to the main vision of the seven trumpets of the reference is designed to strike a note of mystery with reference to God's revelatory activities (cf. 2 Cor. 12:4)."[4]

REVELATION 10:5-7

Next, the angel swears an oath, pronounces an end to the delay for divine justice, and says that the coming seventh trumpet will complete the mystery of God. The specifics of this passage have been explored previously under the seventh trumpet.

REVELATION 10:8-11

Reminiscent of one of Ezekiel's experiences, John is directed to eat the little book.

The voice from heaven that John had heard earlier speaks to him again and tells him to go and to take the little book from the angel. John does as directed, the angel tells John to eat the little book, and that it will taste sweet, but it will be bitter to his stomach. Again, John does as he is told and immediately the angel's prophecy is fulfilled. Precedents for something like this can be found in Ezekiel 2:9-10; 3:1-4, 14; Jeremiah 15:16-18.

The logical question that occurs is, why would John be asked to eat a little book? Obviously, there must be meaning and a purpose for such an action, however, the passage does not disclose such. It seems that the little book is symbolic of the Word of God, and it is sweet in the sense that reveals the promises and grace of God. Eating the book suggests the partaking of the sweetness of the Word, in spite of some of the bitterness that John will have to endure, suggesting trials and Christian persecutions. "Receiving the Word of God is a great joy; but since the Word is an oracle of judgment, it results in the unpleasant experience of proclaiming a message of wrath and woe (cf. Jer. 15:16, 19)."[5]

Finally, after eating the little book, John is directed to continue prophesying to the many peoples, nations, languages, and kings.

39.2	THE PROCLAMATIONS OF COMING CONCLUSIONS

In Revelation 14, John is shown a series of proclamations that will be made as the opening acts immediately before the most severe of God's wrath, the seven bowl judgments, descend on Israel, the Unholy Trinity, the Gentile nations and peoples, and finally, the earth itself.

The intent of the inclusion of the pronouncements is to assure "… the reader of the ultimate triumph of Christ and the judgment of the wicked."[6] Fruchtenbaum[7] proposes three prophetic purposes for the proclamations of Revelation 14:
- To predict the failure of the Unholy Trinity's program.
- To announce the results of the forthcoming Bowl Judgments.
- To assure, encourage, and comfort the saints living at the time.

The following is a summary of the proclamations:

The Seven Proclamations	
First	About the Lamb and the 144,000 Jews
Second	About the angel declaring the Gospel

Third	About the angel declaring the fall of Babylon
Fourth	About the angel declaring the doom of the beast worshippers
Fifth	About the voice declaring blessings on the faithful saints
Sixth	About the Son of Man reaping a harvest
Seventh	About the angel with the sickle

FIRST PROCLAMATION - THE LAMB AND THE 144,000 JEWS

Core Scripture: Revelation 14:1-5

The 144,000 Jews that will be selected and supernaturally protected during the course of Daniel's 70th Week (Revelation 7:1-8) are now seen by John at their ultimate destiny standing with the Lamb, their Lord and Messiah Jesus Christ, on Mount Zion in the Millennium Kingdom. This has been previously explored in Section 33.6.

SECOND PROCLAMATION - THE ANGEL DECLARES THE GOSPEL

Core Scripture: Revelation 14:6-7

In a final altar call of sorts combined with an announcement of coming attractions, another angel (the first in this series, and apparently different from the angels previously mentioned) flying overhead tells the world what God's judgment has arrived, time has run out, and the moment of decision between God and Satan is at hand. There are a number of interesting aspects of these two verses that should be noticed:

- The sense of this passage is that the time has come in which things will be decided between Jesus Christ and Satan, and their respective followers.
- The angel is flying high in the sky (literally mid-heaven), apparently so that all that live in the world can see him and no one will miss this final call.
- The information that the angel is announcing is the good news about *an eternal gospel* (the KJV uses the phrase *the everlasting gospel*), and, "… seems to be neither the gospel of grace nor the gospel of the kingdom, but rather the good news that god at last is about to deal with the world in righteousness and establish that God's righteousness is ageless."[8]

- The angel's announcement is to *those who live on the earth, and to every nation and tribe and tongue and people* - a wordy description to emphasize that everyone on the earth will hear the invitation to accept Jesus Christ.
- The message the angel proclaims to a world following the Unholy Trinity's scheme includes the following eternal truths:
  + *Fear God, and give Him glory*: The True God in heaven is the One to be known, obeyed, worshipped, and glorified, not the false god of the earth.
  + *the hour of His judgement has come*: The sense of this part of the message is emphatic, the time of judgment is no longer coming, the hour of His judgment is here. The fact of every person will be judged has arrived, it is no longer an event at some time in the future.
  + *and worship Him who made the heaven and the earth and sea and springs of water*: The final call acknowledges that the One that the world was created for and through, Jesus Christ, is the One to be worshipped, not the one that the world is focused on at the time.

"This proclamation is a final call to the world to accept the Gospel in light of the Revelation 13 problem where the Antichrist declares himself to be god, and the False Prophet is calling all men to take upon themselves the Mark of the Beast and thus show their submissive acceptance of the deity of the Antichrist."[9]

THIRD PROCLAMATION - THE ANGEL DECLARING THE FALL OF BABYLON

Core Scripture: Revelation 14:8

Another angel (the second is this series), by implication also flying in mid-heaven, declares that Babylon, the one that has brought immorality to the world, the seat of all that stands in opposition to holiness and righteousness has fallen and is no more. Victory is the Lord's. Because the context of this passage seems to be at a time late in the Great Tribulation, the reference to Babylon seems to be to a literal city; throughout the Bible, Babylon can refer to a political or religious system, in addition to the literal ancient city so the idea here is a restored city.

FOURTH PROCLAMATION - THE ANGEL DECLARING THE DOOM OF THE BEAST WORSHIPPERS

Core Scripture: Revelation 14:9-12

Another angel (the third in a series) announces those that worship the Antichrist, or has taken his mark, will partake of the full strength of the wine of God's wrath, and will be eternally tormented. The statement in verse 11 indicating that there will be no rest day or night from the torment stands in stark contrast to believers being brought into God's rest for eternity. "The stern warning addressed to all worshippers of the beast is also an encouragement to those who put their trust in Christ in the time of great tribulation. Though some of them will face martyrdom and others will need to go into hiding, they are assured that their lot is far preferable to those who accept the easy way out and worship the beast."[10]

FIFTH PROCLAMATION - THE VOICE DECLARING BLESSING ON THE FAITHFUL SAINTS

Core Scripture: Revelation 14:13

For this pronouncement, John hears a voice from heaven, rather than seeing a flying angel, declare that those who are martyred in the name of the Lord, are blessed, and they will now be able to rest from their faithful work. The sense of this blessing is for those saints that die during, rather than prior to, the Great Tribulation. The voice is believed to be that of the Holy Spirit.

SIXTH PROCLAMATION - THE SON OF MAN REAPING A HARVEST

Core Scripture: Revelation 14:14-16

John sees One seated on a white cloud, identified as the Son of Man, with a golden crown on His head and a sharp sickle in His hand. Many believe this being to be Jesus Christ who appears to be ready to harvest the earth, with an emphasis placed on the idea that the time for harvesting has come. Another angel (the fourth in this series), this time seen exiting the Temple, shouts out to the One on the cloud to start reaping because the earth's harvest is ripe and ready for reaping, at which point the One seated on the cloud proceeds to do so. The Greek word used for ripe, suggests a fruit or vegetable that is almost too ripe.

SEVENTH PROCLAMATION - THE ANGEL WITH THE SICKLE

Core Scripture: Revelation 14:17-20

Then another angel (the fifth in this series) comes out of the Temple with a sickle of his own, is then exhorted by another angel (the sixth in this series), coming from the altar, to also reap the harvest on the earth. The angel passes his sickle over the earth and throws the harvest into the winepress of the wrath of God. The word used for ripe in this passage suggest fully grown and in prime condition. Because they were fully grown, and filled with juice, when they are trampled in the winepress there is so much juice that it splatters as high as the horses' bridles, rather than floods to the height of the bridles. The idea here is that unbelievers were given over to God's wrath.

39.3   WRATH OF GOD - THE BOWL JUDGMENTS

And the wrath of God continues with the pouring of the seventh bowl concluding just before the Second Advent of Christ.

GENERAL OBSERVATIONS OF THE BOWLS

Previously under the discussion of the trumpets we have seen that the fifth, sixth, and seventh trumpet judgments were also identified as the three woe judgments. Therefore, these seven bowl judgments, contained within the seventh trumpet, are all part of the third woe. Comparatively, the seven bowl judgments are simplistically deadly when set in contrast to the three woe judgments which are complicatedly deadly.

Revelation 15 – 16 records the last earthly events to occur before, and will be followed immediately by, the Second Coming of Jesus Christ to the earth to begin His Thousand-Year Kingdom – long-awaited by the saints for centuries. As God's Plan has marched down through time to this point, people have had the opportunity to choose belief in Jesus Christ as the Son of God and the Messiah or not, however, now that God's long-suffering has worn out, the time for unrepentant Jews and Gentiles is quickly drawing to a close. There is very little time left to get right with God, as the sense of the bowl judgments is that they are immediately before the Second Advent of Christ, and the seven judgments will come about in rapid succession. In fact, verse 15:1 indicates that these seven plagues are the last things to occur in order for God's anger to be completed. In Revelation 16 the seven bowls are poured out onto the earth, and then Christ returns (the last verse of Revelation 16 is followed chronologically by Revelation 19:11 and following because Revelation 17:1 – 19:10 are a parenthetical interval as indicated below).

We previously examined the seven angelic proclamations that will also occur immediately before the bowl judgments that will be the conclusion of God's anger. "What has already been anticipated under the three figures of the divine eschatological judgment – the cup of wine (14:10), the harvest of the earth (14:14-16), and the vintage (14:17-20) – is now further described under the symbolism of the seven bowls."[11]

Notice that even though God is having His final judgments poured out on a wicked world, He still desires for those that remain to repent and turn to Him. The notion further substantiates the fact that God is a forgiving and patient sovereign. However, as will be seen in Revelation 16, none will turn to Him during these last calamities.

Some contend that Revelation 15:2 indicates that there are no believers on the earth during the time of the bowl judgments, however, this cannot be accurate because there has to be believers of Jesus Christ on earth at the time of the Lord's return, and since Revelation 16:21 suggests that there are none that repent as a result of the bowl judgments, then there would have been no new believers.

Revelation 10:7 indicates that after the angel sounds the seventh trumpet, resulting in the seven bowl judgments poured out on the world, the mysteries of God will be completed.

Some theologians contend that the seven bowl judgements are an amplification of the seven trumpet judgments because they both follow a particular sequence of realms affected by the judgments: (1) the earth, (2) the sea, (3) the rivers and fountains of water, (4) the sun, (5) the darkness, (6) the Euphrates River, and (7) lightnings, thunders, and a great earthquake. The notion that there are similarities does not mean that they are the same things, because a detailed examination reveals irresolvable differences, the principle of which is that the trumpet judgments deal with one-third of things, while the bowl judgments deal with the whole thing.

As is somewhat the case with the seal and trumpet judgments, the means by which the seal judgments are accomplished is not disclosed. The Scriptures simply state that each bowl that is held by an angel is poured out and devastation results. What is contained within the bowl is not disclosed. It seems more plausible that it will be events of nature that will cause death and destruction rather than some supernatural effect as usually seen in a science fiction movie. The obvious example might be a nuclear bomb blast, or a nuclear exchange between nations, which causes a blood-like poisoning of the salt and fresh water of the earth instead of the world waking up one morning only to find that the water has inexplicably changed into actual blood. Other than the ten plague judgments on Egypt, which could have been events of nature as well, the sense of devastating judgments in the Bible is more consistent with events of nature than science fiction.

Just as experienced by some that follow Jesus Christ who are purified, as silver is refined by heat and working, ultimate human rebellion approaches its own purity through the refining caused by the bowl judgments. Interestingly, evil reaches its own almost pure conclusion in the form of a rebellious human society, just as good has already achieved absolute purity in the form of God, Jesus Christ and the Holy Spirit.

The following is a summary of the bowl judgments:

The Seven Bowl Judgments	
First	Brings painful sores on those who worship the Antichrist
Second	Destroys the sea with blood and killing all in it
Third	Poisons the earth's fresh water with blood
Fourth	Brings scorching heat and fire from the sun
Fifth	Brings darkness on the Antichrist's global empire
Sixth	Deceives the nations to come to Armageddon
Seventh	Brings earthquakes and hailstones

THE PRELUDE TO THE SEVEN BOWLS

Just as there is an introductory prelude to the seven-seal judgments (Revelation 5 – the determination that Jesus Christ is the one that is worthy to open the sealed scroll held by God) and another to the seven trumpet judgments (Revelation 8:3-5 – an angel holding a golden censer at the altar who throws it, full of fire, to the earth), there is also an introductory prelude to the seven bowl judgments that consumes all of Chapter 15 of Revelation and the first verse of Chapter 16. In this heavenly scene, John witnesses the worship of the sovereign Lord and the seven angels, each holding a bowl filled with plagues preparing to pour out the contents of the bowls onto an unrepentant world (Revelation 16).

Revelation 15:1
John sees another sign, this time however, it is qualified with the adjectives *great* and *astounding*. This time what John witnesses are seven angels that possess seven plagues, and they are identified as the last plagues before God determines that His anger is completed. John seeing *another sign in heaven* is a reference to two signs that he has seen previously – the woman recorded in Revelation 12:1 which was a *great sign*, and the *great red dragon* recorded in Revelation 12:3 which was a sign without a qualifying adjective. Walvoord has this to say about these three signs: "The three signs taken together represent important elements in the prophetic scene: (1) Israel, that is, the woman; (2) the final world empire under the control of Satan and the beast, that is the great red dragon; and (3) the seven angels having the seven last plagues, that is, divine judgment upon the satanic system and political power of the beast."[12]

An important aspect of this passage is the sense of finality that is being conveyed in the words.
- The plagues are identified as the last plagues which suggests two things: first, they are a continuation of the several plagues of the previous judgments, and second, there will either be no more plagues or no more judgments to come from God. "This implies that the previous judgments were also plagues, that is, divine judgments of God pouring out affliction upon a

wicked world. … That they are described as the last plagues shows that they are the final judgments preceding the second coming itself."[13]

- That these are the last judgments are conditioned on the fact that the last part of the verse indicates that after the plagues are let loose, then God's anger will have been completed. "In view is not divine wrath as an attitude, but divine judgment as the expression of God's wrath."[14] Also, as pointed out above, after the seven bowls are poured out the next chronological event is the return of Christ.

The focus of what John sees are seven angles, mostly like new angels that have not been seen before, who are in possession of seven plagues. On numerous occasions throughout the Bible, and not restricted to Israel, plagues have been used as one of God's instruments of judgment to bring the disobedient back to righteous behavior and living. Ten plagues are recorded in the Book of Exodus as having been used on the Egyptians to force them to release the Israelites so that they could return to their land. During the wandering itself, God used plagues as judgments on the Jews for their disobedience. Therefore, there is a harmonious consistency with God's use of plagues as part of His final judgments on a wicked world.

Revelation 15:2
John then sees another celestial scene similar to the other such scenes earlier in the Book of Revelation, especially Chapters 4 and 5, that stands in stark contrast to the scene of deadly judgments ensuing around this passage.

- While not specifically stated as such, the setting of this scene is probably the Throne Room of God for two reasons: first, the other instance of seeing a sea of glass found in Revelation 4:6 is taking place in the Throne Room; and second, the later part of Chapter 15 refers to the temple thereby suggesting all of the events of Chapter 15 take place in the presence of the Throne of God.
- The sea of glass seems to be the same as was seen in Revelation 4:6, except this time rather than looking like crystal, it seems to be mixed with fire. Because of the words used in the description and the context, the sea does not appear to be an actual body of water, but instead something that replicates the visual attitudes of a large body of water. Walvoord seems to think that the sea that looks like crystal in Revelation 4, "… speaks of the holiness of God…," where the "… fire speaks of divine judgment proceeding from God's holiness."[15]
- Either standing by the sea or standing on the sea is what appears to be a large collection of people that have conquers, or overcome, the beast of Revelation 13, or the Antichrist. It seems without reservation that the ones standing are those that had been martyred for their testimony by the beast. It is not certain if this is the same group of martyrs as found in Revelation 7:9 or if it is a different group; the sense is that it is probably a different group.
- Those that are standing are holding harps that had been given to them by God.

Revelation 15:3-4

The martyrs are singing two hymns of praise. "The former recounts the faithfulness of God to Israel as a nation in recognition that large number of Israelites are among these martyred dead. The song of the Lamb speaks of redemption from sin made possible by the sacrifice of the Lamb of God, and would include all the saints."[16]

Revelation 15:5-8

Then John looks again and sees the temple and the angels preparing for their assignments. The temple that John sees is thought to be the inner sanctuary of the tabernacle, or the Holy of Holies, the place where the ark, containing the stone tablets of the Ten Commandments, was kept during Israel's time. The tabernacle of testimony (or, the tent of the tabernacle in the NET) is in reference to the whole tentlike tabernacle structure, the Holy of Holies of which only occupying a portion thereof. John sees that the curtain separating the Holy of Holies from the remainder of the tabernacle is parted, and seven majestically dressed angels are coming out carrying the seven plagues.

While there is no threat to the theology of the scene, there is a lack of clarity regarding the plagues and bowls at this point.

- First, verses 15:1 and 15:6 indicate that the seven angels are in possession of seven plagues, the idea being that they are holding a vessel containing the plagues. The verse further intimates that the plagues are the last judgments to be poured out on the world, after which God's anger will be completed. The logical conclusion is that seven bowl judgments recorded in Revelation 16 are the same as the seven plagues.
- Second, verse 15:7 indicates that one of the four living creatures gives each of the seven angels a golden bowl that is filled with the wrath, or more literally the anger of God. There is no recording that the angels placed the plagues within the bowls, the passage only says that the bowls containing the wrath are given to the angels. The implication is that the plagues and the wrathful content of the bowls are the same.

The "smoke" that filled the temple refers to the Shekinah cloud first associated with the tabernacle and then with the temple. It symbolizes God's special presence and that he is the source of the judgments (Exod. 10:34ff; 1 Kings 8:10-11; Ezek. 11:23)."[17]

"Access into the sanctuary is made impossible by the smoke until the judgments contained in the seven plagues are fulfilled. It is an ominous sign of impending doom for those who persist in their blasphemous disregard of the sovereignty and holiness of God."[18]

Revelation 16:1

The John hears a loud voice, undoubtedly God's, from the temple commanding the seven angels to proceed with pouring out the bowls of divine judgment onto the earth.

FIRST BOWL

Core Scripture: Revelation 16:2

Interpretation

While the passage in the NASB shown here seems to suggest a singularity of affliction (the word *sore* is singular as well in the KJV and the NKJV), the NIV and the NET uses the plural sense of the word. As the bowl of judgment is poured out on the earth, which the affliction extends to everyone in the world seems more consistent with the nature of the bowl judgments being for the entire world.

The Physical Affliction: The word sore can also be described as an ulcer or a wound, however, even though it is not identified, it is described with two qualifiers. See the adjacent table for how the sores are described in various translations. The words used in these translations indicate the sores are bad, possibly even evil, in the sense of injurious or baneful, and, pain due to a sore inflicted retributively. Whatever the affliction

Revelation 16:2	
NIV	*ugly, festering*
NASB	*loathsome and malignant*
NET	*ugly and painful*
KJV	*noisome and grievous*
NKJV	*foul and loathsome*
AMP	*foul and painful*

will be it will physically affect those living at the time and in a manner that is consistent with all the other tragedies of that time. It should also be pointed out the passage makes no indication as to how long the affliction will last, therefore, the implication is that it will last until the Lord's Coming.

The People Afflicted: As has been pointed out throughout this book, whenever the mark of the beast is offered to humankind, anyone accepting the mark will pass a point of no return with the Lord. The sense is that the mark of the beast will be the final 'line in the sand' and whoever crosses the line will be lost forever. They will have made their decision about Christ and 'there will be no going back' - the implication is that they will not be able to recant and seek forgiveness from the Lord.

What This Bowl Means

This bowl means that those the world over who have accepted the mark of the beast, and who subsequently worship the beast will be afflicted with painful sores that will result in terrible suffering. This obviously results in a catastrophic impact on humankind.

PARENTHETICAL COMMENTS

The sad events that have been seen thus far, and the weight of expectation of the events still to come, give rise to an observation that should be mentioned.

The most dramatic and unexpected aspect of all of the events of this time in human history is not so much that the entire world is being subjected to unprecedented physical occurrences and human suffering, but it lies in the fact that in the midst of the overwhelming chaos, the horrifying amount of death, the unbelievable extent of destruction, and the insane levels of confusion, the most dramatic and unexpected aspect of all this is, when the evidence clearly points to the Living God, millions of created human beings will in the end shake their collective fist in the face of the Triune Creator. This is the true depth and full measure of human capacity for evilness - that many individuals will allow themselves to be corporately susceptible to the opposite of good and goodness. "It is amazing how blind humanity will become, how superstitious and spiritually ignorant. For they will turn to an image rather than to God."[19]

It never ceases to be amazing that when confronted with truth and untruth, and incredible number of people will, for whatever logical or illogical reason, turn to untruth too many times! What is it about the human intellect and psyche that does not let one person accept truth while another does? Why is it that some will choose to walk in darkness rather than in the light (John 1:5; 3:19; 8:12; 12:35)? Why is it that some will not grasp, comprehend, understand, or seize what many others clearly grasp, comprehend, understand, or seize? The only explanation is that it is precisely the quality of the human design that allows choices to be made from among a range of options, even the ability to not choose one's Creator. This is the true measure of human dignity - which a Creator God would design a creature, in His own image that includes intelligence, which has the freedom to choose any other belief than the truth that the Creator Himself has provided. Notice the contrast in images. Human beings are created in the specific image of their Creator, but during the course of fulfilling their purpose by living a life on the earth with the potential of an eternal life with Creator, they instead choose to place their faith and hope in an image that they themselves create because they permitted themselves to be influenced by the antithesis of their Creator. Interestingly, the Creator that had the choice of whether to create creatures or not, allows those creatures He chose to create, to choose whether to believe he or she was created by the Creator … or not.

SECOND BOWL

Core Scripture: Revelation 16:3

Interpretation
Like the second trumpet, this bowl judgment will cause the water of the sea to change into blood, how this judgment occurs is not disclosed in the passage. Also, unlike the second trumpet where one third of the sea creatures die, all sea creatures die under this judgment.

What This Bowl Means
This bowl means that something will cause all of the salt water bodies to either change into blood, resulting in the death of everything that lives in the water. This obviously results in a catastrophic impact on humankind.

THIRD BOWL

Core Scripture: Revelation 16:4-7

Interpretation
Like the third trumpet, this bowl judgment will cause the water of the rivers and springs to either change into blood. Unlike the third trumpet where a great burning star, identified as Wormwood, falls into the sea, how the judgment occurs is not disclosed in the passage. Also, unlike the third trumpet where one third of the water is poisoned, there is no disclosure as to the number of dead under this judgment, however, there is a statement that John recorded that was made by the angel of the waters.

Identity of the Angel: This angel is apparently a holy angel that has responsibility and jurisdiction over the waters, and quite possibly in response to the effect that previous seal and trumpet judgments have had on the seas, rivers, and springs; this angel provides justification for God's judgment. First, the angel praises the Lord by acknowledging His righteousness, His eternality, and His holiness for having judged those that have dishonored Him in history past by rejecting His messengers. Second, the angel acknowledges that God had previously sent saints and prophets to earth as emissaries to guide the creatures to their Creator, but they were killed instead of being accepted. Because sinful humankind had poured out the blood of God's earlier emissaries, now God will pour out the blood of sinful humankind at the end. God exercises His justifiable revenge by now giving sinners what they deserved, which was what they had given Him earlier. "Even as the saints are worthy of rest and reward, so the wicked are worthy of divine chastening and judgment."[20]

What the Altar Said: After the angel of the waters has spoken, the altar voices agreement. While the passage indicates that the altar was the one that spoke, most likely, it was another angel that spoke.

What This Bowl Means
This bowl means that something will cause all of the fresh water sources, rivers, and springs, to change into blood. While it is not recorded, this most likely will result in the death of everything in the water, as well as much of humankind. This obviously results in a catastrophic impact on humankind. In addition to the second and third trumpets, "combining the judgment of the second and third vials, it appears that all the water is turned into blood, constituting a universal testimony to all men that God will avenge his martyred saints."[21]

FOURTH BOWL

Core Scripture: Revelation 16:8-9

Interpretation
Continuing the trend of similarities with the trumpet judgments, the fourth bowl involves the light of the sun, however, rather than decreasing the amount of sun, moon, and star light penetrating the atmosphere and striking the earth as is the case with the fourth trumpet, the amount of sunlight increases to the point where human beings are scorched with fierce heat. How this occurs is not indicated, however, while the effect is worldwide, the means must be somewhat sporadic or disproportionate because some people will either not be affected by the event, or else they will not die from the effects.

This in one of the judgments that it is easy to speculate about its means. It seems very plausible that weapons of mass destruction, nuclear, chemical, or biological, could be the source of so much of the death and destruction described in this and the various other judgments. While it is not a justification for this interpretation, the sense of the descriptive details of earthly and human devastation appear to be consistent with what humankind has learned to expect from either, the explosion of nuclear device, or, the release of a chemical or biological agent. This notion is supported by the fact that the nature of the end times is that the world is warring and is in great distress and turmoil, and it seems logical that if there is worldwide warfare then weapons of mass destruction will inevitably be used. Humankind unfortunately already possesses the technology by which to destroy itself, and the world political condition is already unstable enough for some political entities to use weapons of mass destruction for their own misguided purposes. God must have a sense of irony about Himself; it does not seem uncommon for Him to use the very creations of the human mind originally conceived as to serve God and fellow man, but changed into instruments by which humankind can be abused by those bent on evil rebellion because they have succumbed to the influence of the Unholy Trinity.

Interestingly, returning to the condition of human society for a moment, the applicable passages of this and the following bowl judgments both end with a three-part insightful observation by John.

- First, humankind blasphemies and curses God, this acknowledging His very existence - \which stands in complete contrast to humankind generally ignoring Him for centuries.
- Second, humankind understands that the distress that the world is experiencing is originating as judgments by God.
- Third, in the midst of the most terrible times on the earth since the beginning of human history, humankind will not repent of their sinfulness, nor will they worship and glorify God, even for no other reason than to bring an end to their personal suffering, unbearable pain and individual misery. Unbelievable!

"The divine judgment thus inflicted ... does not bring men to repentance but only increases their blasphemy, even though they recognize that the plague comes from God whom they reject."[22]

What This Bowl Means
This bowl means that something will happen that will cause the sun to scorch humankind, most likely with a staggering quantity of death and devastation. This obviously results in a catastrophic impact on humankind. However, acknowledgement of God is admitted by the world, but human rebellion is becoming more purified with each judgment because humankind rejects Him for judging them.

FIFTH BOWL

Core Scripture: Revelation 16:10-11

Interpretation
As in the fifth trumpet that includes darkness and human suffering to the point of desiring death, this bowl judgment includes the same plus the additional idea that humankind continues to reject the one causing their torment. Unlike the fifth trumpet, where darkness covered the entire earth, the focus of the darkness here is on the beast, or the Antichrist, and his dominion. While the size or extent of the satanic kingdom is not disclosed, the darkness is not worldwide as it is limited to this kingdom. While the literal interpretation indicates that this is a literal darkness, the possibility that the darkness is symbolic for something else is not to be readily dismissed from possibility. It is hard to see how darkness could cause the torment described, however, the suffering could be the residual from

previous judgments. While we see these judgments as sequential events in time, one starts then finishes before another starts, in all likelihood the reality may be that one starts, causes significant death and destruction, but the affect lasts longer than the time that the following judgment starts. The entire time is a continuous time of distress, trouble, pain, suffering, agony, and misery, not a happy time.

As discussed above under the fourth bowl, this judgment also ends with an observation by John of humankind continuing to reject God.

What This Bowl Means
This bowl means that, in a similar fashion as the previous bowl judgments, a single event causes the time to increase in terribleness, the time it is the evil empire that is directly affected. This obviously results in a catastrophic impact on humankind.

SIXTH BOWL

Core Scripture: Revelation 16:12-16

Interpretation
"The sixth vial [bowl] has occasioned more comment on the part of expositors than any of the preceding vials, and numerous interpretations have been offered."[24] Just as the sixth trumpet focused on the Euphrates River, part of this bowl also focuses on that great river, but this time it is the drying of the waters that is predicted. "But while the sixth trumpet releases demonic hordes to inflict death on the earth dwellers, the sixth bowl effects the assembling of the rulers (kings) from the East to meet the Lord God Almighty in battle."[25]

The Euphrates River: Because of what follows this bowl, this judgment proceeds to prepare the region, as well as the world, for the great confrontation about to take place, which may be just a matter of a few days or a few weeks away from the time of this judgment. This judgment indicates that the waters of the Euphrates River will be dried up, the obvious implication of the context being that the absence of water will allow for easy crossing of what would otherwise be a barrier for an organized land movement of humankind, which, in this case is an invading force coming from the east of the Euphrates River.
- Throughout the Bible, the great Euphrates River is seen as the eastern boundary for a variety of national entities; it served as the boundary for the nation of Israel during their ancient history, and it served as the eastern limit of the Roman Empire centuries later.
- "[B]y mentioning the Euphrates by name, John is suggesting that the unseen rulers of this world are being prepared to enter into a final and fatal battle with the Sovereign of the universe."[26]

Kings of the East: There is much debate about the identity of the kings of the east, literally the kings from the sunrising. One matter that seems to be consistent is that theologians do not see the army of 200 million recorded in the sixth trumpet as being the force referred to here under the kings of the east. This is supported by the belief that the trumpet judgments and the bowl judgments are distinct, and separated by a period of time, thus taking the sixth trumpet (army of 200 million) an event separated from the sixth bowl (kings of the east).

- Fruchtenbaum: After making a strong case that the army of 200 million is a military force of demons, and not an army from China, on the basis that the Scriptural context indicates that the four bound angels are demonic angels and they command an enormous force of demons, Fruchtenbaum contends that the kings of the east are Mesopotamian (Assyrian and Babylonian) in origin, and not from any further east. "The fact that the Antichrist's capital city of Babylon will sit on the banks of the Euphrates River further attests to the fact that the kings who come from the east will be Mesopotamian kings. Thus, consistency of interpretation also militates against matching this reference to China. Consistency of interpretation and not current events must be the basis of determining the meaning of any given text."[27]
- Walvoord: After surveying one hundred commentaries on the Book of Revelation, Walvoord has identified that, "… as many as fifty different interpretations have been advanced."[28] He concludes with this: "The passage is best understood as referring to the kings of the East, literally, of the 'sunrising,' referring to Oriental rulers who will descend upon the Middle East in connection with the final world conflict described a few verses later. The reasons seem to be weak for taking this prediction in other than its literal meaning. The rising power of the Orient in our day in countries such as Japan, China, India, as well as lesser nations, makes such an invasion a reasonable prediction."[29]

Three Unclean Spirits and the Kings of the Whole World: John then sees three unclean spirits like frogs, one each coming out of the mouths of the dragon (Satan), the first beast (Antichrist), and the second beast (False Prophet).

- Unclean Spirits like Frogs: Frogs were considered unclean animals by the Jews and sometimes used as a metaphor for something demonic and evil. "Frogs are dwellers in the deep, or the mire, and here we have pictured that which comes out of the pit itself as the manifestation of the purpose and plan of Satan."[30] That the spirits are specifically identified as demonic emissaries of the Unholy Trinity removes the possibility that they will be actual people living at the time that will go about as ambassadors of the Antichrist.
- Purpose of the Spirits: The demonic spirits are commanded to go the kings of the world and summon them to gather their respective military forces into one place in preparation for a military confrontation.
- The Extent of the World: According to Vine[31], the Greek word for *earth* in this passage is *oikoumene*, and it means the whole inhabited earth; this

word is also used in this same sense in Matthew 24:14, Revelation 3:10 and 12:9. Therefore, the summons extends beyond the Imperialistic (Roman) Empire ruled by the Antichrist to all of the nations of the inhabited world.

- The Cause for the Summons: The cause for the summons request is not disclosed, nor is there even an allusion to a reason - it just says that the kings are to come to form a force *for the war of the great day of God, the Almighty*. The following observations can be made:
  + That the summons request is directed to the kings of the world does not establish that the nations summoned are either allies of the Antichrist, or his enemies. The fact that demonic spirits are to use what appears to be deception and trickery suggests that the kings of the world will be brought to Har Magedon under false pretenses.
  + Interestingly, the Antichrist summons the kings of the earth to join with him to battle the returning Lord. While the Jews are not specifically mentioned as the object of a coordinated attack, it seems obvious that they will be the people that will be caught in the middle and will be the prize for the victor. This indicates that Satan knows how history will play through, and he truly believes he can be victorious over the Lord.
  + There is no evidence as to when this summons request is issued. There are many possibilities, with the following being just two:
    o Will it be issued to the King of the South and the Kings of the North prior to their Daniel 11:40 invasion of Israel? Since the Antichrist is the world ruler and he has established himself as the only god in the Jewish Temple, is this an excuse for him to destroy these nations in his pursuit of global domination? If so, this could explain the need for the deceiving spirits to extend the invitation.
    o Will it be issued to the kings of the earth after the King of the South and the Kings of the North have been destroyed in order to assist in meeting the coming Kings of the East?
  + As the sense of the political and/or economic condition of the world at this time is characterized as being tumultuous at best, and in the process of collapsing at worst, under the rulership of the Antichrist, the point of total collapse could be at hand and there is rebellion among nations because the government of the Antichrist is rapidly dissolving.
  + Some geo-political crisis, not related to Biblical prophecy, could precipitate the need for a military response and the Antichrist is responsible by force as is typical for him.
  + It could be a gathering that has the specific purpose of going against the Jews in order to destroy them forever - another Final Solution effort.
  + The preferred interpretation for this book is that when the Antichrist summons the kings of the earth to Har Magedon, it is an invitation to a military confrontation that is sent to some or all the Kings of the

North (Daniel 11:40), the King of the South (Daniel 11:40), and the Kings of the East (Daniel 11:44 and Revelation 16:12).

- The Need for Deception: Interestingly, the passage indicates that it is necessary for the demonic spirits to perform signs and miracles for the kings. While it might be stretching the passage a bit, Fruchtenbaum makes the following observation: "The summons will be reinforced by demonic activity to make sure that the nations will indeed cooperate in assembling their armies together. These demonic messengers will be empowered to perform signs in order to assure compliance and defeat any reluctance on the part of the other kings."[32]

Great Day of God, the Almighty: This is a reference to the Day of the Lord, and suggests that the coming battle will be the final battle for the prize of humankind, which as we already know is won by the Lord. This will be the time in which the Lord demonstrates, for the last time and for all of humankind to witness, His sovereignty and His omnipotence. Most Christians associate the end of history with a massive battle at Armageddon, but in fact, as will be seen later, there is actually no military confrontation at Armageddon, and the gathering referred to in this passage is only one of eight stages of how the Great Tribulation ends and the Lord returns.

Coming as a Thief, Nakedness, and Shame: As He has said before, the Lord again utters words that sends excitement down the spines of believers and fear down the spines of non-believers. *Behold, I am coming like a thief.* Its inclusion in this passage suggests that believers that are living at the time will be encouraged and comforted by the words as they watch the results of the seal, trumpet, and bowl judgments come about. They are reminded that the imminency of Christ's return is mentioned a number of times in the New Testament - Matthew 24:43; Luke 12:39; 1 Thessalonians 5:2, 4; 2 Peter 3:120; and Revelation 3:3. The picture painted here is that the Lord will come suddenly and without prior notice, and those that are prepared, symbolically clothed, will go with Him into eternity, while those that are not prepared, symbolically naked, will spend eternity in shame, separated from God. While it can be taken as a universal warning and not limited to this particular time, those that are alert to deception, untruth, disloyalty to Jesus, and are ready will take the trip into divine rest and security, while those that are not ready will only take a trip into eternal damnation.

The Place Called Har Magedon: Ironically, in spite of the fact that when the armies of the various kings of the world move to a place called Har Magedon they will fulfill God's predictions. There is a broad range of interpretations among scholars, theologians, and interpreters, as to the actual meaning of the Hebrew word, Har Magedon, Armageddon in Greek, as can be seen from the following options:

- A Symbolic Name: Johnson[33] contends that in the Hebrew, Har Magedon essentially indicates, "a place of gathering in troops", and he acknowledges that it has no connection to a literal and specific place. He indicates that

233

har means hill or mountain, and that *magedon* could mean Megiddo, a Canaanite stronghold captured by the Israelites, on the western edge of the Esdraelon Plain. He then takes the position that Megiddo is not a mountain, nor even a hill, and is never designated as such, therefore, he dismisses the probability that Har Magedon is a reference to the place.

- The Literal Place: Without denying the symbolism of Har Magedon as meaning a place of gathering in troops, Walvoord[34] contends that it is also a literal and specific place, and that there is agreement that the location is near the Mount of Megiddo (in the northern part of Israel). Part of Walvoord's reasoning is that the final battle between good and evil will involve this place as a gathering place because there is a long history of battles that have been waged by Israel that has taken place at this location.

What This Bowl Means

This bowl means that the unholy Trinity will prepare the rebellious nations of the world to first battle each other, but as will be seen, they will join forces to mutually but unsuccessfully go against the Lord. This obviously will result in a catastrophic impact on humankind.

SEVENTH BOWL

Core Scripture: Revelation 16:17-21

Interpretation

Before the various aspects of this passage are examined, it should be noticed that in their totality, these verses announce and record the wrathful judgment that the saints of all time have waited for so long. The picture painted by this passage, as well as many others, describing the end of time is one of universal and comprehensive global coverage so that no thing or no person can escape from its implications and effects. This becomes the "… final act of God preceding the second coming of Christ."[35]

Bowl Poured Into the Air: Just as the contents of the first six bowls of judgment are not identified, neither is the bowl of this judgment, and after the initial mention, it is not mentioned again. Those Bible students that are naturally curious have to resist speculating as to what the contents of this bowl, as well as the seals, trumpets, and other bowls will be. Suffice it to say that whatever it will be will lead to a magnitude of catastrophic results as never seen by the earth or its inhabitants. There are several speculative observations that can be made here:

- The judgment being poured into the air could be in an allusion to Paul's statement in Ephesians 2:2 where Satan is identified as the ruler of the kingdom of the air (cf. Ephesians 6:12). This at least has some connection to the Bible in general.

- Another allusion might be the idea, which has precedence in Ezekiel 38:9 and 16 during Daniel's 70th Week, where the Lord comes as a storm coming that covers the earth.
- A truly speculative, and far-fetched, view is that this is a reference to military activities in the air because control of the skies (and space?) usually determines the victor in a conflict.

Loud Voice Saying, *It is done*: Just as the seventh trumpet sounded and a voice announced that the world belonged to the Lord, as soon as the contents of the seventh bowl is poured out, a voice is heard introducing the conclusion to history. This time the voice originates from the heavenly temple, presumably from the Lord Himself, loudly and emphatically announcing that the end is now present and that the release of His wrathful anger will be accomplished with the current judgment. All the anger that the Lord has suppressed for the centuries of rebellious human history has now been released, and as will be seen and is characteristic of the Lord, it is now (dispensationally) time to restart His program with humankind in another manner.

Lightning and Thunder: Just as the seventh seal was broken and the seventh trumpet sounded, as soon as the contents of the seventh bowl is poured out, flashes of lightning are seen and peals of thunder are heard introducing the judgment. It is without reservation that this display of natural forces in all likelihood will be overwhelmingly intense and fearfully demonstrable that something very unnatural is about to happen – quite possibly the ultimate and quintessential display of natural force.

Great and Mighty Earthquake: With a voice from the heavenly temple, flashes of lightning and peals of thunder as the prelude, and again as with the breaking of the seventh seal and the sounding of the seventh trumpet, as soon as the contents of the seventh bowl are poured out, a great and mighty earthquake occurs introducing this express judgment of God. This time the earthquake is described, as would be expected, the earth convulses, shakes, moves, and collapses on itself as never before – quite possibly the ultimate and quintessential an earthquake of unbelievable topographical change and awesome destruction and devastation.

Great City Split into Three Parts: The fact that an actual, literal earthquake causes destruction of a city strongly suggests that an actual, literal city will be destroyed. However, there is dispute as to which city will be the one that will be split into three parts, with there being three possibilities:
- Babylon: The most likely reference of this passage is that Babylon will be the great city that will be split apart. There are several reasons for taking this position:
  + Babylon is specifically identified in the same verse and is also referred to as a great city. It is further qualified as the special object of God's

235

wrath with the statement, *to give her the cup of the wine of His fierce wrath.*

+ There are numerous passages in the Old Testament prophets that very emphatically state that Babylon will be destroyed to such an extent someday that only animals will live in its ruins – a condition that has not occurred thus far.
+ The picture the prophecy paints of the global destruction is that it will be Gentile cities that are destroyed, as there is really only one real Jewish city of any significance – Jerusalem – and it will not be totally destroyed.
+ One of the more interesting reasons is that the Babylon is being rebuilt over its ancient ruins in southern Iraq, or at least it was in the process until the fall of the Hussein despotic government.

- Jerusalem: While it is true that Jerusalem is called a great city in Revelation 11:8, and will experience some amount of significant topographical changes in connection with the end time events as indicated in Zechariah 14:4, it does not appear to be totally destroyed as seems to be the clear implication of the seventh bowl judgment.
- Rome: The probability that the city of Rome will fulfill any end time prophecy is remote, and it does not seem to be in harmony with this passage.

Cities of the Nations Fall: Every city of the world will apparently be left in shambles, which, if the cities are destroyed, then the social, economic, cultural, and political infrastructure will be gone as well. The idea is that if something managed to survive earlier judgmental destructions, then it will be destroyed as a result of the seventh bowl.

Babylon the Great: Throughout the Bible, Babylon has been the antithesis of the holy city of Jerusalem, or God's city. Babylon represents all that opposes the Lord and that for which He stands. The destiny of Babylon is total annihilation because she has represented apostasy and rebellion for centuries.

Cup of the Wine of His Fierce Wrath: As has been pointed out since the beginning of this Chapter, the wrath that will be experienced by the earth is God's anger manifested in the form of wrathful judgments dispensed onto the world.

Demise of Islands and Mountains: In contrast to the sixth seal, which indicates that every island and mountain will be moved from its place, the impact of the seventh bowl is that every island and every mountain will be radically and violently changed to the point that it disappears. It is very possible that the appearance of the earth will not even begin to resemble the form that existed just before the seventh bowl.

One Hundred Pound Hailstones: And if all of this is not enough, giant hailstones, weighing approximately one hundred pounds each, will fall from heaven and will shred the surface of the earth. This aspect of the judgment is of the order of magnitude that is comparable to the devastation that fell on Sodom and Gomorrah centuries earlier, but instead it is universal, the hailstones fall over the entire earth.

Humankind Blasphemes God: In spite of indescribable death and unrealistic destruction, and the total and complete devastation of anything and everything human and natural, many of those people that somehow have managed to survive the horror will still remain unrepentant and will blaspheme and curse God, and will continue to shake their collective fist in His face. A portion of God's creation has now achieved ultimate apostasy. On a number of occasions in the Bible, God has demonstrated that He will have only just so much patience with rebellious humanity, at which time He will go no further with them, but instead will give them over to their destiny of eternal damnation.

Severity of the Plagues: One of the reasons that there will be some that blaspheme God in the end will be because He actually poured out severe punishments onto the earth and humankind. Ironically, God will not be rejected because some say He does not exist or other that He is not relevant, but because in their arrogance and pride, they will reject God because He did precisely what He said He would do, He judged them with plagues. It is very possible that they did not believe God would not do what He had been saying He would do for centuries.

What This Bowl Means

This bowl means that humankind has the willing ability to suffer and endure overwhelming tribulation of terrifying severity as has never existed on earth before, but yet, after all the evidence to the contrary they will remain unrepentant and pridefully defiant. Humankind is clearly divided into those that are for God and those that are against Him.

40

THE CAMPAIGN OF ARMAGEDDON

We are now at one of the most important milestone events (actually a series of events) in not only world human history, but in God's entire Plan for Israel, the Church, and the world. The logical and ultimate conclusion to the history of humankind's collective, universal, and continuing efforts to carve out individual and national lives without God will be detailed, which is the gathering of the apostate world for the war of the great day of God, the almighty – the Campaign of Armageddon. All the centuries of the twisting and turning of human existence converges at this single defining period of time in human history – when rebellious human and demonic beings, in spite of the fact that they are created in the image of their Creator, achieve ultimate apostasy by recognizing the existence of God but fully rejecting Him – and then as unbelievable as it may seem, attempt to kill the very One that created them.

Among the many observations that can be made and understandings that can be concluded about these events is that humankind, having reached its utmost apostate, sinful, and evil state of existence, will go out to meet the Lord Jesus Christ, the ultimately good, holy, and divine being, not to welcome His coming, but instead to arrogantly try to blot Him from their existence. Humankind, influenced and aided by Satan as he expends effort to accomplish divinity, reaches the ultimate point where there is nothing beyond divine self-declaration for which to strive which is the place where they can become their own god in order to determine their own earthly and final destiny. This is precisely why the times in which we live are so crucial – the world society seems to be reaching that very point.

One of the most difficult obstacles to a deep understanding of the grand plan of God that is revealed in Biblical prophecy is in what manner will Daniel's 70th Week terminate – it is obvious from even a casual reading of the Bible that there will be a final last battle between humankind and the returning Messiah, however, the Bible also reveals a number of other events and happenings that will occur about the same time the final battle occurs. A deeper understanding of God's revelation of this particular time in history begs an answer to the question: What is the chronological arrangement of the various movements of nations, military clashes, and major events presented in Scripture of what will happen during the Campaign of Armageddon that culminates in the return of Jesus Christ? Before we can develop a "best guess" sequence of events that would detail the Campaign of Armageddon, it is necessary to establish a basic understanding of the elements of the campaign first, by examining the primary passages associated with the campaign, then, by establishing the nature of the campaign, and finally, by exploring several theories of the sequence of end time events proposed by several trusted theologians.

40.1	THE PRIMARY PASSAGES

There are a number of passages that provide information regarding the Campaign of Armageddon, and it takes all of them to provide the details necessary to assemble a sequence of events.

DANIEL

The prophet Daniel provides the most detail about the various events associated with the Campaign of Armageddon in Chapter 11.

- 11:1-35: Daniel 11 reveals numerous predictions about selective parts of the history of Israel beginning with Darius the Mede (539 BC) and extending up to the last Gentile ruler of the revived Roman Empire which is still in the future.
  + The predictions in verses 1-35 involve about 200 years of Israel's history, and all of the predictions have been historically verified. "[V]erses 1-35, describes the major rulers of the Persian Empire and then gives in great detail some of the major events of the third empire following Alexander the Great, concluding with Antiochus Epiphanes (175-164 BC)."[1]
  + Daniel 11 is one of the reasons that Daniel, is a controversial book, because there are some who believe the book was written years after the events recorded had transpired thereby eliminating the prophetic character of the book (they see it as a book of history instead of as a book of prophecy about the future). Without going into considerable detail, there is sufficient justification for the book to have been written decades before the events transpired.
  + "The entire period from the death of Antiochus Epiphanes to the time of the end is skipped over with no reference to events of the present church age ..."[2]
- 11:36-45: There is an interesting point here that supports the fact of Israel's future existence. When Israel ceased to exist in 70 AD, the predictions in Daniel 11:36-45 remained unfulfilled, and as we already know, because God is reliable, then all promises, good and bad, have to be fulfilled eventually, therefore, Israel has to exist again as a nation in order for the events of verses 36-45 to take place. The events have no confirmation with any historical events including Antiochus Epiphanes therefore they are considered prophetic revelation of events yet future in Israel's history. "[V]erses 36-45 deals with the last Gentile ruler who will be in power when Christ comes in His second advent."[3]

+ 11:36-39: The last Gentile ruler that is mentioned cannot be Antiochus Epiphanes because the information after verse 35 is not substantiated by his role in history; also, it does not match any other ruler since Antiochus. This passage provides insight into the nature of this last Gentile ruler.
  o Four characteristics are recorded by Daniel, which will distinguish this king from the other kings:
    - This last Gentile ruler will assume the role of absolute authority.
    - This last Gentile ruler will consider himself to be the only god, supreme above others.
    - This last Gentile ruler will blaspheme the True God.
    - This last Gentile ruler will prosper until the things that are decreed for him come to an end when the wrath is completed.
  o Other characteristics that will be found in this last Gentile ruler include the following:
    - This last Gentile ruler will not give any credibility to the gods worshipped by his fathers. It should be noted that the Hebrew word used here for gods is *Elohim*, which in this context is a general reference to all deity – the last Gentile ruler rejects the True God as well as false gods. Also, the last Gentile ruler will not regard the god of women, which is a difficult phrase to interpret; it probably has much to do with the normal desire of Jewish women to be the mother of the Messiah. Finally, this last Gentile ruler will exalt himself above all other gods.
    - This last Gentile ruler will honor the military might and the ability to make war – he is a leader of war.
    - This last Gentile ruler will not follow the tradition of previous generations, and instead of desiring divine qualities, he will be materialistic and will be attracted to expensive things.
    - This last Gentile ruler will honor, or perhaps reward, those that are loyal to him with positions of authority, or with gifts of land probably taken by earlier conquests, especially if they are accompanied by money or brides.
  o "Taking the passage Daniel 11:36-39 as a whole, it is apparent that the revelation provides an incisive analysis of the combination of materialism, militarism, and religion, all of which will be embodied in the final world ruler."[4]
  o The various prophecies of the end times are in harmony if this last Gentile ruler is the same as the little horn of Daniel 7:8, 20-25, the king of the revived Fourth Empire – The Imperialist (Roman) Empire, and at the same time the beast out of the sea in Revelation 13:1-10 – the Antichrist.

+ 11:40-45: This passage provides insight into the personality of the last Gentile ruler. As will be seen below, these verses will provide revelation of the various military exploits that will occur between this ruler and other nations.

  o The words *he, him,* and *his*: There is debate about the identification of the antecedent for the words *he, him,* and *his* of this passage. Some believe that once the *king of the north,* 11:40b, appears, then all the occurrences of *he, him,* and *his* are to this king; and, it is the king of the north that establishes a camp in the land of Israel as indicated in 11:45. "[I]t is preferable to take the "he" as referring to the king of 11:36, the world ruler ..." which "... seems to be most in keeping to the entire tenor of this passage ..."[5]

  o 11:40-43: The nations move against each other and the final world war erupts over the land of Israel.

    - Verse 40 begins with an indication that military conflicts involving many of the nations of the world at that time, described in the verses that follow, will occur at the time of the end. This connects verses 36-45, which are about events that are still future to our time, with those of 2-35, which describe events that have happened in our past (but future to Daniel when he wrote the book). Daniel seems to skip from time to time that history has recorded the fulfillment of the prophecies that were recorded (Antiochus Epiphanes persecuted the Jews), ending about 150 years before Christ, to a monumental event that will be a very short time before Christ returns a second time – could it be that this indicative of a time period that interrupts the flow of God's relationship with Israel, the Church age? This also indicates another very important characteristic regarding Biblical prophecy. The prophetic statements enumerate in verses 2 through 35, numbering approximately 135 according to Walvoord[6], have been recorded by history to have been literally fulfilled in the manner described, therefore, there is every expectation that the prophetic statements listed in verses 36 through 45 will also come to pass.

    - It is conceivable that the earlier invasion by the Ezekiel 38 – 39, the Northern Confederacy just before the mid-point of Daniel's 70th Week is the reason that the forces of the Antichrist are present in the land to prevent another similar occurrence when the Kings of the South and the North come against him

    - The final conflict at the end of Daniel's 70th Week begins with an initial attack by the King of the South against the Antichrist located in the land of Israel; the sense is that the attacker will "engage in thrusting" against the attacked. Then, the kings of the North will storm against the Antichrist with what might be a force large than possessed by the force from the south. The passage lists three methods of attack, chariots, horsemen, and many ships. As seen so many times in the detailed study of the Book of Revelation, caution has to be exercised before these methods of attack are interpreted, and care is necessary so that newspaper interpretation is avoided. Suffice it to say that the attack will be a multifaceted attack utilizing land and sea resources. The fact that the Kings of the North not only appear to have considerable military resources, the Antichrist must have many more resources.

- There seems to be a disagreement within verse 40. First, the passage says that the two Kings will *collide* (in the case of the King of the South) and *storm* (in the case of the King of the North) against *him* (the Antichrist), however later in the verse, it says that he will *enter, overflow*, and *pass through* many lands, or according to the NET Bible *will invade lands, passing through them like an overflowing river*. The sense is that the Antichrist's forces, while they appear to be present in the land of Israel may be in the form of bases, apparently are not an occupying force within Israel. When the Antichrist and/or the protected nation of Israel are the target of a coordinated attack by the other major world powers, the Antichrist responds militarily by counterattacking the surrounding countries. The implication is that the Antichrist successfully defends the kingdom he rules, the revived Imperialistic (Roman) Empire, as well as the nation of Israel, by invading the invaders; while the Scriptures do not indicate specifically, the invaders are defeated and conquered.

- In addition to the successful defeat of the invading forces, the Antichrist will then turn his attention to the *Beautiful Land*. He will enter the surrounding lands (nations) and many will fall, with the exception of the lands of Edom, Moab, and Ammon. The Antichrist will extend his power (political control?) over these lands, and he will possess the monetary wealth of Egypt, which was indicated to have been hidden for an unexplained reason.

- The implication is that a conquering force occupies an amount of the Middle East region that is not quantified in the passage beyond the mention of several nations. The occupancy of nations will be considerable.

- The *Beautiful Land* is identified in Ezekiel 20:6, as the land that God would bring the Israelites to out of Egypt, a land *selected for them, flowing with milk and honey, with is the*

243

glory of all lands. In Malachi 3:12, God tells Israel that the land He gives to Israel is a *delightful land*. Finally, Daniel himself used this reference in two other verses, 8:9 and 11:16, to indicate that others will invade and occupy the land given them by God.

- There will be three countries that are not invaded, Edom, Moab, and Ammon, which are part of modern-day Jordan.
- Apparently after all of this, additional nations will submit to the Antichrist's formidable power, including Libya and Ethiopia (identified as the Nubians in the NIV).

+ 11:44-45: This passage sets the stage for what will be the final confrontation among the world's nations.

 o Apparently at such time that the previous activities have been completed to some extent, the Antichrist receives reports (NIV and NET), or hears of rumors (NASB), that there is a military force moving in his direction this time from the east and again from the north.

 - The implication is that these forces must be considerable, otherwise why would the Antichrist become concerned. Actually, concerned is an understatement – this passage indicates that the Antichrist *will go forth with great wrath to destroy and annihilate many* (*great rage* in the NIV and *tremendous rage* in the NET). However, the passage does not indicate what lands, nations or peoples will be the object of his rage, nor does it say that his rage will be focused on the new invading forces.

 - "The tidings out of the east probably refer to the gigantic invasion described in Revelation 9:13-21; cf. 16:12."[7] Revelation 16:12 indicates that as the result of the pouring out of the sixth bowl judgment, the Euphrates River will dry up to allow for the Kings of the East to cross unimpeded. Earlier, in Revelation 9:16, an army of two hundred millions soldiers are seen within the context of the sixth trumpet judgment regarding events associated with the Euphrates River.

 - This particular passage does not provide details regarding the confrontation between the Antichrist's forces and these forces from the East and the North.

 o The Antichrist will locate his headquarters, his center of operations, or his base, between the Mediterranean Sea and the Dead Sea, at or near the beautiful Holy Mountain, the Temple Mount in the Old City of Jerusalem.

 o Finally, Daniel closes with the observation that the Antichrist will come to his end at this place, and no one will come to his aid when he is conquered for the obvious reason that it will be the Son of God that will do away with him.

ZECHARIAH

The Prophet Zechariah contributes to the Campaign of Armageddon the fact that the city of Jerusalem will be made a burden to the world.
- 12:1-9: The God that creates the world, the universe, and human beings, says that He will use the city of Jerusalem as the centerpiece cause for His judgments of the nations of the world.
  + In this passage, five times it is mentioned that these events will take place *in that day*, or at the time of the Day of the Lord, which will be at the Campaign of Armageddon.
  + The nations that surround Jerusalem will be made dizzy, as if they were intoxicated, because of the heavy burden that God's city has become to them.
  + In spite of the fact that the city belongs to God, the nations of the world will try to destroy it however all that they will succeed in doing is invoking God's anger and wrath as He in turn destroys them.
  + However, during that time of death and destruction, God will protect the inhabitants of the city from harm.
- 14:1-8: Again, the Lord indicates that He will gather nations against the city of Jerusalem.
  + In this passage, seven times it is mentioned that these events will take place *in that day*, or at the time of the Day of the Lord, which will be the Campaign of Armageddon.
  + At first, the nations will appear to be conquering the city because of the violence and plundering. One-half of Jerusalem's inhabitants will go into exile, while the remainder will stay in the city.
  + Then the Lord will go to battle for Jerusalem against the nations that have attacked her. When Jesus Christ stands once again on the Mount of Olives, He will do so as Israel's Savior and Messiah.
  + Then an earthquake will split Jerusalem in half, east and west, centered on the Mount of Olives, with one side going to the north and the other side going to the south. The valley created will be the path that the inhabitants of Jerusalem will use to escape the siege.

REVELATION
- 12:13-17: Throughout the Bible it has been Satan's intent to pursue and make every effort to attack and destroy God's chosen nation of Israel. When he is cast out of heaven at the midpoint of Daniel's 70th Week, and he realizes that he only has a short time left to do his evil work, he increases his pursuit to the point of worldwide persecution. "Thus, we find that the middle of the seven-year Tribulation period, or three and a half years before the Lord Jesus Christ comes back to earth, there is going to be a movement of unprecedented fierceness and wrath that will try to exterminate every Jew who is living at that time."[8]

- 16:13: As part of the sixth bowl judgment, three demonic spirits, described *as three unclean spirits like frogs*, which go out from the Unholy Trinity to gather the nations of the world to battle against Israel. Pentecost[9] astutely puts the purposes of Satan into sharp perspective: "The Lord Jesus Christ is coming to reign on the earth over the seed of Abraham and the seed of David. If Jesus Christ reigns, it is evident that Satan is no longer a world ruler. Satan's purpose is to wipe out every Jew so there will be no kingdom people over whom Jesus Christ can reign. And if Christ has no Jewish nation over which He can reign, Satan could continue as the world ruler. To defeat God's purpose of setting His Son Jesus Christ on the throne of this earth to reign, Satan attempts to wipe out the people of the throne so there can be no earthly kingdom."

40.2	THE NATURE OF THE CAMPAIGN OF ARMAGEDDON

THE CHARACTER OF THE CAMPAIGN OF ARMAGEDDON

Actually the title of this chapter is somewhat inaccurate on several points, and a bit of clarification is necessary.

- First, while all conclusions are essentially ultimate, the march of time will actually prove that all "conclusions" prior to the Second Coming of Jesus Christ will be anything but ultimate - they will be semi-ultimate. Nations, tribes, and peoples - the basic structure of the division of human beings into groupings to form human civilization - that were thought to have "concluded" in reality only changed form - one civilization turned into another civilization, and so on, and the only thing that really changes is the political, economic, or social conditions under which the people live. Human civilization as a whole does not change; it evolves, in spite of the finality that seems to be recorded by history. But the Campaign of Armageddon is different. It will be the event that will conclude all other conclusions - human civilization as it has been known from its beginning will fundamentally terminate as all that have lived will face the Creator and be judged. Thus, the ultimate conclusion.
- Second, as has been indicated throughout this book, the Campaign of Armageddon will be the ultimate form of human civilization attempting to live without God. The conditions that will exist on earth at the time will be such that humankind, the creation of a Creator, will not be able to reject the creator to any extent beyond what they will have and it will not be possible to be any more defiant than what they will be. It will be the logical and ultimate conclusion to human existence without God.
- Third, while it is true that the vast majority of Christianity believers that the ultimate conclusion of apostate human history will occur at a place identified as Armageddon in an isolated military conflict between good and

evil, it is also more accurate to understand that the place Armageddon is only one part of a series of end times events that culminates with the Lord Jesus Christ standing permanently and victoriously on the earth forever. As will be discussed below, Armageddon is the place where the campaign comes together and from where the campaign against the Jews is launched that ends in the final battle, hence the reason for the identification as the "Campaign" of Armageddon, the implication being that it will be a series of related events," Pentecost[10] makes the observation that the Greek word for *battle* is *polemos* in Revelation 16:14 is more accurately interpreted as the word for campaign - thus, the demon spirits are to go to the kings of the earth and bring them into a campaign that will end with *the war of the great day of God, the Almighty*.

THE VARIOUS LOCATIONS ASSOCIATED WITH THE CAMPAIGN

Har Magedon, or the Mount of Megiddo
Core Scripture: Revelation 16:16

The location of the gathering will be in the valley on the west side of *Har Magedon*, or the Mount of Megiddo, a valley which is part of the Esdraelon Plain and the Valley of Jezreel geographical complex. A commanding view of the valley below is possible for this mount, or more accurately, a hilltop.
- This valley has a long history of being either the gathering place or the site of numerous military campaigns between the nations of antiquity. Indeed, Israel has been involved, successfully and unsuccessfully, in many battles in this area throughout the nations' history. In fact, military experts have described the valley at the location of the gathering as the perfect location for a massive military battle.
- According to Baly[11] regarding the geography of the Middle East, the area around and in Israel was crucial to the travel between the nations of the known world. God placed His chosen nation in the very place that represented one of the only land connections between Asia, to the north and everything beyond, and the entire African continent. Keeping in mind that the tiny nation of Israel is bracketed between the Mediterranean Sea, on the west, and the great desert, on the east and south, until the advent of mechanized transportation, the only path of travel north and south was over this tiny land bridge. Interestingly, *Har Magedon* itself is located at one of the only places where there was a crossing of two of the major routes of the ancient world.
  + Dominant Route: The most pronounced path of travel was via the Great Trunk Road, which passes through Gaza in the south, Ascalon, Megiddon, Hazor, and Damascus in the north.

247

> + Subdominant Road: Probably the second most pronounced path of travel was via the Water-Parting Route, which passes through Beersheba in the south, Hebron, Jerusalem, Megiddon, Tyre, and Sidon in the north. The point is, as Israel can be established to be at the "center" of the earth, Har Magedon can be seen as the crossroads of the nations of the earth.

- While Scripture does not specifically indicate that a military confrontation will actually occur at this location, it is not beyond the realm of that possibility because when the conflict does starts it will be spread over two hundred miles of Israel, with *Har Magedon* being at the north most end.

Jerusalem
Core Scripture: Zechariah 12:2-11 and 14:2

The city of Jerusalem will play the center, around which the Campaign of Armageddon plays out.

Babylon
Core Scripture: Revelation 17 - 18

As has been indicated throughout this book, the Bible seems to indicate that the ancient city of Babylon will one day exist as a functioning city again and will be very important to the Antichrist and his empire.

Valley of Jehoshaphat
Core Scripture: Joel 3:2 and 12

As indicated elsewhere in this chapter, this valley will be the place that the Lord will bring the enemies of Israel in order to judge them. While there are some who believe the mention of this valley is symbolic because its name means "the Lord judges," there are many others that believe that this judgment will be in an actual valley with that name, as is the position of this book.

In ancient Israel, there was a valley that extended east from Jerusalem over to the east of Jordan and then northward. There was a trade route that followed this valley that connected Jerusalem to Assyria in the north. Today, this valley is identified with the Kidron Valley and is used by the Jews as burial grounds.

Edom or Idumea
Core Scripture: Isaiah 34:5-17 and 63:1-6

Edom, southeast of Jerusalem, is mentioned as one of the places in which there will be a battle between Christ and the nations. Because of its history of conflict with Israel (descendants from Jacob), Edom (descendants from Esau) symbolically represents all the heathen nations that attempt to harm Israel. As the counterpoint to Israel, Isaac told Esau that he would live in an infertile land (Genesis 27:39-40) and would be a perpetual enemy of Israel (refer to Ezekiel 35 and 26:5). The Bible speaks of this nation being destroyed and desolated at the time of the Day of the Lord.

THE POWERS PARTICIPATING IN THE CAMPAIGN

The Bible clearly identifies the various groups of powers that will be arrayed in battle during the latter part of Daniel's 70th Week.

- The Antichrist and His Forces, or the King of the West: While the title the "King of the West" does not appear in Scripture, it is used here to distinguish the Antichrist from the other kings. The passages that are pertinent to the Campaign of Armageddon do not specifically mention the Ten Nation Confederacy by name, however, the Bible does indicate, and this book has established that, there will be a political world power that will have evolved out of the earlier Roman Empire, that will be led by the Antichrist who will have political, economic, and military control.
- The Kings of the Earth: In Revelation 16:13-16, as part of the sixth bowl judgment the Unholy Trinity sends out three demonic emissaries to bring the Kings of the Earth, presumably their military forces, to the place in north Israel called *Har Magedon*. These kings are political rulers over the whole known inhabited earth. In the absence of more Scriptural information, this phrase is held to be a plural reference to all the other powers that will participate in the campaign other than the Antichrist's empire.
- The Kings of the North: While many theologians believe that the Kings of the North is the same force as the Northern Confederacy of Ezekiel 38 - 39, which will be led by Gog/Magog (Russia), near the end of Daniel's 70th Week, there is at least one scholar that believes otherwise.
    + Walvoord contends that two separate events are being indicated. "The chronology of Daniel 11:36-39 refers to the period of world rule, and, therefore, is later than Ezekiel 38 and 39. Hence, it may be concluded that the battle described here, beginning with verse 40, is a later development. If Russian forces are involved in the phrase, "the king of the north," it would indicate that, in the period between the two battles, Russia is able to reassemble an army and once again participates in a military way in this great war."[12]
    + It is interesting to note the belief of Pentecost[13] who contends that, immediately before the midpoint of Daniel's 70th Week the King of the South will initiate a military action against Israel and will be joined by the Kings of the North who is also the Northern Confederacy of Ezekiel 38 - 39. The Lord will supernaturally eliminate the Kings of the North, the Ezekiel passage makes no mention of a force from the south, nor does it indicate if the King of the South is eliminated as well.
- The Kings of the East: While referenced in Revelation 16:12, not much is known about this confederacy. It appears to be a coalition of unidentified

Asiatic nations that will originate from beyond (east of) the Euphrates River, or more literally, from the land of the sunrising. Fruchtenbaum contends that these kings will be Mesopotamian in origin.

- The King of the South: Mentioned in Daniel 11:40, unlike the Kings of the North and the Kings of the East which appear to be alliances, coalitions, or confederations, this unidentified nation is singular in reference and it is typically Egypt. There is the likelihood that like the other powers, this King may be nations or forces in addition to Egypt; in fact, some believe it will be a grouping of some sort of African nations. Because of the coordinated invasion, this power will probably be allied to some extent with the Kings of the North.
- The Lord and His Army: As will be explored in the next chapter, when Jesus Christ returns to the earth, He will come in kingly power and He will bring His heavenly army of saints when He comes.

40.3 THE CAMPAIGN SEQUENCE OF EVENTS

Fruchtenbaum[14] has proposed a specific sequence of events that he identifies as The Eight Stages of the Campaign of Armageddon.

- Prelude to the Eight Stages: Daniel 11:40-45 is said to occur immediately prior to the end of Daniel's 70th Week, as a world war between the Antichrist, seeking to consolidate rulership of the world into a one world government with him as the self-declared leader, and the Ten Nation Confederacy, first allies with the Antichrist, but now in opposition to him. The Antichrist and his forces will be headquartered in the land between the Mediterranean Sea and the Temple Mount.

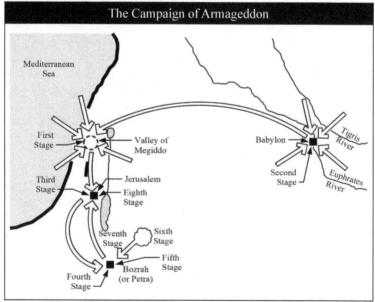

- First Stage – The Assembling of the Allies of the Antichrist:
    + According to Revelation 16:12-16, the sixth bowl judgment causes the Euphrates River to dry up, in order for the kings of the East to move against Babylon and on toward Israel.
    + Satan, the Antichrist, and the False Prophet each send out an impure, demonic spirit, which will look like frogs, to collectively command the kings of the earth to be gathered at Armageddon to prepare for the final world war. Consequently, the kings of the world will gather their armies at Armageddon. The kings in this passage are believed to the seven kings that have been under the authority of the Antichrist since the middle of Daniel's 70th Week.
    + Regarding the two hundred million mounted troops mentioned in Revelation 9:16-17, many believe they are the armies that come from the East (popular belief is that they originate in China who publicly announced they can field an army of two hundred million soldiers) to participate in the Campaign. However, this is not Scriptural. The two hundred million mounted troops are part of the sixth trumpet judgment and are told to kill one third of humankind on earth. And the drying up of the Euphrates River is part of the sixth bowl judgment. As discussed in Section 38.3, the two hundred million of the sixth trumpet judgment are believed to be demonic hordes, while the armies of the East of the sixth bowl judgment are human beings. These are two distinct and separate prophecies.
- Second Stage – The Destruction of Babylon: With Zechariah 5:5-11 as the justification, Babylon will be literally rebuilt and will function as the political and economic center as well as the capital city for the Antichrist; see Chapter 41. As the kings of the east move to the west, they are responsible for the destruction of Babylon after the Antichrist has left his capital city bound for *Har Magedon*, as recorded in Isaiah 13:1 – 14:23, Jeremiah 50 – 51, and Revelation 18:1-24.
- Third Stage – The Fall of Jerusalem: Based on Zechariah 12:1-9 and 14:1-2, the armies of the Antichrist will move south to go against Jerusalem for the purpose of destroying it, however, the victory will not come easily due to Jewish resistance and losses to the Antichrist's forces, however, Jerusalem will fall and there will be brutality, plundering, and half the population will go into exile. Thus, Jerusalem will be a burdensome stone to the nations of the world as predicted, and Gentile domination of the city will continue.
- Fourth Stage – The Armies of the Antichrist at Bozrah: By this time the main concentration of Jews will not be in Israel or Jerusalem, but instead will be in the land of Edom at a place called Bozrah according to Jeremiah 49:13-14 and Micah 2:12.
- Fifth Stage – The National Regeneration of Israel: Before the Lord's return, the nation of Israel must satisfy two requirements. First, they must confess of their national sin which will last for two days (Leviticus 26:40-42; Jeremiah 3:11-18; Hosea 5:15 – 6:3), by confessing their earlier attitude

toward Jesus Christ (Isaiah 53:1-9), thus saving the entire nation (Romans 11:25-27). Second, they must plead for the Lord's return, which will last for one day (Psalm 79:1-13; 80:1-19; Isaiah 64:1-12; Zechariah 12:10 – 13:1; Matthew 23:37-39). Israel will be regenerated (Joel 2:28-32), false prophets will be executed (Zechariah 13:2-6); and the basic reason for the tribulation is explained (Zechariah 13:7-9).

- Sixth Stage – The Second Coming of Jesus Christ: At the request of the nation of Israel, Jesus Christ will return to earth (Psalm 18:8-16; Habakkuk 3:1-19). First, He will go to Bozrah (Isaiah 34:1-7; 63:1-6; Habakkuk 3:3; Micah 2;12-13; and possibly Judges 5;4-5), and He will arrive as being in the clouds of heaven (Matthew 24:30; Acts 1:9-11; Revelation 19:1-16) and accompanied by armies (Matthew 16:27; Jude 14-15) to judge the rebellious (Ezekiel 39:17-20; Revelation 19:17-21).

- Seventh Stage – The Battle from Bozrah to the Valley of Jehoshaphet: The battle between the Antichrist and Christ, while it will begin at Bozrah, it will apparently extend all the way back to the Valley of Jehoshaphet, which is on the eastern side of the old city of Jerusalem, and also known as the Kidron Valley. The Antichrist will be among the first causalities (Habakkuk 3:13b and 2 Thessalonians 2:8), he will enter into hell (Isaiah 14:3-11), and his dead body will be viewed on earth (Isaiah 14:16-21). Then so many of the Antichrist's army will be killed (Joel 3:12-13 and Zechariah 14:12-15) that massive quantities of blood will fill the landscape for 200 miles (Jeremiah 49:20-22). Thus, ends the fighting and dying of rebellious humankind.

- Eighth Stage – The Victor's Ascent up upon the Mount of Olives: Jesus Christ ascends up to the Mount of Olives (Zechariah 14:3-4a), and at the same time the seventh bowl judgment is poured out onto the earth (Revelation 16:17-21) that includes an earthquake that splits Jerusalem into a northern part and a secondary part, with a river running between the two (Joel 3:14-17; Zechariah 14:4b-5; and Matthew 24:29). And thus ends the Great Tribulation.

40.4 THE BATTLE FROM BOZRAH TO THE VALLEY OF JEHOSHAPHAT

The very first place that Jesus Christ goes upon His return to earth is in the land of Edom, more specifically the city of Bozrah, to rescue those Jews that were among the one-half of the population that fled Jerusalem when the Antichrist's armies were about to crush the city. Among the major theologians cited in this book, Fruchtenbaum stands alone in the belief that Bozrah is the first stop on Christ's return itinerary. So, in an effort to understand a possible sequence of events that seems to be consistent with the various individual activities described in the Bible, we will explore the view of Fruchtenbaum.

The Antichrist has moved his armies to the area around the place of refuge and the Jews are at risk of being attacked again. "Since the main purpose of the

Campaign of Armageddon is the annihilation of the Jews, the armies of the world will move southward from Jerusalem to Bozrah as Jeremiah 49:13-14 makes clear."[15] Fruchtenbaum also believes that Micah 2:12 supports the notion that the Antichrist will move against Bozrah.

Upon the appearance of Jesus Christ and His divine forces, they will proceed immediately to Bozrah and engage in battle with the Antichrist and his forces to rescue the Jews that are in refuge. In spite of the fact that he has attempted to rule the world with tyrannical force, the Antichrist himself is said to be one of the first causalities of the conflict.

- The one that the world worshipped as having more power than anyone could stand up to, now becomes powerless and immediately falls before the all-powerful Lord Jesus Christ. Habakkuk 3:13b anticipates a divine warrior that will strike down the wicked leader, and Paul's description of the lawless one in 2 Thessalonians 2:8 includes the fact that he will be destroyed by the breath of the Lord. "The one who has claimed to be god, the one who has been able to perform all kinds of miracles, signs, and wonders, the one who exercised all the authority of Satan as he ruled the world, will be quickly dispensed with by the word of the Lord Jesus Christ."[16]
- The spirit of the Antichrist descends into hell and is detailed in Isaiah 14:3-11 that makes the point that the Jews will taunt him about the strength of the Lord being greater than his, about how the world rejoices over his death even though be ruled the world at one time, and how he will pompously enter hell at the surprise of all the other previously powerful rulers that are now eternal residents of the fiery thereafter.
- The body of the dead Antichrist will be viewed by the world in utter disbelief that he died as easily as described in Isaiah 14:16-21. The body will not be buried, in fact the Antichrist's armies will trample it, and the families of the Antichrist's armies will trample it, and the family of the Antichrist will be destroyed to prevent another such person from coming from them.
- The Lord and His armies will continue to battle and will slaughter the remaining forces of the world as can be seen from Zechariah 14:12-15 which describes a horrible death for both warriors and their animals of burden. There will be three weapons used against the Antichrist's armies:
- Zechariah 14:12 and 15 - A Plague: The Lord will strike the combatants with a disease of sickness that will be so devastating as to seemingly cause death due to physical deterioration: their flesh will decay, their eyes will rot, and their tongues will dissolve. There are some interpreters that try to justify that nuclear weapons will be used during the Campaign based on this passage. While there are other passages that certainly leave open the possibility that some form of nuclear explosion could cause the magnitude of destruction described, especially in the Book of Revelation, this passage is talking about the method of destruction that will be used by the Lord. It does not seem plausible that the Lord would need to use nuclear weapons

if He is able to destroy by the word of His mouth. It could be that the effect of His word will be as also made by a nuclear blast.

- Zechariah 14:13 - A Great Confusion: While the nature is not revealed, the Lord will strike the armies with a great panic (see adjacent table for word used in various translations) that will cause the combatants to turn on each other. Those that have had the

Zechariah 14:13	
NIV	*great panic*
NASB	*great panic*
NET	*great confusion*
KJV	*great tumult*
NKJV	*great panic*
AMP	*A great confusion, comfiture, and panic*

unfortunate distinction of having participated in warfare know just how easily it is for confusion to run rampant across a battlefield.
- Zechariah 14:14 - The Jews Fight Back: While it is a matter of speculation whether the Jews will be supernaturally empowered to fight back again their enemies as some believe, this verse certainly indicates that Judah will fight alongside Jerusalem against their oppressors, possible rallied by the Lord and His armies. The Jews will take much plunder that is possibly the plunder that the Gentiles originally took from them.

The battle between the forces of righteousness and the forces of unrighteousness will extend from the area of Bozrah, in the south, to the north to the Valley of Jehoshaphat on the east side of Jerusalem as detailed in Joel 3:12-13. Set within the context of a call to war for the purpose of judgment, this passage indicates that nations that are the enemies of God are to be roused and will participate in a battle of judgment from the Lord in the Valley of Jehoshaphat. Agricultural imagery is used to describe the manner of judgment that will be a part of the Campaign of Armageddon:
- Harvesting with a Sickle: The nations will be judged by the same type of judgment as described in Revelation 14:15-20.
- Stomping on Grapes: A common metaphor for the judgment of wickedness, the stomping of grapes in a winepress clearly indicates that the lifeblood of living creatures will be crushed out of them in the same sense as in Revelation 14:17-20.

Joel 2:12 specifically mentions the Valley of Jehoshaphat as the place where there will be harvesting of grapes and stomping of them in the winepress, and Revelation 14:20 refers to the same activity will occur outside of the city. The city is considered to be Jerusalem, and the place outside of the city would be the Valley of Jehoshaphat. So, the sense of the final great battle between the Antichrist's armies and the Lord and His armies could take the following form:
- When Jerusalem is conquered by the Antichrist, one-half of the Jews will evacuate the city and will go to Bozrah as their place of refuge.
- The Antichrist will apparently pursue them with his armies.

- The armies of the Antichrist and his allies will probably be arrayed in one of two ways in order for the magnitude of carnage described in Revelation 14:20 to be possible:
  + Some or all of the forces all move from Jerusalem to Bozrah and the final battle occurs as the armies retreat back from Bozrah to Jerusalem.
  + The forces are arrayed throughout the land between the Valley of Jehoshaphat and Bozrah, and the final battle occurs all along this distance.

We come finally to a concluding verse of sorts that describes an especially horrendous scene that will be the result of all this judgment. Revelation 14:20 says that the depth of blood that will be poured out of the winepress will be about four or five feet in depth for a distance of about two hundred miles. We know that the Lord and His divine forces will be victorious and all of the blood will be from the allied armies that banded together to oppose the Lord. We also know that as implied by Zechariah 14:16 there will be survivors of this battle. There are several theories of the extent of the land mass that will be covered by the blood, all of which are about two hundred miles in length.

- It will extend from the Valley of Jehoshaphat in the north, as the original gathering place of the allied forces, to the area around Bozrah south of Jerusalem, where the battle begins. However, there is no mention in the Bible of any combat occurring north of Jerusalem.
- "… [I]t refers to the round-trip distance between Jerusalem and Bozrah. The fighting will begin at Jerusalem and move to Bozrah (100 miles), and with the second coming of Christ, will return back from Bozrah to the Valley of Jehoshaphat (another 100 miles)."[17]
- Fruchtenbaum[18] also proposes that Jeremiah 49:20-22 indicates that the blood will extend from Bozrah to the south to empty into the Red Sea near present-day cities of Eilat and Akaba, which is about two hundred miles south of Jerusalem.

40.5 THE DEFEAT OF THE ANTICHRIST AND THE ARMIES OF THE WORLD

Several aspects of the defeat of the Antichrist have already been examined, however, the central passage of the conflict between the good forces and the evil forces, Revelation 19:17-21, needs to be explored in more detail.

- Revelation 19:17: Immediately after detailing the vision of the Glorious Return that he sees, John turns to a description of the battle that begins with an angel standing in the sun calling for the birds of the sky to come and feast at the great banquet of God that is about to happen.
  + Angel Standing in the Sun: The occurrence could very well be a supernatural event, however, it is more likely that the angel is standing in the light of the sun, possibly a ray of the sun, or maybe the angel is actually projecting light as is seen in other instances in the Bible.

The effect is probably one of brilliance while the word of the Lord is being spoken.

+ Shouting in a Loud Voice: There have been a number of times in the Book of Revelation where an angel has made a vocal pronouncement in a loud, or shouting, voice, signifying something of importance. This time the call is to the birds of the sky, most likely to carrion birds, which are like vultures, which fly high in the sky and circle around places of food.

+ Gather Around the Great Banquet of God: The angel is calling the birds to gather around so that they may feast on those of the Antichrist's armies that are about to die.

- Revelation 19:18: The birds of prey (symbolically used as evidence of death) are invited to feast on the forthcoming flesh, to be made available by the Lord, of a wide range of people that are present for the battle: generals, powerful people, horses and riders, free and enslaved people, and great and small people. "The divine judgment upon the wicked is not a respecter of persons or station, and is the great equalizer of all."[19] Jesus includes a similar reference to this future scene in Matthew 24:28.

- Revelation 19:19: John sees the beast, the Antichrist, and the kings of the earth and their armies, the forces allied with the Antichrist, arrayed for the battle with the Lord and His forces.

- Revelation 19:20: The great and final battle between good and evil that has long been anticipated is at hand. While there is no indication of how long the battle will last, or the nature of the skirmish, the Antichrist and the false prophet, the ones convicted by Jesus as being deceivers of those human beings that accepted the mark of the beast and worshipped evilness, are seized and together are thrown into the lake of fire burning with sulfur, or brimstone. In response to why they were not thrown into Sheol, or hell, Walvoord offers this explanation: "comparison with other scripture, it seems that the beast and the false prophet are the first to inhabit the lake of fire. Unsaved who die prior to this time are cast into Hades, a place of torment, but not into the lake of fire, which is reserved for those who have been finally judged as unworthy of eternal life."[20]

- Revelation 19:21: This last verse concludes the chapter with the point that the remainder of the armies will be killed by the sword from Jesus' mouth, and the birds of prey feasted on their dead flesh. Thus, the judging warfare associated with the Campaign of Armageddon comes to an end. "There is no evidence that the armies of earth prevail in any sense against the armies of heaven, but there is total defeat of man at the height of his satanic power when brought into conflict with the omnipotence of God."[21]

40.6 THE VICTORY ASCENT UP TO THE MOUNT OF OLIVES

For all practical purposes, the sequence of events of the formal return of Jesus Christ will finish when He ascends upon the Mount of Olives to fulfill the angels words recorded in Acts 1:11. The Bible does not mention nor disclose the amount of time that will elapse between the beginning of Christ's glorious return and the completion of the battles of the Campaign of Armageddon. Likely it will be a few hours or maybe a couple of days. Nevertheless, after the final battle is completed and the armies of the world are defeated, Jesus Christ will stand on the Mount of Olives as described in Zechariah 14:3-4a. Note that the sense of the timing expressed in this passage suggests all will happen in the span of a single day.

While it is not a major theological issue, there is some debate as to if Jesus Christ comes to the Mount of Olives as His very first stop, or if it will be later in the sequence of events. It seems that the perception of most Christians is that He will set foot on the Mount first according to Acts 1:11, however, the verse does not specifically indicate that this will be so. As already indicated, Fruchtenbaum[22] takes this position that the Mount of Olives will not be the first stop on the return itinerary based on the following:

- Zechariah 12:7: Set within a larger passage about how Judah will be caught up in the Campaign of Armageddon just as Jerusalem, this verse records the fact that Judah will be saved before the Jews in Jerusalem.
- The passage identified in the above descriptions of Christ going to Bozrah to engage in battle with the Antichrist armies, especially Zechariah 14:3.

At some time around the time when Christ arrives at, and ascends the Mount of Olives in victory, a tremendous earthquake will devastate the entire earth, according to Revelation 16:18, and will rip through the city of Jerusalem. There are two passages that provide slightly differing accounts of the effect of the earthquake on the city, and Fruchtenbaum harmonizes them in the following manner:

- Revelation 16:18-19: The city of Jerusalem will be split into three parts.
- Zechariah 14:4: The Mount of Olives will split from east to west dividing it into a northern part and a southern part in order to provide a means of escape from the earthquake that destroys the city.

41

THE DESTRUCTION OF BABYLON

Revelation 16:19 indicates that there will be two events that will be part of the pouring out the seventh bowl judgment: first, the city of Jerusalem will be split into three parts by a tremendous earthquake, and second, the wrath of God will come upon the city of Babylon, and the implication is that it will be utterly destroyed.

41.1 THE SIGNIFICANCE OF BABYLON

"Scholars differ on the interpretation of this chapter [Revelation 18], some taking it as a reference to Rome being destroyed, some taking it in a nonliteral sense, and others referring to it as a literal Babylon that has been made the capital city of the world government during the Great Tribulation. There is much to support and commend the interpretation that this is a literal prophecy referring to a literal city even though it is given the symbolic name Babylon, which ties it in to both the political and religion qualities that have characterized Babylon in history."[1] There are three reasons to believe that Babylon will once again be a literal city, at or very near its original location, and that it will be prominent during the latter time of Daniel's 70th Week:

- Zechariah predicts that Babylon will be rebuilt so that the full extent of evilness will be represented at the time of the final confrontation between good and evil. Just as God has His own city, Jerusalem, Satan has to have his, Babylon, because Satan and the Antichrist are characterized during this time as mimics of God and Jesus Christ.
- There are numerous Old Testament prophecies that describe a final and complete destruction of Babylon that are, as of today, unfulfilled.
- The most literal and harmonious view of prophecy and end times dictates that Babylon be a literal, functioning city again so that it will be counted among the two most important cities to the Antichrist, Jerusalem and Babylon. Some believe that Babylon will be the seat of the Antichrist's world government, however, as there is no direct revelation of this possibility. Jerusalem seems to have a more secure foundation as the center of his operations, based on the implications of Scripture. Suffice it to say that Babylon will be of great political and commercial importance to the Antichrist, regardless if he actually resides within its confines or not.

41.2 BABYLON WILL BE REBUILT

Core Scripture: Zechariah 5:5-11

Zechariah 5:5-11 strongly suggests that Babylon, as the representative city of the antithesis of goodness, which is wickedness, will be rebuilt when its time is here. While this passage has previously been explored, it will be examined here in more detail.

- 5:5-7: After an angel tells Zechariah to look at what is going forth, he questions what he is seeing and is told by the angel that it is a basket (or an ephah), which is, "… a measure of weight and became the symbol of economy … in this case a corrupted one …"[2] The ephah is further described as representing the wickedness of the people. Sitting inside the ephah, the material of which it is made is not identified however there is a lead cover, is a woman. The sense is that the cover provides a secure confinement for the woman inside.

- 5:8: The angel identifies the woman as the personification of corporate idolatrous wickedness (the Hebrew word used is a general word that is an antonym for righteousness, which suggests civil, ethical, and religious evilness), throws her down into the ephah and places the cover, identified as a lead weight, over the mouth of the ephah.

- 5:9-11: Zechariah sees two-winged, stork-like women fly over, pick up the ephah, and lift it into the sky in preparation for flying off with it. Zechariah questions the angel once again and inquires as to where the ephah is being taken, and the angel responds that it is being taken, to the land of Shinar (Babylonia), or returned to its original locations, where she will be placed on a pedestal, in a temple that will be built for her, when her time is ready as part of the final judgment on Babylon and wickedness. The land of Shinar has always represented rebellion and idolatry in ancient history, and will again represent them in future history.

There will be a future time for an actual rebuilt Babylon to be the representation of evilness. "Because Babylon was uniformly represented in Scripture as the source of much evil, the return of the basket and the woman in the basket symbolized that evil will be removed from Israel and returned to Babylonia where it will become part of their apostate religious system. The language indicating that the basket will be set in a place in the house probably means that it will be an object of worship as an idol in Babylon."[3] Also, the idea here is that wickedness has to be removed from the land of Israel prior to their regeneration. And it will be moved onto Babylon, in order to prepare Israel to receive their Messiah.

41.3 THE UNFULFILLED PROPHECIES OF BABYLON'S DESTRUCTION

Most of the Old Testament passages predicting the destruction of Babylon have been briefly summarized in Section 23.4, and the following are the key points that are made by those passages:

- The Antichrist will apparently not be present in Babylon when it is destroyed because he will have to be told that his enemies have destroyed his political/commercial center.
- The Jews living in Babylon at the time will be given several warnings that they are to leave the city before it is too late, or God's vengeance will come upon them as well. They will go to Jerusalem to announce that Babylon has been destroyed.
- The Lord will judge and destroy Babylon using military forces from all over the world. This will be another gathering of many peoples that is different from the gathering predicted in the sixth bowl judgment of Revelation 16:12-16 and discussed above under the first stage. "Whereas the gathering in the first stage will be the pro-Babylon or pro-Antichrist forces, these will be anti-Babylon or anti-Antichrist. Their purpose will be to destroy Babylon."[4]
- The destruction of Babylon indicated by the Old Testament prophets has not been accomplished to be considered complete. Ancient Babylon was not destroyed, it slowly died and became a ghost town.
- Babylon's destruction will be associated with the final redemption, regeneration and restoration of Israel.
- Babylon's destruction will occur as part of the Day of the Lord that will be global in scope.
- The destruction of Babylon will be ruthless and will be so total and final that only wild animals of the desert will live there, it will never be fit for human habitation again. Babylon's destruction will be especially severe because of the centuries of evil treatment against the people of Israel, which will be met with rejoicing by the Jews.
- With the exception of those that leave the city when requested, there will be no surviving remnant from the destruction of Babylon.

41.4 THE FALL OF BABYLON ANNOUNCED

Core Scripture: Revelation 18:1-3

A brilliantly radiant angel (apparently not the same angel of Revelation 17, but of similar stature), possessing the necessary authority to act, comes down out of heaven and announces, in the verb tense indicating a future event yet to occur but seen as completed, that the Great City of Babylon has fallen.

- As a result of its destruction, Babylon becomes the place where fallen angels, as characterized by the following, reside during the Messianic Age:

+ A habitation, dwelling place for every unclean (evil) spirit or demon.
+ A prison cage for every unclean and hated bird.
+ A hold for unclean and detested beasts.

As the final judged condition of destroyed Babylon, the city is abandoned to the demonic realm because of its utter wickedness.

- The relationship of Babylon with all the other nations is characterized as evil because the political kings of those nations have committed *adultery* (see the adjacent table for other words used by various translations) with Babylon. The idea here is that there has been an evil association between Babylon and the other nations of the world.

- Because of the evil associations, economic prosperity has come to merchants, and the pursuit of economic gain has caused them to abandon God, and all that is righteous in the world. "Just as the church had grown rich in proportion as it had been wicked, so the nations have likewise prospered, as they have abandoned God and sought to

Revelation 18:3	
NIV	*her adulteries*
NASB	*passion of her immorality*
NET	*her immoral passions*
KJV	*her fornication*
NKJV	*her fornication*
AMP	*her passionate unchastity*

accumulate wealth of this world. The wealth originally collected through the influence of the apostate church is taken over by the political systems in the great tribulation which with universal political power is able to exploit to the full its accumulation of wealth."[5]

41.5 THE JEWS CALLED TO LEAVE BABYLON

Core Scripture: Revelation 18:4-5

An unidentified voice from heaven calls for the people of God, the Jews, living in Babylon (remember at times of the return from the Babylonian Exile, many Jews living comfortably in Babylon chose not to return, cf. Jeremiah 51:45) to come out:

- First, so that they will not be taken over by the wickedness prevalent in the city of sinful humankind, the magnitude of which is described as extending all the way up to heaven (the imagery is one of bricks piled on one another as in a building, which is an allusion to the Tower of Babel and its attempt to reach heaven).
- Second, so that the plagues (the seven bowls of Revelation 16, especially the seventh bowl where the destruction of Babylon occurs) will not be inflicted on them.

41.6 THE INDICTMENT AGAINST BABYLON

Core Scripture: Revelation 18:6-8

The heavenly voice calls on God to reward Babylon just as the people of God will be rewarded, and based on the power of the Lord, He will 'reward' Babylon in judgment according to the following indictment:

- The debt created by Babylon is to be repaid (to give back what is due) double for the deeds she did to others, the magnitude of Babylon's sin justifies double retribution as the standard of judgment.

- To the extent that Babylon exalted herself in self-glorification, and revealed in sensual luxurious living, she is to be tormented; and because she boasted arrogantly of her pride in her identity, she is to be affected to the point of grief, anguish, and sorrow.

- For all her evilness, she is to receive the plagues of disease, mourning, and famine, all in a single day, it will come on the city all of a sudden; and finally, she will be consumed by fire to the point of utter destruction as punishment. "When it is time for God's judgment, it descends with unwavering directness."[6]

41.7 THE KINGS OF THE EARTH LAMENT BABYLON'S DESTRUCTION

Core Scripture: Revelation 18:9-10

The kings that were party to, and participated in, the immorality of Babylon's wickedness and became rich and worthy, as stated in the indictment, weep, mourn and wail at the sight of the smoke going up into the sky from her fiery destruction. But for self-preservation so as to not receive any of Babylon's torment, they will stand at a distance and watch the doom that falls suddenly on her, it falls in one hour. "[T]he burning of the city is a symbol of the fall of its political and economic might, and the kings of the earth marvel at the destruction of the seemingly infinite power of the capital of the world empire."[7]

41.8 THE MERCHANTS OF THE EARTH LAMENT BABYLON'S DESTRUCTION

Core Scripture: Revelation 18:11-19

The merchants (in verse 23, they are called *the great men of the earth* in the NASB, NIV, and KJV; and tycoons in the NET) that benefited from Babylon's prosperity now mourn the destruction of the source of their prosperity, which is a testament of Babylon's economic standing in the world. The mourning is not about the city, however, instead it is for their loss of income and the fact that they face failure of their businesses because they cannot trade their cargo with the luxury-hungry people of the city,

The goods traded with Babylon are listed in the passage, and they are characterized as for the wealthy that live a life of luxury, and it is stated that those living in the city lust after them. The list includes, precious stones, expensive metals, fine fabrics, costly raw materials for building structures and making vessels, expensive perfumes, spices and ointments, an abundance of foods and food sources, vehicles for transportation and finally slaves, all of which are normally available only to the wealthy.

Just as the kings did, the merchants will stand at a distance to mourn because they are afraid of being tormented as well. Until verse 17b, the merchants are identified in general, however, at this point a very interesting and unexpected group of merchants are specifically identified as mourning to a great extent - captains and seamen of merchant ships. Why would this group be singled out in the vision being shown John? It seems unexpected that the shipping industry would suffer from Babylon's destruction. It is proposed that one of the reasons this group was identified is that, in addition to the shipping necessary for the goods listed in the passage, the shipping of oil might be greatly affected as well because of its importance to the entire world. It does not seem to be a coincident that the place of economic wealth in the world of the end times is also the current center of the world's oil reserves that even now drives the world economy.

The expression of sadness and mourning economic loss by the kings and merchants seems to fly in the face of Jesus' pronouncement in Matthew 6:19-21, where He commanded that the goal of people was not to accumulate material possessions that could be stolen, lost, or destroyed, but instead to accumulate treasures in heaven where they could not be stolen, lost, or destroyed, "In contrast to the transitory wealth of their world, which are here consumed by a great judgment from God, are the true riches of faith, devotions, and services for God laid up in heaven beyond the destructive hands of man and protected by the righteous power of God."[8]

41.9 REJOICING IN HEAVEN

Core Scripture: Revelation 18:20

The heavenly saints, apostles and prophets are called to rejoice over the destruction of the quintessential representation of wickedness, the earthly city of Babylon, because God has judged it for what had been done to His children throughout history.

41.10 THE UTTER DESTRUCTION OF BABYLON

Core Scripture: Revelation 18:21-24

In an act that is reminiscent of, and parallel to, the closing of the prophecy by Jeremiah 51:61-64 of the destruction of Babylon, a powerful angel picks up a stone, identified as a milestone, and throws it into the seas, then states that it is symbolic for the violent downfall of Babylon, with violent force, the city will be destroyed, just as the force of the throw to deposit the stone in the water allows the stone to sink out of sight. Just as the stone disappears from existence to be found no more, so shall Babylon also.

No longer in the city of Babylon will there be luxurious living found in the festiveness manifested in music, the crafting of fine products of luxury, the milling of grain for foodstuffs, light shining from a lamp, nor happiness derived from marriage. The city will be cold, dead, and very silent - never to live again.

Summarizing the indictment, the passage indicated that all is gone because the merchants, the tycoons, the great men of the world sought personal wealth and possessions above service to the Lord, and in the process lost their souls because of their deceptive practices against the nations of the world, and the martyrdom of saints and prophets that spoke out against them, in the God-given effort to save them

41.11 A FINAL THOUGHT

"There is an obvious parallel in the rise and fall of Babylon in its varied forms in Scripture. As introduced in Genesis 1:1-9, Babylon, historically symbolized by the tower reaching to heaven, proposed to maintain the union of the world through a common worship and a common tongue. God defeated this purpose by confusing the language and scattering the people. Babylon, ecclesiastically symbolized by the woman in Revelation 17, proposes a common worship and a common religion through uniting in a world church. This is destroyed by the beast in Revelation 17:16 who thus fulfills the will of God (Rev. 17:17). Babylon, politically symbolized by the great city of Revelation 18, attempts to achieve its domination of the world by a world common market and a world government. Christ destroys these at His Second Coming (Rev. 19:11-21). The triumph of God is therefore witnessed historically in the scattering of the people and the unfinished tower of Genesis 11 and prophetically in the destruction of the world church by the killing of the harlot of Revelation 17 and in the destruction of the city of Revelation 18."[9]

42

REVELATION OF CHRIST'S SECOND ADVENT

Both the Old Testament and the New Testament include passages predicting the Second Advent of Jesus Christ. The return of Jesus Christ for a second time is a major subject of the Bible. "Through the precise phrase "the Second Coming" does not occur in either the Old or New Testament, many passages bear witness to the fact that Christ who came once to provide salvation is coming a second time to rule. … Just as the first coming of Christ accomplished the major purpose of God to provide salvation, so the Second Coming of Christ will accomplish the major purpose of God to place everything in subjection to Jesus Christ as King of Kings and Lord of Lords. This is a prominent element of references to his Second Coming in both the Old and New Testament."[1]

42.1   THE SECOND ADVENT - OLD TESTAMENT

"The second coming of Christ, along with the kingdom which follows is in fact, the very heart of the progress of Scripture and is the major theme of Old Testament prophecy."[2] As will be seen below, there is a considerable amount of Scripture that directly and indirectly establishes that Jesus Christ will not only come to the earth once, but will come to earth a second time in order to fulfill all of the Old Testament prophecies that remain unfulfilled.

The passages in the Old Testament that point to the Second Coming of Jesus Christ are of several general characterizations:
- A Second Coming reference will sometimes be intertwined with the first coming reference and the passage has to be analyzed in order to determine which part was fulfilled by the first coming and which part will be fulfilled by the Second Coming.
- A passage that points to an advent of the Messiah in which a particular aspect or activity that was not documented to having been fulfilled at the first advent will be at the Second Advent.
- A passage that describes some aspect of Christ's office of king or describes His rulership of the nation of Israel or the world in the one-thousand-year Millennium refers to the Second Advent.
- As is true of much of prophecy, there are prophetic passages that appear to have been fulfilled at some point in the past, however its ultimate fulfillment will be at the Second Coming of Christ.
- Some of the passages regarding the Second Coming are provided in the context of the Campaign for Armageddon.

GENESIS

- 3:15: In addition to God's judgment on Adam and Eve for allowing sin to enter into human existence, an act of which brought physical death to them and the entire human race as a subsequent inheritance, God also provided a plan for the redemption of the same human race that included a promised redeemer who would come and ultimately be victorious over Satan. God would bring judgment of sin to Satan and those of humankind who follow, and who would eventually rule those of the human race who would recognize their personal sinfulness and seek to be saved from it. As Jesus has come to earth the first time to defeat Satan, He has yet to come to be the ruler and king of humankind, thus He is to come again to complete God's intentions. God's judgment resulting from the Fall sets the stage for the history of humankind's kicking and screaming struggle against the tendency to be sinful, and the provision of a gracious means of a promised seed that would conquer the tendency to sin and its resulting behavior, the earlier acts of which have been written down in the Bible so that subsequent generations of people would know the entire story.
- 12:1-3; 17:15-19; 22:15-18: As we have seen on numerous occasions in this book, God made unconditional and covenantal promises with Abram that extended to the entire human race in the Abrahamic Covenant which has not been fulfilled as of today, and can only be fulfilled by the return of the Son of God at some time in the future.
- 49:10: As part of his remarks to his sons immediately before his death, in addition to Jacob's disclosure of the future of each son, he also tells them that there will be one that will come from his son Judah who will permanently possess the scepter as the ruler of the sons of Jacob, or Israel. As Jesus has yet to rule Israel on earth as of today, He can only do so if He comes to earth a second time.

DEUTERONOMY

- 30:1-10: God reaffirms to Israel that their blessings as a result of obedience to the covenantal promises would include being gathered from all the lands to which they had been dispersed because of earlier disobedience to be ruled over by God Himself. Thus the return of Jesus Christ is directly related to the delivery of Israel. "It is most significant that … Christ's return is related to Israel's restoration, regathering, and installation in the Promised Land. This is a prominent theme of the Old Testament and a major factor in prophecies concerning the Second Coming."[3]

2 SAMUEL

- 7:12-16: In the Davidic Covenant, God promises that the throne of David will permanently and eternally reside with the house of Israel. As this has not been fulfilled as of today, Jesus Christ has to return again in order to occupy the throne over Israel as the son of David.

JOB
- 19:25-27: In spite of living prior to any written revelation, and in prophetic anticipation of final judgment and vindication of his personal innocence, Job knew that in the end his Redeemer (or "my Vindicator"; the Hebrew word used is identified as the kinsman-redeemer, also found in the Book of Ruth) would descend from heaven and stand on the earth to mete out justice.[4] Job also understand that he would be in a place, after his physical death, where he would see God.

THE PSALMS
- 2:1-12: Written by David as a royal psalm, this is one of the most often cited passages that anticipates Christ's ultimate exaltation over the entire world despite opposition from the rulers of the thrones. David indicates that God has anointed the One that will sit on the throne and rule with a rod of iron, and all the nations should stop their rebellion and submit to the authority of the ruler. While there does not seem to be a direct theological connection acknowledged by scholars with Campaign of Armageddon, notice the sense of verses 1 through 3 and how the language tends to describe the nations that rise up first against each other, and then later against the Lord as He comes from heaven to earth.
- 24:1-10: This psalm indicates that God owns the earth an all that is in it, and it will be God's king that will enter into the earth in glory to rule; only those who are godly will be allowed to enter into the kingdom, which will result.
- 72:7-19: Verses 7 through 11 describe the state of the king's rule over the earthly realm, and is considered to be Christ's rule during the Millennium. Also, verse 15 through 19, the one that will rule will be favored by God will be eternal, and the nations will worship him, another vision of Christ's rule during the Millennium.
- 89:1-52: This psalm makes several references to aspects of the Davidic Covenant that are unfulfilled, therefore it essentially affirms that a descendent of David will eventually sit on the throne and rule over Israel.
- 96:1-13: When the Lord comes to rule the nations of the earth, there will be rejoicing.
- 97.1-12. With a foundation of equity and justice, the Sovereign Lord will judge His sinful enemies and will rule the earth from His throne; and there is joy in the world.
- 98:1-9: The entire world watches and praises the Lord as He demonstrates His faithfulness by delivering Israel.

- 99:1-9: An obvious picture of the Millennium, this psalm presents the vision that praise is due the Almighty Lord who reigns from His throne in Zion, as the earth and the nations tremble and shake.
- 110:1-7: This psalm is clearly a messianic psalm that prophetically looks forward to Jesus Christ reigning as the King in the order of Melchizedek as He judges apparently at the time of His second advent and just before the Millennium begins. Jesus used verse 1 to indicate that He, as David's Lord and Master, was to be the one that would fulfill the prophecy of sitting at the right hand of God and having His enemies presented to as a footstool (Matthew 22:44; Mark 12:36; and Luke 20:42).

ISAIAH

- 2:1-3: The prophet foresees the future of Jerusalem and Judah, and indicates that Jerusalem will be the capital of the world in, according to the Hebrew, the end of days, which according to other passages indicates that this will be during the Millennium. The passage also indicates that nations will stream to the new capital and to the Temple to learn of God's moral standards (the Lord will teach and the people will want to learn). Jerusalem and the Millennial Temple rebuilt on the Temple Mount, will be the place from which the God of Jacob will issue edicts, in other words, it will be the seat of the Lord's preeminent government of humankind (mountains denote governmental authority in the Bible).
- 2:11-18: This passage details the changes that will occur when the Lord comes to govern humankind. Idolatry, and those who practice it, will be eliminated, and the proud and arrogant will be humiliated. Again, another indication that the Lord will be on the earth to rule.
- 2:6: The Lord will cleanse Israel's sin from her, will restore her glory, and will be present with her.
- 6 - 7: This passage very clearly makes a connection between Jesus Christ and each of His two advents: He comes as a child born to us, and He comes as King. He was born to use *as a King* at His first advent, but because His Kingship was rejected, Christ did not fulfill the prophecy of being the King on earth at His first advent, therefore, while He will not be physically born a second time, He has to come again in order to fulfill the prophecy *as the King*. "Throughout the Old Testament the Second Coming is associated with Christ's future reign on David's throne, as well as His universal government over all nations."[5]
- 11:10-12: Like the many other similar verses, in fulfillment of the Abrahamic, Palestinian, Davidic, and New Covenants, Israel will be restored, all those that are dispersed will be regathered back to her land, and the Lord will stand like a signal flag before the nations, who will seek guidance from Him.
- 17 - 19: This extended passage indicates that when the Lord is resident on earth, He will judge the various nations surrounding Israel.

- 25 - 27: This passage contrasts what life was like prior to the Lord's coming to earth with the way of life will be for those that wait upon Him after He comes and judges the nations.
- 28:16: The Lord lays a precious cornerstone down in Zion, which is Christ in His Kingdom.
- 34:1-17: The prophet Isaiah contributes to the Campaign of Armageddon with information about events that will happen in the ancient nation of Edom. The Lord indicates that He will have a day of vengeance when He will judge the nations of the world, and Edom is specifically called out for judgment.
    + He calls for everyone in the world to listen to His announcement that He is angry and furious with the nations and He is going to annihilate them and the dead will lay unburied and will rot in the sun.
    + There will be celestial events that are similar to those found in Joel 3:15, Matthew 24:29, and Revelation 16:18.
    + Then the Lord turns His anger toward Edom where the slaughter with His sward will be seen as a great sacrifice in Bozrah because the Lord must uphold the cause of Zion.
    + The land of Edom will be destroyed to the point that, for generations, only wild animals will be there because there will be no people living there.
- 40:1-31: The Lord's coming is heralded, He returns to Israel, and the One that comes is the Almighty God.
- 42:1-13: The One that is to deliver and govern Israel will be the Servant chosen, and given authority, by God.
- 49:1-26: The Servant of the Lord that comes will be a blessing to Israel and the Gentile nations.
- 52:7-12: Jews and Gentiles will see the reign of the Lord when He returns to earth.
- 52:13 - 53:12: God will vindicate His Suffering Servant and will exalt Him on earth.
- 59:1-21: The Lord will still send the promised Redeemer even though Israel is sinful, which is confirmed by Paul in Romans 11:26-27.
- 61:1-2: In this oft referenced passage, Isaiah points out what the Lord will do when He comes to Israel. When Jesus is here the first time, He reads from Isaiah 61, but stops before reading the portion about God seeking vengeance as recorded in Luke 4:18-19. Jesus then tells those in the synagogue that He had come to fulfill the portion of Isaiah that He read which implied that the remaining portion will be fulfilled at a later time in human history.
- 63:1-3: When Jesus Christ returns to Jerusalem He will be asked why He has bloodstained clothes. His response is that He has been in Bozrah, and in a raging anger, destroying the enemies of Israel, those nations that oppose God, and blood from the slaughter has splattered onto His clothing.
- 63:4-19: When the Lord comes, He will judge the wicked.

- 66:1-24: The Lord says through Isaiah that He will come to judge the sinfulness of the world and establish His ruling Kingdom.

JEREMIAH

- 23:5-8: The prophet Jeremiah records the Lord saying that He promises that a time will come when He will raise up a descendant of David, who will rule over Israel justly, and will restore the people to their land and allow them to live in peace and security.
- 25:15-38: The divine judgment on the nations in verses 15-29, and the world in verses 20-38, is described, and as it has not occurred yet to the magnitude detailed, the Lord will come to the earth to do so.
- 31:31-40: This, the New Covenant, will be accomplished at a future time when the Lord will be present with an eternal Israel and a fully restored and permanent Jerusalem.

EZEKIEL

- 34:11-31: Similar to Jeremiah 23:5-8 except explained using the common metaphor of a shepherd and his sheep, this passage indicates that the Lord will restore His people to their land, He establish His servant shepherd from the house of David, and the people will live in safety and security in a place that fulfills their needs.
- 37:21-22: In the prophecy of the restoration of the people and land of Israel, Ezekiel indicates that the Lord will raise up one king to rule over them.

DANIEL

- 2:34-35 and 2:44-45: At the conclusion of Nebuchadnezzar's dream, He sees a stone, uncut by human hands, essentially pulverize the great statue that Daniel interprets to be a divine kingdom that will come some day and do away with human government. Obviously, this has not occurred to date, and this kingdom has to have a ruling King that will be Jesus Christ. Notice the symbolic contrast between materials: the metal of Nebuchadnezzar's statue are natural materials that have been manipulated and given relative value by humankind, while stone is a natural material untouched by human manipulation and without any human determined value.
- At the conclusion to his dream about the future of Israel in the context of the world, Daniel sees a scene, that is prophetically foreshadowing of a similar scene described in Revelation 4 and 5, where the Son of Man, Jesus Christ, is escorted before the Ancient of Days, God, and is given all the authority, honor, and sovereignty needed for Jesus to permanently rule all the peoples, nations, and language groups of the world.

HOSEA
- 3:4-5: As a result of the Lord's judgment of sin, Israel will seek out her God and their Davidic King.

JOEL
- 3:1-3: The prophet Joel has much to say about the nations of the world and God's coming judgments, and advises that the Lord has plans to judge the nations of the world who are accused or the abusive treatment and persecution of the Jews and the land of Israel - they had been scattered, they had been enslaved, and the land had been divided. As promised by God, and reaffirmed frequently in the Old Testament, God will restore His covenant people, identified in verse 2 as His inheritance, form their captivities and scatterings according to Moses' promise recorded in Deuteronomy 30:3. At the same time, He will gather all the nations together, He will bring them to the Valley of Jehoshaphat, and then He will enter into judgment with them. As this has obviously not happened in history, it can only still be in the future.
- 3:9-16: Joel is the only one that identifies the Valley of Jehoshaphat in its relation to the Campaign of Armageddon, and he proclaims that the nations of the world are to prepare for holy war with God who is calling down His warriors. It should be noted that the magnitude of this prophecy does not adequately connect to anything else except the Campaign of Armageddon.
    + The people of the nations are to convert their farming implements into weapons; they are to assemble at the appointed place at the Valley of Jehoshaphat.
    + Using imagery drawn from agriculture, God commands His warriors to harvest what is ripe and to tread in a winepress what is ready - they are to destroy the enemy.
    + A large mass of humanity will be gathered in the Valley of Jehoshaphat, identified here as the valley of decision.
    + There will be celestial events that seem to be the same sort of events found in other passages, such as Isaiah 34:4, Matthew 24:29, and Revelation 16:18.
    + The Lord will come out of Jerusalem accompanied by earthquakes and heavenly rumblings, and demonstrate His ability to be the refuge for Israel and her stronghold. The implication is that God destroys the forces gathered in the Valley of Jehoshaphat.

MICAH
- 4:1-3: This passage is very similar to Isaiah 2:1-3.
- 4:7: There will come a day when Israel will be made into a great nation again, and she will be ruled over by the Lord from Mount Zion.

- 5:2: This verse foretells that the One that will eventually rule over Israel will come from Bethlehem.

ZECHARIAH

- 2:10-12: "The Lord's coming to live among His people is messianic, referring to the time when He comes to rule on the throne of David. Possibly, however, both of Christ's advents are in view here as in passages such as Isaiah 9:6-7; 61:1-2. But the emphasis here is on Second Advent when God's blessings on Israel will overflow to the nations."[6]
- 6:12-13: Yet another passage proclaiming that Christ, here identified with the messianic title of *Branch*, who will ultimately and harmoniously unite in Himself.
- 9:9: This is another passage in which both advents can be seen. At His first advent, Jesus came to Israel as the legitimate and victorious King riding on a donkey, however, He was rejected. As so much of the Old Testament anticipates the coming of a messiah and a king, this passage can be applied to the Second Advent as well when Jesus will come again, but not riding on a donkey at that time, and will be accepted as the King.
- 12:10: God tells Zechariah that He will determine the dynasty of the Davidic line to the king, and that He will extend His grace to those of the Jews that look upon Him, the One that they had pierced; in other words, the One that would come as Israel's Messiah would be the One that had been previously pierced.
- 14:1-9: This passage contributes a significant portion of the details regarding major aspects of the Campaign of Armageddon and Christ's Second Advent.
    - + A Day of the Lord will come upon Israel in which the restored nation will be attacked by the nations of the world that will result in what appears to be urban combat in the City of Jerusalem. This will result in half of the city going into exile while the remainder stays in the city. The picture painted by verses 1 and 2 is that there will be much death, destruction, violence, and crimes against people, chaos, and thievery within the ancient city.
    - + Then the Lord will come to the earth to go into battle with all the enemies of Israel and will stand on the Mount of Olives at the time it splits into two parts with a valley between the parts which will allow those remaining in Jerusalem to escape.
    - + Finally, verse 9 confirms that the Lord will be the undisputed King over the earth and will be seen as One with a single name.
- 14:16: After all the events associated with the Lord's coming and the destruction of the nation's standing against Israel, those that survive will go up to the Temple annually.

42.2   THE SECOND ADVENT - NEW TESTAMENT

The Old Testament characterizes the relationship between the people of Israel and God, as including a promise that on a future day, God will come to them as their Deliverer, Protector, and Sustainer – or, in other words, God will come to His children to be their God, and they will be His people. Thus, there is a Jewish anticipation of the coming of God to establish His Kingdom. As we have just seen, the nature of the applicable passages identify God only as God and makes no specific mention that the One that is to come will be Jesus of Nazareth. Also, the applicable passages examined do not clearly indicate or anticipate that there will be two comings of God to the earth separated by a significant amount of time – a fact that is only made apparent when studied from the vantage point of two thousand years into the Church Age. The New Testament, without doubt, establishes that Jesus of Nazareth was the One that was anticipated by the Old Testament to come as God, and it further establishes that His coming would be cut short but that he would come again. While not anticipated by the Old Testament, the New Testament indicates that another program, different from God's program with Israel, will occupy the time between the two comings. So we come to today, where the One anticipated by the Jews to come as God the first time, is the very same One that is anticipated by the Church to come as God a second time.

MATTHEW

- 13:40-42: Set within the context of the Parable of the Wheat and the Tares to explain that there will be those that believe in Jesus Christ living amongst those that do not believe. Jesus indicates that He will send His angels (implication is at some time in the future) to collect all those that practice evilness in order to throw them into a fiery furnace as punishment for disobedience. This is a clear indication that God will someday judge all people.
- 24:15-31 (cf. Mark 13:14-27): In this portion of Christ's Sermon on the Mount of Olives, Jesus advises the disciples that a time will come in which there will be unprecedented suffering by Israel (the time of the Great Tribulation, or the second half of Daniel's 70th Week), and following this description He makes a number of statements regarding the events that occurs immediately at the end of that time:
  + There will be false sightings of the Messiah (Matthew 24:23-26 and Mark 13:21-23), however as pointed out in the following verse, no one will have to wonder when Christ comes, it will very obvious.
  + Jesus says that just as lightning is seen all across the sky, His return will be visible to all (Matthew 24:27).
  + Accompanying Jesus' return will be heavenly and celestial events that will be unmistakable as to their awesomeness (Matthew 24:29-39 and Mark 13:24-25).

- + When Jesus appears in the sky, the people of the nations that had not believed He would come will be terrified in their realization that the anticipation fueled by the Bible is being fulfilled (Matthew 24:30).
  + Jesus will direct His angels to collect all the believers from all over the earth (Matthew 24:31 and Mark 13:27).
  + The sense of the passage paints the picture that the time of suffering followed by the coming of God will be of unsurpassable importance and significance.
- 25:31: As part of His Sermon on the Mount, Jesus Himself indicates that the Son of Man will come (again) in His glory with the angels and will sit on His throne.
- 26:64 (cf. Mark 14:62): When, as a prisoner unjustly charged by Caiaphas, the high priest and the Sanhedrin and admonished to swear before God that He was the Son of God, Jesus responded by pointing out that he would soon sit at the right hand of the very God of Israel and, in a probable reference to Daniel 7:13, He would come (return) in the clouds of the sky.

LUKE
- 21:25-28: The physician more eloquently describes the coming of Jesus than does Matthew and Mark. Immediately prior to the coming of Jesus, there will be distress and anxiety in the world because of the celestial events and the chaos ensuing among the people. Then, the Messiah will come in power and glory, and in a manner that cannot be ignored.

ACTS
- 1:6-11: Try to imagine the scene described in this passage that perhaps only lasted a few moments.
  + Jesus Christ and the apostles are standing on the Mount of Olives (as we know from other passages), for a reason that is not disclosed.
  + It would not seem surprising if we were to learn that each apostle present is spiritually and intellectually exhausted because of all that has been witnessed in the several weeks since Jesus entered Jerusalem on a donkey. They might be standing there in some amount of uncertainty over recent events as well as concern over what is yet to come. Remember, the very human and weak apostles have been with the Son of the Living God, in His divine state, for just short of two months, and they would have to be emotionally spent at this point.
  + After all that the apostles had seen and heard, the possibility that they still did not understand all that Jesus had been telling them, seems to be more like a certainty because they ask Jesus what seems to be an unusual, but logical, question: *Lord, are you at this time going to restore the kingdom to Israel?*

+ Jesus responds by telling them that they are not to know of all the details and the timing of God's program with humankind, only God the Father knows. Also, He discloses to them a mandate to evangelize the world, the responsibilities, implications, and significance of which they probably may not have perceived at the time.
+ After having given them what will eventually be understood to be the central mandate for Christianity, the body of Christ, Jesus Christ ascends from their presence into the sky and into heaven.
+ Most likely, the apostles were standing there utterly amazed at what they had been witnessed, shocked at the supernatural event that had just occurred, and awestruck at the fact that they were part of something they may not have understood fully.
+ As the apostles stand there starring into the sky, two angels snap them back to reality by telling them that the very One that had just ascended into heaven would return one day in the very same manner, through the sky from heaven.
+ Thus the fact that Jesus would come again is firmly established by the passage.
• 3:19-21: The message taught by Peter on the day of Pentecost was focused around the fact that the Jesus that had been born to the Jews was indeed the Messiah promised by God and recorded in the Old Testament Scriptures; and for the first time preached the Gospel to the world, notwithstanding that it was only to a few thousand people in Jerusalem. Peter succinctly put it in perspective, the fulfillment of the Old Testament promise would be that the kingdom would come at a future time and would only be for those that repented of their sin by their confession of faith in the One that fulfilled the Old Testament.

1 THESSALONIANS
• 3:13: In an admonishment to increase in love for one another, Paul tells the Thessalonians that there will be a time in the future when the Lord Jesus will come with all of His saints.

2 THESSALONIANS
• 1:6-10: Again, Paul advises the Thessalonians that the Lord Jesus will be revealed (or return) from heaven someday to judge the disobedient and punish the unrighteous with eternal destruction away from the presence and glory of God.
• 2:8: Paul further discloses that there will someday be a lawless person that will defy God but will be destroyed by the word of Jesus and his existence will be erased – another indication of a future return and judgment.

277

HEBREWS

- 9:27-28: This is the only passage in which there is a specific indication that Jesus Christ will come to earth a second time. Several observations may be made of these two verses:
  + This passage clearly and succinctly presents the purpose for each of Christ's advents: He came the first time to bear the whole weight of human sinfulness, and notice the implied qualifications, once and for all; and He will come a second time to bring the promised and assured salvation to those that eagerly await His coming.
  + Notice what is said about dying once and then facing judgment: a major part of the identification between finite human beings and the infinite God is the fact that, just as humans, Jesus Christ also was appointed to die once, but instead of facing judgment as humans do, He will bring judgment on evil.
  + The second verse makes clear that there is a period of time between the two advents because there will be some that will eagerly await Him.

1 PETER

- 4:12-13: By acknowledging that believers should not be surprised when they are persecuted, Peter comforts them by pointing out that the persecution identifies them with the suffering of Jesus Christ, so that when He comes again, His glory revealed, those that are persecuted will rejoice and be glad of their commitment to, and sacrifice for, their Lord.

2 PETER

- 3:1-14: The Apostle Peter characterizes the last times as including the Lord's return being questioned by scoffers. Peter reminds his readers to remember the teachings of both the prophets and the apostles and to not be deceived by those bent on distracting attention from the anticipation of, and deliberately suppressing the knowledge of, the Lord's return. Peter continues by reminding them that God created the earth, that He destroyed it once by flood and will destroy it again by fire, and that there will be future judgments and destruction of the ungodly. Also, they are further reminded that God is timeless and longsuffering, and the event schedule for His Plan is not aligned with human understanding of time. Peter then describes the supernatural and cataclysmic celestial events that will transpire when the Day of the Lord comes over the world and He encourages believers to put their personal lives in godly order while they wait for the coming Day of the Lord that will result in the new heavens and new earth.

JUDE

- 14-15: Jude points out that from the beginning of humankind Enoch, among the earliest generations to live on earth and even before God called out a chosen people understood that the Lord would come to the earth with thousands of His holy ones to execute judgment on the ungodly. The implication of this passage is that there is a divine Creator God who provided humankind the opportunity to make moral choices with some resulting in ungodly behavior and lifestyles that would reject the Creator, which would be concluded with a worldwide judgment between godliness and evilness.

REVELATION

- 1:7: Again in a probable reference to Daniel 7:13, as well as Matthew 26:64 and Mark 14:62; John made the observation that Christ's return to earth will be in the sky and will be seen by everyone, including the ones that pierced Him, Israel, and all the nations will mourn because of Him.
- 12:5: In the succinct summary of the worldly relationship between Israel, Jesus Christ, and Satan of the first six verses of Revelation 12, John indicates that the woman, Israel, gives birth to the child, Jesus Christ, who is suddenly caught up to heaven to His throne, before it could be devoured by the dragon, Satan. In the definition of the child's role, John points out the child will also rule over the nations with a rod of iron, which implies that he will have to come to heaven to do so.
- 19:11 – 20:6: This most significant passage will be examined in greater detail below and in further chapters.
- 22:7, 12, and 20: As the Apostle John concludes what will be the last book of God's written revelation, he records Christ saying three times I am coming soon which from the last words spoken by Christ to whoever reads the Scriptures.

43

CHRIST'S SECOND ADVENT

The progression of the human race down through not less than sixty centuries is now poised on the cusp of the single most important event of human history. In the absence of a restraint of evil, humankind has reached the logical conclusion of idolatry and apostasy - that of believing, not so much that God may or may not exist, but of believing that He was unnecessary. In fact, the implication is that the condition on earth is that it is not possible for humankind to get farther away from the righteousness of God than they are in the minutes before Christ's arrives - humankind is capable of no greater depravity, pride, and arrogance than exists at this time. Try imagining the scene: Vast numbers of human beings collected in numerous apostate nations, some of which are dominated by a single satanically-possessed man, all fighting amongst themselves for control, possessions, power, or dominance. Then, when the Son of God makes His glorious entrance into the skies above the earth, which will be seen by all, these same feuding people will join forces to go into battle with the Almighty Son of God in the futile hope of eliminating the Creator God.

The One promised to the nation of Israel that has been expected and anticipated for more than four millennia, and, the One that the True Church, prior to being snatched away, looked forward to the return of for at least two millennia will come to the earth within a matter of a few hours. The One that comes to Israel as their Messiah - the eternal covenantal promises, predictions, and prophecies made by God, and recorded in the Scriptures to the nation are about to be finally and fully completed. People living at this time will only have one of two emotions, either, one will be filled with overwhelming hatred for God that will be focused on eliminating Him, or, one will be filled with overwhelming excitement because of the realization that the prophecies of the Bible were right after all, and if they then believe, the pain and suffering of human life on earth will be exchanged for eternal peace in the presence of the Creator of everything. Notice that those that hate God will, by their hatred, acknowledge the existence of God, but will not believe in Him.

Jesus Christ is the dominant theme of the Bible, with His first coming being primarily focused on bringing a means of eternal salvation to all people, and the second coming primarily focused on judging all people for what they did or did not do with the means of salvation brought the first time. However, before we begin to complete the sequence of events of the Campaign of Armageddon, we will examine what the Bible has to say about the Second Coming of Jesus Christ.

43.1 THE IMPORTANCE OF THE SECOND ADVENT

The foundation of God's Plan for Humankind, as detailed in the Bible, revolves around the significance of Jesus Christ. He is the very center around which creation rotates. He is the deliverer that the Old Testament looked toward, however, he was unknown at the time. He is the One that was destined to come to humankind not once, but twice. And the New Testament reinforces this fact because it also looks toward the deliverer coming as well as acknowledging the earlier visit. The Holy Trinity has made many promises and commitments that have to be fulfilled and completed, and Christ's Second Coming is necessary to conclude the story of humankind.

"The second coming of Christ, along with the kingdom which follows it, is in fact, the very heart of the progress of Scripture and is the major theme of Old Testament prophecy. The great covenants of Scripture relate to God's program - especially these covenants with Abraham, Israel, David, and the new covenant. Much of the revelation of the Psalms and the major and minor prophets revolves around this great theme. Great prophetic books like Daniel, Zechariah, and Revelation focus on the subject of the Second Coming of Christ and the consummation of history and the kingdom. For this reason, the doctrine of the Second Coming in large measure determines the total theology of the interpreter of the Bible and justifies the attempt to order prophetic events yet to be fulfilled in considerable detail in faithfulness to the extent of scriptural revelation."[1]

That the Second Coming of Jesus Christ is of tantamount importance to those that believe in the Bible is attested to by its inclusion as an essential doctrine in numerous creeds developed down through the centuries of Christian history, as well as its inclusion as uncompromising doctrine in many churches today. Without God's inspired revelation, Jesus' claim to be the Son of God, His first advent as the suffering servant, His resurrection, His ascension to the right hand of God, and His eventual return to earth as king, Biblical Christianity would have no possibility of being a legitimate religion or having a spiritual and saving claim on the lives of human beings. Thus for those that live today, the coming of Jesus Christ, first for His church and then as the kingly ruler of the earth, stand unopposed in magnitude and significance to humankind.

43.2 WHY TWO ADVENTS?

The true depth of the answer to this question is founded in the infinite mind of God, however, the finite mind of humankind can see its inclusion in His reasoning for creating the universe, the world, and human beings in His image and likeness in the first place. While the Bible does provide somewhat of an answer to the questions, we are all going to have to wait until our own personal presence with the Lord before we will know why God did all that He did. Without the clarity provided by the New Testament, it is doubtful that believers in this present age, two thousand years after Christ's First Advent, would have recognized the first visit by Jesus as being the Messiah anticipated by the Old Testament any better than the Jews. Nevertheless, God purposed to have His Son come to earth at two different times in order to fulfill the several roles of suffering servant, advocating priest and righteous king,

Among the many perspectives that are conceivable regarding why two advents are necessary, is the idea that God choose from among the nations of the world a people to be His people and the ones to which He would be their God, and gave them a mandate to be His representatives to the other nations. However, due to human weakness and the propensity of turning to evil rather than to good, God's chosen people did not honor or obey the mandate to be His representatives to the nations. After they rejected the offer of the anticipated kingdom by rejecting His royal emissary, Jesus Christ, God determined to temporarily remove the mandate from the Jews and give it to another chosen people, the True Church, to represent Him to the nations of the world. Thus, the Messiah has to visit the earth two times, first to offer the kingdom to God's chosen nation so that when they rejected it, partial aspects of the kingdom could be given to a people now chosen by Christ; the people of which would be delivered from the wrath that God would eventually bestow on His chosen nation. The notion of two advents is further substantiated by the fact that Jesus did not fulfill all the Old Testament prophecies regarding His offices of servant, priest, and king during His first advent.

As we know, Jesus is the primary focus of the Bible, and there are many passages about His Second Coming that are obvious in the New Testament (He had already come once, so references to Him coming would be a second time since the references were written after His visit), and while much more difficult to discern, there are many passages in the Old Testament as well. The only reference in the Bible that specifically states that Jesus Christ will come a second time occurs in Hebrews 9:27-28, where the writer indicates that *Christ was sacrificed once to take away the sins of many; and he will appear a second time, not to bear sin, but to bring salvation to those who are waiting for him.*

43.3	THE SECOND ADVENT IN CHURCH HISTORY

The Old and New Testament passages discussed above substantially document that the Second Coming of Jesus Christ is the most major prophetic theme of the entire Bible, however, how has this doctrine fared down through two thousand years of church history? Citing various historical writings, MacLeod observed that they indicate the Second Coming has been, "... the historic faith of the Christian church."[2] Consider other observations made by MacLeod:

- "The early church fathers certainly believed in the Second Coming."[3] The following all anticipated the Lord's return and wrote about some aspect of that time:

+ " … The Epistle of Barnabas, probably written by Alexander between AD 70 and 100…"[4] indicates that the Son will come to destroy the wicked one, to judge the godless, and to change the universe.
+ "Clement of Rome, probably writing about AD 96…"[5] advises that the Lord will come and will bring His reward.
+ Justin Martyr, writing about AD 155, acknowledged that Jesus had ascended to heaven and will return again.
+ Irenaeus, who lived about AD 130 to 200, wrote that the Antichrist will reign for three and one-half years and will devastate all things in the world, after which the Lord will come down from heaven in glory and cast him into the lake of fire.
+ Tertullian, who lived about AD 160 to 225, made a reference to church saints meeting the Lord in the air.
- "In similar fashion the great Reformers eagerly anticipated the return of Christ."[6]
  + Martin Luther (1483-1546) acknowledged that the prophets of the Bible anticipated the Second Return of Jesus Christ, and that it was his belief that the angels were preparing for battle. It is also interesting that Luther's students, Erasmus Alber and Nikolaus Herman, also wrote about the coming of the Lord.
  + John Calvin (1509-1564) wrote that we are to await the Redeemer who will come down from heaven to appear to all in divine glory, and to judge the living and dead.
- "In the same way the great creeds and confessions of the church all express the conviction that Jesus Christ will someday return bodily and visibly to this earth."[7] The divinity and glory of Jesus, His provision of eternal salvation, His authority to judge, and the anticipation of His return can be found to the following:
  + The Apostles' Creed.
  + The Nicene Creed.
  + The Augsburg Confession (1530; Lutheran church).
  + The Belgic Confession (Flemish and Dutch Reformation churches).
  + "The Thirty-Nine Articles (1571) of the Church of England of Anglican Church (Episcopal Church of North American) …"[8]
  + The Westminster Confession (1647; Presbyterian churches).
  + The Confession of the Congregational Union of England and Wales (1833).
  + The New Hampshire Confession (1833; Baptist churches).
- MacLeod draws five analytical observations from the writings of the prophets, the apostles, the early church fathers, and the great teachers of church history that provides the prophetic dimensions of the Second Coming of Jesus Christ:
  + First, Jesus will come to rescue His people, including raising those that have died.

+ Second, He will come to judge His people, evaluating their faithfulness and watchfulness during the time of His absence …"[9]
+ Third, at His first coming, Jesus lived in "obscurity and weakness," yet at His Second Coming, "… there will be an open manifestation of the character and splendor of the Lord Jesus Christ."[10]
+ Fourth, Jesus will come to transform everything into a hew heaven and a new earth.
+ "Fifth, He will come to conquer all that is evil, whether human or demonic."[11]

43.4 THE SECOND ADVENT COMPARED TO THE FIRST ADVENT

The distinctions between the Second Coming of Jesus and the First Coming are fairly well established, Walvoord and Chafer[12] provides the following summary of the Two Advents:

First Advent	Second Advent
Christ came as the Redeemer from sin, which purpose demanded His death, His resurrection, and His present ministry	Christ comes to rescue Israel from her persecutors and restore her as a nation (Rom. 11:26-27)
Christ came "Gentle and riding on a donkey" (Zech. 9:9) and on the earth was born, lived, and died	Christ comes with power and great glory (Rev. 19:11-16)
Christ was rejected of men	Christ comes as King of kings and Lord of lords and is the Judge and Ruler of men (Rev. 19:16)
Christ provided salvation for individual Jews and Gentiles	Christ comes to judge both Jews and Gentiles (Ezek. 20:34-38 and Matt. 25:31-46)
Christ merely judged and resisted Satan (Col. 2:15)	Christ binds Satan and conquers the forces of evil (Rev. 20:1-3)

43.5 THE SECOND ADVENT COMPARED TO THE RAPTURE

The Rapture has been discussed at considerable length in Chapter 28, and the conclusion was that a literal interpretation of the Bible supports the idea that Christ will come to gather His bride, the Church, at some unknown time prior to the beginning of Daniel's 70th Week that will be not less than seven years before He comes a second time in fulfillment of all of the Old and New Testament prophecies regarding His return to earth as King Messiah, Savior, and Judge to bring justice to the earth and humankind. LeHaye[13] has developed a comparative table that is instructive in understanding the distinctiveness of the Second Coming and the Rapture.

Rapture / Blessed Hope	Second Coming / Glorious Appearing
Christ comes in the air for His own	Christ comes with His own to earth
Rapture of all Christians of the True Church	No one raptured
Christians taken to Father's house	Resurrected saints do not see Father's house
No judgment on earth	Christ judges inhabitants of earth
Church taken to heaven	Christ sits up His kingdom on earth
Imminent - could happen any moment	Cannot occur for at least seven years
No signs	Many signs for Christ's physical coming
For believers only	Affects all humanity
Time of joy	Time of mourning
Before the "day of wrath" (Tribulation)	Immediately after Tribulation (Matthew 24)
No mention of Satan	Satan bound in abyss for 1,000 years
The judgment seat of Christ	No time or place for judgment seat
Marriage of the Lamb	His bride descends with Him
Only His own see Him	Every eye will see Him
Tribulation begins	1,000-year kingdom of Christ begins

Another comparative table offered by Hindson[14]:

Rapture	Second Coming
Christ comes *for* His own (John 14:3; 1 Thess. 14:17; 2 Thess. 2:1)	Christ comes *with* His own (1 Thess. 3:13; Jude 14; Rev. 19:14)
He comes in the *air* (1 Thess.4:17)	He comes to the *earth* (Zech. 14:4; Acts 1:11)
He *claims* His bride (2Thess. 4:16-17)	He comes *with* His bride (Rev. 19:6-14)
Removal of *believers* (1 Thess. 4:17)	Manifestation of Christ (Mal. 4:2)
Only His own see Him (1 Thess. 4:13-18)	*Every eye* shall see Him (Rev. 1:7)
Tribulation begins (2 Thess. 1:6-9)	Millennial *kingdom* begins (Rev. 20:1-7)
Saved are *delivered from wrath* (1 Thess. 1:10; 5:9)	Unsaved *experience the wrath* of God (Rev. 6:12-17)
No signs precede rapture (1 Thess. 5:1-3)	Signs precede second coming (Luke 21:11, 15)
Focus: *Lord and church* (1 Thess. 4:13-18)	Focus: *Israel and kingdom* (Matt. 24:14)

43.6	BACKGROUND – THE OFFER OF THE KINGDOM AND THE REJECTION OF THE MESSIAH

Before the Second Advent of Jesus is examined in detail, it would be helpful to review the offer of the kingdom to Israel and its rejection at the First Advent of Jesus. The offer / rejection of the kingdom at the First Advent sets the stage for the events of the Second Advent.

As we have seen, one of the purposes for the seven yearlong Daniel's 70th Week is to prepare Israel to accept Jesus Christ, first, as the Son of the God of Abraham, Isaac, and Jacob, and second, as their Saving Messiah anticipated by the Old Testament Scriptures. Notwithstanding the offer of the kingdom by Jesus as Son and Messiah had to be rejected two thousand years ago so that the Gentiles could be grafted in, the leadership of Israel did indeed reject the offer by rejecting Jesus Himself. But now as history approaches the end of the age, and the appropriate number of Gentiles have accepted and believed Jesus Christ, God is bringing Israel to the point where her century's long spiritual blindness is removed and there will be clarity of spiritual understanding that Jesus is Israel's Messiah and King.

THE OFFER OF THE KINGDOM AND THE REJECTION OF THE MESSIAHSHIP OF CHRIST

An important aspect of Christ's First Advent regards the offer of Israel's Messiah and the promised kingdom to Israel which was rejected by the Jewish leadership.
- Based on Old Testament prophecies there was a heightened anticipation and expectation by Israel that the Lord would someday come to them and bring in the long-awaited kingdom that would deliver them from their plights. While Israel understood there would be a kingdom someday, they most certainly did not know when it would come, nor by what manner it would come. The Bible tells us that the anticipation of the kingdom was still on the minds of the apostles because the question that was asked in Acts 1:6.
- John the Baptist proclaimed that the kingdom was at hand in Matthew 3:1-2, and Jesus proclaimed its nearness as well in Matthew 4:17. Interestingly, none of the Gospels record John the Baptist, Jesus, or anyone else for that matter, explaining what was meant by the kingdom, therefore, the deduction is that "… the common Jewish understanding of the kingdom in first century Israel was that of a literal earthly kingdom centered in Jerusalem and ruled by the Messiah."[15]
- As indicated in Matthew 4:23 and 9:35, as Jesus traveled throughout Jerusalem and among the towns and communities surrounding the city, He preached the gospel of the kingdom, by which access was granted by repentance, as well as performing miracles. Therefore, the kingdom was

available to Israel however it was contingent on Israel accepting the One making the offer as the promised Messiah.

- In Acts 3:19-21, during the Pentecost perhaps Peter recognized that Israel had rejected the kingdom because Jesus had been rejected as the Messiah, however, he understood that the kingdom had not been permanently rejected because there would be another opportunity for the kingdom to come to Israel, and in the meantime, people could receive an earthly portion of the heavenly kingdom by repenting of their sins.
- Matthew 11:12-14 records Jesus making an interesting observation about the offer of the kingdom. He indicates that John the Baptist would be the Elijah of the Malachi 4:5-6 prophecy if Israel were to accept Him as the promised Messiah. He also sort of suggests that John the Baptist was the concluding aspect of the prophecies of the law and prophets.
- However, as we know, Israel rejected John the Baptist as the Elijah to come, and more importantly, Israel rejected Jesus as the promised Messiah thereby postponing the coming of the kingdom.

There are several passages that should be examined regarding the offer and the rejection of the kingdom to Israel.

First Public Rejection of Jesus
Core Scripture: Matthew 12:22-45

Matthew 4 – 12 records Jesus going about the Jewish nation proclaiming His Messiahship and preaching the gospel of the kingdom using miracles as signs to authenticate His identity and His message. It is in this passage that Jesus changes His ministry focus (from preaching and proclaiming the gospel of the kingdom to training the apostles for His absence) because of the events that transpire - He will consider the kingdom offer rejected because of His rejection by the leadership of Israel.

- Matthew 12:22-29: A demon-possessed man that is also blind and mute is brought to Jesus, who then miraculously heals his sight and restores his voice, and (by implication because it is not specifically stated) commands the demon to leave its host. This results in the people asking if Jesus could really be the Messiah, because the purpose of the miracle was to get the people to see Him as the Son of David. While this was not an unusual miracle for Jesus to perform, the Pharisees made the wrong conclusion (notice that the people waited for the leadership to determine if Jesus was the Messiah or not) regarding the authority by which Jesus acted and, instead of seeing it as a demonstration of the power of their Lord God, they conclude that it was a demonstration of the power of the prince of demons, Beelzebul. The Pharisees "… refused to accept Jesus as the Messiah because He did not fit the Pharisaic mold of what Messiah was supposed to say and do (Luke 7:30-35)."[16] Verse 24 is the pivotal passage - it became obvious to Jesus that His work, and therefore His identity, was not being associated with the power of the God of Abraham, Isaac, and Jacob, but with the power of the opposition, Satan. Jesus now changes His ministry and begins by responding to the Pharisees with two rational arguments: first, if He were of Satan, then why would He exorcise a demon from a human being which would be an act contrary to the satanic cause, and the second, if He is accused of being of the power of exorcising demons, then according to what power did those among them claim to be of when they exorcised demons? He also presents the logical conclusion that since He is not of Satan, then He must be of the power of God, which then can be concluded that is standing before them.

- Matthew 12:30-37: In immediate spoken response to His rejection, Jesus symbolically 'draws the line in the sand' by advising all that can hear that if one is not with Him, then they are against Him. He goes on to say that all sins and blasphemies can be forgiven accept those made against the Holy Spirit, which is an unpardonable national blasphemy against the generation committing the sin. "The content and definition of the unpardonable sin is the national rejection of the Messiahship of Jesus by Israel while He was physically present on the basis that He was demon possessed. This sin was unpardonable, and the judgment was set. The judgment came in the year AD 70 with the destruction of Jerusalem and the Temple and the worldwide dispersion of the Jewish people."[17] Fruchtenbaum provides further explanation of the unpardonable sin by pointing out four ramifications:
  + First, the unpardonable sin is national in scope and not individual, however, personal repentance could remove the individual from the coming judgment, but could not remove the nation from the judgment.
  + Second, the sin was limited to the generation present when the blasphemy occurred.
- Third, an unpardonable sin cannot be committed by a nation today because Jesus is not physically or viably present before any nation with an offer of bringing in the kingdom.
  + Fourth, commitment of the unpardonable sin by that generation at that time carries two implications:
    o That generation was under a special judgment (AD 70 destruction).
    o The kingdom would be offered to, and accepted by, a future Jewish generation (immediately before the Second Coming of Jesus).
- Matthew 12:38-40: As if Jesus had not already been performing miracles to authenticate His identity, the Pharisees incredibly asks for a sign not to mention the just completed miraculous healing and exorcism of the blind and mute demon-possessed man of verse 22. How much more offensive could they have been? However, because the Jewish leadership had accused Him of being demon-possessed thus causing Jesus to change His ministry activities. He advised the Pharisees that the only sign that will no longer be any signs for the nation to demonstrate His identity. Rather, "… [f]or the nation there would be no sign but one: the sign of Jonah, which is the sign

of resurrection. It is a sign that would come to Israel on three occasions: first, at the resurrection of Lazarus; second, at Jesus' own resurrection: and third, at the resurrection of the Two Witnesses in the Tribulation. The first two were rejected, but the third will be accepted."[18]

- Matthew 12:41-45: Jesus judged the Jewish generation that rejected His offer of a kingdom and Messiahship. Using the examples of Nineveh and the Queen of Sheba, Jesus pointed out that they believed in God with much less revelation than what had been provided to Israel. "Christ closed the story with the point that what was true of the man was also true of that particular generation. When that generation began, it began with the preaching of John the Baptist. John's ministry was essentially a clean-up ministry, for he was to prepare the people for the reception of the Messiah. By means of the preaching of John, that generation was swept and garnished. Now that Messiah had come, they rejected Him on the basis of their perception of demon possession. That generation, swept and garnished, now remained empty, the last state of that generation was to be worse than the first."[20]

It is fitting then that when Jesus was asked again by the Pharisees for a sign, recorded in Matthew 16:1-4, Jesus responded in the same manner as described in Matthew 12:39: *A wicked and adulterous generation asks for a sign! But none will be given it except the sign of the prophet Jonah.*

First Sign of Jonah
Core Scripture: John 11:1-57

After the Jewish leadership had rejected Jesus as the Messiah sent by God, Matthew 12:39 records Jesus telling the Pharisees that the only sign that would be given to the nation was the sign of Jonah, and the death of Lazarus became an opportunity for Jesus to perform the miracle of resurrection to demonstrate His power over death. Jesus provides the reason for the miracle in verse 42, and that being so that the crowd (which included Jewish people from Jerusalem) standing and watching Him would then believe that God had sent Him. The response from the crowd after they witnessed Lazarus come out of the tomb alive was divided. Some people believed God had sent Jesus, while others needed an 'official' response from the chief priests and the Pharisees, who called a council to decide the matter. Not surprisingly, Caiaphas, the high priest at the time, conspired to do away with Jesus out of fear of Roman reprisal for religious division with the land of Israel: *So from that day on they plotted to take his life* (John 11:53*).* "The rejection of the Messiahship of Jesus was not complete. Going beyond the rejection of His Messiahship, they now condemned Him to death."[21] As the time for Jesus' death was not at hand, He removed Himself from public exposure to avoid being arrested prior to the proper time, while the people of Israel debated His identity, His miracles, and His claims.

Jesus' Judgment of Jerusalem
Core Scripture: Luke 19:41-44

As part of His triumphal entry, while thousands of people proclaimed His Messiahship, Jesus wept over Jerusalem and thought about what could have been had the Jewish leadership accepted His Messiahship. However, because He had been rejected and the unpardonable sin had been committed by that generation, Jesus passes the inevitable judgment over the nation. The judgment was literally fulfilled forty years later in the destruction of the city and the Temple, and the dispersal of the survivors to the four corners of the earth.

Jesus' Indictment of the Jewish Leadership
Core Scripture: Matthew 23:1-36

After having His authority officially challenged by the chief priests, teachers of the law, elders, Pharisees, Herodians, and the Sadducees, Jesus responds to the challenge with a scathing indictment, denunciation, and condemnation of the sinfulness of the Jewish leadership. After pronouncing seven woes on them, Jesus closes His public ministry. "The Pharisees are held accountable not only for their rejection of the Messiahship of Jesus, but also for leading the nation to the same rejection as well. …. The judgment is primarily upon the leaders, but also upon the nation whom the leaders led in the rejection of His Messiahship."[22] He was also going to hold them accountable for killing the Old Testament prophets.

The Second Sign of Jonah: Several days later, Jesus was crucified, buried, and was resurrected after three days, thus completing the second sign of Jonah. However, the Jewish leadership also rejected this sign by stoning Stephen because of his testimony of the true identity of Jesus as recorded in Acts 7. Thus, beginning in Acts 8, the gospel of the kingdom is extended to the non-Jewish peoples.

THE RESULTS AND CONSEQUENCES OF THE REJECTION

"When Jesus was rejected, the offer of the Messianic Kingdom was rescinded and the Mystery Kingdom replaced it."[24]

An interesting question arises at this point: What would have happened had the Jewish leadership accepted the Messiahship of Jesus and the offer of the kingdom? As the rejection of Jesus and His subsequent death were already foretold by Old Testament prophecies (and keep in mind the anticipation of a second coming by the same One as would come the first time; based on the passages discussed above), a likely scenario might have been that the Roman government would have seen Jesus and His kingdom as a treasonous rebellion against Caesar, which would have led to Jesus' death and resurrection anyway. What would have happened after His resurrection is speculative at best.

After the rejection of His Messiahship in Matthew 12 resulting in the unpardonable sin, Jesus radically changed His ministry in four ways:
- First - The Purposes of Miracles:
  + Before Matthew 12: Jesus performed miracles for the purpose of authenticating His identity.
  + After Matthew 12: He trained the apostles for their forthcoming ministry as recorded in the Book of Acts.
- Second - The People for whom He Performed Miracles:
  + Before Matthew 12: Without requiring faith first, Jesus performed miracles for the masses; those He healed to proclaim what Jesus had done.
  + After Matthew 12: Requiring faith first, Jesus performed miracles for those with a specific need for a miracle; Jesus required those being healed to tell anyone of the miracle.
- Third - The Message that was Proclaimed:
  + Before Matthew 12: Jesus and the apostles went about the land proclaiming Jesus to be the Messiah.
  + After Matthew 12: Jesus required the apostles to be silent regarding His identity until it was rescinded by the Great Commission in Matthew 28:18-20.
- Fourth - Jesus' Teaching Method:
  + Before Matthew 12: Messages that were taught were clearly understandable by the masses.
  + After Matthew 12: As a sign of judgment, messages to the masses were taught in parables for three reasons to fulfill Isaiah 6:9-20 and Matthew 13:34-35 (which included a reference from Psalm 78:2):
    o The parabolic method would be used to illustrate the truth.
    o So that the masses would not understand the truth.
    o To fulfill prophecy as foretold.
  + Mark 4:33-34 adds the additional fact that when Jesus was alone with the disciples, He explained the meaning of the parables taught to the masses.

43.7   THE BASIS OF THE SECOND ADVENT

The Bible teaches that there are no preconditions for the Rapture of the Church, however, there are two major preconditions that must be met specifically by Israel before Christ can come to establish the Millennial Kingdom. The following passages delineate the two preconditions necessary for Christ's return.
- Leviticus 26:40-42: Like Exodus 23:22-33, Deuteronomy 28, and Joshua 24:20, this passage describes the covenant blessings for Israel's obedience as well as their curses for disobedience. The history of Israel remarkably

follows the sequence of God's words. The verse before the passage being examined, Leviticus 26:39, seems to suggest that Israel has been scattered to the nations of the world, thus setting the stage for the passage that follows. According to verse 42, God intends to fulfill His covenant promises to Israel. As indicated in verse 40, before Israel can enjoy the blessings of the covenant promises, she must *confess their sins of their ancestors unfaithfulness and their hostility toward me.*

- Jeremiah 3:11-18: This passage looks forward to when God will restore Israel and Judah as one nation and bless them in their land in the kingdom ruled by their Messiah from the Temple, however, the blessings are contingent on verse 13 where they must confess their wrongdoing and rebellion, they must confess their idolatry with foreign gods because of their disobedience.
- Zechariah 12 - 14: These three chapters form one unit of thought regarding the events associated with Christ's Second Return, with Chapter 13 indicating that Israel will be cleansed from their sin, and Chapter 14 indicating events in Jerusalem, the coming of the Messiah, and the establishment of the kingdom. However, these are all conditioned on verse 12:10, "... Israel must first look unto the One whom they have pierced and must plead for His return."[25]
- Hosea 5:15: "The national offense of Israel was in the rejection of His Messiahship. According to this verse, only when this offence is acknowledged or confessed will Christ come back to the earth."[26]
- Matthew 23:37-39: Immediately following Jesus' indictment of the Jewish leadership, Christ indicates His desire to gather the Jews unto Himself if they would only accept Him, however, because of their rejection of His Messiahship, they will be scattered and their house (the Temple) will be left desolated. Jesus declares that they will not see Him again until they say, *Blessed is he who comes in the name of the Lord!* (Matthew 23:39)

Thus the observation that can be developed from these five passages is that, "Jesus will not come back to earth until the Jews and the Jewish leaders ask Him to come back. Just as the Jewish leaders led the nation to the rejection of the Messiahship of Jesus, they must someday lead the nation to the acceptance of the Messiahship of Jesus. This, then, is the twofold basis of the second coming of Christ: Israel must confess her national sin and then plead for Messiah to return, to *mourn for Him as one mourns for an only son.* Until these two things happen, there will be no second coming."[27]

43.8 THE CHANGE IN ISRAEL'S BELIEFS

All of Israel's existence has been spent in the expectation of Her Messiah. When Israel had the chance of accepting the Messiah, she instead rejected Him, and later suffered cataclysmic destruction which set the nation and its people on a course of dispersion that has lasted for two thousand years. All this time Israel was spiritually blind and did not realize that their Messiah was before them. As

Daniel's 70th Week wages on, Israel will eventually realize their spiritual blindness and will confess their national sins and plead for Christ's return.

ISRAEL'S SPIRITUAL BLINDNESS

Isaiah anticipated a time in which the nation would be judicially blinded by a divine judgment in 6:9-10. This Old Testament prophecy is subsequently quoted by Jesus (Matthew 13:14-15; Mark 4:12, Luke 8:10), by John (John 12:37-40), and by Paul (Acts 28:26-27 and 2 Corinthians 3:14-15) to demonstrate Israel's attitude toward Christ thus fulfilling the prophecy. Paul outlines the prophetic nature of this blindness, or hardening, in Romans 11:

- 11:1-24: Paul makes an impassioned presentation that it is according to God's Plan that Israel would be disobedient to the offer of the Messiah and the kingdom so that the Gentiles would have an opportunity to experience the grace that He has for all of those that believe in Him. As a consequence of the rejection of the offer, Israel was blinded and hardened to the salvation work that had been done by Jesus, however, the blindness was to only be partial and temporary, and not complete and final. The partial aspect can be seen in that there will be some Jews who come to saving faith in Jesus during the course of the Church Age, and the temporary aspect can be seen, as discussed above, in that Israel will eventually confess their unpardonable sin and will plead for the return of the very One that they had previously rejected.
- 11:25-26a: Paul emphasizes that he did not want the Roman Jews, and hence all Jews, to be ignorant of the mystery of the church. He indicates that the blindness would not be permanent and would end when the Lord determines that enough Gentiles are set aside as holy (Acts 15:14); … "[i] n other words, God has a set number of Gentiles that He has destined to come into the lace of blessing, the Olive Tree of verses 16-24."[28] After the Church is completely full of believing Gentiles and Jews, God will direct Jesus to remove the Church in the Rapture and will shift His attention from saving individuals to saving the nation of Israel. Fruchtenbaum points out that the use of the word 'all' does not mean that all Jews that have ever lived will be saved; instead, it is limited to only those Jews living in the nation at the end of Daniel's 70th Week that will be saved.
- 11:26b-27: Paul provides a New Testament endorsement of the Old Testament prophetic truth that God will deliver Israel from her ungodliness and will take her away her sins that are recorded in Isaiah 59:20-21 and 27:9. This is also part of the promise of the New Covenant described in Jeremiah 31:33-34.
- 11:28: Paul them makes the analytical observation that in spite of the New Covenant promises and the fact that He has elected Israel to be His covenant people, God hardens and alienates Israel so that she becomes an enemy to the Gospel so that the Gentiles would have the opportunity

to come to Him. Paul also points out that God still dearly loves the nation because of the covenant promises made to the founding fathers of Israel.

- 11:29: In a delineation of God's sovereignty, Paul expresses another Old Testament truth in which God's call of election to holiness is irrevocable, and that the covenant promises are a gift of grace from Him, also which is irrevocable.
- 11:30-32: "… Paul provided the principle for what is going to happen concerning the calling out of the Gentiles and Israel's national salvation. He pointed out that unbelief has given God a chance to reveal His mercy, not on the deserving, but on the undeserving. Once the Gentiles were disobedient but now have obtained mercy. Now Israel is in disobedience but now have been put on the level where they are eligible for mercy, for God has shut up all that He might have mercy on all, and that is the summary of the gospel."[29]
- 11:33-36: Paul closes the passage with a strong doxology that worships the wisdom and glory of God.

THE CONFESSION OF ISRAEL'S NATIONAL SIN

As was seen above in Hosea 5:15, after His rejection the Messiah would return to heaven until the time that was designated for Israel's punishment had taken place, after which they would seek the One that they had rejected. That the Jewish leadership of a presumably future nation will confess of the sinfulness of the earlier nation is recorded in the Old Testament.

- Hosea 6:1-3: While recognizing that God has judged the disobedience of Israel over the course of her history, at some point in time the leadership will confess of their wrongdoing and will call for return to the safety and security of the Lord God. The picture that is painted by the passage is that, first, Israel has experienced the agony of existence without God that has been exacerbated by the judgments of Daniel's 70th Week, second, is now repentant of her lifelong sinfulness and disobedience, and third, recognizes that if they acknowledge and return to Him, He will rescue them from their distress and restore them to a vibrant state of existence in the Lord's blessing. "Just as the Jewish leaders once led the nation to the rejection of the Messiahship of Jesus, they will now lead the nation to the acceptance of His Messiahship by issuing the call of Hosea 6:1-3."[30]
- Isaiah 53:1-9: Fruchtenbaum[31] believes that his passage is the actual words that will be confessed by the Jewish leadership. Whether this will be the actual words or not remains to be seen, however, the nation will finally see the light and will make the following admissions of miscalculation, misinterpretation, and misunderstanding.[32]
  + 53:1-3 - Isaiah's Confession of Rejection: Isaiah indicates that Israel did not value the Servant Jesus, she considered Him to be an ordinary man.

- o 53:1: Israel will lament the fact that they did not believe anyone who would believe that their message about Jesus would have been from God.
- o 53:2: Israel will admit that Jesus did not suit their messiah expectation:
  - He did not have the physical appearance that they wanted to follow and believe.
  - He lacked the royal and majestic bearing that they wanted the messiah to have had when he appeared.
- o 53:3: Israel will confess that while Jesus was acquainted with pain, sorrow, and suffering, they despised and rejected Him, they were repulsed by Him, and they considered Him to be insignificant.
- + 53:4-6 - Israel's Realization of His Substitutionary Death: Israel will finally realize the significance of the death and resurrection of Jesus.
  - o 53:4: Israel will acknowledge that they misinterpreted the significance of the death of Jesus. Originally believing His death was punishment by God for something else He had done, Israel will later realize that His death was the consequences of their sinfulness. "The Servant vicariously took on Himself all the sins (and spiritual anguish caused by sin) of the nation (and the whole world) and carried ... them to Himself."[33]
  - o 53:5: Israel will confess that Jesus was pierced through for their rebellion, crushed for their sinfulness, and eternal punishment all for them; and because of His suffering they will be spiritually healed and will have internal peace.
  - o 53:6: Israel will admit that the nation behaved like a herd of sheep that tend to follow the leading sheep and go where he goes without knowing if it is a right way or a wrong way. The admission will be for having taken a wrong path of rebellion that caused the need for a sacrifice for sinfulness.
- + 53:7-9 - Israel's Account of the Death of the Servant: Israel will acknowledge Jesus' willful and sacrificial death.
  - o Isaiah 53:7: Israel will acknowledge that Jesus willingly and silently submitted Himself to a harsh death to bear the burden of people's sin.
  - o Isaiah 53:8: Israel will admit to having subjected Jesus to a false and unjust trial that resulted in His death, not for anything that He had done, but for what they themselves had done.
  - o Isaiah 53:9: Israel will recognize that even though they intended to bury Jesus with criminals, He ended up in the tomb of a rich man because He had not committed any act that justified His burial with criminals.

PLEADING FOR THE MESSIAH TO RETURN

There are a number of passages that reveal that a day will come in which Israel will plead for the Messiah to return to save them from their enemies. The enemies will be the several armies of the world that will be battling within the land of Israel as part of the Campaign of Armageddon.

- The Psalms: While there are a number of Psalm that expresses Israel's poetic pleadings for the Lord's deliverance from trouble, there are two that merit a closer look.
    + 79:1-13: An invasion by foreigners, a defiled temple, a ruined Jerusalem, the death of many, and a nation despised by its neighbors, all converge to cause the surviving remnant to plead for the Lord to come to their aid and to judge the nations that are resistant to following God. The nation seeks forgiveness from the sovereign Master that has the power to forgive and the strength to judge the enemies of the people.
    + 80:1-19: Israel pleads for their Shepherd to come to them and deliver them from their distress and to no longer be angry with them. They asked the Lord to restore them to the place of peace and security that they had been at before and have been promised to be at again someday.
- Isaiah 64:1-12: Israel pleads for the Lord to tear apart the sky and let the nations know that He is like no other god of powerful and awesome ability that has ever been seen before. Israel recognizes that their Lord distinguishes between righteous deeds, for which He blesses, and unrighteous deeds, for which He punishes. The nation admits to the futility of their disobedience that has caused God to reject them. They also understand that their God is like a potter, and they are like the clay, and if they submit it to the potter, he will form them into a vessel of incredible value that will be treasured by the potter. The nation pleads with God to deliver them from their unrighteousness, from the distress of a desolate land and destroyed cities, from the agony of a burned and defiled temple in the midst of a ruined Jerusalem.
- Joel 2:28-32: The prophet says that everyone that calls on the name of the Lord will be given the Holy Spirit to regenerate and deliver them from the terrible and dark days of the end of history.
- Zechariah 12:10 - 13:1: Israel will look to the One they had pierced and by great lamentation will plead for deliverance that will result in the cleansing of their sin.
- Zechariah 13:7-9: The Lord indicates that He will direct the death of His Associate, the Shepherd, after which the flock will be scattered (most likely fulfilled by the destruction of Jerusalem in AD 70). Persecution of the saints will happen throughout the age, however two-thirds of the Jewish Christians will perish during Daniel's 70th Week. The one-third that survives will be refined and purified under the trials of Daniel's 70th Week in the same manner as precious metals are purified. Finally, they will call on the Lord, who will then answer.

SO WHAT DOES THIS ALL MEAN?

We can see that the state of affairs at the end of Daniel's 70ᵗʰ Week will be such that the leadership of the nation of Israel will recognize the sins of the current nation as well as the sin of Israel throughout her history, will confess of that sin, and will plead for the return of the One that was crucified two millennia ago. For all intents and purposes, the six purposes for the Daniel's 70ᵗʰ Week of these seven years, enumerated in Chapter 28, have all been accomplished.

- First Purpose: Israel has now been sufficiently punished for her rejection of the Messiah, and her judicial hardening has been removed.
- Second Purpose: Because of all that has happened to her over the seven years of Daniel's 70ᵗʰ Week, Israel's will, is now broken and she is prepared to receive her Messiah.
- Third Purpose: Again, because of all of the unprecedented measures or troubles that have prevailed over Israel over the past seven years which essentially serves as the capstone of an edifice of rebellion, Israel finds that she needs the Messiah to come to restore her to her divinely intended state by providing provision, protection, and rule.
- Fourth Purpose: Because of all those who, at great personal risk, have diligently evangelized the world in the midst of her darkest hour, humankind has now had its last chance to hear the Gospel and turn from sinfulness to follow the Lord - the last revival has now occurred.
- Fifth Purpose: With the Gentile armies of the world converging onto the Jewish nation with a specific focus on Jerusalem, part of the reason for Israel's pleading for the return of the Messiah is the realization that the covenant promises imply that deliverance from Gentile domination will be fulfilled as part of God's restoration of the nation.
- Sixth Purpose: While only affecting Israel indirectly, the multitude of judgments that have been poured out on an unbelieving world for the last seven years has convinced Israel that she is ready to accept the Messiah.

43.9 THE SECOND ADVENT OF JESUS

DANIEL'S CONTRIBUTION

Do you remember Daniel's interpretation of the statue of Nebuchadnezzar's dream? Do you remember the stone that will destroy the statue? Who do you believe the stone represents, and, what does the mountain represent? Let's continue with the examination of the Times of the Gentiles started in Chapter 20 where God had given Nebuchadnezzar a dual-purpose dream. In addition to teaching Nebuchadnezzar a lesson in power, the dream was given for the purpose of providing the Biblical canon with an outline of the remaining history of the world that would see something destroy the greatest nations of the world. We pick up the story in Daniel 2, more in verses 34, 35, 44, and 45.

- After seeing an impressive statue of a man composed of various metals, gold, silver, bronze, iron and clay, in a dream, Nebuchadnezzar also sees a stone, uncut by human hands, hit the statue in its feet, and smash it into so many small pieces that they will be blown away by the wind. The stone then grows into a mountain that filled the entire earth.
- We have already examined in detail the identity of the powerful nations that are represented by the various metals, which will dominate Israel and have concluded that the dream and Daniel's interpretation also indirectly provides a useful timeline for the remaining history of the world.
- The most accurate interpretation of the stone is that it represents Jesus Christ as can also be seen in Psalm 118:22, Isaiah 8:14. 28:16, and 1 Peter 2:6-8. While not necessarily acknowledging that the stone represents Christ, Walvoord states that it is "… a symbolic picture of political sovereignty. The stone is part and parcel of the sovereignty of God of which it is an effective expression."[35]
- The symbolism of a mountain in Scripture is usually a reference to a kingdom.

Walvoord makes a succinct conclusion of this portion of Scripture: "The effect is that the fifth kingdom (stone turning into a mountain), the kingdom of God, replaces completely all vestiges of the preceding kingdoms, which prophecy can only be fulfilled in any literal sense by a reign of Christ over the earth."[35]

THE GLORIOUS APPEARING

Core Scripture: Revelation 19:11-16

The point between the tenth and eleventh verses of Revelation 19 represents a turning point in the flow of the Bible. While considerable prophetic information of the Lord's Second Advent can be found all over the Bible, it is here that Jesus discloses His revelation to the Apostle John that He will come to earth again to fulfill the covenant promises and to conclude human dominated history. It is here and extending to the end of the Book, which is the end of the Bible that all remaining and outstanding prophecy begins to be fulfilled. It is here that everything anticipated by God's chosen nation Israel, expected by Christ's church, and feared by an unbelieving world, will occur. It is here that the Son of God goes forth to war for His victory over all that stands in rebellion and to gather His own to Himself.

Revelation 19:11
John sees the heavens open up and a white horse come forth, ridden by the One that is Faithful and True and He comes to judge and to go to war.
- Heavens Opened Up: Just as had happened in earlier portions of the Book of Revelation, John is given the opportunity to see inside heaven: John saw a door standing open in 4:1, and he saw the heavenly temple standing open in 11:19. Now, just as Ezekiel (1:1), John sees heaven flung open!

While neither Ezekiel nor John describe what they see, we can hope that the absence of details is that they were too wondrous to describe in human words.

- White Horse and Rider Coming Out: Standing in stark contrast to the white horse that comes forth in Revelation 6:1 which we have identified as the Antichrist mimicking the expected savoir of the world, this time the rider is identified as Faithful and True, an obvious reference to Jesus Christ who comes riding out on a white horse in the custom of a Roman general riding in ceremonial procession in the main street of Rome, the Via Sacra, to signify conquest, triumph, and victory. Interestingly, the interpretation of the Greek words *pistos* (meaning to be trusted, reliable, said of God) and *alethinos* (meaning true in the sense of real, ideal, genuine) as Faithful and True is consistently found in the KJV, the NASB, the NIV, the NKJV, the AMP, and the NET Bibles. The sense of this reference is to stand in opposition to the false messiah that claimed to be the Savior earlier.
- In Righteousness He Judges: The rider, obviously Jesus Christ, comes to bring the judgment that had long been promised to the unbelieving.
- Goes to War: In what seems to be answer to the question asked in Revelation 13:4 by the followers of the Antichrist as to who can stand up to the beast. Christ comes forth as the One who can not only stand up to him, but can and will be victorious over him as foretold in Revelation 17:14.
- Events in the Sky: While it is not recorded here, there are other passages, that have been examined above, that describe the celestial events that will be taking place at the time of, and contributing to the glory of, His Appearing, cf. Matthew 24:27-31.

Revelation 19:12-13
The rider is further described as having eyes like a fiery flame, wearing many crowns on his head, having a name written that is known to no one except Himself, wearing clothing dipped in blood, and called the Word of God.

- Eyes Like a Fiery Flame: This is the third time in Revelation, the others being 1:14 and 2:18, in which Jesus is identified as having eyes like a fiery flame. This description suggests that He is able to see into the souls of humans in order to see their true nature and to righteously judge their sin.
- Crowns: While not specifying the exact number as seen elsewhere in Revelation for other reasons, Jesus is seen wearing many crowns identified as diadems, the sovereign crowns of royalty. Perhaps the number is not mentioned because no matter how many crowns may be worn by a human imposter, Jesus will always be able to rightfully possess more.
- Unknown Name: While this aspect of Jesus Christ's description is somewhat mysterious, a possible interpretation is that it is a name not seen before for Him because of how and who He is coming at this time. Keep in mind that there are numerous names used for God and Jesus throughout the Bible that is usually in reference to what He is doing at the time. Johnson makes an interesting comment: "Knowledge of the name is in antiquity

associated with the power of the god. When a name becomes known, then the power is shared with those to whom the disclosure is mad ... it may conclude that the exclusive power of Christ over all creation is now to be shared with his faithful followers ..."[36]

- Clothing Dipped in Blood: This particular description of Christ can be interpreted in one of two ways that are instrumental in determining exactly where Christ goes first:
  + The Blood is Christ's Own: "Some think this refers to Christ's blood, which he shed for humanity at the cross."[37]
  + The Blood is from Christ's Enemies: There are actually two schools of thought for this view:
    o Walvoord: While not identifying the source of the blood, Walvoord believes the blood symbolically represents divine judgment on wickedness, and Christ comes from heaven with the blood already on His robe.[38]
    o Fruchtenbaum: As Christ comes from heaven He goes first to Bozrah, where the one-half of the Jews who fled Jerusalem have gone when the city was attacked. There, Jesus will engage in combat to destroy the enemies of Israel and by the time He gets to Israel He will be stained with the blood of God's enemies as anticipated by Isaiah in 63:1-6.[39]

Revelation 19:14
Along with Jesus come heavenly armies, finely dressed in white and riding on white horses.

- Heavenly Armies: Some believe that those that come with Jesus are angelic armies because there are so many other references to the angels being the soldiers and armies of heaven, however, why is it necessary for angels to ride horses, and why would they need to be victorious over the wicked armies of the Antichrist. Because of the proximity of Revelation 19:6-10 that immediately precedes this passage, the more probable interpretation is that these armies are the saints of the Church that were raptured before Daniel's 70th Week. This is further confirmed by Revelation 17:14 where the beast will make war against the Lamb and the chosen, faithful followers. Walvoord[40] tend to not limit the heavenly armies to the Church; he believes the armies could include angelic hosts.
- Dressed in White: White clothing traditionally represents purity and righteousness in the Bible.

Revelation 19:15
Jesus strikes down the nations (the Gentiles) with a sharp sword that extends from his mouth, and declares that He will rule with an iron rod, and He stomps the winepress exercising the fury and wrath of the All Present God.

- (The Nations) The Gentiles: Notice that this initial action by Christ is taken against the nations of the earth rather than wicked individuals.

- Sharp Sword Extending from His Mouth: This image is hard to interpret and army be as a possible fulfillment of Isaiah 49:1-7, Jesus will use the Word of God as the instrument of war to strike down unrighteous nations in order to establish His sovereign rule. Notice that there is no Old Testament parallel to this imagery, and it seems to be exclusively used by the Apostle John.
- Rule with Iron Rod: Quoting from Psalm 2:9, this seems to represent and "... unyielding, absolute government under which men are required to conform to the righteous standards of God."[41]
- Stomps the Winepress: Anticipated in Isaiah 63:1-6, Jesus will exercise divine judgment on those that have rejected grace - it is too late for the mercy of God.

Revelation 19:16

The rider of the white horse has a name on His clothing and His thigh that says King of kings and Lord of lords. "Here at last has come One who has a right to rule the earth, One whose power and majesty will demonstrate His authority as He brings to bear His sovereign judgment on a wicked world.[42]

43.10 THE OBSERVATIONS OF THE SECOND COMING

THE MULTIFACETED FULFILLMENT

The Bible still has much to say about the Lord Jesus Christ's return to earth.
- First and Last Biblical Prophecies of Christ's Second Advent:
  + First: Jude 14-15 indicates that Enoch, the seventh in line from Adam, is the first Biblical figure to anticipate a future coming of the Lord along with thousands, to bring judgment on the ungodly.
  + Second: Jesus Himself provides the last prophetic statement of the Bible of His coming in Revelation 22:20-21.
- At the End of Daniel's 70th Week: Matthew 24:21-29 and the many passages listed above reveal that it will be at the end of the seven-year time of Daniel's 70th Week when Christ will return.
- Premillennial: The Lord's return will be prior to the one-thousand-year Millennium.
- Literal Event: In order to fulfill Acts 1:11, Jesus will literally return to earth.
- Personal Event: Acts 1:11 reveals that Jesus Himself will personally come to earth.
- A Bodily Return: Zechariah 14:4 reveals that Christ will return in His resurrection body that will occupy a single physical, three-dimensional (Euclidian) space. Some believe that Ephesians 4:10 teaches that Christ becomes omnipresent at His resurrection and fills all things and is in everything. While He is certainly omnipresent, this is not a valid interpretation of the passage, and Scripture does not support that He is in everything.

- A Full and Visible Return:
  + Matthew 24:30: *Then will appear the sign of the Son of Man in heaven. And then all the peoples of the earth will mourn when they see the Son of Man coming on the clouds of heaven, with power and great glory.*
  + Acts 1:11: Jesus visibly ascended into heaven, therefore, if He returns as He ascended, He will return visibly as well.
  + Revelation 1:7: Jesus' return will be witnessed by humankind the world over.
- A Geographical Presence: The following passages predict that the Deliverer will come to, and out of, Jerusalem:
  + Job 19:25: Jesus Christ will stand on earth.
  + The Psalms:
    ○ 14:7: *Oh, that salvation for Israel would come from Zion!*
    ○ 20:2: *and grant you support from Zion."*
    ○ 53:6: *Oh, that salvation for Israel would come out of Zion!*
    ○ 110:2: *The Lord will extend your mighty scepter from Zion, saying "Rule in the midst of your enemies!"*
    ○ 128:5: *May the Lord bless you from Zion; may you see the prosperity of Jerusalem all the days of your life.*
    ○ 134:3: *May the Lord bless you from Zion, he who is the Maker of heaven and earth.*
    ○ 135:21: *Praise be to the Lord from Zion, to him who dwells in Jerusalem. Praise the Lord.*
  + Isaiah 2:3: *Many people will come and say, "Come, let us go up to the mountain of the Lord, to the temples of the god of Jacob. He will teach us his ways, so that we may walk in his paths." The law will go out from Zion, the word of the Lord from Jerusalem.*
  + Joel 3:16: *The Lord will roar from Zion and thunder from Jerusalem; the earth and the heavens will tremble. But the Lord will be a refuge for his people, a stronghold for the people of Israel.*
  + Amos 1:2: *He said: "The Lord roars from Zion and thunders from Jerusalem; the pastures of the shepherds dry up, and the top of Carmel withers."*
  + Zechariah 14:3-4: He will stand on the Mount of Olives.
  + Romans 11:26: *... The deliverer will come from Zion ...*
  + Matthew 24:30 (cf. Revelation 1:7): He will return in the clouds
- A Glorious and Powerful Return:
  + Matthew 16:27 and 25:31: He will come in glory with His angels and will sit on His throne.
  + 2 Thessalonians:
    ○ 1:8: Jesus will come with flaming fire.
    ○ 1:10: Jesus will come to be glorified in His holy saints.
  + 1 Peter 1:7 and 4:13: The revelation of the glory of Christ's return will glorify the suffering of believers.
  + Revelation:

303

- o 1:12-17: Provides details of His glorious state of being
- o 14:7 and 19:1: The act of Christ's return will glorify God the Father.
- o 19:11-16: Description of the glory of Christ's appearance and the procession from heaven.
- Accompanied by the Angels and Saints:
  - + Matthew 25:31: Jesus will come with His angels.
  - + 1 Thessalonians 3:13: Paul encourages the Thessalonians by telling them: *May he strengthen your hearts so that you will be blameless and holy in the presence of our God and Father when our Lord Jesus comes with all his holy ones.*
    - o Jude 14-15: ... *the Lord is coming with thousands upon thousands of his holy ones to judge everyone* ...
    - o Revelation 19:11-21: In the passage about Christ's Second Return, the following is found: *The armies of heaven were following him, riding on white horses and dressed in fine linen, white and clean.*
- Will Deliver the Elect:
  - + Matthew 24:22: Christ's return will cut short the final battle for the sake of the elect.
  - + Luke 21:28: Redemption draws near.
  - + John 5:28: The dead will hear Christ's voice.
  - + Romans 11:26-27: Israel will be saved.
- Will Be Mourned by Unbelievers: Matthew 24:30 (cf. Revelation 1:7) indicates that all the people on earth will mourn over Him, the sense being that many will realize that Jesus really does exist and they have not accepted His offer of salvation.
- Will Fight and Destroy the Enemies of Israel:
  - + Zechariah 14:3: *Then the Lord will go out and fight against those nations, as he fights on a day of battle.*
  - + Revelation 19:17-21: ... *the beast and the kings of the earth and their armies gathered together to wage war against* Jesus Christ and His armies. The beast (Antichrist) and the false prophet *were thrown alive into the fiery lake of burning sulfur. The rest were killed with the sword coming out of the mouth of the rider on the horse* ...
- Will Judge the Earth:
  - + Matthew:
    - o 19:28: The apostles will judge the tribes of Israel.
    - o 24:29 - 25:46: Gentiles and Jews will be judged.
  - + Luke 17:29-30: Judgment will be like that of Sodom.
  - + 2 Thessalonians:
    - o 1:8-9: *He will punish those who do not know God and do not obey the gospel of our Lord Jesus. They will be punished with everlasting destruction and shut out from the presence of the Lord and the glory of his might.*
    - o 2:8: The lawless one, the Antichrist, will be judged.

+ Jude 15: The ungodly will be convicted.
+ Revelation:
  ○ 2:27: In addition to His iron rule, Jesus will break the wicked.
  ○ 19:11-21: The participants of the Campaign of Armageddon will be judged.

THE NECESSITY OF THE LORD'S RETURN

Throughout this book, the point has been made, and it most like certainly is applicable here as well, that in order for God to have the credibility that He says He has in the Bible, it is absolutely essential that Jesus Christ return to earth in glory to fulfill all of the covenant promises to Israel, as well as to fulfill all of the outstanding prophecies of the Bible. If He does not return, then the Bible as the foundation of God's revelation to humankind will not be reliable and all that we believe will be like chaff blowing in the wind. Finally, the Lord's return is necessary because He has to be on earth so that He can rule during the one-thousand-year Millennium.

THE EXHORTATIONS ASSOCIATED
WITH THE SECOND ADVENT

Pentecost[43] has assembled an extensive listing of various passages where an exhortation is made in the context of the Lord's return;
* Matthew 24:42-44; 25:13 (cf. Mark 13:32-37; Luke 12:35-38; and Revelation 16:15): To watchfulness.
* 1 Thessalonians 5:2-6 (cf. 1 Peter 1:13; 4:7, and 5:8): To sobriety.
* Acts 3:19-21 (cf. Revelation 3:3): To repentance.
* Matthew 25:19-21 (cf. Luke 12:42-44; and 19:12-13): To fidelity.
* Mark 8:38: To be unashamed of Christ.
* Matthew 16:26-27: To be against worldliness.
* Philippians 4:5: To moderation.
* Hebrews 10:36-37 (cf. James 5:7-9:8): To patience.
* Colossians 3:3-5: To mortification of the flesh.
* Philippians 1:9-10: To sincerity.
* 1 Thessalonians 5:23: To practice sanctification.
* 2 Timothy 4:1-2: To ministerial faithfulness.
* 1 Timothy 6.13-14: To incite obedience to the apostles' injunctions.
* 1 Peter 5:2-4: To pastoral diligence and purity.
* 1 John 3:2-3: To purity.
* 1 John 2:28: To abide in Christ.
* 1 Peter 1:7: To endure manifold temptations and the severest trials of faith.
* 1 Peter 4:13: To bear persecutions.
* 2 Peter 3:11-13: To holiness and godliness.

- 1 Thessalonians 3:12-13: To brotherly love.
- Philippians 3:20-21: To keep in mind our heavenly citizenship.
- 2 Timothy 4:7-8: To love the second coming.
- Hebrews 9:27-28: To look for Him.
- Philippians 1:6: To have confidence that Christ will finish the work.
- Revelation 2:25 and 3:11: To hold fast the hope firm unto the end.
- Titus 2:11-13: To separation from worldly lusts and to live godly.
- Luke 17:24-30: To watchfulness because of its suddenness.
- 1 Corinthians 4:5: To guard against hasty judgment.
- Matthew 19:27-28: To the hope of a rich reward.
- 2 Corinthians 1:14 (cf. Philippians 2:16 and 1 Thessalonians 2:19): To assure the disciples of a time of rejoicing.
- John 14:3 (cf. Acts 1:11): To comfort the apostles in view of Christ's departure.
- 1 Thessalonians 1:9-10: The principal events for which the believer awaits.
- 1 Corinthians 1:4-8: A crowning grace and assurance of blamelessness in the day of the Lord.
- Matthew 25:19: The time of reckoning with the servants.
- Matthew 25:31-46: The time of judgment of the living Gentiles.
- 1 Corinthians 15:23: The time of completion of the resurrection program for the saved.
- 2 Corinthians 5:10 (cf. Colossians 3:4): The time of the manifestation of the saints.
- 1 Thessalonians 4:14-18: A source of consolation.
- 2 Thessalonians 1:7-9: Associated with tribulation and judgment for the unsaved.
- 1 Corinthians 11:26: Proclaimed at the Lord's Table.

44

THE RESURRECTIONS

Walvoord has this to say about the several resurrections that have occurred or will occur: "From Genesis through Revelation the testimony of Scripture is that physical death does not end human existence, but that in one form or another life will go on. After death the soul of every human being continues its existence. Accountability for what has happened in life becomes a major issue in existence after death. In addition to the teaching that life goes on after death, the Scripture teach that at one time or another all will receive bodies suited for eternal existence. This is standard biblical doctrine."[1]

44.1	THE NATURE OF RESURRECTION

In previous chapters, we have seen that the Bible has much to say about the nature of human life and death. In addition to a complex but perishable physical human body we possess a spiritual soul that, while distinctly human and imperishable, is also complex on the basis that it is not composed of material matter. Our soul is something that even science in its infinite wisdom is unable to explain, define, or determine as to its origin or its destiny after physical death. The Bible effectively paints the picture that God originally created human beings with the capability to live eternally, but because of a spiritual separation from God resulting from sin, death of the physical body was introduced, but not death (annihilation) of the soul. The Bible also tells us that at a future date, our physical body will be resurrected and will be rejoined with our surviving spiritual soul and will become a recreated being to go to our eternal destiny.

There are some that believe that there will be one general resurrection at some time in the future of human history, however, this is not scripturally supported. The chronological study of the various resurrections in the Bible will establish the necessary doctrine. As you will notice, some are historical and some are still in the future.

THE REFERENCES TO RESURRECTION

- Job 19:25-26: Job understands that a Redeemer, in which he believes, lives and he will once again stand on the earth and that even though he will deteriorate after death, he will live again in his body (resurrection?) to see his Redeemer. "The Book of Job, probably written several hundred years before the rest of the Old Testament, presents substantial proof that the doctrine of resurrection was part of God's original revelation to the human race, carried forth by tradition and embodied here in the Scriptures."[2]

- Psalms 11:7 and 17:15: David recognizes that he, and other righteous people, will someday see the face of God, the sense being, long after their own physical death.
- Isaiah 26:19: The prophet Isaiah anticipates the dead of Judah will be raised from the grave to joyfully celebrate God.
- Daniel 12:1-2: The angel Michael discloses to Daniel the knowledge that everyone will be raised from the dead, with some going to eternal paradise and others going to eternal punishment.
- Ezekiel 37:24: While Ezekiel's prophecy about the restoration of Israel in the Valley of Dry Bones is not an example of resurrection, verse 24 does anticipate the resurrection of David as the ruling prince under the Messiah.
- Matthew:
  + 22:30 (cf. Luke 20:35-36): Jesus indicates that there will not be marriage among the resurrected people because they will be like angels.
  + 22:31-32: Jesus, answering the Sadducees that were trying to trick Him, indicates that there is and will be resurrection of the dead, because God is the God of the living, especially Israel's patriarchs, who yet physically are dead but still live.
- Luke 14:13-14: Jesus indicates that those that perform good works for the unfortunate will be repaid with blessing at the resurrection of the righteous.
- John 11:21-27: The story of the death of Lazarus reveals that those who believe in Jesus and the fact that He lives, or will live, after His own physical death, will never die.

44.2 FIRST AND SECOND RESURRECTIONS DEFINED

The New Testament distinguishes between a first resurrection and a second resurrection that needs to be clarified.

- John 5:24-30: As part of His response to persecution by the Jewish authorities for the work that He is doing, Jesus indicates that there will come a day when He will call out for those among the dead that believe in the message of the salvation He has provided and the One that sent Him to perform the work in order to provide the salvation, to rise from the grave to live again. In verse 29, He clarifies that there are two resurrections – those that have done what is good will be resurrected to life, while those that have done what is evil will be resurrected to condemnation. Thus, this passage clearly indicates that all people will one day live again after physical death.
- 1 Corinthians 15:23: Indicates that there will be an ordering of at least two resurrections.
- Revelation 20:4-6: Teaches the distinction between the two resurrections originally identified in the passage from John and it also indicates that there will be a second death that follows resurrection:

+ Revelation 20:4: The resurrected Tribulation Saints that John sees in heaven are identified as the "first" resurrection by verse 5.
+ Revelation 20:5: There are two parts to this verse that are important to see. The first part, the portion in parenthesis, implies that there is a group of people that are not raised (resurrected) at the same time as the Tribulation Saints. The reference to the first resurrection in the second part of the verse refers to those identified in verse 4, those in heaven, rather than those identified in the parenthetical portion of the first part of this verse. Furthermore, this implies that those that will not be resurrected at this time but will be at the end of the one-thousand-year period will constitute the "second" resurrection.
+ Revelation 20:6: The Lord says that those that are resurrected in the first resurrection will be blessed, which implies those of the second resurrection will not be blessed. The verse also indicates that the second death will have no power over those that will be of the first resurrection; this indicates several things:
  o A reference to a second death obviously indicates that human beings will live again after their own personal physical death.
  o If the second death has no power over the blessed of the first resurrection, then this suggests that the second death is one of punishment.
  o The implication for those resurrected as part of the second resurrection, is that the second death is associated with them.
• These several passages combined indicate that there will two categories of resurrections and two kinds of death:
  + The First Death: Physical death ultimately awaits every human being regardless if they are good (except, of course those that will be alive at the time of the Rapture) or evil.
  + The First Resurrection: Those that are righteous (good) will be resurrected separately from those that are unrighteous (evil), the implication being that they are raised immediately prior to the Millennium. As will be seen in the discussion below, the first resurrection of the saved will occur as different events over the course of history:
    o Resurrection of Jesus Christ: Almost two thousand years ago.
    o Resurrection of First-Fruits: At the same time as Christ's resurrection.
    o Resurrections at Rapture: At some undisclosed time in the future before Daniel's 70th Week.
    o Resurrection of Two Witnesses: During Daniel's 70th Week.
    o Resurrection of Tribulation Saints: During the 75-day interval.
    o Resurrection of Old Testament Saints: During the 75-day interval.
    o Resurrection of Millennium Saints: Not disclosed in the Bible.

+ The Second Resurrection: Those that are unrighteous (evil) are not resurrected until the end of the Millennium. The second resurrection will be a single event at the end of human history.
+ The Second Death: The blessed of the first resurrection *will not* experience this death, indicating that the righteous will spend eternity in the state of blessing in the presence of the Lord, however, the unblessed of the second resurrection *will* experience this death indicating that they will spend eternity in punishment separated from God.
- Walvoord concludes that the "... descriptions of the resurrections show that before the Millennium all the righteous dead will have been raised in one resurrection or another and will enter the millennial kingdom in their resurrection bodies. Only the wicked will remain in their graves to be subject to resurrection at the end of the millennial kingdom."[3]

44.3	**FIRST EVENT OF THE FIRST RESURRECTION – JESUS CHRIST**

There is considerable evidence in the Bible, mostly the New Testament, of Jesus willingly submitting Himself to the physical pain of earth, burial in an earthly grave, all in order to allow God to then resurrect Him, and to be witnessed by multitudes of people. Also, Jesus taught that resurrection from the dead was a future event for all human beings that would precede their judgment, and His own resurrection became the testimony for many others to believe in Him. Finally, Paul and the other New Testament authors reinforced this fact in the letters and books of the New Testament.

- Psalm 24:7-10: This Psalm of David anticipates the entry of the Messiah through the gates of Jerusalem, which is believed to be a reference to His entry into the Millennial Kingdom.
- Isaiah 11:3-5 and many others: There are many passages in the Bible like this passage that indicates that the Lord will someday rule over the nation of Israel, and if Jesus is the Lord, and was resurrected, then logic indicates that the one that will rule Israel will have been raised from the dead.
- Matthew 16:21; 17:22-23; and 20:17-19: Toward the end of His ministry, Jesus repeatedly said He would be betrayed, put to death, but then will be raised from the dead after three days.
- John:
  + 5:21: Jesus advises the Jewish authorities that He gives eternal life to whomever He wishes, just like God the Father raises the dead and gives life to them.
  + 5:28-29: Jesus very clearly says that the dead will be resurrected with those who have done well and will live eternally, and those that have done evil will be condemned to eternal punishment.
  + 6:29-40, 44, and 54: When Jesus is telling the multitudes that He is the Bread of life, He also says that it is God's will to draw certain individuals to Himself by having them believe in Jesus Christ as the Son of God

and in turn blessing them with eternal life by raising them from their own physical death and bestowing upon them resurrection bodies.

- Acts:
    + 1:22: When the apostles were electing the replacement for Judas, the primary criteria was that it had to be someone who had personally witnessed the resurrection of Jesus just as they had earlier.
    + 2:24: As part of the first sermon of the Church, Peter professes to those present that he witnessed, and consequently believes, that God raised Jesus from the dead and that death was not capable of holding Him.
    + 2:31-32: Also, during the first sermon, Peter related the Old Testament testimony that David believed that his descendent that would occupy the throne would do so after having been released from the grip of death.
    + 3:15 and 26: When confronting a crowd in the temple, Peter tells them that he and others had witnessed how they, the leadership of the nation, had killed the Founder of life who had come to serve them, but that God had raised Him from death.
    + 4:2 and 10: Peter is arrested by the priests, temple guards, and Sadducees because they were angry that he was teaching the people that Jesus had been resurrected from the dead.
    + 5:30: Again when in trouble with the Jewish authorities, Peter points out that the One that they have seized and killed was raised from the dead by the God of their forefathers.
    + 10:40: When witnessing to Cornelius and his household, Peter includes the testimony that Jesus was seen alive by witnesses three days after His resurrection.
    + 13:30, 34, and 37: Paul and Barnabas include Jesus' resurrection by God, as part of their testimony at Pisidian Antioch, in order to fulfill the promises made to David.
    + 17:18: Paul is criticized by the Athenian elites for having taught the Gospel that Jesus Christ once lived, was crucified, and then resurrected from the dead.
    + 17:31-32: Continuing his discourse before the Athenians, Paul advises them that God has set a day in the future when He will authorize a designated man to judge the people of the world, a man who He has been authenticated by raising him from death.
    + 23:6: While on trial before the Sanhedrin, Paul shouts at the council that he is one of them, a Pharisee, and that he is being tried for his belief in the One that was resurrected from the dead.
    + 24.15 and 21: When standing before Felix, Paul defends himself by pointing out that his hope in God was based on the fact that there will be a future day of resurrections for the just and the unjust.
    + 26:8: Another part of Paul's defense is his questioning of the accusers as to their lack of belief that God is capable of raising the dead.
- Romans:

+ 1:4: In Paul's salutation to the Romans, he says he is enslaved to the descendent of David, who, as the Son of God, is the same one that has been resurrected.
+ 4:23-25: As part of his illustration of justification, Paul concludes with the fact that the righteousness that was credited to Abraham is also credited to those who believe in the One that resurrected Jesus who was given to be the payment for the sinfulness of those that believe.
+ 6:4-5, and 9: Paul taught that those that believe in Jesus' death and resurrection for their personal sin are united with Him, and will be blessed with a resurrected body that will live eternally.
+ 7:4: Paul explains to the listeners that being united with Christ means they are dead to the Law, and that in unity, believers will bear fruit for God.
+ 8:11 and 34: Belief that Jesus was resurrected from the dead that will assure that believers will also be raised from the dead, because He sits at the right hand of God interceding for those that believe.
+ 10:9: Paul very clearly states that salvation is based on confession and heartfelt belief in Jesus, the Son of God, who was resurrected by God.
- 1 Corinthians:
  + 6:14: Paul indicates that if God has the power to raise Jesus from the dead, then He has sufficient power to raise people from the dead.
  + 15:4 and 15-20: In his retort to the Corinthians' lack of belief in resurrection, Paul logically establishes that the resurrection of Jesus, and the resurrection of those people that believe in Jesus' resurrection, is central to the fullness of faith in God. He continues by pointing out that without the resurrection of Jesus then he and others are guilty, first of having falsely witnessed about God, and second, of having an empty and useless faith. He also makes the point that those who believed in Jesus and have already died, their bodies would remain dead until a future resurrection.
  + 15:23: Jesus will be the first fruits of those that will be resurrected later.
- 2 Corinthians:
  + 1:9: Paul reveals his own security by writing to the Corinthians that he does not fear death because he is confident that God will also raise him from the dead.
  + 4:14: As he does so many times in his epistles, Paul discloses that the same God that raised Jesus from the dead will also raise those who believe in Jesus from the dead and bring them into His presence.
  + 5:15: Paul's message of reconciliation includes the fact that those who believe in Jesus' resurrection no longer live for themselves, but instead they live for Christ.
- Galatians 1:1: Paul's salutation to the Galatians includes the fact that he was a personal witness, therefore an apostle, of the basis that he had seen Jesus in His resurrected body.

- Ephesians 1:20 and 2:6: Paul says that Jesus was resurrected by the power of God, who then seated Him at His right hand in the heavenly realm; and those that believe in this fact will also be resurrected and seated with Christ.
- Philippians 3:10-11: Paul says that his personal goal is to believe in and to share in Jesus' experiences, including suffering, so that he will be resurrected from the dead.
- Colossians:
    + 1:18: As well as being the head of the body, the True Church, Jesus is the firstborn of those that will ultimately be raised from the dead.
    + 2:12: Paul tells the Colossians that baptism identifies a believer with Jesus and is symbolic of being buried, and faith in the power of God results in being raised from the dead.
- 1 Thessalonians 1:10: In his response to the deterioration of the Thessalonians belief in the return of Jesus Christ, Paul indicates first, that the One who will return is also the One that God raised from the dead, and second, the One that will return is the One that will deliver believers from the wrath that is to come.
- 2 Timothy 2:8: Paul indicates that the Gospel he preaches is based on the descendent of David that was raised from the dead.
- Hebrews 6:2: The author of Hebrews indicates that the resurrection from the dead is foundational to belief in Jesus Christ.
- 1 Peter:
    + 1:3 and 21: In an eloquent description of the hope enjoyed by believers, Paul blesses God for His great mercy given to those people who have trust in, have faith in, and have a living hope in the One that God resurrected.
    + 3:21: Paul explains that baptism is not the washing off of dirt but is a symbolic pledge to God of belief in the resurrection of Jesus.
- Revelation 1:18: One of the first scenes John the Apostle encounters during his experiences that led him to write the Book of Revelation of Jesus Christ, is the Lord Himself proclaiming that He was once dead, but now is alive and will live forever.

44.4	**SECOND EVENT OF THE FIRST RESURRECTION - FIRST-FRUITS**

Matthew records an interesting event that occurs at the time of Jesus' death and resurrection that is not recorded by Mark, Luke, or John or any other New Testament author.

- Matthew 27:50-56: This passage documents the sequence of events that occurs beginning at the moment Christ breathes His last breath as a human.
    + 27:50: Jesus the Messiah, hanging in agony on the crude wooden cross, cries out for the second and last time words that are not revealed, but are most likely a repetition of His first day of asking God the Father why He has forsaken His son; He then dies.

+ 27:51: While Luke 23:45 records that the sun stopped shining, two other unexpected events occur at the moment of His death:
  ○ Torn Curtain: Also recorded by Mark and Luke, the heavy curtain that separates the holy of holies from the holy place in the Jewish Temple was torn apart, beginning at the top and extending full height to the bottom, signifying that access to God was no longer restricted. "As the divine commentary in Hebrews 10:19-22 signifies, the death of Jesus opened the way for ordinary believers to go into the holy of holies, where formerly only the Jewish high priests could go."[4]
  ○ Earthquake: Only recorded by Matthew, and all that is stated, is that the earth shook and the rocks split obviously indicating an earthquake of an undefined magnitude, however, it was of sufficient strength to open many tombs in the surrounding rock filled land.
+ 27:52-53: This passage indicates that the resurrection of saints occurs at the exact moment of Christ's death (the implication being that Christ would not have been the first resurrection as indicated by 1 Corinthians 15:23). However, what the passage actually says is that the tombs of many people, an undisclosed number of saints probably at a nearby cemetery, were opened by the earthquake, but, the saints within those tombs were not resurrected until after Christ's resurrection, at which time they went into the holy city of Jerusalem where they were seen by many people. The significance of this particular event is nowhere found in the Bible, however, two observations may be made:
  ○ The Distinction between Resurrection and Resuscitation (Restoration): "This token resurrection needs to be distinguished from restorations to life. The Bible records seven such miraculous restorations: a boy raised by Elijah; a boy raised by Elisha; three raised by Jesus (Jarius' daughter, the son of a widow of Nain, and Lazarus); Dorcas raised by Peter; and Eurtychus raised by Paul. However, these individuals were not given resurrection bodies, so they died a second time."[5]
  ○ The Possible Implication of the Token Resurrections: Many theologians and scholars believe the purpose for this event is to be a symbol of Israel's Feast of the First Fruits. Leviticus 23:9-14 details the Old Testament ceremony where the Israelites were to bring a sheaf of grain to the priest before the harvest begins, who will then wave it before the Lord as a token of the harvest to come. This view would substantiate Christ as the first fruits as stated in 1 Corinthians 15:23. "It may be that the resurrection of the saints in Jerusalem on the day of Christ's resurrection was, like the firstfruits offering, a token of the "harvest" to come when other saints will be raised."[6]

44.5 THIRD EVENT OF THE FIRST RESURRECTION – RAPTURE

There awaits at some yet to be determined time in history when the True Church will be snatched up, taken out of this world to meet the Lord in the air, given resurrection bodies, and taken into the eternal presence of God the Father. 1 Corinthians 15:51 and 1 Thessalonians 4:17 very clearly indicates that this will include those who are alive at the time who will be translated into resurrected bodies, as well as those who have previously died, whose bodies will be resurrected from the grave.

44.6 FOURTH EVENT OF THE FIRST RESURRECTION – TWO WITNESSES

The life of God's two witnesses described in Revelation 11:3-11 will serve God's purposes for forty-two months by standing in Jerusalem during Daniel's 70th Week witnessing about the surrounding events taking place and heralding the coming of Jesus Christ. The Antichrist will kill them, and they will remain where they fell and will be seen by the entire world. After three and one-half days, God will resurrect them by breathing new life into them, they will stand to be seen by the world, and then God will call them to heaven.

44.7 FIFTH EVENT OF THE FIRST RESURRECTION - TRIBULATION SAINTS

The Apostle John's Revelation tells us that there will be people that will not follow the Antichrist during Daniel's 70th Week, instead they will become believers in Jesus Christ, but many will be martyred for their new found faith.

The picture painted by the Bible is one in which the earth and those that live during the time between the Rapture and the Second Coming will experience unprecedented and unspeakable terror, difficulty, and horror, and those that become new believers will experience the worst of it. Not only will they experience the judgment catastrophes falling on earth, they will have to endure the tragedy of being pursued relentlessly by the Antichrist simply because of what they believe.

Revelation 20:4 reveals that those who will be martyred for not worshipping the Antichrist, as seen in Revelation 6:9-11 and 7:9-17, will reign with Christ in the Millennium, therefore, they will have to be resurrected in order to do so. Several observations are made by Walvoord[7] from these passages:
• First, this is a resurrection of a particular group of people and not the resurrection of all saints.
• Second, since the passage says that the resurrected martyred will reign with Christ for one thousand years; this resurrection has to occur before, or at the immediate beginning of the Messianic Millennium.

- Third, because Revelation 20:4 follows the Second Advent of Christ as described in 19:11-21, the implication is that this resurrection has to occur after Christ comes again. This fact is an obstacle to those that believe the rapture will be at the end of Daniel's 70th Week (Posttribulationism); why would Christ rapture the Church just a few days before He returns to earth and resurrects these saints?
- Fourth, these passages provide convincing evidence that Christ will come before the one-thousand-year millennial period thus supporting the Premillennial view of Christ's return.

	SIXTH EVENT OF THE FIRST
44.8	**RESURRECTION – OLD TESTAMENT SAINTS**

The Old Testament does not contain much about the resurrection of those who become saints prior to Christ's First Advent. However, in the progression of the doctrinal development of the resurrection of all living human beings after death, the pattern that has been revealed is that all those who are considered righteous will be resurrected to live during the one-thousand-year Millennial Kingdom. Scripture is the most at harmony regarding the Old Testament Saints, if the conclusion of a literal interpretation of Isaiah 26:19, Daniel 12;1-2, and John 5;28-29 has them resurrected during the 75-day Interval so that they will enter the Millennial Kingdom along with the Rapture Church and the Tribulation Saints. This is also substantiated by the fact that the covenantal promises of a restored Israel for the righteous will be fulfilled in the Millennium and if the Old Testament Saints are to receive their part of the promises they will need to be present during the Millennium.

	SEVENTH EVENT OF THE FIRST
44.9	**RESURRECTION - MILLENNIUM SAINTS?**

One piece of information about the various resurrections that is not found in the Bible is what will happen to those righteous human beings that physically die during the Millennium – we are left to speculate what might be most consistent with other aspects of this portion of God's Plan. It seems logical, and not beyond the realm of divine possibility, that when a righteous human being dies during the Millennium, they are immediately translated into their resurrected body and continue living. Keep in mind that the Millennium will be inhabited simultaneously by resurrected saints, the righteous that lived before the Millennium, and those human beings that will have survived the terrors of Daniel's 70th Week and exited as righteous. If the immediate translation of the ones then die was not to be the case, then they would not be able to experience the blessed fullness of the one-thousand-year Messianic Kingdom as all the other resurrected righteous will do. Another notion that lends credibility to this speculation is that the Bible does not say anything about human death in the Millennium.

44.10 ONLY EVENT OF THE SECOND RESURRECTION – THE WICKED

The resurrection of the wicked will be examined in greater depth in a later chapter, however, suffice it to say at this point Scripture is the most at harmony regarding the wicked, if the conclusion of a literal interpretation of Isaiah 26:19, Daniel 12:1-2, John 5:28-29; and Revelation 20:5 has them resurrected at the end of the Millennial Kingdom immediately before the Great White Throne Judgment. This is also substantiated by the fact that the covenantal promises of a restored Israel for the righteous will be fulfilled in the Millennium and if the wicked are not to receive their part of the promises they cannot be present during the millennium.

45

THE JUDGMENTS

The Bible is very clear throughout its broad sweep of God's revelation that humankind is made up of two groups of people, first, those that are with, for, and of God, and, second, those that are without, against, and not for God. There is no middle ground; it is one or the other. The Bible is also clear that each group has distinctly different destinies;

- Unbelievers: The judgment for unbelievers is that they have been found to be guilty of not accepting God and Jesus Christ, and so are condemned to a second death of eternal punishment. Since they did not accept God and Jesus Christ and are not saved, it is not necessary to judge the effectiveness of their work while on earth.
- Believers: The eternal salvation of each believer was assured when each person accepted Jesus Christ as their personal Savior and Lord. Therefore, they will avoid the second death of eternal punishment, but instead will be judged for the effectiveness of their work on earth, or, what they did with what they were given by Christ.

There are many believers, theologians, and scholars who believe that at some time in the history of humankind there will be only one, all-encompassing, grand judgment by God of all human beings that have ever lived on the earth. However, an inductive study of the Bible teaches something entirely different; as will be seen below, there will be several distinctly different judgments with God assigning different times for the different judgments of different groups of people. Another consideration is that, as we have just seen above in the various resurrections, the Bible teaches that there are a number of times in history when people are resurrected so how could there only be one judgment?

It should be noted that these judgments, when combined, are characterized by several aspects:

- As is hopefully becoming apparent, these various judgments are integrally intertwined with the various resurrections that has been discussed in Chapter 44. These judgments determine if a person is to experience the second death, after their first death.
- The focus of these various judgments is on the entirety of humankind regardless of when they lived in history.
- These are permanent judgments of individual people, not temporal judgments that occur as part of other events.

- The purpose of these various judgments is to determine the eternal destiny of each individual person based on what they decided about their personal relationship with their Creator and what they did about their sin nature.
- As previously stated, these judgments are individually based, and are made necessary because of the consequences of original sin that occurred at the Fall resulting in physical death.

Before the details of each respective judgment is examined in detail, what about the Judge Himself? Who will it be? Where does His authority originate? What are His qualifications?

- First, the Judge will be the One to whom authority to do so has been bestowed by God – Jesus Christ – as very clearly and unobjectionably stated in John 5:22 and 27.
- Walvoord describes the nature of the Judge in this concise and succinct manner: "As "THE JUDGE OF ALL THE EARTH" (Gen. 18:25; see 1 Sam. 2:10) and "all men" (Heb. 12:23), God judges with equity (Ps. 96:10), justice (Acts 17:31), impartially (1 Pet. 1:17), righteousness (Ps. 9:8), and truth (Rom. 2:2). The Scriptures affirm that God is the Judge of all activities on the earth. His authority is without limit in heaven and earth, and there is no possibility of questioning the accuracy of His judgments (Pss. 58:11; 99:4). His judgments are based on His absolute justice, as the Scriptures often affirm (Gen.18:25; Deut. 32:4; Pss. 33:5; 89:14; Jer. 11:20; 33:15; Ezek. 33:20; Rom.3:5-6; 1 Pet. 2:23; Rev. 16:7; 19:2). He "loves justice" (Pss. 11:7; 99:4), and He has the power to carry out His judgment because of His omnipotence."[1]

| 45.1 | **EVERY PERSON STANDS BEFORE FINAL JUDGMENT** |

Hebrews 9:27 teaches that every person who has ever lived is *destined to die once, and after that to face judgment* before Jesus Christ, the Judge authorized by God, the Creator, to exercise judgment of the peoples of all time. After the physical death of every person, each is to be judged for what he or she did or did not do with the knowledge that Jesus is the Son of God and gave His life as the one and only sacrifice for the sins of each individual in the world that believes in Him. The sense of the profound and sobering passage is if it says every person must stand before his or her Creator, then that also includes every saved and righteous person as well.

As discussed, all people who have lived throughout time will stand before the Triune God and be judged for their personal standing with their Creator. What is not always understood by believers is that judgment will not occur as one single event for all people; instead it will be several different events that occur at different times and in different places depending on each person's individual salvation, the time of their death, or when they lived.

- Unbelievers: Unbelievers will be judged at the Great White Throne Judgment (see Chapter 55) which will confirm that they rejected God's offer of salvation in His Son.
- Believers: Believers will be judged at the Bema, or Judgment Seat, of Christ (see Section 29.1 below) which will confirm their security in God's Son.

One of the many themes that run through the full length of the Bible is the certainty that every person will die (except those that are living at the time of the Rapture and at the end of the Millennium), face a judgment before God, and spend eternity in a particular place.
- Hebrews 6:1-2: The author of Hebrews lists resurrection from death and eternal judgment as two of the several things that are included in a mature understanding of Christ.
- Jeremiah:
  + 17:10: *I the Lord search the heart and examine the mind, to reward each person according to their conduct, according to what their deeds deserve.*
  + 32:19: In Jeremiah's prayer to God, he said, *great are your purposes and mighty are your deeds. Your eyes are open to the ways of all mankind, you reward each person according to their conduct and as their heeds deserve.*
- Hebrews 9:27-28: The author says that all people are destined to die once and then face judgment. The context of these verses suggests that the *people* in verse 27 refers to all people, all who have lived; while the *many* and *those who eagerly await Him* in verse 28 are those that have trusted in Jesus Christ who, at the First Advent, paid the price for their human sinfulness, and who, at the Second Advent, will come to deliver their eternal salvation.

45.2 FIRST JUDGMENT – JUDGMENT OF CHRIST ON THE CROSS

"Christ's death on the cross was a divine judgment on the sin of the whole world."[2] One of the most significant questions that confront humankind concerns why and for what did Jesus die and be resurrected? This question is answered by the following passages:
- John 3:16: The classic passage says it all. God loved the world to such an extent, that He provided His only son to be the substitutionary sacrifice for the sinfulness of those people so they could have everlasting life. While not every person will be saved, Jesus' death on the cross and His resurrection is available to anyone who believes at which time that person is changed from being hopelessly condemned to possessing joyful assurance of eternal life.
- Romans 5:8: Jesus, demonstrating God's love for sinners, died for them.
- 2 Corinthians 5:19-21: The means by which God reconciles the world back to Himself is by Jesus being the message of reconciliation that is

proclaimed by His ambassadors to sinners so that they can exchange their sin for righteousness.
- 1 Timothy 2:4, 6: (In spite of the fact that not all will,) God desires all people to be saved by coming to realize the truth is that Jesus gave Himself as a ransom for all.
- 1 Peter:
    + 2:24: Jesus took human sinfulness onto His body as He died on the cross, so that the unrighteous could leave it behind and become righteous.
    + 3:18: Jesus, the just that is spiritually alive, suffered death of the flesh one time for the sins of the unjust, humankind, in order to make God available through a substitution.
- 2 Peter 3:9: God is patiently waiting for everyone to come to repentance (even though not all will).

While the death and resurrection of Jesus Christ may not "seem" like a judgment, it nevertheless is the most profound judgment, because He unselfishly sacrificed Himself as the payment for a crime of which, while He was not guilty, all human beings are guilty. Jesus made it possible for unmerited divine grace is made available to undeserving sinful people.

45.3 SECOND JUDGMENT – JUDGMENT SEAT, BEMA, OF CHRIST

As discussed in more detail in Section 29.1, this judgment is not so much a judgment as much as it is an examination. After the time when the Church Age believers are raptured off the earth and taken to heaven, this is the occasion when each believer stands before Jesus Christ and is examined, not for their personal salvation which is assured, but for what they did and did not do with the spiritual gifts and abilities that they were given as part of the blessing of salvation, as can be seen in Romans 14:10-12 and 2 Corinthians 5:10.

45.4 THIRD JUDGMENT – ANTICHRIST AND FALSE PROPHET

As a consequence of the defeat of the Antichrist and the world's armies upon His Advent, Jesus Christ will seize the Antichrist and the False Prophet and will cast them alive into the fiery lake of burning sulfur, as clearly indicated in Revelation 19:20, which has been unoccupied until these two demonic beings are cast into it. The fiery lake of burning sulfur will be studied in a later chapter, where it is the final destiny of all the wicked people that will have ever lived.

45.5 FOURTH JUDGMENT - SATAN

After Jesus Christ dispenses with the Antichrist and the False Prophet, He will complete His judgment of the Unholy Trinity by turning His attention to the ancient

serpent, the devil, Satan himself. It is an interesting irony that the one that thought
he could replace God for thousands of years and had actively attempted to do so
for the previous three- and one-half years, will himself be first temporarily set
aside in the abyss before he is eternally cast aside into the fiery lake of burning
sulfur one thousand years later. It is also an interesting fact that for the entire one
thousand years of the Millennium, Satan will be unable to exert his influence on
humankind for the duration of his time in the Abyss.

Walvoord points out that the "… dramatic prophecy contained in these three
verse has been the subject of endless dispute because to some extent the whole
controversy between premillennialism and amillennialism hangs upon it. The
passage yields to patient exegesis, and there is no solid reason for taking it in
other than its ordinary sense."[3] Walvoord then proceeds to detail both views and
concludes that the premillennial view is most consistent with the Scriptures.

Revelation 20:1-3 describes the sequence of activities that will transpire for the
judgment of Satan:
- Revelation 20:1: The Apostle John sees an angel descend from heaven
  with a chain and the keys to the abyss in his hand.
    + The Angel: While there are some who believe that the angel here is
      Jesus, since the passage does not specifically identify nor suggest that
      the angle is Jesus, it is better to conclude that it is a heavenly being.
    + The Chain: There is no evidence elsewhere to suggest that the chain
      in this passage is anything other than an actual chain. The other New
      Testament instances of when a chain is part of the narrative indicated
      that it is a general description of being bound.
        o Mark 5:3: A man possessed of demons that, once bound, could
          no longer be bound even with chains.
        o Acts 12:7: When Peter is delivered from a prison by an angel,
          the chains by which he had been bound dropped off of him.
        o Acts 28:20: When in Rome, Paul associates his being bound by
          chains for his belief in Jesus as also being bound by chains for
          the hope of Israel to believe in Jesus.
        o 2 Timothy 1:16: Paul makes another reference to being imprisoned
          by chains to signify the extent that he would go to serve Christ.
    + The Keys to the Abyss: Normally in the Bible, possession of the keys
      to something signified the holder has authority to do something.
    + The Abyss: Essentially, the abyss is first the normal place of detention
      for the wicked angels (fallen demons), and then second, is a temporary
      place of confinement for those whose ultimate destiny will be the fiery
      lake of burning sulfur.
        o The English word abyss is the transliteration of the Greek word
          abussos which literally means bottomless or boundless, which
          only appears in the Book of Revelation in the passage currently
          being examined as well as the following passages:

- Revelation 9:1-2, 11: In the first glimpse of the nature of the abyss, or the bottomless pit, John records that it is a place, presumably within the earth, that has an access shaft with some sort of operable covering that is normally kept closed and locked. When it is opened, an excessive amount of smoke erupts out like from a giant furnace, suggesting it is a punishing place of intense heat. Also, the passage indicates that there is at least one king in the abyss and that is a fallen angel whose name is *Abaddon* in Hebrew and *Apollyon* in Greek, which both means 'destroyer.' Thus we can see some of the true character of the unmasked satanic and evil world. "Satan and the demons are seen as the destroyers of the souls of men and as those who can only bring affliction. When divine restraint is released, as in this instance, the true character of the evil one is manifested immediately."[4]
- Revelation 11:7: The beast that ascends from the abyss is none other than Satan.
- Revelation 17:8: Another reference to one of the three beasts of the Book of Revelation having originated in the abyss.
  - Also, the following passages reference the abyss as well:
    - Luke 8:31: When Jesus encountered the demoniac, the demons that possessed the man begged Jesus not to send them to the abyss indicating that the abyss was the normal abode for demons.
    - Romans 10:7: In the context of a large narrative, Paul makes reference to Jesus having descended to the abyss after death and before resurrection.
- Revelation 20:2: The angel will seize Satan and will bind him, presumably with the chain for a period of one thousand years. This binding will render him inactive and unable to deceive humankind as he will have done for the previous several millennia. Nowhere in the Bible is there any evidence that Satan will be present at any time in the future kingdom.
- Revelation 20:3: The angel will then throw Satan into the abyss and will lock and seal it behind him so that he can deceive the nations no longer until the one-thousand-year penalty is completed. Parenthetically, John mentions that Satan will then have to be released for a short time after the one thousand years are completed.

45.6   FIFTH JUDGMENT – MARTYRS OF DANIEL'S 70ᵀᴴ WEEK

Revelation 20:4 describes a group of saints that will be determined by an unidentified group sitting on thrones, possibly the apostles who are given authority to judge on the basis of Luke 22:30, to be worthy of being resurrected (given resurrection bodies) in order to reign with Christ for a thousand years. Because of the references to these saints having resisted worshipping the beast or his image, nor having received the mark of the beast, it is fairly obvious that these will be saints that will be martyred during the Great Tribulation. This seems to be a particular group from a designated time period and should not be thought as being the larger body of believers.

45.7 | SIXTH JUDGMENT – LIVING JEWS AT JESUS' SECOND ADVENT

The first of the two judgments of those people that will survive the horrific Daniel's 70th Week will be the judgment of living Jews immediately after Christ's Second Coming and, most certainly before the start of the Millennial Kingdom, and the 75-day interval seems to provide the most probable opportunity.

The covenantal promises made by God to the patriarchs of Israel, while unconditional in the sense that God will fulfill the promises regardless of what Israel does or does not do throughout her long and tumultuous history, they are conditional on the requirement that all Jews have to be obedient to and remain righteous before the Lord in order to obtain the promised blessing of entering the long-awaited kingdom. Remaining holy applies even to those Jews that will live in the greatest distress ever to happen. So when the end of that time comes, Jesus Christ, as authorized by God, will judge whether the surviving Jews will enter the soon-to-start eternal kingdom, or whether they will be set aside for eternal punishment.

If the end times are indeed upon us, the current nation of Israel provides the unbelieving portion of the two-stage restoration process (the first stage gathered in belief during Daniel's 70th Week, and the second stage gathered in belief in the time of their Messiah's presence) to form the Jewish nation that will be present during Daniel's 70th Week. This also facilitates, for judgement by Christ when He comes, a nationally identifiable Jewish people that will include a portion that comes to belief in Jesus shortly before or at the time of His reappearance, as well as a portion that will never come to belief. The regathering for judgment can be seen in the following passages:

- Isaiah 11:12: The Messiah will signal for the reclamation and reunification of the banished and exiled - the dispersed of Israel and the scattered of Judah to be gathered from the four corners of the earth.
- Jeremiah 23:7-8: Just as the God of Israel is known for delivering His people out of Egypt, the same God will be known for having delivered the people of Israel from all the lands and places from which He banished them in order for them to live in their own land.

Just as the Jews will be gathered nationally back in the land in unbelief in order for the order for Daniel's 70th Week to take place, they will be also be gathered again at the end of Daniel's 70th Week for judgment as can be seen in the following passages:

- Ezekiel 20:33-38: Again, and so that they will know that He is their God, the God that judged Israel after having brought them out of Egypt will again judge them - the following being the characteristics of His judgment.
  + God will be the Sovereign King over Israel in power and might with fury being poured out.
  + Again, in power and might with fury poured out, God will bring the people out from the lands in which they were scattered.
  + God will bring the people to the place of judgment, the wilderness of the peoples, and will enter into individual, face-to-face judgment just as He had done in the wilderness after the nation's delivery from Egypt.
  + The people will pass under the rod before Him. "This pictures a shepherd holding out his rod and forcing the sheep to pass under it single file for counting (cf. Jer. 33:13). The shepherd would let those sheep that were actually his enter the fold, a place of protection. In this instance the fold was the 'the bond of the covenant.' The 'covenant' could refer to the Mosaic Covenant, which Israel had broken (cf. Ezek. 16:59), but this does not seem likely since Israel invalidated the Mosaic Covenant by her unbelief. Therefore God will make a New Covenant with her when He restores her to Himself (Jer. 31:31-33)."[5]
  + God will eliminate those that are rebellious before Him or transgress against Him, and He will not bring them to the promised land - they will be purged and not allowed to enter the Millennial Kingdom.
- Romans 11:26: Paul's reference to all Israel being saved indicates that, like all through the Church Age, those that believe in Jesus at the end of Daniel's 70th Week will be saved and will enter the Millennial Kingdom without physically dying first. Also, Paul indicates that the rebels that are living in the land at the time of Christ's return will be purged out in judgment so that only the righteous remain.
- Ezekiel 39:25-28: In a demonstration of His righteous justice, His almighty power, and His longsuffering grace, God tells the prophet Ezekiel that since Israel has been disobedience and has not maintained His sovereign holiness before the world voluntarily, then He will cause them to do so involuntarily. However, He will be merciful to someday bring them out of the countries of their enemies, will restore their fortunes, and will sanctify them before the nations of the world.

Thus, during the 75-day Interval, Jesus will bring all of scattered Israel together and judge them and determine which Jews have been faithful that will enter the Millennial Kingdom and which Jews have not been faithful and will not enter the Kingdom.

45.8	**SEVENTH JUDGMENT – LIVING GENTILES AT JESUS' SECOND ADVENT**

Core Scripture: Matthew 25:31-46

The second of the two judgments of those people that will survive the horrific Daniel's 70th Week will be the judgment of the living Gentiles immediately after Christ's Second Coming and immediately before the start of the Messianic Kingdom. The 75-day interval seems the most probable time for this judgment. The principal passage that explains this judgmental event is Matthew 25:31-46, which is commonly called the "Judgment of the Sheep and Goats" or the "Judgment of Nations," and is the only time when sinners *and* believers are judged as part of the same judgment event, while the other judgments discussed above and below are events where either sinners *or* believers are judged and sent to their respective destinies. The absence of one classification of people at a judgment event certainly does not diminish the significance of the judgment; it just means that all the judgment events deal with only one classification, while this judgment deals with both classifications of people. Also, in the end of earthly time, all people will have been judged regardless of which classification they belong.

An immediate observation that may be made about the Lord's Coming and His judgment of the living Gentiles is that the Times of the Gentiles ends with this judgmental event. "… [I]t is fitting that a judgment of the Gentiles should take place as a preparation for the millennial kingdom."[6]

There are several Old Testament passages that provide broad details of this judgment:
- Psalm 2: This is one of the classic passages that anticipates a judgment of the peoples and nations of the world as they demonstrate their overwhelming ineptitude to control their own destiny much less govern themselves.
- Isaiah 63:1-6: One of the few graphic descriptions of the events that will transpire when Jesus comes to earth and exercises His divine judgment on the world and the Gentiles. It pictures Christ coming from Edom with blood splattered clothing because of His judgment on an unbelieving and unrighteous people.
- Joel 3:1-2, 12: The Lord indicates that He will enter into judgment against the nations of the world in the valley of Jehoshaphat, outside Jerusalem.
- Zephaniah 3:8: God says He will gather the Gentile nations and kingdoms together, and in anger will pour out His fury which will consume the whole earth.
- Zechariah 14:1-19: The Lord says He will gather the nations against Jerusalem and then He will go to battle against them and will fight for His people. As part of this day, the Lord will stand on the Mount of Olives, immediately east of Old City of Jerusalem, as the city is split apart by an earthquake. The Lord will strike Jerusalem, but after the judgment the city will return to being a secure place.

Before the Matthew passages are studied, the time in which this judgment occurs should be clearly established. There are not less than three views available for consideration.

- First View – Judgment at the End of the Millennium: Those that hold to this view tend to be those that believe the judgment of the Gentiles is the same judgment as the Great White Throne Judgment. One of the main objections to this view is that Matthew 25:31-32 specifically indicates that the judgment will occur at the time the Son of Man, Jesus Christ, comes.
- Second View – Judgment After the Millennium Begins: This view is based on there being unbelievers during the Millennium and a rebellion of nations refusing to worship the Lord. The primary objection is that the passages used to support this view are taken out of context.
- Third View – Judgment Before the Millennium Begins: This view has several unarguable aspects:
  + "The interpretation that is most consistent with Matthew 25:31 is that the judgment of the sheep and goats is premillennial."[7]
  + When compared and contrasted to the Great White Throne Judgment, which according to Revelation 20:11-15 clearly occurs at the end of the thousand-year reign of the Lord, it becomes obvious that the Judgment of the Sheep and Goats is entirely different and occurs at an entirely different time.
  + There is an objection to this view on the basis that Matthew 25:34 says that the sheep are said to enter eternal life rather than the millennial kingdom, and the goats are to enter eternal punishment (death resulting in temporary placement?) rather than eternal condemnation in the lake of fire. The response to this objection is that the final destiny for the sheep and goats "… can be inevitable without it being immediate."[8] Stated in another manner, the following scenario would be consistent with Scripture:
    o Sheep: Immediately they go into the Millennial Kingdom, and inevitably at the end of the thousand years they go into eternity in the presence of Christ.
    o Goats: Immediately they are put to death and enter temporary placement, and inevitably at the end of the thousand years they go into eternity in the lake of fire.

As will become obvious in this discussion below there is a distinction between the Judgment of the Sheep and Goats and the Great White Throne Judgment, therefore, the following table[9] compares and contrasts the two judgmental events.

Comparison Between Judgment of the Sheep and Goats and the Great White Throne Judgment		
	Judgment of the Sheep and Goats Matthew 25	Great White Throne Judgment Revelation 20
Who are judged?	All the living people of the nations	Resurrected people
What is the criterion of judgment?	Acts of mercy toward the least of these brothers of mine	A person's works whose name was not found in the book of life
What is the destiny of the judged?	Sheep to eternal life and goats to eternal punishment	Only the condemned are mentioned and they are thrown in the lake of fire
Where does this judgment take place?	On earth	After the heavens and the earth have fled away
What is the method of judgment?	Separated by the Shepherd into two distinct groups	Confirmation that names are not written in the book of life
What is the identity of those judged?	Two classes of people – sheep (good) and goats (evil)	Only the wicked are mentioned
What is the basis of the judgment?	Treatment of the least of these brothers of mine	Their evil works
Who are the actors that are present?	Sheep, goats, the least of these brothers of mine, the Son of Man, angels	God and those whose names are not written in the book of life
What is the time sense of the judgment?	Before the millennium	After the millennium

A detailed examination of the passage yields considerable information about the transition from one historical time to another. Pond[10] identifies the following:

MATTHEW 25:31

This introductory verse makes a definitive statement about the Lord's return and forms the conclusion to Jesus' Olivet Discourse narrative. After having responded to the three questions by the disciples concerning Jesus' return to earth, Jesus finishes by telling them seven parables about the distinctions between believers and unbelievers and what will happen when He does return. The passage indicates that three things will occur: the Son of Man will come in glory, all the angels will come with Him, and He will sit on His glorious throne.
- When the Son of Man Comes: This is a direct reference to the Lord Jesus Christ's Second Advent.
- Son of Man:
  + Of the four ways the phrase "son of man" is used in the Old Testament, the manner in which it is used in Daniel 7:13 is considered the basis that Jesus uses to identify Himself to the Jews. "In Matthew 25:31-46 Jesus applied this title to Himself as the universal King; as the Son of Man He will fulfill God's purpose for man as described in Psalm 8:5-8."[11]

In fact, almost all of the times the phrase "son of man" occurs in the New Testament, Jesus is the one that uses it and He does so because as the fulfillment of the Davidic Covenant, Jesus is the One that the right to reign will be given as indicated in Daniel 7:14.

+ The phrase occurs thirty times in the Gospel of Matthew and again Jesus is the One that uses it in reference to Himself in relation to His ministry, His suffering, death, and resurrection, and His future coming. In Matthew the Son of Man is described as being the rightful earthly authority, He is the ransom for sin, and He is the returning royal Judge.

• Coming in His Glory: The first time that Jesus came to earth, he came to suffer because He emptied Himself of His glory as stated in Philippians 2:5-8, however in Matthew 16:27 Jesus says that He will come again in the glory of His Father, or more precisely, the glory of the Father will be transferred to Him (cf. John 17:4-5). Also, numerous passages indicate that glory will accompany Jesus as He establishes His Kingdom, as can be seen in the following passages:

+ Numbers 14:21: *and as surely as the glory of the Lord fills the whole earth.*

+ Isaiah:
    ○ 60:1-3: In spite of the Lord calling Israel to be the light to the nations, she was yet still in darkness. In this passage, Isaiah is calling for Israel to rise up and shine because her light had arrived because God's glory had risen like the sun on her. There was thick darkness of sin and wickedness over Israel and the people of the earth. This was true before the First Advent and will be true of the Second Advent. Jesus Christ will bring the Lord's glory to Israel and the nations again. The nations will just seek the light they will look to Israel for righteousness and illumination.
    ○ 66:18: *And I, because of what they have planned and done, am about to come and gather the people of all nations and languages, and they will come and see my glory.*

+ Habakkuk 2:14: *For the earth will be filled with the knowledge and the glory of the Lord as the waters cover the sea.*

+ Matthew:
    ○ 16:27: *For the Son of Man is going to come in his Father's glory with his angels ...*
    ○ 19:28: Jesus tells His disciples, "*Truly I tell you, at the renewal of all things, when the Son of Man sits on his glorious throne, you who have followed me will also sit on twelve thrones, judging the twelve tribes of Israel.*

+ Romans 8:18: Paul writes, *I consider that our present sufferings are not worth comparing with the glory that will be revealed in us.*

- + Colossians 3:4: *When Christ, who is your life, appears, then you also will appear with him in glory.*
- + 2 Thessalonians 1:7-10: *and give relief to you who are troubled, and to us as well. This will happen when the Lord Jesus is revealed from heaven in blazing fire with his powerful angels. He will punish those who do not know God and do not obey the gospel of our Lord Jesus. They will be punished with everlasting destruction and shout out from the presence of the Lord and from the glory of his might on the day he comes to be glorified in his holy people and to be marveled at among all those who have believed. This includes you, because you believed our testimony to you.*
- + 1 Peter 4:13: *But rejoice inasmuch as you participate in the sufferings of Christ, so that you may be overjoyed when his glory is revealed.*
- Angels will Come with Him: In Matthew 16:27, and in both the Parables of the Wheat and Tares, Matthew 13:34-43, and the Parable of the Dragnet, Matthew 13:47-50, Jesus indicates that when He comes He will be accompanied by the holy angels who will be sent by Jesus as reapers to collect and dispose of the wicked.
- He will Sit on His Throne: Subsequent to Jesus' return, He will sit on His throne on earth thus exercising His right to reign in royal authority over the earth. "The Son of Man sitting on His glorious throne is the beginning of the ultimate fulfillment of the Davidic Covenant and many Old Testament prophecies."[12]

MATTHEW 25:32-33

Upon taking His throne the first thing Jesus does is assemble all the nations of the world before Him and separate them as a shepherd separates sheep, and puts them on his right, from the goats, which he puts on his left.

- Assembly of All the Nations:
  - + Usage in the New Testament: Pond[13] analyzes the different ways in which the phrase "the nation" (singular) and "the nations" (plural) is used inside the Synoptic Gospels and outside and makes the following observations:
    - o "the Nation" (Singular): Outside the Synoptic Gospels, the word means "… a political group, a nation, or a group of citizens …"[14] sometimes in reference to Israel, to all humankind, and sometimes in reference to specified or unspecified nations.
    - o "the Nations" (Plural):
      - - Outside the Synoptic Gospels: Most of the time the plural form is in reference to non-Jewish people, either non-believers or believers. Then it may have another qualification that includes a nation or people from the Old Testament, a descendent of Abraham as the father of many nations, the portion of the

world that would be blessed by Abraham, the nations called to praise God, peoples who stand in opposition to God, or finally people who do not believe in God, but are ruled by Him.

- Inside the Synoptic Gospels: For the most part, when the phrase the nations is used it is a reference to non-Jewish people, all the Gentiles, or all the nations.

- Usage in the Judgment of the Sheep and Goats: Pond[15] proposes three questions that must be answered in order to determine the identity of all the nations:

  + Are "the nations" National Groups?: Some say that the nations that stand before the Lord at this judgment event will be actual national groups, however, if this were true then that would mean that the wicked citizens, which every nation would inevitably have, would enter the Millennium. The answer to this question must be those that are judged are individuals that comprise the various nations. To support this notion, the following passages that speak of end of the age judgments indicate that it is individuals that will be judged:

    o Matthew 13:30, 47-50: In Matthew 13:30, a portion of the Parable of the Wheat and Tares as detailed in Section 26.2, distinguish between the believers (the wheat) and unbelievers (the tares) during harvest. In Matthew 13:47-50, a portion of the Parable of the Net as detailed in Section 26.2, paints the picture of fishermen separating good fish (the righteous) from the bad fish (the wicked).

    o Jude 14-15: *Enoch, the seventh from Adam, prophesied about them: "See, the Lord is coming with thousands upon thousands of his holy ones to judge everyone, and to convict all of them of all the ungodly acts they have committed in their ungodliness, and of all the defiant words ungodly sinners have spoken against him."*

  + Do "the nations" include Resurrected People?: While there is a strong tendency of some to view the Judgment of the Sheep and Goats to represent a universal last judgment, that would demand that some participants would have been resurrected. As can be seen from the table above, the Judgment of Sheep and Goats and the Great White Throne Judgment are two distinct judgmental events, to say they are the same is to be inconsistent with Scripture and to not account for the Millennial Age.

  + What Group of Living People do "the nations" then Represent?: Pond[16] finds that there are four possibilities:

    o All are Heathen: This is based on a way of being provided for those people that have never the Gospel, however, this "... contradicts the exclusiveness of the gospel (John 10:9; 14:6; Acts 4:12) and therefore must be rejected."[17]

- o All are Supposed Believers: This is based on the goats being professors of faith, but not actual believers, however, this "… changes the meaning of … [all nations] … from the targets of evangelism … to the smaller group of professing Christendom."[18] Thus this possibility is rejected.
- o All are Humankind: This is based on those that will be judged will be all individuals that will be living at the time of Christ's Second Coming, however, this overlooks the fact that there will be separate judgment of the living Jews during this time as well. Thus this possibility is rejected.
- o All are Non-Jews: This possibility is consistent with the common meaning of the nations in the New Testament which means believing and non-believing Gentiles.
- o In conclusion, all the nations in this context means individual believing and non-believing Gentiles that are living at the time the Great Tribulation ends and the Lord comes.
- The Separation by the Shepherd: The sense of the separation is consistent with the other uses of the concept in the New Testament where it means to set apart for a particular use. In this verse the reason for the separation is that there are distinctly different destinies for each of the two groups into which the nations are divided. Another aspect is that the separation will be a careful endeavor to individually distinguish one from another.
  - + Sheep: Matthew uses this word in his Gospel "… in a hypothetical situation to illustrate the worth of a person, as a symbol for innocence, and to express the need for a leader."[19]
  - + Goats: "More difficult to ascertain is the meaning of [the goats]… a young goat or kid, often meaning in the Septuagint a goat used for a sacrifice… a payment… an honorarium… or food…"[20]
  - + Right and Left Hand: The Bible is consistently clear about the meaning of being on one side or the other, with the right representing a place of honor. In the imagery the Bible presents for the relationship between God and Jesus, God's right hand is the position of the Lord's power meaning that Jesus is in the position of authority. By contrast, being at the left hand would connote being excluded from experiencing blessing.
  - + Those that are Separated: The sheep and goats will be judged for the manner in which they treat *these brothers of mine, even the least of them* (Matthew 25:40, 45) during the time immediately preceding this judgment event, which is the Great Tribulation. Pond "… examines the nature and basis of the judgment enacted by the Son of Man…"[21] *for these brothers of mine, even the least of them* by analyzing three views that have been proposed by Bible scholars according to four questions. The third view, *the least* are martyred disciples, is the view that is most consistent with Scripture.

Views of the Identity of *these brothers of mine, even the least of them*			
	Jews of the Tribulation	Missionary Disciples	Martyred Disciples
In what way are *the least* Christ's brothers?	Share Jewish nationality/ race with Christ	Committed Disciples: ○ Spiritual brothers and sisters ○ Sacrificial lifestyle in humility ○ Messenger of the Gospel	Committed Disciples willing to die for their faith
In what way are they *the least*?	Intensely persecuted	Sacrificial ministry that could result in death	Evangelistic ministry resulted in martyrdom
In what way do *the least* interact with the sheep and goats?	Missionaries to the Gentiles	Missionaries to the Gentiles	Sheltered and protected by the sheep, but rejected by the goats
Reasons for supporting this view?	Refer to Note A below	Refer to Note B below	Refer to Note C below

Note A:
1. The Jews are the same physical brotherhood as Jesus (as stated by Jesus in Matthew 5:47; Paul in Romans 9:3; and Peter in Acts 2:29).
2. This view is consistent with the Jewish "ministry to and their self-denial for the Messiah." [Eugene W. Pond, "A Study of the Judgment of the Sheep and Goats in Matthew 25," "Biblotheca Sacra," Volume 159, page 438]
3. Commonality with the *little ones* in Matthew 10:40-42 and 18:4-6.
4. Consistent with the 144,000 redeemed remnant as sealed witnesses for the Lord:
   ○ Isaiah 62:10: Like a banner, Israel will draw the nations to God.
   ○ Revelation 7: 144,000 witnesses as the logical choice for *the least*.
   ○ Matthew 10: Shared commonality.
5. Aligns well with *all the nations* as Gentiles.
6. Jews are a persecuted race.
7. Jews are bearers of the Abrahamic blessing.
8. Aligns with the judgment location and intent in Joel 3:2.

Note B: Equivalent to obeying Christ's Great Commission (Matthew 28:19-20) to the nations (Matthew 24:14.

Note C:
1. Related to *little ones* in Matthew 18:6.
2. Forms strong contrast with the King in Matthew 25:34, 40.
3. Most harmonious with the idea that Gentiles that come to faith do so because of these disciples; martyrdom would be a testimony.

MATTHEW 25:34-40

Jesus places the sheep on his right because during the time of distress and suffering, the sheep provided for the needs of these brothers of mine, even to the least of them.

- When the sheep do not understand why Christ places them to His right, they ask what it was that they did to justify their exalted position; this suggests their sincerity, their humility, and their tendency to love without reservation those people that are at a disadvantage, that are wrongly accused, pursued, or persecuted, or simply worse off than themselves. Christ replies by telling them that, by providing for *the least*, the sheep have shown Christ love by:

+ Feeding *the least* when they were hungry.
+ Giving *the least* something to drink when they were thirsty.
+ Showing hospitality when *the least* were strangers.
+ Clothing *the least* when they needed it.
+ Caring for *the least* when they were sick.
+ Visiting *the least* when they were imprisoned.
• As reward for the work that demonstrates their faith, the sheep, are blessed with an inheritance of the eternal kingdom which will be life in the presence of the Lord.
• In a way, what the sheep did during the time of distress was no more than is expected of obedient and loving servants at any time in human history.

MATTHEW 25:41-45

Jesus places the goats on his left because during the time of distress and suffering, the goats did not provide for the needs of *these brothers of mine, even the least of them*. The goats stand in antithesis of the sheep.
• When the goats do not understand why Christ places them to His left, they ask what it was that they did not do to justify their cursed position; this suggests their insincerity, their self-centeredness, and their tendency to ignore those people that are at a disadvantage, that are wrongly accused, pursued, or persecuted, or simply worse off than themselves. Christ replies by telling them that, by not providing for *the least*, the goats have not shown Christ's love by:
+ Not feeding *the least* when they were hungry.
+ Not giving *the least* something to drink when they were thirsty.
+ Not showing hospitality when *the least* were strangers.
+ Not clothing *the least* when they needed it.
+ Not caring for *the least* when they were sick.
+ Not visiting *the least* when they were imprisoned.
• As reward for the work that demonstrates their lack of faith, the goats are cursed with the loss of an inheritance of the eternal kingdom which will not be life in the presence of the Lord.
• In a way, what the goats did during the time of distress is no more than is expected of disobedient, idolatrous, and apostate people at any time in human history.

MATTHEW 25:46

The final destiny is stated, the *these* refers to the previous verses and means the goats who go to eternal punishment, and without specifically identifying them, Jesus states that the sheep will go into eternal life.

45.9 EIGHTH JUDGMENT – THE WICKED

The resurrected wicked will be judged at the Great White Throne, which will be examined in more detail in Chapter 55.

45.10 NINTH JUDGMENT – FALLEN ANGELS

While it is not certain when this judgment will occur, the fallen angels will be judged by both believers (1 Corinthians 6:3) and Jesus Christ (Matthew 25:42 and Revelation 20:10) and then cast into the lake of fire.

45.11 TENTH JUDGMENT – MILLENNIAL SAINTS?

While the Bible answers many of the questions we have, there are so many other questions in which the Bible does not provide us with an answer. There is no Scripture that addresses what happens to those who die during the Millennium. "It is probable the righteous who die in the Millennium will be resurrected, much as the church will be at the Rapture, and that living saints will be given bodies suited for eternity like those living church saints will receive."[22]

46

RESTORATION OF ISRAEL

Standing as an undeniable and unmovable obstacle in the path of those that hold that the Church replaces Israel because Israel no longer has a place in God's Plan, is the Scriptural certainty that God has every intention of restoring Israel, the very nation of people that He chose as the apple of His eye, to a condition and state of glory of having God as their personal protectorate. The restoration of Israel is a major fulfillment of the prophecy of the four unconditional covenants. And to think we may be watching that fulfillment today. The entire structure of the Bible and the giving and fulfillment of prophecy does not indicate another removal from the land.

46.1 GOD'S INTENTION TO RESTORE ISRAEL TO THEIR LAND

It should be noted that God not only intends to restore Israel as a nation, a people, a theocracy, but to do so in a special land He had given them, He intends to restore them to a condition and state that far exceeds the condition and state that has ever existed. Throughout Israel's painful history, the nation has always been significantly flawed and unable to humanly accomplish the state of being desired for them by God, so, God will no longer rely on their feeble efforts and will instead step in and fulfill the unconditional promises made thousands of years ago to the patriarchs and will put them in a higher position than even they imagined. Quite simply, there is a wide chasm of difference between Israel's perceptions of what the Kingdom will be like, and, the actual Kingdom God will provide for them in the Millennium.

The fact that the long dispersed Jewish Diaspora re-established their national identity in the land originally given them by God in the middle of the Twentieth Century rates as one of the most significant events to happen in that century. In terms of Biblical prophecy, it is without a doubt that restoration to the land is the most significance single event to occur since Jesus Christ, the Incarnate Son of God, walked the earth nearly two thousand years ago. In spite of the fact that for two thousand years Israel had not existed nationally, there is currently a politically recognized nation surrounding Jerusalem today that is called Israel, and it is populated by millions of Jews that have come from around the world to start new lives in this land that is only a tiny speck on the world map.

"Israel's awakening from national death in the graveyard of the nations will be the prelude to a glorious place of divine favor in the coming Kingdom

Age. After the long night of unbelief during this present age is over, and the severest of all the nation's chastisements in the Tribulation are past, the resplendent millennial day will dawn for the believing remnant of the chosen people. Nationally and spiritually restored, the nation will be at last ready to be "a kingdom of priests and a holy nation (Exod. 19:6) which was ever God's intent for His ancient people."[1]

Many of the Old Testament prophecies, as well as each of the unconditional covenants (Abrahamic, Palestinian, Davidic, and New) all looked forward to an eternal existence for God's chosen people. Even though the nation only existed as a globally scattered people for centuries, the promise of a regathering to their land as a legitimate nation was an eventuality waiting only for God's timing. While we must be very careful before calling the regathering that happened in 1947 an actual fulfillment of prophecy, when it is seen from the perspective that so many other Biblical prophecies appear to be coming to pass, the re-establishment of Israel seems to be very much the expected fulfillment of the Jewish restoration to the land for the final time.

Certainly the re-establishment of the nation of Israel has changed the face of Biblical prophecy forever. Beginning at the time Israel was utterly destroyed as a viable nation and people, until the 1940s, the study of prophecy was, in all likelihood, greatly impaired because there was a crucial piece of the puzzle - the existence of Israel as a nation - was missing from the prophetic picture being painted by the Bible. Is must have been frustrating to study prophecy prior to 1947, because the absence of the nation of the nation of Israel left far too many loose ends and unconnected dots. The re-establishment of Israel had an enormous impact on theological understandings - it is certain that many theologians and scholars have had to re-examine much of what they thought they understood about Biblical prophecy. For those of us living today and mining the Scriptures, we are actually witnessing major world events that have profound and ever-changing consequences for humankind and the earth.

The theological state of Israel today hardly convinces anyone that they are awaiting the Messiah to fulfill His Second Advent. There are many that are atheists or agnostics, and the general sense is that the nation is not focusing on worshipping God. "The majority of Israelis today are secular Jews, and of course even though religious Jews believe in God they reject Jesus (Yeshua) as their Messiah."

Price[2] makes several unique observations about the restoration of Israel to their land at this time of history.
- God's Intent to Restore Israel: Several passages provide God's reasoning for bringing Israel out of dispersion back into national existence.
  + Zechariah 10:6, 8: God will have compassion on Israel, will bring them back, will forgive and forget, and will restore them to a state as if their sinfulness had not occurred.

+ Jeremiah 3:14: God wants them to return to Him because He is their true husband; as can be seen in the adjacent table, there are various words used in this context.

Jeremiah 3:14	
NIV	*husband*
NASB	*master*
NET	*Master*
KJV	*married to them*
NKJV	*married to you*
AMP	*Lord and Master and Husband*

- Prophetic Facts of Restoration: There are four facts that can be gleaned from the Bible attesting to the restoration of Israel to their land:
  + Fact 1: "... the Bible predicts that Israel would return to the Land in unbelief ..."[3] and is based on the following Biblical logic:
    ○ Isaiah 6:9-13: Israel will remain hardened and unyielding into Daniel's 70th Week up to the time of Christ's Second Advent.
    ○ Ezekiel 36:24-25: Israel will be regenerated while in their land; therefore, they must have returned to their land in unbelief before regeneration.
    ○ Zechariah 12:10 and Matthew 24:30: Israel will repent.
    ○ Romans 11:1-6: Paul writes that God has preserved a faithful remnant at several times of Israel's history, suggesting a remnant throughout Israel's history.
    ○ Revelation 7:1-8: God will commission and supernaturally protect 144,000 Jews during the Great Tribulation to witness for Him.
  + Fact 2: "... the Bible predicts that Israel would return to the Land in stages ..."[4] which will be a process of Jews coming out of the nations to which they are dispersed and going to the land of Israel to start new Jewish lives. The return of the Jews actually started in 1882 and has continued until today, and will continue into the future.
  + Fact 3: "... the Bible predicts that Israel would return to the Land through persecution ..."[5] as can be seen in the following:
    ○ Deuteronomy 4:30: This idea is connected to this Old Testament passage that foresaw distress in Israel's future.
    ○ Jeremiah 16:15-16: Using the analogies of fishing and hunting, the Jews will be targeted during their return to the land.
    ○ Revelation 12:13, 17: Using symbolism, Revelation indicates that Satan will persecute Israel during the Great Tribulation.
    ○ The Twentieth Century: Pogroms, the Holocaust, and Anti-Semitism have resulted in the death of millions of Jews over the last one hundred years.
  + Fact 4: "... the Bible predicts that Israel would return to the Land to set the stage for end-time events ..."[6] as can be seen in Matthew 24:15-20 which implies that the state of Israel must exist again complete with laws and institutions, in order for judgment to occur.

- Two-Stage Return: Price supports these facts by pointing to a number of Old Testament passages that support a two-stage return to the land as can be seen in the table below. He also indicates that Zionist teachings support the idea of a two stage return, "... the first by man, and the second by God. This

First Stage - Physical Restoration to the Land	Second Stage - Spiritual Restoration to the Land
Ezekiel 11:17	Ezekiel 11:18-19
Ezekiel 36:24	Ezekiel 36:25-27
Ezekiel 37:21	Ezekiel 37:23
Jeremiah 23:3	Jeremiah 23:4

corresponds to the Zionist efforts to revive the barren land and reduce the population and build a secular state, which would be followed by God's revival of all Israel, reversal of nature's curse, and building of a spiritual state."[7]

An analysis of the major and minor prophetical books reveals that they collectively disclose God's historical program with the nation of Israel and serves as a microcosm of Israel's history, and have much more than what follows, but this is what is pertinent to this book:
- Israel's spiritual condition is well documented and includes blindness, deafness, sluggishness, disobedience, rebelliousness, indifference, sinfulness, false worship, idolatry, blasphemy, deceitfulness, unjustness, which are all repudiated and forsaken by God.
- The judgment of Israel in the form of temporary chastisement by dispersal from their land.
- A small, believing remnant that will be preserved by divine power as a witness of Jehovah.
- The promise of divine restoration to their land that will be permanent that will fulfill the unconditional covenants.
- The repentance of Israel prior to going into the Millennium.
- The cleansing and redemptive conversion by divine mercy of Israel where she will be made holy, righteous, justified, given a new spirit, and made obedient.
- Israel's dead will be resurrected.
- Israel will be judged and rewarded with blessing in the new heaven and new earth.

Isaiah's References to the Restoration of Israel:
- 11:11-12: After describing the nature of a future time under the Messiah in verses 1-10, the passage indicates that the Sovereign Master will reclaim His remnant from the various nations to which they were scattered.
- 27:12-13: The restoration of the Jews from the Assyrian and Babylonian Captivities also serves as a predictive example of Israel's restoration as part of Daniel's 70th Week.

- 41:8-9: Israel is reminded that they were chosen by God, that they would be brought back from the extremities of the world, and that they would not be rejected.
- 43:1-7: The Lord will protect His people as He rescues them.
- 61:4-11: A description of the condition of Israel implies a restoration and rejuvenation.
- 66:20-22: The destination of those restored will be the new heavens and the new earth

Jeremiah's References to the Restoration of Israel:
- 16:14-16: In verses 1-13, Israel was told that a great disaster would befall them and they would be sent into exile, and in this passage, Jeremiah tells Israel restoration would follow the exile. "God promised that after Judah's coming Captivity there would be a new "Exodus." No longer would the people look back to the first Exodus when God brought the Israelites ... out of bondage in Egypt. Instead they would point back to the time when God brought them from the land of the north (i.e., Babylon; ...) where they had earlier been banished. Thus God reaffirmed His promise ultimately to restore Israel to the land."[8]
- 23:3-4: The Lord promises that He will regather His people that are still alive in the nations of dispersal and bring them back to their homeland. He will increase their number and will provide rulers to govern them. They will have no need to be fearful or terrified.
- 30 - 33: There is considerable detail within these chapters delineating the restoration of Israel and Judah, together in comfort, after a time of great distress. Notice particularly the following:
  + 30:16-24: The Lord says that simultaneously He will restore Israel and He will judge Israel's enemies.
  + 31:31-34: God promises a new covenant with Israel and Judah after their restoration, when the Lord will be their God and all will know Him.
  + 31:35-37: In what might be the ultimate symbol of God's guarantee of continuance, the Lord says that Israel will continue as long as the sun gives light by day and the moon and stars give light by night; and He also indicates that Israel will continue until the full extent of the heavens and the foundations of the earth can be measured and explored.
- 46:27-28: The Lord tells the descendants of Jacob to trust Him because He will return them to peace and safety at some time in the future.

Ezekiel's References to the Restoration of Israel:
- 11:17-21: The Sovereign Lord, who has always been the sanctuary of the Jews while in exile, will gather them from the lands to which they had been scattered; He will give the promised land back to them and they will remove the detestable and abominable things. He will remove their

341

hardened heart of stone and will replace it with a heart of flesh and they will become obedient to the Lord. Those that remain devoted to the detestable and abominable things will be judged.

- 20:33-38: In the same manner as God brought Israel out of Egypt, He will bring them out of the nations in a yet future event.
  + 20:33: The Lord acknowledges that He understands that Israel wants to be like other nations that worship false gods in idolatry, however, He will never let that happen because He will rule over them with the same strength as He did when He delivered them out of Egypt, except this time rather than deliverance, He will bring wrath.
  + 20:34-36: Just as God brought Israel out of Egypt in the first exodus and entered into judgment with the patriarchs while they were in the wilderness (Exodus 32:11; Deuteronomy 4:34; 5:15; 7:19; 11:2; Psalm 136:12). He will bring the scattered nation out of the various lands of dispersal in a second exodus and will enter into judgment with them in *the wilderness of the peoples*. The judgment that is referenced there appears to be the seal, trumpet, and bowl judgments of Revelation.
  + 20:37: God will judge them and uses the analogy of a shepherd allowing only his sheep to pass into an area of protection (cf. Jeremiah 33:13). In this verse the area of protection is a covenant. In all likelihood, it is the New Covenant rather than the Mosaic Covenant because Israel had invalidated it by unbelief (Ezekiel 16:59) - God will bring Israel into covenantal relationship with Himself (Jeremiah 31:31-33).
  + 20:38: God will eliminate those that are rebellious, unbelieving Jews, by not allowing them to enter into the land of promise. This judgement will prepare the nation to enter into the Millennium Kingdom as a purified people. Remember that God purified the nation during the first exodus by having them wander around for forty years until all those that had not trusted the Lord previously died out; thus the nation entered the promised land in a more purified form. "Then it will be a new nation, a regenerated nation, which will be allowed to enter the Land under King Messiah for the final restoration."[9]
- 22:17-22: In a reference to Nebuchadnezzar's invasion of Israel as the Jews retreated to Jerusalem, this passage refers to a regathering in unbelief in preparation of judgment. As the context is to another time, it can be instructive here because of the imagery - Israel is likened to the dross. Dross is a metallurgical term that refers to the useless residue that separates from a pure metal after it is smelted under high temperature in a furnace. Here in this passage, God equates Israel with dross because of her sinful impurity, and He is going to bring them to the crucible of Jerusalem to smelt again with His wrath.
- 28:25-26: The Lord indicates that when He restores the house of Israel from their exile, they will live in security and will see and know their God.

- 34:11-16: The Lord will search for His people in much the same manner a shepherd searches for his lost sheep, and will being them out from their scatterings to the good pasture.
- 36:22-27: The Lord indicates that part of the purpose of restoring Israel is to Judge them for having profaned the Lord's name in front of the nations of the world. Then He will cleanse them, give them a new heart, put a new spirit within them and they will obey Him.
- 37: In this chapter, the famous prophecy of the valley of the dry bones is given. Refer to discussion below.
- 39:25-39: Yet another passage in which God reaffirms His promise to restore Israel from her exile because He is jealous for His name and He will judge them for the sinfulness practiced against Him.

Minor Prophet References to the Restoration of Israel:
- Hosea 1:10-11: This prophecy indicates the divided nation of both Judah and Israel will be called sons of God again as they are gathered together again in national restoration under their ideal ruler - the Messiah.
- Joel 3:17-21: As the Lord dwells in Zion, He will make Jerusalem holy and His people will reside in security as He avenges their blood.
- Amos 9:11-15: God will restore not only the Jews to their land in which they will reclaim, He will restore the rule of David; after they are planted in their land, they will never again be uprooted.
- Micah 4:4-7: The Lord will restore the outcasts and form them into a mighty nation.
- Zephaniah 3:14-20: God will remove the instruments of judgment He sent against Israel, and He will then raise His nation above other nations of the earth.
- Zechariah 8:3-5, 8: God says that He will restore the city of Jerusalem to a condition of peace and calm, and will bring His children back there to live.

"The united testimony of the prophets is all to the same point, that Israel will yet be regathered from the nations of the world and reassembled in their ancient land. The beginnings of this final regathering are already in contemporary history with almost two million Jews, or approximately one in six of all the Jewish population of the world, now living in Palestine [note that the book being referenced was published in 1959]. Scriptures make clear that the regathering will continue until consummated after the second advent of Christ. The promises of regathering linked as they are in Scripture to the original promise of the land as an everlasting possession of Israel, coupled with the fact that no possession of the land in history has approached a complete fulfillment of these Scriptural promises, make it clear that Israel has a future, and in that future will actually possess all the land promised Abraham's seed as long as this present age continues."[10]

46.2	EZEKIEL'S PROPHECY OF THE RESTORATION OF ISRAEL

We should examine Ezekiel 33 - 37 in more detail because in these five chapters we find a comprehensive narrative describing the essential character of the obedience / blessing / disobedience / cursing cycle of suffering described above. When these chapters are combined with Chapters 38 and 39 (to be examined later), they form a unit that outlines a new life to come for Israel that displays God's "… divine grace in restoring the prodigal nation to Himself by the regenerating power of the Spirit, together with the defeat of the last demon-inspired attack of Israel's enemies …"[11]

This extended prophecy is an excellent example of that class of prophecies that have both immediate / near and far applications - the immediate context is set against the drama of the Babylonian Captivity of Israel, yet it also has much to say about the events that are yet still future for Israel. In both applications, during the Captivity (first) and during the Diaspora (second), the twelve tribes are respectfully scattered among the surrounding nations (first), then among the nations of the world (second); thus, the Babylonian Captivity serves as a foreshadow of the future time for Israel in which she will be scattered to the world. Also, as with other near / far prophecies, there are aspects of the near application that were not fulfilled that must be fulfilled in the far application.

The situation that this prophecy addresses is that Israel is out of the land, dead so to speak, the temple is destroyed, the kings are dethroned, and her enemies have triumphed. In order for the Lord to restore the promised blessings accordingly, the false leaders have to be removed, the neighboring countries that decimated her have to be judged, and more critically, the nation itself has to be reborn, or re-established, in the promised land.

INTERPRETATION OF EZEKIEL 33

While the context is based in the law, Feinberg[12] makes the following observations of Ezekiel 33 which emphasizes human responsibility to God's law and the necessity of repentance.

- 33:1-6: During this historical time period, national vigilance was accomplished by charging a watchman with the responsibility to alert the community of an impending enemy attack. Once the alert was sounded, all who heard the alert were responsible for themselves. If the alert was not sounded, the watchman was derelict in his duty and his negligence was considered iniquity.
- 33:7-9: The watchman responsibility given to Ezekiel earlier in Chapter 3 is reaffirmed by God and it is qualified by being a watchman in the spiritual realm. Notice that the watchman concept in verses 1-6 applied to

the watchman alerting the nation, while here the alert is given to a sinful individual.

- 33:10-20: While the people of Israel blamed God for their situation, God directed Ezekiel to make it clear to them that they themselves were to blame for whatever situation they found themselves. God desires to save, and it is the actions of the individual that determine his or her situation - those that are wicked are punished, and those that are obedient are blessed. One's condition is their own responsibility.
- 33:21-22: While in exile, Ezekiel receives news that the event that he had been predicting for years has occurred - Jerusalem had fallen to the Babylonians.
- 33:23-29: Ezekiel gives a prophecy that is directed against those that had remained in the land after it was conquered because they are still living according to their previous wickedness. Ezekiel points out that they had not repented in light of the recent judgment. In a distorted twist of logic, the survivors rationalize that the land promised to Abraham should now be theirs, however, their sin will preclude them form inheriting it.
- 33:30-33: In spite of the fact that they listened to Ezekiel, the people still had no intention of obeying God. "They enjoyed and delighted in his new message of restoration and blessing for Israel and predictions against hostile nations, but they would not obey the moral implications of the prophecies which were prerequisites for personal participations of the blessings."[13]

INTERPRETATION OF EZEKIEL 34

Feinberg[14] observes that Ezekiel concentrated on messages of judgment in Ezekiel 34 and will also focus on promises of blessings.
- 34:1-10: God rebuked the false shepherds (rulers) of Israel who were negligent in caring for, and protecting, the sheep of Israel because they executed their responsibilities only for potential gain. Notice the implied contrast between the false shepherds of downtrodden sheep of that time and the future Shepherd of protected sheep yet to come. Notice also that they are scattered. God will hold the false shepherds accountable for their lack of effectiveness and negligence.
- 34:11-16: This passage describes that God's faithfulness stands in stark contrast to the false shepherds identified in the previous passage. Because of the failure of the Jewish leadership, the Lord will take charge and seek out the sheep that were scattered on a previous dark and cloudy day (i.e., the time of their dispersion). This passage describes, in symbolic language, the restoration of Israel to the land of promise from out of their dispersions. Upon their restoration, God will provide for the sheep, will protect them, will feed them in good pastures, and will care for them. The image of the sheep lying down is in reference to the peace and security that Israel will

enjoy during the Millennial Kingdom. Finally, there will be judgment on those who become prosperous and forget God's provisions.

- 34:17-22: After the false shepherds are judged, God turns His attention to the judgment of individual sheep in the flock. In anticipation of the sheep and great judgment spelled out in Matthew 25:31-46, God will judge between the oppressive (those professing faith) as they followed the false shepherds, and the helpless (those exercising true faith), and the latter will no longer be the prey for the former. Notice that wealth (verse 18) is apparently the qualifier for those that are considered oppressive. While the deliverance was accomplished to some degree in the return from the Babylonian Captivity, it will be completely accomplished in full measure in the Millennial Kingdom.

- 34:23-31: Continuing the shepherd and good pasture imagery, God describes how He will replace the ineffective shepherds with another good Shepherd for His flock, and He will make a covenant of peace with them to provide for peace and security. They and their land will bear fruit, they will not have to fear those that had previously preyed on them, they will not face famine anymore, nor will they be insulted by other nations any longer. The image painted here is the time of the Millennial Kingdom. "Unquestionably the climax is the conversion of Israel when they will recognize the Lord as their God and experience the blessedness of the acknowledgement of them by the Lord as His people."[15]

INTERPRETATION OF EZEKIEL 35

Along with Isaiah, Jeremiah, and Obadiah, Ezekiel here condemns Edom (identified as Mount Seir) because this nation has perpetually been Israel's enemy for centuries. It is possible, because of the context of Ezekiel 33 - 39, that this condemnation "… was listed here to represent the judgment God would inflict on all nations who opposes Israel. Edom was the prototype of all Israel's later foes. The destruction of Edom would signal the beginning of God's judgment on the whole earth based on that nation's signal the beginning of God's judgment in the whole earth based on that nation's treatment of Israel (cf. Gen. 12:3)."[16] Notice that each section of this chapter ends with, *Then you (they* in the third section) *will know that I am the Lord.* In this chapter, hatred of Israel has lasting consequences, as in the case of Edom, perpetual desolation for perpetual enmity. God fulfills His promise made to Abram that He will curse those that curse Israel. Feinberg[17] makes the following observations of Ezekiel 35:

- 35:1-4: The Lord curses Edom and says that He will make its people as desolate as its land, which is desert. This prophecy has been literally fulfilled.
- 35:5-9: Ezekiel expounds on the sins Edom committed against Israel, which included, being an everlasting enmity, and having delivered the people of Israel to the power of the sword. The imagery here is that Edom literally poured out the people of Israel to bloodshed. Responding in retribution in

kind, God will turn them over to bloodshed (because they had not hated bloodshed) and will lay waste to their land and its people. He will also cut the land off from the surrounding nations via war, and He will not provide proper burial for the slain (an indignity in the Orient).
- 35:10-15: Another reason for God's punishment of Edom was the fact that they tried to unite with Israel by possessing the land and people of Israel, in spite of Israel's God, who they insulted and exalted themselves against. If the nations and lands had united under Edom, then Edom would have not only had a territorial advantage, but also it would have taken possession of the land and people, an obvious aggressive move toward the Lord. "The principle of recompense in kind was again set forth, for Edom would receive from the hand of the Lord in direct proportion to her anger, envy and hatred against Israel."[18] Verse 14 suggests that Edom will have no place in the Millennium Kingdom.

INTERPRETATION OF EZEKIEL 36

This chapter strongly supports the literal method of interpretation of Scripture, because it speaks of a literal land and regenerative experience. It should be noted that verses 1 - 15 really belong to Chapter 35. Feinberg[19] points out "[t]his chapter contains the most comprehensive enunciation of the plan of redemption to be found in this book, setting forth all the factors that comprise God's plan of salvation."
- The preeminent motive in their redemption is the glory of God (vv. 22-23).
- Israel will know ultimately that their God is the Lord (v. 28).
- There will be an abhorrence of their sins (vv. 31-32).
- Forgiveness of their sins will be realized (v. 25).
- Regeneration will be effected (11:19; 18:31; and 36:26-27).
- The gift of the Holy Spirit will be granted (v. 27 and 37:14). No prophet before him assigns the ministry of the Holy Spirit in regeneration such a precise place as Ezekiel does.
- Included is obedience to God's love (v. 27 and 11:20)."

Feinberg[20] makes the following observations of Ezekiel 36:
- 36:1-7: God instructs Ezekiel to tell the *mountains of Israel* (the land and people of promise) that because Edom slandered them, preyed on them, and controlled them by making them subject to the surrounding nations do the same to Edom. "It is vital to remember that such action on God's part does not reveal in any sense a partiality toward Israel. It is rather a vindication of God's glory and will, for He has condescended to link His purposes on earth with the people of Israel."[21]
- 36:38-15: In terms descriptive of the Millennial Kingdom, the Lord says He will rescue Israel, He will restore the nation and its people, they will be fruitful and productive, and they will no longer be the prey of nations because they will live in peace.

- 36:16-21: In a succinct manner, the Lord explains His reason for submitting Israel to their suffering. Because of their evil conduct and sinful deeds the Jews defiled the land, God responded by removing them from their land and scattering them to foreign nations, and they profaned the name of the Lord to the world.
- 36:22-31: "In unmistakable language Ezekiel made clear that the basis of all God's dealings in grace are never predicted on man's merit, but rather on His holy character and name."[22] Because the Lord cares about how His name is regarded by the nations of the world, He will take the people of Israel from the nations to which they were scattered, bring them back to their land, cleanse and purify them (notice the reference to washing with water to purify), replace their heart of stone with a heart of flesh, will put His spirit within them (renewal by Holy Spirit), and will provide for their safety, security, and well-being. In short, they will be God's people, and He will be their God; and His name will be glorified because His character will be made evident to the world.
- 36:32-38: God affirms His intent to restore His name by restoring Israel, thus demonstrating His purpose and power.

INTERPRETATION OF EZEKIEL 37

While there are several alternative interpretative views of this chapter that will be detailed later, most conservative scholars believe this chapter of Ezekiel is a classic Biblical description of the literal resurrection and restoration of the long-lost nation of Israel.

- 37:1-6: The Lord sets Ezekiel in the midst of a valley that has a very large quantity of human bones scattered all around (not in heaps), bones that are disconnected from one another and that are dried and bleached (desiccated) from having been exposed to the climate for a long period of time. Emphasizing the hopelessness (from the human standpoint) of the situation, the Lord then asks Ezekiel a rhetorical question regarding if he believes the bones can be resurrected, to which Ezekiel answers the only truthful way he can by responding that only the Lord knows - implying only by a supernatural manner. The Lord tells Ezekiel to write a prophecy over the bones and tell them that the Lord will raise the bones to life again and will cover them with flesh and bring a spirit into them. The identity of the bones is revealed in verse 11 below. It is possible that the reference to the covering of the bones by sinews and flesh could be to the restoration of Israel to the land in unbelief, and the bringing in of a spirit could refer to the conversion of Israel into belief.
- 37:7-10: So Ezekiel did as God had instructed, he prophesied over the bones and they began to come together physically (but not spiritually). "As though superintended from a higher intelligence, they came together in exactly the right way and proportion to form normal human bodies."[24] This

particular portion of the event would suggest the first stage of restoration, Israel returning to the land in a physical, but unconverted, form. Next God instructed Ezekiel to prophesy for the spirit to come into the newly resurrected bodies, he did and it did, and they rose up as a strong army. Notice that in verse 9 the bones are identified as *slain* (NASB) and *corpses* (NET), thus presenting the idea that because they rise up as a great army in verse 10, the bones may have originated from an earlier battle in which Israel was destroyed.

- 37:11-14: God then explains that the dry bones are symbolic of the entire house of Israel, both Judah and Israel (Ephraim), and that He intends to remove them from their scattered among the nations of the world and their being cut off from existence as a viable people. The passage also introduces the notion of the nation being raised from the grave, with the grave representing the locations of their dispersions. Finally, God reaffirms His intentions to restore Israel physically and spiritually so that they will unequivocally know that He is their God.

- 37:15-23: God directs Ezekiel to take two wooden sticks, with one stick being representative of Judah ("... the southern kingdom included, in addition to Judah, the greater part of Benjamin and Simeon, the tribe of Levi, and godly Israelites who had come at different times from the northern kingdom ..."[25] and the other stick being Joseph through Ephraim (and Manasseh, the main body of the northern kingdom), and join them together. The imagery continues with the stick being held by God's hand, and Him declaring that the nation will no longer be divided, but instead will be united together in a pure, clean, and spiritually converted condition, without idolatry, transgression, or anything detestable. Thus the second stage of the restoration to their land is complete - they are spiritually converted. Again God states that they will be His people and He will be their God.

- 37:24-28: The chapter closes with Ezekiel describing what the restored condition of Israel will be like during the Messianic Kingdom. In their purified state, they will be ruled by the Davidic King as a shepherd over them, they will walk according to God's laws, they will live in the land given to their forefathers, there will be a covenant of peace between them and God, their prosperity will be increased, God will dwell among them in His sanctuary, and finally, God will be their God, and they will be His sanctified people. Notice the number of times the word forever, or the concept of perpetuity, is used in this passage. Thus will be the fulfillment of their divine destiny.

OBSERVATIONS OF EZEKIEL 37

Unger[26] has examined Ezekiel 37 and has made the following observations and developed the following conclusions.

General Observations

"This prophetic disclosure, because of its importance and graphic character, places it at once in the forefront of major Old Testament passages, dealing with the return of Israel to its homeland. Indeed, in portions of Scripture abounding in magnificent and glowing accounts of Israel's future hope and glory, the vision of the dry bones stands as one of the most striking and arresting portraitures of the nation's restoration to be found anywhere in the prophetic Word. Its language is compelling and pregnant; its imagery vivid and trenchant; its scope sweeping and expansive; its theme grand and elevated."[27]

"This phenomenon of bones strewn so confusedly over the face of the valley, but coming together and fitting so marvelously each into its proper place, picturesquely bespeaks God's power to bring all the Twelve Tribes together no matter where they are, of in what condition they are."[28]

"The exaltation of Israel, nationally and spiritually, and her establishment to the 'head' of the nations and 'not the tail' (Deut. 28:13) will be the most stupendous vindication of God's goodness and faithfulness the world has ever seen or ever will see. This uplifting will be the most colossal proof that Israel, despite all her backsliding and disobedience, is God's elect nation, His own chosen people."[29]

Dispelling Erroneous Views

Unger[30] points out that there are a number of views of this Ezekiel 37 that are considered as erroneous because they are not consistent with a literal interpretation of Scripture.

- Contrary to what some believe, the vision does not generally describe the physical resurrection of the dead. Ezekiel specifically indicates that the bones are representative of the *whole house of Israel*; there are no indications that it is in reference to humankind. The idea is that it is a physical resurrection of living people that are spiritually and nationally dead because they are scattered among the nations of the earth. Also, this is a vision of a future event and not an actual event itself.
- While the vision depicts the restoration of Israel, it does not depict a physical resurrection from the grave. The use of the word grave is not in reference to places of human burial, but instead to the nations that the Jews were dispersed. Also, the spirit of the prophecy does not include physical, bodily resurrection.
- The vision does not represent spiritual resurrection of the conversion of any individual souls. The prophecy is in reference to the resurrection and conversion of a nation, and not in reference to individuals.
- The subject of this prophecy is exclusively Israel; it does not extend spiritually to the church. As has been pointed out on numerous occasions in the Bible, there is no indication whatsoever of the church replacing Israel. The church can only be made to replace Israel by spiritualizing or allegorizing the text.

The Method of Israel's Restoration

Unger[31] believes "… the true scope and meaning of the passage is the national and spiritual reinstatement of god's chosen people will appear as the prophecy is further interpreted and explained."[32]

- Israel will be Restored by Divine Power: The vision that Ezekiel was shown was of a situation that was humanly impossible to accomplish; only by the supernatural, omnipotent power of God could disconnected, scattered, and dry bones of dead human beings be resurrected.
- Israel will be Restored by Divine Word: Notice the discussion between God and Ezekiel, God tells him to prophesy to the bones to hear the word of the Lord. What God promises by words will be accomplished in reality.
- Israel will be Restored by Divine Life: The bones come together, are covered with flesh, and the breath of life is breathed into them, all to accomplish a divine resurrections of a politically dead nation to come to life within the context of national existence, it is not their spiritual conversion because they have not been regathered back in the land. This prophecy is about the reconstruction of a nation.

The Purpose of Israel's Restoration

Unger[33] continues by describing the reasons God has for restoring Israel.

- To Vindicate God's Divine Word: "The execution of so vast and grand an undertaking, at once so seemingly improbable and impossible of accomplishment, will be with the definite divine end in view of demonstrating to the unbelieving world in general, and proving to Israel in particular, that what God has promised His chosen people … He will most assuredly fulfill."[34] Restoration of the nation of Israel, after two millennia of non-existence, will demonstrate without doubt the power God has for directing the affairs of humankind and fulfilling promises made.
- To Revive the Lost National Hope of Israel: Notice the depths of hopelessness that is depicted by this vision. The conditions are that the bones are dried almost back to the dust of the earth (very dry - powdery), they are scattered in a disorderly fashion in a valley that is a low depression of the face of the earth. The scene appears to be the dead that have been left in an undignified and humiliating manner to deteriorate from the effects of the weather, scavenging animals, and those that steal from the dead. Utter hopelessness. But yet God, in all His powerfulness, will graciously reverse this situation by resurrecting these bones back into the nation of His chosen people.
- To Settle Israel in Her Own Land: God will restore the nation of Israel by bringing them out of the nations to which they were scattered (opening of the graveyards of the nations), into the land that He had given their forefathers, so that they can live as a united nation peaceably in the land. There are two considerations that support the idea that this restoration has not occurred historically. First, the return of less than 50,000 Jews from the Babylonian Captivity hardly qualifies as the return of a nation to its homeland; and second, those that did return at that time were only

members of the previous nation of Israel, people from the nation of Judah did not return. This prophecy refers to the entire house of Israel as being resurrected and returned to their land.

- To Effect Israel's Spiritual Conversion: The resurrection of the dispersed people to re-establish the nation of Israel is necessary in order for God to fulfill His promise to ultimately convert Israel to believing in Jesus Christ as their Messiah. Thus the following sequence can be observed in this prophecy: Resuscitation (Ezekiel 37:4-10, 12, and 13), regathering (Ezekiel 37:12), regeneration (Ezekiel 37:14a), and re-establishment (Ezekiel 37:14b); notice that the vision of Ezekiel 37 only includes resuscitation, and the words of the Lord make reference to the other three events. "The facts presented in the divine interpretation of the vision are these: Israel will be raised to nationhood and regathered to Palestine in unbelief. There she shall be converted as a nation, previous to being established forever in peace and glory in the land during Messiah's Kingdom ..."[34]

- To Demonstrate Israel's Status as an Elect Nation: Notice that on several occasions, God has Ezekiel refer to the resurrected people as His people, a claim that certainly establishes that their election is not because of anything they have done.

The Scope of Israel's Restoration

Unger[35] details that "Israel's awakening from national death in the graveyard of the nations will be the prelude to a glorious place of divine favor in the coming kingdom."[36]

- The Restoration is of the Whole House of Israel: The prophecy specifically indicates that both the tribes of Judah and Israel will be included in the resurrection - all twelve tribes that are living at the time of the event, not those that are physically dead and buried. The godly of Old Testament Israel will be raised immediately before the beginning of the Millennium. Since this is an event of national proportions rather that individual proportions, the sense is that not all dispersed Jews will be resurrected in order to return to the land, but instead only a majority will be resurrected.

- Both Judah and Israel will be United into One Nation. This is evident in the symbol of the two sticks being rejoined and God's instructions to Ezekiel to respond to questions asked of him explaining that it is God's intent to unify the politically divided nation once again - all twelve tribes. It should be remembered that after the Babylonian Captivity only a meager remnant of the two tribes of Judah returned and repossessed the land, and it was those two tribes that occupied the land between the return and the subsequent dispersal in 70 AD. However, the ten tribes of the northern kingdom of Israel never did return from the Assyrian Captivity, thus they have become the Jewish tribes in history. So, where are they now? There has been considerable research dedicated to answering this question, however, it appears to have led only to controversy, therefore, suffice it to conclude that the answer may not be discoverable until later.

The Results of Israel's Restoration
Unger[37] lists the several things that will be forever for Israel.

Will Include a Land Forever:
- God promises of permanent possession of land made in the Abrahamic Covenant (Genesis 12:1; 13:15, 17) and the Palestinian Covenant (Deuteronomy 30:5) will be fulfilled. Also this was affirmed in Isaiah 11:11-12; Jeremiah 23:8; Ezekiel 37:12, 21-22; and Amos 9:15. Israel will now possess the full extent of the land promised according to Genesis 15:18 and Ezekiel 47:13 - 48:35.
- It should be noted that there are other secondary fulfillments associated with the land:
    + Genesis 3:17: When Adam and Eve were judged, God also cursed the productivity of the earth and it was made to present challenge to humankind's effort to subdue it.
    + Deuteronomy 11:13-17: The Lord indicated that if the Jews were obedient then He would bless the fruitfulness of the land. Throughout the Old Testament, it can be seen the land was cursed when the Jews were judged for their disobedience.
    + Isaiah:
        o 11:6-9: The wilderness of the animal world will be tamed.
        o 30:26: Even the light of the sun and moon will increase.
        o 35:1-2: The parched land will be rich and fertile, and will blossom and be fruitful possibly due to climatic changes made by God.
        o 55:13: The land will become less harsh and more conducive to human cultivation.
        o 65:20: Human will live longer.
    + Joel 3:18 (cf. Amos 9:13): Again the land will be productive.
    + Romans 8:21-22: The entire creation groans because of the Fall, however, it will be set free in the future.
- "God is vast and glorious purpose for His "earthly people" will be thus worked out in their earthly inheritance during the Kingdom Age, and then into eternity."[38]

Will Include a King Forever: God's promises of a permanent king made in the Abrahamic Covenant (Genesis 12:2; 13:16; and 17:2-6) and the Davidic Covenant (2 Samuel 7:11, 13, 16) will be fulfilled. Also, this was affirmed in Psalm 89:30-37; 110:1; Jeremiah 33:21; Ezekiel 37:24-25; Luke 1:31-33; Acts 2:29-32; and 15:14-17. Along with the permanent kingship comes a permanent house, throne, and kingdom.

Will Include a Covenant of Peace Forever: God's promise of a permanent peace made with the Abrahamic Covenant (Genesis 12:3 and 22:18) and the New Covenant (Jeremiah 31:31-40) will be fulfilled. The internal spiritual tranquility that will be facilitated by the New Covenant will also cause an outward, or political, peace as there will no longer be conflict between the divided nation because they will be united under the One Shepherd King as indicate in Ezekiel 37:22, 24-26. Other aspects of the permanent peace include the following:

- Isaiah:
  + 9:6-7: The peace that will prevail will be established because the Prince of Peace will be the governing authority.
  + 11:4-5: An enduring peace will extend worldwide.
- Ezekiel 34:25: The creation will also be calm, and there will be security.

Include a Sanctuary Forever: After Israel's resurrection, regathering, unification, and conversion, the Lord will place His sanctuary, or dwelling place, in the midst of Israel, and all will know that God has sanctified her. The sanctuary in which Christ will restore the Judaic system of worship, far in excess of what it has ever been, is described in Ezekiel 40 - 46. "In the Kingdom Age God's own unique presence with Israel in His government of them through David-Messiah, and in the Shekinah presence with their temple worship, will convince the nations that it is Jehovah who "sanctifieth Israel," and who has eternally set them apart for blessing and glory as His own."[39]

47

THE 75-DAY INTERVAL

The long-awaited return of the Lord Jesus Christ has come about. He is present; He has started to fulfill His promises by first destroying His enemies as well as the enemies of the godly, and He is about to begin to fulfill even more of His covenant promises in the days and months to come. Immediately at hand there is a beloved nation that has to be restored, there are ungodly things that have to be dismantled, discarded, or destroyed, there are resurrections that need tending to, and finally there are judgments that are necessary. The Bible provides for a seventy-five-day period that is for the closing of Daniel's 70th Week, and for the preparations for the one-thousand-year Messianic Age and Millennial Kingdom that will shortly begin.

47.1	THE DETERMINATION OF THE 75 DAY TIME PERIOD

Core Scripture: Daniel 12:11-12

The seven years that forms Daniel's 70th Week has been previously established as being two consecutive and distinct time periods – each being, depending on the passage examined (Daniel 7:25 and 12:7, and Revelation 11:2 and 13;5), three and one-half years, forty-two months, or 1,260 days in length. Notwithstanding all the time passages that have been examined thus far, there is one more passage that has to be accommodated as a related part of Daniel's 70th Week – Daniel 12:11-12. In the concluding verses of the Book of Daniel, immediately before Daniel is told that he will sleep so that he can rise to live again in the future, the angel Michael discloses two more time periods that are part of his revelation – 1,290 days and 1,335 days. Notice immediately two things about these periods:

- The 1,290-day period is thirty days longer than the time allowed for each of the two halves of Daniel's 70th Week, and the 1,335-day period is 45 days more than the 30 for a total of 75 days.
- While Daniel does not indicate an exact association, each of the two time periods are loosely related to other things of Daniel's 70th Week.

It should be noted that, "… it is obvious that the second coming of Christ and the establishment of His millennial kingdom requires time …"[1] to clean-up after the events of the death and destruction of the Great Tribulation and make things ready for the continuation of human history into the one-thousand-year Millennium, and the beginning of the Dispensation of the Kingdom.

Daniel 12:11 says that the 1,290-day period that will be the time that is allotted for the Abomination of Desolation:

- Daniel 9:27 indicates that the Abomination of Desolation will occur in the rebuilt and restored Jewish Temple at the midpoint of the seven-year period.
- While there are some that might hold the time of the midpoint to be an approximation, meaning that the event could occur at sometime around the midpoint of Daniel's 70th Week, the absence of further qualifications suggests that the time of the midpoint should be held to be the exact middle day of the seven-year period.
- Therefore, 1,290 days from the midpoint of Daniel's 70th Week will extend thirty days past the day of the Lord's Second Coming at the end of the second half of Daniel's 70th Week. This view would allow for a thirty-day period of time for the removal of the abomination from the Temple and to provide for the preparation of the priests and the Temple for sacrifices.

Daniel 12:12 says that those that are able to wait for the 1,335-day period will be blessed.

- This passage seems to be a continuation of the time and purpose expressed in Verse 11, therefore the time would also be measured from the midpoint of Daniel's 70th Week which would extend 75 days past the Lord's Second coming at the end of the second half of Daniel's 70th Week.
- The sense of this passage is that the people that are most probable to receive this blessing would be those Christ believers that have survived not only the Great Tribulation, but the entire 1,335-day period.
- If people are blessed at the end of the 1,335 days, then the most probable blessing that the believing survivors would receive would be to go as a living human being into the one-thousand-year Messianic Age.

Thus, Daniel 12:11-12 establishes that there will be an interim period of time after the Second Advent of Christ, before the beginning of the Millennium, in which, first, the abomination of the Temple by the Antichrist will be removed and the Temple restored by the thirtieth day after, the Millennial Kingdom will begin by the seventy-fifth day after.

Since the historical progression of humankind and the various aspects of God's Plan, including the fulfillment of prophecies, have occurred in time and space as we know them (as opposed to events in the heavenly realm that we do not really understand very well), then there is every expectation that all future events will also happen on earth in the same time and space. The several topics that will be examined in this chapter will require a period of time in which to resolve or complete the associated events and issues, and this seventy-five-day interval seems to provide that time.

47.2 THE RESTORATION OF THE JEWISH TEMPLE AND REMOVAL OF THE ABOMINATION OF DESOLATION

When the Antichrist desecrates the Jewish Temple with the Abomination of Desolation, it will be done in such a way that the Temple is considered impure and the sacrificial worship will have to cease. As the Antichrist will remain in control of the world for the duration of the second half of Daniel's 70th Week (the Great Tribulation), the implication is that this abomination will continue for the remainder of Daniel's 70th Week. Upon Jesus' return to the earth to deliver God's people from evil and to bring judgment to the unrighteousness, His defeat of the Antichrist will eliminate the need for the Temple to continue to be defiled, therefore it will have to be renovated, in a sense, and will have to be purified so that the sacrificial worship can resume. As discussed above, Daniel 12:11-12 indicates that at the end of the allotted time for the desolation of the Temple, thirty days after Christ's Second Advent, the Temple will again be brought back into its rightful condition in God's Plan.

47.3 THE RESTORATION OF THE NATION OF ISRAEL

Throughout this book, the point has been made numerous times that there are unilateral and many of which are yet to be fulfilled at some time in the future. Among these is the restoration of the nation of Israel which is detailed in Chapter 46. The fulfillment of the Abrahamic, Palestinian, Davidic, and New Covenants are dependent on Israel existing as a viable nation at some time in the future of the history of humankind. Christ's Second Coming will be the event that will start the process of the fulfillment of all of the outstanding promises, with one of the most major promises being the restoration of Israel: the regathering of the nation, to their land, under the rulership of God, as a blessed and chosen people.

Since the restoration process will take time to accomplish, there is the possibility that the specific activities may begin during this 75-day interval – the Bible does not indicate a starting time, however, there is nothing that would prevent its start during this interval.

It seems harmonious with the Scriptures that the 75 days will be a time to get ready for the regathering of the people of the nation (land, government, infrastructure, removal of war debris, etc.), so that the actual regathering would be part of the Millennium. The sense of Daniel 12:11-12 is that it is a prophecy more about Israel, rather than the Gentiles, so if a blessing is to be received 75 days after Christ comes, then the only blessing available will be for a living human being – that has survived Daniel's 70th Week, the last battle, and the Judgment of the Nations because of belief – to go into the Millennium.

47.4	**THE STATE OF THINGS JUST PRIOR TO THE MILLENNIAL KINGDOM**

It is interesting to creatively speculate about what the state of things will be at the end of the 75 Day Interval, which according to Daniel 12:12 will be a time of blessing for those that are able to live until the 1,335 days after the desolation of the Jewish Temple. The following could be possible as a theological global society and culture begin to emerge as the Lord leads the righteous in the construction of the things that will be required in the Millennium:

- The Lord Jesus Christ has logistically established His presence in the world.
- It would seem very likely that the true sense of safety, security, and freedom that is predicted for the one-thousand-year age is beginning to be felt for the first time since before the Fall.
- The abomination that desolated the Jewish Temple has been removed and the Temple has been restored and made ready for Jesus Christ to rule from His throne.
- Civilized order may be making a strong showing as the human condition begins to become organized.
- Whatever form the governmental structure of the world's nations will have, is probably well under way.
- Because of the absence of the evil influence of Satan, respective social, political, economic, and cultural structures may be returning to the various people groups, tribes, and nations, but this time fee of the "garbage" that had characterized them before.
- Removal of the debris and ravaged of the after-effects of a cataclysmic global war is probably well under way.
- Assessments of the damage to the earth caused by the seal, trumpet, and bowl judgments are probably in progress and plans being made to restore the creation to its intended condition.
- Whatever will be normal life in the Millennial Kingdom may be relatively settled.
- The living beings that will be present will consist of only two groups:
  + Those that have physically lived through the Great Tribulation and have been judged as faithful and worthy of living in the presence of the Lord.
  + Those that have lived before and have physically died, but because they have been judged to be righteous have been resurrected and given supernatural resurrection bodies.
- Construction of buildings for habitation and the infrastructure necessary for the collection of human beings in communities and cities is probably in full progress.

47.5 | THE TRANSITION OF THE DISPENSATIONS

It is easy for believers to think that the events of Daniel's 70th Week, the 75 Day Interval, and especially, the Messianic Millennium will be different than the human condition on earth on this side of those times. While it is certain there will be some supernatural aspects that are unique to those times, it is also important to notice that the Bible does not suggest that the natural order of the earth, the sun rises and sets, the wind blows, the seasons change, etc., and the normal order of human life, (unresurrected) human beings will be born, breathe, at, grow old, die, etc., will be no different than now exists. Also, time will be as it has always been and will still be measured in the same manner as today – 24-hour daily cycle, 365 days to the year, etc. What this means is that, with the exception of the presence of the Lord Jesus Christ ruling on earth, resurrected beings, and the changed social and cultural conditions, the earth and human life will pretty much be as they were before.

For all practical purposes, a period of some amount of time will be required for the Dispensation of Grace (the Church) to logistically transition into the Dispensation of the Kingdom. The Dispensation of Grace will end with humankind achieving the ultimate state of apostasy, and the Bible seems to suggest that the Dispensation of the Kingdom will begin in its full glory rather than the first weeks, months, or years being consumed with resolving what is left over from Daniel's 70th Week. Thus, if this be the case, it seems plausible that the 75-day interval will be a time for the practical and pragmatic thing required to start a new dispensation to take place.

48

REVELATION OF THE MILLENNIUM

The only location in the Bible that mentions a one-thousand-year time period is Revelation 20:1-6. This will be a time in which Satan will be bound and thrown into the Abyss, there will be enthroned saints who have been given authority to judge, and that the saints who were martyred during Daniel's 70th Week will be seen. The passage suggests that the resurrected saints and the saints that survived Daniel's 70th Week will live together in the world after Daniel's 70th Week. However, there are many passages in both Testaments that provide more detail about a future time of living in the presence of the Lord Jesus Christ.

48.1 PREDICTIONS OF A MILLENNIUM - THE OLD TESTAMENT

One of the most prolific themes that run consistently throughout the Old Testament is the anticipation of the Jews that there will be a future time when the nation of Israel will exist in a glorious state defined by God's theocratic rule, they will be delivered from their enemies, and they will live righteously in peace, safety and prosperity. For all the ups and downs of ancient Israel's yo-yo-like relationship with God, the evidence and testimony of the Old Testament is that God will permit, allow, and cause the nation to exist as she has never really existed before, as the nation chosen by God from among the many nations, peoples, and tribes of human history to be His chosen. There is a hope for future glory that can be gleaned from the Old Testament that transcends the depressing cycle of with God / without God existence that characterizes Israel's history prior to its third deportation from the land for disobedience. That hope will be realized in the Millennial Reign of Christ and the fulfillment of the covenantal promises made by God, all of which are yet to occur.

THE PSALMS
- 72: While this royal psalm addresses the reign of Solomon during his time, it also paints the picture that the reign of God, in the person of Jesus Christ the royal Son of God, will be universal in a future kingdom. His judgment will be righteous, His presence will be as natural as rain on the grass of the field, kings will bow down to Him, His rule will be over all the earth, and He will care for the needy and the oppressed.
- 89: This psalm clarifies that, in spite of Israel's sinfulness (verses 89:30-32), the Lord's love for her will remain eternally loyal (verse 89:33), and the

361

future reign of the Lord will fulfill the Davidic Covenant promise (verse 89:34) of a throne forever (verses 89:29, 35-37).

DANIEL

It is without doubt that the prophecy-rich Book of Daniel holds in its short twelve chapters the timeline key to the last several thousand years of not only Israel's history but the entire world's history as well. One of the most significant Biblical testimonies that there be a future time when God will reign as King is found in Nebuchadnezzar's bizarre dream of a colossal statue (Chapter 2) and Daniel's strange vision of the four beasts (Chapter 7).

Daniel 2:34-35 and 44-45 indicates that God will destroy the ten-king human government and will bring in His own everlasting kingdom that will be ruled by His appointed Ruler, Jesus Christ.

- It should be noted that the destruction of the ten kings also represents the destruction of all of the human, earthly empires that have ever been. The symbolism of the governmental change is manifested in the God that will terminate human government and will replace it with a theocratic government.
- This new form of government will be further characterized by the fact that it will not ever be replaced, nor will it ever be left to another people as God did with Israel after the rejection of Jesus when He let Israel go into a dispersed and dormant existence. This new government is more aptly identified as a kingdom that will last forever.
- This new kingdom is identified as being a stone cut from a mountain without human hands. The stone is Jesus Christ and the mountain is God, and the reference to human hands indicates that the action is all by God and humankind has no participation in the development and execution of God's Plan.
- The stone will come to earth and will essentially obliterate the ten-king human government. The reference to *the iron, the bronze, the clay, the silver,* and *the gold* indicates there will be a permanent change in government - humankind will no longer rule on the earth, instead, God will send another ruler to establish the government that He has always wanted for Israel and the nations of the world. The stone will then expand and cover the entire earth which leaves little doubt as to the extent of this new form of rule.
- This passage presents a strong case for premillennialism because it indicates God, in the person of Jesus Christ, will come to terminate human rule on earth and establish His own kingdom.

ISAIAH

The prophetic Isaiah writes that there will be a time when an ideal king will establish a particular kind of kingdom that will stand in contrast to the typical governments and empires of humankind. Isaiah 11 has much to contribute to the understanding of the judgements and righteousness of this kingdom which must be in the future still since nothing like it has occurred as of yet in history. The following observations may be made that characterizes that kingdom:

- The shoot from Jesse's root stock is a reference to Jesus who as a royal descendent of Jewish lineage who will be the loyal bearer of the Lord's spirit. He will:
  + Possess extraordinary wisdom, will obey the Lord, and will execute His plans.
  + Exercise righteous and proper judgment and will execute the wicked.
  + Elevate the suffering poor and tear down tyranny.
  + 11:10: *In that day the Root of Jesse will stand as a banner for the peoples; the nations will rally to him, and his resting place will be glorious.*
- There will be changes in the terrorism and violence in the animal and human worlds and no longer will animals or humans need to fear each other.
- There will no longer be rebellion against the Lord and there will be universal submission to His sovereignty.
- The remnant of the Lord's chosen people, Israel, will be regathered from the faraway places, and jealousies and hostilities will cease as the saints are restored to the land given them by God.

JEREMIAH

Jeremiah looks forward to a righteous branch of David ruling over his nation.

- 23:5-6, 8 and 33:16: The Lord will raise up a righteous Branch of David, we know it to be Jesus Christ, who will rule justly with wisdom and understanding; and when He does, Israel will live safely and securely in their own land.
- 30:9: Israel's most favorite king, David, will also rule over them. It should be noted that the Bible indicates that David will be resurrected in order to reign with Jesus Christ to fulfill the promise that David will be Israel's eternal ruler. While Jesus is sometimes referred to as David, it is always as the Son of David or the Seed of David, never as just David alone. "The only explanation that follows any literal understanding of these prophecies is that they picture David in his resurrected state reigning over the house of Israel with Christ on earth."[1] Refer also to Ezekiel 34:23-24 where David is identified as the prince that will shepherd over Israel in the future kingdom under the Lord.

EZEKIEL
- 37:21-25: This passage records again the often-repeated promise that the Lord will gather the children of Israel from all the corners of the earth, will restore them as a nation in their own land, will place one king (David) over the never-again-to-be-divided nation as her shepherd, and a harmonious relationship will persist forever. See also Psalm 89:36, Daniel 7:27, Ezekiel 37:25, and Luke 1:33.

MINOR PROPHETS

Not to be any less important than the Major Prophets, the Minor Prophets also contribute to the significant body of testimony that there will be a future kingdom:
- Joel 3:20: *Judah will be inhabited forever and Jerusalem through all generations.*
- Amos 9:13-15: The *days are coming* when the Lord *will bring* His *people back from exile* and they will live in rebuilt cities forever.
- Micah 5:4: In the future, Jesus Christ will shepherd Israel who will live securely.
- Zechariah 14:9-11: *The Lord will be king over the whole earth.* Then there is a description of the *whole land* that also emphasizes that Jerusalem *will be inhabited, never again will it be destroyed*; *Jerusalem will be secure.*

In closing this discussion of the Old Testament predictions of the Millennium it should be noted that the Old Testament looks toward a future time when God's kingdom will be on earth and life will be different for what it is today or has been throughout human history. The length of time for this future kingdom is only described as eternal; there is no mention of a one-thousand-year span of time.

48.2	PREDICTIONS OF A MILLENNIUM - THE NEW TESTAMENT

In opening the discussion of the New Testament predictions of the Millennium it should be noted that the New Testament also looks forward to a future time when God's Kingdom will exist, however, in this Testament it is referred to as Christ's Kingdom that will be on earth for one thousand years according to Revelation 20:1-7. As previously discussed, most conservative Biblical scholars believe the one-thousand-year Millennium is distinct from, but similar to, the Universal, or Eternal Kingdom. Interestingly, Walvoord[2] makes the analogous observation that since the Bible indicates that God's Kingdom will endure forever; the 1,000-year millennium will be like the "vestibule" to God's Eternal Kingdom.

MATTHEW
- 19:28: Jesus promised the apostles that they would sit on thrones to judge the twelve tribes of Israel.
- 20:20-23: The mother of James and John was not corrected by Jesus when she requested her sons be permitted to sit on either side of Jesus when He brought in the kingdom.
- 14:3: Jesus did not correct the apostles when they asked Him if He would bring in the kingdom, instead they were told to continue to anticipate His coming again when He would rule as God on earth.

LUKE
- 1:31-33: In the account of Jesus' conception, the angel Gabriel told Mary, and like most devout Jews of the time, she believed that the child she was to bear would be the expected Messiah that would reign forever over the house of Israel. She understood that the covenantal promises would be fulfilled through her son.

ACTS
- 1:6: When the apostles asked Jesus immediately prior to His Ascension when the kingdom would begin, as He did on several occasions during His earthly life He again did not correct their anticipation of it, but instead gave them instructions of what to do as they waited for it.
- 8:12; 14:22; 19:8; 20:25; 28:23, 31: Just as Jesus did in Acts 1:3, many Biblical scholars believe that the preaching and teaching of the Kingdom of God described in these passages are in reference to the Millennial Kingdom.

REVELATION

Details of the Apostle John's visions of the future described in the Book of Revelation have been examined previously, but suffice the current discussion to point out that Revelation 20:1-7 has much to say about the future Millennium that includes the following:
- The length of the kingdom time period is mentioned six times in seven verses as being one thousand years.
- Satan will be bound for one thousand years.
- Those that have died for Christ will be resurrected and reign with Him.
- At the end of the time period, Satan will be released, there will be a final rebellion, and the wicked will be resurrected (for judgment as described elsewhere).

PAUL'S WRITINGS

While kingdom details are not really prominent in Paul's writings, he does provide a number of pieces of information that help to construct the millennial doctrine.

- Romans 11:13-32: Israel will be delivered back to their land.
- 1 Corinthians:
  + 6:9-10: A list of those who will not inherit the kingdom is given.
  + 15:50: A distinction is made between those that will inherit the kingdom, the imperishable, and those that will not, the perishable.
  + 15:24: When all earthly human rule, authority, and power have been brought to an end, Jesus will then hand the Kingdom of righteous saints to God.
- 1 Corinthians 15:51-52 (cf. 1 Thessalonians 4:13-18): The Rapture is clearly delineated, and other passages indicate that the rapture will be one of the events that signal the beginning of the end of this present age.
- Galatians 5:21 (cf. Ephesians 5:5): Several lists of those that will not inherit the kingdom are given.
- 2 Timothy:
  + 2:12: Believers will reign with Christ.
  + 4:1: Christ is associated with a kingdom.
- 1 Thessalonians 2:12: A call to live in a particular way in order to be called by God to live in the Kingdom.
- 2 Thessalonians 1:5: Righteous suffering for the Lord makes one worthy.

49

THE 1,000-YEAR MILLENNIUM

For centuries, a hopeful and seemingly achievable future expectation has intrigued humankind and has challenged the tribes, cultures, peoples, and nations that have developed religiously, philosophically, and intellectually. That expectation, which is timeless and universal, concerns whether or not there will be a time in the future when earthly life will be in a perpetual state of peace, and in a kind of social, economic, ecological, political, familial, and cultural harmony that has never existed before. Recorded history and archeological evidence has substantiated instances of this expectation among many of the cultures and civilizations that have existed throughout the span of human existence.

Even today, among secular society there is an innate desire deep within the soul of every person to find or achieve some type of nirvana, utopia, or that condition of human existence that stands in direct contrast to the conditions they encounter in everyday living. In fact, those that live in civilized, organized, and technically astute modern societies consistently strive for a personal lifestyle that will be more aligned with their perception of what nirvana or utopia is supposed to be like. Thus, it would not be surprising if science could prove what students of the Bible already know: every human being has an internal tendency or inclination to want to live in a safe and secure place, without want or need.

The interesting aspect of this expectation is that far too many people believe that the place of peace and perfection is achievable during this life on earth, and do not realize that what the Bible is teaching is that the place of perfection will be at a time in the future and in a state that is uniquely different than what existed in their earthly life. Today people try to create, to search for, to purchase, or to rationalize that place instead of understanding that it will be a result of the decisions they make in this life about the One that makes that state of perfection available to them. They also fail to realize that belief in such a future will reward this life with a supernatural spiritual, emotional, and intellectual power to find happiness, albeit limited to some extent, on this side of death. The first part of the true place of perfection is the subject of this chapter: life on earth in Jesus Christ's Kingdom, and the second part is the subject of a future chapter regarding the eternal state in the heavenly presence of the Triune God.

So, just what exactly is ahead for humankind? Does the Bible say very much about a time as just described? Or, is the Bible silent on such matters? The Bible has a great deal to say about a future kingdom on earth that will be before the eternal state. However, there are those that believe in other views: some that there will

be no earthly kingdom at all, and some that believe we are living in the kingdom now. So the crucial questions are these:
- Will there be an earthly kingdom?
- If there will be, will it be in the future, or was it in the past?
- Or if not, is it going on now?

The millennium will be populated by the following groups:
- The Old Testament Saints.
- Christians of the True Church.
- Tribulation Saints.
- The Sheep from the Judgement of the Sheep and Goats.

49.1 THE IMPORTANCE OF THE MILLENNIAL DOCTRINE

Is a millennial doctrine important to the Church today? Yes, it is of utmost importance not only to the Church, but to those believers that want to have an intellectual understanding of Scripture, and it is especially important to those that are entrusted with responsibility of shepherding portions of the body of Christ by maintaining doctrinal purity. One of the reasons for its importance is that today the millennial question is one of the several theological lightning rods pointing to the sky to protect the vast human investment that has been made in the local church by the Lord from lightning bolts that electrify opposition.

Walvoord[1] has made several interesting observations:
- "There remains today a tendency to dismiss the whole subject [millennialism] as belonging to another age and as being foreign to intellectual studies of our day …"[2] with some saying that the question is obsolete, unnecessary, or irrelevant. When liberal theologians do write about anything resembling the millennium, the search for understanding usually involves ultimate ethical values rather than prophecy.
- The millennial question has become the rallying point between two significantly different views of the relationship between an earthly kingdom and the Lord's Second Advent, and what should be expected from each, which is evidenced by the fact that there have been numerous books that have been written and published in the attempt to say the question is not important, but in reality acknowledging the necessity of having a well-developed doctrine of belief.
- It seems that during the twentieth century premillennialism has advanced involuntarily from a doctrine of theology into a system of theology which carries all the implications required of such a development with that being the necessity to stand on veracity of the Scriptures by taking the offense rather than falling back on the defense (it should be understood, that God really does not need us to defend the Bible, it can defend itself and survive

any scrutiny thrown at it by puny human beings). This is attributed to the following reasons:

+ The Roman Catholic Church has for centuries controlled (word specifically used) access to the Bible by the laity and has built its church-empire around priestly leadership as being the only ones that are capable of interpreting Scripture.

+ Liberal theology, to which the Bible is not authoritative, and should be interpreted spiritually (allegorically), is intellectually and theologically challenged by premillennialism.

• Premillennialism as a system of theology has achieved this principled view largely because of three movements - the Bible institute movement, the Bible study movement, and the prophetic conference movement - that swept the country in the first half of the twentieth century (and continues to do so today) which has been, for the most part, premillennially grounded. One of the historical lines of conflict that has been aided by the millennial question, and these movements, is the question if the Bible should be interpreted literally or allegorically. One's view on the millennial question tends to also be one's view on many, many of the other available views on the other aspects of eschatology. "It is not too much to say that millennialism is a determining factor in Biblical interpretation of comparable importance to the doctrines of verbal inspiration, the deity of Christ, substitutionary atonement, and bodily resurrection."[3]

49.2 THE PURPOSE OF THE MILLENNIUM

Why would God find it necessary to include a one-thousand-year period of time after Christ's Second Advent? What purpose will it fulfill? Hitchcock[4] proposes there are three reasons for the Millennium:

• "To Reward the Faithful:" After the armies of the Antichrist are defeated at the close of Daniel's 70th Week and at Christ's Second Advent, God will establish His kingdom on earth. "While the Millennium will include things like worshipping and serving our Lord, Scripture emphasizes our ruling and reigning with Christ. The Bible says that all believers from every age will reign with Christ for a thousand years."[5] Consider the following passages about what God's people will do during the Millennium:

+ Daniel 7:18, 22, and 27: The holy people of the Most High will be rewarded with the kingdom which they will possess forever.

+ Luke 19:11-26: "This parable ... sums up Jesus' teaching to the disciples. Each disciple had duties given to him by Jesus, and each was to carry out his responsibilities. But the parable was addressed not only to the disciples. It was also addressed to the nation at large to show that it too had responsibilities."[6]

+ 1 Corinthians 6:2-3: The *Lord's people will judge the world*, including *trivial cases*.

+ Revelation:

      ○ 2:26-28: Jesus promises the faithful that they will join Him in His millennial rule. *To the one that is victorious and does* the Lord's *will until the end will be given authority over the nations, that one will rule them with an iron scepter and will dash them to pieces like pottery* – just as He *received authority from* the *Father*.

      ○ 20:4: John saw two things: first, *thrones on which were seated those who had been given authority to judge*, and second, those that had been martyred during Daniel's 70th Week reigning *with Christ for a thousand years*.

      ○ 20:6: Those that the second death has no power over *will be priests of God and of Christ and will reign with him for a thousand years*.

- "To Redeem Creation:" God wants to reverse His curse on creation as recorded in Genesis 3:14-19, and to fulfill His original intentions for the earth. The world is not at all what it was supposed to be, and Scripture says it will be someday. "God's original purpose was to bring all things under the dominion of humankind and to submit all things to Himself through human beings (Genesis 1:26-27)."[7]
- "To Realize the Biblical Covenants:" God made very specific promises to Israel that are recorded in the four, great, unconditional covenants, see Chapter 18. These covenants remain unfulfilled, but they will be fulfilled in the Millennium.

49.3   THE MILLENNIUM DEFINED

Revelation 20:1-6 establishes the Millennium and is the only place in the Bible that states the Millennium will be one thousand years in length.

THE TIME OF THE MILLENNIUM

Core Scripture: Revelation 20:1-6.

The essential New Testament passage that establishes the doctrine of the Millennium is found in Revelation 20:1-6. Notwithstanding the fact that this is the only passage in the Bible that identifies the time period for the Millennium as being one thousand years, it is emphatically stated six times in verses 1 through 7 in association with several different aspects of the future time that share the same span of duration.

- Literalness of the Millennium: It is common among liberal Biblical theologians and scholars not to hold a literal interpretation of the Book of Revelation, but instead to allegorize the entire book on the basis that the extreme use of symbols and apocalyptical language demands anything but a literal interpretation. This is particularly true for this passage; if the entire book is symbolic, then there is no reason to believe there will be a time in the future that will take place as described. It is this interpretation that leads to the other views that the millennium has already occurred or it is only symbolic of something else completely unrelated to what Revelation 20:1-6 says. As is true with the literal, grammatical, historical interpretative method used in this book, there is no reason to take the literalness of a future Millennium in any other way than literally stated.

• Duration of the Millennium:

  + Pentecost makes the point that if, "… the angels, heaven, the pit, Satan, the nations, the resurrections mentioned in this chapter are literal … [i]t would be folly to accept the literalness of those and deny the literalness of the time element."[6] Invoking the interpretative principle that if there is no reason to take a passage otherwise, then the literal interpretation is dictated, supports the notion that there is no reason not to believe that there will be a future time period that will be one thousand years in length.

  + Pentecost also responds to the question, naturally raised, regarding the conflict between a one-thousand-year reign by Jesus Christ and the numerous Old and New Testament passages that speak to the fact that Christ will reign over an endless kingdom, such as found in Ezekiel 43:7-9; Daniel 7:13-14, 27; 9:24; Luke 1:30-33; and Revelation 11:5 among many others. Pentecost points out that John Calvin did not hold to a premillennial view because these passages do not allow for a fixed one-thousand-year reign. 1 Corinthians 15:24-28 provides the appropriate response to this conflict. God has given Jesus the mediatorial right to rule until all things are in subjection to Him, at which time Jesus will then subject Himself and the eternal kingdom to the Lord God. "God's original purpose was to manifest His absolute authority and this purpose is realized when Christ unities the earthly theocracy with the eternal kingdom of God. Thus, while Christ's earthly theocratic rule is limited to one thousand years, which is sufficient time to manifest God's perfect theocracy on the earth, His reign is eternal."[9]

  + "There is no good reason for taking the thousand years in other than their literal sense."[10]

THE BINDING OF SATAN FOR THE ENTIRE MILLENNIUM

Core Scripture: Revelation 20:1-3.

"Satan, as the god of this age (2 Cor. 4:4), has carried on this work to defeat the purpose and program of God. The Millennial age is to be the age in which divine righteousness is to be displayed (Isa. 11:5; 32:1; Jer. 23:6; Dan. 9:24). It is also to be God's final test of fallen humanity under the most ideal circumstances. All outward sources of temptation must be removed so that man will demonstrate what he is apart from Satanic influence. So that there can be the full manifestation of righteousness and a test of humanity apart from external temptation, Satan must be removed from the sphere. Therefore, at the second advent he will be bound and removed from the scene for the entirety of that millennial period."[11]

The sense of the passage indicates that Satan is more than restricted, he is physically restrained thus rendering him inactive, and then confined by being locked in the abyss thus separating him from the world of humankind. "The fact that Satan is bound for a thousand years is confirmed by the multitude of passages dealing with the kingdom period in which Satan is never found working in the world."[12]

THE ENTHRONEMENT OF JUDGES

Core Scripture: Revelation 20:4a.

After he witnesses the binding and confinement of Satan, the Apostle John then sees in his vision those who have been given authority to judge sitting on thrones. One of the difficulties of this portion of this verse is the lack of a specific identity for those that are sitting on the thrones. "The most probable interpretation is that they are the twenty-four elders who are said to reign on earth (5:10). This correlates with the prophecy of Christ recorded in Luke 22:29-30 ..." and "... Matthew 19:28 ..."[13] regarding the promises by Jesus to the twelve apostles, that as members of the true Body of Christ, they will be present on earth with Christ during His Messianic Kingdom in some responsible capacity to assist His rule of the world and the nation of Israel.

That the twelve apostles will be present in their resurrected bodies on the earth during the Millennial supports the notion that the resurrected Church saints will be on the earth (rather than in heaven as some suggest) during the Millennium.

THE RESURRECTION OF TRIBULATION SAINTS

Core Scripture: Revelation 20:4a.

John then sees a sight that must bring him comfort. He sees those resurrected that were martyred during Daniel's 70th Week because they testified for Jesus Christ and refused to worship the beast (the Antichrist) or his beast, and had refused to bear the mark of the beast as described in Revelation 13:15-17. He also understands that they will participate in some responsible capacity in Jesus' theocratic government that will rule during the one-thousand-year Millennium. This is also the group that John had seen earlier souls below the heavenly altar in the Fifth Seal, Revelation 6:9-11 and as the enormous crowd before the Lord in Revelation 7:9-17.

"Those who were the special objects of Satan's hatred and the beast's persecution are now exalted, reworked, and blessed."[14]

Because of what is stated in the following verse, an important truth is established. Verse 5 indicates that the wicked dead will not be brought back to life until after the thousand years, thus establishing the truth of several things:

- Both the righteous dead and the wicked dead will be physically and bodily resurrected to live again thereby supporting the truth that all people will live again in the future with some to face judgment and others to go into the presence of the Lord.
- The resurrection of the religious and the wicked is separated by the one-thousand-year period, with the righteous enjoying the blessings of the Messianic Age, but the wicked delayed until after the time of blessing to face the final judgment before being eternal condemned.

FIRST AND SECOND RESURRECTIONS DEFINED

Core Scripture: Revelation 20:4b-6.

This is the central passage that legitimately establishes the relationship between the first death, the first resurrection, second death, and the second resurrection that has previously been examined in Section 44.2.

49.4	**THE RELATIONSHIP BETWEEN OLD TESTAMENT EXPECTATION OF A JEWISH KINGDOM AND NEW TESTAMENT EXPECTATION OF A ONE-THOUSAND-YEAR MESSIANIC REIGN**

A logical question occurs at this point, how do we know that a future restoration in glory for the nation of Israel as repetitively indicated in the Old Testament is the same thing as the one-thousand-year period of time spoken of in Revelation 20? While there are no Scriptural passages that attest to this specific relationship, there are other facts that support this conclusion.

- While the Church is mentioned in Chapters 2 and 3 of the Book of Revelation, it is not mentioned at any point after Chapter 3. Also, it has been concluded that Chapters 4 through 19 relate to the seven-year time of Daniel's 70th Week, which is directed at the nation of Israel, which is then concluded by the Campaign of Armageddon and the return of Jesus Christ. Chapters 20 through 22 clearly indicate that there will be a one-thousand-year period of blessing for those that believe in Christ, followed by a final judgment of the wicked, which is then followed by the eternal age. It is fairly obvious that the one-thousand-year period of blessing has to include Israel as a physical nation on the physical earth, because if it does not then God will not have been able to fulfill all of His promises that are as yet unfulfilled, and life in eternity is described as being vastly different than what is known on earth. The Book of Revelation does not leave any other substantial period of time between this present age and the eternal age except the one-thousand-year Messianic reign of Christ. If the expected Jewish Kingdom does not occur during this time, then when will it?

- A literal interpretation of a significant portion of the Old Testament teaches that Israel will someday live in a peaceful kingdom that will be ruled by their Messiah on the throne of David. If Jesus Christ is their Messiah, then the New Testament indicates that there will be a one-thousand-year age when He rules. These two reigns must be the same.

It is the conclusion of this book that the promises by God of a future time of Israel's restoration physically, nationally, culturally, and spiritually will be the same period of time as will be the one-thousand-year messianic reign of Jesus Christ. The Messiah that is expected by the Jews is the same God-man as presented in Revelation 20.

49.5	**THE FINAL RESTORATION OF ISRAEL – FULFILLMENT OF THE EVERLASTING COVENANTS**

The one-thousand-year Millennium will be all, and more, of what the nation of Israel has yearned for centuries. It will be Israel's time of glory, when the nation is what it was intended to be, when God is their God, when all that is anticipated and expected is accomplished and fulfilled. The four everlasting covenants made by God unconditionally with Israel include the Abrahamic, Palestinian, Davidic, and New Covenants. Pentecost15 has this to say about the Millennium and Israel, "… the kingdom on earth is viewed as the complete fulfillment of those covenants, and that the millennial age is instituted out of necessity in order to fulfill the covenants. … It will thus be observed that the millennial age finds the complete fulfillment of all that God promised to the nation Israel."

One of the principles of interpretation of prophetic and eschatological passages that is evidenced in the Bible is to be aware that some prophetic fulfillments will be immediate (at the time the prophecy is given and within its context), in the immediate future (at some time after the prophecy is given, but not as part of the context in which it is given, but still recorded in biblical or extra-biblical history), or it can be fulfilled in the future yet to occur (largely based on the fact that some features have never occurred or been recorded in history). This is certainly true of these four covenants; fulfillments have been scattered down through history since the founding covenant was made by God with Abram. While many fulfillments have been recorded to have occurred, there are still others outstanding.

From the study of these four covenants there are five features which can be developed regarding the implications of Israel's future. While these have previously been examined in Chapter 22, it is helpful to review them here. Keep in mind that the covenants formally record God's promises to the nation Israel, but the Old Testament contains an enormous amount of information that supports and explains the specific of the covenants.

- First Feature – A Nation Forever: God promised Abram in the Abrahamic Covenant that He would provide a land, a seed, and a blessing for Abram himself, for his descendants, and for the world at large. Of particular interest here is the fact that God promised to make Abram the father of a nation of great and innumerable people, and He promised that the nation would be everlasting. The Old Testament tells us that Abram is the father of the nation of Israel. We know from the Bible, and from recorded history, that Israel has survived through dozens of centuries in spite of the fact that they were judged by God and removed from their land on several occasions, the last time for almost two thousand years. And yet, here we are in the first few years of another millennium and the nation of Israel exists and continues to exist in the face of overwhelming obstacles – another testimony to God's sovereignty. We have seen that Israel will exist as an unbelieving nation during the seven years of Daniel's 70th Week, will be rescued by Jesus upon His return to earth, and will exist as a legitimate nation during the Millennial Age.

- Second Feature – A Land Forever: Expanding upon the Abrahamic Covenant, God promised Abram a land for his descendants who would turn into a nation, and that the title deed for the land would pass down through the generations descending from Abram, thus causing the land to belong to Israel forever. The Palestinian Covenant expanded the promise and provided more detail. Also, associated with this feature are several other dimensions that require mention:
  + The promise of a land eternally did not preclude God from removing Israel from the land for disobedience, which He has done three times now, and restoring them to the land when it serves His purposes, which He has done twice so far, and the current restoration possible being the third.
  + The implication of an eternal deed to a parcel of land is that there will eventually be a permanent restoration to that land and a regeneration of the Jews that will live there that is part of the other aspects of the covenantal promises.
  + Another implication of an eternal deed to a parcel of land is that Israel's Messiah will eventually be their God within their midst in the land as well. We know from the Bible, that Christ will take up residence in the restored nation of Israel.
  + When Israel occupies the land in the kingdom age, it will be as the nation that is restored to her God.

+ When Israel lives in their land in the kingdom age, they will do so as a nation fully converted to Jesus Christ.
+ When Israel is in their land in the kingdom age, the restored and regenerated nation will have no enemies nor will they ever be oppressed again.
+ Finally, when Israel lives permanently in the full extent of their God-given land, all the nations of the earth will be blessed by the Lord. There will no longer be people and nations that are disobedient, only those that are obedient.
- Third Feature - A King Forever / A Throne Forever / A Kingdom Forever: God promised David in the Davidic Covenant that Israel would forever have a king from his lineage that would sit on Israel's throne ruling a Jewish kingdom. This promise is accomplished in the Millennial Kingdom when Jesus sits on the throne of Israel, within the new temple constructed on the Temple Mount, as the rightful and eternal king of Israel.
- Fourth Feature – A New Covenant: Throughout the Old Testament, there are a considerable number of passages that describes the state in which Israel will live in their land during the time of their kingdom. In the Millennial Age, Israel will be a restored nation that has been regenerated, forgiven by God for all of her transgressions, and justified to be the holy children of God.
- Fifth Feature – Abiding Blessings: Finally, Israel is promised considerable blessing in their future kingdom and during the Millennial Age God will bestow overwhelming blessing onto the nation by caring for her people by providing a way of life that is unsurpassed in quality of living.

49.6 THE REIGN OF JESUS CHRIST ON EARTH

"It is evident that there can and will be no earthly theocratic kingdom apart from the personal manifested presence of the Lord Jesus Christ."[16] This statement, while straightforward and succinct, describes a condition time when there will be no human beings on earth, except those that live in the presence of the Lord Jesus Christ. Jesus Christ will live on earth and will rule global humankind during the Millennial Kingdom.

Pentecost[17] has identified a large number of Biblical references to Jesus Christ that describes His essence during the Millennial Kingdom:
- The Names and Titles Applied to Christ in the Millennium: "Something of the manifold relationship which Christ sustains to the millennium is to be observed in the many names and titles given to Him during that period, each suggesting some facts of His person and work in that day."[18]
  + Those Describing Him as the Branch:
    o Isaiah:
      - 4:2: The Branch of Jehovah.
      - 11:1 (cf. Jeremiah 23:5, 33:15): The Branch of David.
    o Zechariah:

- 3:8: Jehovah's Servant.
- 6:12, 13: The Man whose name is the Branch.

+ Those Describing Him as the True God and Rightful Ruler:
  o Isaiah:
    - 2:2-4; 7:14; 9:6; 12:6; 25:7-10; 33:20-22; 40:9-11 (cf. Jeremiah 3:17; 23:5-6; Ezekiel 43:5-7; 44:1-2; Joel 3:21; Micah 4:1-3, 7; Zechariah 14:9, 16-17): Jehovah.
    - 9:6 (cf. Daniel 3:25; Hosea 11:1): The Son of God.
    - 24:23; 44:6: The Lord of Hosts.
    - 52:7: Thy God.
  o Jeremiah 23:6; 33:16: The Lord our Righteousness.
  o Daniel:
    - 7:13: The Ancient of Days.
    - 7:22-24: The Most High.
  o Micah 4:7 (cf. Zechariah 14:9): The Lord.

+ Those Describing Him as the "… Messiah to emphasize His humanity, and His right to rule over men because of His relation with them."[19]:
  o Daniel 7:13: The Son of Man.
  o Isaiah:
    - 11:1, 11: The rod of Jesse.
    - 42:1-6; 49:1-7; 53:11: The Servant.
    - 53:2; Ezekiel 17:22-24: The Tender Plant.

+ Those Describing Him "… in which His right to the throne and the royal powers associated with the throne are attributed to Him."[20]:
  o Isaiah 33:17, 22; 44:6; 2:2-4; 9:3-7; 11:1-10; 16:5; 24:21 – 26:15; 31;4 – 32:2; 42:1-6; 49:1-9; 51:4-5; 60:12 (cf. Daniel 2:44; 7:15-28; Obadiah 17-21; Micah 4:1-8; 5:2-5, 15; Zephaniah 3:9-10; 3:18-19 (cf. Zechariah 9:10-15; 14:16-17): The King.
  o Isaiah:
    - 11:3-4; 16:5; 33:22; 51:4-5; Ezekiel 34:17, 20; Joel 3:1-2; Micah 4:2-3: The Judge.
    - 33:22: The Lawgiver.
  o Daniel:
    - 9:25-26: Messiah the Prince.
    - 8:25: The Prince of Princes.
  o Revelation 21:3: He will be manifested as the Tabernacle of God with Men.

+ Those Describing Him as the "… Messiah, through His names, is presented as the Son of God and Son of man who redeems and reigns throughout the kingdom age."[21]:
  o Isaiah:
    - 28:16 (cf. Zechariah 3:9): The Stone.
    - 40:10-22 (cf. Jeremiah 23:1, 3; Ezekiel 34:11-31; 37:24; Micah 4:5; 7:14): The Shepherd.
    - 59:20: The Redeemer.

377

- 60:1-3: The Light.
  - ○ Jeremiah 23:6; 33:16: The Lord our Righteousness.
  - ○ Micah 2:13: The Wall Breaker.
  - ○ Malachi 4:2: The Sun of Righteousness.
- The Manifestations of Christ in the Millennium: "The prophetic Scriptures state a number of ministries and manifestations associated with the Messiah at His second advent."[22]
  - + Genesis 17:8 (cf. Matthew 1:1 and Galatians 3:16): He will be manifested as the Son of Abraham to possess the land and institute the kingdom.
  - + Isaiah:
    - ○ 9:6 (cf. Psalm 134:3 and Hebrews 1:8-10): He will be manifested as Son of God.
    - ○ 60:2; 61:2 (cf. Ezekiel 21:27; Daniel 7:22; Habakkuk 2:3; Haggai 2:7; Zechariah 2:8; and Malachi 3:1): His Second Advent is clearly established.
  - + Luke 1:32-33 (cf. Matthew 1:1 and Isaiah 9:7): He will be manifested as the Son of David as the rightful heir to the throne.
  - + Acts 1:11 (John 5:27): He will be manifested as the Son of Man and will execute judgment.
  - + Jesus Christ will be manifested as God's Theocratic King so that:
    - ○ Isaiah 32:1: He will be the King of Righteousness.
    - ○ Zechariah 14:9 (cf. Philippians 2:10): He will be the King over the Earth.
    - ○ John 12:13: He will be the King over Israel.
    - ○ Revelation 19:16: He will be the King of Kings.
  - + In all the manifestations listed above, Jesus Christ will be:
    - ○ Deuteronomy 18:15, 18: Prophet.
    - ○ Isaiah:
      - 2:3 (cf. Zechariah 8:22): Teacher.
      - 33:17-22; 40:9-11; 52:6 (cf. Daniel 2:45; 7:25-27; Micah 5:2-5; and Zephaniah 3:15): King.
      - 33:22 (cf. Genesis 49:10): Lawgiver.
      - 40:10-11 (cf. Jeremiah 23:1, 3 and Micah 4:5; 7:14): Shepherd.
      - 59:20-21; 62:11 (cf. Malachi 4:2): Redeemer.
      - 61:2; 62:11 (cf. Daniel 2:44-45; 7:9-10): Judge.
      - 62:12: Rewarder of the Saints.

49.7 THE RELATIONSHIP BETWEEN THE LIVING AND THE RESURRECTED

There will be many unique aspects of the Millennium, and one of the more interesting aspects will be that there will be normal human beings that will live alongside saints that have been resurrected from the various dispensations of the history of humankind. While at the first this may seem strange, keep in mind that for several weeks after Christ's own resurrection, He walked among and interacted with the Jews of Jerusalem without difficulty on either His part or the part of the human beings. This is significant in that it indicates that it is possible for the earthly human realm and the spiritual resurrected realm to coexist in the presence of each other.

While the Bible in not particularly clear about as many details as we would like, the sense is that there will be a variety of mortal and resurrected beings that will live together on the earth in the physical presence of Jesus Christ that will include the following groups:
- The resurrected and translated church age saints that accompany Jesus Christ at His Second Advent that will reign as the Bride of Christ,
- Those saints martyred during Daniel's 70th Week.
- Those Gentiles that live through Daniel's 70th Week and are judged to be sheep.
- Those Jews that live through Daniel's 70th Week and are judged to be righteous.
- The Old Testament saints that are resurrected after Christ's return and before the Millennium to inherit their reward of blessing.

"There has been no specific delineation as to the positions these various groups would occupy, their spheres of activity, their relation to the rule of the King, their relation to the earth, nor their relationship to each other."23

There are some, Pentecost[24] among them, who hold to the idea that the resurrected saints will not actually live on earth along with the living human beings, but instead will reside in the New Jerusalem of Revelation 21.

49.8   JERUSALEM IN THE MILLENNIUM

Since the city of Jerusalem is the place where God chose to focus the people He would call His own, it is not surprising that Jerusalem would then play crucially central role in the Millennium. Jerusalem is one of the oldest roles in human history and has had significant meaning to humankind as God's city for the duration of that history. Pentecost[25] provides a list of the millennial attributes that are described in the Bible concerning Jerusalem's place.
- Jerusalem Will Be the Center of the Millennial Earth: Because the Messiah will have His throne in the city, and the purpose of the thousand-year period is for the King to rule humankind, Jerusalem will be the figurative, if not literal, center of the world.
  + Isaiah 2:2-4: The *Lord's Temple will be established* and will be at the *top* of the highest *mountain* and *will be exalted. Many people will come and say, come, let us go up to the mountain of the Lord to the temple of the God of Jacob.*

+ Jeremiah 31:6: *Watchmen on the hills of Ephraim* will *cry out* for Israel to come *up to Zion to the Lord our God.*
+ Micah 4:1-2: Similar to Isaiah 2:2-4 above.
+ Zechariah 2:10-11: The Lord says He is coming to live among Zion who will be joined with many nations and will be His people.
- Jerusalem Will Be Center of Kingdom Rule: As the city was the government center of David's rule at the height of Israel's history, Jerusalem will again be the center of the kingdom rule for David's Greater Son.
  + Jeremiah:
    o 3:17: *Jerusalem* will be called *The Throne of the Lord,* and *all nations will gather in Jerusalem to honor the name of the Lord.*
    o 30:16-17: The Lord says that all of Israel's enemies will be devoured and *will go into exile,* those who plundered will themselves be plundered, those that made spoil of you will be despoiled themselves. The Lord says that He *will restore Israel to health and heal their wounds.*
    o 31:6: *There will be a day when watchmen will call out* to *go up to Zion, to the Lord our God.*
  + Ezekiel 43:5-6: *The Spirit* lifted Ezekiel *up and brought* him *into the inner court, and the glory of the Lord filled the temple.*
  + Joel 3:17: *Then you will know that I, the Lord your God, dwell in Zion, my holy hill. Jerusalem will be holy; never again will foreigners invade her.*
  + Micah 4:7: From *Mount Zion,* the Lord *will make the lame* His *remnant and those driven away a strong nation.*
  + Zechariah 8:2-3: *This is what the Lord Almighty says: I am very jealous for Zion, I am burning with jealousy for her. This is what the Lord says, I will return to Zion and dwell in Jerusalem. Then Jerusalem will be called the Faithful City, and the mountain of the Lord Almighty will be called the Holy Mountain.*
- The Lord Will Bring Glory to Jerusalem: Because the Lord will be present in the city, Jerusalem will participate in His glory, thus bringing honor to Him.
  + Isaiah:
    o 52:1-12: Jerusalem will awake from her exile and will never to be invaded again. The unrighteous will be gone, and the city will be rebuilt. There is to be no more mourning and the city will be freed because she will be redeemed. The Lord will return to Jerusalem, the city will be blessed, and the Messiah returns to rule.
    o 60:14-21: Even though Jerusalem had a hard time during the several dispersions, the Lord will once again make her an everlasting pride of the nation. The city will be blessed in many ways. The people will be righteous and will possess the land forever.
    o 61:3: The Lord will *bestow* a *crown of beauty* on those in *Zion who grieve, and a garment of praise. They will be called oaks*

of righteousness, a planting of the Lord for the display of his splendor.

- o 62:1-12: The nations will see the preparations for Jerusalem's restoration and the coming of the Lord. God announces that He will work to restore Jerusalem's righteousness, salvation, and glory. While it is not recorded, Jerusalem will be given a new name which suggests a new righteous character. Jerusalem will display the splendor of the Lord.
- o 66:10-14: Like a mother comforts her child, the Lord will comfort Jerusalem. Peace will come to her, and wealth will flow to her. The people will rejoice and prosper, and God will judge her enemies.
- + Jeremiah:
  - o 30:18: *This is what the Lord says: "I will restore the fortunes of Jacob's tents and have compassion on his dwellings; the city will be rebuilt on her ruins, and the palace will stand in its proper place.*
  - o 33:16: *In those days Judah will be saved and Jerusalem will live in safety.*
- + Joel 3:17: *Then you will know that I, the Lord your God, dwell in Zion, my holy hill. Jerusalem will be holy; never again will foreigners invade her.*
- + Zechariah 2:1-13: Zechariah sees a young man with a measuring line with the intent on measuring Jerusalem. An angel directs Zechariah to tell the young man that Jerusalem will be a great city without walls. The Lord says He will come to Jerusalem and live among the people.
- • The Lord Will Protect Jerusalem: Because of the presence of the Lord in the city, Jerusalem will be protected by His power and need never again fear for its safety.
  - + Isaiah:
    - o 14:32: *The Lord has established Zion, and in her his afflicted people will find refuge.*
    - o 25:4: The city of Jerusalem has *been a refuge for the poor, a refuge for the needy in their distress, a shelter from the storm and a shade from the heat. The breath of the ruthless is like a storm driving against a wall.*
    - o 26:1-4: Isaiah wrote a song picturing himself standing in the redeemed land in the Millennium that first emphasizes the reversal of fortunes, the humble will be exalted, and the oppressors vanquished. Jerusalem will be the strong city in which the redeemed will live.
    - o 33:20-24: Jerusalem will be peaceful.
- • Jerusalem Will Be Greatly Enlarged: In contrast to its size at any point in history, Jerusalem will be enlarged.
  - + Jeremiah 31:38-40: Jerusalem was destroyed by the Babylonians, but even before the destruction, God had promised to rebuild it. Four

locations are given that form the extent of the new city: *the Tower of Hananel*, at the northeast corner and *the Corner Gate*, probably at the northwest corner forming the northern boundary, and *the hill of Gareb* and *Goah*, locations of which are unknown, but probably forms the western boundary. The southern boundary is defined as the *whole valley where dead bodies and ashes are thrown*, the Hinnom Valley and the eastern boundary are *the terraces out to the Kidron Valley*. The southwest tip of the city, where the Kidron Valley and the Hinnom Valley unite is probably where this will extend. The city will be holy and set apart and the city will no longer *be uprooted or demolished*.

+ Ezekiel 48:30-35: This passage describes the gates of the new Jerusalem, refer to Section 53.5.

+ Zechariah 14:10: *The whole land, from Geba to Rimmon, south of Jerusalem, will become like the Aradah. But Jerusalem will be raised up high from the Benjamin Gate to the site of the First Gate, to the Corner Gate, and from the Tower of Hananel to the royal winepresses, and will remain secure.*

• Jerusalem Will Be Accessible: For all that seek an audience with the King, they will find an audience within Jerusalem.

+ Isaiah 35:8-9: A *highway, called the Way of Holiness*, will safely lead to God's city. *The unclean will not journey on it, but only the redeemed will walk there.*

• Jerusalem Will Be the Center of Worship: Because the Lord will have His throne in the Temple in the city, Jerusalem will be the center for the worship of Him.

+ Jeremiah:

  ○ 30:16-21: "Israel's condition appeared hopeless, but God promised to reverse her misfortunes. ... At the same time God promised to restore Israel to spiritual *health*. ... God's restoration will involve a physical rebuilding. ... God will increase Judah's numerically ... The *leader* of Israel will again *be one of their own* instead of some foreign despot ... Only at that future date when the city, its inhabitants, and their ruler have been restored to God will someone be able to declare that Israel is God's *people* and that He is her *God*."[26]

  ○ 31:6, 23: *There will be a day when watchmen cry out ... come, let us go up to Zion, to the Lord our God ... the Lord Almighty, the God of Israel, says: When I bring them back from captivity, the people in the land of Judah and in its towns will once again use these words: The Lord bless you, you prosperous city, you sacred mountain!*

+ Joel 3:17: *Then you will know that I, the Lord your God, dwell in Zion, my holy hill. Jerusalem will be holy; never again will foreigners invade her.*

- + Zechariah 8:8, 20-22: *I will bring them back to live in Jerusalem; they will be my people, and I will be faithful and righteous to them as their God ... And many peoples and powerful nations will come to Jerusalem to seek the Lord Almighty and to entreat him.*
- • Jerusalem Will Be Forever: For all that seek an audience with the King, they will find an audience within Jerusalem
  - + Isaiah:
    - ○ 9:7: *Of the greatness of his government and peace there will be no end. He will reign on David's throne and over his kingdom, establishing and upholding it with justice and righteousness from that time on and forever. The zeal of the Lord Almighty will accomplish this.*
    - ○ 33:20-21: *Jerusalem* will be *peaceful* and those that live there will not be displaced and no warship will attack them.
    - ○ 60:15: Even though Israel was once *forsaken* and hated, God *will make* them *the everlasting pride and the joy of all generations.*
  - + Joel 3:19-21: Because of *the violence done to Judah* and the shedding of *innocent blood, Egypt will be desolate* and *Edom a desert waste.* But the Lord says that *Judah will be inhabited forever* and *Jerusalem through all generations* because God will not let the *innocent blood* go unavenged. *The Lord dwells in Zion!*
  - + Zechariah 8:4: *This is what the Lord Almighty says: "Once again men and women of ripe old age will sit in the streets of Jerusalem, each of them with cane in hand because of their age. The city streets will be filled with boys and girls playing there."*

49.9 ISRAEL WILL BE THE CENTER OF GENTILE ATTENTION

Once Israel is restored nationally and regathered to live in the land provided by God, the eyes of the world will be upon the nation as can be seen from the following passages taken from Fruchtenbaum[27]:

- • Isaiah:
  - + 14:1-2: Gentiles will assist in the Jews returning to their land, they will join Israel to worship the Lord, and they will serve the restored nation.
  - + 49:22-23: As the Gentiles will be servants of Israel, Israel will no longer be ashamed of them,
  - + 60:1-3: Nations will come to Israel because the Shechinah Glory will once again abide over Israel.
  - + 61:4-9: The cities of Israel will be rebuilt, and the Jews will be ministers to the Gentiles.
- • Micah 7:14-17: When the Gentiles see how Israel is supernaturally restored, they will no longer reject the Jews, but instead will fear them reverentially.
- • Zephaniah 3:20: When Israel is restored they will become a name for God before the peoples of the earth.

- Zechariah 8:23: Gentiles will respect the Jews because of their relationship with God.

49.10 THE GENTILES IN THE MILLENNIUM

Even though much of what the Bible says about the Millennium concerns the restoration of Israel in a long-awaited kingdom, there is also a considerable amount of information of those that go into the thousand-year period as living Gentile human beings. Consider the following observations made by Fruchtenbaum[28] regarding those that survive the Judgment of the Sheep who were pro-Semitic and will be the ones that repopulate the world.

GENERAL CHARACTERISTICS
- Isaiah:
  + 11:10: The Gentile nations of the Millennium will be attracted to the majesty of the Messiah and will look to Him for guidance.
  + 14:1-2: The Gentile nations will serve the restored nation of Israel.
  + 42:1: The Gentile nations will be in subjection to the One chosen by God for justice.
  + 49:5-7: "… Messiah will be manifested in the most complete sense as the light to the Gentiles, and all the kings of the Gentiles will worship Him …"[29]
  + 56:1-8: All foreigners (Gentiles) of the nations will worship the Messiah alongside the Jews in the Temple.
  + 66:28-24: The Lord will gather all the Gentiles, nations and ethnic groups, to witness His splendor (the Shechinah Glory) and will then send them out into the nations to tell others of God's splendor. From the Gentiles, God will choose some to serve as priests in the Temple.

THE OBLIGATION TO OBSERVE
THE FEAST OF TABENACLES

According to Zechariah 14:16-19, all of the Gentile nations will be obligated to send a delegation to Jerusalem to worship the King at the Feast of Tabernacles (the memorial festival commemorating Israel's deliverance from bondage in Egypt). While it will be mandatory to send a delegation, apparently some nations will not do so with the result being the Lord withholding the rains.

THE RELATIONSHIP WITH THE ARAB STATES

Historic and Universal Hatred for Israel
The Bible confirms a continual hatred that the Arab nations, as descendants of Ishmael and Esau, have has for the sons of Isaac and Jacob that has perpetuated for many centuries and is very evident even today. The Arab nations have stood in opposition to Israel since the days of Isaac and Ishmael played together as the children of Abraham and Sarah. Consider the following passages that describe this animosity:

- Numbers 20:14-21: When Israel was in the exodus out of Egypt in search of the land promised to them by God and they needed to pass through the land of their kindred, the Edomites, the Edomites refused to allow them to do so and in fact turned out a substantial military force to oppose the crossing.
- Psalm 83:1-8: The psalmist describes the conspiratorial goal of unifying the Arab nations surrounding Israel as being the annihilation of the people that follow God to the extent that even the name of Israel is no longer known in the land. The modern-day nations of the nations listed in the passages are as follows:
  + Edom is Southern Jordan.
  + Ishmaelites are those that are descendants of Abraham's son Ishmael.
  + Moab is Central Jordan.
  + Hagarites is Egypt.
  + Gebal is Lebanon.
  + Ammon is Northern Jordan.
  + Amalek is the Sinai Peninsula.
  + Philistia is the Gaza Strip.
  + Tyre is Lebanon.
  + Assyria is Syria and Iraq.
  + Consider just how applicable Psalm 83:1-8 is today. The Arab nations, who are hostile to God, still conspire and plot against Israel, and they are united in the simple goal of annihilating a nation that is many times smaller than their combined area and numbers.
- Ezekiel 35:1-5: The prophet Ezekiel predicts that God will obliterate Mount Seir, the mountain range to the southeast of Israel where Edom is located that is populated by the descendants of Esau. He will be against them, will lay waste to their cities and will make the land desolate. He will do this because of their everlasting enmity and oppression of Israel.
- Obadiah 10-14: God will shame and destroy forever the land of Edom because of their treachery against their brother Israel. God will repay Edom everything that was done to Israel.

The Future of the Arab States
"Ultimately, peace will come between Israel and the various Arab states, but it will come in one of three forms: *First*, by means of occupation; *second*, by means of destruction; or *third*, by means of conversion."[30] It seems logical that

the things that will happen to the Arab states will occur in the days leading up to Christ's Second Advent so that the final disposition of the states is in place at the start of the Millennium.

- Lebanon: Peace will come because the area of Lebanon is included within the land promised by God to Israel and will be settled by some of the northern Jewish tribes.
- Jordan: Modern Jordan comprises the ancient countries of Moab, Ammon, and Edom.
  + Northern Portion: The ancient land of Moab, descended from Abraham's nephew Lot, will be destroyed, but not totally. "For a long season Moab had been permitted to go unpunished. The result was a settling down in haughty carelessness, with utter indifference to the abominations everywhere practiced."[31]
    o Jeremiah 48:1-46: Moab will be destroyed and people will run for their lives and go into exile.
    o Jeremiah 48:47: God will restore Moab in the future.
  + Central Portion: As with Moab, the ancient land of Ammon, also descended from Lot, will be partially destroyed, but a remnant will return also.
    o Jeremiah 49:1-2: Ammon will become a mound of ruins and surrounding villages will be set on fire.
    o Jeremiah 49:6: God will restore the fortunes of the Ammonites.
  + Southern Portion: As indicated above, Edom is much different than Moab and Ammon, it will be completely destroyed as indicated in the following passages:
    o Jeremiah:
      - 49:7-13: The descendants of Esau will not be able to hide from God who will find them and destroy everyone and everything – nothing will remain of the seed of Esau. Edom had been given a chance to trust the Lord, but they refused so now they will have a drink of the cup of God's wrath resulting in the land becoming a waste.
      - 49:19-20: The destruction of Edom will come about by war and military conflict.
    o Ezekiel:
      - 25:12-14: By military conflict will Israel completely destroy Edom because of the sin of vengeance against Israel.
      - 35:6-9: Because Edom has been blood-thirsty during its existence; God will pursue their destruction to the point where dead bodies will fill the mountains, hills, and valleys.
    o Obadiah:
      - 5-9: Edom's total destruction will be influenced by the lack of aid from friends and their own wisdom and military may be of no substantial benefit.

- 17-21: Edom's destroyer will be the very brother that Edom had previously oppressed, Israel, who will sweep through the land as fire does through stubble. Israel will ultimately possess the mountain of Edom.

"So Edom, or present-day southern Jordan, is to suffer desolation, and the destruction of all descendants of Esau will come by means of the people of Israel."[32]

- Egypt: "Peace will come between Israel and Egypt initially by means of destruction and later by means of conversion."[33] and "... will take their place in the ranks of the sheep Gentiles."[34]
  + Isaiah 19:1-22: A description of the punishment that will come over Egypt is provided in this passage that details famine, civil war, and desolation.
    o Leaders will lead the nation to destruction (19:11-15) causing a sense of fear and dread of Israel to develop within the nation (19:16-17). Fruchtenbaum makes the observation that in the second half of the twentieth century the leaders of the nation have brought much destruction and introspective fearfulness to the nation in a manner unlike any other time in history.[35]
    o Eventually as peace prevails, five cities in Egypt will speak the language of the Canaan, or the Hebrew language (19:18), and an altar will be built in the midst of the nation (19:19-20b), which will lead to national conversion (19:19-22).
    o While Egypt will be persecuted by the Antichrist (Daniel 11:42-43), God will prevent the Antichrist from success (19:20b).
    o Egypt will eventually acknowledge the authority of the Lord of Israel and will worship Him with sacrifices, offerings, and vows.
  + Ezekiel 29:1-16: As the Prophet Ezekiel details what the Lord will do to Egypt as punishment for their discretions against Israel, he adds another detail not found in the other passages: Egypt will be desolate for only forty years (apparently the first forty years of the Millennium), then the Lord will graciously regather Egypt's people form the diaspora that He has caused and restore them to their land and fortunes. While Egypt had been a strong and destroying nation at times during Israel's presence in their land, the restored nation will not be powerful again.
  + Joel 3:19: Recalling the fact that those that curse the Hebrews will themselves be cursed, this passage indicates that Egypt and Edom will be punished for their respective mistreatments of Israel. There is a distinction made between the final dispositions of Egypt and Edom in this passage – *Egypt will be a desolate and Edom a desolate wilderness.* Fruchtenbaum[36] suggests that while Edom's final disposition will be a permanent condition, Egypt's will be a temporary condition as will be seen in the following passage.
- Assyria: Peace will come to the modern-day states of Iraq and Syria, as indicated in Isaiah 19:23-25. With Assyria to the immediate north of

Israel and Egypt to the immediate south, the three nations will be joined physically and certainly politically and economically, by a highway that will facilitate movement freely between the three nations, and, they will join together in the worship of the Lord Jesus Christ. Thus Israel will be a blessing to those two nations of the new world. The passage describes their unity as being spiritual:

+ Egypt: A blessed people.
+ Assyria: A work of God's hands.
+ Israel: God's special possession.

- Kedar and Hazor: Peace will come to this area in modern-day Saudi Arabia by means of national destruction. Jeremiah 49:28-33 teaches that Saudi Arabia will be destroyed by war, its people scattered across the earth, never to be restored and the land will remain a permanent desolation.

- Elam (Persia and Iran): While Iran is not technically an Arab state, it is included here for two reasons: it is included in the Bible as a land and people God will judge, and, the people are of the same religion as the Arab States – Islamic. As what befalls Egypt, Iran will be destroyed and its people dispersed as Jeremiah 49:34-39 records, but the Lord will restore a remnant at some undisclosed time in the Millennium.

Two Desolate Spots in the Kingdom

In addition to what the Old Testament has to say about the future conditions of the historical and current Arab States, it also records a special condition that will come over two lands that is not indicated for the others – complete and permanent destruction and desolation to the point the land in not habitable that stands in stark contrast to the fruitful and plentiful conditions that will prevail across the remainder of the earth. Because of centuries of terrorizing the Hebrews, God will judge two peoples and their lands into non-existence. Continual sinfulness against God results in His withdrawal of grace.

- Babylon: The first of the two nations that has historically challenged and oppressed Israel will be completely destroyed to the same extent as the Bible indicated happened to Sodom and Gomorrah – it will be made uninhabitable ruin. During the Millennium, the land of Babylon will be a place of continual burning and smoke and will be the place of residence confinement for demons. There are many passages in the Bible that presents the facts of Babylon's destruction:

  + Isaiah 13:20-22: In a prophecy about Babylon, Isaiah writes, *She will never be inhabited or lived in through all generations, there no nomads will pitch their tents, no shepherds will rest their flocks*. But, *jackals, owls, wild goats*, and *hyenas* will live there. Babylon's *time is at hand*.
  + Jeremiah:
    - 50:39-40: In a passage similar to Isaiah 13:20-22, Jeremiah wrote that no one will live in Babylon after its destruction just like no one lived in *Sodom and Gomorrah* after God destroyed them *along with the neighboring towns*.

- 51:41-43: *How desolate Babylon will be among the nations! The sea will rise over Babylon; its roaring waves will cover her. Her towns will be desolate, a dry and desert land, a land where no one lives, through which no one travels.*
  + Revelation:
    - 18:1-2: John saw an *angel coming down heaven,* who *had great authority* and *the earth was illuminated by his splendor.* The angel *shouted with a mighty voice* and said that *Babylon* had *fallen,* and the only things that will live there will be *demons, every impure spirit, every unclean bird and detestable animal.*
    - 19:3: *The smoke from* fallen Babylon *goes up for ever and ever.*
- Edom: The second of the two nations will also be utterly desolated. Edom will also become an uninhabitable place of burning and smoke and the residence of demons as recorded in the following passages; also notice that the final punishment is for the glee shown by Edom at Israel's times of destruction:
  + Isaiah 34:8-15: As Babylon, Edom will also be desolate and an extensive number of things in this passage describe her state at that time.
  + Jeremiah 49:17-18: The Lord says, "*Edom will become an object of horror … as Sodom and Gomorrah were.*
  + Ezekiel 35:10-15: The Lord said that because Edom says that the land of Israel will be theirs, He will treat Edom *in accordance with the anger and jealousy you* [Edom] *showed in your hatred of them* [Israel]. The Lord further said, *Because you rejoiced when the inheritance of Israel became desolate, that is how I will treat you. You will be desolate …*
  + Joel 3:19: *But Egypt will be desolate, Edom a desert waste, because of violence done to the people of Judah, in whose land they shed innocent blood.*

Thus we find that the Bible indicates there will be two places of continual burning during the Millennium, and the resulting smoke will be visible for the duration. Also, it seems that while Satan is confined to the Abyss, the lands of Babylon and Edom could very well be the place of confinement for the multitude of demons that will be constrained during the one-thousand-year Messianic Age.

49.11 THE STATE OF BEINGS AT THE END OF THE MILLENNIUM

THE RESURRECTED OLD TESTAMENT, CHURCH AND TRIBULATION SAINTS

All the righteous saints that died prior to the beginning of the Millennium, including those that were living at the time of the Rapture and were translated, will still be in their final resurrected form and have been living in their heavenly reward for one thousand years.

MORTAL HUMAN BEINGS

If the Messianic Millennium, which will actually be the third time that God will have given humankind an opportunity to develop a new human civilization, is anything like the first two civilization starts, then at the end there will be millions, if not billions, of mortal human beings living on the earth. There will be Jewish and Gentile human beings that were originally judged by Jesus at the beginning of the Millennium to be His followers and thus eligible to inhabit the earth during the Millennium as well as their natural born descendants. It would not be surprising if those born during the Millennium vastly outnumber the original believers that started the time.

At the end of the one-thousand-year rule by Christ, the Bible paints the picture that there will be two extremes of life on earth:

- The Righteous: There will be many mortal human beings that will remain righteous throughout the Millennium. The Bible does not say anything about what will happen to these at the end, therefore, it is plausible that they will be translated in the same, or similar, manner as those living at the time of the Rapture.
- The Unrighteous: There will also be many mortal human beings that will have given in to the call of their own depravity and will oppose God. In spite of the absence of satanic influence, mortal human beings will still not be capable of managing and controlling their own humanness without the presence of God in their lives. One of the conditions of the Millennium is that Jesus will rule with a rod of iron and will judge iniquity immediately, thus suggesting that many of the wicked will be put to death immediately for their transgressions.

Will Mortals Die During the Millennium?

The Bible does not provide any details or specifics as to if those that enter the Millennium as mortal human beings will live to the end of the one thousand years, or, if they will die at some point during the time. The Bible also does not say if those that are born during the time will live for the remainder of the Millennium. It should be kept in mind that since Death and Hades are not thrown into the lake of fire until the time of the Great White Throne Judgment, it is very possible that they are still operative during the Millennium, and what death there is will be the same as, or similar to, death that happened during the time prior to the Millennium.

The one thing we do know is that mortals will live much longer than they did prior to the Millennium, and in fact, Isaiah 65:20 indicates that a person who dies before the age of one hundred will be considered cursed. It is not clear if people will die of old-age, accidents, or even of illness, notwithstanding all that is said about the almost perfect conditions that will exist during the Millennium. In the absence of Scriptural information, it seems plausible that should there be death during the Millennium the same immediate conditions that exist today might exist at that time, that is, the resurrection of the physical body from the grave that will rejoin the soul at the end of the Millennium.

THE UNRIGHTEOUS DEAD

The bodies of the wicked and unrighteous human beings that died prior to the beginning of the Millennium are still in the grave and their souls are still in Hades. While the Bible does not address the disposition of the unrighteous that die during the Millennium, the most plausible explanation is that their bodies go into the grave and their souls go into Hades along with all the other wicked.

50

LIFE IN THE MILLENNIUM

The Bible has much to say about the human condition that will exist on earth during the Millennium. As will be seen, because the Millennium will be the earthly manifestation of God's intentions for a theocratic kingdom, the human condition for the most part will be one that reflects the worthiness and dignity that is bestowed by God on His created beings, and demonstrates the glory and greatness of His kingdom. Pentecost[1] organized the multitude of passages found in the Bible into a list of attributes that paints a portrait of what life will be like in the Millennium.

50.1   PEACE

There will be no wars so there will be national and individual peace; the kingdoms of the world will be under the rulership of Jesus Christ; since wealth will not be directed to military offensive and defensive capability, then it can be devoted to other peaceful, non-military needs.

- Isaiah:
  + 2:4: *They will beat their swords into plowshares and their spears into pruning hooks. Nation will not take up sword against nation, nor will they train for war anymore.*
  + 9:4-7: Warriors will burn the garments worn in war. A child will be born that will be Jesus. The passage then describes many of the things Jesus will be and will do.
  + 11:6-9: A passage that describes that the animal world will be safe, calm, and non-violent.
  + 32:17-18: *The fruit of that righteousness will be peace; its effect will be quietness and confidence forever. My people will live in peaceful dwelling places, in secure homes, in undisturbed places of rest.*
  + 33:5-6: The Lord ... *will fill Zion with his justice and righteousness.* The Lord *will be the sure foundation* and *a rich store of salvation and wisdom and knowledge. ... the fear of the Lord is the key to this treasure.*
  + 55:12: *You will go out in joy and be led forth in peace.*
  + 60:18: *but you will call your walls Salvation and your gates Praise.*
  + 65:25: *The wolf and the lamb will feed together, and the lion will eat straw like the ox, and dust will be the serpent's food. They will neither harm nor destroy on all my holy mountain." says the Lord.*
  + 66:12: *For this is what the Lord says: "I will extend peace to her like a river and the wealth of nations like a flooding stream.*
- Ezekiel:

+ 28:26: *They will live there in safety and will build houses and plant vineyards; they will live in safety when I inflict punishment on all their neighbors who maligned them. Then they will know that I am the Lord their God.*
+ 34:25, 28: *I will make a covenant of peace with them and rid the land of savage beasts so that they may live in the wilderness and sleep in the forests in safety. ... They will no longer be plundered by the nations, nor will wild animals devour them. They will live in safety and no one will make them afraid.*
- Hosea 2:18: *In that day I will make a covenant for them with the beasts of the field, the birds in the sky and the creatures that move along the ground. Bow and sword and battle I will abolish from the land so that all may lie down in safety.*
- Micah 4:3: *He will judge between many peoples and will settle disputes for strong nations far and wide. They will beat their swords into plowshares and their spears into pruning hooks. Nation will not take up sword against nation, nor will they train for war anymore.*
- Zechariah 9:10: God will take away implements of war and *proclaim peace to the nations. His rule will extend to the ends of the earth.*

50.2 JOY

The fullness of joy marks the time.
- Isaiah:
+ 9:3: God has *enlarged the nation and increased their joy*, and the people rejoice before God, *at the harvest*, and *when dividing the plunder.*
+ 12:3-6: *With joy you will draw water from the wells of salvation. In that day you will say: "Give praise to the Lord, proclaim his name; make known among the nations what he has done, and proclaim that his name is exalted. Sing to the Lord, for he has done glorious things; let this be known to all the world. Shout aloud and sing for joy, people of Zion, for great is the Holy One of Israel among you.'*
+ 14:7-8: The people *break into singing* because *the lands are at rest and at peace.*
+ 25:8-9: The Lord *will swallow up death forever. The Sovereign Lord will wipe away the tears from all faces; he will remove his people's disgrace from all the earth. The Lord has spoken. In that day they will say, Surely this is our God; we trusted in him, and he saved us. This is the Lord, we trusted in him; let us rejoice and be glad in his salvation.*
+ 30:29: *And you will sing ... your hearts will rejoice*
+ 42:1, 10-12: Because His chosen servant *will bring justice to the nations*, the people are encouraged to *sing a new song to the Lord of his praise from the ends of the earth. Let the wilderness and its towns, the settlements where Kedar lives, the people of Sela*, sing and *shout*

from the mountaintops in joy and rejoicing. *Let them give glory to the Lord and proclaim his praise in the islands.*

+ 52:9: *Burst into songs of joy together, you ruins of Jerusalem, for the Lord has comforted his people, he has redeemed Jerusalem.*

+ 60:15: This passage is discussed in more detail above.

+ 61:7, 10: *Instead* of *shame* and *disgrace*, Israel will *inherit a double portion in your land, and everlasting joy will be* theirs. *I delight greatly in the Lord; my soul rejoices in my God.*

+ 65:18-19: *But be glad and rejoice forever in what I will create, for I will create Jerusalem to be a delight and its people a joy. I will rejoice over Jerusalem and take delight in my people; the sound of weeping and of crying will be heard in it no more.*

+ 66:10-14: "Those who love Jerusalem, but who have had reason to mourn her condition, now have reason for great joy. ... Zion's abundance will be a source of strength and courage, a cause for deep contentment and fulfillment. ... It is God who extends these blessings in all times. So he promises to extend *peace like a river*. ... the glory of the nations, which is customarily translated "the wealth of nations."... When he gives them courage, strength, hope, and will (comfort them), these are not merely arm's-length transactions. They are an expression of the intimate, personal involvement of a loving, personal God with his people.[2]

• Jeremiah:
  + 30:18-19: The Lord will have *compassion* on *Jacob's tents* and rebuild them. *From this will come songs of thanksgiving and the sound of rejoicing.*
  + 31: 13-14: *Young women will dance and be glad*, the Lord will *turn their mourning into gladness*, and He will *give them comfort and joy instead of sorrow*. He *will satisfy the priests with abundance.*

• Zephaniah 3:14-17: Israel *should shout aloud* and *be glad and rejoice with all* their *heart. The Lord has taken away your punishment, he has turned back your enemy. The Lord* will be with Israel and they will never again *fear harm. The Lord your God is with you, the Mighty Warrior who saves, He will take great delight in you; in his love he will no longer rebuke you, but will rejoice over you with singing.*

• Zechariah:
  + 8:18-19: *The word of the Lord Almighty came to me. This is what the Lord Almighty says: "The fasts of the fourth, fifth, seventh and tenth months will become joyful and glad occasions and happy festivals for Judah. Therefore love truth and peace."*
  + 10:6-7: *I will strengthen Judah and save the tribes of Joseph. I will restore them because I have compassion on them. They will be as though I had not rejected them, for I am the Lord their God and I will answer them. The Ephraimites will become like warriors, and their*

hearts will be glad as with wine. Their children will see it and be joyful; their hearts will rejoice in the Lord.

50.3	**HOLINESS**

The King and the King's subjects manifest holiness in the form of a theocratic kingdom that includes a land that includes a land that is holy, a city that is holy, and a temple that is holy.

- Isaiah:
  + 1:26-27: The Lord will restore Jerusalem to *the City of Righteousness, the Faithful City. Zion will be delivered with justice, her penitent ones with righteousness.*
  + 4:3-4: *Those who live in Zion, who remains in Jerusalem, will be called holy, all who are recorded among the living in Jerusalem. The Lord will wash away the filth of the women of Zion; he will cleanse the bloodstone from Jerusalem by a spirit of judgment and a spirit of fire.*
  + 35:8-9: "Righteous pilgrims will once again travel to Jerusalem. They will go on *a highway* known as the *Way of holiness*, for it will lead to God's city where His ways will be followed. It will not be traveled by *the unclean* or *wicked fools*. No *ferocious* animal will hinder the travel of *the redeemed* on that highway."[3]
  + 60:21: *Then all your people will be righteous and they will possess the land forever. They are the shoot I have planted, the work of my hand, for the display of my splendor.*
  + 61:10: *I delight greatly in the Lord; my soul rejoices in my God. For he has clothed me with garments of salvation and arrayed me in a role of his righteousness, as a bridegroom adorns his head like a priest, and as a bride adorns herself with her jewels.*
- Jeremiah 31:23: The God of Israel says, He *will restore the nation of Israel from captivity, the people in the land of Judah and in its towns will once again use these words: "'The Lord bless you, you prosperous city, you sacred mountain.*
- Ezekiel:
  + 36:24-31: God will take Israel *out of the nations and bring* her *back to* her *land* and *cleanse* them. He will give them *a new heart and put a new spirit* in them. He will make food *plentiful and will not bring famine upon them* so that they will not *suffer disgrace* before the nations.
  + 37:23-24: *They will no longer defile themselves with their idols and vile images or with any of their offenses, for I will save them from all their sinful backsliding, and I will cleanse them. They will be my people, and I will be their God. " 'My servant David will be king over them, and they will all have one shepherd. They will follow my laws and be careful to keep my decrees.*
  + 43:7-12: God told Ezekiel that the *temple* was *the place of* His *throne* and *for the soles of* His *feet*, and where He *will live among the Israelites*

forever. The people of Israel will never again defile His *holy name by their prostitution and the funeral offerings for their kings at their death.* When Israel *defiled* His *holy name by their prostitution and funeral offerings,* He *destroyed them.* If they obeyed, He would *live among them forever.* So that they would be *ashamed of their sins,* God tells Ezekiel to *describe the temple to the people, its perfection,* its *design, its arrangements, its exits and entrances,* and *all its regulations and laws.*

+ 45:1: " *'When you allot the land as an inheritance, you are to present to the Lord a portion of the land as sacred district, 25,000 cubits long and 20,000 cubits wide; the entire area will be holy.*

- Zephaniah 3:11, 13: God says that *Jerusalem will not be put to shame for all the wrongs* she has done to God but instead she will be restored and she *will do no wrongs, will tell no lies,* and a *deceitful tongue will not be found.* Jerusalem *will eat,* lay down, *and no one will make them afraid.*
- Zechariah:
  + 8:3: *This is what the Lord says: "I will return to Zion and dwell in Jerusalem. Then Jerusalem will be called the Faithful City, and the mountain of the Lord Almighty will be called the Holy Mountains"*
  + 13:1-2: At the Second Advent of Christ *a fountain will be opened* and Israel and Jerusalem will be given the opportunity to spiritually *cleanse* themselves of their *sin and impurity* (idolatry). The Lord *will banish the names of the idols from the land,* apostasy will become extinct, and the idols *will be remembered no more.* He will remove false *prophets and the spirit of impurity from the land.*
  + 14:20-21: "The messianic kingdom will not be like the world is today, with its division between sacred and secular. Everything will be *sacred.* Before Israel conquered the Promised Land, it was inhabited by the vile Canaanites. The promise that *there will no longer be a Canaanite in the house of the Lord* is a euphemistic way of saying that the morally degenerate person will be excluded from entering the millennial temple (Ezek. 44:9)."[4]

50.4 GLORY

God will be glorified in the manifestation of the glorious kingdom.
- Isaiah:
  + 4:2: *In that day the Branch of the Lord will be beautiful and glorious, and the fruit of the land will be the pride and glory of the survivors of Israel.*
  + 24:23: *The moons will be dismayed, the sun ashamed; for the Lord Almighty will reign on Mount Zion and in Jerusalem and before its elder – with great glory.*
  + 35:2: *It will burst into bloom; it will rejoice greatly and shout for joy. The glory of Lebanon will be given to it, the splendor of Carmel and Sharon; they will see the glory of the Lord, the splendor of our God.*

+ 40:5: *And the glory of the Lord will be revealed, and all people will see it together. For the mouth of the Lord has spoken.*
+ 60:1-9: The glory of the Lord rises over Jerusalem.

50.5   COMFORT

The King will minister to the need for the fullness of comfort.
- Isaiah:
    + 12:1: *In that day you will say: "I will praise you, Lord. Although you were angry with me, your anger has turned away and you have comforted me.*
    + 29:22-23: *Therefore this is what the Lord, who redeemed Abraham, says to the descendants of Jacob: "No longer will Jacob be ashamed; no longer will their faces go pale. When they see among them their children, the work of my hands, they will keep my name holy; they will acknowledge the holiness of the Holy One of Jacob and will stand in awe of the God of Israel.*
    + 30:26: *The moon will shine like the sun, and the sunlight will be seven times brighter, like the light of seven full days, when the Lord binds up the bruises of his people and heals the wounds he inflicted.*
    + 40:1-2: *Comfort, comfort my people, says your God. Speak tenderly to Jerusalem, and proclaim to her that her hard service has been completed, that her sin has been paid for, that he has received from the Lord's hand double for all her sins.*
    + 49:13: *Shout for joy, you heavens; rejoice, you earth; burst into song, you mountains! For the Lord comforts his people and will have compassion on his afflicted ones.*
    + 51:3: *The Lord will surely comfort Zion and will look with compassion on all her ruins; he will make her deserts like Eden, her wastelands like the gardens of the Lord. Joy and gladness will be found in her, thanksgiving and the sound of singing.*
    + 61:1-7: All three persons of the Holy Trinity are mentioned in verse 1: *the Spirit, the Sovereign Lord*, and *me*, or the Messiah. Verse 1-2a is about Jesus' First Advent and verse 2b-3 is about His Second Advent and that when He returns He will bring judgment on unbelievers and will comfort Israel. He will then restore Israel in many ways: the people will be uplifted, the city will be rebuilt, they will become wealthy, and *everlasting joy* will be theirs.
    + 66:13: *As a mother comforts her child, so will I comfort you; and you will be comforted over Jerusalem.*
- Jeremiah 31:23-25: *The Lord Almighty, the God of Israel*, will bring Israel *back from captivity* and will bless them. He *will refresh the weary and satisfy the faint.*
- Zephaniah 3:18-20: "*I will remove from you all who mourn over the loss of your appointed festivals, which is a burden and reproach for you. At that*

time I will deal with all who oppressed you, I will rescue the lame; I will gather the exiles, I will give them praise and honor in every land where they have suffered shame. At that time I will gather you; at that time I will bring you home. I will give you honor and praise among all the peoples of the earth when I restore your fortunes before your very eyes," says the Lord.
- Zechariah 9:11-12: This passage is discussed in more detail below.
- Revelation 21:4: '*He will wipe every tear from their eyes. There will be no more death' or mourning or crying or pain, for the old order of things has passed away.*

50.6   JUSTICE

The King will administer perfect justice to and for every individual.
- Isaiah:
    + 9:7: *Of the greatness of his government and peace there will be no end. He will reign on David's throne and over his kingdom, establishing and upholding it with justice and righteousness from that time on and forever. The zeal of the Lord Almighty will accomplish this.*
    + 11:5: The Messiah will judge and *righteousness will be his belt and faithfulness the sash around his waist.*
    + 32:16: *The Lord's justice will dwell in the desert, his righteousness live in the fertile field.*
    + 42:1-4: The Messiah is the *chosen one in whom* God *delights* and *will put* His *Spirit on him and he will bring justice to the nations.* The Messiah will be gentle in His judgments; He will not even break a weak, useless reed. The Messiah *in faithfulness he will bring forth justice* and He will not *be discouraged* until He has established *justice on earth. In his teaching the islands will put their hope.* The islands are people in remote locations.
    + 65:21-23: "In these verses the Lord described the millennial kingdom, which is seemingly identified here with the eternal state (*new heavens and a new earth*). In Revelation, however, the new heavens and new earth (Rev. 21:1) *follow* the Millennium (Rev. 20:4). Most likely Isaiah did not distinguish between these two aspects of God's rule; he saw them together as one."[5] Israel will live in their land in houses and plant vineyards in the millennium and the new earth. They will not be conquered again nor *will not labor in vain, nor will they bear children doomed to misfortune.*
- Jeremiah:
    o 23:5: *"The days are coming," declares the Lord, "when I will raise up for David a righteous branch ...*
    o 31:23: *This is what the Lord Almighty, the God of Israel, says: "When I bring them back from captivity, the people in the land of Judah and in its towns will once again use these words: 'The Lord bless you, you prosperous city, you sacred mountain.'*

50.7 | FULL KNOWLEDGE

Every individual will have full knowledge of the Lord and His ministry through the teaching of the Holy Spirit.
- Isaiah:
  + 11:1-2, 9: *A shoot will come up from the stump of Jesse; from his roots a Branch will bear fruit. The Spirit of the Lord will rest on him – the Spirit of wisdom and of understanding, the Spirit of counsel and of might, the Spirit of the knowledge and fear of the Lord ... They will neither harm nor destroy on all my holy mountain, for the earth will be filled with the knowledge of the Lord as the waters cover the sea.*
  + 54:13: *All your children will be taught by the Lord, and great will be their peace.* Israelites considered the education of their children to be especially important and they wanted them to be true to the Lord.

50.8 | INSTRUCTION

The full knowledge of the Lord will come about through instruction by the King.
- Isaiah:
  + 2:2-3: In the millennium, the Lord's temple will be located on a very high mountain in Israel, and many will go up to be instructed by the Lord.
  + 25:9: When Israel is delivered, she will express her trust in the Lord, and they will *rejoice and be glad in his salvation.*
  + 29:24: *Those who are wayward in spirit will gain understanding; those who complain will accept instruction.*
  + 49:10: *He who has compassion on them will guide them ...*
- Jeremiah:
  + 3:14-15: *"Return, faithless people,"* declares the Lord, *"for I am your husband. I will choose you – one from a town and two from a clan – and bring you to Zion. Then I will give you shepherds after my own heart, who will lead you with knowledge and understanding.*
  + 23:1-4: "Jeremiah summarized the unrighteous kings as being like *shepherds* who were *destroying and scattering* God's *sheep*. The *shepherds* deserved *punishment* because of *the evil* they had *done* (cf. Ezek.34:1-10). But if God removed them, whom would He appoint to regather His sheep? Jeremiah gave a twofold answer. First, God Himself would *gather the remnant* of the people who were dispersed and would *bring them back*. He would assume responsibility for Israel's regathering (cf. Jer. 31:10; Micah 2:12; 5:4; 7:14). Second, God would raise up new *shepherds over them who* would *tend* and care for the people the way God intended."[6]
- Micah 4:2: Similar to Isaiah 2:2-3.

| 50.9 | **REMOVAL OF THE CURSE** |

The curse placed on the earth in Genesis 3:17-19 will be removed and the plant world will become abundant and the animal world will lose its ferocity.

- Isaiah:
    + 11:6-9: This frequently quoted passage speaks to the tranquility that will exist in the millennium because the curse will be lifted and wild as well as tamed animals will live in harmony. *The wolf will live with the lamb, the leopard will lie down with the goat, the calf and the lion and the yearling together; and a little child will lead them. The cow will feed with the bear, their young will lie down together, and the lion will eat straw like the ox. The infant will play near the cobra's den, and the young child will put its hand into the viper's nest. They will neither harm nor destroy on all my holy mountain, for the earth will be filled with the knowledge of the Lord as the waters cover the sea.*
    + 35:9: In the passage about the Way of Holiness highway to the City of Jerusalem we find: *No lion will be there, nor any ravenous beast; they will not be found there. But only the redeemed will walk there ...*
    + 65:25: *The wolf and the lamb will feed together, and the lion will eat straw like the ox, and dust will be the serpent's food. They will neither harm nor destroy on all my holy mountain," says the Lord.* Ferocity will not be found among the wild animals and there will be safety and harmony under God's watchfulness.

| 50.10 | **SICKNESS REMOVED** |

The King will minister as a healer and illness and even death, except as punishment for sinfulness, will be removed.

- Isaiah 33:24: *No one living in Zion will say, "I am ill"*
- Jeremiah 30:17: *I will restore you to health and heal your wounds, declares the Lord*
- Ezekiel 34:16: *I will search for the lost and bring back the strays. I will bind up the injured and strengthen the weak, but the sleek and the strong I will destroy. I will shepherd the flock with justice.*

| 50.11 | **HEALING OF THE DEFORMED** |

The King will heal physical deformities at the beginning.

- Isaiah:
    + 29:18-19: *In that day the deaf will hear the words of the scroll, and out of gloom and darkness the eyes of the blind will see. Once more the humble will rejoice in the Lord; the needy will rejoice in the Holy One of Israel.*
    + 35:3-6: *Strengthen the feeble hands, steady the knees that give way; say to those with fearful hearts, Be strong, do not fear; your God will*

> *come, he will come with vengeance; with divine retribution he will come to save you. Then will the eyes of the blind be opened and the ears of the deaf unstopped. Then will the lame leap like a deer, and the mute tongue shout for joy. Water will gush forth in the wilderness and streams in the desert.*

- + 61:1-2: *The Spirit of the Sovereign Lord is on me, because the Lord has anointed me to proclaim good news to the poor. He has sent me to bind up the brokenhearted, to proclaim freedom for the captives and release from darkness for the prisoners, to proclaim the year of the Lord's favor and the day of vengeance of our God, to comfort all who mourn.*

- Jeremiah 31:8: *See, I will bring them from the land of the north and gather them from the ends of the earth. Among them will be the blind and the lame, expectant mothers and women in labor; a great throng will return.*

- Micah 4:6-7: *"In that day," declares the Lord, I will gather the lame; I will assemble the exiles and those I have brought to grief. I will make the lame my remnant, those driven away a strong nation. The Lord will rule over them in Mount Zion from that day and forever.*

- Zephaniah 3:19: *At that time I will deal with all with all who oppressed you. I will rescue the lame; I will gather the exiles. I will give them praise and honor in every land where they have suffered shame.*

50.12 PROTECTION

The King will supernaturally preserve lives of the Jews and protect their nation from enemies.

- Isaiah:
    - + 41:8-14: The Lord will protect Jerusalem and says those *who rage against you will surely be ashamed and disgraced; those who oppose you will be as nothing and perish.* Jerusalem will no longer have enemies. God says He will help His people.
    - + 62:8-9: The Lord has sworn that never again will He give Israel's food to her enemies, but she will harvest and eat her own crops.

- Jeremiah 23:6: *In his days Judah will be saved and Israel will live in safety. This is the name by which he will be called: The Lord Our Righteous Savior.*

- Ezekiel 34:27: When God rescues Israel *from the hands of those who enslaved them,* they *will be secure in their land,* and the land will produce *fruit* and *crops.*

- Joel 3:16-17: *The Lord will roar from Zion and thunder from Jerusalem; the earth and the heavens will tremble. But the Lord will be a refuge for his people, a stronghold for the people of Israel. "Then you will know that I, the Lord your God, dwell in Zion, my holy hill. Jerusalem will be holy, never again will foreigners invade her.*

- Amos 9:15: *I will plant Israel in their own land, never again to be uprooted from the land I have given them, says the Lord your God.*
- Zechariah:
  + 8:14-15: *This is what the Lord Almighty says: "Just as I had determined to bring disaster on you and showed no pity when your ancestors angered me," says the Lord Almighty, so now I have determined to do good again to Jerusalem and Judah. Do not be afraid.*
  + 9:8: *But I will encamp at my temple to guard it against marauding forces. Never again will an oppressor overrun my people, for now I am keeping watch.*
  + 14:10-11: The land of Israel will be topographically changed; *Jerusalem will be raised up high,* and *it will be inhabited; never again will it be destroyed. Jerusalem will be secure.*

50.13 FREEDOM FROM OPPRESSION

Nether religious, political, nor social oppression will be found in the restored nation.
- Isaiah:
  + 14:3-6: *On the day the Lord gives you relief from your suffering and turmoil and from the harsh labor forced on you, you will take up this taunt against the king of Babylon: How the oppressor has come to an end! How his fury has ended! The Lord has broken the rod of the wicked, the scepter of the rulers, which in anger struck down peoples with unceasing blows, and in fury subdued nations with relentless aggression.*
  + 42:6-7: *"I, the Lord, have called you in righteousness; I will take hold of your hand. I will keep you and will make you to be a covenant for the people and a light for the Gentiles, to open eyes that are blind, to free captives from prison and to release from the dungeon those who sit in darkness.*
  + 49:8-9: *This is what the Lord says: "In the time of my favor I will answer you, and in the day of salvation I will help you; I will keep you and will make you to be a covenant for the people, to restore the land and to reassign its desolate inheritances, to say to captives, 'Come out,' and to those in darkness, 'Be free!'" "They will feed beside the roads and find pasture on every barren hill.*
- Zechariah 9:11-12: "God's faithfulness to His covenants with Israel is His basis for delivering her from worldwide dispersion. The immediate addressees in these verses may have been Jewish exiles till in Babylon, but the covenant-fulfillment theme suggests an ultimate reference to Israel's end-time regathering. At least the nation's future hope (messianic deliverance) was the basis for contemporary encouragement in Zechariah's day. *The blood of My covenant with you* may refer to the sacrifices of the Mosaic Covenant (cf. Ex. 24:8), but could as well relate back to the foundational Abrahamic Covenant which was confirmed with a blood sacrifice (Gen.

15:8-21). *The waterless pit* (an empty cistern used for a dungeon) is probably a figure for the place of exile. The *fortress* refers to Jerusalem. The exiles in Babylon were called prisoners of hope because they had God's promise of being regathered. God *will restore twice as much*, that is, His blessing in the Millennium will far exceed anything Israel has ever known."[7]

50.14 LABOR

It appears there will be a perfect economic system that, guided by the King, will include employment opportunities in industry, manufacturing, and agriculture.

- Isaiah:
  + 62:8-9: This passage is discussed in more detail above.
  + 65:21-23: *They will build houses and dwell in them; they will plant vineyards and eat their fruit. No longer will they build houses and others live in them, or plant and others eat. For as the days of a tree, so will be the days of my people; my chosen ones will long enjoy the work of their hands. They will not labor in vain, nor will they bear children doomed to misfortune, for they will be a people blessed by the Lord, they and their descendants with them.*
- Jeremiah 31:5: Farmers *will plant vineyards on the hills of Samaria* and will *enjoy their fruit*.
- Ezekiel 48:18-19: The farm land in the Sacred District will be farmed by *workers from the city* and *from all the tribes of Israel*.

50.15 UNIFIED WORSHIP

All the world will worship God and His Messiah.

- Isaiah:
  + 45:23: *By myself I have sworn, my mouth has uttered in all integrity a word that will not be revoked: Before me every knee will bow; by me every tongue will swear.*
  + 52:1, 7-10: Zion is to awake and Jerusalem is to put on their garments of splendor, and the *Lord has comforted his people, he has redeemed Jerusalem.*
  + 66:17-23: *all mankind will come and bow down before me.*
- Zechariah:
  + 8:23: *This is what the Lord, Almighty says: "In those days ten people from all languages and nations will take firm hold of one Jew by the hem of his robe and say, 'Let us go with you, because we have heard that God is with you.'"*
  + 13:2: *"On that day, I will banish the names of the idols from the land, and they will be remembered no more," declares the Lord Almighty. "I will remove both the prophets and the spirit of impurity from the land.*

+   14:16: *Then the survivors from all the nations that have attacked Jerusalem will go up year after year to worship the King, the Lord Almighty, and to celebrate the Festival of Tabernacles.*
- Zephaniah 3:9: *Then I will purify the lips of the peoples, that all of them may call on the name of the Lord and serve him shoulder to shoulder.*
- Malachi 1:11: *My name will be great among the nations, from where the sun rises to where it sets. In every place incense and pure offerings will be brought to me, because my name will be great among the nations," says the Lord Almighty.*
- Revelation 5:8-14: The four living creatures, the twenty-four elders, an enormous number of angels, and every creature on, above, or under the earth will sing praises to the Lord in honor and glory.

50.16 GOD WILL BE MANIFESTLY PRESENT

God will be fully recognized and fellowship will be unprecedented.
- Ezekiel 37:27-28: *My dwelling place will be with them, I will be their God, and they will be my people. Then the nations will know that I the Lord make Israel holy, when my sanctuary is among them forever.*
- Zechariah 2:10-13: The Lord will come and live among the Jews. Many nations will join with the Lord to be His people.
- Revelation 21:3: *And I heard a loud voice from the throne saying, Look! God's dwelling place is now among the people, and he will dwell with them. They will be his people, and God himself will be with them and be their God.*

50.17 THE HOLY SPIRIT WILL BE FULLY AVAILABLE

The Holy Spirit will be present and individuals will experience enablement.
- Isaiah:
  +   32:13-15: *... till the Spirit is poured on us from on high ...*
  +   44:3: *... I will pour out my spirit on your offspring ...*
  +   59:21: *"My Spirit, who is on you, will not depart from you ...*
  +   61:1: *The Spirit of the Sovereign Lord is on me ...*
- Ezekiel:
  +   11:19-20: *I will give them an undivided heart and put a new spirit in them, I will remove from them their heart of stone and give them a heart of flesh. Then they will follow my decrees and be careful to keep my laws. They will be my people, and I will be their God.*
  +   36:26-27: *I will give you a new heart and pout a new spirit in you. I will remove from you your heart of stone and give you a heart of flesh. And I will put my Spirit in you and move you to follow my decrees and be careful to keep my laws.*
  +   37:14: *I will put my Spirit in you and you will live ...*

405

- + 39:29: *I will no longer hide my face from them, for I will pour out my Spirit on the people of Israel, declares the Sovereign Lord.*
- Joel 2:28-29: *And afterward, I will pour out my Spirit on all people. Your sons and daughters will prophesy, your old men will dream dreams, your young men will see visions. Even on my servants, both men and women, I will pour out my spirit in those days.*

50.18   THE PERPETUITY OF THE MILLENNIUM

The Millennium is not viewed as temporal, but eternal.
- Isaiah:
    - + 51:6-8: The Lord's salvation and righteousness will last forever
    - + 55:3: *Give ear and come to me; listen, that you may live. I will make an everlasting covenant with you, my faithful love promised to David.*
    - + 56:5: *to them I will give within my temple and its walls a memorial and a name better than sons and daughters; I will give them an everlasting name that will endure forever.*
    - + 60:19-20: This passage is discussed in more detail above.
    - + 61:8: *In my faithfulness I will reward my people and make an everlasting covenant with them.*
- Jeremiah 32:40: *I will make an everlasting covenant with them: I will never stop doing good to them, and I will inspire them to fear me, so that they will never turn away from me.*
- Ezekiel:
    - + 16:60: *Yet I will remember the covenant I made with you in the days of your youth, and I will establish an everlasting covenant with you.*
    - + 37:26-28: *I will make a covenant of peace with them; it will be an everlasting covenant. I will establish them and increase their numbers, and I will put my sanctuary among them forever. My dwelling place will be with them; I will be their God, and they will be my people. Then the nations will know that I the Lord make Israel holy, when my sanctuary is among them forever.*
    - + 43:7-9: This passage is discussed in more detail above.
- Daniel 9:24: *to bring in everlasting righteousness*
- Hosea 2:19-20: *I will betroth you to me forever; I will betroth you in righteousness and justice, in love and compassion. I will betroth you in faithfulness, and you will acknowledge the Lord.*
- Joel 3:20: *Judah* and *Jerusalem will be inhabited forever.*
- Amos 9:15: *I will plant Israel in their own land, never again to be uprooted again from the land I have given them," says the Lord your God.*

51

THE MILLENNIAL GOVERNMENT
OF THE EARTHLY KINGDOM

One of the observations that may be made at this point in the study of the Millennium is that while there will be many differences between the Millennium Kingdom and the human conditions of this present age, there will also be many similarities. Many Christians think that life in the millennium will have the saved floating around on clouds singing and playing harps. In fact, the opposite appears to be true. With the exception of the presence of the Lord Jesus Christ and resurrected saints, the Bible gives every indication that life on the earth for mortal human beings during the one-thousand-year age will be similar to what it was like prior to the end times possibly in the following ways:

- As mortal humans have done for thousands of years, they will give birth, they will be educated, they will work at jobs and will participate in leisure activities, they will eat, sleep, wear clothes, they will age and finally they will die.
- In spite of the fact that Satan will have no influence on humankind, the natural human inclination to depravity will cause sinfulness to some extent, albeit much less than before, that will require the need for some amount of laws and judgment of sins.
- Mortal humans will need houses in which to live.
- There will be diverse nations with political structures.
- After the human community rebuilds itself, there will be economies of various scales, global, regional, national, state, local, community, etc.
- There will be unique and diverse cultures among the many tribes of peoples.
- Various forms of transportation will again be present, probably much as it existed prior to the Lord's return.
- The Bible gives no indication that technological progress will not continue to advance and develop.
- Agriculture will be common and will be more abundant.
- Buildings, highways, urban infrastructure will be constructed as cities reform, and there will be rural communities.

Also, when the human conditions in the Millennium are closely examined it is realized that the Bible paints the picture that a governmental structure will be present during that time. Contrary to the general understanding of the millennium that is current today, millennial civilization will require other positions of ruling responsibilities in order to administer the Lord's theocratic rule. In fact, other than Jesus Christ on the throne, the form of government that will exist does not appear very different from what can be found in the various governmental forms of pre-millennial human nations, tribes, and people at any point in history.

51.1 | THE CHARACTER AND NATURE OF THE MILLENNIAL GOVERNMENT

The Bible has much to say about the nature, form, and organizational structure that will administer the Lord's theocratic rule as He becomes the very manifestation of God's authority on earth. Pentecost[1] makes the following observations.

THE LORD'S GOVERNMENT WILL BE A THEOCRACY

Much of the information presented above attests to the fact that the form of government in the Millennium will be a theocracy. It seems safe to conclude that the millennial government that will be present during the one-thousand-year period will be the form of theocracy that God has wanted for His creation all along. Individual freedoms will be guaranteed by the rule of Jesus Christ, thus it will not be necessary for any human association to create laws with respect to universal rights. The debate and conflict over human rights that has been ever-present in the human condition will no longer be an issue requiring action by human law or rule.

- It will not be a democracy; there will be no need to vote to make decisions on matters.
- It will not be a republic; there will be no reason to elect representatives to look out for constituents.
- It does not appear that there will be any form of legislative, executive, or judicial power vested in the people, however, that does not mean people will be unrepresented.
- It will not be a monarchy in the sense that sovereignty is vested by human heredity.
- It will most certainly not be a dictatorship.

THE LORD'S REIGN WILL BE UNIVERSAL

An observation that will be made of the information presented below is that the reign described by the Bible is reserved for the Jews in their covenant land. Since Jesus will be the King of kings and Lord of lords, the implication is that a somewhat similar form of government will extend to the remainder of the human society that covers the earth - the sense of the Biblical descriptions of the millennium is that the Lord's reign extends to all parts of the earth (there is no reason to conclude that human habitation will only be in the vicinity of Jerusalem). There will be no area of the earth that will not be under the authority of the Lord Jesus Christ as can be seen from the following passages:

- Daniel:
    + 2:35: As part of Nebuchadnezzar's dream interpretation, Daniel says the *iron, clay, bronze, silver,* and *gold* (which represents governments of humankind) will *become like chaff on the threshing floor* that is *swept* away by the *wind without leaving a trace* (human governments will fall apart and be blown away). But the *rock* that struck the *statue became a huge mountain* (Jesus Christ) *and filled the whole earth.* This image represents that while human governments come and go, Christ's reign will be everlasting.
    + 7:14, 27: *He was given authority, glory and sovereign power; all nations and peoples of every language worshiped him. His dominion is an everlasting dominion that will not pass away, and his kingdom is one that will never be destroyed. ... Then the sovereignty, power and greatness of all the kingdoms under heaven will be handed over to the holy people of the Most High. His kingdom will be an everlasting kingdom, and all rulers will worship and obey him.'*
- Micah 4:1-2: *In the last days the mountain of the Lord's temple will be established as the highest of the mountains; it will be exalted above the hills, and peoples will stream to it. Many nations will come and say, "Come, let us go up to the mountain of the Lord, to the temple of the God of Jacob. He will teach us his ways, so that we may walk in his paths." The law will go out from Zion, the word of the Lord from Jerusalem.*
- Zechariah 9:10: *He will proclaim peace to the nations. His rule will extend from sea to sea and from the River to the ends of the earth.*

THE LORD'S RULE WILL BE INFLEXIBLE RIGHTEOUSNESS AND JUSTICE

The battle between good and bad will no longer plague human beings during this time. As seen elsewhere, good will be written on the hearts of many who will walk a righteous life, and for those that are bad, there will be judging, reproving, and smiting. The following passages attest to this fact:
- Isaiah:
    + 11:3-5: As the ruler of the world, Jesus will impartially judge the world in righteousness and faithfulness. Even the poor and needy will no longer be oppressed. The wicked will be slain.
    + 25:2-5: When the Kingdom is established on earth, the Lord's name will be praised and His act of judgment will be marvelous. All the nations of the world will be blessed through Israel.
    + 29:17-21: When the Millennium comes, Lebanon will once again become fertile, and the deaf will hear and the blind will see. Because of what the Lord will do for them, the needy will rejoice in Him.

+ 42:13: The Lord will march out like a champion, like a warrior he will stir up his zeal; with a shout he will raise the battle cry and will triumph over his enemies.
+ 49:25-26: The Lord will protect Israel from her oppressors, then all humankind will know that God is her Savior.
+ 66:14: When you see this, your heart will rejoice and you will flourish like grass; the hand of the Lord will be made known to his servants, but his fury will be shown to his foes.
- Daniel 2:44: *"In the time of those kings, the God of heaven will set up a kingdom that will never be destroyed, nor will it be left to another people. It will crush all those kingdoms and bring them to an end, but it will itself endure forever.*
- Micah 5:5-6, 10-15: In addition to bringing peace to Israel, Christ will enable to her to defeat her enemies. The Ruler will destroy:
+ The horses and chariots.
+ The cities and strongholds.
+ Witchcraft.
+ Idols.
+ Asherah poles.
+ Nations that have not obeyed the Lord.

THE LORD'S RULE WILL DEAL SUMMARILY WITH SIN

The implication here is that while sinfulness will not be completely eliminated from the earth over the course of the Millennium, some unquantified amount will still be present, sinfulness will be brought to an immediate resolution after its commitment. "Any overt act against the authority of the King will be punished with physical death. It seems as though sufficient enablement is given to the saints through the fullness of the Spirit, the universality of the knowledge of the Lord, the removal of Satan, and the manifestation of the King's presence to restrain them from any sin."[2]

- The Psalms:
+ 2:9: *You will break them with a rod of iron; you will dash them to pieces like pottery.*
+ 72:1-4: This Psalm speaks of the millennial reign of the Messiah in which blessings will flow from the righteousness of God.
- Isaiah 11:4: *but with righteousness he will judge the needy, with justice he will give decisions for the poor of the earth. He will strike the earth with the rod of his mouth; with the breath of his lips he will slay the wicked*
- Jeremiah 31:30: *everyone will die for their own sin*
- Zechariah 14:16-21: Survivors of the nations that have attacked Jerusalem will go up to worship the Lord Almighty. Those that do not go to worship the Lord will receive no rain. The Lord will also bring the plague on them.

THE LORD'S REIGN WILL BE IN THE FULLNESS OF THE HOLY SPIRIT

The spirit of the Lord's wisdom, understanding, counsel, might, knowledge, and fear will rest on Jesus Christ.
- Isaiah 11:1-3a: *A shoot will come up from the stump of Jesse; from his roots a Branch will bear fruit. The Spirit of the Lord will rest on him – the Spirit of wisdom and of understanding, the Spirit of counsel and of might, the Spirit of the knowledge and fear of the Lord – and he will delight in the fear of the Lord.*

THE LORD'S GOVERNMENT WILL BE UNIFIED

The Jewish people will no longer be divided into Israel and Judah, nor will the nations be divided against each other as seen in the following verses:
- Ezekiel 37:13-28: God instructs Ezekiel to use a stick to demonstrate that He will bring the two nations back into a single nation that will have one king.
- Hosea 1:11: In Hosea's introductory verse, he said he was active during the reigns of various kings in both Judah and Israel.

THE LORD'S REIGN WILL BE ETERNAL
- Daniel 7:14, 27: The government of the Lord will be an everlasting dominion.

51.2 THE RULERS OF THE MILLENNIAL GOVERNMENT

What may come as a surprise to most Christians is that the Bible tells us that there will be various levels or positions within the millennial government that will be present and will assist the Lord's rulership. This is one of the most significant indicators that the fabric of life on earth during the one-thousand-year millennium will be similar to the nature of human life prior to the end - there will be a bureaucratic structure to the government, the only for which is that there is sufficient enough quantity of administrative matters that requires people to tend to the details. However, while the Bible does not specifically say so, it is apparent from an examination of the various levels that the bureaucracy will be composed of both mortal human beings and resurrected saints. Pentecost[3] makes the following observations:

MESSIAH WILL BE KING

"Scripture makes it clear that the government of the millennium is under the Messiah, the Lord Jesus Christ..."[4] as can be seen in the following passages:

- Psalm 2:6: God has appointed Jesus to the throne and His rule will be universal.
- Isaiah:

  + 9:3-7: In Isaiah's prophecy about a future Savior to be born to Israel, the Savior is said to *be called Wonderful Counselor, Mighty God, Everlasting Father, Prince of Peace.* There will be no end to *the greatness of his government and peace* as the Savior reigns *on David's throne over his kingdom forever.*

  + 11:1-10: Identified as a *branch* of a *shoot* of the *stump of Jesse,* Jesus is characterized in the ways listed in the adjacent table.

  + 16:5: *In love a throne will be established; in faithfulness a man will sit on it – one from the house of David – one who in judging seeks justice and speeds the cause of righteousness.*

Isaiah 11:1-10
the Spirit of the Lord will rest on him
the Spirit of wisdom and of understanding
the Spirit of counsel and of might
the Spirit of the knowledge and fear of the Lord
he will delight in the fear of the Lord
with righteousness he will judge the needy
with justice he will give decisions for the poor of the earth
he will strike the earth with the rod of his mouth
the breath of his lips he will slay the wicked
righteousness will be his belt
faithfulness the sash around his waist

  + 24:21-23: In a prophecy of the Messiah coming as a great future King, Isaiah says, "[w]hen Yahweh brings universal judgment on the world again; He will sovereignly punish all unfaithful authorities both in the heavenly realm... and in the earthly realm.... Rulers are the particular individuals in view.... Before God punishes them, he will confine them in as pit.... The "moon" and "sun," the most glorious rulers of human life, in the physical sense, will be ashamed by the appearance of an even more glorious ruler... ."[5]

  + 32:1-2: In the millennium, the King will reign in righteousness and the appointed rulers will rule with justice.

  + 42:1-9: In the first half of this passage (verses 1 – 4), God presents His servant, the chosen one, who will faithfully bring justice to the nations. Supported by God and His Spirit, the servant, the Messiah, will gently bring forth justice without faltering or being discouraged. "... God's answer to the oppressors of the world is not more oppression, nor is his answer to arrogance more arrogance; rather, in quietness, humility, and simplicity, he will take all of the evil into himself and return only grace. That is power."[6] In the second half of this passage (verses 5 – 9), the Lord's incomparable character is demonstrated by the servant doing God's will.

+ 42:13: *The Lord will march out, stir up his zeal, shout out the battle cry*, and *triumph over his enemies.*
+ 51:4-5: The Lord urges His chosen people to listen to Him because instruction will come out about what God would do to preserve and return them to the land. This would be a lesson to the whole world about fulfilling His promise to the Israelites so that it would lead Gentiles out of their darkness and into His light. The Servant would bring salvation to Gentiles in the furthest reaches of humanity.
- Daniel:
  + 2:44: *In the time of those kings, the God of heaven will set up a kingdom that will never be destroyed, nor will be left to another people. It will crush all those kingdoms and bring them to an end, but it will itself endure forever.*
  + 7:15-28: *Daniel was troubled in spirit* by his dream of the four beasts. He was especially troubled about *the fourth beast*, which unlike the other three beasts, with its *iron teeth, bronze claws, the ten horns,* and *the other horn* which had conquered three of the kings and was waging war with and defeating the holy people, *the Ancient of Days came* and judged *in favor of the holy people* and the time came to possess the kingdom. Its interpretation was that the beast was *a fourth kingdom* on earth that *will devour the whole earth*; the *ten horns are ten kings* from the kingdom; *then another king* will appear that will conquer *three kings* and *speak against the Most High and oppress the holy people.* Then *all kingdoms* will be given over *to the people of the Most High. His kingdom will be an everlasting kingdom, and all rulers will worship and obey him.*
- Micah:
  + 4:1-8: *In the last days the mountain of the Lord's temple will established as the highest of the mountains. Many nations will come* to the Lord's temple because they will want to learn of His laws and His ways. Peace will prevail, and there will be no more war.
  + 5:2-5: One will come out of the small town of *Bethlehem* one will come *who will be ruler over Israel*. He will *shepherd His flock in the strength of the Lord.* They will live securely and His *greatness will reach to the ends of the earth.*
- Zephaniah 3:9-10: *"Then I will purify the lips of the peoples, that all of them may call on the name of the Lord and serve him shoulder to shoulder. From beyond the rivers of Cush my worshippers, my scattered people, will bring me offerings.*
- Zechariah:
  + 9:10-15: This passage describes the implements of war that the Lord will rid Jerusalem of as He restores the nation.
  + 14:16: *Then the survivors from all the nations that have attacked Jerusalem will go up year after year to worship the King, the Lord Almighty, and to celebrate the Festival of Tabernacles.*

DAVID WILL BE A REGENT

A regent is a person that serves in the absence of the sovereign. The Old Testament clearly indicates that there will be a regency of David during this time as can be seen by the following passages:

- Isaiah 55:3-4: When people come to the Lord, God's *everlasting covenant* with David grants them the benefits of the covenant. In the future, David will be the world's *ruler and commander*.
- Jeremiah:
  + 30:9: God will raise David up as the king of those that return to Israel.
  + 33:15: God will *make a righteous Branch sprout from David's line; he will do what is just and right in the land.*
  + 33:17: The Lord says that *David will never fail to have a man sit on the throne of Israel.*
  + 33:20-21: Jeremiah writes that the Lord said that if the days and night can be changed and no longer come at their appointed time, then His covenant with David and the Levities *can be broken and David will no longer have a descendant to reign on his throne.* This was God's way of saying that His covenant with David cannot be broken any more than the days and nights moved off their schedule.
- Ezekiel:
  + 34:23-24: The sovereign Lord has spoken: He will place *one shepherd* over them, His *servant David* who will tend to them; *the Lord will be their God*, and *David will be prince among them.*
  + 37:24-25: When Israel is restored, God has appointed His *servant David* to be the *king over them, and they will all have one shepherd.* Then, God makes three predictions about the state of restored Israel: first, the nation will follow His laws and keep God's decrees, second, Israel will live in the land promised to them forever, and third, they will enjoy David's rule forever.
- Hosea 3:5: Hosea writes that when Israel returns, they will return to David as their king.
- Amos 9:11: God says that when Israel is restored, He *will restore David's fallen shelter*, *repair its broken walls*, *restore it ruins*, and *rebuild it as it used to be.*

The central question is in what capacity Jesus will rule over Israel - directly or indirectly through David as a regent. There are several views that should be reviewed:

- First View - The name of David is used typically and refers to Jesus:
  + Explanation of the View: Because of the close association of David and references to the Son of David, identified in the New Testament as Jesus, some believe that whenever there is a reference to David in the future it is actually referring to Jesus.
  + Objections to the View:

- ○ Jesus is never actually called David in Scripture; however, He is called by the following indicating that Jesus will be a descendant of David:
  - Jeremiah 23:5: Branch of David.
  - Son of David fifteen times.
  - John 7:42 (cf. Romans 1:3 and 2 Timothy 2:8): Seed of David.
  - Revelation 5:5: Root of David.
  - Revelation 22:16: Root and Offspring of David.
- ○ "The appellation "my servant, David" is used repeatedly for the historical David."[7]
- ○ Jehovah is clearly distinguished from David:
  - Isaiah 55:4: If David is who this passage refers to (there are other options), then God has *made him a witness to the peoples* as well as *a ruler and commander to the peoples*.
  - Jeremiah 30:9: After being delivered from those that restrained and enslaved them, Israel *will serve the Lord their God*, and the one that God has raised for them, *David their king*.
  - Ezekiel:
    - 34:24: The Lord says that He will be Israel's God, and His *servant David will be prince*.
    - 37:21-25: *The Sovereign Lord* says that He will *gather* His people and *bring them back into their own land, make them one nation*, and never allow them to be *divided* again. *They will no longer defile themselves with idols and vile images* and God *will save them from all their sinful backsliding* and *cleanse them*. God's servant *David will be king* over them and they will *follow* God's *laws* and *keep* His *decrees. They will live in the land* given to God's *servant Jacob forever* and *David will be their prince forever. God will make* an *everlasting covenant of peace with them*. God will bless them and He *will put* His *sanctuary among them forever*, and will dwell with them forever.
    - Hosea 3:5: The Lord will be Israel's God and David their king.
- ○ David is recorded as having done things that Jesus would not do, such as the following:
  - Ezekiel
    - 45:22: Offering a sin offering for himself.
    - 46:2: Engaging in acts of worship.
    - 46:16: Dividing an inheritance with his sons.
- **Second View** - The name David refers to the literal son of David:
  - + Explanation of the View: A literal male descendant of David would do the things indicated because Jesus cannot do all that is stated.

- o Jeremiah 33:15, 17, 20-21: The Lord will make a righteous Branch sprout from David's Line. The Lord says that David will always have a man available to sit on the throne of Israel.
  + Objections to the View:
    - o Jews are not able to legitimately trace their lineage back to any time before the destruction of Jerusalem in 70 AD.
      - Christ would not be Christ if another one had to come after Him.
      - Literal interpretation requires David to mean just what it implies under normal usage.
- Third View - The name David refers to the literal historical man David:
  + Explanation of the View: The human being identified, in the Bible as the King of Israel at one time, by the name David will be resurrected at the Second Coming of Jesus Christ to rule with Christ in the position as a regent.
  + Support of the View:
    - o It is the most consistent with the principle of literal interpretation.
    - o There would be no violation of the various prophecies of David's future reign if David was a regent to Christ.
    - o Positions of ruling responsibility will be given to many of the saints that will be resurrected as part of the Lord's return.

Thus, it may be concluded that the historical King David will be resurrected to rule over the restored nation of Israel when they live in the land promised by God under the authority of Jesus Christ.

NOBLES AND GOVERNORS WILL REIGN UNDER DAVID

- Old Testament: There are several passages which suggest there will be subordinate rulers under David:
  + Jeremiah 30:21: Restored Israel will have a leader and a ruler.
  + Isaiah 32:1: *See, a king will reign in righteousness and rulers will rule with justice.*
  + Ezekiel 45:8-9: Restored Israel's government will include princes.
- New Testament:
  + Matthew 19:28: The Twelve apostles will rule over the twelve tribes of Israel.
  + Revelation 19:16: The reference to Jesus as King of kings and Lord of lords suggests that there will be subordinate rulers.

LESSER AUTHORITIES

There is evidence that there will be lesser authorities, reporting to the head of the tribe who in turn reports to David, who will be appointed to reign as a reward for their own faithfulness as can be seen in the following passages:

- Zechariah 3:6-7: *The angel of the Lord says that the Lord Almighty* gave a *charge to Joshua* that if he *will walk in obedience* and *keep* His *requirements*, then he will *govern* the Lord's *house* and *have charge* of His *courts*.
- Luke 19:12-28: "This parable of the 10 Minas sums up Jesus' teaching to the disciples. Each disciple had duties given to him by Jesus, and each was to carry out his responsibilities. But the parable was addressed not only to disciples. It was also addressed to the nation at large, to show that it too had responsibilities. If the nation did not turn to Jesus, it would be punished."[8] This passage also demonstrates there will hierarchies of responsibilities in heaven.

JUDGES WILL BE RAISED UP

"As the judges of the Old Testament were of divine appointment and were representatives through whom the theocratic kingdom was administered, so those who rule in the millennium will have the same characterization as judges, so that it may be evident that their authority is a demonstration of theocratic power."[9]

- Isaiah 1:26: The Lord tells Israel that He will *restore your leaders as in days of old, your rulers as at the beginning.* After this, Jerusalem will be known as *the City of Righteousness* and *the Faithful City.*
- Zechariah 3:7: See above.

52

THE LAND TO WHICH ISRAEL
WILL BE RESTORED

As God had promised and reaffirmed so many times in the Old Testament, Israel is now restored to their promised land. After all the dispossessions and restorations to the land, after all the tribulations (especially the Great Tribulation), and after all the times that Israel has been disobedient to the Lord, the Lord has kept a remnant down through the centuries who is now going to inherit the covenant land on behalf of all the Jews that have lived. The land aspect of the Abrahamic Covenant and the Palestinian Covenants will now be fulfilled.

As the Promised Land has never been fully occupied nor fully under Israeli sovereignty to date, even in their current occupancy of a portion of the land, then the implication is that the promise will be fulfilled when the Lord regathers the Jews the last time after His Second Advent. In fact, Zechariah writing after the exile, still looks ahead to the glorious restoration in the future as seen in 10:9-12 and 14:1-21.

52.1	THE OLD TESTAMENT BACKGROUND OF THE PROMISE OF THE LAND

We have previously examined the four everlasting and unconditional covenants made by God with Israel that yielded five prophetic features that were to remain unfulfilled until the anticipated kingdom of Israel was brought in by God – the second feature involved the return of Israel to their promised land. Earlier in this chapter, the conclusion was made that the kingdom anticipated by Israel in the Old Testament and the one-thousand-year Millennium of the New Testament occur simultaneously, thus establishing the unfulfilled promises to Israel will be fulfilled during the Millennium in general, and in particular, that the nation of Israel would be returned to the land from which they were removed earlier.

Before the details of the land of Israel in the Millennium are explored, a review of the Biblical background is necessary. "God promised Abraham that He would give a particular parcel of land to his descendants (Gen.12:7). Later he reiterated this promise and became more specific about its boundaries (Gen.15:7, 18-21; 17:8; Num.34:1-12), He also told the Israelites that they would only be able to occupy the land to the extent that they followed Him faithfully (Deut. 7:12; 8:2). If they proved unfaithful, He would not only limit their possession of the land but even drive them out of it (Deut. 28). Ezekiel prophesied that God would bring the

Israelite back into the land (36:24-30). He would give them a different attitude, and they would follow Him faithfully. Then they would finally, as newer before, enjoy the full extent of the land He had promised their forefathers (cf. Deut. 30). He also promised that they would never lose possession of the land because they would remain faithful to Him (ch.39)."[1]

Regarding the boundaries of the original land gift to Abram, it should be understood that there is adequate information to establish the broad expanse of the land and the approximate boundaries, but there is not enough to be exact. It should also be kept in mind that some of the geographical locations mentioned in the passages have not been determined, of discovered archeologically.

THE BOUNDARIES OF GOD'S PROMISE OF LAND TO ISRAEL

Townsend[2] has studied the topic of God's covenantal promise of a land and he observes that the land is described in three ways in the Old Testament:
- Identified as Canaan: The books of the Old Testament refer to the land promised to Israel by God simply as Canaan, which would apparently be well understood at the time that the Hebrews were moving up to and then into the land to conquer it.
  + Genesis:
    o 17:8: God said to Abram during the making of the covenant that *the whole land of Canaan* will be given to him, and his descendants, *as an everlasting possession*, and He *will be their God*.
    o 48:3-4: Jacob was telling Joseph that while he was *in the land of Canaan God Almighty* was going to bless him.
  + Exodus 6:4: God tells Moses that He previously *appeared to Abraham, to Isaac and to Jacob* and established a covenant with them *to give them the land of Canaan*.
  + Numbers 34:2: *The Lord said to Moses, "Command the Israelites and say to them: 'When you enter Canaan, the land that will be allotted to you as an inheritance.*
  + Deuteronomy 1:7-8: God told the Israelites to break camp and advance against the Canaanites because God has given them the land.
  + Joshua 14:1-2: *As the Lord had commanded*, the individual *inheritance in the land of Canaan* was allotted to the tribe clans by lot.
  + Psalm 105:11: God tells the psalmist that He *will give the land of Canaan as the portion you will inherit*.
- General Description: Also, there are passages that provide a reference to a general area without being specific. This identification can be found in the following passages:

+ Genesis 15:18: After the Lord made the covenant with Abraham, He described in rather extensive terms the boundaries of the Promised Land by first indicating the landmarks that constituted the limits of the land, and by listing the peoples that will need to be removed from the land first.
+ Exodus 23:31: Again the Lord describes the limits of the land by using landmarks, and by delivering the peoples that lived there to Israel to be driven out.
+ Numbers 13:21: Again landmarks are used to describe the land.
+ Deuteronomy 11:24: The land boundaries are described as from one place to another place.
+ 1 Kings 8:65 (cf. 2 Chronicles 7:8): Solomon observed a festival in which people from distant lands attended.
+ Isaiah 27:12: The Lord will gather Israel to the land between two locations.
• Specific Descriptions: "At least three Old Testament passages (Num. 34:1-12; Josh. 15:1-12; Ezek. 47:15-20; cf, Ezek. 46:1, 28) describe the specific borders of the Promised Land. Though these passages were written during different times in Israel's history (pre-Conquest, post-Conquest, exile) and refer to different occupations of the land (the Conquest, glorious restoration), they concur in outlining the historic land of Canaan …"[3]

WAS THE PROPHECY FULFILLED IN THE CONQUEST?

Townsend indicates that while Joshua 21:43-45 and 23:14-15 indicates that the Lord fulfilled the land promise of the Abrahamic Covenant in the Conquest, a closer examination of Joshua 11:16 through Judges 3:6 reveals that while Israel might have occupied the land, the Canaanites had not been completely removed. Therefore, there was "… demoralizing coexistence …"[4] in the land between the Israelites and the Canaanites that is essentially an incomplete fulfillment of the Abrahamic Covenant.

WAS THE PROPHECY FULFILLED IN THE UNITED MONARCH?

Again Townsend indicates that 1 King 8:65 indicates that the promise was fulfilled, however, there are other passages that points out that "… much of the Promised Land was not under direct Israelite sovereignty …"[5] Examples include the area of Philistia as recorded in 1 Kings 4:21 and 2 Chronicles 9:26, and "… it appears that the Phoenician coastal area above Tyre inhabited by the Sidonians was never included under Israelite rule of tribute."[6] Again, this is essentially an incomplete fulfillment of the Abrahamic Covenant.

52.2	THE LAND OF PALESTINE IN THE MILLENNIUM

In addition to substantive changes occurring in Jerusalem, the land of Palestine itself will also experience substantial changes for the better as noticed by Pentecost.[7]

THE LAND WILL BE GREATLY ENLARGED

Israel will possess the full extent of the land that was promised by God to the fathers of Israel (Genesis 15:18-21).
- Isaiah:
    + 26:15: Isaiah states that the Lord has *enlarged the nation* and *extended all the borders of the land.*
    + 33:17: *and view a land that stretches afar.*
- Obadiah 17-21: At the beginning of the Millennium Israel will return to more land than was originally theirs.
- Micah 7:14: *Shepherd your people with your staff, the flock of your inheritance, which lives by itself in a forest, in fertile pasturelands. Let them feed in Bashan and Gilead as in days long ago.*

THE TOPOGRAPHY OF THE LAND WILL BE CHANGED

A great fertile plain will replace the mountainous terrain now found in the land to such an extent to allow for the two rivers to flow east and west out of the city of Jerusalem.
- Ezekiel 47:1-12: Ezekiel describes the water that is coming out from under the temple that turns into a river and eventually discharges into another body of water.
- Joel 3:18: When the Messiah rules in the Millennium the land will be a virtual paradise and will provide agricultural blessing to the Lord's people. Grapes will be plentiful, so much so, that the mountains will appear to drip with wine, milk will be plentiful, and ravines (wadis) will not run dry. All of this are signs of prosperity. A fountain will flow out of the Lord's house which will remind all that God is the source of the land's fertility.
- Zechariah 14:4, 8, 10: When the Lord comes He *will stand on the Mount of Olives, east of Jerusalem, and the Mount of Olives will be split in two from east to west, forming a great valley with half of the mountain moving north and half moving south. Living water will flow out from Jerusalem, half of it east to the Dead Sea an half of it west to the Mediterranean Sea* … A large area southwest of Jerusalem will be leveled to a broad plain.

THERE WILL BE RENEWED FERTILITY AND ABUNDANT PRODUCTIVITY

There will be a level of agricultural fertility and productivity that has not existed before.

- Isaiah:
    + 29:17: *Lebanon* will *be turned into a fertile field* that will *seem like a forest.*
    + 32:15: *and the desert becomes a fertile field, and the fertile field seems like a forest.*
    + 35:1-7: This passage expresses the utopia that humankind has longed for that will come after God judges the world. *The desert and the parched land* will become rich agriculturally because of an increase in rainfall. Isaiah encourages the believing remnant to encourage the depressed (*feeble hands*), those that are terrified (*knees that give way*), and the *fearful* because *God will come* with *divine retribution* to save them. The people will be changed, the *blind* will see, the *deaf* will hear, *the lame* will *leap like a deer*, and the *mute* will *shout for joy.* Water will be plentiful because the dry land will take a well-watered condition.
    + 55:13: The Lord will make the land unusually fertile which will demonstrate that He is in control.
- Ezekiel 36:29-35: The Lord will save Israel from their *uncleanness*, He will make *grain plentiful*, He *will not bring famine* on them, and He *will increase the fruit of the trees and the crops of the field.* The people will *remember* their *evil and wicked deeds* and will *loathe* yourselves for their *sins and detestable practices. On the day* the Lord cleanses Israel, He *will resettle* their *towns and the ruins will be rebuilt. The desolate land will be cultivated.*
- Joel 3:18: Similar to Amos 9:13 below, water will flow from Jehovah's House that will irrigate the fertile valley.
- Amos 9:13: The Lord says a time is coming when the mountains will seem to flow with wine because the land is more fertile.

THERE WILL BE AN ABUNDANCE OF RAINFALL

Historically in the land of Israel, abundant rainfall was a blessing from God for obedience, as well as the lack of rainfall was a curse from God for disobedience; since Israel will be back in her land in obedience, God will provide abundant rainfall again.

- Isaiah:
    + 30:23-33: Isaiah describes what life will be like in the Millennium. He says that God will send rain for the purpose of making the land rich and crops plentiful.

- + 35:6-7: *Then will the lame leap like a deer, and the mute tongue shout for joy. Water will gush forth in the wilderness and streams in the desert. The burning sand will become a pool, the thirsty ground bubbling springs. In the haunts where jackals once lay, grass and reeds and papyrus will grow.*
- + 41:17-18: *The poor and needy search for water, but there is none; their tongues are parched with thirst. But I the Lord will answer them; I, the God of Israel, will not forsake them. I will make rivers flow on barren heights, and springs within the valleys. I will turn the desert into pools of water, and the parched ground into springs.*
- + 49:10: During Israel's restoration, God will *lead* the people *beside springs of water.*
- Ezekiel 34:26: *I will send down showers in season; there will be showers of blessings.*
- Joel 2:23-24: The Lord will send an abundance of showers that will increase the yield of grain, wine, and oil.
- Zechariah 10:1: *it is the Lord who sends the thunderstorms. He gives showers of rain to all people.*

THE LAND WILL BE RECONSTRUCTED

After the destruction caused by the various events and judgments of Daniel's 70th Week, the land will be reconstructed, restored, and made clean inside.
- Isaiah:
  - + 32:16-18: *The Lord's justice will dwell in the desert, his righteousness live in the fertile field. The fruit of that righteousness will be peace; its effect will be quietness and confidence forever. My people will live in peaceful dwelling places, in secure homes, in undisturbed places of rest.*
  - + 49:19: Though the land of Israel was *ruined* and *made desolate* and the *land laid waste,* but *the children born during* their *bereavement* will say that *this place is too small* for them and that they need *more space to live in.*
  - + 61:4-5: *They will rebuild the ancient ruins and restore the places long devastated; they will renew the ruined cities that have been devastated for generations. Strangers will shepherd your flocks; foreigners will work your fields and vineyards.*
- Ezekiel:
  - + 36:33-38: The Sovereign Lord said that He would *cleanse* Israel *from all your sins* and will resettle them in the *rebuilt* cities and in a land that will no longer be *desolate* but instead will be *cultivated* again. *They will say, This land that was laid waste has become like the garden of Eden; the cities that were lying in ruins, desolate and destroyed, are now fortified and inhabited.* The surrounding nations that remain will know that *I the Lord have rebuilt what was destroyed and have*

replanted what was desolate. The Lord will regather the people to the land and will restore the quality of their lives.

+ 39:9: *Then those who live in the towns of Israel will go out and use the weapons for fuel and burn them up – the small and large shield, the bows and arrows, the war clubs and spears. For seven years they will use them for fuel.*

• Amos 9:14-15: After being restored to the land, Israel *will rebuild the ruined cities and live in them.*

52.3	**THE DIVISION OF LAND AMONG THE TRIBES OF ISRAEL**

Core Scripture: Ezekiel 47:13 – 48:7 and 48:23-29

The Lord will now allot portions of the land among the 12 tribes of Jacob as their inheritance. In this portion of Scripture, God describes the boundaries of the land in Ezekiel's time that was originally described in Numbers 34:1-12 during Mosaic times. In Ezekiel 47:13, God indicates that Joseph should get a double portion of land so it goes to his sons, Ephraim and Manasseh. Levi was removed from the territorial allotments because the Lord is their inheritance (Deuteronomy 10:9). Ezekiel 47:15-20 delineates the boundaries of the land of Israel.

"In its reiteration of the command to divide the land as a special grant, v. 14 establishes the standard for the distribution: each of the ancestral brothers.... is to receive an equal share. The declaration also asserts that this apportionment represents the fulfillment of the oath that Yahweh had made to the patriarchal ancestors more than a millennium earlier. Ezekiel's people should have welcomed the news that Yahweh had not forgotten his oath."[8]

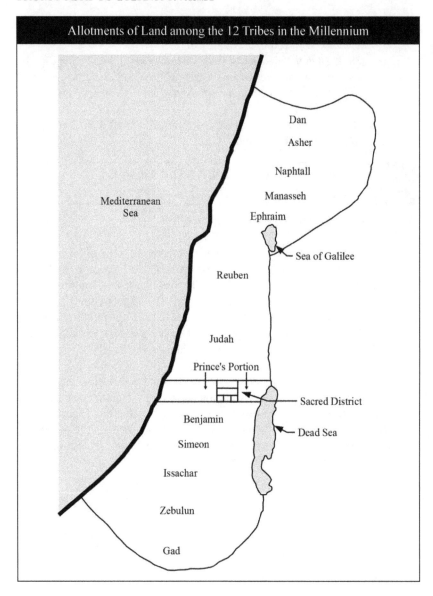

Allotments of Land among the 12 Tribes in the Millennium

53

THE MILLENNIAL MOUNTAIN

During the time of the Second Advent of Christ, a number of significant changes will happen to people and places. Among those things will be dramatic geographical and topographical changes all over the earth. In Israel, a great mountain, identified as the Millennial Mountain, will rise to be the highest mountain in the world. On top of this awesome mountain will be the Sacred District that includes Jehovah Shammah (the Millennial City of New Jerusalem) and the Temple Complex with Jehovah's House (also known as the Millennial Temple).

53.1 THE MILLENNIAL MOUNTAIN

Core Scripture: Isaiah 2:2 and Micah 4:1-2

Among conservative theologians and scholars there are conflicting ideas about what the word *mountain* means in Isaiah 2:2. There are many exceptional scholars who hold to the view that the word *mountain* is symbolic for the kingdom of God and Jesus Christ and not an actual mountain. The other view, held by a smaller group of scholars is that the word *mountain* means an actual, physical mountain. The idea here is that during the Second Coming of Christ, at the end of Daniel's 70th Week, there will be significant geographical and topographical changes that, as the following Scriptures attest, will result in a tremendous mountain rising in the Land of Israel.

Constable says: "[t]he term "mountain" is a symbol of a kingdom or nation elsewhere in the prophetic writings (e.g., Dan.2:35; Amos 4:1). The ancients also regarded mountains as the homes of the gods. If Isaiah was using "mountain" as a figure of speech, he meant that Israel and her God would be the most highly exalted in the earth eventually. This will be the case during Messiah's earthly reign. The reference to "the mountain of the house of Yahweh" (v.2), however, may indicate that the prophet had a more literal meaning in mind. He may have meant that the actual mountain on which the temple stood would be thrust higher in elevation. This may happen (cf. Ezek. 40:2; Zech. 14:4, 10), but the primary implication seems to be that Israel and Yahweh will be exalted in the world."[1]

- Isaiah 2:2-4: The *mountain of the Lord's temple*, which will be the highest in the world will arise and many people and nations will come to the mountain to be taught of the Lord's ways. While the location of the mountain is not mentioned in this passage, it is presumably within the land of Israel. Nations

will be judged, disputes will be settled, weapons of war will be turned into implements of farming, and there will be no more war.
- Micah 4:1-2: In the last days, the *mountain of the Lord's temple* will be established and it will be the highest mountain of the mountains. Many nations will go up to the mountain to learn how to walk in the Lord's ways.

The following passages, among many, provide support for the passages above that describes the mountain as a physical mountain:
- Isaiah:
  + 27:13: Those that are perishing in Assyria and Egypt will come to the *holy mountain in Jerusalem* to worship the Lord.
  + 56:6-8: Israel and redeemed Gentiles will be brought to Lord's *holy mountain* to worship the Lord in prayer and offerings.
  + 65:25: *The wolf and the lamb will feed together, and the lion will eat straw like the ox, and dust will be the serpent's food. They will neither harm nor destroy on all my holy mountain," says the Lord.*
  + 66:20: People and all the nations will be brought to the *holy mountain in Jerusalem* as an offering to the Lord.
- Ezekiel:
  + 20:40-41: The Lord says that on His *holy mountain, the high mountain of Israel*, He will accept those that come to serve Him. He will require their offerings, choice gifts, and holy sacrifices of them. He will accept those He gathers, out of the nations, like fragrant incense. By this action, He will be proved to be holy through those He brings out in the eyes of the nations.
  + 40:1-4: God gave Ezekiel a special revelation of being on a *very high mountain* in Israel and told him to look carefully, listen closely, and pay attention to everything he will be shown by God, and then, to tell the people of Israel what he had seen.

In each of the above passages, *Strong's Exhaustive Concordance* indicates the word *mountain* (number 2022) means a real physical mountain. So, which is it, an actual mountain or a symbol? It is the view of this book that during the Millennium there will be an actual mountain in Israel that will be the highest in the world with the Sacred District, Jehovah Shammah and the Temple Complex with Jehovah's House (also known as the Millennial Temple) on its top. The mountain will be exalted and many people and many nations will come to the Temple to worship God, to make offerings to God, and to learn from God. And finally, the law of God will proceed from the mountain and will attract many to be students of God and His ways.

53.2 THE SACRED DISTRICT

Core Scripture: Ezekiel 45:1-8a; 48:8-22 and 48:30-35

Apparently there will be a plateau at the top of the millennial mountain that will be the location of the Sacred District that will include the Millennium Temple and the Temple Complex, land areas for the Levities and the Zadokites, Jehovah Shammah, and land for growing of food. It will occupy a land allotment, like the other 12 tribes, that will be situated between the land allotments of Judah (to the north) and Benjamin (to the south).

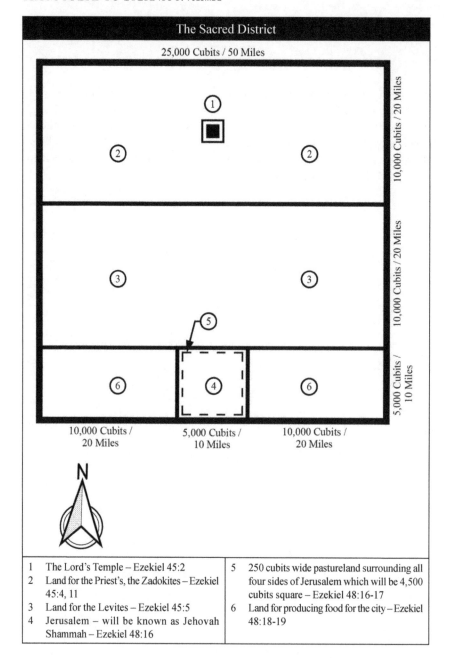

1	The Lord's Temple – Ezekiel 45:2	5	250 cubits wide pastureland surrounding all
2	Land for the Priest's, the Zadokites – Ezekiel 45:4, 11		four sides of Jerusalem which will be 4,500 cubits square – Ezekiel 48:16-17
3	Land for the Levites – Ezekiel 45:5	6	Land for producing food for the city – Ezekiel
4	Jerusalem – will be known as Jehovah Shammah – Ezekiel 48:16		48:18-19

Ezekiel describes the layout for the Sacred District in the following passages (refer to the illustration):

- 45:1: The Lord tells Ezekiel that when the land is allotted as inheritances, the Lord is to be presented with land as a Sacred District that is *25,000 cubits long and 20,000 wide* that *will be holy.*

- 45:2: *A section of 500 cubits square is to be* set aside *for the sanctuary* (temple) that will have a *50-cubit* wide portion of *open land* around all four of the sides.
- 45:3: In the Sacred District, there is to be a *25,000 cubits long and 10,000 cubits wide* portion of land that includes the sanctuary (temple) within it.
- 45:4: The land portion described in the previous verse will be a *sacred portion for the priests* (we know from other passages that this is the Zadokites) *who* will *minister in the sanctuary* and *before the Lord*. The land portion will also be for the *houses* of the *priests*.
- 45:5: Another land portion that is *25,000 cubits long and 10,000 cubits wide* will be established for *the Levites as their possession for towns to live in.*
- 45:6: A land portion of *25,000 cubits long* and *5,000 cubits wide,* that will adjoin with the sacred portions described in earlier passages, will be created for the city (Jerusalem).
- 45:7: *The prince will have the land bordering each side* of the Sacred District. The inheritance will primarily be on the *east side* and *west side* of the Sacred District.
- 45:8a: *This land will be his possession in Israel.*
- 48:8: Israel is to present this Sacred District as a gift to the Lord. The district *will be 25,000 cubits wide* and the length will be equal to the land allotments for one of the tribe members and the temple complex *will be in the center.*
- 48:9: The land allotment for this *special portion* that is to be presented *to the Lord* is to *be 25,000 cubits long and 10,000 cubits wide.*
- 48:10: The portion described in the previous verse is *for the priests.* Then the dimensions are repeated again. The temple complex (*sanctuary of the Lord*) will be *in the center.*
- 48:11: This first portion of the land *will be for the consecrated priests, the Zadokites, who* have been *faithful* to the Lord and *did not go astray when the Levites did when the Israelites went astray.*
- 48:12: This first portion of the land is a *special gift* to the Zadokites priests, which borders the land for *the Levities.*
- 48:13: Alongside the portion of land for the Zadokites will be another portion of land that will be *25,000 cubits long and 10,000 cubits wide* and will be for the *Levities.* For unknown reasons the dimensions are repeated twice in the same verse.
- 48:14: The Levities are instructed not to *sell or exchange* any part of the land because it is the *best of the land, it is holy to the Lord,* and it *must not pass into other hands.*
- 48:15: *The remaining area,* an area that is *5,000 cubits wide and 25,000 long will be for the common use of the city, Jerusalem, for houses and pastureland.* The *city will be in the center* of this portion.
- 48:16: The city will be *4,500 cubits* square.
- 48:17: The area for the *pastureland for the city will be 250 cubits* square.

- 48:18: *What remains*, that borders on *the sacred portion* will be *10,000 cubits on the east side and 10,000 cubits on the west side* which will be used for producing food for the workers of the city.
- 48:19: *The workers from the city who farm* the land will *come from all tribes of Israel.*
- 48:20: *The entire* Sacred District *will be a square that is 25,000 cubits on each side. As a special gift, you* (Israel) *will set aside the sacred portion, along with the property of the city.*
- 48:21: The portion described in the previous verse as *the sacred portion and the property of the city will belong to the prince.* The land on the east side and the west side of the temple complex will belong *to the prince.* Also, the temple complex will be in the center of them.
- 48:22: The *property of the Levites and the property of the city will lie in the center of the area that belongs to the prince. The area belonging to the prince will lie between the border of Judah and the border of Benjamin.*
- 48:30: The city will have *exits.*
- 48:31: *The gates on the north side will be the gate of Reuben, the gate of Judah, and the gate of Levi.*
- 48:32: *On the east side will be the gate of Joseph, the gate of Benjamin, and the gate of Dan.*
- 48:33: *On the south side will be the gate of Simeon, the gate of Issachar, and the gate of Zebulun.*
- 48:34: *On the west side will be the gate of Gad, the gate of Asher, and the gate of Naphtali.*
- 48:35: *The distance all around the city will be 18,000 cubits. And the name of the city from that time on will be: THE LORD IS THERE.*

53.3   THE TEMPLE COMPLEX

Core Scripture: Ezekiel 40:1 – 43:27 and 47:1-2

As can be seen in the illustration about the division of the land of Israel among the twelve tribes, there is a portion of the land at the center (between the land allotments for Judah and Benjamin) that is not inherited by one of Jacob's sons. It is an area of land set aside for the mountain, the Sacred District, and land for the princes.

Ezekiel writes in 40:1-4 that God took Ezekiel by the hand and took him in visions to the land of Israel and set him on a very high mountain (another passage that supports the belief that the mountain is a real, literal mountain). The first thing Ezekiel sees are buildings to the south which suggests that God had placed Ezekiel at the location where Jehovah's House (The Millennial Temple) will be in the Sacred District.

Ezekiel then sees a man whose appearance was like bronze who was standing in the gateway (the gateway is probably the east gate) holding a linen cord and a measuring rod in his hand. The man will lead Ezekiel on a tour of the Jehovah's House (see illustration) and he will act as a surveyor and will take the measurements listed in the Bible. The linen cord would be used in the same way as a surveyor's chain is used for measuring long dimensions and distances, and the measuring rod is similar to a yardstick used for measuring short dimensions.

The man then tells Ezekiel, *"Son of Man, look carefully and listen closely and pay attention to everything I am going to show you, for that is why you have been brought here. Tell the people of Israel everything you see."* (Ezekiel 40:4)

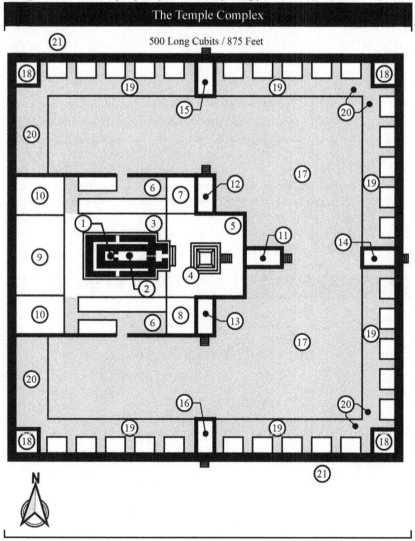

The Temple Complex

500 Long Cubits / 875 Feet

433

1	Holy of Holies – Ezekiel 41:4	11	East Inner Gate – Ezekiel 40:32-34
2	Holy Place – Ezekiel 41:2, 21	12	North Inner Gate – Ezekiel 40:35-37
3	Temple – Ezekiel 40:48 – 41:22, 13-14, 16-26	13	South Inner Gate – Ezekiel 40:28-31
4	Altar – Ezekiel 40:47; 43:13-17	14	East Outer Gate – Ezekiel 40:6-16
5	Inner Court – Ezekiel 40:28-46	15	North Outer Gate – Ezekiel 40:20-23
6	Priest's Chambers and Sacristies – Ezekiel 42:1-14	16	South Outer Gate – Ezekiel 24-27
7	Priest's Who Guard the Temple – Ezekiel 40:44-46	17	Outer Court – Ezekiel 40:6-27
8	Priest's Who Guard the Altar – Ezekiel 40:44-46	18	People's Kitchen (total of four) – Ezekiel 46:21-24
9	The Building of the Separate Place (function not explained) – Ezekiel 41:12-15	19	Outer Court Chambers (total of thirty) – Ezekiel 40:17-19; 41:5-11
10	Priest's Kitchens – Ezekiel 46:29-30	20	The Pavement – Ezekiel 40:18
		21	Outer Wall

The following passages describe what Ezekiel is shown of the Temple Complex by the guide.

+ 40:5 – The Outer Wall: An outer wall surrounds and defines the entire sacred complex.

+ 40:6-16 – The East Gate to the Outer Court: As can be seen from the illustration, the east gate is actually a building instead of just a simple swinging gate. As the guide approaches the gate, he first encounters a series of seven steps and a threshold thereafter. Once inside the gate, in what is probably the gateway, there are three square recesses, alcoves, on each side for a total of six. They serve as guardrooms for security personnel. At the west end of the gate is another threshold which separates the gateway from a portico that included two jambs at the outer court end. While it is unclear, there may be windows in the outside walls. Some portions of the gate were decorated with palm trees.

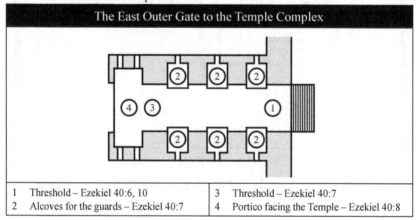

The East Outer Gate to the Temple Complex

1	Threshold – Ezekiel 40:6, 10	3	Threshold – Ezekiel 40:7
2	Alcoves for the guards – Ezekiel 40:7	4	Portico facing the Temple – Ezekiel 40:8

40:17-19 – The Outer Court: Once outside of the east gate and in the outer court, Ezekiel saw thirty rooms, probably chambers, around the perimeter that faced a pavement. The size and shape of the rooms are not recorded. The outer court is for the people.

+ 40:20-23 – The North Gate: This gate is very similar to the east gate.
+ 40:24-27 – The South Gate: This gate is also very similar to the east gate.
+ 40:28-37 – The Gates to the Inner Court: The guide brought Ezekiel to the south gate and said that the gates at the inner court were like the gates at the outer court, except there are eight steps.
+ 40:38-43 – The Rooms for Preparing Sacrifices: By the side of each inner gateway was a doorway that lead to the room to be used for washing the burnt offerings. Within the portico are two tables on each side of the room on which the burnt (primary function was propitiatory, to turn away divine wrath, and expiatory, to atone for sin) purification (also known as a sin offering; primary function was to cleanse sacrificial appurtenances so that other offerings may be received), and reparation (also known as a guilt offering; primary purpose was to make restitution, reparation, for sullying a sacred object or person) offerings were to be slaughtered. The tables, and their respective functions, described in verses 42-42 are somewhat confusing and difficult to visualize. "As one enters the vestibule [portico] one notices four additional tables, two on each side of the doorway, positioned against the inside of the vestibule wall … opposite those visible from the outside. The outside four were probably intended for the actual slaughter of the sacrificial animal (v. 41) and the inside ones for washing. V. 42 describes four of the tables, apparently those visible to the prophet outside."[2] It is also confusing as to which tables were for the utensils.
+ 40:44-46 – The Rooms for the Priests: Two rooms are described, one adjacent to the north gateway that faces south, and the other, adjacent to the south gate facing north. The room facing south is for priests who guard the sanctity of the temple, and the room facing north is for the priests who guard the altar. The only priests that can guard the temple and the altar are the Zadokites, which are of Levitical descent.
+ 40:47 – 41:4 – The Interior Measurements: The guide measured the inner court and found it to be a square, with an altar in front of the temple. The most logical place for the altar is the center of the inner court so that it can be seen through each of the three inner and outer gateways simultaneously. Next, they arrive at the portico of the temple in which the opening between the inner court and the vestibule is wide and it includes two jambs and pillars, and there are stairs that number 10 (possibly). They then moved into the main hall, and after that into the inner sanctum, however, there are no descriptions of decorations, furnishings, or functions of the two rooms.
+ 41:5-12 – The Auxiliary Structures of the Temple: The guide takes measurements of the temple wall and the side rooms in which there are thirty rooms on each of three levels for a total of ninety rooms. Access to the upper floors is by stairs. The temple was on a raised base

which was the foundation for the side rooms. While no other details are given, the building on the west side of the temple was measured.

+ 41:13-15a – The General Dimensions of the Temple Complex: The guide takes more measurements of the temple.

+ 41:15b-26 – The Interior Decorations and Furnishings: Ezekiel describes some of the finishes in the temple. The following were covered in wood: the main hall, the inner sanctuary, the portico facing the court, the thresholds, the narrow windows and galleries, the floor, the wall up to the windows, and the windows. The space above the outside of the entrance to the inner sanctuary was covered with cherubim and palm trees. The walls were covered at regular intervals all around the inner and outer sanctuary with carved cherubim and palm trees with each cherubim having two faces, one face a human being turned to the palm trees on one side and a lion turned to the palm trees on the other side. They were carved all over the temple. The main hall and the Most Holy Place had rectangular door frames and double doors with each door leaf having two hinged doors. There was a wooden altar. There were wooden overhangs and narrow windows.

+ 42:1-14 – The Great Priestly Sacristies: Then the guide led Ezekiel through the north inner gate to the northwestern corner of the outer court among the rooms opposite the outer wall on the north side. This must end the visionary guided tour of the temple complex because there is no further mention of Ezekiel being taken to another place. There was a building that faced north and a gallery that was three levels. Verse 2 to verse 12 is somewhat open to debate because there are references and dimensions of things that cannot be discerned. The subject seems to be the various rooms along the west outer wall. There is an opposite arrangement of rooms north of the south wall. The arrangement of rooms in the illustration is based on the source referenced. However, these rooms were for the priests that approach the Lord (highest order of priests) so that they can eat the most sacred portions of the offerings – the grain offerings, the sin offerings, and the guilt offerings. The priests are not to wear the garments in which they minister into the outer court; they must leave them in these rooms and wear other clothes when they go out into the outer court among the people.

+ 42:15-20 – The Concluding Temple Measurements: After he finished taking measurements, the guide led Ezekiel outside the temple complex through the east outer gateway. The guide then measured the outside dimensions of the temple complex. The functional purpose of the outside walls is that they are "… not constructed to keep enemy forces out … but to protect the sanctity of the sacred area from the pollution of common touch and to prevent the contagion of holiness from touching the people. … In the past priests had failed to maintain the distinction between the holy and profane, but the present structures guard against such abominations under the new order."[3]

+ 43:1-9 – God's Glory Returns to the Temple: The man (presumable the guide) brought Ezekiel to the east gate (most likely the outer gate) and the following happened:

　○ He saw the Glory of the God of Israel coming from the east with a voice like the roar of running water, and the land was radiant with His glory. This was a scene that Ezekiel had seen before in his role as a prophet, except the last time, Ezekiel witnessed the departure of the glory of the Lord form the temple.

　○ The Lord entered the temple through the east gate.

　○ The Spirit of the Lord then lifted Ezekiel up and carried him into the inner court. The glory of the Lord filled the temple.

　○ Ezekiel heard a voice speaking to him from inside the temple, and the voice said:

　　- This is the place of God's throne and the place for the soles of His feet.

　　- This is where He will live among the Israelites forever.

　　- The Israelites, and their kings, will never again defile His holy name, with prostitution and funeral offerings for their kings at their death.

　　- In the past, the Israelites lived adjacent to the temple, they defiled His holy name with detestable things, so He destroyed them in His anger.

　　- If they will put away such practices, God will live among them.

+ 43:10-12 – Epilogue of the Temple Vision: Ezekiel is told to describe the temple to Israel, so that they will be ashamed of their sin. They are to consider the perfection of the temple based on Ezekiel telling them of the whole design, as well as its regulations and laws. Ezekiel is then instructed to write these things down before the Israelites. Ezekiel concludes this portion with the statement: *This is the Torah of the temple. All its surrounding territory at the top of the mountain shall be absolutely holy.*

+ 43:13-17 – The Great Altar Restored: The guide took measurements of the altar that included a lower gutter, a lower ledge, an upper ledge, square altar hearth with an upper gutter around the hearth, four horns projecting upward, and with steps facing east.

+ 43:18-27 – Consecration of the Altar: The Sovereign Lord announces *the regulations for sacrificing burnt offerings and splashing blood against the altar.* The Lord goes on to describe the process of making daily sacrifices, using various animals, for a total of seven days. After the seven-day ritual, the Lord will accept the altar. "This process will mark the full resumption of God's fellowship with His people, as then God will accept them. These sacrifices will point Israelites to Christ who will have given them access to the Father (Heb. 10:19-25)."[4]

+ 47:1-12 – The River from the Temple: The man brought Ezekiel back to the entrance to the temple and he saw water coming out from under the threshold of the temple that flowed east to the south of the altar, the east inner gate, and the east outer gate. After leaving the temple complex, the water flowed south beginning as a trickle that was ankle deep that gradually changed into a river that was too deep and wide to cross except by swimming. At the bank of the river, Ezekiel saw groves of trees on each side of the river as the river flows eastward and eventually empties into the Dead Sea. When it empties, the salty water of the Dead Sea turns fresh. There will be swarms of living creatures that will live in and around the river. Also, fisherman will fish from the abundance of many kinds of fish in the river. Swamps and marshes will remain salty. There will be fruit trees that grow along the banks of the river, and their leaves will not wither, nor will their fruit fail. The fruit trees will bear fruit every month. The leaves will heal and the fruit will serve as food.

Let's take a look at the design of the Temple Complex (see illustration).
- The temple complex is square in plan which speaks to the formality of the complex.
- There is symmetry about the complex on the east to west centerline; the arrangement and sizes of the rooms on the north side are mirror-image on the south side.
- The temple complex is raised on three levels above the surrounding area with each level accessed by stairs. This is somewhat speculation, but the vertical dimension of a stair (known as a riser) is probably about 12 inches which we will use for descriptive purposes. That would make the outer court (7 steps) about 7 feet above the surrounding area, the inner court (8 steps) about 8 feet above the outer court, and the temple (10 steps) about 10 feet above the inner court. This would make the temple about 25 feet above the surrounding area which speaks to the majesty of and reverence for, the temple.
- Through a series of walls and gates, access to the several levels are controlled. The people only have access to the outer court, the Levites and the Zadokites have access to the inner courts, and only the Zadokites have access to the main room of the temple.

53.4 JEHOVAH'S HOUSE –THE MILLENNIAL TEMPLE

Core Scripture: Ezekiel 40:48 – 41:26

During the Millennium, in order for the Lord to live among His chosen people, a temple will be necessary that will become the center of the millennial earth. For reasons that are not disclosed in the Bible, there is Scripture devoted to dimensions of the temple and the description of the rooms, walls, entries, and the temple. The inclusion of so many details raises the question of who will build the temple. If God is going to provide the temple, then the details are not necessary, however, if humans are going to build the temple then the details would be necessary.

The Promise of a Temple
"Several Old Testament prophets predicted that during the millennium, Israelite believers will worship God in a way that requires a new Temple."[5]
- Isaiah:
  - + 2:2-4: Ezekiel saw that, *In the last days the mountain of the Lord's temple will be established; as the highest of the mountains,* and will have the following characteristics:

Characteristics of Jehovah's House - Millennium Temple	
it will be exalted above the hills	*the word of the Lord from Jerusalem*
all nations will stream to it	*He will judge between the nations*
the mountain of the Lord	*will settle disputes for many people*
the temple of the God of Jacob	*they will beat their swords into plowshares*
He will teach us his ways	*and their spears into pruning hooks*
so that we may walk in his paths	*nation will not take up sword against nation*
the law will go out from Zion	*nor will they train for war anymore*

  - + 60:7, 13: The offer of sacrifices and various woods will *adorn the sanctuary.*
- Jeremiah 33:18: In describing loyalty to God, never *will the Levitical priests ever fail to have a man to stand before me continuous to offer burnt offerings, to burn grain offerings and to present sacrifices.*
- Ezekiel:
  - + 37:26-28: God says to Israel, *I will make a covenant of peace with them; it will be an everlasting covenant. I will establish them and increase their numbers, and I will put my sanctuary among them forever. My dwelling place will be with them; I will be their God, and they will be my people. Then the nations will know that I the Lord make Israel holy, when my sanctuary is among them forever.*
  - + 43:1-7: Refer to Ezekiel 37:1-9 and details above.
- Joel 3:18: *A fountain will flow out of the Lord's house as will water the valley of the acacias.*

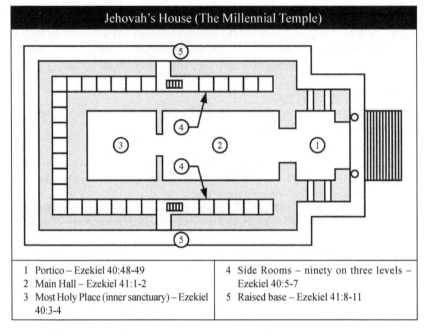

Jehovah's House (The Millennial Temple)

1 Portico – Ezekiel 40:48-49	4 Side Rooms – ninety on three levels –
2 Main Hall – Ezekiel 41:1-2	Ezekiel 40:5-7
3 Most Holy Place (inner sanctuary) – Ezekiel 40:3-4	5 Raised base – Ezekiel 41:8-11

- Haggai 2:9: In discussing the future, the Lord Almighty says *the glory of this present house will be greater than the glory of the former house; and in this place I will grant peace.*

Zechariah 6:12-13: This passage is probably foreseeing that the Branch, Jesus Christ, *will build the* Millennial *Temple of the Lord. He will be clothed with majesty and will sit and rule on his throne, and he will be a priest on his throne. And there will be harmony between the two.*

53.5   JEHOVAH SHAMMAH – THE MILLENNIAL CITY OF NEW JERUSALEM

There is a place in the Sacred District for the millennial city of New Jerusalem. The Bible does not indicate what the relationship will be between the centuries old Jerusalem and Jehovah Shammah (the New Jerusalem). It may not continue to exist because of the millennial mountain or it may continue to exist but under another name. But we do know that the Millennial City of New Jerusalem will be in the Sacred District at the top of the mountain.

According to Ezekiel 48:34, the name of the Millennial City of New Jerusalem will be Jehovah Shammah, which means Jehovah is there. "Since the Messianic God-Man will personally reign from this particular city, the city will not only fulfill its name of Jerusalem (the city of peace), but also Jehovah Shammah (Jehovah is there). For this same reason the city will also be called Jehovah our Righteousness according to Jeremiah 33:16."[6]

The Bible has the following to say about the New Jerusalem:

- The Psalms:
  + 48:1-3: Psalm 48 is a song about Zion, the city of God, and its glory and security. Beautiful in elevation, the city will be the joy of the whole earth. *God has shown himself to be her fortress.*
  + 48:11-13: Mount Zion will rejoice because of His judgments, and its inhabitants are urged to study *the beauty of the city.*
  + 87:1-7: God founded the *city on the holy mountain. Glorious things are said of* the *city of God.* Nations will be gathered to Zion and *Rehab* (representing *Egypt*), *Babylon, Philistia,* Phoenicia (represented by *Tyre*), and *Cush* acknowledged God. God's writing their names in a *register of the peoples* figuratively that they will have a place in Zion.
  + 122:1-9: A song of David in which he expressed *delight in going up to Jerusalem.* David briefly described the city and then acclaimed it for its physical splendor, lauded it as the spiritual center, and cited it as the seat of justice. God instructed them to pray for peace and security for Jerusalem. God will seek prosperity for the sake of the sanctuary.
  + 147:2-3: *The Lord builds up Jerusalem; he gathers the exiles of Israel. He heals the brokenhearted and binds up their wounds.*
  + 147:12-14: Jerusalem is called upon to praise the Lord who gave them security, *peace,* and *the finest of wheat.*
  + 147:15: The Lord *sends His commands* (Kingdom Law) *to the earth; his word runs swiftly.*
  + 147:19-20: God *revealed His word* only *to Jacob* (Israel), *no other nations.*
- Isaiah:
  + 1:26-27: See above.
  + 4:3-6: Surviving Israel will be holy, not marked by wealth or prestige, and their sins will be forgotten. The *filth of the women of Zion* will be washed away by the Lord; God *will cleanse the bloodstains from Jerusalem by a spirit of judgment and a spirit of fire.* In a future time of blessing, God's glory will be visible when the redeemed nation will be their promised land.
  + 14:32: *The Lord has established Zion, and in her his afflicted people will find refuge.*
  + 33:20-24: "Quietness and security will characterize Jerusalem in that day (v. 20), for Jehovah in the Person of the Messiah will dwell in this city (v. 21a). It will be a city of many streams and waters, but without any ships of war ever sailing in them (v. 21b). The Messiah in the midst of the city will serve as the Judge, Lawgiver, King, and Savior (v. 22), and so Israel's sins will be totally forgiven (vv. 23-24)."[7]
  + 52:1: God instructs Zion to awake, and put on their garments of splendor, the holy city of Jerusalem. No longer will the uncircumcised or defiled enter the city again.

+ 52:7-10: This passage foreshadows Messiah's return to Jerusalem to proclaim *salvation* and to bring *peace*. The people of Jerusalem will *shout for joy* because they are *comforted* and *redeemed*. God's grace will show His power to *all the nations* and the *salvation* He offers.

+ 60:10-14: The foremost nation in the economic, social, and religious structures of the world will be Israel. In contrast with His earlier *anger*, evidence of God's *favor and compassion* will be the *foreigners* and *kings* that will contribute to the rebuilding of Jerusalem's *walls*. There will be a constant flow of *wealth* into the city, and any *nation* that might try to rise up against Israel will be defeated by God. Various woods from *Lebanon* will be installed in the temple to *adorn* God's *sanctuary* which is where the Lord resides. Other nations will realize that *Zion* is God's chosen city.

+ 62:1-12: The Lord says that He will continue to work on *Jerusalem* until her *vindication, salvation and glory* can be seen by the nations of the world. Jerusalem will be *called by a new name* which means it will have a new righteous character. Jerusalem will be an adornment to *the Lord* and the city will display His *splendor* and the inhabitants will manifest His character in their conduct. The new name of the city will be Hephzibah (which means My delight is in her) and Beulah (which means married one). Devoutly righteous Israelites will be like *watchmen* (in ancient times, watchmen would be stationed on the wall to watch for enemies) who will be on alert and were to hold God to His promises. *Pass through, pass through* and *build up, build up* suggest a sense of urgency for the people are to prepare for the Lord's coming. When the Lord comes, word is to go throughout the world that God has come to bless Jerusalem.

+ 65:18-19: *But be glad and rejoice forever in what I will create, for I will create Jerusalem to be a delight and its people a joy. I will rejoice over Jerusalem and take delight in my people; the sound of weeping and of crying will be heard in it no more.*

+ 66:10-14: The Lord says to rejoice in the restoration of Jerusalem and to delight in her as an infant does in her mother's sustenance. As said many times in Isaiah, peace will come to Jerusalem and the nations' wealth will flow to her.

• Jeremiah:
  + 3:17: *At that time they will call Jerusalem The Throne of the Lord, and all nations will gather in Jerusalem to honor the name of the Lord. No longer will they follow the stubbornness of their evil hearts.*
  + 31:6: At the time of restoration, *there will be a day when watchmen on the hills of Ephraim, Come, let us go up to Zion to the Lord our God.*
  + 31:38-40: The Lord indicates that in the future, the city of Jerusalem *will be rebuilt* for Him and for His people. There is discussion about the changing of the city boundaries. God then describes two characteristics

of the new city, that it will *be holy to the Lord*, and that it *will never again be uprooted or demolished.*

+ 33:9-11: The Lord says that this city will bring *renown, joy, praise, and honor* to Him *before all nations on earth* because they hear of *all the good things* God does for them; and the nations will be *in awe and will tremble at the abundant prosperity and peace* that God provides. The *Lord says* that *the towns of Judah and the streets of Jerusalem* will once again hear *the sounds of joy and gladness, the voices of bride and bridegroom, and the voices of those who bring thank offerings to the house of the Lord*, and will no longer be *deserted* and without inhabitants. Those that bring thank offerings will say, "*Give thanks to the Lord Almighty, for the Lord is good; his love endures forever.*"

- Joel 3:17: "*Then you will know that I, the Lord your God, dwell in Zion, my holy hill Jerusalem will be holy; never again will foreigners invade her.*"
- Micah 4:6-8: "*In that day,*" the Lord *will gather the lame, will assemble the exiles and those I have brought to grief,* He *will make the lame* His *remnant*, and will make them *a strong nation. The Lord will rule over them in Mount Zion forever.*
- Zephaniah 3:14-17: This passage is one of exaltation and joy; Israel will be joyful because she will have been redeemed in the Millennium. A day will come when the fears of the remnant will become songs of praise. Israel will give praise because her redeemer, the Messiah King, will be in their midst and she will have no *fear*. Calmness will prevail. They will be encouraged to not to be in despair or fearful, but instead hold their hands high as a symbol of triumph because of the Lord's presence. The nation will once again be the object of God's love and not His wrath.
- Zechariah:
  + 1:14-17: *Therefore this is what the Lord says; I will return to Jerusalem with mercy, and there my home will be rebuilt. And the measuring line will be stretched out over Jerusalem, declares the Lord Almighty. Proclaim further: This is what the Lord Almighty says: My towns will again overflow with prosperity, and the Lord will again comfort Zion and choose Jerusalem.*
  + 2:1-5: Isaiah saw *a man with a measuring line* who was going out *to measure Jerusalem, to find out how wide and how long it is*. Isaiah was told by a second angel that *'Jerusalem will be a city without walls because of the great number of people and animals in it. And I myself will be a wall of fire around it,'* declares the Lord, *'and I will be its glory within.'*
  + 2:10-12: "*Shout and be glad, Daughter Zion. For I am coming, and I will live among you,*" declares the Lord. *Many nations will be joined with the Lord in that day and will become my people. I will live among you and you will know that the Lord Almighty has sent me to you. The Lord will inherit Judah as his portion in the holy land and will again choose Jerusalem.*

+ 8:1-8: God is *jealous for Zion* (Jerusalem) and He says when He returns He will *dwell in Jerusalem. Then Jerusalem will be called the Faithful City, and the mountain of the Lord Almighty will be called the Holy Mountain.* People of a *ripe old age will sit in the streets* and they will be filled with children playing. *The Lord* says He will *save* His *people from the countries* in all directions and He *will bring them back to live in Jerusalem* (Israel) and they will be His *people* and He will be *their God.*

+ 8:20-22: The Lord says that *many people and powerful nations will come to Jerusalem to entreat Him.*

+ 14:9-11: *The Lord will be king over the whole earth.* The lands surrounding Jerusalem will be made into a plain, yet Jerusalem in its totality will be *raised up. Jerusalem will be secure* never to be destroyed again.

+ 14:20-21: "In *that day* holiness will characterize millennial life (cf. 8:3) whether it be public life (*the bells of the horses*), religious life (*the cooking pots in the Lord's house*, the millennial temple, Ezek. 40 – 43), or private life (*every pot in Jerusalem and Judah*). Perhaps the general thought is the removal of a dichotomy between secular and sacred. ... Because He is *the Lord Almighty* and the Holy One, He will establish holiness throughout the glorious Millennium!"[8]

53.6   THE PRIESTHOOD AND SACRIFICES IN THE MILLENNIUM RESTORED

Core Scripture: Ezekiel 44:1 – 46:24

Because there will be a new temple during the Millennium, the priesthood and the sacrificial system will need to be restored since it had not existed since 70 AD, except for a short time during Daniel's 70th week. Fruchtenbaum says, "... the millennial system of priesthood and sacrifice must not be viewed as a reinstitution of the Law of Moses, which ended permanently and forever with the death of the Messiah. During the Millennial Kingdom, a whole new system of law, Kingdom Law, will be instituted. There will be no reinstitution of any precious code of law."[9]

The ark of the covenant, while was present in the Solomonic Temple, will not be present in the Millennial Temple, see Jeremiah 3:16, because the tablets that embodied the Law of Moses are no longer necessary because the Mosaic Law is no longer in affect because of the death of Christ on the cross and His resurrection did away with the law. God Himself in the Person of the Messiah will be dwelling in and reigning from Jerusalem.

"... [T]here will be a sacrificial systems instituted in the Millennium that will have some features similar to the Mosaic system, along with some brand-new laws. For that very reason, the sacrificial system of the Millennium must not be viewed as a reinstatement of the Mosaic system, because it is not. It will be a brand-new system that will contain some things old, and some things new, and will be instituted for an entirely different purpose."[10]

- Ezekiel:
    + 44:1-3 – The Regulations of the Outer Eastern Gate: In the Millennium, the Shechinah Glory of the Lord will return to the Millennial Temple and enter through the outer eastern gate, and after which the gate will be closed, never to be opened again. This will symbolize that the Shechinah glory will never leave the Millennial Temple. Then, Ezekiel will explain the relationship the outer eastern gate will have with the prince, which will be the resurrected David who will eat before the gate on the porch of the gate. Since the gate is permanently closed, access to the porch will be via the outer court.
    + 44:4-6a – Give Attention to Instruction: The guide brought Ezekiel to the north gate and Ezekiel looked and saw the Temple filled with the glory of the Lord and he fell facedown. *The Lord said, Son of Man, look carefully, listen closely, and give attention to everything I tell you concerning all the regulations and instructions regarding the temple of the Lord.* The Lord instructed him to give attention go the entrances and exits to the sanctuary.
    + 44:6b-8 – The Violation of Sacred Space: Continuing from the previous verse: *Enough of your detestable practices, people of Israel! In addition to all your other detestable practices, you brought foreigners uncircumcised in heart and flesh into my sanctuary, desecrating my temple while you offered me food, fat and blood, and you broke my covenant. Instead of carrying out your duty in regard to my holy things, you put others in charge of my sanctuary.*
    + 44:9-14 – The Role of the Levites: *This is what the Sovereign Lord says, No foreigner uncircumcised in heart and flesh is to enter my sanctuary, not even the foreigners who live among the Israelites.* He essentially restricted anyone from outside the covenant from entering the Temple. The Lord says that the Levites departed from Him when Israel went astray and followed after their idols; they must bear the consequences of their sins. Therefore, they may serve in God's sanctuary: *Having charge of the gates of the temple and serving* in them (guard duty); slaughtering *the burnt offering and sacrifices for the people and stand before the people and serve them.* However, since they previously *served* the people *in the presence of their idols and made the people of Israel fall into sin*, they must pay the consequences. The Levites are not to approach the Lord, serve Him, or come near any of the Lord's holy things or His most holy offerings. *They must bear the shame of their detestable practices. The Lord will appoint them to guard the temple for all the work that is to be done in it.*
    + 44:15-16 – The Role of the Zadokites: Because of their long-term devotion to the Lord, the Zadokites are allowed to come near the Lord

445

and to minister before Him. They are *to offer sacrifices of fat and blood* to the *Sovereign Lord*. The Zadokites alone can come close to the Lord, to minister at His tables, and serve as guards to Him.

+ 44:17-27 – Practical Instructions for the Zadokites: The Lord provides the following rules (some lifted out of the Mosaic Torah) to demonstrate holiness in their respective conduct and the guard the sanctity of the sacred place:

  o Clothing: They are to wear linen clothes, no woolen garments, inside the temple or out in the inner court, and they are to wear linen turbans and undergarments. The linen garments are to be worn while functioning in an official capacity. *They must not wear anything that makes them perspire.* Like other bodily excrements, sweat was considered defilement (Deuteronomy 23:12-14). When they go out into the outer court, they are to wear another set of clothes and leave their other clothes, worn in the inner court, in the sacred rooms so that people are not consecrated through contact with their garments. " … [W]earing sacred vestments out among the people would violate the holiness of the temple by distributing its sanctity … Just as communicable diseases are spread by germs or viruses, so holiness may attach itself to a person. While the people were charged to live ethically holy lives, contact with holy objects was a strict taboo. … While Ezekiel was undoubtedly aware of the lethal consequences of holy contagion, his present concern is not the potential victims but protecting the sanctity of the sanctuary."[11]

  o Personal Habits: *They must not shave their heads or let their hair grown long,* but in any case their hair must be trimmed. The priest must not drink wine when they enter the inner court (recognition of the debilitating effects of alcohol on the mind). Regarding marriage, they *must not marry widows or divorced women,* but *only virgins of Israelite descent or widows of priests.*

  o Teaching the Israelites: They are to teach God's people the dif*ferences between the holy and the common* and *how to distinguish between the unclean and the clean.*

  o Justice: Charged with the responsibility for the administration of justice, they *are to serve as judges and decide* disputes *according to my ordinances*; they *are to keep* God's *laws and* His *decrees for all the appointed festivals, and they are to keep* His *Sabbath holy.*

  o Defilement: To maintain priestly purity, they *are not to defile himself by going near a dead person,* except defilement is acceptable when the person is a close family member. After cleansing, the priest is to w*ait seven days.* On the seventh day, the priest is to enter *the inner court* and is *to offer a sin offering for himself.*

+ 44:28-31 – The Special Status of the Zadokites: The Lord said, "*I am to be the only inheritance the priest have. You are to give them no possession in Israel; I will be their possession. They will eat the grain offerings, the sin offerings and the guilt offerings; and everything in Israel devoted to the Lord will belong to them. The best of all the firstfruits and of all your special gifts will belong to the priests. You are to give them the first portion of your ground meal so that a blessing may rest on your household. The priests must not eat anything, whether bird or animal, found dead or torn by wild animals.*

+ 45:8b-9 – A Challenge for Princes: *The Sovereign Lord says* the *princes of Israel have gone far enough* and that they should *no longer oppress* God's *people* but instead *allow* them to *possess the land according to their tribes.* The Lord continues: *Give up your violence and oppression and do what is just and right. Stop dispossessing* God's *people.* Political leaders confiscated real estate of the common people. "In v. 9 Yahweh appeals to the princes directly, in the second person, top stop their abusive behavior, specified as violence, oppression, and expulsion of the people from their land. He calls for a new commitment to justice and righteousness, viz., the maintenance of Yahweh's covenant standards, especially the protection of the rights of the weak."[12]

+ 45:10-12 – A Business Ordinance: In that environment, there were a lack of technical standards for weights and measures and thus, there was an economic temptation for merchants to cheat those buying goods by embellishing the readings of the weights and measures through dishonesty. The idea here is that the Lord, through Ezekiel, tells the merchants that they should be honest and use the proper weights and measures.

+ 45:13-17 – An Offering Ordinance: After chastising the princes of Israel for not being honest in their use of weights and measures, Ezekiel turns to describing the future sacrificial rituals and responsibilities. Ezekiel listed the amounts that the people were required to tithe for the use of the prince of Israel. The prince will collect all their gifts and, as their representative, use them *to provide the burnt offerings, grain offerings and drink offerings at the festivals, the New Moons and the Sabbaths – at all the appointed festivals of Israel. He will provide the sin offerings and fellowship offerings, burnt offerings and fellowship offerings to make atonement for the Israelites.*

+ 45:18-25 – The New Passover: The Sovereign Lord provides detailed instructions about which animals were to be sacrificed, the procedures for doing so, and when the sacrifices were to be made for the following festivals:
   ○ The New Year feast (verses 18-20), is to *purify the sanctuary* and to forgive if someone sins unintentionally.
   ○ The Passover/Unleavened Bread feast (verses 21-24), lasting *seven days.*

- o The Feast of Tabernacles (verse 25), lasting *seven days.*
- + 46:1-15 – Other Festivals: Again, *the Sovereign Lord says* several things in this passage. The inner east gate is to be open on *the Sabbath day and on the day of the New Moon.* The prince, David, is allowed to access and move around this gateway. The priests will make offerings for the prince.
- + 46:16-18 – Regulations Regarding Management of Royal Lands: The management of the land is established on the basis that all the land belongs to God that is appropriated to Israel as His stewards. "Another topic related to freewill gifts is the Year of Jubilee. Every 50 years property was to revert to its original owners (Lev. 25:10-13). Ezekiel posed two hypothetical cases based on the generosity of the prince to show that the Year of Jubilee will be in force during the Millennium. *If the prince* will give part of his estate *to one of his sons, it will also belong to his descendants.* Property given to a family member will not be returned in the Year of Jubilee. *However ... a gift* made to a servant will not be permanent; *the servant may keep it until the year of freedom; then it will revert to the prince.* ... This regulation assures that no one individual will gain permanent control of the land."[13]
- + 46:19-24 – The Temple Kitchens: The man guiding Ezekiel around the temple complex brought him first to the priests' kitchens located at the west end of the priests' chambers. *The priests will cook the guilt offering and the sin offering ... to avoid bringing them into the outer court and consecrating the people.* Second, Ezekiel was brought to the *kitchens* for the sacrifices of the people that were *in the four corners of the outer court.* The priests' *will cook* the people's *sacrifices.*

53.7	WHY ANIMAL SACRIFICE IN THE MILLENNIAL AGE?

When Jesus Christ died on the cross as the ultimate sacrifice, the need for animal sacrifice was no longer necessary in the temple. So why would animal sacrifice be necessary in the Millennium to provide an expiation for sin? Fruchtenbaum[14] proposes four reasons to take Ezekiel literally:

- • Dispensationalists take the literal approach consistently and as such takes the position that there will be Millennial Temple and sacrificial system.
- • Other prophets spoke of the Millennial Temple:
  - + Isaiah:
    - o 2:3: *Many people will come and say, Come, let us go up to the mountain of the Lord, to the temple of the God of Jacob. He will teach us his ways, so that we may walk in his paths. The law will go out from Zion, the word of the Lord from Jerusalem.*
    - o 60:13: *The glory of Lebanon will come to you, the juniper, the fir and the cypress together, to adorn my sanctuary; and I will glorify the place for my feet.*

+ Daniel 9:24: *Seventy 'sevens' are decreed for your people and your holy city to finish transgression, to put an end to sin, to atone for wickedness, to seal up vision and prophecy and to anoint the Most Holy Place.*
+ Joel 3:18: This passage is discussed in considerably more detail above.
+ Haggai 2:7, 9: *The Lord says, I will shake all nations, and what is desired by all nations, and what is desired by all nations will come, and I will fill the house with glory, says the Lord Almighty. ... The glory of this present house will be greater than the glory of the former house, says the Lord Almighty. And in this place I will grant peace, declares the Lord Almighty.*
- If what Ezekiel said about the Shechinah Glory leaving the First Temple (Ezekiel 8–11) can be taken literally, then what he said about the Millennial Temple can be taken as literal as well as the return of the Shechinah Glory to the Millennial Temple.
- Ezekiel provides an extensive amount of specific measurements for the Tabernacle and the Millennial Temple which can be taken as literal.

The prophets also saw that animal sacrifice would also be included in the worship at the Millennial Temple.
- Isaiah:
  + 56:6-7: *Burnt offerings and sacrifices will be accepted on* the Lord's *altar* at His house.
  + 60:7: *All Kedar's flocks will be gathered to you, the rams of Nebaioth will serve you; they will be accepted as offerings on my altar, and I will adorn my glorious temple.*
  + 66:18-23: God-sent messengers will bring Israelites that had been scattered to many nations back to God. The messengers will bring them to God's *holy mountain as an offering to the Lord*, just *like the Israelites bring their grain offering to the temple of the Lord* ...
- Jeremiah 33:17-18: *For this is what the Lord says: "David will never fail to have a man to sit on the throne of Israel, nor will the Levitical priests ever fail to have a man to stand before me continually to offer burnt offerings, to burn grain offerings and to present sacrifices.'*
- Malachi 3:3-4: *Then the Lord will have men who will bring offerings in righteousness, and the offerings of Judah and Jerusalem will be acceptable to the Lord, as in days gone by ...*

54

THE LAST REBELLION

We know from the Bible that humankind is sinful both by practice and by nature. There will be people born during the Millennium that will be prone to sinfulness in spite of Jesus being on the throne. "During the Messianic kingdom, people who haven't yet been glorified will still have sinful natures, but the perfect world around them will offer no enticement to sin, nor will Satan and his demons be around to tempt them either."[1] At or very near the end of the one-thousand-year millennium, there will be sufficient sin in the world so that when Satan is released, he will gather the sinful together and will rebel against Jesus and those that are living righteous lives. This will be his last stand.

54.1 SATAN LOOSED FROM IMPRISONMENT

Core Scripture: Revelation 20:3 and 7.

The last three chapters of the book of Revelation describe the manner in which human existence and the physical universe will change and several passages in Revelation 20 details what the Apostle John is shown regarding the final days of Satan, which begins with his release from confinement. While we are told that an angel originally seized, bound, and then threw Satan into the confinement, we are not told who releases him or what the circumstance will be.

- Revelation 20:3: As a parenthetical comment, John footnotes the seizing, binding, and confinement of Satan to the prison abyss as being only for a short period of time, after which he must be released, the implication being that he is restored to something of his former position. It is interesting that the operative word in the passage and this comment is 'must' which speaks to the necessity, divine destiny or unavoidable fate of something.[2]
- Revelation 20:7: John records more specifically that Satan will be released from his confinement after the one-thousand-year reign of Christ is finished and the Theocratic Kingdom has run its allotted time. The sense of the passage indicates that the release is not only physical, but he is allowed to exert his demonic and deceptive influence once again on those mortal human beings that have chosen a life of rebellion rather than a life of righteousness.

54.2 WHY RELEASE SATAN?

The obvious question that arises at this point is: Why would God find it necessary to release Satan from a secure confinement (Revelation 20:3 uses the word *must* which implies God is obligated in some way)? There are many who do not know why God would find it necessary to release Satan from a secure confinement that virtually eliminates his demonic influence. Walvoord[3] summarizes four possible reasons:

- "to demonstrate that man even under the most favorable circumstances will fall into sin if left to his own choice;
- to demonstrate the foreknowledge of God who foretells the acts of men as well as His own acts;
- to demonstrate the incurable wickedness of Satan;
- to justify eternal punishment, that is, to show the unchanged character of wicked people even under divine jurisdiction for a long period of time."

MacLeod makes several observations about what these events demonstrate:

- About Satan: "As soon as he is released, he will demonstrate that neither his plans nor his nature have changed."[4]
- About Humankind: "This final chapter in the world's history will again demonstrate that people perpetually embrace evil unless sustained by sovereign grace."[5]
- About the Continuation of History:
  + "One of the reasons for the continuation of history [into a golden age for humankind after the Lord's Second Advent] is that God is demonstrating man's utter ruin in sin and his responsibility for the evil state of the world."[6]
  + "And so at last, during the millennial kingdom, God will place the human race in a world without Satan. It will be a world in which Jesus Christ will reside on the earth in His physical, visible, glorious body. It will be a perfect environment, with disease curtailed. But the problem of humanity will not be the environment, or chromosomes, or even the devil."[7]
- About Human Sinfulness: "The Apostle Paul wrote that the day will come when "every mouth" will be stopped (Rom. 3:19). Yet up until this very moment people's mouths have not been stopped because they either suppress their sense of sin or else excuse themselves."[8]

Pentecost[9] provides the more formal dispensational answers and observations:

- Pentecost indicates that the purpose for Satan's release is revealed by what he does immediately after his release, to deceive humankind and to revolt against God, which becomes just one more test, albeit the final test this time, to demonstrate the corruption and depravity of the human heart. God has subjected collective humankind to every conceivable test possible - innocence (freedom), conscience (self-determination), human (civil) government, promise (patriarchal rule), law (legalism), grace (church), and now the kingdom (glory) - but each time humankind has failed to develop the kind of kingdom, or governing structure, God wants for His creatures.

- "The purpose for which Satan was released, then, was to demonstrate that, even when tested under the reign of the King and the revelation of His holiness, man is a failure. While those going into the millennium were saved, they were not perfected. The progeny born to them during the millennium age were born with the same fallen sin nature with which their parents were born and consequently needed regeneration. During the administration of the King, in which He ruled with a 'rod of iron,' outward conformity to His law was necessary. The binding of Satan, the removal of external sources of temptation, the fullness of knowledge, the bountiful provision from the King, caused many, whose hearts had not been regenerated, to give this required conformity to the law of the King. There must be a test to determine the true heart condition to the law of the King."[10]

- Nevertheless, after Satan is released, he organizes a militant force from the apparent unrepentant nations of the earth and attempts, one more time, to displace God and steal His throne. This all in spite of the benevolence of God, the benefits of living in God's Theocratic Kingdom, the blessed provision of Jesus Christ, and the golden age for humankind - the human heart of many of Jesus Christ, and the golden age for humankind - the human heart of many will be so corrupt as to metaphorically shake their fist at their Creator.

- However, judgment comes to Satan, and all the people of his forces, and within a short period of time, and to all that had been unrighteous.

So the answer to the question of why God would find it necessary to release Satan is wrapped up, in part, with the reasoning for a golden age for humankind where the Lord is physically present and actively ruling. It is a test to demonstrate to humankind, now for the last time, that while even in His presence without obedience to Him and His gracious provision of divine values, blessed laws, and sovereign authority, humankind is utterly unable and completely incapable of organizing, managing, and governing themselves individually, culturally, socially and corporately - when left to their own humanistic efforts, humankind fails to achieve holiness and righteousness in the sight of the Lord.

54.3   SATAN LEADS THE FINAL REBELLION AGAINST GOD

Core Scripture: Revelation 20:8-9.

" ... God will use Satan in the closing events of world history to demonstrate once and for all the depravity and moral corruption of the human race."[11]

REVELATION 20:8

"On being relieved from his confinement, Satan loses no time in resuming his nefarious activities and plunges into his campaign to deceive the nations of the entire earth."[12] Unreformed, unchanged and certainly unrepentant, Satan aggressively returns to his original state of doing everything in his power to create a counterfeit kingdom to replace God by deceiving the various peoples and nations of the earth.

There are several observations that may be made because of the mention of Gog and Magog and the sense is that they are not the same Gog and Magog of Ezekiel 38 and 39:

- There are no contextual details for rebellious nations to the north in Revelation as there are in Ezekiel.
- There is a one-thousand-year separation between fulfillment of the Ezekiel prophecies and fulfillment of the Revelation prophecies.
- In Ezekiel, Gog is a nation to the north that actually invades Israel, while the use of Gog in Revelation seems to be to nations at large over the entire earth.
- As we have seen in Chapter 35, the people of Gog and Magog in Ezekiel who invade Israel are supernaturally killed, and then buried while within the nation of Israel, while in Revelation they are completely consumed by fire.
- Satan is mentioned as part of the invasion in Revelation, while he is not mentioned in the Ezekiel account.
- The revelation in Revelation is from all directions, while the invasion in Ezekiel is from the north.
- The Ezekiel account is within the context of the greater Campaign of Armageddon, while in Revelation there is no mention of any other conflicts; it stands alone.
- The Ezekiel account is accompanied by earthquakes, hail, and other disaster which are not mentioned in the Revelation account.

The passage indicates that the number of rebels will be *like the sand on the seashore*, giving a clear indication that sin will have grown to such an extent as to be national in significance. This also substantiates the notion that there will be many during the Millennium that will outwardly show obedience to Jesus' rule, but inwardly will be consumed with rebellious ideas of how to resist Him.

The passage does not indicate how Satan will deceive, or mislead, the nations. The implication is that he will probably convince those resisting the Lord's rule, those already unrighteous, and those leaning toward their depraved human nature that if they join his cause (apparently a military effort), they can overthrow the Lord and His government and replace it with their own. Thus, they would receive all the power, glory, and honor that would have gone to the Lord.

REVELATION 20:9

Satan will lead a military force against the beloved city but they will be destroyed.

- The Military Forces of the Nations: "It is amazing to think that human beings who have lived on earth with the King of kings and Lord of lords will actually mobilize for war against Him. But again, this shows the depravity of the human heart."[13] While the participating nations of the invading forces are not identified, the implication is that many of the nations of the earth comprise the forces. The forces are recorded as being numerous therefore they will be of sufficient size and destructive capability for Satan to believe that he can overthrow the Lord and all that is in the city. There is no indication that there will be a military force that will oppose Satan, and as will be seen, there will be no need for one.
- Satan's Invasion Strategy: Satan's military strategy will be to marshal the forces to surround the camp of the saints and the beloved city.
- The Camp of the Saints: The Greek word translated as camp refers to those who are in a battle array such as in a fortress or citadel, or warriors gathered in a camp in anticipation of a battle. This suggests that Satan's military attack will not come as a surprise to Jesus or to the city - they will be prepared in spite of the fact that God the Father will destroy the invaders.
- The Beloved City: The only city that this could be is Jerusalem, most probably because for one thousand years it has been the location of the Lord's throne and the spiritual center of the world.
- Destruction of the Forces: The Apostle John records the outcome of the confrontation; rather than a prolonged battle with death on both sides, God supernaturally destroys Satan's forces by fire From heaven, the extent of which is described as He completely destroys them.

"Thus is shattered the last vain attempt of Satan to claim a place of prominence and worship in attempted usurpation of the prerogatives of God. Thus ends also the false theory that man under perfect environment will willingly serve the God who created and redeemed him. Even in the ideal situation of the millennial reign of Christ, innumerable hosts immediately respond to the first temptation to rebel. This is the end of the road for the nations who rebel against God as well as for the career of Satan."[14]

54.4 SATAN'S FINAL DOOM

Core Scripture: Revelation 20:10.

After the utter destruction of the last military effort to overthrow the Lord's theocratic rule over Israel and humankind, in divine judgment of Satan, identified here as *the devil who deceived them*, into the same place in which the beast (the Antichrist) and the False Prophet have resided for one thousand years, the lake of fire and sulfur, the place of eternal residence prepared for all that are wicked, unrighteous, and rebellious against God (refer to Matthew 25:41).

Once in the lake of dreadful damnation, the three that comprised the False Trinity will be tortured and tormented every day and night forever and ever - the words and phrases used to describe the time aspect emphasizes it eternally as well as it certainty. The "fire denotes the searing holiness of God through which He exacts retribution for sin and rejection (Hebrews 10:30; Revelation 14:9-11)."[15]

Satan's permanent confinement in the lake of fire and sulfur also proves that he is a created being and not a god.

This verse rejects the idea that annihilation follows death: if the Unholy Trinity is not annihilated, then there is nothing to support that the wicked dead will be annihilated either.

55

THE GREAT WHITE THRONE JUDGMENT

The last prophetic revelation, recorded in Revelation 20:11-15, that the Apostle John sees before the creation of the new earth and the new heavens is the wicked and unrighteous dead standing before the Lord who is sitting on the large white throne. As listed in Chapter 45, this will be the eighth of nine judgments to occur in history since Christ's crucifixion.

55.1	SCRIPTURE CONCERNING A FUTURE JUDGMENT

Some of the passages that speak to the future judgment of humankind, or a destiny in heaven or hell, include the following:
- Psalm 96:13: God will someday come to judge fairly the earth, the world and the nations.
- Ecclesiastes 12:14: The Book of Ecclesiastes closed with the verse that says that every good deed or bad deed will be accountable to God someday.
- Daniel 12:2: After death, some will go to everlasting life and some will go to everlasting abhorrence.
- Matthew 25:46: After His return to earth and as the consequence of the judgment of the Gentiles, the Sheep and Goat Judgment, the passage ends with a reiteration that the righteous go to eternal life and the unrighteousness go to eternal punishment.
- Acts 17:31: Paul tells the intellectuals of Athens that God has set a day in which the world will be judged by One designated by Him that was authenticated by the fact that He was raised from an earthly death.
- 2 Timothy 4:1: Again, Paul identifies Jesus Christ as the one that will judge the living and the dead.
- Hebrews 9:27: This passage is discussed in considerably more detail above.

55.2	THE THRONE IN THE BOOK OF REVELATION

Before discussing the Great White Throne, it is helpful to look at the other references to thrones in the Book of Revelation:
- 1:4: John indicates that the authority for his letters to the seven churches is given him by God, Jesus Christ (verse 5), and the seven spirits that stand before God's throne.
- 3:21: In His message to the Church at Laodica, the church accused of being lukewarm and having closed Jesus out, He says that to those that conquer

will be given victory, the implication is the victory will be over the influence of the world, and He gives His permission to sit with God on His throne.
- 4:2-11: The wondrous scene in heaven includes the Lord in His glory on His throne surrounded by a rainbow, the twenty-four elders, the four living creatures, with flashes of lighting and crashes of thunder.
- 5:1-14: This is the scene in which the Lamb takes the scroll from the hand of God on His throne and the heavens declare His worthiness to receive power, wealth, wisdom, might, honor, glory, and praise.
- 6:16: The unbelievers on the earth during the turmoil of the sixth seal judgment seek to have the mountains and rocks fall on them to hide them from the wrath of God, who is seated on the throne, and from Jesus Christ.
- 7:9-17: In a scene similar to that descried in 4:2-11, John sees the Lord sitting on His throne surrounded by the twenty-four elders and the four living creatures.
- 8:3: An altar is seen before the throne.
- 12:5: In the description of the woman, the child, and the dragon, the narrative summaries Jesus' first advent by the fact that He was brought to the throne of God after His earthly life.
- 14:3: After the anointing of the 144,000, John hears singing coming from heaven apparently from those before God's throne, the four living creatures, and the elders.
- 16:17: After the angel pours out the contents of the seventh bowl, John hears a loud voice say, *It is done!* which he understands to be from God on His throne within the temple.
- 19:4-5: After Babylon is destroyed, God, who is seated on His throne, is worshipped by the four living creatures and the twenty-four elders.
- 20:11: This passage is discussed in considerably more detail below.
- 21:5-6: From the throne, Jesus Christ declares that He is reliable, He is the Alpha and the Omega, and He is the One that provides water for those that are thirsty.
- 21:1: The river of the water of life will pour out from the throne of God and the Lamb.
- 21:3: The throne of God will be present in the New Jerusalem where God's servants will worship Him.

55.3 THE GREAT WHITE THRONE

Core Scripture: Revelation 20:11.

John describes the awesome scene as he sees One majestically sitting on a large white throne away from whom flee the earth and heavens.
- The characterization of the throne given by John is that it is a great and it is a white throne, no other details are provided. The scene is noticeably cold and austere and without witnesses - nothing else is apparently necessary to compliment the finality of the Lord passing sentence on the deviant.

- "The fact that the throne is "great," that is, great in size conveys the grandeur of its authority. Its size may also suggest that the occasion is great, for this is the final winding up of the affairs of this earth. The whiteness of the throne points out the purity and complete and invincible justice of the One who sits on it." That it is a "throne" suggests that sovereign decisions will be meted out."[1]
- There is no mention of a throne room, or the immediately surroundings, and the sense is that the throne is not on the earth, but instead either in God's abode in the heaven or else in space.

MacLeod[2] compares the throne in verses 4:2-11 with the throne in 20:11:

Throne in Revelation 4:2-11	Throne in Revelation 20:11
Surrounded by a rainbow as a sign of the covenant promises	No Promises are offered, only justice and retribution
Lightning, thunder, and voice proceed out to threaten judgment	Cold and austere judgment with no further warnings
Surrounded by other thrones of the various glorified saints	Only purpose is judgment and there are no others around
Holy Spirt, symbolized by the seven lamps, is present	Setting is pure retribution and Holy Spirit is not mentioned
Singing and joyful exultation can be heard	Nothing is heard except the administration of retributive justice

There is no indication in the Bible that the various scenes in which the throne is seen is the same throne each time, or if there are several thrones for the different purposes as identified in the various passages, such as one for judgment, one for glory, etc., just as the Bible records different names for God for His different attributes. It is probably reasonable to conclude that there is only one throne of God, and the various details given are only applicable to the immediate surroundings at the time the throne is seen and that are appropriate for the condition seen, such as nothing additional at the Great White Throne Judgment.

While the specific identity of the One sitting on the throne is not indicated in this passage, it is without doubt Jesus Christ (cf. Revelation 3:21). There are numerous other New Testament passages that indicate that God has authorized His Son Jesus Christ to be the judge of the creation:
- Matthew 19:28 and 25:31: After Jesus' Second Advent, He will sit on His glorious throne.
- John:
  + 5:22: Jesus says, *the Father judges no one, but has entrusted all judgment to the Son.*
  + 5:30: Jesus says, *I judge only as I hear, and my judgment is just, for I seek not to please myself but him who sent me.*

- Acts 17:31: Luke says, *For he has set a day when he will judge the world with justice by the man he has appointed. He has given proof of this to everyone by raising him from the dead.*
- 2 Corinthians 5:10: *For we must all appear before the judgment seat of Christ, so that each of us may receive what is due us for the things done while in the body, whether good or bad.*
- 2 Timothy 4:1: ... *Christ Jesus, who will judge the living and the dead* ...

55.4 STANDING BEFORE THE GREAT WHITE THRONE

Core Scripture: Revelation 20:12-13.

The dead, great and small, stand before the throne, the dead are given up by the sea, Death and Hades give up the dead and all are to be judged according to their deeds by what is written in the several books. It should be noted that two times John mentions that those standing before God's throne are judged according to their deeds, and as will be seen, their sinfulness will deserve punishment.

The Dead, Great, and Small: As will occur with various other resurrections, this will be a literal, physical bodily resurrection.
- The resurrected people that are standing before the throne are assumed to be the wicked dead for several reasons:
  + First, they were not raised in the first resurrection and are the ones referred to in Revelation 20:5.
  + Second, as will be seen in verse 15, they will be thrown into the lake of fire.
  The sense is that they are standing before pure righteousness and justice as indicated in Hebrews 9:27.
- The reference to the great and small suggests that all that will be present at the judgment will be equal, wealth makes no difference, intelligence makes no difference, there are now no differences between individuals that matters - all stand without distinction before the Lord to be judged. No one has an advantage over another. "John said that "the great and small" (v. 12) will stand before God: the importance and the unimportant, the powerful and the weak, the educated and the uneducated, the rich and the poor, the old and the young. The wealthy Western nations and the third-world nations will all be represented."[3]
- This is in harmony with what Jesus is recorded as saying in John 5:28-29 that those that are evil will be resurrected that will result in condemnation.

The Sea Gives Up the Dead: For an undisclosed reason, special mention is made for those apparently lost at sea that did not have a formal burial. The possible reason for including the reference to the dead being given up by the sea is to establish the idea that disintegrated bodies, or those scattered in lakes that make them unrecoverable, are still able to be resurrected. "The resurrection of the dead from the sea merely reaffirms that all the dead will be raised regardless of the condition of their bodies."[4]

Death and Hades Gives Up the Dead: An obvious statement that those standing before the throne are resurrected human beings and neither Death nor Hades have the power to hold them against the will of the Lord. "Death and Hades" were agents of judgment. Death was seen as a power stalking the land, and Hades was personified as a monster opening its jaws to receive the dead. Hades is the abode of the unrighteous as they wait for the last judgment."[6] It should be noted that neither Death nor Hades (Sheol in the Old Testament) are permanent states nor do they refer to eternal punishment, but instead are temporary places until the time of persecution.

The Books: As Paul says in Romans 2:6, God will reward each one for the deeds done in their lifetime and in this context the used of the word "reward" does not always mean being rewarded with an award, it can also mean that punishment is the award for defiance and rebellion.
- Those standing before the throne are judged by an examination of what is written in the several books which apparently records information about each person's life. While the passage does not indicate who examines the information contained within the books, the implication is that Christ is the judge that makes the final determination of guilt or innocence.
- There are two classifications of record books involved in this judgment:
  + The (Unnamed) Books: Apparently these unidentified books record what individuals did and/or did not do in their respective earthly lives - the emphasis is on personal and individual works or deeds.
  + The Book of Life: This book seems to be the single record of all human beings whose sins have been forgiven because they have embraced God's offer of grace through Jesus Christ. The implication is that all the people that are listed in the book, while sinners, are yet the redeemed saved and will not be subject to the second death. The absence of one's name in this book indicates that they are the unredeemed lost and are destined for the judgment furnished by the lake of fire, which is the second death.

The relationship between the two books seems to suggest that they are independent accounts of individual people that indicates the person is sinful, based on their deeds recorded in one book, and thus not saved, based on the absence of their names in the other book.
- Macleod makes several interesting observations of what God will know about humans at the time of this judgment:
  + "It is sobering to realize that God has a record of lives of all the billions of human beings who have ever lived, including every thought, every

mean act, every dirty transaction, every dishonest moment, every foul word, every treacherous betrayal, every harsh feeling or remark."[7]

+ "If mere humans can produce instant replay, computer printouts, and a disc capable of storing the entire Encyclopedia Britannica, or, if desired, 50,000 or more photographs, then it should not be surprising that the Creator of the universe should have data on all His creatures."[8]

Interpretative Thought: Walvoord provides an insightful observation as to the nation of the judgment: "The absolute justice of God is revealed in this judgment of works. ... While works are never a ground for salvation, they are, nevertheless, considered important to God. ... Though men are judged according to their works, the book of life is introduced as the deciding factor as to where they will spend eternity."[9]

All the Dead Appear to be the Unrighteous: There is no mention at all of the righteous dead; therefore the implication is that all these before the throne are the unrighteous dead. While we have seen that the righteous dead are given resurrection bodies "... like the holy, immortal, and incorruptible body of Christ in His resurrection ..."[10] Here we see that the wicked dead are apparently given resurrection bodies suitable for eternal punishment.

Individuals Judged as a Group: While the judgment is described in personal and individual terms, the destiny is that the same group will be gathered and placed into punishment.

55.5 THE JUDGMENTS BEFORE THE GREAT WHITE THRONE

Core Scripture: Revelation 20:14-15.

Death, Hades, and all those whose name is not listed in the book of life, which is everyone standing before the throne, will be subject to the second death - cast into the lake of fire to reside in eternal punishment.

The Destruction of Death and Hades: Again, neither have the power to resist being judged by the Lord. They are cast away to symbolize that the thing that has been feared by humankind throughout history is no longer feared - death will never exist again nor will it ever have power over a human being again, and Hades as the receptacle for the dead will not be necessary again.

Interpretative Thought: Walvoord provides another insightful observation: "If the point of view be adopted that the book of life was originally the book of all living from which have been expunged the names of those who departed from life on earth without salvation, it presents a sad picture of a blank space where their names could have been written for all eternity as the objects of divine grace.

THE GREAT WHITE THRONE JUDGMENT

Though they are judged by their works, it is evident that their destiny is determined primarily by their lack of spiritual life. When the fact is contemplated that Jesus Christ in His death reconciled the world for Himself (II Cor. 5:19) and that He died for the reprobate as well as for the elect, it is all the more poignant that these now raised from the dead are cast into the lake of fire. Their ultimate destiny of eternal punishment is not, in the last analysis, because God wished it but because they would not come to God for the grace which He freely offered."[11]

Lake of Fire: While there are some who will allegorize the lake of fire by making it a symbol, or, suggest that it is a form of annihilation for the wicked, the truth is that it is a real place at some literal and physical location within God's creation - it is hell in every sense of the word as we understand it.
- Also, if the chamber for the unsaved in Hades contains flames for the tormenting of its residents, as recorded in Luke 16:24, and the old heaven and old earth will be burned up by fire, then it is not far-fetched to believe that the lake of fire will exist as a place of punishment.
- Keep in mind that, by the time of this confinement of the resurrected wicked are cast into the lake of fire, the Antichrist and the False Prophet have resided there already for one thousand years. Satan will have only recently arrived as well.
- Other passages that include references to the lake of fire include the following:
    + Matthew 13:42: The lake of fire will be like a fiery furnace where there will be weeping and gnashing of teeth.
    + Matthew 25:41 and 46: Those judged unrighteous by Jesus when He returns and judges those that survive Daniel's 70th Week will be cast into the place of eternal fire which had been prepared for the devil and his angels.
    + Revelation 14:11: Those that accept the mark of the beast will be cast into the place that smokes from the torture of the unrighteous.
    + Revelation 21:8: Cowards, unbelievers, detestable people, murderers, the sexually immoral, magicians, idol worshippers, and liars will eventually find their place in the lake of fire and sulfur when subjected to the second death.

Characteristics of the Lake of Fire: An analysis of Scripture reveals the lake of fire has the following characteristics:
- It is a place of torment beyond this life.
- Sulfur (some versions say brimstone) is the fuel that burns.
- The time of confinement is without end; when Satan and the wicked are cast into the lake, they join the Antichrist and the False Prophet who have been there for one thousand years.

56

THE ETERNAL STATE

After God's Plan has worked throughout centuries of human history, it culminates in the eternal state – the final form of God's creation. The eternal state is defined as God's provision of a new earth, a new heaven, and a New Jerusalem for His redeemed children to spend eternity with Him. After the many and varied struggles of human existence, the glories of societies and nations, the tumultuous frictions between civilizations, the astounding human accomplishments and the horrible depths of human depravity, all judgments are now done and all created beings have arrived at their respective final destines. All human history as told through the story of creation, the fall of the created creatures, and their subsequent reach for redemption is now finished; the time God has allotted for the course of the human condition to run its race is now expired; all that is left is for the saints from the broad span of human history to settle in the place prepared for them by their Creator/Savior and to walk, not into the sunset, but into the perpetual sunshine of God's presence.

The sense of this last provision by God for His physical creation and His created beings is that the old order has been done away with and a new order will be bought in. Just as it is a constant theme through the Bible, for the last time God is dismissing the order that facilitated the demise of humankind, and has brought a remnant forward and placed it within a new and better order. All things in the new order will be unmistakably perfect. Just as God's original creation was perfect, so will His final version of His creation be perfect.

56.1 GOD'S INTENTION FOR A NEW EARTH AND A NEW HEAVEN

Throughout Biblical history there has been an expectation that the present earth and the present heavens would someday be destroyed and replaced with a new earth and a new heaven. The applicable passages attesting to this intention of God were presented previously which indicates that while God and Christ are eternal, the current physical creation is not and essentially was never intended to last forever. When human history comes to its end, and God's children stand on the threshold of their eternal reward of being in the presence of the Trinity, then God intends that it begin with everything new, the earth, the heavens, and a new city for His children. The conclusion that the Bible teaches about the present earth and the present heavens is that they will be completely and fully destroyed with nothing remaining. God had created it out of nothing, and to nothing it would return.

56.2	THE PURGING OF CREATION

Core Scripture: 2 Peter 3:10-13.

"The reason God will destroy the present heaven and earth is that He originally made them as the habitat for perfect humanity. However, sin so thoroughly corrupted not only the human race, but the earthly environment, that He will destroy it – and create "a new heaven and a new earth," in which righteousness dwells, this is the final stage in His plans to deliver humanity into the blessing He originally intended people to enjoy."[1]

The second half of Revelation 20:11 says that *the earth and the heaven fled from his* [the one sitting on the throne] *presence, and there was no place for them.* This is within the context of what is said five verses further in Revelation 21:1 where John sees a new heaven and a new earth that has replaced the prior heaven and earth which has passed away from existence - thus the vision suggests a universe-wide, cataclysmic-scale destruction of the present creation. "Further, it would be most natural that the present earth and heaven, the scene of the struggle with Satan and sin, should be displaced by an entirely new order suited for eternity. The whole structure of the universe is operating on the principle of a clock that is running down. Though many billions of years would be required to accomplish this, the natural world would eventually come to a state of total inactivity if the physical laws of the universe as now understood should remain unchanged. What could be simpler than for God to create a new heaven and a new earth by divine fiat in keeping with His purpose for eternity to come?"[2]

Prophecies concerning the purging of creation include the following:
- Isaiah:
  + 34:1-4: *Come near, you nations, and listen*, God invites all nations and peoples to hear his proclamation. Because *the Lord is angry with all nations, He will totally destroy* all the armies, and *dead bodies will stink* and *the mountains will be soaked with their blood.* As part of this judgment of wrath, *stars* will *dissolve, the heavens* will roll up *like a scroll*, the *starry host will fall*, and nature will wither. "Catastrophic events in the sky will accompany the Messiah's return to the earth to establish His millennial reign (cf. Joel 2:10, 30-31, 3:15; Zech.14:6-7; Matt. 24:29). However, Isaiah 34:4 may refer to the judgment of the sixth seal in the Tribulation (Rev. 6:12-13), or to the eternal state, after the Millennium, when the sun will not be needed (Rev. 21:1). Or perhaps Isaiah was speaking figuratively of a change in the whole power structure in the Millennium, when human kings will be done away with and God alone will be in control."[3]
  + 65:17: God told the prophet Isaiah that He is ready to build a new earth and a new heaven, so that the former ones can be discarded not to be remembered.

- Matthew 24:35 (cf. Mark 13:31 and Luke 21:33): Jesus states, in a testimony of His sovereignty, that the heaven and the earth will pass away, but His words will not.
- Luke 16:17: Again, in a variation on the theme of Jesus' eternally, not one jot or tittle of His words will ever change even though the heaven and the earth will pass away.
- 2 Peter 3:10-13: This passage is discussed in more detail below.

THE ORIGINAL CURSE ON EARTH AND PROPHETIC ANTICIPATION OF ITS REMOVAL

Before the purging of creation is examined it would be helpful to explore the divine logic that establishes the need for such a purging.

- Genesis 3:17-19: As a judgmental consequence of the original sinful act perpetrated by Adam and Eve, rather than cursing his physical body as He did in Eve's case, God cursed the ground and made it such that it would resist Adam's stewardship mandate effort, and subsequently all of humankind's efforts, to work it in order to survive. "It was not Adam's body that bore the penalty for his sins; it was the ground, the very substance of which the material universe was made, the very elements God had molded to form his body and those of the other living creatures. The punishment for Adam's sin extended as far as the matter of which he was made and as far as the dominion with whose care he was charged."[4] Quite simply, the earth was corrupted by the sin and the subsequent judgment of Adam and Eve.
- Romans 8:18-25: Set in the context of the suffering of humankind that will eventually change to the salvation of *the children of God*, there are several observations that can be made relative to the curse on the earth:
  + Morris[5] points out that the phrase *the creation was subjected to frustration* in verse 20 is a reference to time and chance entering the realm of the physical creation which evolutionists contend is the permanent condition of the universe.
  + The creation is personified as it eagerly awaits the coming everlasting glory of Jesus Christ, the implication being that the curse will be released and the earth will forever flourish in the way God intended.
  + While the creation did not willfully commit sin nor did it volunteer for its condition, Paul points out that it groans and suffers from the penalty for Adam's willful rebellion.
  + The effect of God's curse is that the earth is subjected to a state of bondage to decay and deterioration, but will be liberated / delivered / redeemed when God's salvation grace is finally enacted for His children, thus bringing the earth into conformity with God.
- Hebrews 1:10-12 (cf. Psalm 102:25-27): In a testimony to the eternality of God, the author of Hebrews quotes a psalmist that speaks about how the ordered systems of the universe will decay and eventually perish.

Thus, the Bible tells us that the world yearns to be released from the bondage of the curse so that it can participate in the glory of God's provision for His children, therefore, it "… becomes necessary to remove the last vestige of this curse from the earth before the manifestation of the eternal kingdom."[6]

THE EARTH AND HEAVEN REPLACED

From the writings of the Apostle Peter, 2 Peter 3:10-13 is at the core of the theological doctrine which says that the present earth and the present heaven will someday be replaced by a new earth and a new heaven; and it provides the necessary detail to interpret Revelation 20:11b. Throughout the study of prophecy and eschatology there are several passages that are not only difficult to interpret prophetically, but are also difficult to pinpoint their respective locations in the span of events allotted for God's Plan for humankind; such as the various movements and battles of the Campaign of Armageddon, and some of the seal, trumpet, and bowl judgments during Daniel's 70th Week. One of the most difficult passages in the New Testament is the passage under consideration here. Overstreet[7] makes the following observations:

- Interpretative Difficulty: Without engaging in a deep technical discussion, the controversy of interpretation is based on what the last word of the Greek text of verse 10 is, or should be, as well as how the various translations have constructed the grammatical structure of the verse and the sense that can be derived.
    - + Word Problem: The basis of the problem lies with differing words used in the various extant Greek manuscripts. The essence of the difficulty is between the following two views, which as can be seen leads to differing conclusions and understanding of the intent of the passage:
        - ○ First View: Does verse 10 say that the earth and its works 'shall be burned up,' which seems to be the most harmonious with the context, however it does not have significant manuscript support?
        - ○ Second View: Does verse 10 say that the earth and its works 'shall be found?' "… [M]ost modern textual critics would regard this reading as having the strongest manuscript support."[8] While this view makes the least sense it is the more reliable conclusion.
- Grammar Problem: Resolution of the grammatical problem will further clarify the interpretation of the passage. Recognizing that the original Greek manuscripts were written without punctuation marks, an appeal to the context and tone of a passage can reveal how a sequence of words can, or ought to, be interpreted. "The context of the passage is speaking of destruction, dissolution, and judgment. This writer [Overstreet] believes that Peter is not making a declarative statement regarding the earth and the works therein, but is asking a solemn and thought-provoking question;

therefore, the verse should be punctuated accordingly. The verse would thus read, "But the day of the Lord will come as a thief; in which the heavens shall pass away with a great noise, and the elements shall be dissolved with fervent heat; *and shall the earth and the works that are therein be found?*"[9]

The Time of the Event

- The Day of the Lord: Verse 10 indicates that when the Day of the Lord comes, then all the cataclysmic events that are described in the passage will also come to pass. The Day of the Lord extends from just after the Pretribulational Rapture through Daniel's 70th Week, through the Millennium, and to the passing away of the present earth and heavens.
- Before or After the Millennium: There are essentially two viewpoints as to when the passing away of the earth and the heavens will occur: the first, before the Millennium, and the second, after the Millennium. An examination by Overstreet[10] of the before Millennium view reveals that there is no Scriptural support for the passing away of the earth and the heavens before the Millennium, therefore, the most viable conclusion, which is more harmonious with the overall context of the Scripture, is that the event occurs after the Millennium.
- The following observations are among the strengths of the passing after the Millennium viewpoint:
    + First and foremost, if the passing of the earth and the heavens in 2 Peter 3:10-13 is the same as Revelation 20:1, then that connection establishes its timing - it will be at the same time as the Great White Throne Judgment at the end of the Millennium.
    + Isaiah 66:22 does not refer to the kingdom in the Millennium, but instead to necessary preparations for eternity.
    + The references to a judgment that includes fire contained in 2 Thessalonians 1:7-8 and Revelation 16:8-9 are not equated to each other nor are they the same as the 2 Peter 3 usage of fire. The Thessalonians passage is in reference to the Lord's Second Coming and His vengeance on those who do not know God, the Revelation passage is in reference to events occurring during Daniel's 70th Week, and the 2 Peter passage is in reference to the entire creation.
    + The full extent of Isaiah 65:17-25 and 66:22-24 are not required to be implemented prior to the beginning of the Millennium. As is true of Jesus' interpretation of Isaiah 61:1-2 recorded in Luke 4:18-19, there are passages that look forward to the future and have applications to two events in one passage. Therefore, in the Isaiah 65 passage, verse 17 refers to new earth and heaven, while verses 18-25 refer to the kingdom. The same is true for the Isaiah 66 passage, verse 22 looks forward to eternity while verses 23-24 look to the millennium.

The Extent of the Event

As with the time of the event, there are two viewpoints as to the extent of the passing away of the earth and the heavens event: the first, it will be a limited renovation of the universe, and the second, it will be an annihilation of the entire universe. Again, an examination by Overstreet[11] reveals that there is no Scriptural support for the limited renovation view, therefore, the most viable conclusion, which is more harmonious with the overall context of the Scripture, is that the event will be a complete replacement of the present earth and the present heaven with a new earth and a new heaven. The following observations are among the strengths of the replacement viewpoint:

- In spite of the fact that Psalms 104:5 and 148:3-6 indicates that the creation will last 'forever,' the word can also mean a time past, or a time future, that had, or will have, a long duration. Essentially, the term is relative to the human understanding of time and could indicate that something could exist for as long as it is allowed to exist and does not necessarily mean it will last in the same manner as God is everlasting.
- Isaiah 13:9-14, 24:19-20, and Nahum 1:5 do not refer to particular portions of this event; instead the Isaiah passages refer to the time of Daniel's 70th Week, and the Nahum passage refers to a prophecy against Nineveh.
- The conditions that the prophets indicate will exist during the Millennium can be accomplished by Jesus and do not require a renovation of the universe by fire.
- The concept of a limited renovation does not fit the context of the passage.
- The extent of the destruction because of the Flood, which was itself a renovation, is not equivalent to the extent of the future destruction indicated to be by fire, which is an annihilation - just because the first was a renovation, it is not automatic that the second be the same. The Greek words used in Peter's mentioning of the Flood in 2 Peter 3:5-7 is best interpreted to mean that even though the earth was flooded, only the world system perished with the earth being spared actual physical destruction. In 2 Peter 3:10 and 13, Peter used the Greek words to indicate that the earth will be physically destroyed.

The Issue of the Elements Being Dissolved in a Fire

2 Peter 3:10 and 12 indicate that the earth and the heavens will be completely destroyed by a fire. The Greek word used for *fire* means, according to Overstreet[12], to "be consumed by heat, burn up;" words used in other versions indicated in the adjacent table. When connected to the next Greek word used for *destroyed* means "to loose, untie," "set free," "destroy, bring to an end, abolish, do away with;" words used in other versions indicated in the adjacent table[13], and also "to dissolve."[14]

2 Peter 3:10 and 12	
NIV	*fire*
NASB	*fire*
NET	*blaze*
KJV	*fervent heat*
NKJV	*fervent heat*
AMP	*fire*

Overstreet poses an interesting and thought-provoking question: "Does not this word, in connection with the "fervent heat," and the "great noise" communicate the same thought as that of nuclear fusion?"[15] While there is absolutely nothing in the Bible that would lead one to believe that nuclear destruction is indicated, it is plausible since God was capable of creating the universe ex nihilo, or out of nothing, in the beginning which involves

2 Peter 3:10 and 12	
NIV	*destroyed*
NASB	*destroyed*
NET	*melt*
KJV	*melt*
NKJV	*melt*
AMP	*dissolve*

the movement, combination, articulation of the elementary particles of matter, atoms, then He is also very capable of deconstructing His creation.

In Revelation 20:11 MacLeod[16] paints an interesting image with the following observations: "And so the throne stands isolated, majestic and terrifying. None of the irrelevancies of this life are left to distract the eye from the spectacle of the Judge and His throne. Everything else will have passed away."

56.3 THE NEW EARTH AND NEW HEAVENS

Core Scripture: Revelation 21:1.

And civilization begins a third time in the eternal state which is what God longed for His children to have for their eternal existence.
- The First Civilization: In the beginning God created the universe, made human beings in His image as the highest form of creation, and gave them dominion over all that He had made. However, the created beings exercised the free will that God had also given them by responding to the influence of a challenger and thus caused a partial separation between the Creator and the created and causing themselves to become flawed. God enabled them to govern themselves, gave them the ability to develop their own civilizational structure but after the beings eventually expanded substantially the magnitude of unrighteousness became so great God destroyed all of the first civilization except a remnant by a worldwide flood.
- The Second Civilization: God delivered a remnant of His created beings from the devastation of the flood and again graciously gave them the ability to govern themselves and they eventually grew into a civilization that covered the earth. However, in a similar manner as the first civilization, they too progressed to a state of unrighteousness as never seen by the world, so much so that God sent His Son to them a first time, and they rejected and killed Him, and then He sent His son a second time to rule them before finally drawing everything to a close because their depraved nature and the influence from a challenger made it obvious to all that the created beings were not capable of making a civilization that could function without God.

Unlike the end of the first civilization, this time the earth and the heavens as well were destroyed but not by a flood but by cataclysmic fire.

- The Third Civilization: The Apostle John essentially sees the third beginning of a civilization for God's created beings. This time however, the civilization will be founded on and governed by God's terms and it will be fulfilled according to His will with a resurrected race of beings, without a challenger to influence the beings.

THE APOSTLE JOHN SEES THE THIRD NEW BEGINNING

John saw a new heaven and a new earth after destruction of the present heaven and earth. While the Bible contains precious few clues as to what John saw, the following observations may be made:

- There is every expectation that the new universe will have been made of new materials out of nothing. If God has already created a universe out of nothing in the past, there is every reason to believe He can do so again. "As God created the present heavens and earth to be the scene of the eternal theocratic kingdom of God."[17]
- Even though John saw new celestial things, he only records that it is a new earth and a new heavens, no other descriptive information is given except the things, known in the present earth and heaven, but will not be found in the new earth and heaven (see below). It seems unlikely that if the new creations were not at least similar to the present creations, that he would have provided more details to ensure clarity in understanding the differences. The brevity of information could be due to the fact that John knew that every reader would immediately understand what was being communicated, if so, there is nothing to prevent our interpretation that the new earth and the new heavens are not very much different than the present forms.
- The heavens refer to the atmosphere around the earth and not to God's abode.
- The description of the earth does not include any landmarks or geographical features that will be present; nor is anything known of its character, conditions, or flora and fauna. The implication is that it is round.
- The implication is the new earth and the new heaven will be the place in which the saved will reside for eternity.
- The following things were recorded by John as evil things not being present in the new earth and new heaven:
    + 21:1: Seas.
    + 21:4: Death, mourning, weeping, and pain.
    + 21:23: Sun and moon.
    + 23:3: The curse.
    + 21:25 and 22:5: Night.
- Concerning the Absence of Seas:

+ "The disappearance of the sea is a reminder of the transience of the present created order. This present order of things will come to an end and nothing more powerfully communications this idea than the statement that "there is no longer any sea.""[18]
+ Macleod makes the point that the seas in the Bible are often associated with evil, and can be seen in the following examples:
  o Psalm 107:25-28: Disorder of nature could cause danger and risk to people.
  o Isaiah 57:20: The wicked comes up out of the sea.
  o Ezekiel 28:8: Violence is associated with the sea.
  o Revelation 13:1: The Antichrist came up out of the sea.

57

THE NEW JERUSALEM

In what may be the most unusual, beyond the imagination, thing to happen in the end times is the appearance of the New Jerusalem coming down out of the sky as part of the Eternal State. It will be enormous, like nothing ever seen before on earth. "The appearance of the New Jerusalem also finally fulfills the divine goal for the earthly Tabernacle and Temple (Exodus 25:8) and the church: It will be a "spiritual temple" (Ephesians2:21-22) where the Creator and His creatures can enjoy a holy relationship. The New Jerusalem is therefore "the tabernacle of God" where God will forever "dwell" among His people (Revelation 21:3; 22:3-4) and a "temple" for "the Lord God, the Almighty and the Lamb" (Revelation 21:22)."[1]

57.1	THE ANTICIPATION OF THE NEW JERUSALEM

THE SENSE OF PLACE

Within the world of architecture one of the objectives of the creative design process for a building is to endeavor to accomplish "a sense of place," something that will embody for the owner and the user several philosophical reasons for which the building exists:

- To provide an identity that is yet unique but fits within the context for which the owner desires to be a part.
- To enclose a spatial environment to facilitate the activities for which the owner wishes to take place.
- To express an image to the world within which the owner operates.
- To hold a hierarchal view within the sphere of influence that the owner is a participant.
- To satisfy the need to have a home that is a place to which the owner can be enveloped by and live, work and play in comfort and safety within it.
- To create a place in which to belong.
- To be sanctuary for the owner.

What this means for the theology of prophecy is that there is a practical application for this idea of a sense of place and it is a part of the Lord's attitude and intention to reside in a heavenly place that represents and embodies His identity that is then replicated on the earth in different forms at different times for different purposes during the course of the history of humankind. First, it was the Garden of Eden, then it was the tabernacle, then the First Temple in Jerusalem, then the Second Temple in Jerusalem, the Tribulation Temple in Jerusalem, the Millennial Temple in Jerusalem, and finally it will be the New Jerusalem which itself will be the temple of the Lord. The Bible expresses the Lord's sense of place in a variety of ways as can be seen in the various passages listed below.

THE OLD TESTAMENT EXPRESSION OF THE NEW JERUSALEM

While the eternal New Jerusalem is not specifically identified in the Old Testament, there are several other concepts and motifs that either prefigure it or function as a substitute. The implication is that if there is a holy temple in heaven, would there not be a heavenly Jerusalem as well as indicated in Hebrew 9:23?

- Exodus 25:9, 40: Moses is shown the heavenly temple and instructed to pattern the earthly tabernacle after it.
- 1 Chronicles 28:11-19: David gave his son Solomon the plan of the temple that God had instructed him to have built.
- The Psalms: Even though the Solomonic (First) Temple had not been built until after David's death, the following references are to the Lord being in His house or temple:
  + 2: To establish the proper image for the divine view that Jesus Christ will be authorized to fulfill as the King, the author identifies earthly Jerusalem as Zion, my holy mountain (NASB), which is the place that God, enthroned in heaven, will install one that He wants as His King.
  + 11:4: *The Lord is in his holy temple.*
  + 23:6: *I will dwell in the house of the Lord forever.*
  + 26:8: *the house where you live, the place where your glory dwells.*
  + 27:4: *dwell in the house of the Lord ... seek him in his temple.*
  + 125:1: Mount Zion is eternal and inviolable.
  + 138:2: *your holy temple.*
- Isaiah:
  + 65:18: The Lord indicates that He will create a New Jerusalem, and it and its occupants will be for His own enjoyment.
  + 66:20: Newly converted believers will be an offering as they come to the holy hill of Jerusalem.
- Ezekiel 28:14 and 16: In the Scriptural narrative regarding the King of Tyre as the representative of Satan, the prophet records the heavenly place of God as the holy mountain of God.

THE NEW TESTAMENT EXPRESSION OF THE NEW JERUSALEM

In addition to the Old Testament references, there are New Testament passages that express the existence of the city of God in several ways:

- Galatians 4:26: In an allegory of Hagar and Sarah representing two covenants, Paul makes the reference that the Jerusalem above is the place in which to place one's hope.
- Hebrews:
  - + 11:8-10: A connection is drawn between Abraham's call to trust God and to leave his original home and go to a land of which he knew nothing with the anticipation of eventually coming to the city of God. It seems very plausible that Abraham did not expect to find such a city on earth but to look forward to living in such a city in the future, a city which must have existed at the time, where the righteous reside in the presence of God.
  - + 11:13-14: The descendants of Abraham all died without receiving their reward for righteousness, a reward that will see them changed from being aliens and foreigners on the earth to being citizens of a future city of God.
  - + 11:16: The spiritual heroes of ancient Israel aspired to live in a heavenly land that they understood would be better than the earthly conditions of their respective times – their hope was focused in a heavenly direction.
  - + 12:22: Interestingly, the author equates Mount Zion, the city of the living God, and the heavenly Jerusalem as being the same.
  - + 13:14: In the final exhortations of the Book, believers are to look forward to the city to come because earthly cities will not last.

As the Divinely Revealed Pattern for Earthly Sanctuaries

- Acts:
  - + 7: As an reference to Exodus 25:8-9, 40, Stephen defends himself by using the history of Israel, he revealed that the Jewish tabernacle, the abode of God while the Hebrews were in the wilderness, was patterned after what Moses was shown and instructed to build for the fledgling nation.
  - + 7:48: Stephen continues his defense by pointing out that God only dwells in a sanctuary built according to His design, not within one built by human hands.
- Hebrews:
  - + 9:23: The author connects the earthly sanctuary with the heavenly sanctuary.
  - + 9:11: This passage indicates that Jesus Christ is the authority from a more perfect sanctuary, the one in heaven, not the one of this creation.

"This [the above passages] should be kept in mind when considering the texts in Revelation that depict the furniture of the heavenly Temple (Revelation 11:19; cf. 4:5; 5:8; 6:9; 8:3; 9:13; 14:18; 15:5-8; 16:7) and the structural elements and dimensions of the New Jerusalem itself (Revelation 21;12-21)."[2]

By Actual Identification as the New Jerusalem

Galatians 4:25-26: Paul distinguishes the heavenly Jerusalem in verse 26 form the earthly Jerusalem of verse 25.

- Hebrews 12:
    + 18-22: The heavenly Jerusalem, as a place of grace, is contrasted with the earthly Jerusalem, which is a place of law.
    + 22-24: The inhabitants of the New Jerusalem are described indicating that heaven is the destiny of believers.
    + 26-28: That that can be shaken, the creation, will be removed from that that cannot be shaken, the indestructible heavenly kingdom.
- Revelation:
    + 3:12: In Christ's message to the Church at Philadelphia, He says that He will make those that overcome the world pillars of the temple of God that will be in the City of My God, which is parenthetically referred to as the New Jerusalem that will come down out of heaven from God.
    + 21 – 22: Refer to discussion below.

57.2   THE NEW JERUSALEM

Core Scripture: Revelation 21:2 – 22:5.

THE DESCENDING APPEARANCE OF THE NEW JERUSALEM

Core Scripture: Revelation 21:2.

After John sees the present heaven and earth pass away and the new heaven and earth appear, he sees a magnificent new city descend down from out of heaven from God. He indicates that the New Jerusalem is beautifully dressed for her husband but what is included is not recorded.

THE CITY OF THE NEW JERUSALEM

One can only image John's emotional state at this point having witnessed all he had witnessed about, not only his future, but the future of all believes and unbelievers as well. After seeing the old heavens and earth pass away and the new heavens and earth come into being, John now sees this enormous object come down out of the sky.

- The first descriptive term that John uses of the descending city is that it is holy which signifies that it is the city that God wants for Himself as well as for those that are the righteous citizens of His new world.

- The reference to the heavenly Jerusalem being a holy city stands in opposition to the description of the earthly Jerusalem in Revelation 11:8 as being Sodom.
- Other passages that refer to Jerusalem as the Lord's holy city include:
  - Matthew 4:5 and 27:53: *holy city*.
  - Galatians 4:26: *Jerusalem that is above is free.*
  - Hebrews 12:22: *the city of the living God, the heavenly Jerusalem.*
  - Revelation 3:12: *the temple of my God ... the city of my God, the new Jerusalem.*
- The passage that is the most in harmony with the prophetic nature of God's Plan and the various things said in the Bible about eternity is found in John 14:2 where Jesus reveals that He has to leave in order to prepare a place for His disciples and followers. While no other specific information is given in the New Testament about the special place that Jesus is to build, the New Jerusalem in Revelation is the only references given that could fit the prophecy. So, is the New Jerusalem the place Jesus prepares for those that belong to Him?
- Descends Out of Heaven: There are a number of observations that may be made regarding this city:
  + There is nothing said about the city being created. The language of Revelation 21 and 22 give the impression that the city existed and was functional prior to its descent.
  + The practical matter of just how such a large physical structure can be held within the atmosphere surrounding the earth is not explained, therefore, it is appropriate that our understanding of the passage should be that nothing is impossible for God and there is no reason not to believe it is a literal city, as we will see shortly, composed of precious stones.
- A Bride Adorned for Her Husband: John describes the New Jerusalem as a bride on her wedding day ready to be received by her husband. While the passage does make a specific connection, because of the context of the passage and specifically verse 21:9 it is obvious the reference is that Jesus Christ is the husband.
  + The emphasis here is on the appearance quality, the righteousness, and the importance of the new city in the same manner as the attention of the attendees at a wedding ceremony is always on the beauty of the bride.
  + While a wedding ceremony is of great importance to the groom, bride, families, and friends, not to mention God's intentions for the continuation of His Plan for humankind, the physical presentation of the bride, and the moment she appears, symbolizes the supreme significance of a new intimate relationship that is about to begin and the new life of the intimate bond in which it will be spent. Upon her appearance, thoughts are usually directed to a bride's beauty, her purity, and what she represents about a new life.

479

- + "This beautiful picture is used to describe that eternal abode of God's people. This suggests the purity of Christ's redeemed and glorified people, the intimacy they will enjoy with Him, and the fact that they will live together in peace and joy."[3]
- + Another picture painted by the Bible is that the passage is the descent of heaven. Most Christians have the inaccurate perception that life in the eternal presence of God as taking place somewhere in the sky, up in the air or in the clouds, and that heaven is somewhere in the earth's atmosphere or in space outside the atmosphere. Because of what the last several chapters of the Book of Revelation teaches, life in eternity will be an existence on the new earth and/or in the New Jerusalem.
- • Could the New Jerusalem have existed during the Millennium? As has already been mentioned, there are some who believe the New Jerusalem will exist and be present during the Millennium.
  - + Concerning the question if the New Jerusalem is present in the Millennium, Walvoord does allow for the possibility of it being present: "If the New Jerusalem is in existence throughout the millennial reign of Christ, it is possible that it is a satellite city suspended over the earth during the thousand-year reign of Christ as the dwelling place of resurrected and translated bodies and living ordinary lives. … The possibility of the New Jerusalem being a satellite city over the earth during the millennium is not specifically taught in any scripture and at best is an inference based on the implication that it has been in existence prior to its introduction in Revelation 21. Its character as presented here, however, are related to the eternal state rather than to the millennial kingdom."[3]
  - + One of the strongest arguments for the New Jerusalem being present during the Millennium is that it has to be present for the 1,000 years as the place in which the resurrected saints will live. While there are no specific Scriptural passages that attest to this arrangement, it is based on the presumption that resurrected and translated saints cannot live in the same place, or maybe realm is a better word, as mortal human beings. If this were true then why was Jesus Christ able to spend the 50 days with His disciples and the 500 other witnesses and be seen by them, walk among them, sit and eat with them? It seems this argument is without merit.

THE BENEFITS OF GOD'S NEW ORDER

Core Scripture: Revelation 21:3-4.

Finally, after centuries of His gracious efforts to redeem His creation back to Himself, God and His elect will exist forever in harmony together.

- God's Residence: John points out another characteristic of the New Jerusalem - His place of residents will be among His creatures.

Revelation 21:3	
NIV	*dwelling*
NASB	*tabernacle*
NET	*residence*
KJV	*dwell*
NKJV	*tabernacle*
AMP	*abode of God*

  + The Greek word translated by various Biblical translations for the place of God's residence in Revelation 21:3 is shown in the adjacent table comparison. The better interpretation of the intent of the word is to take the meaning as God permanently dwelling among men; or to tabernacle among men without the temporary aspect that it was a portable abode for God when Israel was in the wilderness.
  + The relationship God desired so many times with the Hebrews will have come in, the resurrected people will live in the new city as His people and He will be their God.
- Pain, Suffering, and Death No Longer Exists: One of the literary techniques that can be used to describe what something is, or will be like, is to include in the description what the something is not. Therefore, another characteristic of the New Jerusalem will be what is absent: there will be no more sadness, weeping, crying, mourning; there will no longer be any pain, nor will there be any more death - there will no longer be any suffering that causes human misery. All that existed before to separate the creatures from their Creator will no longer exist. Consider what is in the old world that causes tears but will not be found in the new world - persecution, sorrow, evil, oppression, tyranny, misfortune, terror, disappointment, tragedy, fear, war, famine, paralyzing effects of sin, and death.

THE PROMISE OF GOD – ALL THINGS MADE NEW – AND IT'S GUARANTEED

Core Scripture: Revelation 21:5-6.
- The Promise of Newness: Probably for the first time in the Book of Revelation, the One sitting on the throne, Jesus, speaks and says that He is making all things new. It is possible that this passage was intended to bring comfort to the churches of Asia Minor that were struggling against their respective cultures and governments.
- The Guarantee for the Promise: The passage adds that the promise of making all things new is secured by the power, sovereignty, and faithfulness of Jesus as the Son of God the Father because His words are reliable and true - a promise is being made by the Triune Creator of the universe who cannot lie (cf. Titus 1:2 and Hebrews 6:18). Also, Jesus guarantees the promise by reminding John and hence the reader, that He is the Alpha (the first letter of the Greek alphabet), who initiated creation and is the source and origin

of all things, and that He is the promises made; and, the implication if that He is everything in between.

- It is Done: When God states that it is done, He is proclaiming that all He intended to do with His active participation in His creation and in human history is fulfilled; it seems more along the lines of a declaration statement rather than an observation of conditions when He says He has directed the course of human history to the conclusion He desired.
- Thirst and the Water of Life:
  + As he will do in Revelation 22:17 in His final invitation for the reader to accept His grace, Jesus once again testifies that He is the source of what every individual human being needs for survival - He is the One that can provide the most precious substance necessary to sustain life, liquid water for the thirst of mortals and spiritual water for the justification of immortality in the presence of the Creator God. The reason for the statement about there being no cost is to emphasize that the divine offer is freely given, and the human acceptance is freely received.
  + In Isaiah 55, especially 1-2, God extends an invitation to Israel to obediently follow Him so as to be a joy in the coming kingdom. He introduces the idea that His grace is as desirable to those who are spiritually lost as water is to those who are physically thirsty. The same motif will be used by Jesus during His earthly ministry as one of the most effective means of explaining Himself to those that yearn spiritually, as He did with the woman at the well recorded in John 4:10-14.
  + The most important promise is of a personal nature - *I will be his God and he will be my son* - which says all that needs to be said about the relationship between the Creator and His created in eternity. "This promise of sonship continues a long-established pattern of covenant faithfulness and close identification between God and His own."[4]

OVERCOMERS INHERIT HEAVEN

Core Scripture: Revelation 21:7-8.

There are seven passages in the Book of Revelation that state that Jesus will bless those that overcome some aspect of the world that is pulling them away from the Lord (1:3; 14:13; 16:15; 19:9; 20:6; 22:7; 22:14). In this passage, Jesus says that to the one that conquers, or overcomes, these things will inherit things promised by Him. To overcome something, one has to be steady, faithful, and assured that whatever temptation comes their way, they can resist, reject, or not be influenced by it because of their faith in the object in which they trust to assist them in overcoming.

- Conquers: This word is used in the sense of a personal victory over something, in this case the acceptance of the offer of salvation written in verse 6 as overcoming, of those things specifically listed in verse 8.
- Inherit these Things and Child of God: The inheritance is all that is given to those that believe in Jesus Christ as the Son of the Living God, and the One that can be trusted to deliver, accomplish, and fulfill all that He offers or says He will do. Part of the promise that will be inherited by believers is that they will become a son of God, or a child of God, and will be eligible for all that is inheritable from the Father. Human beings that believe in Jesus as the Christ are identified as the children of God and shall share in the inheritance from God the Father, as detailed in the following passages:
  + John 1:12: *to those who believed in his name, he gave the right to become children of God.*
  + Romans:
    o 8:14: Children (sons) of God are being led by the Spirit of God.
    o 8:15: The Spirit does not enslave us as sin does. We do not have to live in fear and we are not forced to do God's will. Our sonship is through the Spirit. Adoption is a legal term that indicates a permanent legal standing with God.
    o 8:16: The Holy Spirit and our own spirit witnesses that we are children of God.
    o 8:17: Since we are children of God that makes us heirs of God and co-heirs of Christ and we share in the sufferings of Christ and the riches of God's Kingdom with Christ in His glory.
    o 8:18: Our present sufferings are much less than the glory in God's Kingdom.
    o 8:19: The view of glorification is expanded by Paul to include the creation who awaits the revealing of the children of God.
    o 8:20: As a consequence of the Fall, the creation was subjected to futility; therefore it never achieved the level of perfection desired by God.
    o 8:21: Creation will be released from its bondage and will join the children of God in freedom and glory.
  + Galatians 4:6-7: In the Holy Spirit our hearts receive adoption to sonship, and we are not slaves, instead we are heirs of God.
  + Hebrews:
    o 12:5: We should not lose heart when the Lord rebukes us regarding our discipline in the Lord.
    o 12:6: The Lord disciplines those that He loves, and as His sons we are chastened.
    o 12:7: We should endure discipline from the Lord just as we did from our own fathers.
    o 12:8: We are not legitimate sons and daughters unless we are disciplined.

- o 12:9: As we respected our *human fathers who disciplined us*, then we should respect the Lord more for His discipline.
- o 12:10: Our own fathers disciplined us *as they thought best, but God disciplines us for our good* so *that we may share in the Lord's holiness.*
- o 12:11: Discipline is not pleasant and it is painful at times, but *it produces a harvest of righteousness and peace for those who have been trained by it.*
- o 12:12: strengthen our *feeble arms and weak knees.*
- o 12:13: We should travel level paths, so that the lame are healed and not disabled.
- + 1 John 3:1-2: The Lord has lavished great love on us so that *we should be called children of God.* The *world does not know us* because they do not know Him. What we will be in the future is not known, but we know that when Christ appears, *we shall be like him, for we shall see him as he is.*
- + 1 Peter 1:13-17: With alert and sober minds, we should set our hope on the grace when Jesus Christ is revealed. As obedient children we should not conform to evil desires, and we should be holy, because the Lord is holy. "There is no greater honor in all the universe than what will be bestowed on people who are true to the Lord."[5]
- • Behavior to Overcome: After emphasizing the inheritance for those that believe, the passage continues by identifying what constitutes wicked behavior and concludes what will be the destiny for those that participate in those things that develop from having rejected the One that offers the water of life. As pointed out above, to understand the significance of something, it is important to understand what is contrary to the somethings (i.e., the brightness of daylight is also understood to be the opposite of the darkness of night). "For salvation to be "good news" there must be "bad news" from which to be saved. If all of life's roads lead to the same place, it makes no ultimate difference which road a person chooses. But if they lead to opposite places, to infinite bliss or infinite misery, then this is a life-or-death matter, a razor's edge, and one's choice of roads is infinitely important."[6]
  - + The things listed in the passage will be some of the things that will not be allowed as part of the new earth, new heaven, and New Jerusalem.
  - + Wicked Behavior: Revelation 21:8 lists eight patterns of sinful behavior that will cause the unbeliever to be cast into the fiery lake of burning sulfur:
    - o *cowards*: Those who fear Satan more than they can have faith in Jesus; those that lack the virtue of courage to believe Jesus; those that profess without actual belief.
    - o *unbelievers*: Those who refuse to accept the person and work of Jesus.

- o *detestable persons*: Those who are attracted to the dark, impure, and demonic side of the human condition.
  - o *murderers*: Those who take human life, especially those who persecute believers.
  - o *the sexually immoral*: Those who participate in sexual sinfulness and prostitution.
  - o *those who practice magic spells*: Those who mix potions or mind-altering drugs (the literal meaning of sorcery) and claim to be able to communicate with the spirits of dead people. "In Old Testament times, communicating with evil spirits was a capital offense (Exod. 22:18; Lev. 19:26, 31; 20:6; Deut. 18:9-11). The lake of fire is God's appointed doom for all who practice witchcraft, spiritualism, channeling to spirits, devil worship, and other forms of sorcery."[7]
  - o *idol worshipers*: Those who worship other gods. Could those that could be obsessed with materialism and pleasure be part of this group?
  - o *all those who*: Those who emulate Satan, the father of lies (John 8:44), instead of following God's truth. Also, keep in mind that God specifically says one of the seven things that are an abomination to Him (i.e. He hates) is a lying tongue as recorded in Proverbs 6:6-17.
- The Lake of Fire: This in one of the Biblical terms that is used to refer to the permanent place of eternal punishment for the enemies of God, and it is used only five times in the Book of Revelation (19:20; 20:14, 25; 21:8).
  - + While the lake of fire may seem the same as Sheol in the Old Testament / Hades (hell) in the New Testament, it is not.
  - + The residents of the lake of fire include the following:
    - o Matthew 25:41: Those judged to be goats at the judgment of the Living Gentiles at Jesus' Second Coming (Judgment of the Sheep and Goats).
    - o Revelation 19:20: The Antichrist and the False Prophet.
    - o Implied by Revelation 20:10: The unimprisoned (Revelation 12:7-9) and imprisoned angels (2 Peter 2:4; Jude 1:6; and possibly those recorded in Genesis 6:1-2) who left their heavenly habitation and followed Satan.
    - o Revelation 20:10: Satan.
    - o Revelation 20:11: The spiritually loss of humankind.
- The Second Death: Refer to Section 44.2.

THE NEW JERUSALEM AS THE LAMB'S BRIDE

Core Scripture: Revelation 21:9-11.

An angel invites John to see *the bride, the wife of the Lamb*, and is then taken away in the spirit to a mountain and shown the New Jerusalem, descending out of heaven, and is described as brilliantly possessing the glory of God.

- John's Words of Description: It should be remembered that while John is shown many things that he could not have ever seen before, therefore, he would not have the appropriate vernacular vocabulary to describe the scenes in any other manner than what he was accustomed for the time in which he lived. "Obviously what he saw transcended any earthly experience, and it was necessary for him to describe what he saw in terms that were meaningful to him."[8]
- The Sequence of this Event within the Book of Revelation: There is an important consideration that needs to be examined and that is to determine which view should be held as to when this event occurs within the span of events recorded in the Book of Revelation. This issue is founded on the premise that the Book of Revelation is not written in chronological sequence, i.e. things in later passages happen before things in earlier passages, and a study of the content and the context of each event is required to determine when that event occurs in the overall order of events. As pointed out throughout this book, the multitude of events that comprise God's Plan for humankind is contained in the Bible and a timeless, or an ordered sequence of events, can be assembled as the events are discovered by study and arranged in juxtaposition to each other.
  - \+ A View of Eternity - Chronological Subsequent to Revelation 21:1-8: The view is based on the premise that the New Jerusalem is part of the eternal state because the passages that describe it are subsequent to the passage in Revelation that describes the new heaven and the new earth that follows the final revolt by Satan and the Great White Throne Judgement at the end of the 1,000-year Millennium.
- Walvoord[9] points out that many expositors "… have concluded that there is not sufficient justification for returning to the millennial scene after the tremendous events portraying the close of the millennium and the introduction of the new heaven and the new earth. For these scholars Revelation 21:9 through 22:7 is a description of the New Jerusalem as it will be established in the new earth in eternity to come. In other words this passage would refer to eternity rather than to the Millennium."
- There is Scriptural support for taking the various events of the last major section of Revelation, Chapters 19 through 22, as being chronologically sequential and as forming the transition from finite time, as known by humankind, to infinite time, as known by God.
  - \+ The description of the new city in 21:2 is essentially identical to that given in 21:9, therefore, there is every reason to believe they are

descriptions of the same New Jerusalem therefore, if 21:2 is seen as part of the eternal state, as is held by many theologians, then there is every reason to hold that 21:9 refers to the eternal state as well.

+ The implications of the passage indicates that the New Jerusalem arrives on a new earth, and the earth during the Millennium, while it will be restored and reconstructed to some extent, it will be far from being new in the same sense.

+ The details of the New Jerusalem indicate that there will not be a temple within because the presence of the Lord is the temple. This stands in direct contrast to the earthly city of Jerusalem and the surrounding area, described in Ezekiel 40 - 48, that will be present during the Millennium as the location of the Lord's throne. If the New Jerusalem was present during the Millennium, then is there not a location and purpose conflict regarding the Lord and His seat of ruling power?

+ As will be detailed below, there is sufficient explanation for the various aspects of the New Jerusalem, the mention of nations, kings of the earth, and the healing of the nations, that while they seem out of place in the context of the eternal state, they do not demand that they belong to the Millennium.

+ A Retrospective of the Millennium: This view is based on the premise that the New Jerusalem is part of the Millennium because of some of the particular things that are recorded in Revelation 21. This view is supported by those theologians and scholars that believe the New Jerusalem is an integral part of the Millennium and is the location where the resurrected saints live during the 1,000 years. One of the justifications of this view is the reference in Revelation 22:2 that the leaves for the healing of the nations is believed to be most applicable to the reconstruction and restoration conditions found in the Millennium.

• The Angel: The angel is described as the angel that held the seven bowls of God's wrath. The sense is that it is the angel that previously held the bowls, since this verse is after the pouring out of the bowl contents, as opposed to holding the bowls at the time John is taken to the mountain to see the New Jerusalem.

• The Bride, the Wife of the Lamb: Again, as in verse 21:2, the New Jerusalem is referred to as a bride, however unlike verse 21:2 where is it generally identified as a bride adorned for her husband, in verse 21:9 it is referred to as the Bride, the Wife of the Lamb. By personifying the body of believers in their place of eternal residence as a bride, the term is a used as a figure of speech to characterize the intimate relationship Jesus Christ will have with His believers.

• What John Sees and the Place from which He Sees It: Just as in Revelation 17:3, an angel takes John away in spirit and is shown something that in all likelihood is beyond anything John could have imagined. While the theologians will always debate if John was actually taken to a physical place or he only experiences the scene spiritually, he nevertheless is taken

487

to a huge and majestic mountain, possibly to stand on top of it, so that he has an appropriate vantage-point to see the descent of the New Jerusalem down from heaven to earth.

- The City of New Jerusalem: As stated in 21:2, John continues to describe the city descending from heaven, and in this passage he adds more detailed observations to the growing body of information:
  + It is again referred to as a holy city.
  + It is again described as descending out of heaven.
  + The city possesses the glory of God, and according to Walvoord[10], "the glory of God is the sum of His infinite perfections in their manifestations, so the New Jerusalem reflects all that God is."
  + Descriptions of the physical appearance of the New Jerusalem begins and John first says there is a kind of brilliance about the city that is like that of a precious stone, more specifically like a crystal-clear jasper stone. While later passages record John seeing actual precious stones that comprise architectural elements of the New Jerusalem, here the passage indicates that the brilliance is like a precious stone not that it is a precious stone. Again Walvoord[11]: "The city ablaze with light compared to the brightness of a precious stone such as jasper, and clear as crystal. The stone here described as a jasper has its name transliterated from a similar word in the original (Gr. *iaspsi*), a name used for stones of various colors, but here specifying the qualities "precious" and "clear as crystal". The mention of this stone which is costly to men but used lavishly in the New Jerusalem (cf. 21:19) is destined to manifest the glory of God."

THE WALLS, GATES, AND FOUNDATION OF THE NEW JERUSALEM

Core Scripture: Revelation 21:12-14.

The Apostle John now begins a detailed description of the physical aspects of this colossal structure that he has seen descend from heaven that includes a perimeter wall penetrated by gates, named for the twelve tribes of Israel, that are guarded by angels, and is supported on foundations, named for the twelve apostles.

- The Massive Walls: The first portion that John details is the great and high wall that surrounds the city (a fact that is not specifically stated).
  + Typically, throughout history a wall has served several purposes for a city or a tribe:
    o First and primarily, it was for protection from enemy forces, wild animals, and marauding thieves and killers.
    o Second, it was to exclude the unworthy, to keep undesirable people out from the midst of the community.

- ○ Third, in later centuries it came to represent the nature and might of the people that it surrounded.
  - + In this context, as will be implied in later verses, it seems that the wall here is to serve as a symbolic reminder that only those that are qualified are allowed to enter the city by passing through the gates in the wall.
- The Twelve Gates: Next John indicates that there are twelve gates that pierce the massive wall to allow access into the city. The word that is used suggests the gate is similar to that found at the entrances of temples and palaces, implying that there will be a grandeur, or majesty, about the gates.
  - + While the size, scale, or nature of the gates are not detailed, it seems logical that if the wall in which they are located is great and high then the gates as well might be great and high.
  - + In spite of the fact that John has not disclosed the square shape or plan of the city, he describes that there are three gates on each of the four walls of the city.
- The Twelve Angels: While not specifically stated as such, the implication is that there is an angel positioned at each of the twelve gates, apparently as an honor guard.
- The Twelve Tribe Names on the Gates: The passage indicates that the names of the twelve tribes of Israel are written on the gates, however, it does not indicate if all twelve names are written on each gate, or, if a particular tribe is associated with a particular gate. Even though the heavenly New Jerusalem will be much different than the earthly Millennial Temple described by the prophet Ezekiel, it is always possible that the names on the gates of the New Jerusalem will have only one tribe name recorded on it much as was the case on the gates in the Millennial Temple (cf. Ezekiel 48:31-34).
- The Twelve Foundations: John records that the wall of the city has twelve foundations *and on them were the names of the twelve apostles of the Lamb*.
  - + It should be noted that the foundation referred to here is the foundation for the wall surrounding the city and is not the foundation for the city itself.
  - + There is debate regarding the inclusion of the twelve apostles in the context of the foundation for the wall surrounding the New Jerusalem. The significance for the inclusion of the twelve apostles as part of the New Jerusalem is that, as Jewish leaders called to be the founding leaders of the New Testament Church, they serve to bind the Church and Israel together into one unified body.

THE PHYSICAL SIZE OF THE CITY

Core Scripture: Revelation 21:15-17.

After describing the wall, John then provides factual details regarding the dimensions of the city, the foundation and the wall as measured by the angel.

489

- Golden Measuring Rod: The angel uses a reed which is an ancient instrument that was commonly used for measuring length that was about ten feet long.
- Dimensions of the City: The angel measures the city and determines it to be square in plan, with each side being 12,000 furlongs (a furlong being 582 feet in length), which is 1,342 miles – commonly spoken of as being fifteen hundred miles. The city is also indicated to be fifteen hundred miles in height.
- Dimensions of the Wall: The angel then measures the wall and determines it to be 144 cubits (a cubit being 18 inches in length), which is 216 feet tall.

Regardless of the shape (see distinction below), the massive size of the city will be such that all saints will exist eternally in comfort within the physical parameters of the New Jerusalem.

THE MATERIALS OF WHICH THE CITY IS BUILT

Core Scripture: Revelation 21:18-21.

John now describes the beauty of the city by identifying the various precious stones that comprise the physical structure of the city.
- The Wall and the City: As John recorded in 21:11 where he indicated that the brilliance of the city was like crystal-clear jasper, he reiterates here that the wall is made of jasper and the city is made of gold, refined to the point that both are pure and as transparent as glass. While John says that the city is made of gold, the fact that it is transparent which is not possible for humans to accomplish could mean one of two things: either through God's power the gold is made transparent (the preferred view since it is what is literally stated), or it is a transparent materials that has the appearances of gold. "Employing the language of semblance, John is endeavoring to give a description of a scene which in most respects transcends earthly experience. The constant mention of transparency indicates that the city is designed to transmit the glory of God in the form of light without hinderance."[12]
- The Foundation of the Wall: John observes that the foundation of the wall is adorned with all kinds of precious stones of a multitude of colors however note that he does not say that the foundation is made of these stones, only that they are garnished with them. He then proceeds to list them, for an undisclosed reason, in a particular order however, it is not clear if he is listing them from the top down or from the bottom up:
  + Jasper, probably as the other instances it is mentioned it is crystal clear.
  + Sapphire, blue.
  + Agate (or chalcedony), thought to be sky-blue with stripes of other colors running through it.
  + Emerald, a bright green color.
  + Onyx (or sardonyx), a red and white stone.

+ Ruby, a red colored jewel.
+ Chrysolite, a transparent stone that is thought to be golden in color.
+ Beryl, sea-green.
+ Topaz, transparent yellow-green.
+ Turquoise, another shade of green.
+ Jacinth, a violet color.
+ Amethyst, commonly purple.

"Though the precise colors of these stones in some cases are not certain, the general picture here described by John is one of unmistakable beauty, designed to reflect the glory of God in a spectrum of brilliant color. ... The city is undoubtedly far more beautiful to the eye than anything that man has ever been able to create, and it reflects not only the infinite wisdom and power of God but also His grace as extended to the objects of His salvation."[13]

- The Gates: While it is mind-boggling to try to picture it, the twelve gates are each described to be formed from just one single pearl!
- The Street: As is stated earlier about the wall and the city, the main street is made of pure and transparent gold. The mention of a street suggests that the city will have an infrastructure somewhat similar to the sort of the patterns that are known by humankind – if there are streets, there may be other things such as houses and buildings.

THE TEMPLE OF THE NEW JERUSALEM

Core Scripture: Revelation 21:22.

In contrast to the history of Israel that included first a tabernacle and then a temple during the Millennium, there will be no temple as the place to worship God, to the temple that exists during Daniel's 70th Week, and the temple during the Millennium, there will be no temple in the New Jerusalem because the Lord God Himself and Jesus the Lamb will be the only temple that will be necessary. As was the case during human history, an intermediate structure for the formal worship of God is not required because the saints live in the physical presence of the Lord.

GOD IS THE LIGHT OF THE CITY

Core Scripture: Revelation 21:23-24.

John notices, or is shown, that the shining light of the sun and the moon are not necessary to provide light to the New Jerusalem, all that is required is provided by the glory of God and the Lamb. It should be noted that the passage does not

say that there is no sun or moon (which would not be consistent with the newly created heavens), but that light from either celestial body is required.
- The Light of the Lord is all that is Necessary:
    + That the Lord is frequently referred to throughout the Old Testament as being the equivalent of light, the condition in eternity is that a metaphor in the human history of God's program is given actual manifestation.
    + Also, in the New Testament Jesus is equated with the light as can be seen in the following passages of John's Gospel:
        ○ 1:7-9: *He came as a witness to testify concerning that light, so that through him all might believe. He himself was not the light; he came only as a witness to the light.*
        ○ 3:19: Even though *Light has come into the world*, there are still people who love the *darkness*.
        ○ 8:12: *When Jesus spoke again to the people, he said, I am the light of the world. Whoever follows me will never walk in darkness, but will have the light of life.*
        ○ 12:35: *Then Jesus tells them, You are going to have the light just a little while longer. Walk while you have the light, before darkness overtakes you. Whoever walks in the dark does not know where they are going.*
    + See also Revelation 22:5.
- The Nations: The concept that God is the light continues by indicating that the nations that reside in the New Jerusalem will walk in the light provided by God. The Greek word used, which can mean nations of Gentiles, more than likely refers to the class of Gentiles as the non-Jewish peoples rather than the Gentiles as political entities or nations. The idea here is that they may still be national identities and they as well as their leaders will bring their glory to the presence of the Lord in His glory.

ACCESS TO THE NEW JERUSALEM

Core Scripture: Revelation 21:25-27.

John closes his description of the city itself by noting that the gates will never close, there will never be night, and only the clean will enter the city.
- The Gates Never Close: Even though there will be gates that provide access into and out of the city, they are said to never be closed during the day, and since there is no night, the gates will never be closed. This calls into question the need for gates for the wall for that matter. The best explanation, as implied above, is that the wall represents the spiritual boundary as a reminder for those that are faithful, and the gates represent the spiritual portal in which only the qualified may enter.
- There will be no Light: If the Lord is the source of the light for the city and its inhabitant, then there obviously can be no darkness within the city.

- The Wealth of Nations Will Come: John reiterates that the Gentiles will bring their glory and wealth to the Lord.
- No Unclean Will Enter: This passage is somewhat difficult because it gives the impression that there will be unclean people in the vicinity of the New Jerusalem who are not eligible to enter the city. Rather than this being a description of the time of the New Jerusalem, this probably is for the reader to point out that only those that are spiritual clean in their human life will enter the eternal city in their future life. There is no indication that there will be anyone other than the saints in and around the New Jerusalem in eternity. All of the unfaithful have been judged and confined to eternal punishment in the lake of burning fire.

THE RIVER OF THE WATER OF LIFE AND THE TREE OF LIFE

Core Scripture: Revelation 22:1-2.

John's attention is turned away from the city to the things emanating from the Lord's throne.

- The River of the Water of Life: The river of the water of life is said to pour out from the throne of God and the Lamb which emphasizes the purity and holiness of God. This is similar to, but not the same as, the river that flowed out from the Millennial Temple (Ezekiel 47:1, 12) or from Jerusalem (Zechariah 14:8). The river runs down the middle of the main street of the city. The idea here is that the thing that God's creatures need to sustain eternal life in imperishable bodies is what is provided by God and is symbolized in the form of water that flows from God to His creatures. This is the manifestation of Jesus' words on earth about Him being the source to quench eternal thirst.
- The Throne of God and the Lamb: The references to the throne of God is qualified by the fact that, while the word throne is singular, it belongs to both the Lord God and Jesus Christ the Lamb.
- The Tree of Life: The tree of life serves as Biblical bookends of truth – it is one of the first mentioned in the Bible and is one of the last things mentioned. It seems likely that the tree of life in Revelation is the same tree of life of Genesis, and it also seems to close the loops to speak by bringing God's creation back to its original state. While the fruit of the tree for eternal life in Genesis, here in Revelation it is the leaves of the tree that are for the healing of the nations. The Greek word used means therapeutic in English and is best understood in this context as health-giving, serving, and ministering. It is not likely that actual healing will be necessary in the New Jerusalem during eternity, so it is probably a symbolic representation that conditions requiring healing will never occur, instead the contribution that the tree and its leaves makes is for the nations to enjoy the blessings of the eternal state.

THE THRONE AND WORSHIP OF
GOD AND THE LAMB

Core Scripture: Revelation 22:3-5.

The verse begins with the statement of fact that there will no longer be anything that is cursed in the future city because the throne of God and the Lamb will be in the midst of the New Jerusalem, and, the Lord's servants will worship Him face to face and His name will be written on their foreheads. The curse, bestowed by God on Adam, Eve, and the earth after the Fall, will be completely lifted – everything will be delivered from the tumult brought on by human sinfulness. This lifting can only be possible by the fact that everything not worthy has been judged and sent to its destiny. John closes the details of the New Jerusalem by summarizing the character of the eternal state: the Lord will shine on His children and the saints will worship their Lord forever and ever.

GENERAL OBSERVATION OF THE NEW JERUSALEM

There are observations that may be made about the New Jerusalem that are either, not evident in a verse-by-verse analysis, or, may be seen from inductive reasoning.
- Nature of John's Descriptions: As has been discussed in chapters before, it should be kept in mind that the future city that is recorded in last verses of the Bible is described by John using words and concepts that are unique to him and his place in history.
  + In spite of the few details included in the above passages, not much is really available to get a sense of what the New Jerusalem will be like. When we read these last two chapters of Revelation, like John we can only think about it only as far as our imaginations and intellectual sophistication can take us. Thus, the picture we mentally paint uses images of which we are familiar and that familiarity only to the architectural and environmental scenes in which we have lived, worked, and visited. Also, the physical, built architectural and urban landscape of which we are familiar will in all likelihood be elementary when compared to the New Jerusalem that the Lord has prepared for His body of believers.
  + John, like any other human being, would have no way of understanding, much less describing or explaining, an object or artifact from the future. This would certainly be true for something as massively large and complex as a city, not to mention the fact it may be hovering in the sky. John's uses of precious stones to describe the city could only have been done for one of two reasons, the city is actually composed of these same precious stones, or, the only way John could explain what he saw was to describe precious stones that the city appeared to be like.

- + The New Jerusalem will be an edifice that will most probably far surpass any building created by humankind in form, function, use of materials, aesthetic design quality, and finally in excellence. The New Jerusalem will be a city that will be nothing even remotely resembling any architecture designed by a human. The contrast will be extreme – the greatest achievements of humankind are particular houses and commercial buildings chosen by the peers of its designer as works worthy of recognition because of the skill involved in its design will be insignificant when set beside the city that will have been designed and constructed by the same God that created the universe, the earth, and the creatures that walk the earth, human beings.

- Only Place in the New Order?: The New Jerusalem is the only place of habitation that is identified within the new heaven and new earth and, because of God's historical connection with the city of the same name on earth as well as Jerusalem being the Lord's capital during the Millennium, the New Jerusalem will be the capital of the "world" in which the saved will live in eternity.

- Will the New Jerusalem be Literal?: While the scene that John sees is astonishingly impressive and beyond not only John's imagination, but almost beyond our own notwithstanding the state that technology exists today, there are differences between students of Biblical prophecy in theological interpretation and opinion as to if the structure John describes is a literal city, or is the scene he sees will receive in eternity. Walvoord responds this way: "There does not seem to be any solid objection to the concept that the saints in the new heaven and the new earth will have as their home precisely such a city, glorious in every respect, reaching to tremendous heights into the new heaven, and embodying characteristics to remind them of their spiritual heritage."[14]

- Relationship with the Earth: It is not clear where the New Jerusalem stops its descent from heaven, above the earth's surface in the clouds, or, resting on the earth's surface.
  - + Why would it have been necessary for there to be a new earth if the New Jerusalem was not to be associated with it? In the absence of any other information, if the earth is renovated to a condition identical or similar to the current condition with geography, flora, fauna, atmosphere, climate, etc., the New Jerusalem may be the only structure on the earth's surface. Could it be that the remainder of the earth not covered by the New Jerusalem is a garden paradise in the same manner as the Garden of Eden for the saints to enjoy?
  - + Another condition that is not answered by the Bible is what the relationship will be between the earth and the New Jerusalem regarding the saints and whether they will live on one or the other and how they will travel between the two. As will be discussed in the next chapter about heaven, the Bible seems to imply that heaven will be on earth.

- Shape of the City, or is it a Planet? Jesus's revelation identifies the New Jerusalem as a city, however, its physical size makes it more along the lines of a very small planet. While the New Jerusalem is square in plan, nothing is mentioned regarding the shape of the city. Based on our limited human imagination, which we cannot conceive of the massive New Jerusalem coming down out of heaven in the first place, the only shapes that come to mind include the following:
  + It could be a cube and have any of the following interior organizations and arrangements:
    o It will probably have many levels, passageways going in many directions, an atria, or openings between the levels. This shape would make sense if the heavenly position was such that earth's gravity still exerted an influence. This would make the city similar to a modern building despite its planet size.
    o It could be like a box with communities, houses, buildings "floating" in the space confined by the outside walls of the city with movement between things like flying through the air. This seems plausible since the saints will probably not be bound by physical limitation any longer (which brings into question the influence of gravity).
    o Rather than living inside the city, saints could live on the outside much like humankind currently lives on the earth's surface.
    o It could be a pyramid on the same order as the Egyptian pyramids. This shape would also allow levels, passageways, multiple atriums as well and as of the living arrangements described previously. "... [T]his shape provides a vehicle for the river of life to proceed out of the throne of God, which seems to be at the top, to find its way to the bottom, assuming our experience of gravity will be somewhat normal also in the new earth."[15]
    o It could be a formless or irregular shape defined by functions rather than the necessity to have a pre-determined form.
    o Interestingly it could be nothing like any city of ancient or modern times. When we read these passages, we tend to think in terms of either an urban environment of which we are accustomed, or, we try to imagine the texture and pattern of an ancient city. Because of the physical size of the New Jerusalem, it could be a gigantic earthlike mountain on the basis that mountains are Biblical metaphors for power and majesty, and the Millennial Jerusalem sits atop a mountain with Jesus's Temple being the highest part. This would fit with other aspects of the descriptions, especially those that indicate the river of life flows down from the throne of God.

One thing is certain however, the city will anthropomorphically accommodate the physical form of the saints as resurrected human beings having eternal bodies. We have an insight into that form from what the Bible says about Jesus when He was in His resurrected form between His resurrection from death and His ascension to heaven. At that time, He was still in the bodily form of a human being, He was recognizable, He moved through physical space, He talked, ate, interacted with mortals, and finally He moved through the sky when He ascended.

- Frequency of the Number Twelve: The number twelve is common in the description of the New Jerusalem in addition to its frequent use in the Book of Revelation, not to mention all the other instances it occurs in spiritual things. Most scholars believe the use of the number twelve signifies the completeness of things, as according to some, eternal perfection. The instances of the number twelve, especially in prophecy and in the Book of Revelation, include the following:
  + Twelve tribes of Israel.
  + Twelve apostles of Jesus Christ.
  + Twenty-four elders around the throne (a double twelve).
  + Twelve stars in the crown of the woman.
  + Twelve types of fruit on the tree of life.
  + Twelve pearly gates in the wall around the New Jerusalem guarded by twelve angels.
  + Twelve foundations adorned with twelve precious stones on the wall around the New Jerusalem.
  + Twelve tribes of Israel each contributing 12,000 members to the 144,000 Jews sealed by God during Daniel's 70th Week.
  + Twelve-cubit thickness of the wall around the New Jerusalem.
  + Twelve thousand furlongs as the length, height, and width of the New Jerusalem.

57.3 RELATIONSHIP BETWEEN THE NEW HEAVENS AND EARTH AND THE NEW JERUSALEM

First, the old heavens and old earth will be purged and burned away and replaced with the new heavens and the new earth. As we will see in the next chapter, heaven will take place in the new heavens and on the new earth. Otherwise, if heaven is not on the new earth, then what is the reason for creating a new earth? Second, the New Jerusalem will descend from heaven and will hover above the earth and is the place that Christ told the world before His ascension that He is going to prepare a place for believers. The New Jerusalem will be enormous and will probably have a dwelling place for every believer. Both of these are described as such in the Bible.

But what the Bible does not indicate is exactly where the saints will live. They are said to live with God in the new heaven however, it is implied that they will dwell on the new earth, and it is implied that they will live in the New Jerusalem. What exactly will happen?

58

HEAVEN

We now arrive at the ultimate destiny of all saints – Heaven. At this point, there will be no evil and nothing left to happen to people or the earth except eternal life with God in an entirely new creation. All will be new. Heaven is that state of being that all believers eagerly long for. Since there are very few books about heaven and it is only preached from the pulpit in a very general sense, most believers have little understanding of what heaven will be like. So we long for heaven but we only know that it is a promise from God and it will be a perfect state of existence. Throughout this book we have studied a considerable number of topics, both past and future, and now we are going to examine the nature of heaven and what it will be like for those who live in eternity.

The first big question is: Where will heaven be? It is the contention of this book that heaven will be on the restored earth with the New Jerusalem in the sky above. "What would be the point of the earth being liberated if not to play host, once again, to God's family as it did in the beginning? … When we consider the glory of heaven, we can use this earth as a paradigm. It is as if this world is a blueprint of what's to come; it will be similar but infinitely better."[1]

The second big question is: What will heaven be like? Many believers have the unsubstantiated perception that we will all just be singing while sitting on a floating cloud. But that can't possibly be the answer. God designed and caused an entire universe to come into being. That creation included an earth that was especially suited for His created beings. He then created His masterpiece, human beings, and allotted them a purpose and a time to live on the earth. While there were times in which life on earth was tough for some humans, God's desire is for all humans to live a good and righteousness life. He has allowed humans an unlimited ability to grow intellectually, culturally, socially, and spiritually. He has also allowed humans to create "things" that improve life on earth.

So, if God created humans to have a fruitful experience during their time on earth, what more would He do for them in eternity? He has given us so much, so why would we expect anything less in heaven? It is the contention of this book to hold the belief that God will reward His faithful with an eternity that is much more than what life was like on earth. The Scripture that is considered below paints a picture that life in heaven will be somewhat similar to life on earth, but in a much greater way. Think of it this way: life for the faithful on earth is an imperfect, limited trial run for a life spent in a perfect, eternal heaven.

"God poured himself, his creativity, and his love into making Eden for his creatures. But at that time, that's all we were: his creatures, his image-bearers. Now that we are both his children and his *bride*, chosen out of the human race to live with him forever, would we expect more or less than Eden? More, of course, and that's exactly what the New Earth will be."[2] "The purpose of heaven is to restore the glory of God's relationship with His creation, with humans as the pinnacle."[3]

It should be noted the resurrected beings that will populate heaven will be those that have come out of the Millennium. The Bible does not speak to there being any differences between the Millennium beings and the heavenly beings. The only difference there could possibly be is that the heavenly beings might be more perfect than the Millennium beings.

58.1	**THE RELATIONSHIP BETWEEN THE MILLENNIUM AND THE NEW HEAVENS AND THE NEW EARTH**

The relationship between the millennium and heaven is that they are both distinctly different times in God's Plan. The sequence of events after Daniel's 70th Week is: Christ's Second Advent, the Millennium, the Great White Throne Judgement, the purging and destruction of the old earth and old heaven and creation of a new earth and new heavens, and then eternity.

The Bible does not speak to if there will be any improvements to the resurrected body we had in the Millennium in preparation for eternity. It seems logical that since the human body is resurrected once, that that state is sufficient for both the millennium and the new earth. Heaven will be populated by the following groups:
- The human saints coming out of the millennium who will be given body and a soul equivalent to the body and soul given at others at resurrection.
- The resurrected saints coming out of the millennium.

THE PASSAGES ABOUT THE MILLENNIUM OR THE NEW HEAVENS AND THE NEW EARTH

The Bible contains a considerable number of passages that are believed to refer to the conditions in the millennium, while there seems to be few verses that refer to the conditions that will exist in the new heavens and the new earth. Since heaven is the future we long for, it seems incongruous of the Bible to not have verses about life in eternity when it has so many that reference the millennium. It could very well be that some of the verses referring to the millennium could just as easily apply to the new heavens and new earth; so that leaves us with a question: do the passages refer to the millennium exclusively, or, do they qualify under the law of double reference discussed in Section 3.11 and apply to the new heavens and new earth as well? While no theologian or scholar has been found that directly supports the notion of double references, it seems that it is plausible.

The only place in the Bible that deals with the 1,000-year millennial rule by Jesus Christ is Revelation 21:1-6; there is no mention of this time in the Old Testament. We base our belief of the millennium on these six verses and the many Old Testament verses that speak about a future time when things will be significantly better. These verses state many things about the future, that Israel will be restored to her promised land, that the world will live in peace, that Jesus Christ will reign as King, and that the people will enjoy many blessings.

58.2   THE EXISTENCE OF HEAVEN

It is obvious to believers that heaven exists however it might be instructive to review some of the numerous passages that give support to the existence of heaven as a place of existence:

- Daniel 7:13: In Daniel's vision, he saw the *son of man, coming with the clouds of heaven,* approach *the Ancient of Days and was led into his presence.*
- Matthew 5:16, 34, 45; 6:1, 9-10, 20; 7:11, 21; 10:32-33; 11:25; 12:50; 16:17, 19; 18:10, 14, 18-19; 21:25; 23:9; 24:35-36; 28:18: The testimony of Christ confirms that heaven is the residence of God the Father.
- Acts 1:11: The angels tell the men of Galilee that Jesus, *who has been taken from you into heaven, will come back in the same way you have seen him go into heaven.*
- 2 Corinthians:
  + 5:8: Paul wrote that being in heaven as being *away from the body* and being in heaven *at home with the Lord.* It is far better to be in heaven.
  + 5:17: *Therefore, if anyone is in Christ, the new creation has come.* This means Jews and Gentiles that believe in Christ will form a new body.
- Philippians 1:23: Paul states that being *with Christ* is *better by far* than being on earth.
- 1 Thessalonians 4:17: This passage describes a portion of the Rapture: *After that, we who are still alive and are left will be caught up together with them in the clouds to meet the Lord in the air. And so we will be with the Lord forever.*
- Revelation:
  + 4 – 5: John saw a revelation of heaven.
  + 22:2: In the New Jerusalem, the leaves of the tree of life are for healing.
  + 22:5: Heaven will last forever and ever.

58.3   TERMS USED TO DESCRIBE HEAVEN

The Greek word used for paradise is *paradeisos*, which is the same Greek word transliterated in the Septuagint in Genesis 2:8-9 for garden (containing the tree of life and tree of knowledge of good and evil), in Nehemiah 2:8 for forest (belonging to King Artaxerxes), in Ecclesiastes 2:5 for parks (one of Solomon's royal projects), and in Song of Songs 4:13 for orchards (part of Solomon's description of his lover's beauty). We can see that the word came to mean the ultimate place of beauty, peace, and security, owned by royalty. At the time of the New Testament, the use of paradeisos was extended to include the idea that the dead that were blessed would be in such a place. "… to the oriented mind it (paradise) expressed the sum total of blessedness."[4]

- Luke 23:43: At the crucifixion, Jesus tells one of the two criminals also being crucified that, because of his recognition that Jesus was the Son of God as recorded in verse 39, and his repentant confession of faith recorded in verse 42, the criminal would be in paradise with the Lord Jesus Christ that very day.
- 2 Corinthians 12:2-4: Paul equates paradise with the third heaven, which is a common reference for the abode of God that Paul uses in his books.
- Revelation 2:7: Paradise is used to symbolize the place where the pre-Fall harmony will once again exist between God and His creation for those that overcome the world.

58.4 BELIEVERS BELONG IN HEAVEN

When a believer dies, the soul goes to the intermediate state for a time until the resurrection, and then comes to heaven, that place in which the believer belongs. As believers in Christ, we are already living in heaven in a sense and enjoying some of the benefits such as the knowledge our lives will be eternal. Our citizenship is in heaven, everything of eternal value is there. The Christian life we live on earth is meant to be like heaven on earth and one that emulates the Lord Jesus Christ.

- Matthew:
  + 5:12: Jesus says, *Rejoice and be glad, because great is your reward in heaven, for in the same way they persecuted the prophets who were before you.*
  + 6:19-20: Jesus says, *Do not store up for yourselves treasures on earth … But store up for yourselves treasures in heaven …*
- John 14:2: Jesus says, *My Father's house has many rooms; if that were not so, would I have told you that I am going there to prepare a place for you?*
- 2 Corinthians 5:1-2: *For we know that if the earthly tent we live in is destroyed, we have a building from God, an eternal house in heaven, not built by human hands. Meanwhile we groan, longing to be clothed instead with our heavenly dwelling.*
- Ephesians:
  + 1:3: *Praise be to the God and Father of our Lord Jesus Christ, who has blessed us in the heavenly realms with every spiritual blessing in Christ.*
  + 2:5-6: *made us alive with Christ even when we were dead in transgressions – it is by grace you have been saved.*

- Philippians 3:20: *But our citizenship is in heaven. And we eagerly await a Savior from there, the Lord Jesus Christ*
- Colossians 1:5: *the faith and love that spring from the hope stored up for you in heaven and about which you have already heard in the true message of the gospel* …
- Hebrews 11:13: *All these people were still living by faith when they died. They did not receive the things promised; they only saw them and welcomed them for a distance, admitting that they were foreigners and strangers on earth.*
- 2 Peter 3:13: *But in keeping with his promise we are looking forward to a new heaven and a new earth, where righteousness dwells.*

The Glory of Heaven

"We aren't yet in heaven bodily. But positionally, we are seated with Christ in the heavenlies. Because of our spiritual union with Him, we have already entered into the heavenly realm. We already possess eternal life, and the spiritual riches of heaven are ours in Jesus Christ. … Everything that is truly precious to us as Christians is in heaven."[5]

- God the Father dwells in heaven:
  + Matthew 6:9: The Lord's Prayer begins with *"This, then, is how you should pray: " 'Our, Father in heaven, hallowed be your name* …..
- Jesus Christ sits at the right hand of God where He intercedes for us:
  + Hebrews:
    o 7:25: Christ … *always lives to intercede for them.*
    o 9:24: Christ … *entered heaven itself, now to appear for us in God's presence.*
- God keeps the records of human history in heaven and our names are recorded there because we have an inheritance there and a title deed to property:
  + Luke:
    o 10:20: *rejoice that your names are written in heaven.*
    o 12:33: *a treasure in heaven that will never fail*
  + 1 Peter 1:4: *and into an inheritance that can never perish, spoil, or fade. This inheritance is kept in heaven for you*
- Believers belong in heaven:
  + Philippians 3:20: *our citizenship is in heaven*
  + Hebrews 11:13: Believers *are foreigners and strangers on earth.* The adjacent table lists the passage as it appears in other translations.
- Many of our spiritual brothers and sisters, our departed loved ones, and the Old Testament and New Testament believers who have died are in heaven:
  + Hebrews 12:23: *to the church of the firstborn, whose names*

Hebrews 11:13	
NIV	*foreigners and strangers*
NASB	*strangers and exiles*
NET	*strangers and foreigners*
KJV	*strangers and pilgrims*
NKJV	*strangers and pilgrims*
AMP	*strangers and temporary residents and exiles*

are written in heaven. You have come to God, the Judge of all, to the spirits of the righteous made perfect.

58.5 THE KINDS OF HEAVEN

History, both Christian and secular, has recognized three kinds of heaven and it is the third kind that is of interest to this study.

FIRST HEAVEN – ATMOSPHERIC HEAVEN

This kind of heaven includes that that is immediately above us, the sky and the region of breathable air in the atmospheric realm known as the troposphere which surrounds us and extends to about 20 miles into the sky. The things the Bible records as happening in the sky is usually within 10 miles of the earth's surface.

- Deuteronomy:
  + 11:11, 17: When Israel obeys God he will send *rain from heaven*; when they disobey, He will cut off the rain and their land ill *yield no produce.*
  + 28:12, 24: Moses told Israel: *The Lord will open the heavens, the storehouse of his bounty, to send rain on your land in season and to bless all the work of your hands.* ... but then later he told them if they are disobedient, *The Lord will turn the rain of your country into dust and powder; it will come down from the skies until you are destroyed.*
  + 33:13: ... *May the Lord bless his land with the precious dew from heaven above* ...
- Psalm 147:8: *He covers the sky with clouds; he supplies the earth with rain and makes grass grow on the hills.*
- Joshua 10:11: ... *the Lord hurled large hailstone down on them* ...
- The Psalms:
  + 18:13: *The Lord thundered from heaven* ...
  + 78:26: *He let loose the east wind from the heavens and by his power made the south wind blow.*
  + 147:8: *He covers the sky with clouds; he supplies the earth with rain and makes grass grow on the hills.*
- Proverbs 23:5: *fly off to the sky like an eagle.*
- Isaiah 55:9-10: *As the heavens are higher than the earth, so are my ways higher than your ways and my thoughts than your thoughts. As the rain and the snow come down from heaven, and do not return to it without watering the earth and making it bud and flourish, so that it yields seed for the sower and bread for the eater.*
- Daniel 7:2: *the four winds of heaven churning up the great sea* ...
- Zechariah 6:5: *The angel answered me. "There are the four spirits of heaven, going out from standing in the presence of the Lord of the whole world.*

- Matthew 24:30: *When Christ comes again, all the peoples of the earth will mourn when they see the Son of Man coming on the clouds of heaven, with power and great glory.*
- Acts 1:9: Jesus was taken up to heaven *and a cloud hid him.*
- Ephesians 2:2: *when you followed the ways of the world and of the ruler of the kingdom of the air, the spirit who is now at work in those who are disobedient.*
- 2 Thessalonians 4:17: *we who are still alive and are left will be caught up together with them in the clouds to meet the Lord forever.*

SECOND HEAVEN – CELESTIAL HEAVEN

This kind of heaven includes the stellar realm, the sun, stars and the planets.
- Genesis 1:14: *And God said, "Let there be lights in the vault of the sky to separate the day from the night …*
- Exodus 20:4: As one of the ten commandments, Israel was given a warning not to make an image (idol) *in the form of anything in heaven above …*
- Deuteronomy 4:19: *And when you look up to the sky and see the sun, the moon and the stars – all the heavenly array – do not be enticed into bowing down to them and worshipping things the Lord your God has apportioned to all the nations under heaven.*
- Nehemiah 9:23: *You made their children as numerous as the stars in the sky …*
- Isaiah 47:13 (cf. Jeremiah 10:2): Israel is warned not to use the movements of celestial bodies to predict the future.
- Hebrews:
  + 1:10: *"In the beginning, Lord, you laid the foundations of the earth, and the heavens are the work of our hands.*
  + 11:12: *… came descendants as numerous as the stars in the sky …*
- 2 Peter 3:5: *… by God's word the heaven came into being …*

THIRD HEAVEN – THE ABODE OF GOD

This kind of heaven is the heaven of heavens where God, the Creator of all things, lives with His holy angels and where His throne is located. This is also the ultimate destination of believers. "Even though we are told in the Scriptures that the "heaven of heavens cannot contain God" (1Kings 8:27; 2 Chron. 2:6), and that God is everywhere present, on the earth as well as in heaven (Deut. 4:39; Joshua 2:11), nevertheless, the same Scriptures clearly teach that God does dwell particularly in heaven, a place often designated as *His habitation.*"[6]
- 1 Kings 8: 30, 32, 34, 36, 39, 43, 45, and 49: Solomon, in his great dedicatory prayer, pled for Israel to *hear from heaven.*

- Psalm 33:13-14: *From heaven the Lord looks down and sees all mankind; from his dwelling place he watches all who live on earth …*
- Isaiah:
  + 57:15: *For this is what the high and exalted One says – he who lives forever, whose name is holy: I live in a high and holy place, but also with the one who is contrite and lowly in spirit, to revive the spirit of the lowly and to revive the heart of the contrite.*
  + 63:15: *Look down from heaven and see, from your lofty throne, holy and glorious.*
  + 66:1: *This is what the Lord says: "Heaven is my throne, and the earth is my footstool.*
- Matthew:
  + 5:45: Jesus says, *that you may be children of your Father in heaven.*
  + 7:21: Jesus says, *"Not everyone who says to me, 'Lord, Lord, will enter the kingdom of heaven, but only the one who does the will of my Father who is in heaven.*
  + 10:32-33: Jesus says, *"Whoever acknowledges me before others, I will also acknowledge before my Father in heaven. But whoever disowns me before others, I will disown before my Father in heaven.*
  + 18:10: Jesus says, *"See that you do not despise one of these little ones. For I tell you that their angels in heaven always see the face of my Father in heaven.*
- Luke 22:34: *An angel from heaven appeared to him and strengthened him.*
- Revelation:
  + 3:12: Jesus says, *the new Jerusalem, which is coming down out of heaven from my God.*
  + 4:2: *At once I was in the Spirit, and there before me was a throne in heaven with someone sitting on it.*
  + 15:5: *I saw in heaven the temple – that is, the tabernacle of the covenant law – and it was opened.*
  + 21:10: *the Holy City, Jerusalem, coming down out of heaven from God.*

58.6   WHERE WILL THE SAINTS LIVE?

So, just where will the saints live in eternity?

While we use the word heaven to mean the place where we will spend eternity, there are actually three realms that will be available: the New Earth, the New Heavens, and the New Jerusalem. If God and all the saints live on the New Earth, then what is the purpose of the New Heavens, and the New Jerusalem? The Bible speaks frequently about the saints living on the New Earth, but it does not say much about who will live in the New Heavens. What's more, in the description of the New Jerusalem there is not much said about who the inhabitants will be, in spite of all the details they the saints will probably be distributed among all three realms. This implies that all saints will have the ability to move between any of the realms without restriction or limitation.

58.7 | THE RELATIONSHIP WITH GOD

While the Bible reveals a great deal about God, it will be only a drop in the bucket of what it will be like to see him personally and be in His presence. Take a moment to think about this: in our future there will be a time when we will each have the opportunity of being in the presence of the Awesome God Almighty, the Creator of all things. God's greatest gift to His human creatures is Himself. He wants us to draw closer to Him and to recognize Him as the source of all our joys. "Beholding and knowing God, we will spend eternity worshipping, exploring, and serving him, seeing his magnificent beauty in everything and everyone around us."[7]

As shocking it is to us now, we will see the face of God in heaven. During human life on earth, God did not allow His face to be seen by humans who would die if they saw it. But in heaven we will be able to see His face because of our holiness. To see our Lord face-to-face is a wonder of our redemption.
- Hebrews 12:14: *Make every effort to live in peace with everyone and to be holy; without holiness no one will see the Lord.*
- Matthew 22:4: *They will see his face, and his name will be on their foreheads.*

When the Son became Jesus and walked the earth, He said that if his face is seen, then the face of God has been seen. Whenever we see Jesus we also see God.
- Matthew 1:23: *and give birth to a son, and they will call him Immanuel (which means "God with us").*
- John:
  + 1:14: *The Word became flesh and made his dwelling among us. We have seen his glory, the glory of the one and only Son, who came from the Father, full of grace and truth.*
  + 14:9: *Anyone who has seen me has seen the Father?*

Another way we can see the invisible qualities of God is that we can see the wonders of the earth, animals, flowers, the many forms of weather, the sun, moon, and stars, and the people all around us.
- Romans 1:20: *For since the creation of the world God's invisible qualities – his eternal power and divine nature – have been clearly seen, being understood from what has been made, so that people are without excuse.*

58.8 | LIFE IN ETERNITY

The operative question to be considered is: will life in heaven be a reset back to the Garden of Eden, or will it be a continuation of life on earth? Based on the Bible, it appears it will be a continuation of life on earth that will include all the good that civilization has developed. The Bible does not suggest a reset back to the Garden of Eden for the transition from Daniel's 70th Week to the Millennium, so why would there be the expectation of a reset for the transition from the millennium to eternity? The answer is, in both situations, there is no reset, life will continue as it was, with the stipulation that some things will be different, such as Satan will not be in the millennium or eternity, and the curse ends with Christ's Second Advent. But keep in mind, a new earth and new heaven will replace the old earth and old heaven because they will be destroyed, so, in that sense the earth and heaven will be reset.

INDIVIDUAL IDENTITIES OF THE SAINTS

Saints in heaven will continue to have the names and identities they had while on earth as can be seen in the following passages:

- Job 19:26-27: *And after my skin has been destroyed, yet in the flesh I will see God; I myself will see him with my own eyes – I, and not another. How my heart yearns within me!* Job is saying that no matter how he dies, he will continue in a conscious existence and will see God.
- Matthew 8:11: While in eternal heaven, Abraham, Isaac, and Jacob retained their respective names, and thus their identities.
- Luke 15:4-7, 10: There is more *rejoicing in heaven over one sinner who repents than over ninety-nine righteous persons who do not need to repent.* This verse affirms that each person is a separate individual whose life is observed from heaven.
- Luke 16:25: While Lazarus was in the intermediate heaven, Jesus called him by name.

The name of a specific individual means that the individual has a distinct identity. This suggests that having the same name as on earth implies that we are the same people; there are no passages in the Bible that indicates we will have different names and identities. God's Plan has included individual identities since the beginning. If God was not interested in the diversity of His creatures as individuals, then He would have only created one creature. Individuals will retain their "memory, personality, traits, gifts, passions, preferences, and interests. In the final resurrection, I believe all of these facets will be restored and amplified, untarnished by sin and the Curse."[8]

We should remember that Jesus did not have another identity when He got to heaven after His resurrection – Jesus was still Jesus in all His glory. Consider the following passages where Jesus appeared separately to Mary and Peter in His resurrected body and had previous knowledge of them from the times prior to His crucifixion and resurrection:

- Luke 24:39: After having just appeared to His startled apostles, Jesus says to them, *"Look at my hands and my feet. It is I myself! Touch me and see; a ghost does not have flesh and bones, as you see I have."*

- John:
  + 20:10-18: After Mary saw that Jesus was not in the tomb, she began crying. Then Jesus appeared beside her and she did not realize it was Him. He asked why she was crying and then she recognized Him. He tells about the things that will occur soon. So, Jesus appeared to Mary in His resurrected body and they had a conversation.
  + 24-29: Thomas was not present when Jesus appeared to the apostles, and he was doubting the apostles account of meeting with Jesus. Then Jesus appeared to Thomas and challenged him to put his fingers into the wounds.
  + 21:15-22: Jesus appeared to Peter and asked if Peter loved Him. Each time Peter responded that he did love Him. Jesus then instructed Peter to feed His sheep and to follow Him.

If our identity in heaven is not the same as it was on earth, then how can we be held accountable for what we did and did not do in this life – the judgment would be meaningless. Our own personal identity will endure from life on earth to heaven.

- Isaiah 66:22: *"As the new heaven and the new earth that I make will endure before me," declares the Lord, "so will your name and descendants."*
- Matthew:
  + 8:11: *I say to you that many will come from the east and the west, and will take their places at the fest with Abraham, Isaac, and Jacob in the kingdom of heaven.*
  + 26:29: At the Last Supper, Jesus says to His apostles, *"I tell you, I will not drink from this fruit of the vine from now on until that day when I drink it new with you in my Father's house."*

The Lamb's Book of Life will contain the written names of God's children.

- Revelation:
  + 20:15: *Anyone whose name was not found written in the book of life was thrown into the lake of fire.*
  + 21:27: *Nothing impure will enter it, nor will anyone who does what is shameful or deceitful, but only those whose names are written in the Lamb's book of life.*
  + 21:12-14: Jesus says, *"Look, I am coming soon! My reward is with me, and I will give to each person according to what they have done. I am the Alpha and the Omega, the First and the Last, the Beginning and the End. Blessed are those who wash their robes, that they may have the right to the tree of life and may go through the gates into the city.*

We will receive new names in heaven, which will not invalidate our earthly names, but will be in addition to our earthly names.

- Isaiah 62:2: *you will be called by a new name that the mouth of the Lord will bestow.*
- Revelation:

+ 2:17: *I will also give that person a white stone with a new name written on it, known only to the one who receives it.*
+ 3:12: *I will write on them the name of my god and the name of the city of my God ... I will also write on them my new name.*

BODIES OF THE SAINTS

The best image of what our bodies will be like in eternity is Jesus Christ's body immediately after His resurrection. "Our resurrection bodies will be free of the curse of sin, redeemed, and restored to their original beauty and purpose that goes back to Eden. The only bodies we've ever known are weak and diseased remnants of the original bodies God made for humans. But the bodies we'll have on the New Earth, in our resurrection, will be even more glorious than those of Adam and Eve."[9]

It seems logical that our bodies will have a natural beauty and will be of an appropriate size, not obese or sculpted as is popular in our society. The bodies of the saints will no longer be under the Curse but will be perfect and glorified as God intended by His original design. Since the saints will retain their original identity and name, implying distinctiveness and uniqueness, it seems that we will also retain our distinct and unique appearance. We will all look like we do on earth, only better. If we look like we do on earth, which will include racial identities, genetic make-up and healthiness, untouched by disease. We will be pleasing to God, and our inner beauty will extend to our outer beauty.

- Revelation:
  + 5:9: When John was shown the vision of the scroll and the Lamb, *the four living creatures and the twenty-four elders sang a song*, part of which included the words ... *because you were slain, and with your blood you purchased for God persons from every tribe and language and people and nation.*
  + 7:9: *and there before me was a great multitude that no one could count, from every nation, tribe, people, and language, standing before the throne and before the Lamb.*

Since our bodies will be as described above, it seems probable that we will have our five senses. We will see the new earth and new heavens, as well as hear its sounds, smell it, taste it, and feel it. Remember that before His ascension, Jesus saw the people He was interacting with, talked with them and heard them talking, felt things, smelled the fish cooking and tasted the cooked fish. It may be that our five senses will be even more acute since we are in perfect, resurrected bodies; they may function at levels we never thought possible on earth. God will continually give us more to discover and experience.

As shown by the passages below Jesus had an extraordinary ability (at least on earth terms) to moving through a locked door, disappearing, and flying. This demonstrates that in His risen body He was able to defy the laws of nature. Whether we will have these same abilities is yet to be seen however, we are told our resurrection bodies will be like the risen Christ's body. So the possibilities in this regard is that we will only have the same abilities as we do on earth, the abilities Adam and Eve had, or the abilities Jesus has.

- Luke 24:31: On the road to Emmaus, Jesus disappeared from the presence of those walking the road.
- John 20:19: After His resurrection, Jesus moved through a lock door, or the wall for that matter, to be with the apostles.
- Acts 1:9: On the day of ascension and after Jesus addressed the crowd, *he was taken up before their very eyes, and a cloud hid him from their sight.*

Other features of our bodies in heaven might include the following:

- An unprecedented harmony between the mind and body is a very good possibility.
- Those that are physically handicapped, those that are paraplegics or quadriplegics, those that are mentally handicapped, and those that have all sorts of painful maladies will all receive perfect bodies.
- There is no reason to think we will be genderless; we will retain our own individual gender.
- It appears that we will wear clothes and will not be naked.
- The Bible never teaches sameness among people or saints.
- There will be a continuity of being between the earth, the millennium, and heaven.

EMOTIONS AND DESIRES

Our emotions are derived from, and are a reflection on, the Lord. Our emotions of gladness, anger, rejoicing, enjoyment, delight, love, happiness, jealousy, and love that we have in our earthly life will carry over into heaven. The following passages express some of the emotions that will be found in heaven.

- Luke 6:21: *Blessed are you who weep now, for you will laugh.*
- Revelation:
    + 6:10: An emotional question by the tribulation martyred souls under the altar, revealed by the fifth seal, asking God how much longer they have to wait until God avenges their blood.
    + 7:10: The *great multitude* dressed in *white robes cried out in a loud voice: "Salvation belongs to our god, who sits on the throne, and by the Lamb."*
    + 18:1-24: An emotional lament over fallen Babylon.

+ 21:4: *He will wipe every tear from their eyes. There will be no more death or mourning or crying or pain, for the old order of things has passed away.*

In heaven, we will experience many desires, but they will not be unholy desires – they will please God. We will not have to struggle with desires, they will always be pure. Anticipation of a desire is part of joy. Is it wrong to desire something? Not according to Christianity which teaches that Christ removes our sins while redeeming our desires. Like other emotions built in since creation, we desire things, relationships, and abilities.

- Psalm 37:4: *Take delight in the Lord, and he will give you the desires of your heart.*
- Hebrews 8:10: God will make a *covenant with the people of Israel* that he *will put His laws in their minds and write them on their hearts.*

EATING AND DRINKING

In the Bible, there are numerous occurrences of such words as drinking, eating, meals, and feasts. Feasting in the Bible is an important event, especially for the Jews in the Old Testament. Even today, the Jews celebrate feasts that draw attention to God, His redemptive power, and His greatness. Feasting is important because it brings people together for a common reason and there is laughter, relationship building, and conversation during the meal.

Some of the passages that include references to eating and drinking include the following:

- Psalm 78:25: It is interesting that during the Exodus, the manna from heaven was called *the bread of angels.*
- Isaiah 25:6: On this mountain the Lord Almighty will prepare a feast of rich food for all peoples, a banquet of aged wine – the best of meals and the finest of wines.
- Luke 14:15: *"Blessed is the one who will eat at the feast in the kingdom of God."*
- Luke 22:18: Jesus says, *For I tell you I will not drink again from the fruit of the vine until the kingdom of God comes.*
- Luke 22:29-30: Jesus says, *And I confer on you a kingdom, just as my Father conferred one on me, so that you may eat and drink at my table in my kingdom ...*
- John 21:4-14: Jesus prepares breakfast for His disciples and then ate bread and fish with them.
- Revelation 19:9: *Blessed are those who are invited to the wedding supper of the Lamb! ...*

KNOWING AND KNOWLEDGE

When discussing the topic of knowledge, we should remember that only God is omniscient. Even though we will be in our resurrection body, we will never know as much as God because we will still be finite. In heaven, we will see more clearly, but not as clearly as God. When we see God for the first time, we will know Him in ways we have never comprehended and will continue to learn about Him throughout eternity.

When we get to heaven, we will probably begin with the knowledge we had on earth and what was learned in the millennium. It's possible that God could infuse additional knowledge into us as we make the transition from one place to the next. He might also correct perceptions that we have that are wrong, confused or convoluted. We will most likely study because sometimes the desire to learn becomes the goal of learning. Of course, we will study truth, which being an attribute of God is inexhaustible.

In heaven we will continue to learn about God and growing in more understanding. We will be learning forever. The Bible seems to indicate that we will not have the same level of knowledge as God has, but instead we will continue to learn as we do on the earth.
- Jeremiah 31:34: *No longer will they teach their neighbor, or say to one another, 'Know the Lord, because they will all know me, form the least to the greatest," declares the Lord.*
- Matthew:
  + 10:26: Jesus says, *there is nothing concealed that will not be disclosed, or hidden that will not be made known.*
  + 11:29: Jesus says, *Take my yoke upon you and learn from me, for I am gentle and humble in heart, and you will find rest for your souls.*

DAILY LIFE

Rest
From the very beginning of creation, the concept of rest has been part of God's Plan, God rested on the seventh day of creation, God set aside days and weeks of rest, and He wanted the earth to rest every seven years. "Eden is a picture of rest – work that's meaningful and enjoyable, abundant food, a beautiful environment, unhindered friendship with God and other people and animals. Even with Eden's restful perfection, one day was set aside for special rest and worship. Work will be refreshing on the New Earth, yet regular rest will be built into our lives."[10] Since God included rest in Eden, and to life on earth, it is reasonable to expect we will rest in heaven.

Sleep

Sleep is not an imperfection because it was included in the original creation of human being, so again, it is reasonable to expect we will sleep in heaven. One of the grand pleasures of life on earth is sleep until rested so it would be expected in heaven.

Work

Work was part of the original design of humankind. Work was not caused by the Curse but it was made menial and tedious; also it was not caused by sin. In heaven, work will be redeemed and made into what it was intended to be. God performs work in heaven, such as creating all that He has. It seems logical that it takes a lot of work for God to take care of His children on earth. So if God works in heaven, why shouldn't we?

RELATIONSHIPS

While all our needs can be satisfied by Jesus Christ, at creation God said that it was not good for man to be alone. God created humans to need human companionship. It does not offend God for us to have relationships with other image-bearers. Remember Jesus' commandment to love God, yet He also commanded us to love our neighbors. The second commandment flows from the first commandment. Loving other people is one of the ways we show our love for God. It is comforting to love people and to look forward to seeing them in heaven.

- Genesis 2:18: *The Lord God said, "It is not good for the man to be alone …*
- Matthew 6:19-21: Jesus says, *"Do not store up for yourselves treasures on earth, where moths and vermin destroy, and where thieves break in and steal. But store up for yourselves treasures in heaven, where moths and vermin do not destroy, and where thieves do not break in and steal. For where your treasure is, there your heart will be also.*
- Matthew 22:37-39: Jesus replied: *" 'Love the Lord with all your heart and with all your soul and with all your mind.' This is the first and greatest commandment. And the second is like it: 'Love your neighbor as yourself.' All the Law and the Prophets hang on these two commandments. "*

Regarding the question of if we will recognize family and friends in heaven; we just have to remember Jesus Christ was recognizable in many instances after His resurrection: Mary, His disciples on several occasions, His appearance to Thomas, and the five hundred people. So since the risen Jesus Christ was recognized by people it is reasonable to expect that we will be recognized and will recognize our family and friends. There is no evidence in the Bible to the contrary.

- Luke 24:15-16, 31: *As they talked and discussed these things with each other, Jesus himself came up and walked along with them; but they were kept from recognizing him. … Their eyes were opened and they recognized him, and he disappeared from their sight.*

- John:
    + 20:15-16: *He asked her, "Woman, why are you crying? Who is it you are looking for? Thinking he was the gardener, she said, "Sir, if you have carried him away, tell me where you put him, and I will get him. Jesus said to her, "Mary." She turned toward him and cried out in Aramaic, "Rabboni!" (which means "Teacher").*
    + 20:24-29: *Now Thomas (also known as Didymus), one of the Twelve, was not with the disciples when Jesus came. So the other disciples told him, "We have seen the Lord!" But he said to them, "Unless I see the nail marks in his hands and put my finger where the nails were, and put my hand into his side. I will not believe." A week later his disciples were in the house again and Thomas was with them. Though the doors were locked, Jesus came and stood among them and said, "Peace be with you!" Then he said to Thomas, Put your finger here, see my hands. Reach out your hand and put it into my side. Stop doubting and believe.*
    + John 21:1-14: *Afterward Jesus appeared again to his disciples, by the Sea of Galilee. It happened this way: Simon Peter, Thomas (also known as Didymus), Nathanael from Cana in Galilee, the sons of Zebedee, and two other disciples were together. "I'm going out to fish." Simon Peter told them, and they said, "We'll go with you." So they went out and got into the boat, but that night they caught nothing. Early in the morning, Jesus stood on the shore, but the disciples did not realize that it was Jesus. He called out to them, "Friends, haven't you any fish?" "No," they answered. He said, "Throw your net on the right side of the boat and you will find some." When they did, they were unable to haul the net in because of the large number of fish. Then the disciples whom Jesus loved said to Peter, "It is the Lord!" As soon as Simon Peter heard him say, "It is the Lord," he wrapped his outer garment around him (for he had taken it off) and jumped into the water. The other disciples followed in the boat, towing the net full of fish, for they were not far from the shore, about a hundred yards. When they landed, they saw a fire of burning coals there with fish on it, and some bread. Jesus said to them, "Bring some of the fish you have just caught." So Simon Peter climbed back into the boat and dragged the net ashore. It was full of large fish, 153, but even with so many the net was not torn. Jesus said to them, "Come and have breakfast." None of the disciples dared ask him, "Who are you?" They knew it was the Lord, Jesus came, took the bread and gave it to them, and did the same with the fish. This was now the third time Jesus appeared to his disciples after he was raised from the dead.*
- 1 Corinthians 15:6: *After that, he appeared to more than five hundred of the brothers and sister at the same time, most of whom are still living, though some have fallen away.*

CONCLUSION

And so, we come to the end of our journey through what the Bible says about prophecy and end times. It is my prayer that this book was helpful in your pursuit to understand what God has set before the world. I'm sure you will agree that it is exciting to see the path those of us who are believers will take which ultimately ends with each of us standing before the Lord Jesus Christ and then living an eternal life.

Amazing things are predicted by God when it is time to draw earthly history to a close. We should be overjoyed that Jesus will remove us from the world in the Rapture so that we will not experience the horror occurring after the Rapture during Daniel's 70th Week. It will be awesome to be part of Jesus Christ's Second Advent and then live through the Millennium and then eternity in our immortal, resurrected bodies.

Hopefully you have worked your way through both volumes of this book prayerfully examining each personality, each judgment, each group of people, each event, and that this book has been sufficient for you to develop, or increase, your understanding of prophecy and end times. You should be able to see through the fog of complexity and clearly see how all of the Biblical components fall into place to form a program that fulfills God's purposes for His creation. Not many believers ever get to this point of understanding God's program and timeline.

See you in heaven.

SOURCES

28 - The Rapture

1   John F. Walvoord, *The Rapture Question*, page 12

2   John F. Walvoord, *The Rapture Question*, page 181

3   John F. Walvoord, *The Rapture Question*, pages 79-81

4   John F. Walvoord, *The Rapture Question*, page 85

5   John F. Walvoord, *The Rapture Question*, page 89

6   John F. Walvoord, *The Rapture Question*, page 90

7   John F. Walvoord, *The Rapture Question*, page 92

8   John F. Walvoord, *The Rapture Question*, page 13

9   John F. Walvoord, *The Rapture Question*, page 156

10   John F. Walvoord, *The Rapture Question*, page 156

11   John F. Walvoord, *The Rapture Question*, page 71

12   John F. Walvoord, *The Rapture Question*, page 74

13   Thomas, The Doctrine of Imminence in Two Recent Eschatological Systems, *Bibliotheca Sacra*, Volume 157, Number 628

14   Nestle-Marshall, *The Interlinear Greek-English New Testament*

15   John F. Walvoord, *The Rapture Question*, page 75

16   John F. Walvoord, *The Rapture Question*, page 49

17   J. Dwight Pentecost, *Things to Come*, page 193

18   John F. Walvoord, *The Rapture Question*, page 51

19   John F. Walvoord, *The Rapture Question*, pages 53-54

20   John F. Walvoord, *The Rapture Question*, page 184

21   John F. Walvoord, *The Rapture Question*, page 189

22   John F. Walvoord, *The Rapture Question*, page 193

23   John F. Walvoord, *The Rapture Question*, page 246

24   John F. Walvoord, *The Rapture Question*, page 206

25   John F. Walvoord, *The Rapture Question*, pages 212-213

26   John F. Walvoord, *The Rapture Question*, page 214

27   John F. Walvoord, *The Rapture Question*, page 224

28   John F. Walvoord, *The Rapture Question*, pages 227-228

29   John F. Walvoord, *The Rapture Question*, page 231

30   John F. Walvoord, *The Rapture Question*, page 231

31   John F. Walvoord, *The Rapture Question*, page 244

32   John F. Walvoord, *The Rapture Question*, page 242

33   John F. Walvoord, *The Rapture Question*, page 244

34   John F. Walvoord, *The Rapture Question*, page 246

35   John F. Walvoord, *The Rapture Question*, pages 249-250

36   John F. Walvoord, *The Rapture Question*, pages 251-252

37   John F. Walvoord, *The Rapture Question*, page 254

38   John F. Walvoord, *The Rapture Question*, page 258

39   J. Dwight Pentecost, *Things to Come*, page 215

40   John F. Walvoord, *The Rapture Question*, page 268

29 - The Church After the Rapture

1   J. Dwight Pentecost, *Things to Come*, page 220

2   J. Dwight Pentecost, *Things to Come*, page 220

3   Mark Hitchcock, *The End*, pages 218-219

4   Mark Bailey, Judgment Seat of Christ, in Tim LeHaye and Ed Hindson, *The Popular Encyclopedia of Bible Prophecy*, page 177

5   J. Dwight Pentecost, *Things to Come*, page 222

6   J. Dwight Pentecost, *Things to Come*, page 226

7   J. Dwight Pentecost, *Things to Come*, page 228

30 - The Seven Great Personages of the End Times

1   John F. Walvoord, *The Revelation of Jesus Christ*, page 187

2   J. Dwight Pentecost, *Things to Come*, page 286-290

3   John F. Walvoord, *The Revelation of Jesus Christ*, page 188

4   J. Dwight Pentecost, *Things to Come*, page 288

5   J. Dwight Pentecost, *Things to Come*, page 288

6   J. Dwight Pentecost, *Things to Come*, page 290

7   Arnold G. Fruchtenbaum, *The Footsteps of the Messiah*, Revised Edition, page 260

8   J. Dwight Pentecost, *Things to Come*, page 286

9   John F. Walvoord, *Prophecy Knowledge Handbook*, page 579

10   Arnold G. Fruchtenbaum, *The Footsteps of the Messiah*, Revised Edition, page 242

11   John F. Walvoord, *The Revelation of Jesus Christ*, page 166

12   John F. Walvoord, *The Revelation of Jesus Christ*, page 194

13   John F. Walvoord, *The Revelation of Jesus Christ*, page 195

14   Arnold G. Fruchtenbaum, *The Footsteps of the Messiah*, Revised Edition, pages 290-293

15   Arnold G. Fruchtenbaum, *The Footsteps of the Messiah*, Revised Edition, pages 292-293

16   Arnold G. Fruchtenbaum, *The Footsteps of the Messiah*, Revised Edition, page 293

31 - Introduction to Daniel's 70ᵗʰ Week

1   John F. Walvoord, *Major Bible Prophecies*, page 346

2   Lewis Sperry Chafer, revised by John F. Walvoord, *Major Bible Themes*, Revised Edition, page 320

3   John F. Walvoord, *Prophecy*, page 118

4   Richard L. Mayhue, Day of the Lord in Tim LeHaye and Ed Hindson (General Editors), *The Popular Encyclopedia of Bible Prophecy*, page 73

5   J. Dwight Pentecost, *Things to Come*, page 230-231

6   Arnold G. Fruchtenbaum, *The Footsteps of the Messiah*, Revised Edition, page 181

7   John F. Walvoord, *Major Bible Prophecies*, page 350

8   David Jeremiah, *The Jeremiah Study Bible*, footnote for 2 Thessalonians 2:2, page 1689

9   J. Dwight Pentecost, *Things to Come*, page 232

10   J. Dwight Pentecost, *Things to Come*, pages 236-237

11   Randall Price, *Jerusalem in Prophecy*, page 136

12   J. Dwight Pentecost, *Things to Come*, pages 237-238

13   Randall Price, *Jerusalem in Prophecy*, page 136

14   Arnold G. Fruchtenbaum, *The Footsteps of the Messiah*, Revised Edition, pages175-178

15   John F. Walvoord, *The Rapture Question*, page 59

16   John F. Walvoord, *The Rapture Question*, page 65

17   John F. Walvoord, *The Rapture Question*, page 67

18   John F. Walvoord, *The Rapture Question*, page 67

19   John F. Walvoord, *The Rapture Question*, page 66

20   Thomas Ice and Timothy Demy, *Fast Facts on Bible Prophecy*, "Restrainer", page 166

21   Charles C. Ryrie, *Dispensationalism Today*, page 123

22   Charles C. Ryrie, *Dispensationalism Today*, page 131

23   John F. Walvoord, *The Revelation of Jesus Christ*, page 104

24   John F. Walvoord, *The Revelation of Jesus Christ*, page 109

25   John F. Walvoord, *The Revelation of Jesus Christ*, pages 109-110

26   J. Dwight Pentecost, *Things to Come*, page 252

27   J. Dwight Pentecost, *Things to Come*, page 258

32 - The Gentiles in Daniel's 70th Week

1   John F. Walvoord, *Nations in Prophecy*, pages 88-89

2   John F. Walvoord, *Nations in Prophecy*, pages 88-89

3   J. Dwight Pentecost, *Things to Come*, pages 324-326

4   Ed Hindson and Lee Fredrickson, *Future Wave*, pages 142-143

5   John F. Walvoord, *Daniel, The Key to Prophetic Revelation*, page 71

6   Mal Couch (General Editor), *A Bible Handbook to Revelation*, page 280

7   John F. Walvoord, *The Nations in Prophecy*, page 90

8   Mal Couch (General Editor), *A Bible Handbook in Revelation*, page 235

9   Ed Hindson, False Prophet in Tim LeHaye and Ed Hindson (General Editors), *The Popular Encyclopedia of Bible Prophecy*, page 102

10   Grant Jeffrey, *Prince of Darkness*, page 268

11   Grant Jeffrey, *Prince of Darkness*, page 270

33 - Israel in Daniel's 70th Week

1   Charles H. Dyer, Jerusalem, Eye of the Storm, *Storm Clouds on the Horizon*, page 71

2   John F. Walvoord, *Armageddon, Oil and the Middle East Crisis*, page 105

3   Arnold G. Fruchtenbaum, *The Footsteps of the Messiah*, Revised Edition, page 130

4   Arnold G. Fruchtenbaum, *The Footsteps of the Messiah*, Revised Edition, page 286

5   Charles H. Dyer, Jerusalem, the Eye of the Storm, *Storm Clouds on the Horizon*, page 73

6   John F. Walvoord, *Daniel, The Key to Prophetic Revelation*, page 233

7   John F. Walvoord, *Major Bible Prophecies*, page 319

8   Randal Price, *Jerusalem in Prophecy*, pages 138, 152, and 258-259

9   J. Dwight Pentecost, *Things to Come*, page 250

10   J. Dwight Pentecost, *Things to Come*, page 214

11   John F. Walvoord, *The Revelation of Jesus Christ*, page 139

12	John F. Walvoord, *Prophecy Knowledge Handbook*, page 588
13	John F. Walvoord, *Prophecy Knowledge Handbook*, page 588
14	John F. Walvoord, *Prophecy Knowledge Handbook*, page 589
15	John F. Walvoord, *Prophecy Knowledge Handbook*, page 561
16	John F. Walvoord, *Prophecy Knowledge Handbook*, page 572
17	John F. Walvoord, *Prophecy Knowledge Handbook*, page 573
18	John F. Walvoord, *The Revelation of Jesus Christ*, page 178
19	J. Dwight Pentecost, *Things to Come*, page 308
20	John F. Walvoord, *Prophecy Knowledge Handbook*, page 574
21	Arnold G. Fruchtenbaum, *The Footstep of the Messiah*, Revised Edition, page 232
22	John F. Walvoord, *The Revelation of Jesus Christ*, page 180
23	John F. Walvoord, *Prophecy Knowledge Handbook*, page 575
24	John F. Walvoord, *The Revelation of Jesus Christ*, page 181
25	John F. Walvoord, *Daniel, The Key to Prophetic Revelation*, page 252
26	John F. Walvoord, *Daniel, The Key to Prophetic Revelation*, page 252
27	John F. Walvoord, *Daniel, The Key to Prophetic Revelation*, page 252
28	John F. Walvoord, *Daniel, The Key to Prophetic Revelation*, page 252
29	John F. Walvoord, *Daniel, The Key to Prophetic Revelation*, pages 277-280
30	John F. Walvoord, *Daniel, The Key to Prophetic Revelation*, page 280

34 - The Third Jewish Temple

1	Randall Price, *The Temple in Bible Prophecy*, page 35
2	Randall Price, *The Temple in Bible Prophecy*, page 39
3	Randall Price, *The Temple in Bible Prophecy*, page 39

35 - The Invasion of Israel by a Confederacy

1	Charles L. Feinberg, *The Prophecy of Ezekiel*, page 225
2	J. Dwight Pentecost, *Things to Come*, pages 346-355
3	Arnold G. Fruchtenbaum, *The Footsteps of the Messiah*, Revised Edition, pages 117-124
4	John F. Walvoord, *Prophecy Knowledge Handbook*, page 190
5	Arnold G. Fruchtenbaum. *The Footsteps of the Messiah*, Revised Edition, page 121
6	Arnold G. Fruchtenbaum. *The Footsteps of the Messiah*, Revised Edition, page 121
7	Arnold G. Fruchtenbaum, *The Footsteps of the Messiah*, Revised Edition, page 123
8	J. Dwight Pentecost, *Things to Come*, page 344
9	J. Dwight Pentecost, *Things to Come*, page 351
10	J. Dwight Pentecost, *Things to Come*, page 351
11	J. Dwight Pentecost, *Things to Come*, page 352
12	J. Dwight Pentecost, *Things to Come*, pages 344-345
13	Charles H. Dyer, Ezekiel, in John F. Walvoord and Roy B. Zuck, *Bible Knowledge Handbook - Old Testament*, page 1300
14	Randall Price, *The Temple in Bible Prophecy*. page 456
15	Randall Price, *The Coming Last Days Temple*, page 457
16	Randall Price, *The Coming Last Days Temple*, page 457
17	Mal Couch, Gog and Magog, *Dictionary of Premillennial Theology*, pages 124-125

18   Arnold G. Fruchtenbaum, *The Footsteps of the Messiah*, Revised Edition, pages 111-112

19   Charles L. Feinberg, *The Prophecy of Ezekiel*, page 225

20   Charles L. Feinberg, *The Prophecy of Ezekiel*, page 231

21   Charles L. Feinberg, *The Prophecy of Ezekiel*, page 239

36 - The Abomination of Desolation

1   Randall Price, *The Temple and Bible Prophecy*, page 475

2   Randall Price, *The Temple and Bible Prophecy*, page 482

3   Randall Price, *The Temple and Bible Prophecy*, page 482

4   Randall Price, *The Temple and Bible Prophecy*, page 484

5   Randall Price, *The Temple and Bible Prophecy*, page 484

6   Randall Price, *The Temple and Bible Prophecy*, page 485

7   Randall Price, *The Temple and Bible Prophecy*, page 485

8   Randall Price, *The Temple and Bible Prophecy*, page 485

9   Randall Price, *The Temple and Bible Prophecy*, page 485

10   Randall Price, *The Temple and Bible Prophecy*, page 487

11   Randall Price, *The Temple and Bible Prophecy*, page 487

12   Randall Price, *The Temple and Bible Prophecy*, page 488

13   Randall Price, *The Temple and Bible Prophecy*, page 490

14   Randall Price, *The Temple and Bible Prophecy*, pages 488-489

15   John F. Walvoord, *Daniel, The Key to Prophetic Revelation*, pages 264-270

16   Randall Price, *The Coming Last Days Temple*, page 490

17   Randall Price, *The Temple and Bible Prophecy*, page 494

18   Randall Price, *The Temple and Bible Prophecy*, page 495

19   Randall Price, *The Temple and Bible Prophecy*, pages 495-496

37 - The Seven Sealed Scroll and Seal Judgments

1   Alan F. Johnson, *The Expositor's Bible Commentary - Revelation*, pages 69-70

2   John F. Walvoord, *The Revelation of Jesus Christ*, page 113, references a book by Ethelbert Stauffer, which indicates that seven seals were necessary

3   John F. Walvoord, *The Revelation of Jesus Christ*, page 70

4   Tim LeHaye, *Revelation Unveiled*, page 124

5   John F. Walvoord, *The Revelation of Jesus Christ*, page 115

6   John F. Walvoord, *The Revelation of Jesus Christ*, page 115

7   Alan F. Johnson, *The Expositor's Bible Commentary - Revelation*, page 72

8   John F. Walvoord, *The Revelation of Jesus Christ*, page 115

9   Tim LeHaye, *Revelation Unveiled*, page 125

10   Alan F. Johnson, *The Expositor's Bible Commentary - Revelation*, page 72

11   John F. Walvoord, *The Revelation of Jesus Christ*, page 125

12   John F. Walvoord, *Prophecy Knowledge Handbook*, page 552

13   John F. Walvoord, *Prophecy Knowledge Handbook*, page 552

14   John F. Walvoord, *The Revelation of Jesus Christ*, page 123

15   Mal Couch (General Editor), *A Bible Handbook to Revelation*, page 234

16   Alan F. Johnson, *The Expositor's Bible Commentary - Revelation*, page 76

17   John F. Walvoord, *The Revelation of Jesus Christ*, page 123

18   Clarence Larkin, *The Book of Revelation*, page 53

19   NET Bible, page 2318

20   John F. Walvoord, *The Revelation of Jesus Christ*, page 132

21   John F. Walvoord, *The Revelation of Jesus Christ*, page 134

22   Tim LeHaye, *Revelation Unveiled*, page 147

23   Alan F. Johnson, *The Expositor's Bible Commentary - Revelation*, page 93

38 - Intervals and Trumpet Judgments

1   Mal Couch (General Editor), *A Bible Handbook to Revelation*, page 242

2   John F. Walvoord, *The Revelation of Jesus Christ*, page 155

3   Alan F. Johnson, *The Expositor's Bible Commentary - Revelation*, page 96

4   Mal Couch (General Editor), *A Bible Handbook to Revelation*, page 244

5   John F. Walvoord, *The Revelation of Jesus Christ*, page 159

6   John F. Walvoord, *The Revelation of Jesus Christ*, page 159

7   John F. Walvoord, *Prophecy Knowledge Handbook*, page 566

8   Alan F. Johnson, *The Expositor's Bible Commentary - Revelation*, page 97

9   John F. Walvoord, *The Revelation of Jesus Christ*, page 160

10   Mal Couch (General Editor), *A Bible Handbook to Revelation*, page 159

11   John F. Walvoord, *The Revelation of Jesus Christ*, page 161

12   John F. Walvoord, *Prophecy Knowledge Handbook*, page 566

13   John F. Walvoord, *The Revelation of Jesus Christ*, pages 163-164

14   Tim LeHaye, *Revelation Unveiled*, page 174

15   Alan F. Johnson, *The Expositor's Bible Commentary - Revelation*, page 98

16   Alan F. Johnson, *The Expositor's Bible Commentary - Revelation*, page 99

17   Alan F. Johnson, *The Expositor's Bible Commentary - Revelation*, page 99

18   John F. Walvoord, *The Revelation of Jesus Christ*, page 168

19   John F. Walvoord, *Prophecy Knowledge Handbook*, page 571

20   John F. Walvoord, Revelation, in John F. Walvoord and Roy B. Zuck *The Bible Knowledge Commentary - New Testament*, page 954

21   John F. Walvoord, *The Revelation of Jesus Christ*, page 172

39 - The Little Book, Pronouncements, and Bowl Judgments

1   John F. Walvoord, *The Revelation of Jesus Christ*, page 170

2   Arnold G. Fruchtenbaum, *The Footsteps of the Messiah*, Revised Edition, page 239

3   John F. Walvoord, *The Revelation of Jesus Christ*, page 173

4   Alan F. Johnson, *The Expositor's Bible Commentary - Revelation*, page 101

5   Alan F. Johnson, *The Expositor's Bible Commentary - Revelation*, page 101

6   John F. Walvoord, *The Revelation of Jesus Christ*, page 213

7   Arnold G. Fruchtenbaum, *The Footsteps of the Messiah*, Revised Edition, page 183

8   John F. Walvoord, *The Revelation of Jesus Christ*, page 217

9   Arnold G. Fruchtenbaum, *The Footsteps of the Messiah*, Revised Edition, page 266

10   John F. Walvoord, *The Revelation of Jesus Christ*, page 220

11   Alan F. Johnson, *The Expositor's Bible Commentary - Revelation*, page 148

12   John F. Walvoord, *The Revelation of Jesus Christ*, pages 225-226

13   John F. Walvoord, *The Revelation of Jesus Christ*, page 226

14   John F. Walvoord, *The Revelation of Jesus Christ*, page 226

15   John F. Walvoord, *The Revelation of Jesus Christ*, page 227

16   John F. Walvoord, *The Revelation of Jesus Christ*, page 228

17   Alan F. Johnson, *The Expositor's Bible Commentary - Revelation*, page 151

18   John F. Walvoord, *The Revelation of Jesus Christ*, page 230

19   Mal Couch (General Editor), *A Bible Handbook to Revelation*, page 275

20   John F. Walvoord, *The Revelation of Jesus Christ*, page 234

21   John F. Walvoord, *The Revelation of Jesus Christ*, page 234

22   John F. Walvoord, *The Revelation of Jesus Christ*, page 234

24   John F. Walvoord, *The Revelation of Jesus Christ*, pages 235-236

25   Alan F. Johnson, *The Expositor's Bible Commentary - Revelation*, page 154

26   Alan F. Johnson, *The Expositor's Bible Commentary - Revelation*, page 154

27   Arnold G. Fruchtenbaum, *The Footsteps of the Messiah*, Revised Edition, page 310

28   John F. Walvoord, *The Revelation of Jesus Christ*, page 236

29   John F. Walvoord, *The Revelation of Jesus Christ*, page 236

30   J. Dwight Pentecost, *Prophecy For Today*, Page 116

31   W. E. Vine, *An Expository Dictionary of New Testament Words*, "World", page 234

32   Arnold G. Fruchtenbaum, *The Footsteps of the Messiah*, Revised Edition, page 311

33   Alan F. Johnson, *The Expositor's Bible Commentary - Revelation*, pages 155-156

34   John F. Walvoord, *The Revelation of Jesus Christ*, pages 238-239

35   John F. Walvoord, *The Revelation of Jesus Christ*, page 240

40 - Campaign of Armageddon

1   John F. Walvoord, *Daniel, The Key to Prophetic Revelation*, page 252

2   John F. Walvoord, *Daniel, The Key to Prophetic Revelation*, page 252

3   John F. Walvoord, *Daniel, The Key to Prophetic Revelation*, page 252

4   John F. Walvoord, *Daniel, The Key to Prophetic Revelation*, page 276

5   John F. Walvoord, *Daniel, The Key to Prophetic Revelation*, page 278

6   John F. Walvoord, *Daniel, The Key to Prophetic Revelation*, page 269

7   John F. Walvoord, *Daniel, The Key to Prophetic Revelation*, page 279

8   J. Dwight Pentecost, *Prophecy for Today*, page 115

9   J. Dwight Pentecost, *Prophecy for Today*, page 116

10   J. Dwight Pentecost, *Things to Come*, page 338

11   Denis Baly, *The Geography of the Bible*, pages 112-113

12   John F. Walvoord, *Daniel, the Key to Prophetic Revelation*, page 278

13   J. Dwight Pentecost, *Things to Come*, pages 350-355

14   Arnold G. Fruchtenbaum, *The Footsteps of the Messiah*, Revised Edition, Chapter 14

15   Arnold G. Fruchtenbaum, *The Footsteps of the Messiah*, Revised Edition, page 330

16   Arnold G. Fruchtenbaum, *The Footsteps of the Messiah*, Revised Edition, pages 351-352

17   Arnold G. Fruchtenbaum, *The Footsteps of the Messiah*, Revised Edition, page 354

18   Arnold G. Fruchtenbaum, *The Footsteps of the Messiah*, Revised Edition, page 355

19   John F. Walvoord, *The Revelation of Jesus Christ*, page 279

20   John F. Walvoord, *The Revelation of Jesus Christ*, page 281

21   John F. Walvoord, *The Revelation of Jesus Christ*, page 281

22   Arnold G. Fruchtenbaum, *Footsteps of the Messiah*, Revised Edition, pages 355-357

41 - The Destruction of Babylon

1   John F. Walvoord, *Major Bible Prophecies*, page 358

2   Arnold G. Fruchtenbaum, *The Footsteps of the Messiah*, Revised Edition, page 314

3   John F. Walvoord, *Prophecy Knowledge Handbook*, page 323

4   Arnold G. Fruchtenbaum, *The Footsteps of the Messiah*, Revised Edition, page 314

5   John F. Walvoord, *The Revelation of Jesus Christ*, page 259-260

6   John F. Walvoord, *The Revelation of Jesus Christ*, page 261

7   John F. Walvoord, *The Revelation of Jesus Christ*, page 262

8   John F. Walvoord, *The Revelation of Jesus Christ*, page 265

9   John F. Walvoord, *The Revelation of Jesus Christ*, page 267

42 - Revelation of Christ's Second Advent

1   John F. Walvoord, *Major Bible Prophecies*, page 360

2   Lewis Sperry Chafer, revised by John F. Walvoord, *Major Bible Themes*, page 328

3   John F. Walvoord, *Prophecy*, pages 132-133

4   According to a text note on page 851 of the New English Translation Bible (NET), the "Hebrew has "and he will rise/stand upon [the] dust" " making an implied reference to resurrection of his Redeemer

5   John F. Walvoord, *Prophecy*, page 133

6   F. Duane Lindsey, Zechariah, in John F Walvoord and Roy B. Zuck, *The Bible Knowledge Commentary - New Testament*, page 1553

43 - Christ's Second Advent

1   Lewis Sperry Chafer, revised by John F. Walvoord, *Major Bible Themes*, page 328

2   David J. MacLeod, "Expositional Studies of the Seven 'Last Things' in the Book of Revelation," *Bibliotheca Sacra*, Volume 156, Number 622, April-June 1999, page 205

3   David J. MacLeod, "Expositional Studies of the Seven 'Last Things' in the Book of Revelation," *Bibliotheca Sacra*, Volume 156, Number 622, April-June 1999, page 205

4   David J. MacLeod, "Expositional Studies of the Seven 'Last Things' in the Book of Revelation," *Bibliotheca Sacra*, Volume 156, Number 622, April-June 1999, page 205

5   David J. MacLeod, "Expositional Studies of the Seven 'Last Things' in the Book of Revelation," *Bibliotheca Sacra*, Volume 156, Number 622, April-June 1999, page 205

6   David J. MacLeod, "Expositional Studies of the Seven 'Last Things' in the Book of Revelation," *Bibliotheca Sacra*, Volume 156, Number 622, April-June 1999, page 205

7   David J. MacLeod, "Expositional Studies of the Seven 'Last Things' in the Book of Revelation," *Bibliotheca Sacra*, Volume 156, Number 622, April-June 1999, page 206

8   David J. MacLeod, "Expositional Studies of the Seven 'Last Things' in the Book of Revelation," *Bibliotheca Sacra*, Volume 156, Number 622, April-June 1999, page 207

9   David J. MacLeod, "Expositional Studies of the Seven 'Last Things' in the Book of Revelation," *Bibliotheca Sacra*, Volume 156, Number 622, April-June 1999, page 208

10   David J. MacLeod, "Expositional Studies of the Seven 'Last Things' in the Book of Revelation," *Bibliotheca Sacra*, Volume 156, Number 622, April-June 1999, page 208

11   David J. MacLeod, "Expositional Studies of the Seven 'Last Things' in the Book of Revelation," *Bibliotheca Sacra*, Volume 156, Number 622, April-June 1999, page 208

12   John F. Walvoord (Editor), *Lewis Sperry Chafer Systematic Theology Volume Two* - Abridged Edition, page 424

13   Tim LeHaye, *Understanding Bible Prophecy for Yourself*, page 47, and, *Charting the End Times*, page 112

14   Edward E. Hindson, "The Rapture and the Return: Two Aspects of Christ's Coming," Thomas Ice and Timothy J. Demy, General Editors, *The Return - Understanding Christ's Second Coming and the End Times*, pages 95-106

15   Arnold G. Fruchtenbaum, *Israelology, The Missing Link in Systematic Theology*, page 614

16   Arnold G. Fruchtenbaum, *Israelology, The Missing Link in Systematic Theology*, page 617

17   Arnold G. Fruchtenbaum, *Israelology, The Missing Link in Systematic Theology*, page 617

18   Arnold G. Fruchtenbaum, *Israelology, The Missing Link in Systematic Theology*, pages 618-619

19   Arnold G. Fruchtenbaum, *Israelology, The Missing Link in Systematic Theology*, page 620

20   Arnold G. Fruchtenbaum, *Israelology, The Missing Link in Systematic Theology*, page 620

21   Arnold G. Fruchtenbaum, *Israelology, The Missing Link in Systematic Theology*, page 621

22   Arnold G. Fruchtenbaum, *Israelology, The Missing Link in Systematic Theology*, page 623

24   Arnold G. Fruchtenbaum, *Israelology, The Missing Link in Systematic Theology*, page 624

25   Arnold G. Fruchtenbaum, *Israelology, The Missing Link in Systematic Theology*, page 782

26   Arnold G. Fruchtenbaum, *Israelology, The Missing Link in Systematic Theology*, page 783

27   Arnold G. Fruchtenbaum, *Israelology, The Missing Link in Systematic Theology*, page 783

28   Arnold G. Fruchtenbaum, *Israelology, The Missing Link in Systematic Theology*, page 785

29   Arnold G. Fruchtenbaum, *Israelology, The Missing Link in Systematic Theology*, page 786

30   Arnold G. Fruchtenbaum, *Israelology, The Missing Link in Systematic Theology*, page 784

31   Arnold G. Fruchtenbaum, *Israelology, The Missing Link in Systematic Theology*, page 331

32   John A. Martin, Isaiah, in John F. Walvoord and Roy B. Zuck, *The Bible Knowledge Commentary - Old Testament*, pages 1107-1108

33   John A. Martin, Isaiah, in John F. Walvoord and Roy B. Zuck, *The Bible Knowledge Commentary - Old Testament*, page 1108

34   John F. Walvoord, *Daniel, The Key to Prophetic Revelation*, page 76
35   John F. Walvoord, *Daniel, The Key to Prophetic Revelation*, page 76
36   Alan F. Johnson, *The Expositor's Bible Commentary - Revelation*, page 178
37   Mal Couch (General Editor), *A Bible Handbook to Revelation*, page 290
38   John F. Walvoord, *The Revelation of Jesus Christ*, page 277
39   Arnold G. Fruchtenbaum, *The Footsteps of the Messiah*, Revised Edition, pages 339-342
40   John F. Walvoord, *The Revelation of Jesus Christ*, page 277
41   John F. Walvoord, *The Revelation of Jesus Christ*, page 278
42   John F. Walvoord, *The Revelation of Jesus Christ*, page 278
43   J. Dwight Pentecost, *Things to Come*, pages 393-394

44 - The Resurrections

1   John F. Walvoord, *End Times*, page 153
2   John F. Walvoord, *End Times*, page 154
3   John F. Walvoord, *End Times*, page 163
4   John F. Walvoord, *Matthew – Thy Kingdom Come*, page 235
5   John F. Walvoord, *End Times*, page 157
6   John F. Walvoord, *End Times*, page 157
7   John F. Walvoord, *End Times*, pages 161-162

45 - The Judgments

1   Don Campbell, Wendell Johnston, John Walvoord, John Witmer, *The Theological Wordbook*, "Judgment", page 198
2   John F. Walvoord, *End Times*, page 168
3   John F. Walvoord, *The Revelation of Jesus Christ*, pages 290-295
4   John F. Walvoord, *The Revelation of Jesus Christ*, page 163
5   Charles H. Dyer, Ezekiel, in John F. Walvoord and Roy B. Zuck, *The Bible Knowledge Commentary - Old Testament*, page 1265
6   John F. Walvoord, *The Millennial Kingdom*, page 284
7   Eugene W. Pond, "A Study of the Judgment of the Sheep and Goats in Matthew 25, Biblotheca Sacra, Volume 159, page 219
8   Eugene W. Pond, "A Study of the Judgment of the Sheep and Goats in Matthew 25, Biblotheca Sacra, Volume 159, page 219
9   Eugene W. Pond, "A Study of the Judgment of the Sheep and Goats in Matthew 25, Biblotheca Sacra, Volume 159, pages 219 and 299
10   Eugene W. Pond, "A Study of the Judgment of the Sheep and Goats in Matthew 25, Biblotheca Sacra, Volume 159, pages 219 and 299
11   Eugene W. Pond, "A Study of the Judgment of the Sheep and Goats in Matthew 25, Biblotheca Sacra, Volume 159, page 203
12   Eugene W. Pond, "A Study of the Judgment of the Sheep and Goats in Matthew 25, Biblotheca Sacra, Volume 159, pages 214-215
13   Eugene W. Pond, "A Study of the Judgment of the Sheep and Goats in Matthew 25, Biblotheca Sacra, Volume 159, pages 293-297

14	Eugene W. Pond, "A Study of the Judgment of the Sheep and Goats in Matthew 25, Biblotheca Sacra, Volume 159, page 293
15	Eugene W. Pond, "A Study of the Judgment of the Sheep and Goats in Matthew 25, Biblotheca Sacra, Volume 159, pages 297-301
16	Eugene W. Pond, "A Study of the Judgment of the Sheep and Goats in Matthew 25, Biblotheca Sacra, Volume 159, pages 300-301
17	Eugene W. Pond, "A Study of the Judgment of the Sheep and Goats in Matthew 25, Biblotheca Sacra, Volume 159, page 301
18	Eugene W. Pond, "A Study of the Judgment of the Sheep and Goats in Matthew 25, Biblotheca Sacra, Volume 159, page 301
19	Eugene W. Pond, "A Study of the Judgment of the Sheep and Goats in Matthew 25, Biblotheca Sacra, Volume 159, page 290
20	Eugene W. Pond, "A Study of the Judgment of the Sheep and Goats in Matthew 25, Biblotheca Sacra, Volume 159, page 290
21	Eugene W. Pond, "A Study of the Judgment of the Sheep and Goats in Matthew 25, Biblotheca Sacra, Volume 159, pages 436-444
22	John F. Walvoord, *End Times*, page 178

46 - Restoration of Israel

1	Merrill F. Unger, *Great Neglected Bible Prophecies*, page 42
2	Randall Price, *Jerusalem in Prophecy*, pages 203-212
3	Randall Price, *Jerusalem in Prophecy*, page 205
4	Randall Price, *Jerusalem in Prophecy*, page 205
5	Randall Price, *Jerusalem in Prophecy*, page 205
6	Randall Price, *Jerusalem in Prophecy*, page 206
7	Randall Price, *Jerusalem in Prophecy*, pages 207-208
8	Charles H. Dyer, Jeremiah, in John F. Walvoord and Roy B. Zuck, *Bible Knowledge Commentary - Old Testament*, page 1150
9	Arnold G. Fruchtenbaum, *The Footsteps of the Messiah*, Revised Edition, page 101
10	John F. Walvoord, *The Millennial Kingdom*, page 182
11	Merrill F. Unger, *Great Neglected Bible Prophecies*, page 80
12	Charles L, Finberg, *The Prophecy of Ezekiel*, pages 188-194
13	Charles L, Finberg, *The Prophecy of Ezekiel*, page 193
14	Charles L, Finberg, *The Prophecy of Ezekiel*, pages 195-200
15	Charles L, Feinberg, *The Prophecy of Ezekiel*, page 199
16	Charles H. Dyer, Ezekiel, in John F. Walvoord and Roy B. Zuck, *Bible Knowledge Commentary - Old Testament*, page 1295
17	Charles L, Finberg, *The Prophecy of Ezekiel*, pages 201-204
18	Charles L, Feinberg, *The Prophecy of Ezekiel*, page 203
19	Charles L, Feinberg, *The Prophecy of Ezekiel*, page 205
20	Charles L, Feinberg, *The Prophecy of Ezekiel*, pages 205-211
21	Charles L, Feinberg, *The Prophecy of Ezekiel*, page 206
22	Charles L, Feinberg, *The Prophecy of Ezekiel*, page 208
24	Charles L, Feinberg, *The Prophecy of Ezekiel*, page 213
25	Charles L, Feinberg, *The Prophecy of Ezekiel*, page 215

26   Merrill F. Unger, *Great Neglected Bible Prophecies*, pages 15-54

27   Merrill F. Unger, *Great Neglected Bible Prophecies*, page 15

28   Merrill F. Unger, *Great Neglected Bible Prophecies*, page 29

29   Merrill F. Unger, *Great Neglected Bible Prophecies*, page 41

30   Merrill F. Unger, *Great Neglected Bible Prophecies*, pages 16-27

31   Merrill F. Unger, *Great Neglected Bible Prophecies*, pages 28-31

32   Merrill F. Unger, *Great Neglected Bible Prophecies*, pages 28

33   Merrill F. Unger, *Great Neglected Bible Prophecies*, pages 31-41

34   Merrill F. Unger, *Great Neglected Bible Prophecies*, page 31

35   Merrill F. Unger, *Great Neglected Bible Prophecies*, pages 42-48

36   Merrill F. Unger, *Great Neglected Bible Prophecies*, pages 42

37   Merrill F. Unger, *Great Neglected Bible Prophecies*, pages 48-54

38   Merrill F. Unger, *Great Neglected Bible Prophecies*, page 49

39   Merrill F. Unger, *Great Neglected Bible Prophecies*, pages 53-54

47 - 75 Day Interval

1   John F. Walvoord, *Daniel, The Key to Prophetic Revelation*, page 295

48 – Revelation of the Millennium

1   John F. Walvoord, *End Times*, page 195

2   John F. Walvoord, *End Times*, page 195

49 - The 1000 Year Millennium

1   John F. Walvoord, *The Millennial Kingdom*, pages 15-17

2   John F. Walvoord, *The Millennial Kingdom*, pages 15

3   John F. Walvoord, *The Millennial Kingdom*, pages 16

4   Mark Hitchcock, *The End*, pages 417-421

5   Mark Hitchcock, *The End*, page 418

6   John A. Martin, Luke, in John F Walvoord and Roy B. Zuck, *The Bible Knowledge Commentary - New Testament*, page 252

7   Mark Hitchcock, *The End*, page 420

8   J. Dwight Pentecost, *Things to Come*, page 491

9   J. Dwight Pentecost, *Things to Come*, page 493

10   John F. Walvoord, *The Revelation of Jesus Christ*, page 295

11   J. Dwight Pentecost, *Things to Come*, page 477

12   John F. Walvoord, *The Revelation of Jesus Christ*, page 292

13   John F. Walvoord, *The Revelation of Jesus Christ*, page 296

14   John F. Walvoord, *The Revelation of Jesus Christ*, page 297

15   J. Dwight Pentecost, *Things To Come*, page 476

16   J. Dwight Pentecost, *Things To Come*, page 478

17   J. Dwight Pentecost, *Things to Come*, pages 478-481

18   J. Dwight Pentecost, *Things to Come*, page 478

19   J. Dwight Pentecost, *Things to Come*, page 479

20   J. Dwight Pentecost, *Things to Come*, page 479

21   J. Dwight Pentecost, *Things to Come*, page 479

22   J. Dwight Pentecost, *Things to Come*, page 480

23   J. Dwight Pentecost, *Things to Come*, page 532

24   J. Dwight Pentecost, *Things to Come*, pages 539-546

25   J. Dwight Pentecost, *Things To Come*, pages 508-509

26   Charles H. Dyer, Jeremiah, in John F Walvoord and Roy B. Zuck, *The Bible Knowledge Commentary - Old Testament*, pages 1168-1169

27   Arnold G. Fruchtenbaum, *Footsteps of the Messiah*, Revised Edition, pages 439-441

28   Arnold G. Fruchtenbaum, *The Footsteps of the Messiah*, Revised Edition, pages 485-507

29   Arnold G. Fruchtenbaum, *The Footsteps of the Messiah*, Revised Edition, page 341

30   Arnold G. Fruchtenbaum, *The Footsteps of the Messiah*, Revised Edition, page 492

31   H. A. Ironside, *Notes on the Prophecy and Lamentations of Jeremiah*, page 262

32   Arnold G. Fruchtenbaum, *The Footsteps of the Messiah*, Revised Edition, page 496

33   Arnold G. Fruchtenbaum, *The Footsteps of the Messiah*, Revised Edition, page 497

34   Arnold G. Fruchtenbaum, *The Footsteps of the Messiah*, Revised Edition, page 497

35   Arnold G. Fruchtenbaum, *The Footsteps of the Messiah*, Revised Edition, page 497

36   Arnold G. Fruchtenbaum, *The Footsteps of the Messiah*, Revised Edition, 499-501

50 - Life in the Millennium

1   J. Dwight Pentecost, *Things to Come*, pages 487-490

2   John N. Oswalt, *The Book of Isiah, Chapters 40-66*, pages 676-679

3   John A. Martin, Isaiah, in John F Walvoord and Roy B. Zuck, *The Bible Knowledge Commentary - Old Testament*, page 1085

4   David Jeremiah, *The Jeremiah Study Bible*, footnotes at page 1266

5   John A. Martin, Isaiah, in John F Walvoord and Roy B. Zuck, *The Bible Knowledge Commentary - Old Testament*, page 1120

6   Charles H. Dyer, Jeremiah, in John F Walvoord and Roy B. Zuck, *The Bible Knowledge Commentary - Old Testament*, page 1158

7   F. Duane Lindsey, Zechariah, John F Walvoord and Roy B. Zuck, *The Bible Knowledge Commentary - Old Testament*, page 1563

51 - The Millennial Government of the Earthly Kingdom

1   J. Dwight Pentecost, *Things to Come*, pages 495-496 and 502-503

2   J. Dwight Pentecost, *Things to Come*, page 503

3   J. Dwight Pentecost, *Things to Come*, pages 496- 502

4   J. Dwight Pentecost, *Things to Come*, pages 496-497

5   Thomas L. Constable, *Dr. Constable's Expository (Bible Study) Notes*, Isaiah, pages 115-116, accessed on 11/14/17 at www.soniclight.com/constable/notes.htm

6   John N. Oswalt, *The Book of Isaiah Chapters 40 – 66*, page 111

7   J. Dwight Pentecost, *Things to Come*, page 499

8   John A. Martin, Luke, in John F. Walvoord and Roy B. Zuck, *The Bible Knowledge Commentary - New Testament*, page 252

9   J. Dwight Pentecost, *Things to Come*, page 502

52 - The Land to which Israel will be Restored

1   Thomas L. Constable, *Dr. Constable's Expository (Bible Study) Notes,* Ezekiel, pages 259-260, accessed on 11/16/17 at www.soniclight.com/constable/notes.htm

2   Jeffrey L. Townsend, "Fulfillment of the Land Promise in the Old Testament" "Bibliotheca Sacra," Volume 142, Number 568 (October – December 1985), pages 320-337

3   Jeffrey L. Townsend, "Fulfillment of the Land Promise in the Old Testament." "Biblotheca Sacra," Volume 142, Number 568 (October – December 1985), pages 326

4   Jeffrey L. Townsend, "Fulfillment of the Land Promise in the Old Testament." "Biblotheca Sacra," Volume 142, Number 568 (October – December 1985, pages 329

5   Jeffrey L. Townsend, "Fulfillment of the Land Promise in the Old Testament." "Biblotheca Sacra," Volume 142, Number 568 (October – December 1985, pages 330

6   Jeffrey L. Townsend, "Fulfillment of the Land Promise in the Old Testament." "Biblotheca Sacra," Volume 142, Number 568 (October – December 1985, pages 329

7   J. Dwight Pentecost, *Things to Come*, pages 509-510

8   Daniel I. Block, *The Book of Ezekiel – Chapters 25-48*, pages 709-710

53 - The Millennial Mountain

1   Thomas L. Constable, *Dr. Constable's Expository (Bible Study) Notes*, Isaiah, page 20, accessed on 11/17/17 at www.soniclight.com/constable/notes.htm

2   Daniel I. Block, *The Book of Ezekiel – Chapters 25-48*, page 533

3   Daniel I. Block, *The Book of Ezekiel – Chapters 25-48*, pages 570-571

4   Charles H. Dyer, Ezekiel, in John F Walvoord and Roy B. Zuck, *The Bible Knowledge Commentary - Old Testament*, page 1309

5   Tim LaHaye and Ed Hindson, *The Popular Encyclopedia of Bible Prophecy*, page 228

6   Arnold G. Fruchtenbaum, *The Footsteps of the Messiah*, Revised Edition, page 468

7   Arnold G. Fruchtenbaum, *The Footsteps of the Messiah*, Revised Edition, page 472

8   F. Duane Lindsey, Zechariah, in John F Walvoord and Roy B. Zuck, *The Bible Knowledge Commentary - Old Testament* pages 1571-1572

9   Arnold G. Fruchtenbaum, *The Footsteps of the Messiah*, Revised Edition, page 452

10   Arnold G. Fruchtenbaum, *The Footsteps of the Messiah*, Revised Edition, page 454

11   Daniel I. Block, *The Book of Ezekiel – Chapters 25-48*, pages 640-641

12   Daniel I. Block, *The Book of Ezekiel – Chapters 25-48*, page 655

13   Charles H. Dyer, Ezekiel, in John F Walvoord and Roy B. Zuck, *The Bible Knowledge Commentary - Old Testament,* pages 1312-1313

14   Arnold G. Fruchtenbaum, *The Footsteps of the Messiah*, Revised Edition, pages 455-456

54 - The Last Rebellion

1   Mark Hitchcock, *The End*, page 432

2   David J. MacLeod, "The Fifth "Last Thing:" The Release of Satan and Man's Final Rebellion (Rev. 20:7-10)," *Bibliotheca Sacra*, Volume 157, Number 626 (April - June 2000), pages 203-204

3   John F. Walvoord, *The Revelation of Jesus Christ*, page 303 taken from a book by Robert Govett, *The Apocalypse Expounded*, pages 506-508

4   David J. MacLeod, "The Fifth "Last Thing:" The Release of Satan and Man's Final Rebellion (Rev. 20:7-10)," *Biblotheca Sacra*, Volume 157, Number 626 (April - June 2000), page 204

5   David J. MacLeod, "The Fifth "Last Thing:" The Release of Satan and Man's Final Rebellion (Rev. 20:7-10)," *Biblotheca Sacra*, Volume 157, Number 626 (April - June 2000), page 205

6   David J. MacLeod, "The Fifth "Last Thing:" The Release of Satan and Man's Final Rebellion (Rev. 20:7-10)," *Biblotheca Sacra*, Volume 157, Number 626 (April - June 2000), page 205

7   David J. MacLeod, "The Fifth "Last Thing:" The Release of Satan and Man's Final Rebellion (Rev. 20:7-10)," *Biblotheca Sacra*, Volume 157, Number 626 (April - June 2000), page 207

8   David J. MacLeod, "The Fifth "Last Thing:" The Release of Satan and Man's Final Rebellion (Rev. 20:7-10)," *Biblotheca Sacra*, Volume 157, Number 626 (April - June 2000), page 205

9   J. Dwight Pentecost, *Things to Come*, pages 548-551

10   J. Dwight Pentecost, *Things to Come*, pages 548-549

11   David J. MacLeod, "The Fifth "Last Thing:" The Release of Satan and Man's Final Rebellion (Rev. 20:7-10)," *Biblotheca Sacra*, Volume 157, Number 626 (April - June 2000), page 202

12   John F. Walvoord, *The Revelation of Jesus Christ*, page 302

13   David J. MacLeod, "The Fifth "Last Thing:" The Release of Satan and Man's Final Rebellion (Rev. 20:7-10)," *Biblotheca Sacra*, Volume 157, Number 626 (April - June 2000), page 209

14   John F. Walvoord, *The Revelation of Jesus Christ*, page 304

15   Timothy J. Demy, Lake of Fire in Tim LeHaye and Ed Hindson (General Editors), *The Popular Encyclopedia of Bible Knowledge*, page 193

55 - The Great White Throne Judgment

1   David J. MacLeod, "The Fifth "Last Thing:" The Release of Satan and Man's Final Rebellion (Rev. 20:7-10)," *Biblotheca Sacra*, Volume 157, Number 626 (April - June 2000), page 318

2   David J. MacLeod, "The Fifth "Last Thing:" The Release of Satan and Man's Final Rebellion (Rev. 20:7-10)," *Biblotheca Sacra*, Volume 157, Number 626 (April - June 2000), pages 317-318, Footnote 13

3   David J. MacLeod, "The Fifth "Last Thing:" The Release of Satan and Man's Final Rebellion (Rev. 20:7-10)," *Biblotheca Sacra*, Volume 157, Number 626 (April - June 2000), page 322

4   John F. Walvoord, *The Revelation of Jesus Christ*, page 3085

6   David J. MacLeod, "The Fifth "Last Thing:" The Release of Satan and Man's Final Rebellion (Rev. 20:7-10)," *Biblotheca Sacra*, Volume 157, Number 626 (April - June 2000), page 322

7   David J. MacLeod, "The Fifth "Last Thing:" The Release of Satan and Man's Final Rebellion (Rev. 20:7-10)," *Biblotheca Sacra*, Volume 157, Number 626 (April - June 2000), page 323

8   David J. MacLeod, "The Fifth "Last Thing:" The Release of Satan and Man's Final
        Rebellion (Rev. 20:7-10)," *Biblotheca Sacra*, Volume 157, Number 626 (April - June
        2000), page 323

9   John F. Walvoord, *The Revelation of Jesus Christ*, page 307

10   John F. Walvoord, *The Revelation of Jesus Christ*, page 308

11   John F. Walvoord, *The Revelation of Jesus Christ*, page 309

56 - The Eternal State

1   Thomas L. Constable, *Dr. Constable's Expository (Bible Study) Notes*, Revelation,
        page 233, accessed on 11/18/17 at www.soniclight.com/constable/notes.htm

2   John F. Walvoord, *The Revelation of Jesus Christ*, page 306

3   John A. Martin, Isaiah, in John F Walvoord and Roy B. Zuck, *The Bible Knowledge
        Commentary - Old Testament*, page 1084

4   Henry Morris III, *After Eden*, page 140

5   Henry Morris III, *After Eden*, page 141

6   J. Dwight Pentecost, *Things to Come*, page 551

7   R. Larry Overstreet, "2 Peter 3:10-13," Bibliotheca Sacra, Volume 137, Number 548
        (October - December 1980, pages 354-368

8   R. Larry Overstreet, "2 Peter 3:10-13," Bibliotheca Sacra, Volume 137, Number 548
        (October - December 1980, page 354

9   R. Larry Overstreet, "2 Peter 3:10-13," Bibliotheca Sacra, volume 137, Number 548
        (October - December 1980, pages 357-358

10   Based on George N. H. Peters, *The Theocratic Kingdom*, and Robert D. Culver, *Daniel
        and the Latter Days*

11   Based on Robert D. Culver, *Daniel and the Latter Days*, and John Gill, *Body of Divinity*

12   Arndt and Gingrich, *A Greek-English Lexicon*, page 426

13   Arndt and Gingrich, *A Greek-English Lexicon*, pages 484-485

14   Thayer, *A Greek-English Lexicon*, page 384

15   R. Larry Overstreet, "2 Peter 3:10-13," Bibliotheca Sacra, Volume 137, Number 548
        (October - December 1980), page 365

16   David J. Macleod, "The Seven "Last Thing": The New Heaven and the New Earth
        (Rev. 21:1-8)", Biblotheca Sacra, Volume 157, Number 628 (October – December
        2000), page 320

17   J. Dwight Pentecost, *Things to Come*, page 561

18   David J. Macleod, "The Seven "Last Thing": The New Heaven and the New Earth
        (Rev. 21:1-8)", Biblotheca Sacra, Volume 157, Number 628 (October – December
        2000), page 442

57 – The New Jerusalem

1   Randall Price in Tim LaHaye and Ed Hindson (General Editors), *The Popular
        Encyclopedia of Bible Prophecy*, page 245

2   Tim LeHaye and Ed Hindson, General Editors, *The Popular Encyclopedia of Bible
        Prophecy*, Randall Price, "The New Jerusalem", page 244

3   David J. Macleod, "The Seven "Last Thing": The New Heaven and the New Earth (Rev. 21:1-8)", Biblotheca Sacra, Volume 157, Number 628 (October – December 2000), page 444

4   David J. Macleod, "The Seven "Last Thing": The New Heaven and the New Earth (Rev. 21:1-8)", Biblotheca Sacra, Volume 157, Number 628 (October – December 2000), page 448

5   David J. Macleod, "The Seven "Last Thing": The New Heaven and the New Earth (Rev. 21:1-8)", Biblotheca Sacra, Volume 157, Number 628 (October – December 2000), page 449

6   David J. Macleod, "The Seven "Last Thing": The New Heaven and the New Earth (Rev. 21:1-8)", Biblotheca Sacra, Volume 157, Number 628 (October – December 2000), page 448

7   David J. Macleod, "The Seven "Last Thing": The New Heaven and the New Earth (Rev. 21:1-8)", Biblotheca Sacra, Volume 157, Number 628 (October – December 2000), page 450

8   John F. Walvoord, *The Revelation of Jesus Christ*, pages 319-320

9   John F. Walvoord, *The Revelation of Jesus Christ*, page 318

10   John F. Walvoord, *The Revelation of Jesus Christ*, pages 320

11   John F. Walvoord, *The Revelation of Jesus Christ*, pages 320

12   John F. Walvoord, *The Revelation of Jesus Christ*, pages 325

13   John F. Walvoord, *The Revelation of Jesus Christ*, pages 325

14   John F. Walvoord, *The Revelation of Jesus Christ*, pages 321

15   John F. Walvoord, *The Revelation of Jesus Christ*, pages 323

58 - Heaven

1   David Jeremiah, *The Jeremiah Study Bible*, page 967

2   Randy Alcorn, *Heaven*, page 234

3   David Jeremiah, *The Jeremiah Study Bible*, page 957

4   Vine, "Paradise", *An Expository Dictionary of New Testament Words*

5   Tim LaHaye and Ed Hindson, Heaven in *The Popular Encyclopedia of Bible Prophecy*, page 130

6   Wilbur M. Smith, *The Biblical Doctrine of Heaven*, page 50

7   Randy Alcorn, *Heaven*, page 173

8   Randy Alcorn, *Heaven*, page 274

9   Randy Alcorn, *Heaven*, page 281

10   Randy Alcorn, *Heaven*, page 317

BIBLIOGRAPHY

Alcorn, Randy, *Heaven*, Wheaton, Illinois: Tyndale House Publishers, Inc., 2004.

Arndt and Gingrich, *A Greek-English Lexicon of the New Testament and Other Early Christian Literature,* The University of Chicago Press, 1963.

Baker's Dictionary of Theology, Grand Rapids, Michigan: Baker Book House, 1960.

Baly, Denis, *The Geography of the Bible,* Harper & Row, 1974.

Bauman, Paul et al, *The Prophetic Word in Crisis Days*, Findlay, Ohio: Dunham Publishing Company, 1961.

Benware, Paul N., *Understanding End Times Prophecy*, Chicago, Illinois: Moody Press, 2006.

Block, Daniel I., The New International Commentary on the Old Testament, *The Book of Ezekiel – Chapters 25-48*, Grand Rapids, Michigan: William B. Eerdmans Publishing Company, 1998.

Burns, Cathy, *A One World Order is Coming – Who Will Rule?*, Mt. Carmel, Pennsylvania: Sharing, 1997.

Chafer, Lewis Sperry, Revised by John F. Walvoord, *Major Bible Themes*, Grand Rapids, Michigan: Zondervan Publishing House, 1974.

Constable, Thomas L., Online, *Dr. Constable's Expository (Bible Study Notes)*, Accessed Exodus, Isaiah, Jeremiah, Ezekiel, Matthew, Ephesians, Hebrews, 1 John, Revelation.

Couch, Mal, General Editor, *Dictionary of Premillennial Theology*, Grand Rapids, Michigan: Kregel Publications, 1996.

Couch, Mal, General Editor, *A Bible Handbook to Revelation*, Grand Rapids, Michigan: Kregel Publications, 2001.

Dyer, Charles H., *World News and Bible Prophecy*, Wheaton, Illinois: Tyndale House Publishers, Inc., 1995.

Dyer, Charles H. with Angela Elwell Hunt, *The Rise of Babylon, Sign of the End Times*, Wheaton, Illinois: Tyndale House Publishers, Inc., 1991.

Dyer, Charles H., General Editor, *Storm Clouds on the Horizon – Bible Prophecy and the Current Middle East Crisis*, Chicago, Illinois: Moody Press, 2001

Evans, Mike, *Jerusalem Betrayed*, Dallas, Texas: Word Publishing, 1997.

Feinberg, Charles L., *The Prophecy of Ezekiel – The Glory of the Lord*, Chicago, Illinois: Moody Press, 1969.

Feinberg, Charles L., *Israel in the Spotlight*, Chicago, Illinois: Scripture Press Book Division, 1956.

Feinberg, Charles L., *Premillennialism or Amillennialism?*, Wheaton, Illinois: Van Kampen Press, Inc., 1954.

Fruchtenbaum, Arnold G., *Israelology: The Missing Link in Systematic Theology*, Tustin, California: Ariel Ministries, 1989.

Fruchtenbaum, Arnold G., *The Footsteps of the Messiah*, Revised Edition, Tustin, California: Ariel Ministries, 2003.

Geisler, Norman L. and Paul D. Feinberg, *Introduction to Philosophy – A Christian Perspective*, Grand Rapids, Michigan: Baker Book House, 1980.

Hendricks, Howard G. and William D. Hendricks, *Living by the Book*, Chicago, Illinois: Moody Press, 1991.

Hindson, Ed and Lee Fredrickson, *Future Wave*, Eugene, Oregon: Harvest House Publishers, 2001.

Hitchcock, Mark, *The End*, Carol Stream, Illinois: Tyndale House Publishers, Inc., 2012.

Hitchcock, Mark, *The Complete Book of Bible Prophecy*, Wheaton, Illinois: Tyndale House Publishers, Inc., 1999.

Hoehner, Harold W., *Ephesians – An Exegetical Commentary*, Grand Rapids, Michigan: Baker Academic, 2002.

Ice, Thomas and Kenneth L. Gentry, Jr., *The Great Tribulation – Past or Future?*, Grand Rapids, Michigan: Kregel Publications, 1999.

Ice, Thomas and Timothy Demy, *Fast Facts on Bible Prophecy*, Eugene, Oregon: Harvest House Publishers, 1997.

Ice, Thomas and Timothy J. Demy, General Editors, *The Return - Understanding Christ's Second Coming and the End Times,* Grand Rapids, Michigan: Kregel Publications, 1999.

Ironside, H. A., *Notes on the Prophecy and Lamentations of Jeremiah*, New York, New York: Loizeaux Brothers, Inc., 1952.

Jeffrey, Grant R., *Prince of Darkness*, Toronto, Ontario: Frontier Research Publications, 1994.

Jensen, Irving, *Enjoy Your Bible*, World Wide Publications, 1969.

Jeremiah, David, *Jesus' Final Warning – Hearing the Savior's Voice in the Midst of Chaos*, Nashville, Tennessee: Word Publishing, 1999.

Jeremiah, David, *The Jeremiah Study Bible*, Worthy Publishing, 2016.

Johnson, Alan F., *The Expositor's Bible Commentary – Revelation*, Grand Rapids, Michigan: Zondervan Publishing House, 1996.

Larkin, Clarence, *Dispensational Truth*, Rev. Clarence Larkin Estate, 1918.

Larkin, Clarence, *The Book of Revelation – A Study of the Last Prophetic Book of the Holy Scripture*, Rev. Clarence Larkin Estate, 1919.

LeHaye, Tim, *Understanding Bible Prophecy for Yourself,* Eugene, Oregon: Harvest House Publishers, 2001.

LeHaye, Tim, *Revelation Unveiled*, Grand Rapids, Michigan: Zondervan Publishing House, 1999.

LeHaye, Tim and Thomas Ice, *Charting the End Times*, Eugene, Oregon: Harvest House Publishers, 2001.

LeHaye, Tim and Ed Hindson (General Editors), *The Popular Encyclopedia of Bible Prophecy*, Eugene, Oregon: Harvest House Publishers, 2004.

LaHaye, Tim and Ed Hindson, *Exploring Bible Prophecy from Genesis to Revelation*, Eugene, Oregon: Harvest House Publishers, 2006.

Lockyer, Herbert, *All the Messianic Prophecies of the Bible*, Grand Rapids, Michigan: Zondervan Publishing House, 1973.

MacLeod, David J., "Expositional Studies of the Seven 'Last Things' in the Book of Revelation," Bibliotheca Sacra, Volume 156.

McDowell, Josh, *Evidence That Demands a Verdict*, Campus Crusade for Christ, Inc., 1972.

Merrill, Eugene H., *An Historical Survey of the Old Testament*, Grand Rapids, Michigan: Baker Book House, 1991.

Morey, Robert A., *Death and the Afterlife*, Minneapolis, Minnesota: Bethany House Publishers, 1984.

Morris III, Henry, *After Eden*, Green Forest, Arizona: Master Books, Inc., 2003.

Nelson, Tom, *The Big Picture – From Eternity to Eternity*, Friendswood, Texas: Baxter Press, 1996.

Nestle-Marshall, *The Interlinear Greek-English New Testament,* London, England: Samuel Bagster and Sons Limited, 1960.

Oswalt, John N., The New International Commentary on the Old Testament, *The Book of Isaiah – Chapters 40 – 66*, Grand Rapids, Michigan: William B. Eerdmans Publishing Company, 1998.

Payne, J. Barton, *Encyclopedia of Biblical Prophecy*, New York, New York: Harper & Row, Publishers, 1973.

Pentecost, J. Dwight, *Prophecy for Today*, Grand Rapids, Michigan: Zondervan Publishing House, 1961.

Pentecost, J. Dwight, *Things to Come*, Grand Rapids, Michigan: Academie Books an imprint of Zondervan Publishing House, 1958.

Pentecost, J. Dwight, *Thy Kingdom Come*, Grand Rapids, Michigan: Kregel Publications, 1995.

Pink, Arthur W., *The Attributes of God*, Grand Rapids, Michigan: Baker Book House, 1975.

Pink, Arthur W., *The Antichrist*, Grand Rapids, Michigan: Kregel Publications, 1988.

Pond, Eugene W., A Study of the Judgment of the Sheep and Goats in Matthew 25, "Biblotheca Sacra," Volume 159.

Price, Randall, *Jerusalem in Prophecy*, Eugene, Oregon: Harvest House Publishers, 1998.

Price, Randall, *The Temple and Bible Prophecy*, Eugene, Oregon: Harvest House Publishers, 2005.

Rhodes, Ron, *The End Times in Chronological Order*, Eugene Oregon: Harvest House Publishers, 2012.

Rhodes, Ron, *Unmasking the Antichrist*, Eugene, Oregon: Harvest House Publishers, 2012.

Ryrie, Charles Caldwell, *Dispensationalism Today*, Chicago, Illinois: Moody Press, 1965.

Smith, Gary V., *Broadening Your Biblical Horizons – Old Testament Survey – Part II: Job-Malachi*, Wheaton, Illinois, Evangelical Training Association, 1991.

Smith, Wilbur, *The Biblical Doctrine of Heaven*, Chicago, Illinois: Moody Press, 1968.

Sterrett, T. Norton, *How to Understand Your Bible*, Downers Grove, Illinois: InterVarsity Press, 1974.

Stewart, Don, *The Jews, Jerusalem, and the Next Temple*, San Clemente, California, Eternity Bound, 1998.

Strong, James, *The Exhaustive Concordance of the Bible*, New York, New York: Abingdon Press, 1890.

Swindoll, Charles R. and Roy B. Zuck, Understanding Christian Theology, Nashville, Tennessee: Thomas Nelson Publishers, 2003.

Swindoll, Charles R., John F. Walvoord, and J. Dwight Pentecost, *The Road to Armageddon*, Nashville, Tennessee: Word Publishing, 1999.

Tan, Paul Lee, *The Interpretation of Prophecy*, Hong Kong: Nordica International, Ltd., 1974.

Thayer, Joseph H., *Thayer's Greek-English Lexicon of the New Testament*, Hendrickson Publishers, Inc., 1981.

Townsend, Jeffrey L., "Fulfillment of the Land Promise in the Old Testament." Biblotheca Sacra, Volume 142.

Walvoord, John F., Donald K. Campbell, John A. Witmer, et al, *The Theological Wordbook*, W Pub Group, 2000.

Walvoord, John F., *Daniel – The Key to Prophetic Revelation*, Chicago, Illinois: Moody Press, 1971.

Walvoord, John F., *End Times*, Nashville, Tennessee: Word Publishing, 1998.

Walvoord, John F., *Israel in Prophecy*, Grand Rapids, Michigan: Zondervan Publishing House, 1962.

Walvoord, John F., *The Church in Prophecy*, Grand Rapids, Michigan: Kregel Publications, 1999.

Walvoord, John F., *The Nations in Prophecy*, Grand Rapids, Michigan: Zondervan Publishing House, 1967.

Walvoord, John F., *Armageddon, Oil, and the Middle East Crisis*, Grand Rapids, Michigan: Zondervan Publishing House, 1990.

Walvoord, John F., *Jesus Christ our Lord*, Chicago, Illinois: Moody Press, 1969.

Walvoord, John F., Editor, *Lewis Sperry Chafer Systematic Theology – Volume One*, Abridged Edition, Wheaton, Illinois: Victor Books, 1988.

Walvoord, John F., Editor, *Lewis Sperry Chafer Systematic Theology – Volume Two*, Abridged Edition, Wheaton, Illinois: Victor Books, 1988.

Walvoord, John F., *Major Bible Prophecies*, Grand Rapids, Michigan: Zondervan Publishing House, 1991.

Walvoord, John F., *Prophecy*, Nashville, Tennessee: Thomas Nelson, 1993.

Walvoord, John F., *The Rapture Question* – Revised and Enlarged Edition, Grand Rapids, Michigan: Zondervan Publishing House, 1979.

Walvoord, John F., *Matthew – Thy Kingdom Come*, Chicago, Illinois: Moody Press, 1974.

Walvoord, John F., *The Millennial Kingdom*, Grand Rapids, Michigan: Zondervan Publishing House, 1959.

Walvoord, John F., *The Prophecy Knowledge Handbook*, Wheaton, Illinois: Victor Books, 1990.

Walvoord, John F., *The Revelation of Jesus Christ*, Chicago, Illinois: Moody Press, 1966.

Walvoord, John F. and Roy B. Zuck, *The Bible Knowledge Commentary – New Testament*, Wheaton, Illinois: Victor Books, 1983.

Walvoord, John F. and Roy B. Zuck, *The Bible Knowledge Commentary – Old Testament*, Wheaton, Illinois: Victor Books, 1983.

Unger, Merrill F., *Unger's Bible Dictionary,* Moody Press, 1996.

Unger, Merrill F., *Great Neglected Bible Prophecies*, Chicago, Illinois: Scripture Press Book Division, 1955.

Van Kampen, Robert, *The Sign*, Wheaton, Illinois: Crossway Books, 1992.

Vine, W. E., *An Expository Dictionary of New Testament Meanings*, Westwood, New Jersey, 1940.

Zeller, George, *"Pre-Wrath Confusion: Does the Pre-Wrath Rapture Vile Line Up with the Teachings of God's Word, the Bible?"* Middletown Bible Church, 1997.

Zuck, Roy B., *Basic Bible Interpretation*, Wheaton, Illinois: Victor Books, 1991.

Zuck, Roy, *Teaching as Paul Taught*, Grand Rapids, Michigan: Baker Books, 1998.

ABOUT THE AUTHOR

First, I must confess that I do not have a theological degree (although I wish I did), nor am I a pastor or a theology professor. I am an architect with more than 40 years of experience in the technical aspects required to build buildings. I have produced construction drawings, I have worked with contractors during the construction of buildings, and I have written specifications for hundreds of projects, from very small to very large.

I am a committed believer and have served as a teacher, deacon and elder. I have been interested in prophecy and end times my entire adult life. Early on I tried to study the topic but was continually frustrated because I did not feel like I was really learning enough nor was I progressing at the pace I wanted. I needed something to drive me to learn the Biblical revelation more in-depth and at a faster pace. As an architect, my professional work has always been project based, so I decided to treat the study of prophecy and end times as a project where component would be built on component that would end in something tangible. After that, I began learning at a faster pace.

During the 1990's I was part of a very small men's fellowship that met every other Saturday morning. In mid-1998, I asked the other attendees if I could teach about prophecy and end times and they graciously accepted the idea, so I started studying and writing in earnest. In October of that year I started teaching and much to everyone's surprise, the study lasted for over six years. By the end of the study, I had written about 850 pages of narrative that I used as handouts. Looking back, I realized I had essentially written a first draft of a book. In September of 2016 I decided to build a book from these handouts.

Why did I write this book? I have always believed that if a person really wanted to know in depth about a subject such as prophecy and end times, then he or she had to write a book about that subject. Hence, the book in your hands is the conclusion of my study of prophecy and end times.

My wife and I live in the Dallas suburb of Allen, Texas and we have three grown sons and one grandson. I can be reached at scarborough8616@gmail.com.

Walter R. Scarborough

September 2024

What picture does the Bible

paint about the future?

Many Christians are scared, worried and anxious about the future. They are in a spiritual fog and are baffled by the many prophecies and events of the end times and what they mean. They really do not know that the Bible has much to say about that future; in fact, one-fourth of the Bible is about prophecy and end time events. This book will provide insight into questions such as the following:

- How does the panorama of prophecies and events fit together?
- What are all the various viewpoints of the future?
- What is my place in the future?
- Will I be raptured?
- What will be Antichrist be like?
- What are the conditions of the end of the world?
- Will I have to live through Daniel's 70th Week (Tribulation)?
- Will there be a one-thousand-year Millennium?
- Biblical prophecy and end times – are they understandable?
- What does the Bible say about Christ's Second Coming?
- What will life be like in heaven?

This book will challenge you, it will help you understand Biblical prophecy and end times, and it will bring you hope that the future is fully ordered and will occur in a specific sequence as described in the Bible. It will help you develop a solid foundation on the future of God's Plan for Humankind.

VIEWPOINTS:
LITERAL INTERPRETATION
FUTURISTIC
DISPENSATIONAL
PRETRIBULATIONAL
PREMILLENNIAL
CHURCH DOES NOT REPLACE ISRAEL